THE
ABC-CLIO
COMPANION TO

The
Disability
Rights
Movement

An early issue of This Brain Has a Mouth, *which has since been renamed* Mouth: Voice of the Disability Nation. *Like* Mainstream: Magazine of the Able-Disabled, *and* The Ragged Edge, Mouth *is written by and for people with disabilities to provide information and commentary on developments of interest to the disability rights movement.* (Copyright 1992 *Mouth* magazine. Reprinted with permission.)

THE
ABC-CLIO
COMPANION TO

*The
Disability
Rights
Movement*

Fred Pelka

ABC-CLIO

Library of Congress Cataloging-in-Publication Data

Pelka, Fred, 1954–
    The ABC-CLIO companion to the disability rights movement / Fred Pelka.
        p.   cm. — (ABC-CLIO companions to key issues in American history and life)
    Includes bibliographical references and index.
    ISBN 0-87436-834-0 (alk. paper)
    1. Handicapped—Civil rights—United States. 2. Handicapped—
Legal status, laws, etc.—United States. 3. United States.
Americans with Disabilities Act of 1990. I. Title. II. Series.
HV1553.P42   1997
323.3—dc21   97-7662
03   02   01   00   99 98 97   10 9 8 7 6 5 4 3 2 1

ABC-CLIO, Inc.
130 Cremona Drive, P.O. Box 1911
Santa Barbara, California 93116-1911

To Denise Anne Karuth

ABC-CLIO Companions to Key Issues in American History and Life

Contents

Preface

This book is intended as a general introduction to the people and organizations that have contributed to the disability rights movement. Also included are landmark laws and court cases, as well as key figures and concepts important to an understanding of disability rights. Some of the people profiled are familiar to the general public, for example, Franklin Roosevelt and Helen Keller. In most cases, however, individuals of extreme importance—Edward Roberts, Judith Heumann, Howard Geld, to name just a few—are virtually unknown outside the communities they have so profoundly affected. Most of the biographies are of people who are disabled, but I have also included nondisabled people whose lives have influenced the struggle for disability rights. Events of particular importance and centers of disability culture and education are also included.

A one-volume work on such a broad topic cannot help but be superficial and have gaps. As in any movement for social justice, there are thousands of unsung heroes. It is inevitable too that there be mistakes. I apologize to those whose names I have not mentioned or whose work I have slighted.

I would like to thank all those who so graciously helped with this project.

Those who submitted to extended interviews are listed in the bibliography; many dozens more took time out to answer my questions and send materials. The reference librarians at the Forbes Library, the Hampshire County Law Library, and the Clarke School for the Deaf Library, all in Northampton, and at the N. Neal Pike Institute on Law and Disability at Boston University, were especially helpful. Thank you, Woody Kay, for your friendship, support, and your database searches at the Library of Congress. Thanks to Robert Griss for editing my entry on health care access and to Paul Longmore for providing all of the information contained in the entry on the League of the Physically Handicapped. I would especially like to thank those generous souls who volunteered to read drafts of my manuscript: Frank Bowe, Fred Fay, Hugh Gregory Gallagher, Thomas K. Gilhool, Amy Hasbrouck, Cyndi Jones, Bonnie O'Day, Heidi Reed, Andrea Schein, Bill Stothers, Hartmut Teuber, and Patrisha Wright. Your comments, corrections and suggestions were invaluable. Finally, I would like to thank my best friend, companion, and mentor, Denise Karuth, to whom this work is dedicated, for her suggestions, editing, and loving encouragement.

Introduction

That people with disabilities are an oppressed minority in the midst of a liberation movement is for many a new and startling idea. Throughout history, people with disabilities have been defined as many things: deserving victims of divine punishment, objects of scorn, sideshow freaks, medical case studies, recipients of charity, and poster children. In literature and in movies, in plays and children's stories, disability is used as a metaphor for evil or childlike innocence, and disabled people are portrayed as malevolent or comical, or as victims of a fate worse than death. Americans with disabilities have been routinely incarcerated, sometimes for life, in institutions and nursing homes, solely because of their disability. In the nineteenth and early twentieth centuries, many states passed laws forbidding people with particular disabilities to marry, and some disabled people—adults and children—were forcibly sterilized. A Chicago city ordinance went so far as to make it a crime for anyone who was "in any way deformed so as to be an unsightly or disgusting object" to appear in public.

Disabled Americans have been organizing for more than a century to change all this. As early as the 1850s, deaf people had established local organizations to advocate for their interests, merging into the National Association of the Deaf in 1880. During the Depression, the League of the Physically Handicapped staged sit-ins at federal offices to protest antidisability discrimination by government programs. The National Federation of the Blind and the American Federation of the Physically Handicapped were organized in the early 1940s, while disabled soldiers, returning home after World War II, founded the Paralyzed Veterans of America. At the same time, parents of disabled children formed self-help groups that, in the 1950s, grew into national advocacy organizations. In the 1960s, polio and spinal cord injury survivors asserted their right to study, work, and live in the community, while people with psychiatric disabilities protested their treatment in massive custodial institutions. Through it all, a small but dedicated cadre of visionary rehabilitation professionals devoted themselves to bringing people with disabilities into the mainstream of American life. Finally, in the early 1970s, a series of disability rights cases, first and foremost *PARC v. Pennsylvania*, crystalized disability as a civil rights issue. Inspired by the African-American civil rights movement and the women's movement of the 1960s, the various disability communities began to coalesce to give rise to the modern disability rights movement.

Introduction

In the decades since, disability rights advocates have scored significant legal and legislative victories, culminating in passage of the Americans with Disabilities Act of 1990. Alongside this political movement has been the growth of a disability culture that challenges the notion of disability as a source of shame and the definition of people with disabilities as less than human. Disabled artists, writers, performers, and activists now celebrate disability as a vital facet of human diversity. They have achieved nothing less than a revolution in how society perceives disabled people and how people with disabilities perceive themselves.

Much, however, remains to be done. Millions of disabled Americans remain locked in poverty. Millions more are unnecessarily consigned to nursing homes or institutions, while the majority of American homes, workplaces, and houses of worship remain inaccessible to a vast portion of our population.

The disability community has been called "an open minority" because almost everyone will become disabled at some point in his or her life. For this reason alone, the ongoing struggle for disability rights is significant to all Americans, but its importance doesn't end there. The disability rights movement is a powerful affirmation of the worth and integrity of each individual human being and arises from what is best in the American tradition.

As the Rev. Martin Luther King Jr. once wrote, "Oppressed people cannot remain oppressed forever. The urge for freedom will eventually come." For Americans with disabilities, the urge for freedom has arrived. Whatever the difficulties, there can be no turning back.

THE
ABC-CLIO
COMPANION TO

*The
Disability
Rights
Movement*

Ableism

Upon his retirement, the head of the Spastic Society of Britain was asked if he could envision the day when a person with spasticity would head that charity. "That'd be like putting dogs and cats in charge of the Humane Society," he quipped.

—Quoted in the November/December 1993 issue of *Mouth: The Voice of Disability Rights*.

Ableism is that set of often contradictory stereotypes about people with disabilities that acts as a barrier to keep them from achieving their full potential as equal citizens in society. Among these are the beliefs that people with disabilities are inherently unable to manage their own lives, that they are embittered and malevolent, and that they are, by reason of their disability, morally, intellectually, and spiritually inferior to temporarily able-bodied people, or, conversely, that people with disabilities are saintlike, ever cheerful, asexual, childlike, and unusually heroic. Ultimately, it is the belief that people with disabilities are different from "normal" people, and that their lives are inherently less worthwhile than those of people without disabilities. It is the "ism" at the root of discrimination against people with disabilities on the job, in school, and in the community.

Ableism can be subtle, as when a bus driver radios his dispatcher that he has just picked up "a wheelchair," meaning someone who uses a wheelchair for mobility. Or it can be overt, as when a Myrtle Beach, South Carolina, motel in 1995 refused to allow two women with cerebral palsy to rent rooms. Pushed to its ultimate extreme it can result in violence, as in March 1989 when a group of youths gang-raped a developmentally disabled woman in Glen Ridge, New Jersey. Ableism in Nazi Germany led to the murder of hundreds of thousands of people with disabilities. Ableist attitudes also result in the patronizing policies that keep people with disabilities in institutions and nursing homes, or dependent on charity, denying them freedom and dignity "for their own good."

Although the disability rights movement has made great progress in confronting and debunking ableist attitudes, these beliefs still permeate our society.

See also Audism; Glen Ridge Case; Hate Crimes and Violence against People with Disabilities; Media Images of People with Disabilities; T-4.

References Bowe, Frank, *Handicapping America* (1978); Golfus, Billy, "Disconfirmation," in Barrett Shaw, ed., *The Ragged Edge: The Disability Experience from the Pages of the First Fifteen Years of* The Disability Rag (1994).

Abortion and Reproductive Rights

In 1991, a Los Angeles radio talk show host led a discussion about whether or not Bree Walker Lampley, a local television news anchorwoman, should abort her fetus because it had a 50-50 chance of sharing her disability. Walker Lampley has a condition called ectrodactyly—the fusing of bones in her toes and fingers. Lisa Blumberg, writing in *The Disability Rag & Resource*, saw the incident as evidence of a "growing social conviction that it is irresponsible to bring children who may have disabilities into the world."

The debate over abortion has divided American political life like no other, and so it should come as no surprise that it has also divided the disability community. What concerns disability rights activists from both sides of the debate is that abortion, linked to prenatal and genetic testing, is being used more and more often to screen out "defective fetuses," that is, those with disabilities. Advances in medical technology that have, for example, enabled infants with spina bifida to survive into adulthood and live independently have also enabled parents to detect and abort fetuses with spina bifida before birth.

"Our discomfort," writes sociologist Adrienne Asch, "arises out of the knowledge that when information about life with a disability is described at all, it usually is a description filled with gloom and tragedy and limited opportunities completely at odds with the views of the disability rights movement." Asch considers "women who refrain from childbearing...[because a fetus may have a disability] to be misguided, possibly depriving themselves of the joys of parenthood by their unthinking acceptance of the values of a society still deeply . . . ambivalent about people with disabilities."

Some disability rights activists have responded by taking a "pro-life" or antichoice position, forging alliances with nondisabled antiabortion activists. Others have sought to educate the pro-choice and feminist communities, whose rhetoric on the necessity of abortion in cases where the fetus is "deformed" they consider offensive and ableist.

"The solution," writes Blumberg, "is for the movement to carefully define the issues that should concern us as disability rights activists. As a movement, we should not take any position on the rights of a fetus versus the rights of a pregnant woman. However, what we can and must do is take a position against any medical, legal or social policy that is based on the attitude that people who have disabilities are categorically inferior to others and therefore would be better off if they did not exist."

See also Baby Doe Case; Baby Jane Doe Case; Eugenics; Forced Sterilization.

Reference Blumberg, Lisa, "Eugenics and Reproductive Choice," in Barrett Shaw, ed., *The Ragged Edge: The Disability Experience from the Pages of the First Fifteen Years of* The Disability Rag (1994).

ACCENT on Living

ACCENT on Living was founded in 1956 by Ray and Grace Cheever as a *Consumer Reports* for people with disabilities. Originally called *Polio Living*, the magazine was born out of Ray Cheever's frustration, after contracting polio in 1952, in trying to find a wheelchair he could use. After searching for months, the chair he purchased, despite its expense, fell apart after only one year. Cheever's background in business led him to think of disability in terms of markets, products, and advertising.

The magazine today presents information on new products and input from readers about their experiences. Issues in the 1990s have featured articles on such topics as discrimination against wheelchair users in retirement communities, comparison shopping for electric scooters, dealing with "burnout" among political activists, and making national wilderness areas more accessible. *ACCENT* has approximately 20,000 paid subscribers.

See also Assistive Technology.

ADAPT

See American Disabled for Attendant Programs Today.

Adaptive Environments Center

The Adaptive Environments Center, established in Boston in 1978, consults with schools, businesses, and government agencies on architectural access to private and public buildings. It was founded by accessible design advocates/educators Elaine Ostroff and Cora Beth Able, who were interested in establishing an information and design center dedicated to promoting the integration of people with disabilities into the community. Adaptive Environments performs site surveys, reviews building plans, and drafts solutions to access problems and provides estimates on how much they will cost. It has helped to bring access to hundreds of schools, libraries, museums, and town halls and has helped hundreds of families to make their homes accessible.

A nonprofit organization, Adaptive Environments also publishes books and materials on access, including *A Consumer's Guide to Home Adaptation* (1995), *Universal Design Resource Notebook* (1993), and *Teaching Strategies for Universal Design* (1995). It has received funding through the U.S. Office of Special Education and Rehabilitation Services (OSERS), the U.S. Department of Justice, the National Institute on Disability and Rehabilitation Research, the National Endowment for the Arts, and a variety of other public and private sources.

See also Architectural Access; Universal Design.

Administration on Developmental Disabilities (ADD)

The U.S. Administration on Developmental Disabilities (ADD) is the agency responsible for programs designed to protect the rights and promote the independence of people with developmental disabilities. Included under its administration are the Protection and Advocacy for Persons with Developmental Disabilities Program and the Projects of National Significance (PNS) program, which provides funds to public and private nonprofit institutions seeking to enhance the independence of and community integration of people with developmental disabilities. The ADD also awards grants to the state Developmental Disabilities Councils to develop and coordinate social service programs for developmentally disabled people and their families. The ADD is housed within the Department of Health and Human Services Administration for Children and Families.

See also Developmental Disabilities; Protection and Advocacy for Persons with Developmental Disabilities Program; Williams, Robert.

Advocado Press

See The Disability Rag & Resource.

AIDS

See HIV/AIDS and Disability.

Air Carrier Access Act of 1986

The Air Carrier Access Act of 1986 amends the Federal Aviation Act of 1958 to prohibit discrimination by airlines against "any otherwise qualified handicapped individual, by reason of such handicap, in the provision of air transportation." It anticipated the Americans with Disabilities Act of 1990 and goes further than Section 504 of the Rehabilitation Act of 1973 in that it prohibits discrimination not only by entities receiving federal funds but also by private businesses serving the general public.

Air carriers have a history of discriminating against people with disabilities. For many years, wheelchair users were entirely prohibited from flying, or they were required to bring an attendant (and pay double fare) whether or not such an attendant was needed. The decision as to who could or could not fly was often left to individual pilots, ticket agents, or flight attendants and was thus arbitrary and capricious. Passengers who refused to comply with these restrictions were sometimes physically mistreated and arrested.

The Air Carrier Access Act was passed in response to *Department of Transportation v. Paralyzed Veterans of America*, a 1986 decision handed down by the U.S. Supreme Court upholding the government's contention that Section 504 of the Rehabilitation Act of 1973 applied only to entities that are direct recipients of federal aid. Thus, although airports that receive federal assistance were required to be accessible, individual aircraft owned by airlines not receiving such aid were not. Someone using a wheelchair could get to the gate, but frequently was still not allowed to board the plane.

Sen. Robert Dole (R–KS), working with attorneys for Paralyzed Veterans of America, introduced legislation designed to reverse the effects of this decision. Similar legislation was introduced in the House of Representatives by John Paul Hammerschmidt (R–AR) and Norman Mineta (D–CA). The bill was signed into law by President Ronald Reagan on 2 October 1986. The rapid progress of the bill, which was introduced, passed, and signed within four months of the Supreme Court decision, was seen as a sign of the growing influence and sophistication of the disability rights lobby in Washington. It also brought together representatives of many of the constituencies that would be crucial for passage of the Americans with Disabilities Act (ADA) four years later.

The regulations promulgated for use with the Air Carrier Access Act prohibit airlines from limiting the number of persons with disabilities on a flight. Airlines, however, are still allowed to require some people (such as someone with a severe mental disability) to be accompanied by an attendant. Airport facilities and aircraft built after 1992 are required to have wheelchair accessible bathrooms, and the aircraft must have movable aisle arm-rests and on-board wheelchairs for movement inside the plane. Airlines can still refuse to board a traveler if they feel he or she would compromise the safety of the aircraft, but they must produce a written explanation to the passenger within ten days of the flight. They cannot require special advance notice for disabled travelers, but they can require notice for special equipment. Airlines are also required to provide assistance when necessary with boarding and luggage.

The ADA did not include air travel in its provisions, because its authors felt that the Air Carrier Access Act of 1986 provided sufficient protection to disabled air travelers.

See also Dole, Robert Joseph; Paralyzed Veterans of America (PVA).

References Gostin, Lawrence O., and Henry A. Beyer, eds., *Implementing the Americans with Disabilities Act* (1993); Treanor, Bryant, *We Overcame: The Story of Civil Rights for Disabled People* (1993).

Alcoholism and Drug Dependence

Federal disability rights law, beginning with the regulations promulgated for implementing the Rehabilitation Act of 1973, recognizes alcoholism and drug dependence as disabilities. The U.S. Attorney General's Office, in 1977, noted that there "is a medical and legal consensus that alcoholism and drug addiction are diseases, although there is disagreement as to whether they are primarily mental or physical." The Americans with Disabilities Act of 1990 (ADA), however, contained a provision that ended protections for anyone using illegal drugs. People with active drug dependence were thus the only disabled individuals to see their rights diminished by passage of the ADA.

Social attitudes toward drug and alcohol dependence have long been colored by prejudice. The possession, use, and sale of alcohol and a wide variety of drugs have all been illegal at various times in American history, and alcoholism and drug dependence have often been regarded as moral failings rather than as diseases or disabilities. These punitive attitudes continue to prevail, despite the fact that most medical authorities believe that drug and alcohol dependence can best be treated through individual and group counseling, medication, and sometimes in-patient hospitalization, as opposed to incarceration. Various authorities have postulated a genetic predisposition toward dependency; others outline a range of factors that can place an individual at greater risk, including a family history of dependence. Like people with other disabilities, individuals who are drug or alcohol dependent are often capable of working, given reasonable accommodation. A person enrolled in a methadone maintenance program, for example, may be perfectly capable of gainful employment. Furthermore, many authorities believe that a person's ability to recover from alcohol or drug dependence is greatly enhanced by having a job.

Dependence as disability has been tested in several federal court decisions since passage of the Rehabilitation Act of 1973, with varying and often confusing results. The first reported litigation involving Section 504 of the Rehabilitation Act and drug dependence was *Davis v. Bucher* (1978), in which the federal court concluded that it "is undisputed that drug addiction substantially affects an addict's ability to perform major life activities . . ." and is thus a disability as defined by the Rehabilitation Act. In *Wallace v. Veterans Administration* (1988), the court ruled that a recovering drug addict denied a job as an intensive care nurse was qualified for the position, and that her inability to administer narcotics could be managed through reasonable accommodation. By contrast, the court in *LeMere v. Burnley* (1988) ruled that current alcoholics were *not* covered by Section 504. The U.S. Supreme Court, in *Traynor v. Turnage* and *McKelvey v. Turnage* (both 1988), upheld a Veterans Administration regulation defining "primary alcoholism" not as a disability, but as "willful misconduct."

A further setback for people with drug dependence came in 1990 during Senate deliberations on the proposed Americans with Disabilities Act (ADA). Sen. Jesse Helms (R–NC) introduced language into the ADA that amended the Rehabilitation Act so that "the term 'individual with handicaps' does not include an individual who is currently engaged in illegal use of drugs." The language was incorporated into the final version of the ADA as signed into law in 1990. Since all federal disability rights law is based on this definition of disability, the Helms amendment effectively ended all civil rights protection for people who are active drug users. However, people who have successfully completed a drug rehabilitation program and are no longer using illegal drugs, or are erroneously regarded as engaging or having engaged in such use, continue to be protected.

Most recently, changes in Social Security law have further eroded the rights of people who are or have been alcohol or drug dependent. As of 1 January 1997, the Contract with America Advancement Act of 1996 ended Supplemental Security Income (SSI) and Social Security Disability Insurance (SSDI) benefits, as well as federal Medicaid and Medicare coverage, for individuals whose drug or alcohol dependence is "material" to their disability. The Housing Opportunity Program Extension Act of 1996 gave public housing authorities broad discretion to exclude and evict individuals with drug or alcohol problems with criminal justice records from public housing.

See also Americans with Disabilities Act of 1990; Legal Action Center; Rehabilitation Act of 1973; Section 504 of the Rehabilitation Act of 1973; *Traynor v. Turnage* and *McKelvey v. Turnage*.

References Burgdorf, Robert L., Jr., *Disability Discrimination in Employment Law* (1995).

Alexander v. Choate
105 S. Ct. 712 (1985)

Disabled Medicaid recipients in Tennessee brought suit when the state government decided to lower the number of hospital in-patient days its Medicaid program would cover from 20 to 14 per year. They argued that, under Section 504 of the Rehabilitation Act of 1973, such an action by a federally funded program was prohibited because it would disproportionately affect people with disabilities, who on average need more medical care and hospital days than people without disabilities. The plaintiffs also argued that Tennessee had other options for lowering its Medicaid budget (the purpose of the cut) that would not have such a discriminatory impact on that state's disabled poor. Under Section 504, according to the plaintiffs, the state was required to pursue such options.

In 1985, the U.S. Supreme Court rejected both of these arguments, ruling that Section 504 was not intended to be "a National Environmental Policy Act for the handicapped, requiring the preparation of 'Handicapped Impact Statements.'" The Court decided that neither increasing the number of in-patient hospital days covered under Medicaid nor adapting some other cost-cutting measure that would impact disabled and nondisabled recipients alike was required under Section 504.

Although the decision was a setback for disability rights, advocates were able to use portions of the Court's dicta—the justices' nonbinding comments related to the decision—as the basis for legislative victories in the 1980s. For example, in its dicta, the Court maintained that ending discrimination against people with disabilities included making efforts to remove architectural barriers. This language was cited during the debate over passage of the Fair Housing Amendments Act of 1988.

See also Fair Housing Amendments Act of 1988; Section 504 of the Rehabilitation Act of 1973.

Alliance for Technology Access (ATA)

The Alliance for Technology Access (ATA), founded in 1987, is a network of 43 regional centers set up to help people with disabilities find and use assistive technology, especially computers and computer software. It was organized through the efforts of the Disabled Children's Computer Group (founded in 1983 in Berkeley, California, by parents of children with disabilities, together with interested professionals) and the Office of Special Education at Apple Computer. The ATA remained a project of Apple Computer until 1989, when the independent Foundation for Technology Access was organized as its sponsor. Each ATA center is an independent, nonprofit organization, incorporating consumers, teachers and rehabilitation specialists, service providers, software and technology vendors, and professional and community agencies. In 1993, the ATA provided services to more than 100,000 people.

See also Assistive Technology.

Altered States of the Arts

Altered States of the Arts describes itself as "a nationwide network of creative people who are survivors of the psychiatric system." It seeks to "promote the arts as a vehicle for social change" for ending discrimination and prejudice against people labeled mentally ill. To this end, Altered States of the Arts publishes the quarterly *Altered States*, sponsors conferences, workshops, a talent show, and a troupe of performers, and compiles regional resource lists for use by creative artists "who have been through some sort of psychiatric experience."

Altered States of the Arts was founded in 1990 in Pittsburgh by disability activists Gayle Bluebird, Howie Geld, Dianne

Côté, and Sally Clay to offer people labeled mentally ill a forum for their work. They "believe that the 'madness' of our altered states is a part of human nature to be validated rather than suppressed."

See also Geld, Howard; Psychiatric Survivor Movement.

American Association of People with Disabilities (AAPD)

The formation of the AAPD was announced in July 1995 by Paul Hearne, John Kemp, and Justin Dart Jr., at a gathering in Washington, D.C., to commemorate the fifth anniversary of the signing of the Americans with Disabilities Act (ADA). Its organizers hope that the AAPD will become a mass membership national organization representing the interests of people with disabilities on both a local and national level. Dart has stated that his goal is to have 2 million members enrolled by the year 2000. It is currently headquartered in Washington, D.C.

American Association of the Deaf-Blind (AADB)

The American Association of the Deaf-Blind (AADB) was founded in the 1930s as a correspondence club for people who are both deaf and blind. It grew into a support and service system, providing the loan of braille books, braille-to-print and print-to-braille transcription of personal papers, assistance with shopping, and other essential services.

In 1975, 38 members met at a recreation center managed by the Cleveland Society for the Blind for the first ever AADB convention. Besides socializing and exchanging information, the delegates agreed to pursue an advocacy agenda. The 1994 convention, held at the University of North Carolina in Greensboro, was attended by 240 deaf-blind delegates and more than 400 other participants.

The AADB describes its mission as assuring "that a comprehensive, coordinated system of services is accessible to all deaf-blind persons enabling them to achieve their maximum potential through increased independence, productivity and integration into the community." The AADB also serves as a clearinghouse on information concerning new communication technologies, education, mobility, and other issues of concern to people who are deaf-blind, and it publishes the monthly *Deaf-Blind American*.

The AADB is based in Silver Spring, Maryland, at the headquarters of the National Association of the Deaf. It is a not-for-profit organization. Its membership as of early 1997 was approximately 2,000.

American Coalition of Citizens with Disabilities (ACCD)

The American Coalition of Citizens with Disabilities, Inc., founded in 1975, was one of the nation's preeminent national disability rights groups of the 1970s and early 1980s. The ACCD spearheaded the effort to force the Carter administration to issue regulations implementing Section 504 of the Rehabilitation Act of 1973, used those regulations to push for broad changes in American society, lobbied for passage of the Education for All Handicapped Children Act of 1975, and assisted with the formation of statewide coalitions all across the country. At the height of its activity, the ACCD included more than 80 national, state, and local organizations of and for people with almost every sort of disability.

The major impetus behind the founding of the ACCD came from a group of activists, including Fred Fay and Eunice Fiorito, who met in Washington, D.C., in late 1973. In 1974, Fay, Fiorito, and 150 other advocates met during the annual conference of the President's Committee on Employment of the Handicapped to discuss their proposal for a national cross-disability political organization. A steering committee was formed to draft by-laws, with Deaf activist Al Pimentel elected board chair. Fred C. Schreiber, executive director of the National Association of the Deaf, and Durward McDaniel, co-founder

of the American Council of the Blind, were both early participants in the ACCD, with Schreiber becoming the group's first vice president.

The ACCD began life as a coalition of 19 disability groups with no paid staff and only a small annual budget. One of the first decisions of its new board was to approach the federal Rehabilitation Services Administration (RSA) for funding. Ostensibly, the money was to prepare "a feasibility study to develop a national model for cross-disability communication and cooperation." Fiorito was later quoted in Richard K. Scotch's *From Good Will to Civil Rights* (1984) as saying how this was, in fact, "a pretext to get some money for the coalition to get going." The money raised from the RSA and other sources enabled the ACCD both to set up its own national office in Washington, D.C., and to ask Frank Bowe, a deaf educational psychologist, to become the group's full-time executive director.

The first issue confronted by ACCD was the refusal by the Ford and the Carter administration to issue regulations, drawn up by the Office of Civil Rights within the Department of Health, Education, and Welfare, implementing Section 504 of the Rehabilitation Act of 1973. ACCD called for sit-in demonstrations at HEW offices across the nation to bring public attention to the issue and to put pressure on the Carter administration to approve the regulations. At the end of April 1977, after sit-ins and demonstrations in Boston, Washington, Denver, Atlanta, Chicago, New York, San Francisco, and elsewhere, Secretary Califano relented and published the regulations.

The ACCD then lobbied for passage of the Education for All Handicapped Children Act of 1975 (PL94-142) and the production of the wheelchair accessible Transbus. The former tested the cohesion of ACCD and the notion of cross-disability politics. Advocates in the deaf community were concerned that "mainstreaming" under the act would lead to a return to "oralism," where deaf children would again be forced to reject American Sign

Language in order to assimilate into class-rooms of hearing children. Taking these and other concerns into account, ACCD advocated for an education act that required sign language interpreters to be included as part of making public school education accessible to all disabled children.

The ACCD was not nearly so successful convincing American auto-makers to produce the Transbus, or in forcing federal and state governments to make the nation's mass transit systems accessible. Though Section 504 theoretically covered mass transit systems that receive federal funding and although the Architectural Barriers Act of 1968 covered all new construction using federal funds, the federal government, through the Architectural and Transportation Barriers Compliance Board, routinely granted waivers to transit authorities, allowing them to "fulfill" the requirements of 504 by maintaining segregated paratransit systems for disabled users. These special Dial-a-Ride van programs were almost always underfunded and entirely inadequate in providing service to people with disabilities.

Critics maintained that ACCD was "never the viable national membership group it claimed to be," but rather a "coalition of coalitions." They complained that ACCD's complicated by-laws, designed to limit the clout of member organizations run by nondisabled people, made it difficult to make decisions and set policy, and they had the effect of allowing "paper organizations" with only a few members an equal say with mass membership groups such as the National Association of the Deaf or the Paralyzed Veterans of America. Finally, ACCD's reliance on government and corporate money proved to be a fatal flaw when such funding dried up under the Reagan administration and the recession of the late 1970s and early 1980s. Given these problems, and deep in debt, the ACCD dissolved in 1983.

Despite its demise, ACCD is seen as making a lasting contribution to the disability rights movement. Section 504 and other sections of the Rehabilitation Act remained the most significant civil rights instruments for disabled people until the passage of the Americans with Disabilities Act in 1990. The Education for All Handicapped Children Act (renamed the Individuals with Disabilities Education Act in 1990) opened the doors to a quality education for millions of disabled children. And many of the statewide coalitions sponsored by the ACCD have survived its dissolution and continue to advocate for disability rights.

See also Architectural and Transportation Barriers Compliance Board; Bowe, Frank; Cross-Disability Awareness/Cross-Disability Sensitivity; Education for All Handicapped Children Act of 1975; Fay, Frederick A.; Fiorito, Eunice; HEW Demonstrations; McDaniel, Durwood K.; Section 504 of the Rehabilitation Act of 1973; Schreiber, Frederick C.; Transbus.

References Bowe, Frank. *Changing the Rules* (1986); Scotch, Richard K. *From Good Will to Civil Rights: Transforming Federal Disability Policy* (1984).

American Council of the Blind (ACB)

The American Council of the Blind (ACB) had its origins at the National Federation of the Blind (NFB) annual convention in July 1958. Several delegates felt that the NFB had become too centralized, with policies decided by the leadership without sufficient input from the grassroots membership. There were also differences in editorial policy at NFB publications. Finally, there was a concern that too much of the money raised by local chapters was going to support the national organization.

Over the next two years, a group dubbed the Four Insurgent Generals—Durward K. McDaniel, Marie Boring, Lemar Archibald, and Bradley Burson—outlined a plan for an organization composed primarily of local and special interest affiliates, loosely allied to a central office that would represent them on national issues. The ACB was formally organized according to that plan in 1961.

Today, the ACB has more than 42,000 members organized into 70 state and special interest affiliates. Its annual conventions attract more than 2,000 delegates from all across the United States and several foreign countries. The majority of ACB members are blind or visually disabled; however, membership is also open to persons who are sighted. The focus is on local and grassroots organizing, with affiliates keeping the vast majority of any funds they raise.

Founded in Kansas City, Missouri, the ACB has its headquarters in Washington, D.C. The organization was small at first, with only a few dozen members, but membership expanded dramatically after 1969. The national headquarters lobbies the federal government on legislation and policies dealing with civil rights, employment, rehabilitation services, public transportation, and Social Security. It also serves as an information clearinghouse. The ACB was a member organization of the American Coalition of Citizens with Disabilities and an early supporter of the Americans with Disabilities Act.

ACB's 19 special interest affiliates include such organizations as the American Blind Lawyers Association (ABLA), the Council of Citizens with Low Vision International, Guide Dog Users, Inc., Visually Impaired Veterans of America (VIVA), and the National Alliance of Blind Students. *The Braille Forum*, ACB's monthly newsmagazine, is published in braille, large print, audiocassette, and MS-DOS computer disk. The ACB also has an Electronic Bulletin Board Service and a Washington Connection legislative and employment news hotline.

See also McDaniel, Durwood K.; National Federation of the Blind.

American Disabled for Accessible Public Transit v. Skinner 881 F.2d 1184 3rd Cir. (1989)

At issue in *American Disabled for Accessible Public Transit v. Skinner* (*ADAPT v. Skinner*) was whether or not public transit authorities were required to make their mainline systems accessible to people with disabilities. The case was the result of the controversy over a series of regulations promulgated by the federal Department of

Transportation (DOT) laying out the requirements of public transit authorities under Section 504 of the Rehabilitation Act of 1973 and other federal laws governing their operations.

Accessible mass transit had long been a key issue for disability rights activists. In 1978, the federal Department of Health, Education, and Welfare (HEW) issued guidelines requiring that public transit authorities, all of which received federal funds, make their systems "readily accessible to and usable by handicapped persons." DOT regulations, issued in 1979, required across-the-board alterations to ensure access. These regulations were challenged by the American Public Transit Association (APTA); in 1981, the federal court in *APTA v. Lewis* invalidated the retrofitting requirements. DOT then promulgated a new set of interim regulations, requiring only that transit authorities make "special efforts" for accessibility and giving them a "local option" as to how they might meet their access obligations. Authorities could choose to make their buses accessible by installing wheelchair lifts, to establish a paratransit system using lift-equipped vans separate from the mainline system, or to develop a mixture of the two, using accessible buses for some parts of the system and paratransit for others. The interim regulations also contained a "safe harbor" for transit authorities: there would be no federal oversight of access as long as an authority spent 3.5 percent of federal funds on accessible services. Final regulations issued on 20 May 1986 set minimum standards for paratransit service, restated the "local option," and reset the "safe harbor" requirement at 3 percent of total authority revenues. A coalition of groups, including Disabled in Action of Pennsylvania, the Chicago Council for Disability Rights, the Wisconsin Disability Coalition, and the Coalition of Texans with Disabilities, joined ADAPT and Eastern Paralyzed Veterans of America in filing suit to contest the regulations. After a series of lower court rulings, *ADAPT v. Skinner* was heard by the U.S. Court of Appeals for the Third

Circuit on 5 October 1988, reargued on 15 May 1989, and decided on 24 July 1989.

The appeals court decision was mixed. On the plus side for disability rights advocates it ruled that the 3 percent "safe harbor" was arbitrary and violated federal law and that certain minimum standards of access had to be met, regardless of how much or how little an authority was prepared to spend. The court, however, rejected the argument that Section 504 and other federal laws required transit authorities to provide mainline access, deciding that paratransit was an acceptable alternative, even though it segregated people with disabilities into a separate and, in many respects, unequal system.

The decision in *ADAPT* did not decide the accessible bus issue. Advocates, therefore, pressed for passage of the Americans with Disabilities Act of 1990, with its Title II requirements for accessible mainline public transit.

See also American Disabled for Attendant Programs Today; Paratransit; Public Transportation.

American Disabled for Attendant Programs Today (ADAPT)

The beginnings of American Disabled for Attendant Programs Today (ADAPT) can be traced to a small demonstration in Colorado. At 10 A.M. on 5 July 1978, 19 disability rights activists using wheelchairs surrounded two Regional Transit District (RTD) buses at the intersection of Colfax and Broadway in Denver. The buses, like almost every other bus in the United States at that time, were not equipped to accommodate people who could not use steps. The demonstrators kept them surrounded all day and night, keeping them out of service, and announced the next morning that disability activists would use nonviolent civil disobedience to disrupt Denver bus service until the system made a serious effort to become accessible. Today there is a plaque at the site of this demonstration, erected by the city, to commemorate the courage of these original protesters.

The Denver demonstration and the campaign that followed were organized by the Atlantis Community, Inc., a disability cooperative and independent living center founded in 1975. In addition to disrupting bus service, the group's actions included protesters holding signs as buses rolled by, saying "Why can't I ride too?" and "crawl-ins" where wheelchair users would attempt to crawl up the steps of a bus. They disrupted RTD board meetings, occupied the RTD executive director's office, and spearheaded a ballot initiative changing the city code so that the RTD board would be elected by the general public. Atlantis then lobbied everyone running for a seat on the board. In the fall of 1982, the RTD ordered 89 accessible buses, and, in 1983, the RTD committed to lifts on all buses on all of its routes.

Soon after this victory, Atlantis activists learned that the American Public Transit Association (APTA) would be holding its annual meeting in Denver in October 1983. In July, they convened a meeting of disability activists from around the country to organize a demonstration. It was at this meeting that American Disabled for Accessible Public Transit (later it became American Disabled for Attendant Programs Today) was founded under the slogan "We will ride!"

ADAPT chose the issue of accessible mass transportation for both practical and symbolic reasons. Many people with disabilities are unable to drive or to afford their own cars or modified vans, so they must rely on public transit. Accessible homes, workplaces, churches, and schools are of little use if there is no way to get from one to the other. Symbolically, the call by people with disabilities to ride the bus as equal citizens harkens back to the black civil rights movement of the 1950s. ADAPT organizers repeatedly cited Rosa Parks and the Reverend Martin Luther King, Jr., as direct inspirations. A major part of the group's energy from October 1983 to October 1989 was directed at confronting APTA, with protesters appearing at every APTA convention for six years

John Clayton of ADAPT locks his neck to the door at the Richard B. Russell Federal Building in Atlanta, Georgia, as he and about 100 protesters block the doors to the building on 3 October 1990. ADAPT demanded a telephone meeting with the U.S. Department of Health and Human Services director in order to discuss increased funding for personal assistance services.

straight. At each of these actions people with disabilities attempted to block access into and out of the convention sites and to disrupt business as usual. In ten years ADAPT sponsored 40 major actions and many more smaller events, marches, and vigils.

In 1990, ADAPT shifted its focus to a major effort on behalf of the Americans with Disabilities Act (ADA). In March, ADAPT organized the Wheels of Justice march from the White House to the Capitol, in which between 500 and 1,000 people participated. On 12 March, ADAPT staged a "crawl-up" at the Capitol building, where more than 100 demonstrators left their wheelchairs to crawl up the building's front steps. On 13 March, some 150 ADAPT demonstrators took over the Capitol rotunda. More than 100 demon-

strators were arrested at this action alone, and many believe this demonstration helped to push the ADA through at a crucial moment when disability rights advocates feared that it might be stalled or weakened by unfriendly amendments. Among the 2,000 disability activists invited by President Bush to witness the signing of the Americans with Disabilities Act on 26 July 1990 were ADAPT representatives from 25 states.

With the passage of the ADA, ADAPT's main priority became the struggle for personal assistance services (PAS). ADAPT's strategy in this new campaign has been to target nursing home owners and representatives, the American Medical Association (AMA), and officials of the U.S. Department of Health and Human Services for demonstrations and civil disobedience, and to demand that the federal government redirect 25 percent of the money it spends on nursing homes into PAS. It is also urging investors to divest themselves of their interest in nursing homes.

See also American Disabled for Accessible Public Transit v. Skinner; Americans with Disabilities Act of 1990; Atlantis Community, Inc.; Auberger, Mike; Blank, Wade; Kafka, Robert; Personal Assistance Services; Public Transportation; Thomas, Stephanie; Wheels of Justice.

References Hershey, Laura, "Wade Blank's Liberated Community," in Barrett Shaw, ed., *The Ragged Edge: The Disability Experience from the Pages of the First Fifteen Years of* The Disability Rag (1994); Johnson, Mary, "On the Barricades with ADAPT," in Barrett Shaw, ed., *The Ragged Edge* (1994).

American Federation of the Physically Handicapped (AFPH)

The American Federation of the Physically Handicapped (AFPH) was a national, cross-disability political advocacy organization active in the 1940s and 1950s. It was founded in 1940 by Paul A. Strachan (1894–1972), a hearing-disabled labor activist and special assistant to the U.S. Secretary of Labor. At its height the organization had more than 200 local chapters, called lodges, all across the country. It was officially chartered in Washington, D.C., on 20 August 1942.

The AFPH was most successful in its campaign to convince Congress to establish a National Employ the Physically Handicapped Week. Strachan and the AFPH first approached Congress in 1942, and the legislation passed in 1945. These annual Hire the Handicapped campaigns brought together disability advocates, business leaders, and government officials. In 1952, the group in charge of overseeing these campaigns on a national level became the President's Committee on Employment of the Physically Handicapped. The AFPH remained integrally involved in the early work of the president's committee, pushing for greater efforts by government and business to break down barriers to employment and for inclusion in the workplace of people with the most severe disabilities. The AFPH also advocated for passage of the Vocational Rehabilitation Amendments of 1954, expanding federal rehabilitation services, and the Social Security Amendments of 1956, creating the Social Security Disability Insurance (SSDI) program. It was less successful in its campaign for legislation bringing all federal disability programs into one agency.

Strachan and other AFPH members were outspoken in their criticisms of "do-gooders" who offered pity rather than meaningful opportunities for rehabilitation and employment. In 1950, Strachan wrote that there "should be real Handicapped people on the Governor's Committees [to Employ the Physically Handicapped]" as opposed to only nondisabled "experts." Editorials in the AFPH newsletter *Valor* castigated nondisabled rehabilitation professionals with "their out-worn theories that the Handicapped—because of disability—are useless, as self-supporting citizens." "How many Handicapped have ever had 'Liberty'? How many have felt that they have been and are free from the yoke of those who have a say on their futures...?" The AFPH criticized public assistance programs that penalized disabled people for seeking work or rehabilitation, calling for an end to what modern disability activists call "disincentives." It also convinced the federal government to allow disabled applicants to take civil service exams. At the AFPH 1952 National Conference on Placement of Severely Handicapped, however, Strachan noted that this "had very little effect upon government personnel policies, because, although the Handicapped may have passed such examinations, with good marks, yet respective agencies would refuse to appoint them."

The AFPH cultivated strong ties with organized labor, particularly with the American Federation of Labor (AFL), and received funds from the AFL to lobby for legislation of importance to disabled workers, including reforms in the state Worker's Compensation programs. The AFPH also worked closely with Disabled American Veterans, calling for research into the development of better artificial limbs.

The demise of the AFPH began with disagreements over Strachan's proposal to found a community in Florida for people with severe disabilities. By the mid-1950s it had also run into financial difficulties. A convention called at Grand Rapids, Michigan, in 1958 failed to reach agreement on these issues, and the American Federation of the Physically Handicapped was officially dissolved. About 100 of the conferees joined together to found the National Association of the Physically Handicapped, Inc. (NAPH), which today continues to advocate for the rights of people with disabilities.

See also Disincentives; National Association of the Physically Handicapped, Inc.; President's Committee on Employment of People with Disabilities; Social Security, Social Security Disability Insurance, Supplemental Security Income; Vocational Rehabilitation.

American Foundation for the Blind (AFB)

The American Foundation for the Blind (AFB) was founded in 1921. It came out of a call by the leading blindness organizations of the day—the American Association for the Instruction of the Blind (AAIB) and the American Association of Workers for the Blind (AAWB)—for a central clearinghouse for information and advocacy related to blindness. The AFB's first president was Major Moses Charles Migel, who had donated $7,000 of the $10,000 needed to establish the new organization's first office. Fund-raising for the AFB was a principal cause of Helen Keller, who became closely identified with the organization in the 1920s, until the time of her retirement in 1961. Robert Irwin was its leader throughout the 1920s and 1930s. Irwin and the AFB advocated self-reliance and opposed pensions or special schools for blind people.

Today, the AFB publishes books, pamphlets, videos, and periodicals about blindness, both for blind individuals and for sighted people who work in the field. It publishes the *Journal of Visual Impairment & Blindness*, the leading professional journal on the subject of visual disability, and it provides information on areas such as education, employment, aging, technology, and access. The AFB advocates on issues of concern to people with visual disabilities and was a supporter of the Americans with Disabilities Act of 1990.

See also Irwin, Robert Benjamin; Keller, Helen Adams.

American Indian Disability Legislation Project (AIDL)

There are approximately 1.9 million American Indians and Native Alaskans living in the United States, about half of whom live on or near one of 547 state or federally recognized reservations. According to a 1987 study by the U.S. Department of Education (DOE), the prevalence of disability among American Indians, particularly those who live on reservations, is among the highest of any ethnic group in the country. Even so, federal disability civil rights legislation, for example the Americans with Disabilities Act of 1990 (ADA), does not extend to Indian reservations, which are administered by independent tribal governments.

The American Indian Disability Legislation Project (AIDL) was established in 1993 to collect data "as to whether such laws [as the ADA] and regulations exist among the tribes or whether tribes even view these laws as potentially valuable or culturally relevant." The AIDL pulled together an advisory panel representing 11 tribes, which included American Indian disability rights advocates and researchers such as Michael Blatchford (Navajo), Julie Clay (Omaha), Sidney Claymore (Lakota, Standing Rock Sioux), Stephen Clincher (Fort Peck Sioux), and Jene McCovey (Yurok, Tolowa, Hupa). Working under the auspices of the Rural Institute on Disabilities at the University of Montana and with the endorsement of the National Congress of American Indians, the AIDL collected information from members of tribes in 29 of the lower 48 states and Alaska. Among other results, the data showed that buildings used by the federal government and the U.S. Bureau of Indian Affairs, together with tribal courts and jails, were among those public buildings least likely to be accessible. Only one tribe among the 143 surveyed was reported to have adopted the ADA. "Several others have said that while they have discussed access and employment issues, they do not have a written policy. As such, disability legislation among the tribes remains an unaddressed issue of importance."

See also Clay, Julie Anna; Multicultural Issues; Minority Persons with Disabilities; Rural Institute on Disabilities.

References Clay, Julie, Carol Locust, Tom Seekins, et al., *American Indian Disability Legislation Project: Findings of a National Survey of Tribal Governments* (1995).

American National Standards Institute (ANSI)
See Architectural Access.

American School for the Deaf
The American School for the Deaf in Hartford, Connecticut, was the first public school for deaf people in the United States and the first permanent school for children with disabilities anywhere in the Western Hemisphere. Thomas Hopkins Gallaudet (for whom Gallaudet University in Washington, D.C., is named) traveled to Europe in 1815 to study methods of teaching deaf children. While there, he became acquainted with the system of sign language developed by deaf people in France and codified by Abbé Charles Michel de l'Epée at the Royal Institution for Deaf-Mutes in Paris and by his successor, Abbé Roch Ambriose Sicard. Laurent Clerc, a deaf student of Sicard's, traveled with Gallaudet when he returned to the United States, and they founded what was then called the Connecticut Asylum for the Education of Deaf and Dumb Persons in April 1817. The school became a center of deaf life, and the signs brought over from France by Clerc

had a tremendous influence on the evolution of American Sign Language (ASL).

The school was also host for the nation's oldest educational periodical *The American Annals of the Deaf*, which began publication in 1847. John Vickrey Van Cleve and Barry A. Crouch, in *A Place of Their Own: Creating the Deaf Community in America* (1989), identify the New England Gallaudet Association of the Deaf, formally established in 1854 in Montpelier, Vermont, by alumni of the school, as the first regional organization of deaf people in America.

See also American Sign Language; Clerc, Laurent; Gallaudet, Thomas Hopkins; Gallaudet University; New England Gallaudet Association of the Deaf.

References Gannon, Jack R., *Deaf Heritage: A Narrative History of the Deaf* (1981); Lane, Harlan, *When the Mind Hears: A History of the Deaf* (1984); Schein, Jerome D., *At Home among Strangers* (1989); Van Cleve, John Vickrey, and Barry A. Crouch, *A Place of Their Own: Creating the Deaf Community in America* (1989).

American Sign Language (ASL)
American Sign Language (ASL) is the language of American Deaf culture. Contrary to the widely held view among hearing people that it is simply English rendered into signs, ASL is considered by linguists to be an entirely separate language, with its own grammar, vocabulary, idioms, dialects, and artistic forms. It is a visual language, using the hands and face to articulate and the eyes as receptors, while its grammar uses three-dimensional space. Like any other language, it evolves over time so that differences can be seen between films of signers made in the early part of this century and signers today. For almost 100 years ASL was a suppressed and denigrated language, and the struggle to bring ASL "out of the closet" is perhaps the central struggle of the civil rights movement for Deaf Americans to date.

Sign language has been used throughout recorded history. Arden Neisser, in *The Other Side of Silence* (1983), cites references to sign language in the Talmud and in the literature of classical Greece. A group of Benedictine monks in Italy used

A sign language interpreter addresses the deaf audience during a commencement ceremony at the University of Michigan in 1991. Although sign language has been used throughout history, the struggle to bring the language of American deaf culture "out of the closet" has been the largest battle of the civil rights movement for deaf Americans to date.

signs, in approximately A.D. 530, as a way to communicate after they had taken vows of silence, while a one-handed signing system was in use in Spain during the sixteenth century. Pedro (or Pablo) Ponce de Leon, a Benedictine monk credited as being the first (circa 1550) instructor of deaf children, is also cited as the first to use sign language as a teaching tool. It can be assumed, however, that deaf people had been using signs long before this. When the Abbé Charles Michel de l'Epée opened his school for deaf children in Paris in 1755 (the first such school in the world), there was already a French sign language, which he learned and then modified to be an approximation of spoken French. His work was carried on by his successor at the Royal

Institution for Deaf-Mutes, the Abbé Roch Ambriose Sicard.

Thomas Hopkins Gallaudet, intent on opening a school for deaf people in the United States, visited Europe in 1815 and was introduced to the French sign language by Sicard. When Gallaudet returned to the United States to found the American School for the Deaf in 1817, he brought with him Laurent Clerc, a deaf man who became his assistant and principal instructor at the school. The school in Hartford, Connecticut, became a focal point for the American Deaf community, and French and American signing blended so that, according to linguist James Woodward, roughly 60 percent of American signs today can be traced to a French origin.

In the 1860s, American schools for the deaf began to switch over from the "manual" or "combined" methods of instruction to "oralism"—the use of speech and lipreading to the exclusion of sign language. ASL was denigrated as "pidgin" English, and oralists went to great lengths to keep their students from learning or using sign, even sponsoring legislation prohibiting its instruction in state funded schools. Few hearing scholars were interested in learning ASL, fewer still in studying it as a serious language in its own right.

All this changed in 1960, when a hearing linguist at Gallaudet College (now Gallaudet University) in Washington, D.C., William C. Stokoe, Jr., published the first linguistic analysis of ASL. In 1965, with his deaf colleagues Carl Croneberg and Dorothy Casterline, Stokoe published *A Dictionary of American Sign Language on Linguistic Principles*. At first there was little interest among the Deaf community itself. Instead, hearing linguists and scholars, followed by hearing graduate and undergraduate college students, began studying what for them was an entirely new and esoteric language. Suddenly, there was an explosion of books about and classes in ASL, and deaf users found themselves in the entirely new position of being asked to teach and explain their language.

"The discovery of American Sign Language as a true language," writes historian Jack R. Gannon, "has led to the identification of deaf culture as a rich, untapped field of study. . . . [and] has influenced the attitudes of deaf persons toward themselves, their language, their culture and made them take a closer look at their rights as American citizens" (1981).

It is estimated that 200,000 to 400,000 Americans and Canadians use American Sign Language as their first language.

See also Bell, Alexander Graham; Deaf Culture; Gallaudet, Edward Miner; Oral School, Oralism.

References Gannon, Jack R., *Deaf Heritage: A Narrative History of Deaf America* (1981); Neisser, Arden, *The Other Side of Silence: Sign Language and the Deaf Community in America* (1983); Schein, Jerome D., *At Home among Strangers* (1989).

Americans with Disabilities Act of 1990 (ADA)

The Americans with Disability Act of 1990 (ADA) marks the greatest single achievement of the disability rights movement to date. It offers, for the first time in history, broad civil rights protection for disabled Americans, and its passage was the culmination of work by thousands of committed individuals.

As early as 1977, the White House Conference on Handicapped Individuals passed a resolution calling on Congress to amend the Civil Rights Act of 1964 and the Voting Rights Act of 1965 to include people with disabilities. The defeat of Jimmy Carter by Ronald Reagan in 1980 was seen by some as a setback for such legislation. Furthermore, not everyone in the disability community thought that a push for a single, all-inclusive law was the best course to take. Justin Dart Jr., disability rights advocate, remembers how "the consensus was for advocating legislation that provided services and partial rights in incremental steps." When the idea of major new civil rights legislation came up, some disability rights activists would ask, "We can't even enforce Section 504 [of the Rehabilitation Act], why waste time talking about more?"

The first step toward changing that consensus came in 1982, when Joseph Dusenbury, chair of the National Council on the Handicapped (NCH), authorized Vicechair Dart to pull together recommendations for federal policy in the field of disability law. The council's attorney, Robert L. Burgdorf Jr., had long harbored the idea of a single, sweeping, federal disability rights act, and eagerly took up the challenge. Dart met with disability leaders in every state, and, in 1983, issued a report calling for Congress to "act forthwith to include persons with disabilities in the Civil Rights Act of 1964 and other civil and voting rights legislation and regulations." Over the next three years Dart, newly appointed NCH chair Sandra Parrino, NCH director Lex Frieden, and Burgdorf drafted *Toward Independence*, a report to Congress and the president recommending passage

President George Bush and Barbara Bush receive applause by some of the 2,000 people from major disability groups that gathered to witness the signing of the Americans with Disabilities Act (ADA) on 26 July 1990. The landmark civil rights legislation for people with disabilities is the greatest achievement of the disability rights movement to date.

of "a comprehensive law requiring equal opportunity for individuals with disabilities." Burgdorf drafted such a law, and Sen. Lowell Weicker (R–CT) and Rep. Tony Coelho (D–CA) introduced the bill into Congress in April 1988. Although it won the endorsement of many members, as well as presidential candidates George Bush and Michael Dukakis, the bill died at the end of the session.

The bill was redrafted in 1989 by staff working for Senators Edward M. Kennedy (D–MA) and Thomas Harkin (D–IA), most notably Robert Silverstein and Carolyn Ossolinik, with the direct input of a committee of disability rights attorneys coordinated by Patrisha A. Wright, director of the Washington office of the Disability Rights Education and Defense Fund (DREDF). Robert Funk, representing the White House, John Wodatch from the

Department of Justice, and Maureen West from the office of Sen. Robert Dole (R–KS) were also involved in the later stages of this revision. The new draft changed some of the original bill's provisions, eliminating requirements that older structures be retrofitted for access and that insurance companies be prohibited from discriminating against people with disabilities, but it expanded the bill's protections to cover public accommodations. It also made the section on public transportation more explicit.

After Weicker's defeat in the 1988 elections and Coelho's resignation in 1990, advocacy for the ADA in the House was directed by Rep. Steny Hoyer (D–MD) and Rep. Hamilton Fish Jr. (R–NY), while Senate leadership passed to Harkin, Kennedy, and John S. McCain (R-AR). Patrisha Wright became the coordinator and chief strategist of the community campaign to pass the ADA. The multipronged effort included a grassroots campaign, coordinated on the national level by Justin Dart Jr. at the National Council and Marilyn Golden at DREDF. The legislative campaign in Washington was managed by Wright and Elizabeth Savage at the Epilepsy Foundation of America, who oversaw the lobbying efforts of some 75 national disability, civil rights, religious, and civic organizations.

The ADA was now at the top of the agenda for the largest coalition of disability rights organizations ever assembled, including American Disabled for Attendant Programs Today (ADAPT), the American Council of the Blind, the National Association for Retarded Citizens (ARC), United Cerebral Palsy Associations, DREDF, the National Association of the Deaf, Paralyzed Veterans of America, and the National Council on Independent Living. In all, the bill was endorsed by some 180 national organizations. Justin Dart Jr. and Elizabeth Boggs, co-chairs of the Task Force on the Rights and Empowerment of Americans with Disabilities, established by Rep. Major R. Owens (D–NY), traveled across the country, speaking to and gathering testimony from thousands of people at dozens of events. People with disabilities were encouraged to keep diaries of their day-to-day experiences of discrimination, which they then sent to their representatives in Congress. Organizations advocating for people with HIV/AIDS, as well as nondisability civil rights groups, most notably the Leadership Conference on Civil Rights, also supported the ADA.

There were various attempts in the House to derail or weaken the bill, including efforts to limit its protections for people with HIV/AIDS and psychiatric disabilities. Advocates put together a letter writing and phone campaign, while ADAPT organized its Wheels of Justice march on Washington, at one point occupying the Capitol rotunda. During the final days of deliberation, congressional conservatives offered an amendment that would have removed antidiscrimination

protection for food handlers who were HIV positive. Wright called for a meeting of disability and gay and lesbian advocates at the White House, where they told Boyden Gray, legal counsel to President George Bush, that they would rather lose entirely than pass a bill that left people with HIV/AIDS unprotected. The limiting amendment was defeated. The ADA was approved by the House of Representatives on 12 July 1990, by a vote of 377 to 28. The next day it passed the Senate, 91 to 6. President Bush signed the ADA into law on 26 July 1990, in a ceremony on the White House lawn that was witnessed by more than 2,000 disability rights advocates.

The ADA as passed borrowed from the concepts generated by Section 504 of the Rehabilitation Act of 1973 as well as from the Civil Rights Act of 1964. Title I prohibits businesses with 15 or more employees from discriminating against qualified individuals with disabilities. Employers must provide "reasonable accommodation" for people with disabilities who are otherwise qualified to do the job in question, unless "an undue hardship" would result. Employers may reject or fire employees who pose a direct threat to the health or safety of other individuals in the workplace. People who are current users of illegal drugs are excluded from protection. Religious organizations may give preference in employment to their own members and may require employees to conform to the organization's tenets. Complaints by employees may be filed with the federal Equal Employment Opportunity Commission (EEOC). Complainants may also file suit in federal court to stop discrimination and to recover back pay.

Title II prohibits discrimination in public services provided by state and local governments and by the National Railroad Passenger Corporation (Amtrak). All government facilities, services, and communications must be accessible. Title II uses the regulations promulgated under Section 504 of the Rehabilitation Act as its standard for accessibility, and those promulgated under Section 505 to define "remedies, procedures, and rights" provided to people alleging discrimination because of their disability by state or local governments. Title II also prohibits discrimination in public mass transportation. All new buses must be accessible, and drivers must announce stops at key intersections and transfer points. New bus and rail stations must be accessible, and alterations of existing stations must be made so as to render them accessible. In addition, transit authorities must provide a paratransit service to individuals who cannot use fixed route service, unless this would result in an undue burden, that is, an action requiring substantial and disproportionate difficulty or expense, to be determined on a case-by-case basis. "Key stations" in older transit systems were to be made accessible by July 1993, but transit authorities could apply for extensions of up to 30 years. Title II gave railway transit authorities five years to ensure that one car per train was accessible. Complaints of violations of Title II can be filed with the federal Department of Transportation (DOT). A complainant can also bring a private lawsuit. Standards on accessible vehicles and stations are issued by the Architectural and Transportation Barriers Compliance Board, a free-standing federal board appointed by the president, while regulations regarding services are promulgated by the U.S. Department of Transportation.

Title III prohibits discrimination against people with disabilities in public accommodations, such as restaurants, hotels, theaters, pharmacies, retail stores, health clubs, museums, libraries, parks, private schools, and day care centers. Private clubs and religious organizations are exempt. All entities covered under this title are required to make "reasonable modifications" in policies, practices, and procedures in order to avoid or end discrimination. Auxiliary aids and services to increase effective communication must be provided to individuals with vision, hearing, or other impairments, unless this provision would pose an undue burden. Efforts to remove physical barriers must be made, providing such removal is "readily achievable." All new

constructions in public accommodations and commercial facilities must be accessible, as must alterations, as long as the added costs of making the facilities accessible are not disproportionate to the overall cost of the alterations. Individuals bringing lawsuits under Title III may not collect monetary damages.

Title IV deals with telecommunications. The nation's telephone system is for the most part inaccessible to people who are deaf or speech disabled. Even with the advent of the TDD (telecommunications device for the deaf, commonly called a TTY), users are able to have conversations only with those whose phones are similarly equipped. Title IV mandates that "common carriers"—telephone and telecommunications companies—make available to TTY users access to relay systems that enable them to communicate with phone users who do not have a TTY. A TTY user can phone a hearing and speaking TTY user at a relay center, who then transmits the message via an ordinary telephone to the intended recipient. Title IV also requires federally funded television programming to be closed captioned. Complaints by individuals can be filed with the Federal Communications Commission (FCC).

Title V contains various miscellaneous provisions. For example, it provides exemptions to insurance providers, allowing them to use disability as a factor in refusing insurance or setting premiums. It "reaffirms that nothing in the Wilderness Act" prohibits "the use of a wheelchair in a wilderness area. . . ." It excludes transvestites from protection, as well as transsexuals, pedophiles, exhibitionists, voyeurs, people with "gender identity disorders not resulting from physical impairments, or other sexual disorders," compulsive gamblers, kleptomaniacs, pyromaniacs, and people with psychoactive disorders "resulting from current illegal use of drugs." It also stipulates that nothing in the ADA should be seen as negating or limiting protections provided by previous disability rights laws, on either the federal or state level.

Although critics of the ADA had predicted a flood of litigation to be brought under the act, in the first five years after its passage only 600 to 700 lawsuits were filed. A Harris Poll commissioned by the National Council on Disability in 1995 found that more than 90 percent of business executives supported the antidiscrimination provisions of the ADA. Nevertheless, after the 1994 congressional elections, a number of members of Congress, among them House Speaker Newt Gingrich (R–GA) and House Majority Leader Dick Armey (R-TX), condemned the ADA as wasteful, unnecessary, and absurd. Alarmed disability rights advocates organized to fight this anti-ADA backlash.

Passage of the ADA brought with it some disillusionment. People who expected to see an overnight change in the way society treated those with disabilities were disappointed. Some protested that it contained too many loopholes for those wishing to avoid providing access. Especially troublesome were the provisions exempting insurance companies and religious organizations. It is clear, however, that the ADA has had a significant impact. Its passage has made disability rights a part of the national agenda and has raised people with disabilities to full citizenship under the law for the first time in American history.

See also American Disabled for Attendant Programs Today; Architectural and Transportation Barriers Compliance Board; Burgdorf, Robert L., Jr.; Coelho, Tony; Dart, Justin, Jr.; Disability Rights Education and Defense Fund; Fay, Frederick A.; Funk, Robert J.; Kemp, Evan, Jr.; National Council on Disability; Reasonable Accommodation/Reasonable Modification; Savage, Elizabeth; Section 504 of the Rehabilitation Act of 1973; Telecommunications Devices for the Deaf, Teletypewriters, and Text Telephones; Undue Hardship/Undue Burden; Wheels of Justice March; White House Conference on Handicapped Individuals; Wright, Patrisha A.

References Gostin, Lawrence O., and Beyer, Henry A., eds., *Implementing the Americans with Disabilities Act* (1993); National Council on the Handicapped, *On the Threshold of Independence: Progress on Legislative Recommendations from "Toward Independence"* (1988); Shapiro, Joseph P., *No Pity: People with Disabilities Forging a New Civil Rights Movement* (1993); Treanor, Richard Bryant, *We Overcame: The Story of Civil Rights for Disabled People* (1993).

Americans with Disabilities Newsletter

Americans with Disabilities Newsletter was founded in 1994 and is a publication of Positive Workforce for America, Inc. Based in Hillsdale, New York, the newsletter describes itself as "a comprehensive and affordable source of information on all the issues that have an impact on people with disabilities." A 1996 issue included stories on proposed changes in federal Medicaid regulations, the lack of affordable health insurance for people with disabilities, and "New Ramps to Cyberspace: Access Is Promised, Not Guaranteed," on access to the Internet for people with disabilities. Each issue summarizes the most recent federal court decisions and comments on prominent media stories about people with disabilities. The circulation of the ADA newsletter is approximately 2,600.

Ameslan

See American Sign Language.

The Arc

The Arc (formerly, National Association for Retarded Children, National Association for Retarded Citizens, known as NARC or ARC) was founded in 1950 as a national organization of parents of children with cognitive disabilities. Its mission is to secure "for all people with mental retardation the opportunity to choose and realize their goals of where and how they learn, live, work, and play" and to reduce the incidence of and limit "the consequence of mental retardation through education, research, advocacy and the support of families, friends and community." The Arc, along with United Cerebral Palsy Associations, was the major organization in the American parents' movement of the 1950s and 1960s.

At the time The Arc was founded, the vast majority of Americans believed that mental retardation was a shameful thing. Parents of children labeled mentally retarded were encouraged to feel guilty about their "failure" to have a "normal" child, and physicians routinely recommended that these children be incarcerated in state institutions. The eugenics movement during the first decades of the century ostracized the "feeble minded" as threats to society. At the annual meeting of the American Association on Mental Retardation in 1930, for example, there was discussion of whether or not mentally retarded adults and children should be sterilized, with a majority favoring at least some program of selective involuntary sterilization. In the late 1940s, when a mother in Bergen, New Jersey, wrote a letter to her local paper, asking to hear from parents of other institutionalized children, the editor at first refused to publish it, fearing that the mother would file a lawsuit once she experienced the shame associated with being publicly identified as the parent of a retarded child. (The group sparked by this letter became the nucleus of what would become the New Jersey chapter of ARC). Institutions built to incarcerate people who were developmentally disabled were generally massive, forbidding places where over-crowding, malnutrition, poor sanitary conditions, violence, and neglect were rife. Many people spent their entire lives in such state "schools," where there was generally no schooling, only "custodial" care. Parents who attempted to raise their developmentally disabled children at home had little or no community support, even though they were often denied the right to send their children to public school.

In the 1930s, these parents began to organize small support groups that would later grow into citywide and then statewide associations. Among the earliest were groups in Cleveland, Ohio, (founded in 1933) and Washington State (founded in 1936). Originally, such support groups had no staff, offices, or funds, but met informally in parents' homes to discuss their mutual concerns. By the end of the 1940s, there were more than 80 such associations in cities and towns across the country. Five local associations, from Washington, California, Massachusetts, Ohio, and New York, called for an organizing convention

to be held in Minneapolis, 28 September–1 October 1950, at which the National Association for Retarded Children (NARC) was founded.

During its first four years, NARC had no paid staff and no central office. That situation changed when actress Dale Evans Rogers donated the royalties from her bestseller, *Angel Unaware* (1953), the story of her cognitively disabled child. NARC opened its first headquarters in New York City in 1954, with Salvatore DiMichael as the organization's first executive director. By 1955, the association had some 29,000 members organized into 412 local chapters.

Much of the early work done by NARC chapters focused on education. Parents, seeing their children rejected by the public schools, formed their own schools in church basements and private homes, and they worked to pressure their elected representatives to make changes in state laws and funding. Elizabeth Boggs, one of NARC's founders and chair of its Education Committee, drafted the Educational Bill of Rights for the Retarded Child, which was adopted by NARC in 1953, becoming the framework for the organization's education advocacy.

In 1957, Gunnar Dybwad became NARC's executive director. Dybwad, an attorney who had worked as the director of state programs for juvenile offenders, strongly believed that the oppression of people with mental disabilities was a political and legal issue. Inspired by the U.S. Supreme Court decision in *Brown v. Board of Education* (1954), he looked to the black civil rights movement as a model for effective action. Even after stepping down as executive director in 1963, Dybwad continued to be a consultant to NARC and to local association chapters, and his perspective had a crucial impact on the evolution of their advocacy.

The 1960s brought changes in the public's attitude toward mental retardation, changes for which ARC was largely responsible. A major step forward came when the Kennedy family publicly acknowledged that the president's sister was cognitively disabled. In 1961, President Kennedy appointed a Presidential Panel on Mental Retardation, with Elizabeth Boggs as one of its members. As a result of the panel's recommendations, Congress passed the Maternal and Child Health and Mental Retardation Planning Amendments as well as the Mental Retardation Facilities and Community Mental Health Centers Construction Act in 1963. ARC also successfully lobbied for passage of the Primary and Secondary Education Act of 1965, which represented an unprecedented federal commitment to special education. By this time, ARC membership totaled more than 100,000.

Many ARC members, however, were impatient with the pace of these changes. In particular, they were frustrated at the continuing exclusion of their children from public schools and appalled at the inhumane conditions inside the state institutions. In the fall of 1968, a delegation from the Pennsylvania ARC (PARC) met with Dybwad to discuss the problem. Dybwad believed that the time had come to seek radical change through the federal courts, and after some hesitation, PARC agreed to file a class action suit. PARC hired attorney Thomas K. Gilhool and brought suit in 1969.

Although the particular issue in *PARC v. Pennsylania* (1972) was the unconstitutionality of certain state laws that acted to bar "retarded" children from the public schools, the case had ramifications far beyond Pennsylvania. In striking down these laws, the federal courts for the first time established the right of children with all manner of disabilities to receive a public education. Perhaps of even more significance, *PARC*, together with other lawsuits brought by other ARC chapters and mental patient advocates such as Kenneth Donaldson and Bruce Ennis, established federal litigation as a powerful tool in the struggle for disability rights. "Litigation," wrote Gilhool in a report to the PARC Board of Directors, "has inevitably not only the function of securing a particular result, but of displaying facts and conditions clearly and precisely both before the public and before decision makers. . . ." Indeed, the evidence in PARC was so compelling that after only one day of testimony the federal court recommended that the state enter into a consent agreement prohibiting the exclusion of children labeled mentally retarded from the public schools, a recommendation that the state followed.

The effects of this legal victory cannot be overstated. *PARC*, together with *Wyatt v. Stickney* (1974), *Mills v. Board of Education* (1972), and other lawsuits that followed, opened a floodgate of revelations about the inhumanity of state institutions and the injustice of excluding disabled children from the public schools. This led directly to the shift toward deinstitutionalization in the 1970s and 1980s and to the establishment of community-based programs such as supported living and supported employment. Congressional sponsors of the Education for All Handicapped Children Act of 1975 (Pub. Law 94-142), of which ARC was an important supporter, cited the testimony produced during *PARC* and *Mills* to support their argument that a federal right-to-education law was needed. ARC, together with United Cerebral Palsy Associations, also lobbied for passage of the Developmental Disabilities Act of 1970 and the Developmentally Disabled Assistance and Bill of Rights Act of 1975. These two laws became cornerstones relating to the rights of and programs for children with "developmental disabilities," a term which had not previously existed.

In 1974, the Association for Retarded Children changed its name to the Association for Retarded Citizens, to reflect the fact that many of the "children" were now adults and to counteract the stereotype that people with cognitive disabilities were "perpetual children" "who never grew." The 1970s also saw the founding of People First, a grassroots organization not of parents, but of people who themselves have cognitive disabilities. Members of People First and other self-advocacy groups saw ARC as paternalistic. Indeed, an early ARC brochure was titled *We Speak for*

Them, an assertion that angered many people with cognitive disabilities. ARC changed its name again, in October 1991, because "members, chapter leaders, young parents and people who have mental retardation had become increasingly uncomfortable over careless, inappropriate and too-frequent use of the label 'retarded.' The word therefore became unacceptable in the association's name." The organization's name is no longer an acronym, but simply "The Arc," with the tag line, "a national association on mental retardation."

The Arc was a supporter of the Americans with Disabilities Act of 1990. During the 1990s it also advocated on behalf of criminal defendants and offenders with cognitive disabilities, undertook an AIDS education program, and sponsored numerous research, advocacy, and educational programs and projects. It continues to publish a wide range of materials on the subject of cognitive disability.

In 1996, The Arc had 140,000 members organized into 1,200 state and local chapters. Its national headquarters is in Arlington, Texas.

See also Boggs, Elizabeth; Developmental Disabilities; Developmentally Disabled Assistance and Bill of Rights Act of 1975; Dybwad, Gunnar; Education for All Handicapped Children Act of 1975; Gilhool, Thomas K.; *Mills v. Board of Education;* Parents' Movement; *Pennsylvania Association for Retarded Children v. Commonwealth of Pennsylvania;* People First, People First International; President's Panel/President's Committee on Mental Retardation; *Wyatt v. Stickney.*

References Dybwad, Gunnar, and Hank Bersani, Jr., eds., *New Voices: Self-Advocacy by People with Disabilities* (1996); Thomson, Mildred, *Prologue: A Minnesota Story of Mental Retardation Showing Changing Attitudes and Philosophies Prior to September 1, 1959* (1963); Trent, James W., Jr., *Inventing the Feeble Mind: A History of Mental Retardation in the United States* (1994).

Architectural Access

It is estimated that some 15 percent of the world's people have some form of disability and that in the United States perhaps 12 percent of the population is disabled. While the exact percentages may have changed over time, it is clear that people with disabilities have always been a substantial part of the population. And yet, buildings all over the world have been and continue to be built as if people with disabilities do not exist. Stairs, narrow doorways and corridors, high thresholds between rooms, inaccessible bathrooms, and various other architectural traditions are all barriers to the participation of people with disabilities in society.

The first serious look at the problem of architectural access began following World War II, with the return to civilian life of thousands of disabled veterans. The G.I. Bill provided the opportunity for many of these disabled veterans to enter or continue college. They soon discovered, however, that their campuses, like the rest of America, were not built to accommodate people with disabilities. To address this problem, the U.S. Veterans Administration published a set of construction and criteria standards for campuses receiving federal funds under the G.I. Bill. Two early pioneers of architectural access were architect Leon Chatelain Jr., president of the American Institute of Architects in Washington, D.C., and Timothy Nugent, director of the Rehabilitation Education Center at the University of Illinois. In 1959, Nugent became director of research and development for the American National Standards Institute, Inc. (ANSI) Project A-117, a committee of architects, builders, industry and government representatives, rehabilitation professionals, and disability rights groups such as Paralyzed Veterans of America, formed under the aegis of the President's Committee on the Employment of the Physically Handicapped (now the President's Committee on Employment of People with Disabilities) and the National Society for Crippled Children and Adults (now the Easter Seals Society) to develop access standards to be used by architects and builders all across the country. In 1961, Project A-117 published its landmark *American Standard Specifications for Making Buildings Accessible to, and Usable by, the Physically Handicapped.* These specifications became the basis for all subsequent legislation and standards relating to architectural access, including the Architectural Barriers Act of 1968 and, ultimately, the Americans with Disabilities Act of 1990.

Federal efforts to encourage access continued with the formation in 1965 of the National Commission on Architectural Barriers, which published a report demonstrating that the cost of making a new building accessible generally amounted to less than one-tenth of 1 percent of the total cost of construction. Later studies upped this estimate to one-half of 1 percent, or $5,000 for every $1 million in construction costs. These estimates contradicted the widely held belief of architectural and construction trade associations, which have generally opposed requirements for access as either overly expensive or aesthetically distasteful. Chief among the groups opposed to enforcement of access standards has been the National Association of Homebuilders, though many prestigious architectural firms have also resisted incorporating access into their designs.

Along with the development of federal access legislation and standards, individual states have also adopted access codes and guidelines. The first of these was signed by the governor of South Carolina in 1963. The code was limited, however, in that it only addressed buildings owned by the state or built with public funds, and it contained no provision for enforcement. Of much greater utility was the statewide access code in North Carolina developed by disabled architect Ronald Mace and passed into law in 1974. This legislation covered all buildings and facilities in the state, with the exception of private homes and particular industrial structures such as the catwalks in oil refineries and sewage treatment plants. Since then, architectural access legislation has been passed by most of the states and territories of the United States. The passage of the Rehabilitation Act of 1973, the establishment of the federal Architectural and Transportation Barriers Compliance Board, and the passage of the Fair Housing Amendments Act of 1988 all expanded the government's commitment to eliminating architectural barriers. The Americans with Disabilities Act of 1990 (ADA) marked a culmination of the push to incorporate access requirements into federal law. The ADA requires that the owners/operators of new public spaces make efforts to incorporate access into their design.

In spite of the enormous progress made since 1945, enforcement of the various access codes has been sporadic at best, and most buildings and public spaces remain inaccessible to people with significant disabilities. In response to this lack of enforcement, access advocates in recent years have stressed the concept of universal, or barrier free, design. Whereas "access" and "accessibility" have come to imply making special efforts to accommodate people with disabilities, particularly wheelchair users, universal design addresses the needs of all individuals, making access the standard rather than the exception.

See also Adaptive Environments Center; Americans with Disabilities Act of 1990; Architectural and Transportation Barriers Compliance Board; Architectural Barriers Act of 1968; Barrier Free Environments; Concrete Change; Fair Housing Amendments Act of 1988; Mace, Ronald L.; Nugent, Timothy J.; Universal Design.

References Barrier Free Environments, *The Accessible Housing Design File* (1991); Laurie, Gini, *Housing and Home Services for the Disabled: Guidelines and Experiences in Independent Living* (1977); Lebovich, William L., *Design for Dignity: Accessible Environments for People with Disabilities* (1993); Welch, Polly, ed., *Strategies for Teaching Universal Design* (1995).

Architectural and Transportation Barriers Compliance Board (ATBCB)

The Architectural and Transportation Barriers Compliance Board (ATBCB) was established under Section 502 of the Rehabilitation Act of 1973. Its original purpose was to ensure compliance with the standards prescribed pursuant to the Architectural Barriers Act of 1968, requiring that buildings belonging to, occupied by, and financed through the federal government be accessible to people with disabilities. Its role was further defined under the Rehabilitation, Comprehensive Services, and

Developmental Disabilities Amendments of 1978, which gave it authority to review communications as well as architectural access; for example, the amendments authorized it to review the provision of telecommunications devices for people with communications disabilities. The ATBCB is composed of eleven members appointed by the president, of whom five must be disabled. ATBCB members also include representatives from various federal agencies, including the Departments of Transportation, Labor, the Interior, and Defense.

The ATBCB develops pilot programs and provides technical assistance on meeting accessibility requirements under federal law. Its activities encompass such areas as reviewing and revising accessibility guidelines for federal facilities, developing standards for detectable warnings for people with visual and hearing disabilities, and creating access standards for over-the-road buses and water transportation. The ATBCB is required to issue guidelines for enforcement of Title II and III of the Americans with Disabilities Act of 1990 (ADA). In 1991, it published the *ADA Accessibility Guidelines (ADAAG) for Buildings and Facilities*, and the *ADA Accessibility Guidelines for Transportation Vehicles*.

See also Americans with Disabilities Act of 1990; Architectural Access; Architectural Barriers Act of 1968; Housing; Rehabilitation Act of 1973.

Architectural Barriers Act of 1968 (ABA)

The Architectural Barriers Act of 1968 (ABA) required that all buildings constructed, altered, or financed by the federal government after 1969 be accessible to people with disabilities. The law made the same stipulation for buildings leased or purchased by the federal government after that date and authorized the General Services Administration (GSA) to establish standards for accessibility. The ABA covered not only federal office buildings but also recreational, medical, and educational facilities run or financed by the federal

government. Specifically excluded were buildings intended primarily for nondisabled military personnel.

The ABA, drafted by Hugh Gregory Gallagher, marked the first time that the federal government acted to require architectural access; however, the act was severely limited in what it could do. Frank Bowe, in *Handicapping America* (1978), noted that it "contained no provision for enforcement and compliance." The Architectural and Transportation Barriers Compliance Board (ATBCB), established by Congress in 1973 to enforce the act, was criticized early on for granting waivers to entities seeking exemptions to the act's access requirements. The ATBCB was chronically underfunded, and its efforts focused more on mediation and persuasion than on enforcement. The Reagan administration, in the early 1980s, attempted to abolish the ATBCB entirely. Pressure by access advocates prevented its demise, and the ATBCB has subsequently become much tougher in its enforcement. Because of this crackdown, Bowe and others now see the ABA as an important part of federal guarantees of architectural access.

Enforced or not, the ABA applied only to newer federally occupied or funded buildings. The vast majority of the nation's public buildings and virtually all of its private buildings remained uncovered by any federal accessibility mandate, until passage first of the Rehabilitation Act of 1973, then the Fair Housing Amendments Act of 1988, and finally the Americans with Disabilities Act of 1990.

See also Architectural Access; Architectural and Transportation Barriers Compliance Board; Fair Housing Amendments Act of 1988; Gallagher, Hugh Gregory; Housing.

References Bowe, Frank, *Handicapping America* (1978).

Asch, Adrienne (b. 1946)

Adrienne Asch is a psychotherapist, activist, and disability rights scholar. She is the author or editor of such groundbreaking works as *Women with Disabilities: Essays in Psychology, Culture, and Politics* (edited with Michelle Fine, 1988) and *After Baby M: The Legal, Ethical and Social Dimensions of Surrogacy* (with co-author A. R. Schiff, 1992), as well as numerous articles and book chapters related to the sociology of disability.

Asch was born on 17 September 1946 in New York City. She received her B.A. in philosophy from Swarthmore College in Pennsylvania in 1969. She went on to receive her master's in social work in 1973 and her Ph.D. in social psychology in 1992, both from Columbia University. Asch joined the National Federation of the Blind (NFB) in 1970, becoming a leader in efforts by the New York chapter of the NFB to confront the paternalism and abuses of social service agencies run by nondisabled service providers. She met disability rights activist Judy Heumann in the spring of 1972 and joined Disabled in Action (DIA) soon thereafter. In 1973, Asch joined members of the NFB, DIA, and other disability rights activists to introduce a bill into the New York State legislature adding people with disabilities to the groups protected by that state's antidiscrimination law. The bill was enacted in 1974. From 1974 to 1985, she worked with the New York State Division of Human Rights as a field representative and then as a senior human rights specialist, proposing legislation, writing agency guidelines, and investigating complaints of discrimination.

More recently, Asch has focused on scholarship related to various aspects of the social realities of disability and disability oppression. Her writing has been a catalyst in opening discussion between disability rights and feminist activists and scholars on such issues as abortion and reproductive rights. She has written about "the double oppression" of women with disabilities, the relationship between populism and disability rights, and the ethical questions that arise from the ability to identify and screen "defective" genes as part of the Human Genome Project (the multibillion dollar, federally funded effort to map and understand the human genetic code).

Asch has taught at Barnard College (affiliated with Columbia University in New York), the University of Oregon, City College of New York, and Boston University. In 1994, she became the Henry R. Luce Professor in Biology, Ethics and the Politics of Human Reproduction at Wellesley College in Massachusetts.

See also Abortion and Reproduction Rights; Disabled in Action; National Federation of the Blind.

References Fine, Michelle, and Adrienne Asch, eds., *Women with Disabilities: Essays in Psychology, Culture, and Politics* (1988).

ASL
See American Sign Language.

Assistance Animals
Assistance animals are animals used to aid people with disabilities. The most familiar and widely used assistance animals are dogs, which have been trained to assist people with sensory and mobility disabilities. Donkeys and burros are used in developing countries to transport people with mobility disabilities. Monkeys are trained to assist people with quadriplegia in everything from assisting with feeding to operating a VCR.

People using assistance animals have often experienced discrimination. People using dog-guides, for example, have been refused service in restaurants or forbidden to board buses or airliners. Beginning in the 1960s, the National Federation of the Blind (NFB) worked to pass state laws prohibiting such discrimination. The Americans with Disabilities Act of 1990 (ADA) requires access to public places and workplaces for people using assistance animals, but the courts have interpreted this requirement in different ways. In 1996, the U.S. Court of Appeals for the Ninth Circuit ruled that the 120-day quarantine for guide and service dogs traveling to the state of Hawaii was a violation of the ADA, as long as the owners could provide certification that the animals had been vaccinated for rabies. A U.S. district court in Kansas, however, ruled in 1995 that a

A blind man is assisted onto a bus in 1932 by his dog-guide, one of the first graduates of the "Seeing Eye" dog-guide school. Established in 1929, Seeing Eye was the first school of its kind in the United States.

woman's service dog could not accompany her when she went to visit her fiance in a hospital emergency room, holding that the ADA "does not create a blanket, absolute right of universal access for all assistance dogs" and that it "specifically provides that a public accommodation may impose necessary and legitimate safety requirements." The International Association of Assistance Dog Partners, based in Sterling Heights, Michigan, advocates for the rights of people using assistance dogs, and it publishes the quarterly newsletter *Partner's Forum*.

See also National Federation of the Blind.

Assisted Suicide

See Euthanasia and Assisted Suicide.

Assistive Technology

The Technology Related Assistance for Individuals with Disabilities Act of 1988 defines assistive technology as "any item, piece of equipment, or product system . . . that is used to increase, maintain, or improve functional capabilities of individuals with disabilities." Assistive technology includes speech synthesizers, which enable blind computer users to read what is on a computer screen and people with speech disabilities to speak; sip and puff controls for power wheelchairs; reachers, which allow wheelchair users to pick up something off the floor; lifts to transfer physically disabled people from a wheelchair to a shower chair; foam rubber pen collars, which enable individuals with limited dexterity to write; Computer Aided Real-Time Transcription (CART), which gives deaf persons access to spoken information; and books on tape for people unable to read print.

Assistive technology, designed for use by people with disabilities, often ends up enriching the lives of people who are not currently disabled. The typewriter, for example, was invented to enable blind people to write for sighted readers without translation from braille, while the recent explosion of "virtual reality" computer software is, in part, a result of research into making computer software interfaces accessible to people with severe disabilities. Deaf physicist Robert H. Weitbrecht's "acoustic coupler," developed in the early 1960s, was originally intended to enable deaf people to send teletypewriter (TTY) messages over standard phone lines. It was the forerunner of the computer modem, which today enables tens of millions of people, disabled and not, to use the Internet.

See also Technology Related Assistance for Individuals with Disabilities Act.

References Brummel, Susan, *People with Disabilities and the National Information Infrastructure: Agenda for Action* (1993).

The Association for Persons with Severe Handicaps (TASH)

The Association for Persons with Severe Handicaps (TASH) was informally established in November 1974, and officially founded a year later, as an organization of special education and rehabilitation professionals who wanted to share the latest developments in their field. Its creation was to a great extent a response to the successful conclusion of *Pennsylvania Association for Retarded Children (PARC) v. Pennsylvania*, the landmark right-to-education lawsuit of 1972. Today, TASH is an international association of people with disabilities, their family members, and people who work in the disability field. It helps to shape federal legislation, files lawsuits, disseminates information, and calls for "the full inclusion and participation of persons with disabilities in all aspects of life." In 1995, TASH, a nonprofit organization, had 38 chapters and more than 5,000 members worldwide.

In 1978, TASH became the first national organization to call for the complete end to institutions for persons with disabilities. It pressed Congress to amend the Rehabilitation Act of 1973 to better serve people with severe disabilities, who had previously been denied services under state vocational rehabilitation programs. TASH played a leading role in the development of the Handicapped Children's Protection Act of 1986 and supported passage of the Americans with Disabilities Act of 1990 (ADA). It was also the first national organization to call for legislation prohibiting the use of "aversive procedures" to control the behavior of adults and children with disabilities. TASH researchers have documented the use of electric shock, forced inhalation of ammonia, hitting, and other abuses in the name of "treatment."

TASH publishes a monthly newsletter (called the *TASH Newsletter*) and the *Journal of the Association of Persons with Severe Handicaps* (*JASH*). The newsletter features articles about legislation and congressional action and editorials by disability rights activists. *JASH* is a scholarly journal, published quarterly. TASH, based in Baltimore, Maryland, holds an annual conference, maintains an information/referral department, and sponsors regional workshops for advocacy training.

See also Aversives; *Pennsylvania Association for Retarded Children v. Pennsylvania*; Sheltered Workshops; *Smith v. Robinson*.

Association for Retarded Children, Association for Retarded Citizens
See The Arc.

Association of Late-Deafened Adults (ALDA)

The Association of Late-Deafened Adults (ALDA), a nonprofit organization, was founded in 1987 in Chicago. Among its principal organizers were Kathie Skyer Hering, who had started an informal support group of late-deafened adults in 1985, and Bill Graham, who began attending its meetings the following year. As of 1996, there were 23 chapters in the United States and Canada. Its membership is composed of people who are "post-lingually" deaf, that is, those whose deafness occurred after they had acquired speech and language. The organization runs self-help support groups, sponsors social activities, and advocates on behalf of late-deafened adults for relevant legislation, rehabilitation programs, employment training, and employer awareness. It publishes the quarterly *ALDA News*.

Atascadero State Hospital v. Scanlon 105 S. Ct. 3142 (1985)

The U.S. Supreme Court, in *Atascadero State Hospital v. Scanlon*, ruled that people with disabilities could not bring suit in federal court against state governments for violations of Section 504 of the Rehabilitation Act of 1973. The decision was a major setback for disability rights advocates, who counted on Section 504 as the single most important piece of civil rights protection for people with disabilities prior to the Americans with Disabilities Act of 1990 (ADA).

Douglas James Scanlon sued the Atascadero State Hospital and the California Department of Mental Health in November 1979, after he was denied a job as a graduate student assistant recreational therapist solely because of his disabilities. Scanlon was diabetic and blind in one eye but contended that he was able to fulfill the job requirements regardless. He alleged that the hospital's refusal to hire him was a violation of Section 504, which prohibited entities receiving federal funds from discriminating against individuals on the basis of their disability. In January 1980, a U.S. district court dismissed Scanlon's complaint, arguing that such lawsuits were barred under the Eleventh Amendment, which prohibits federal court action by private citizens against state governments. Scanlon appealed and, after further litigation, the case was argued before the U.S. Supreme Court on 25 March 1985. On 28

June 1985, in a controversial five-to-four decision, the Court upheld the lower court, ruling that "Congress must express its intention to abrogate the Eleventh Amendment in unmistakable language" in each individual law that it passes in order for a state's sovereign immunity to be set aside. In other words, simply accepting federal funds did not mean a state waived its protection from federal suits and thus could not be used to force states to comply with Section 504.

In response to *Atascadero State Hospital v. Scanlon*, Patrisha Wright and Arlene Mayerson at the Disability Rights Education and Defense Fund, Ralph Neas at the Leadership Conference on Civil Rights, and assistant attorney general for Civil Rights under the Reagan administration Brad Reynolds, approached Sen. Alan Cranston (D-CA), who attached a special amendment to legislation passed in 1985. The amendment clarified the congressional intent, allowing suits such as Scanlon's to move forward.

See also Civil Rights Restoration Act of 1987; Section 504 of the Rehabilitation Act of 1973.

Atlantis Community, Inc.

Atlantis Community, Inc. was founded in 1975 when 14 disabled young adults moved out of a nursing home and rented seven apartments at Las Casitas, an apartment complex managed by the Denver Housing Authority. The Atlantis Early Action Program (AEAP), under the direction of Ingo Antonitch, had the support of the Denver chapter of the National Paraplegia Foundation, as well as members of the United Cerebral Palsy Associations, the Young Disabled Adults from Life Center, the Denver Community Design Center, and the Denver Mayor's Commission on the Disabled. Advocates worked out a plan with the Welfare Department and the Colorado legislature to provide funding for home care services.

Atlantis gained national recognition in 1978 when it began a series of demonstrations to protest the inaccessibility of

Atlantis-organized protesters picket at the entrance of a Denver, Colorado, polling station in 1988 to draw attention to the several flights of stairs that make the voting booths inaccessible.

Denver's Regional Transit Authority (RTD) buses. This campaign led to the founding, in 1983, of the direct-action national disability rights organization American Disabled for Attendant Programs Today (ADAPT) (originally founded as American Disabled for Accessible Public Transit). That same year the Denver RTD made a commitment to install lifts on all of its buses, thereby creating a truly integrated mass transit system. Atlantis advocates then organized a campaign of pickets and protests that resulted in 100 percent access to Denver polling places by 1990. A similar campaign led local McDonald's restaurants to improve access for customers who use wheelchairs. When petitions and meetings failed to produce an increase in the number of curb-cuts, or ramps, Atlantis activists used sledgehammers to create their own. As a result, all

curbs in Denver were scheduled to be ramped by 1997. Although completion of this project was hampered by bad weather and other factors, by March 1997 fully 80 percent of Denver's curbs were ramped.

Atlantis offers a variety of services to people with disabilities in the Denver area, including assistance with housing issues, daily living and home management, transportation, life education, and medical services.

See also American Disabled for Attendant Programs Today; Auberger, Michael W.; Blank, Wade.

Auberger, Michael W. (b. 1955)

Michael Auberger is a co-founder of American Disabled for Attendant Programs Today (ADAPT) and has been its national organizer and spokesperson since its formation in 1983. The director of

Atlantis Community, Inc. in Denver since 1986, Auberger is known for his organizing skills, his impassioned public speaking, and his espousal of nonviolent civil disobedience in the pursuit of disability rights.

Auberger was born on 12 May 1955 and is a native of Cincinnati, Ohio. He was spinal cord injured in a bobsled accident in 1971. He earned a B.S. in accounting from Xavier University in Cincinnati in 1978, becoming a tax accountant and then an auditor for the Internal Revenue Service (IRS). He left his job at the IRS to move to Denver, where he joined the Rev. Wade Blank and Atlantis Community Inc.

Auberger's best-known speech was made at the bottom of the U.S. Capitol steps during the Wheels of Justice demonstration in Washington, D.C., in March 1990. "The steps we sit before represent a long history of discrimination and indignities heaped upon disabled Americans. We have faced what these steps have represented. Among us are those who have been institutionalized against our will. There are those among us who have had our children taken away solely because we are disabled. We have been denied housing, jobs. . . . We will not permit these steps to continue to be a barrier to our rights and equality. . . . The preamble to the Constitution does not say, 'We, the able bodied people.' It says, 'We the people.' We are the people."

After passage of the ADA in 1990, Auberger turned his energies to the fight for personal assistance services (PAS) and for an end to the incarceration of people with disabilities in nursing homes.

See also American Disabled for Attendant Programs Today; Atlantis Community, Inc.; Personal Assistance Services (PAS); Wheels of Justice.

Audism

Audism is the belief that life without hearing is futile and miserable, that hearing loss is a tragedy and "the scourge of mankind," and that deaf people should struggle to be as much like hearing people as possible. Deaf activists Heidi Reed and Hartmut Teuber at D.E.A.F. Inc., a community service and advocacy organization in Boston, consider audism to be "a special case of ableism." Audists, hearing or deaf, shun Deaf culture and the use of sign language, and have what Reed and Teuber describe as an "obsession with the use of residual hearing, speech, and lip-reading by deaf people."

See also Ableism; Cochlear Implants; Oralism, Oral School. ·

Autism National Committee

The Autism National Committee, a nonprofit organization based in Ardmore, Pennsylvania, was founded in 1990 to advance the civil rights of people with autism. It endorses the rights of all people with autism, pervasive developmental disorders, and related disabilities to education, residences, jobs and job training, and adequate consumer and family support services. The committee opposes institutionalization and the use of "aversive therapy" such as electric shock and chemical restraints.

The committee publishes *The Communicator*, a quarterly newsletter highlighting committee events and issues of concern. The spring 1995 issue, for example, featured stories on efforts to enact legislation in Massachusetts banning the use of "aversives" and on a lawsuit filed by the family of a 19-year-old woman who died allegedly as a result of "aversive therapy" while a resident at a privately run institution. The committee also publishes brochures such as *Social Justice for all Citizens with Autism*. It holds an annual conference for people with autism, their families, friends, and interested professionals.

See also Aversive Procedures; Grandin, Temple.

Autism Society of America (ASA)

The Autism Society of America (ASA) was founded in 1965 as an information, referral, support, and advocacy organization by a group of parents of children with autism. It was organized in large part in response to the negative attitudes of the medical profession, which considered autism a psychological condition brought on by uncaring, "refrigerator" mothers. It is now generally acknowledged that autism is a neurological disability.

The ASA, a nonprofit organization based in Bethesda, Maryland, has more than 17,000 members organized into 215 chapters in 48 states. Its mission is to "promote lifelong access and opportunity for all individuals within the autism spectrum, and their families, to be fully participating, included members of their community." The ASA publishes the bimonthly newsletter *Advocate*, sponsors an annual conference and an information hotline, and alerts its members to issues of concern, such as pending legislation in Congress.

See also Autism National Committee; Aversive Procedures; Grandin, Temple.

Aversive Procedures

Nancy R. Weiss, executive director of The Association for Persons with Severe Handicaps (TASH), defines "aversive therapy" as the use of "painful stimuli in response to behaviors that are deemed unacceptable. Aversive procedures are often used as part of a systematic program for decreasing certain behaviors" among people with developmental disabilities, particularly those with cognitive disabilities and/or autism.

Disability rights advocates such as Weiss view the use of aversives as a violation of human rights. They note that some procedures routinely used in facilities for people with disabilities are prohibited by the courts for use on convicted felons as "cruel and unusual punishment." Weiss details instances at facilities such as those managed by the Behavioral Research Institute (BRI) (now known as the Judge Rotenberg Educational Center, based in Rhode Island), where a state inspector found one student who, in the course of single day, received "173 spanks to the thighs, 50 spanks to the buttocks, 98 muscle squeezes to the thighs, shoulders and triceps, 88 finger pinches to the buttocks, 47 finger pinches to the thighs, approximately 527

finger pinches to the feet, and 78 finger pinches to the hand." Another BRI student, 22-year-old Vincent Milletich, died on 24 July 1985, after being handcuffed and helmeted with his head forced between an attendant's legs. Milletich was reportedly being "consequated" for making "inappropriate" sounds.

Proponents of aversive procedures claim that it is more harmful to allow developmentally disabled people to continue self-destructive behaviors, such as head banging and face slapping, than to use ammonia sprays or electric shock to stop them. Weiss, though, documents how aversives are often used to control behaviors that are merely inconvenient for staff, such as sheltered workshop clients attempting to stretch their legs. She lists examples of aversive "therapy" being used to control such behaviors as allowing eyes to wander, shaking heads, or muttering under the breath. Even the most self-destructive behaviors, she contends, can be altered without inflicting pain. These behaviors are often attempts by disabled people, who cannot talk and may have cognitive difficulties, to protest the stifling and inhumane conditions under which they are forced to live. It would be better, she says, to deal with the stultifying conditions endured by people with developmental disabilities who remain in institutions than to torture these people into being compliant and uncomplaining.

Several major disability rights organizations have passed resolutions condemning the use of aversives, including TASH, The Arc, the Center on Human Policy, and the Autism Society of America, as well as professional organizations such as the National Association of Private Residential Resources and the American Association on Mental Retardation. There have also been several lawsuits brought against facilities that use aversives, but these cases have been unsuccessful in stopping the practices.

"People who are institutionalized or subjected to painful procedures," concludes Weiss, "are no less political prisoners than some of their counterparts in third world countries....Their plight is magnified by the nature of their condition which hinders their ability to speak out against mistreatment and makes them vulnerable to this abuse. We cannot condone treating persons with disabilities in a manner that would not be tolerated if applied to other segments of the population. Anyone who is concerned with human dignity and with the ethical treatment of all people should express outrage at the continued use of behavior change procedures that cause pain" (Weiss 1991).

See also The Association for Persons with Severe Handicaps; Autism Society of America; Center on Human Policy.

References Campbell, Philippa, ed., *Use of Aversive Procedures with Persons Who Are Disabled: An Historical Overview and Critical Analysis* (1987); Weiss, Nancy R., *The Application of Aversive Procedures to Individuals with Developmental Disabilities: A Call to Action* (1991).

Baby Doe Case

Baby Doe was born in Bloomington, Indiana, in April 1982, with Down syndrome and a blocked esophagus. Her parents, acting under their doctor's advice, decided to withhold the medical procedure necessary to remove the esophogal blockage, thus making the infant's death by starvation inevitable. Advocates with developmental disabilities, particularly groups such as People First, believed that the decision to withhold treatment was made because Baby Doe's physicians and parents held the stereotypical view that life with a developmental disability is bleak and not worth living. They urged the courts to intervene to save the infant's life. Although several couples volunteered to adopt her, Baby Doe died before legal action could be taken.

As a result of the case, and the publicity it received, the Reagan administration issued regulations calling for the formation of "Baby Doe squads"—groups of advocates set up to monitor the care of disabled infants—and for the establishment of a hotline where suspected cases of infanticide could be reported. The administration argued that to deny medical care to a disabled infant on the basis of his or her disability was a violation of Section 504 of the Rehabilitation Act of 1973. The federal courts, including the U.S. Supreme Court, rejected this argument, and ultimately struck down the regulations.

In response to the Baby Doe case, and the Baby Jane Doe case that followed, disability advocates, the right-to-life movement, and the Reagan administration worked together to pass the Child Abuse Prevention and Treatment Act Amendments of 1984.

See also Baby Jane Doe Case; *Bowen v. American Hospital Association*; Child Abuse Prevention and Treatment Act Amendments of 1984; Euthanasia and Assisted Suicide; T-4.

Reference Hentoff, Nat, "The Awful Privacy of Baby Doe," in Alan Gartner and Tom Joe, eds., *Images of the Disabled, Disabling Images* (1987).

Baby Jane Doe Case

Baby Jane Doe was born on Long Island, New York, on 11 October 1983 with spina bifida and hydroencephalus. As in the Baby Doe case a year and a half earlier, her parents, acting on their doctors' advice, refused permission to perform the surgery necessary to keep her alive. As with Baby Doe, disability rights activists saw the case as representative of society's ignorance of and hostility toward disability and its belief that life with a disability is not worth living.

Much of the media coverage of the case emphasized the alleged hopelessness of Jane Doe's condition. The *New York Times* reported that "with surgery she could survive into her 20s but would be severely retarded and bedridden." This was in contrast to the opinion of David G. McLone, chief of neurosurgery at Children's Memorial Hospital in Chicago, who said that, with surgery, Jane Doe could grow up with "normal" intelligence, would probably be able to walk using braces, and could easily live a long life. In order for this to happen, however, the surgery had to be performed as soon after birth as possible. McLone, having treated more than 1,000 children with the condition, was probably the nation's leading medical expert on spina bifida, but his opinion was rarely solicited by the mainstream media.

The Reagan administration, concerned lawmakers, and right-to-life and disability rights activists all sought to save Jane Doe. When the U.S. Justice Department demanded to see Jane Doe's medical records to determine whether physicians, in denying her treatment, had violated Section

504 of the Rehabilitation Act of 1973, the New York Civil Liberties Union, together with the New York State Attorney General, the American Hospital Association, the American Academy of Pediatrics, and other medical groups, protested that this was an intrusion by the federal government into physician-patient confidentiality. The Association for Retarded Citizens, the Association for Persons with Severe Handicaps, the Disability Rights Education and Defense Fund, and Disabled in Action in New York all supported the Justice Department's request. The subsequent court action (*United States v. University Hospital, State University of New York at Stony Brook*, 1983) went against the federal government, which appealed the case. On 23 February 1984, the United States Court of Appeals for the Second Circuit ruled that the privacy rights of the parents and their baby took precedence over Section 504. The spokesman for the New York State Attorney General hailed the decision as barring the federal government "from conducting any investigation of medical decisions regarding defective newborns." However, Judge Ralph Winter, in his dissent, wrote that denying a disabled child food, water, or medical treatment because of his or her disability is a discriminatory, not a medical, decision, just as a decision "not to perform certain surgery because a person is black is not a bona fide medical judgement." As a result of Baby Jane Doe and similar cases, Congress passed the Child Abuse Prevention and Treatment Act Amendments of 1984.

In June 1986, the U.S. Supreme Court, in *Bowen v. American Hospital Association*, ruled that to deny a disabled infant needed medical treatment was not necessarily a violation of its rights under Section 504. In the meantime, Baby Jane Doe's parents had changed their minds, and surgery was performed to relieve the pressure on her brain. Seven years later, a reporter visiting her family reported that, though moderately retarded and using a wheelchair, the child was active and happy and "learning at a level far beyond what doctors testified she would." Some advocates noted the possibility the child might have been less disabled had the surgery been performed sooner.

See also Baby Doe Case; *Bowen v. American Hospital Association;* Child Abuse Prevention and Treatment Act Amendments of 1984; Euthanasia and Assisted Suicide; T-4.

References Biklen, Douglas, "Framed: Print Journalism's Treatment of Disability Issues," in Alan Gartner and Tom Joe, eds., *Images of the Disabled: Disabling Images* (1987); Hentoff, Nat, "The Awful Privacy of Baby Doe," in Alan Gartner and Tom Joe, eds. *Images of the Disabled: Disabling Images* (1987).

Baptiste, Gerald, Sr. (b. 1934)

Gerald Baptiste Sr. is a nationally known advocate for people of color with disabilities. In 1986, he co-founded the Multi-Cultural Committee of the National Council on Independent Living, seeking to add issues of concern to black Americans with disabilities to the agenda of the general disability rights movement. Since the early 1990s, he has taken the lead in attempting to form a national grassroots movement for minority people with disabilities.

Born on 10 February 1934 in Beaumont, Texas, Baptiste has a B.A. in sociology from Prairie View A&M University in Prairie View, Texas. In 1979, he joined the Center for Independent Living (CIL) in Berkeley as a peer counselor, becoming the CIL coordinator for Blind Services in 1981, and the associate director in 1985. He was a grassroots organizer and coordinator for the western United States during the struggle for passage of the Americans with Disabilities Act of 1990, and has conducted training sessions in political organizing and independent living all across the United States and in several foreign countries. He assisted in founding the first independent living center in Japan and is a leader in African-American efforts to establish links with disability rights activists in Africa.

See also Center for Independent Living; National Council on Independent Living; Multicultural Issues, Minority Persons with Disabilities.

Barrier Free Environments (BFE)

Founded in 1974 by architect Ronald L. Mace, Barrier Free Environments (BFE) is an architecture and product design firm that works with individuals, businesses, and the government to design buildings that are accessible to all and to modify those that are not. It provides research and development services to help companies ensure that their products are usable to everyone. BFE and its staff have been involved in the development of national and federal architectural design standards, along with regulations and standards related to Section 504 of the Rehabilitation Act of 1973, the Fair Housing Amendments Act of 1988, and the Americans with Disabilities Act of 1990. Among its publications are *Adaptable Housing: A Technical Manual for Implementing Adaptable Dwelling Unit Specifications* (1987) and the *Accessible Housing Design File* (1991). Barrier Free Environments is based in Raleigh, North Carolina.

See also Architectural Access; Center for Universal Design; Fair Housing Amendments Act of 1988; Housing; Mace, Ronald L.; Universal Design.

Bartels, Elmer C. (b. 1938)

Elmer C. Bartels became commissioner of the Massachusetts Rehabilitation Commission in 1977. He was one of the first severely disabled people to rise to an executive position in a state rehabilitation agency.

Born on 10 June 1938, Bartels was halfway through his senior year at Colby College in Maine in 1961 when he broke his neck during a hockey game, becoming quadriplegic. He graduated the next year with a B.S. in physics and mathematics and, in 1964, earned an M.S. in nuclear physics from Tufts University in Massachusetts. From 1964 to 1968, he worked at the Massachusetts Institute of Technology's Laboratory for Nuclear Science, and, from 1968 to 1977, at Honeywell Information Systems. While working in these capacities, Bartels was also an officer and board member of the National Paraplegia

Foundation and a leader of the Massachusetts Association of Paraplegics and the Massachusetts Council of Organizations of the Handicapped, the precursor to the Massachusetts Coalition of Citizens with Disabilities.

After his appointment as commissioner in 1977, Bartels worked to make Massachusetts' rehabilitation program more responsive to the needs of its clients. He is the author of numerous articles and book chapters on disability and rehabilitation and is a member of a variety of organizations, including the U.S. Sports and Fitness Center for the Disabled and the Disabilities Issues Committee of the Boston Private Industry Council.

See also Vocational Rehabilitation, Vocational Rehabilitation Acts and Amendments.

Bazelon Center

See Judge David L. Bazelon Center for Mental Health Law.

Beers, Clifford Whittingham (1876–1943)

Clifford Beers is best known as the author of *A Mind That Found Itself* (1908), his autobiographical account of life as a mental patient in turn-of-the-century America. He spent his life working to remove the stigma of mental illness and to eliminate abuses in the treatment of people with mental disabilities.

Clifford Beers was born on 30 March 1876, in New Haven, Connecticut. He entered Yale in September 1894. That same year, his older brother developed symptoms of what was at first thought to be epilepsy. Ironically, the first clear symptom of Beers' disability was his obsession with the possibility that he might, like his brother, become disabled, and his depression deepened as his brother's condition deteriorated. On the afternoon of 23 June 1900, Beers threw himself out of a fourth floor window. Taken to the hospital, his first words were, "I thought I had epilepsy." On 4 July 1900, his older

Clifford Whittingham Beers, pioneer in the disability rights movement, pictured in 1933.

brother died of a brain tumor.

Beers was taken to an asylum near Hartford, Connecticut, where conditions were very poor. The food was barely edible. Even in winter, patients were kept naked in unheated rooms, with a thin mat for a bed. Those who complained or were distracted or aggressive were wrapped in cold, wet sheets, strapped into straitjackets, or drugged for days on end. Some were beaten. Beers spent three years at three different hospitals, and at each of these institutions he saw patients brutalized. He began surreptitiously recording his impressions (inmates were forbidden pencil and paper), interviewing other inmates and staff, and sending letters to the authorities. Beers described how women were dragged along the floor by their hair, and he documented the case of one man whose arm was broken in a beating, of another man

sexually assaulted by the attendant-in-charge. "Bear in mind," he concluded, "that everything bad and disagreeable is possible in an Insane Asylum."

Beers was discharged on 10 September 1903 and began to outline both his book and his plans for a national organization. *A Mind That Found Itself* was published in March 1908, and, on 6 May 1908, Beers, his surviving older brother, his father, and 11 others founded the Connecticut Committee for Mental Hygiene. The National Committee for Mental Hygiene was officially organized in New York City on 19 February 1909.

Beers devoted the rest of his life to the national committee, financing the organization during its first days by taking out a personal loan. Twenty-five years after the launching of the Connecticut chapter, there were Committees for Mental Hygiene in nearly 30 other states as well as national committees in 30 countries. During this time, the national and state committees collected data on conditions inside the institutions and on the resources and methods available for the treatment of mental disability. After 1918, the National Committee for Mental Hygiene, together with the American Legion, pushed the federal government into providing psychiatric care for World War I veterans suffering from "shell shock"—now known as post-traumatic stress disorder. In the 1920s, the committee began a campaign for the founding of children's community mental health (or "child guidance") clinics. By 1937, there were 631 such clinics across the country. The most significant legislative achievement of the committee was the passage of the National Mental Health Act of 1946, which dramatically increased the availability of federal funding for mental health programs.

Beers, however, was seemingly never interested in forming a grassroots organization of mental patients, such as were founded by the psychiatric survivor movement of the 1970s. The National Committee for Mental Hygiene remained, instead, a group dominated by mental health professionals. Rather than calling for an end to institutions or offering a radical critique of the psychiatric and medical establishments, Beers advocated only for better hospitals and more humane staff. Roy Porter, in *A Social History of Madness* (1989), writes that Beers even attempted to distance himself from other mentally disabled people and that "on occasion he could display a coolness towards their plight which seems to verge on the callous," refusing, for example, to help a former patient get a job. In addition, the committee was tainted by the involvement of some members in eugenics—the pseudoscience that sought to prevent people with disabilities (and poor and nonwhite people) from having children.

Toward the end of his life, Beers again became depressed. His older brother William, also suffering from depression, committed suicide, and Beers was himself reinstitutionalized. He died on 9 July 1943. The National Committee for Mental Hygiene merged with the National Mental Health Foundation and the Psychiatric Foundation in September 1950 to form the National Association for Mental Health.

See also Chemical Restraint; Eugenics; National Mental Health Foundation; Psychiatric Survivor Movement.

References Beers, Clifford Whittingham, *A Mind That Found Itself* (1908, 1953); Porter, Roy, *A Social History of Madness: The World through the Eyes of the Insane* (1989).

Bell, Alexander Graham (1847–1922)

Alexander Graham Bell began his professional life as an educator of deaf people, and his work had a profound impact on deaf people worldwide. Indeed, Bell first conceptualized his most famous invention, the telephone, as an instrument for educating deaf children. Ironically, the telephone instead contributed to the social isolation of the very people he was hoping to assist, while his lifelong advocacy of oralism would make him an enemy of much of America's Deaf community.

Bell was born on 3 March 1847, in Edinburgh, Scotland. His mother, Eliza Grace Symonds, had lost much of her hearing as a child. His father, Alexander Melville Bell, was a speech teacher of deaf children and an early advocate of Visible Speech, a system of written symbols for oral sounds. As a young man, Bell toured with his father to demonstrate the system. His own work with deaf people began in May 1868 with two pupils at a school in South Kensington in England. In 1870, he immigrated to Canada, and, in 1871, traveled to the United States, where he taught Visible Speech at the Boston School for Deaf Mutes. In 1873, he became the tutor of 15-year-old Mabel Hubbard, the deaf daughter of millionaire Gardiner Greene Hubbard. Bell and Mabel were married in 1877.

Bell was the world's best-known advocate of oralism—the teaching of speech and lip-reading to the exclusion of sign. He condemned the use of American Sign Language and urged that deaf teachers not be allowed to teach deaf students. At the time, the accepted method of educating deaf children was at residential schools, through the use of sign. These schools, such as the American School for the Deaf in Hartford, Connecticut, were also centers of Deaf social life and culture. In 1877, Bell began advocating for the establishment of day schools, so that deaf children could attend school by day but continue to live with their families. Bell's interest was in integrating deaf children into the hearing community, and he believed day schools would be more conducive to this end as well as to using the oral approach. In 1878, Bell opened one of the first day programs, in Greencock, Scotland, and over the next decades was a tireless proponent of day schools.

At the same time, through the writing of such tracts as "Memoir upon the Formation of a Deaf Variety of the Human Race" (published by the Government Printing Office in 1884) and "How To Improve the Race" (published in the *Journal of Heredity* in 1914), Bell sought to prohibit deaf people from marrying each other, so as to prevent the birth of deaf children. On one occasion he actually made this argument in a speech at the commencement of Gallaudet College (now Gallaudet University) in Washington, D.C., to the disgust of his deaf audience. Though stopping short of urging that marriages between deaf people be made illegal, he did call on their hearing friends "to prevent undesirable intermarriages." "It never occurred to him," writes O. Perier in the *Gallaudet Encyclopedia of Deaf People and Deafness* (Van Cleve 1987), "that there were some deaf people who were satisfied with their condition, who considered themselves normal, and who saw nothing wrong with having deaf children." It is little wonder that community leader George William Veditz labeled Bell "the American most feared by deaf people." Bell also advocated prohibiting disabled people from working for the government, arguing that government appointments should be "so made as to encourage the production of offspring from the healthy and strong." A Social Darwinist, Bell also supported restricting immigration into the United States by "undesireable ethnical elements," such as southern Europeans.

In 1886, Bell established the Volta Bureau to sponsor research and programs on deafness and to proselytize for oralism. In 1890, he contributed funds to establish the American Association for the Promotion of the Teaching of Speech to the Deaf (renamed the Alexander Graham Bell Association for the Deaf in 1956). Bell died on 2 August 1922.

See also Eugenics; Gallaudet, Edward Miner; Oralism, Oral School.

References Bruce, Robert V., *Bell: Alexander Graham Bell and the Conquest of Solitude* (1973); Van Cleve, John V., ed., *Gallaudet Encyclopedia of Deaf People and Deafness* (1987); Van Cleve, John Vickrey, and Barry A. Crouch, *A Place of Their Own: Creating the Deaf Community in America* (1989); Winefield, Richard, *Never the Twain Shall Meet: The Communications Debate* (1987).

The Best Years of Our Lives

Based upon the novel in verse *Glory for Me* (1945) by MacKinlay Kantor, *The Best Years of Our Lives* was one of the first Hollywood films to depict with some degree of realism a character with a disability. Released in 1946, the film won seven Academy Awards and was seen by an estimated 60 million people worldwide.

The movie recounts the trials and eventual triumphs of three returning World War II veterans as they struggle to reorient themselves to civilian life. One of these is Homer Parish, a sailor who has lost both his arms below the elbow and uses prosthetic hands. Parish was played by real-life double amputee Harold Russell, one of the first and only times Hollywood has used an actor with a disability to depict a disabled character. Though the acting might seem sentimental by today's standards, the movie marked one of the first times that the general public saw a disabled character not as evil or "bizarre" (as in *Freaks* [1932] or *Treasure Island* [1934 and 1950] or any of a hundred other films) nor as a mawkish "supercrip" (as in *Deliverance* [1919], the romanticized silent film story of Helen Keller), but as an altogether average human being.

The film was less realistic in its treatment of society's view of disability. Historian Paul Longmore notes how *The Best Years of Our Lives* and other "dramas of adjustment" of the post-war era typically "put the responsibility for any problems squarely and almost exclusively on the disabled individual. If they are socially isolated, it is not because . . . society has rejected them" but because "they have chosen isolation." Parish, like other disabled characters to follow, has a chip on his shoulder and needs his nondisabled friends to straighten him out.

Russell received two Academy Awards for his role. In 1947, he was appointed to the President's Committee on Employment of the Physically Handicapped and was named Committee Chair by President Lyndon Johnson in 1964.

See also Disability Blackface; Media Images of People with Disabilities; President's Committee on the Employment of People with Disabilities; Russell, Harold.

References Gartner, Alan, and Tom Joe, eds., *Images of the Disabled, Disabling Images* (1987); Norden, Martin F., *The Cinema of Isolation: A History of Physical Disability in the Movies* (1994); Russell, Harold, *Victory in My Hands* (1949).

Biklen, Douglas
See Facilitated Communication.

Birnbaum, David
See Deaf President Now Campaign.

Blank, Wade (1940–1993)

The Reverend Wade Blank was one of the founding members of American Disabled for Attendant Programs Today (ADAPT), formerly American Disabled for Accessible Public Transit, and an advocate of the use of civil disobedience and nonviolent mass confrontation. He was himself arrested on numerous occasions at nonviolent protests. Although not disabled himself, Blank's commitment to the struggle made him one of the most important disability rights leaders of the 1980s and early 1990s.

Blank was born on 4 December 1940 in Pittsburgh, Pennsylvania. He was educated as a Presbyterian minister and was called, in 1966, to serve a congregation in Akron, Ohio. This, he said later, was where he first learned political organizing from "the [Martin Luther] King people," although he had already participated in the civil rights movement and had marched in Selma, Alabama, in 1965. As a member of the Kent State chapter of the Students for a Democratic Society (SDS) in 1971, he helped smuggle anti–Vietnam War draft resisters into Canada.

In December 1971, Blank arrived in Denver, Colorado, where he took a job as an attendant at the Heritage House nursing home. From his first night on the job, he was shocked by what he witnessed. "I remember for dinner that night, we had baked potatoes, applesauce, and scrambled eggs, and this was near Christmas. The place was like a morgue. The food was cold." Blank discovered that the nursing home administration was illegally expropriating the residents' Social Security

checks. "I was going to work every day and asking myself, if I was disabled, is this the way I'd want to live the rest of my life?" It was at this time that Blank met some of the people who would later become ADAPT organizers. Blank arranged for meetings of the nursing home's younger residents. "They wanted co-ed living. They wanted to have pets. . . . Every morning at 7:30, they'd get dressed and get on a school bus, and go to a workshop and count fish hooks. [The nursing home] called it [a] work activities program." After four years working for reform, Blank was fired when he suggested that some of the residents could leave the nursing home and live independently in the community. With Blank gone, Heritage House erased all his reforms. "They came in and they took all the stereos and TVs...had the dog pound come by and get all the animals, and in one day it went from everything I'd built for four years—to that."

Within six months of being fired, Blank had helped 18 people leave the nursing home, moving them into apartments and taking personal responsibility for their care. They formed the nucleus of the Atlantis Community, Inc., a disability rights collective and one of the first independent living centers in the country. In the meantime, Heritage House was sued by its residents and their families for fraud and abuse, and its administration settled out of court for $2.6 million.

In January 1975, the Atlantis Community demanded that the Denver Regional Transportation District (RTD) bus system be made accessible. This demand was the beginning of what was to become a decade-long struggle to gain accessible mass transportation, first in Denver, and then all across the United States. Blank helped to mastermind a series of lawsuits and demonstrations, including the now-famous demonstration of 5 July 1978, when 19 activists using wheelchairs surrounded and immobilized two buses at an intersection in downtown Denver for two days.

ADAPT was founded in July 1983 at a meeting in the Atlantis office of disability activists from across the country. From the start, ADAPT focused on the most dispossessed of people with disabilities—those incarcerated in institutions and nursing homes. Again, Blank's model was the Reverend Martin Luther King, Jr. Activist Laura Hershey, in her eulogy to Blank in 1993, remembers him telling her how "King involved the poorest in the community, and a movement cannot really change things unless they address the poorest, the least. When King was shot, he was beginning to attack the ghettos. . . . Our ghettos are the nursing homes." ADAPT grew in numbers and influence throughout the 1980s, first taking on the American Public Transit Association (APTA), and then the U.S. Congress when it balked in passing the Americans with Disabilities Act of 1990 (ADA). After passage of the ADA, Blank and ADAPT decided to focus on personal assistance services (PAS) as their primary issue.

Blank died at age 52 on 15 February 1993, in a swimming accident in Todos Santos, Mexico, while attempting to rescue his 8-year-old son Lincoln, who also drowned. His memorial service in Denver was attended by more than 1,000 people.

See also Americans Disabled for Attendant Programs Today; Personal Assistance Services; Wheels of Justice.

References Hershey, Laura, "Wade Blank's Liberated Community," in Barrett Shaw, ed., *The Ragged Edge* (1994); Maddox, Sam, *Spinal Network: The Total Resource for the Wheelchair Community* (1987).

Blinded Veterans Association (BVA)

The Blinded Veterans Association (BVA) was founded in 1945 at the Avon Old Farms Army Convalescent Hospital in Avon, Connecticut. Although the BVA's founding members had all been blinded during military service in World War II, the BVA also advocates on behalf of veterans blinded since their military discharge. The bulk of the BVA's work is done through its Field Service Program. All BVA field representatives are blinded veterans, who link veterans with services, rehabilitation training, and other benefits.

The BVA also sponsors regional recreational and social groups for blinded veterans and their families, offers scholarships, and publishes a newsletter, *The BVA Bulletin*. Its headquarters are in Washington, D.C.

Board of Education of the Hendrick Hudson Central School District v. Rowley 102 S. Ct. 3034 (1982)

Board of Education of the Hendrick Hudson Central School District v. Rowley (also *Board of Education v. Rowley*) was the first case decided by the U.S. Supreme Court regarding the Education for All Handicapped Children Act of 1975. In its 1982 decision, the Court limited the educational services a school district could be required to provide to disabled children and the judiciary's ability to review those services when challenged by parents.

Amy Rowley was a 12-year-old deaf student at the Furnace Woods School in Peekskill, New York. Her parents filed suit after school administrators turned down their request for a sign language interpreter to accompany Amy to her classes. School officials argued that Amy's hearing aide, provided by the school, and her ability to lip-read, were adequate to enable her to understand her lessons. They pointed to other services, such as the tutors they provided for several hours of instruction per week, as sufficient to meet the requirements of the Education for All Handicapped Children Act for "a free appropriate public education." They noted that Amy had better than average grades and was advancing easily from grade to grade. The Rowleys argued that Amy had the potential to do much better and offered to exchange the special instruction already being provided for the use of an interpreter. The U.S. District Court for the Southern District of New York ruled in favor of the Rowleys, as did the U.S. Court of Appeals for the Second Circuit.

The U.S. Supreme Court, however, decided against the Rowleys on 28 June 1982. The act, according to the Court, did not require states to maximize the potential of disabled children commensurate with opportunity provided nondisabled children, but only to meet minimal state education standards. The court further ruled that the judiciary could intervene in special education decisions only if school administrators did not follow due process, as laid out in the act, for writing the Individualized Education Program (IEP) or resolving differences with parents. At first, advocates feared that *Rowley* would drastically limit the scope of the Education for All Handicapped Children Act, but, according to John Parry, editor of *Mental Disability Law: A Primer* (1984), "the actual impact of the decision has been less severe than was expected."

The case did, however, have another sort of impact. The *Rowley* case marked the first time that a deaf attorney had argued before the Supreme Court. Michael A. Chatoff, representing the Rowleys, had graduated from the New York University School of Law with an L.L.M. in 1978. Chatoff was the author of the original Court Interpreters Act of 1978, requiring that interpreter services be made available to deaf and hard-of-hearing people involved in a federal case. Prior to *Rowley*, he had filed a number of deaf rights cases, including suits against the New York Telephone Company and the New York State Public Service Commission, winning a rate reduction for deaf phone users. Chatoff's appearance before the Supreme Court sparked considerable comment, with the Court allowing, for the first time, electronic devices such as Real Time Graphic Display to be used by an arguing attorney. It also inspired other deaf people to enter law school and to become legal advocates for deaf rights.

See also Education for All Handicapped Children Act of 1975.

References Moore, Matthew Scott, and Robert F. Panara, *Great Deaf Americans: The Second Edition* (1996); Parry, John, ed., *Mental Disability Law: A Primer* (1984).

The Body's Memory
See Stewart, Jean.

Boggs, Elizabeth Monroe (1913–1996)
Elizabeth Monroe Boggs was one of the founders of the Association for Retarded Children (ARC, but now The Arc) and a prime mover in the parents' movement of the 1950s and 1960s. A mathematician and theoretical chemist by training, she abandoned her career in the sciences after the birth of her son Jonathan David, becoming instead an advocate for disability rights.

Boggs was born Elizabeth Monroe on 5 April 1913, in Cleveland, Ohio. She graduated from Bryn Mawr College in Pennsylvania in 1935, summa cum laude with a distinction in mathematics. In 1941, she was awarded her doctorate in theoretical chemistry from Cambridge University in England. That same year, she married Fitzhugh Willets Boggs, and the couple settled in Cleveland. Their son Jonathan was born in 1945, and at ten days old he suffered a high fever that left him severely brain damaged. The family moved to New Jersey, and as Jonathan grew older he and his family experienced society's prejudice against children with disabilities and their families. Disabled children were routinely denied access to public schools, while the prevailing medical advice of the time was to institutionalize developmentally disabled children. Boggs, after taking Jonathan to a variety of medical "experts," soon became dissatisfied with the advice she was getting, and, as a scientist, realized that much of it was based on myth and stereotype.

Boggs returned to college to study special education and social work. Her work with other parents of cognitively disabled children resulted in the founding of the ARC in 1950, with Boggs becoming its first woman president in 1958. She was a member of its Governmental Affairs Committee from 1965 to 1979. In that position she helped draft, or lobbied for passage of, such landmark legislation as the Developmental Disabilities Services and Facilities Construction Amendments of 1970 and the Developmentally Disabled Assistance and Bill of Rights Act of 1975. Indeed, the very term *developmental disabilities* was in large part one of Boggs's innovations.

In 1961, Boggs was appointed to be the only advocate on President Kennedy's Panel on Mental Retardation, which among other measures was instrumental in the passage of the Mental Retardation Facilities and Community Mental Health Centers Construction Act of 1963. Boggs was also a member of the National Child Health and Human Development Council at the National Institutes of Health from 1967 to 1971 and of the President's Committee on Mental Retardation from 1975 to 1976. She was an early advocate of group homes and independent living as alternatives to institutionalization, spoke extensively at seminars and conferences around the world, and was the primary author of the United Nations Declaration of General and Specific Rights of the Mentally Retarded (1971). In 1988, she became co-chair, with Justin Dart Jr., of the Task Force on the Rights and Empowerment of Americans with Disabilities and an advocate for passage of the Americans with Disabilities Act of 1990. Also in 1988, Boggs became acting director of the New Jersey Office of Prevention of Mental Retardation and Developmental Disabilities, her first paid disability-related position, and in the late 1980s and early 1990s, she worked for the reform of the Social Security disabilities programs, serving as a member of both the SSI Modernization Project and the Social Security Administration's Task Force on Representative Payees.

Boggs received many awards and honorary degrees, among them the Kennedy International Award for Leadership, the Distinguished Service Award of United Cerebral Palsy Associations, and the N. Neal Pike Award for Service to People with Disabilities. She died on 27 January 1996.

See also The Arc; Developmental Disabilities; Developmental Disabilities Assistance and Bill of Rights Act of 1975; Parents' Movement; President's Panel/President's Committee on Mental Retardation.

Boston Center for Independent Living (BCIL)

The Boston Center for Independent Living (BCIL), the first independent living center to be established on the East Coast, was founded in October 1974 by Paul Corcoran, a doctor of rehabilitation medicine; Fred Fay, a disability rights activist; and Robert McHugh, a vocational counselor with the Massachusetts Rehabilitation Commission. Their efforts were opposed by the federal government, which did not want money for personal assistance services to go directly to disabled consumers, and by medical and rehabilitation professionals, who felt that people with severe disabilities would be unable to handle life in the community.

BCIL started a direct advocacy program in 1979. Among its components were a transportation committee that organized consumers to push the regional transit authority to expand its paratransit and accessible mainline transit. BCIL also joined the Boston Disability Law Center in a suit (*Karuth v. Boston*, 1991) filed against the city of Boston, prompting it to issue medallions for 40 accessible taxis. BCIL advocates participated in the occupation of the Massachusetts State House in 1991, forcing Governor William Weld to reconsider threatened cutbacks in the Massachusetts personal assistance services program. BCIL activists were also instrumental in organizing the first of Boston's Disability Pride Day celebrations in October 1990.

See also Fay, Frederick A.; Independent Living and the Independent Living Movement.

Boston Self Help Center

The Boston Self Help Center was founded in 1977 as a cooperative, nonprofit organization by and for people with a disability or chronic illness, growing out of a series of support groups organized by people with disabilities in the early 1970s. The services it offers are centered on peer counseling and education, and on breaking down distinctions between "client" and "counselor." The center also has had a marked political focus, sponsoring or co-sponsoring a great deal of advocacy in the late 1970s and the 1980s. In 1990, it became one of the first organizations in North America to provide specialized services for persons with multiple chemical sensitivities, also known as environmental illness.

Among the founders and board members of the Boston Self Help Center were Gunnar Dybwad, David Pfeiffer, Marsha Saxton, and Irving Zola. Connie Panzarino, a board member in the 1990s, was a leader in advocacy efforts to free Sharon Kowalski, a disabled lesbian who was kept in a nursing home for eight years against her will.

See also Kowalski, Sharon, and Thompson, Karen; Multiple Chemical Sensitivities; Peer Counseling.

Bourne, Bridgetta
See Deaf President Now Campaign.

Bouvia, Elizabeth
See Euthanasia and Assisted Suicide.

Bowe, Frank G. (b. 1947)
Frank G. Bowe is known for his writing on disability, for his work as the executive director of the American Coalition of Citizens with Disabilities, and for his advocacy for telecommunications access. His book *Handicapping America* (1978), a survey of the attitudinal, architectural, and legal barriers faced by Americans with disabilities in the 1970s, was a major text of the emerging disability rights movement.

Bowe was born on 29 March 1947 in Lewisburg, Pennsylvania. He began to lose his hearing when he was 15 months old, possibly due to the use of the antibiotic streptomycin. Like many deaf children of his generation, Bowe was forbidden to use American Sign Language (ASL), because of the belief that it would interfere with his ability to speak and read lips. He graduated from Lewisburg Joint High School in 1965 and received his B.A from Western

Maryland College in 1969. As an undergraduate, Bowe became interested in the black civil rights movement and worked in an antipoverty program in rural West Virginia. Bowe wanted to be a reporter like his idols Drew Pearson and Jack Anderson, but his deafness interfered with his ability to do interviews and use the telephone. "Teaching was out. Business was out. And now it seemed writing, the thing I did well, was also out." Bowe later described this period in his life as one of "feeling very alone, very much a stranger in my own country."

The situation changed when Bowe began graduate work at Gallaudet College in Washington, D.C., in 1969. For the first time, Bowe was in a community of Deaf people, where ASL was not only accepted but celebrated. Bowe received his master's degree in special education in 1971, and he returned to Pennsylvania, where he created a program for children with multiple disabilities in Bloomsburg, taught disabled children, and trained future teachers. From there he moved to New York City, where he received his Ph.D. in educational psychology from New York University in 1976. He also made his first contact with the cross-disability rights movement in the person of Eunice Fiorito, co-founder and president of the American Coalition of Citizens with Disabilities (ACCD). At that time, the organization had "no office and a budget of little more than a hundred dollars." Shortly after receiving his doctorate, Bowe moved to Washington, D.C., to become the ACCD's first executive director.

One of Bowe's first acts was to conduct a survey of the situation faced by people with disabilities in 1976, accumulating "demographic statistics, judicial decisions, unpublished studies, sensitive memoranda, and hundreds of newspaper clippings detailing the concrete reality of discrimination against disabled people in twentieth century America." Much of this material would appear in his book *Handicapping America*. Bowe's research convinced him that "the key to equality of opportunity for handicapped people in our country" was Section 504 of the Rehabilitation Act of

1973. The problem was that Joseph Califano, President Jimmy Carter's Secretary of Health, Education, and Welfare (HEW), refused to release regulations to govern its application. Bowe and the ACCD first attempted to negotiate with the administration. When negotiations failed, the ACCD called for public demonstrations. On 4 April 1977, disability rights activists occupied HEW offices in Washington, New York, San Francisco, and elsewhere. On 28 April, Califano announced that he had signed the 504 regulations at 7:30 that morning. The HEW demonstrations brought the ACCD and the disability rights movement to general national attention. For ACCD it meant rapid expansion. In addition to using the new 504 regulations to press for disability rights, Bowe and the ACCD were involved in the fight for the development and manufacture of Transbus, a revolutionary design for an accessible mass transit vehicle.

During his years at ACCD, Bowe was also a prolific writer. *Handicapping America* was one of the first and most successful books to lay out a disability rights perspective. Other works from this period include *Rehabilitating America* (1980), *Planning Effective Advocacy Programs* (with J. Williams, 1979), *Access to Transportation* (1980), and *Disabled and Elderly People: What Role for the Corporation?* (1981).

Bowe left ACCD in 1981, but he continued to be an important voice in the national disability rights movement. He was the U.S. representative during the planning of the United Nation's International Year of Disabled Persons in 1981, and has been a consultant to the United Nations in years since. From 1978 to 1983, he was a consultant to the U.S. Congressional Office of Technology Assessment and a member, from 1989 to 1990, of the Task Force on the Rights and Empowerment of Americans with Disabilities. Bowe has been on the editorial board of numerous journals and a consultant to many public agencies. From 1987 to 1989, he was also a regional commissioner for the Rehabilitation Services Administration. From 1991 to 1996, he worked with Deborah Kaplan to insert language into the Telecommunications Act of 1996 calling for a study of telecommunications access issues, and requiring the Federal Communications Commission to promulgate regulations ensuring closed caption access to video programming.

Among Bowe's more recent books are *Disabled Adults in America* and *Disabled Women in America* (both published in 1984), *Black Adults with Disabilities* (1985), *Approaching Equality* (1991), *Equal Rights for Americans with Disabilities* (1992), and *Birth to Five: Early Childhood Special Education* (1995). Bowe is also the author of dozens of articles and book chapters on disability and disability rights.

Since 1989, Bowe has been a professor at the Counseling, Special Education and Rehabilitation Department at Hofstra University, on Long Island in New York.

See also American Coalition of Citizens with Disabilities; HEW Demonstrations; International Year, International Decade of Disabled Persons; Kaplan, Deborah; President's Committee on Employment of People with Disabilities; Section 504 of the Rehabilitation Act of 1973; Task Force on Rights and Empowerment of Americans with Disabilities.

References Bowe, Frank, *Handicapping America* (1978); ———, *Changing the Rules* (1986).

Bowen v. American Hospital Association et al. 106 S. Ct. 2101 (1986)

In *Bowen v. American Hospital Association et al.*, the U.S. Supreme Court ruled that regulations promulgated by Health and Human Services (HHS) during the Reagan administration to protect disabled infants from being denied medical care were invalid. The Court took the position that because it was the parents who had decided to deny the care, and not the hospital receiving federal funds, such infants were not protected under Section 504 of the Rehabilitation Act of 1973. Disability rights advocates supporting the regulations argued that parents often withheld consent for needed medical treatment for their disabled infants on the basis of their doctors' recommendations, and that such recommendations were often made as a result of erroneous and prejudicial attitudes about the value of life with a disability.

Responding to the immediate emergency of disabled infants being denied medical care, HHS in May 1982 issued a temporary, or "interim," regulation defining such denial as "instances of unlawful neglect of handicapped infants" under Section 504, which prohibits discrimination against people with disabilities by entities, such as hospitals and medical programs, receiving federal funds. The regulation required federally funded health care providers to post, "in a conspicuous place" in hospital delivery wards, a notice outlining the protection offered by Section 504 as well as the number of a telephone hotline for those wishing to report suspected abuse of disabled infants. The regulation was intended to remain in place until HHS could draft a more refined "final rule." The American Hospital Association and the American Academy of Pediatrics filed suit against HHS in federal court in April 1983, resulting in a decision by the Federal District Court for the District of Columbia that struck down the interim regulation as "arbitrary and capricious."

HHS then issued a new set of rules, drafted with the same intent as the interim regulation but rewritten to address the concerns of the court. These "Final Rules" took effect on 13 February 1984. On March 12, the American Hospital Association, the American Medical Association, the American College of Obstetricians and Gynecologists, and other organizations and individual physicians filed suit, asking that the court strike down the new regulation as well. The Federal District Court for the Southern District of New York suspended the new rules, and its judgment was affirmed by the U.S. Court of Appeals for the Second Circuit. The government appealed, and the case was argued before the U.S. Supreme Court on 15 January 1986. On 9 June 1986, the Court affirmed the appeals court ruling.

In the meantime, Congress passed and President Reagan signed the Child Abuse Prevention and Treatment Act of 1984, broadening the definition of abuse in the original Child Abuse Prevention and Treatment Act of 1974 to include medical infanticide of disabled children. The act was intended to provide the same protections HHS sought to extend under Section 504.

See also Baby Doe Case; Baby Jane Doe Case; Child Abuse Prevention and Treatment Act of 1984.

Braille

Braille is a system of writing that translates letters, symbols, and digits into a pattern of raised dots legible to blind readers by touch. It was first unveiled in France by Louis Braille in 1829. Braille was brought to the United States in 1860 by Simon Pollak of the Missouri School for the Blind.

The new method had obvious advantages over the system then in use—embossed or raised print, which most blind people found extremely difficult to read. Sighted instructors, however, were skeptical, until William Bell Wait, the sighted superintendent of the New York Institution for the Blind, created and published his own system. New York Point, as the new system came to be called, used raised dots like braille, but organized them differently. The advantage of New York Point was that it was less bulky than braille. New York Point, however, had numerous problems that braille did not, and blind readers complained that Wait's system was much more difficult to read. Wait's method of capitalization, for example, was so unwieldy that most books and pamphlets were published entirely in lower case. Nevertheless, New York Point was endorsed by the American Association of Instructors of the Blind (AAIB) in 1871 as the system of choice.

Joel W. Smith, a blind teacher at the Perkins Institution for the Blind in Boston, was the first to attempt to persuade the association to reconsider. Smith had refined Braille's original system, and he devised a list of common English contractions to make the system less bulky. He dubbed his approach Modified Braille, and presented it to the AAIB in 1878. Blind activist Robert Irwin described how "Mr. Wait and his friends gave the young mild-mannered Smith pretty harsh treatment...." The AAIB refused to reconsider, and New York Point retained its place as the only system sanctioned for use by professional educators of blind students.

What followed was a "war of the dots," somewhat analogous to the struggle between Deaf advocates and oralists over the legitimacy of American Sign Language (ASL). Like ASL, Modified Braille became an "underground" or "people's language" used for personal letters, shopping lists, diaries, and other day-to-day needs, while books and materials published by the American Printing House for the Blind were printed exclusively in New York Point. Sighted instructors and school superintendents attempted to suppress Modified Braille, prohibiting its use in classrooms and confiscating the appliances (slates and styluses) used to write it. Some schools continued to use the old embossed methods, as did several printing houses in different cities.

In 1892, a group of superintendents of schools for the blind, chaired by Michael Anagnos, the director of Perkins School for the Blind, met to discuss their dissatisfaction with this state of affairs, and with New York Point in particular. They formed a subcommittee to determine once and for all which system was easier to read and write. After hundreds of tests and interviews, the group recommended Modified Braille, and the Perkins School and several others converted to the system. Most schools, however, continued to use New York Point. In 1900, Modified Braille was renamed American Braille, at the suggestion of John T. Sibley, a member of the Anagnos committee.

The tide finally began to turn in 1909, when the New York City Public Schools held public hearings to determine which of the systems it would use in its newly established day program for blind students. The hearings were heavily attended by advo-

With her dog-guide at her feet, Martha Villa reads the instructions at New York's first braille automatic teller.

cates from both sides. Helen Keller, fluent in both systems, sent a letter detailing the various problems with New York Point, concluding that it was "much harder for me to read than American Braille" and was "a provincialism." The New York City Board of Education decided in favor of American Braille. At the 1910 annual meeting of the board of directors of the American Printing House for the Blind, a hotly debated resolution to allocate 40 percent of its funds for the printing of American Braille books passed by one vote. From then on, the victory of American Braille was a foregone conclusion, with schools across the country abandoning New York Point.

The next step for braille advocates was to standardize the British and American systems, so that each was understandable to readers of the other. Efforts to accomplish this culminated in 1932 in the "Treaty of London," signed by representatives of the blind communities of Great Britain and the United States. It modified American Braille in order to conform to British strictures, while requiring British Braille to drop many of the contractions American readers found confusing. Some differences between the two systems, however, remain to this day, making for some confusion for readers of one attempting to understand the other.

Today, the survival of American Braille is again being challenged, this time by advances in technology such as portable cassette recorders, enabling blind students to tape lectures and notes, and more esoteric (and expensive) devices such as the Kurtweil Reading Machine (a computer scanner attached to a speech synthesizer, enabling a blind user to read print text). The advent of Talking Books from the Library of Congress and then taped books from such services as Recordings for the Blind and Dyslexic brought about a decline in the number of braille readers. With blind students increasingly being mainstreamed into general public school classes (particularly since passage of the Education for All Handicapped Children Act of 1975), fewer educators are being trained in braille teaching, leading advocates in the blindness community to warn of a crisis in braille literacy. The availability of titles in braille, always a problem, has declined to the point where blind students often have to wait months to receive a needed book. Both the National Federation of the Blind and the American Council of the Blind have, in recent years, advocated for state legislation to ensure that all students who might benefit are offered a chance to become braille literate.

See also American Council of the Blind; Irwin, Robert B.; Keller, Helen Adams; National Federation of the Blind; Perkins School for the Blind; Oralism, Oral School.

References Irwin, Robert B., *As I Saw It* (1955); Spungin, Susan J., *Braille Literacy: Issues for Blind Persons, Families, Professionals, and Producers of Braille* (1989).

The Braille Forum
See American Council of the Blind.

Breaking New Ground
Farming and ranching have the highest rate of disabling injury of any industry in the United States. The Breaking New Ground Resource Center (BNG) was founded in 1979 to assist farmers and ranchers who have become disabled to continue in their profession. Although the organization focuses primarily on assisting residents of rural Indiana, the BNG also publishes a free newsletter that reaches 8,000 farmers, rehabilitation professionals, and others across the United States and in several foreign countries. The BNG helps to establish support groups for disabled farmers, provides help in finding appropriate adaptive technology to assist them with work and daily living, and develops publications and videotapes of benefit to farmers with disabilities.

The BNG is housed at Purdue University in West Lafayette, Indiana. It is funded by the USDA Extension Service and the Indiana Easter Seal Society.

See also Assistive Technology.

Breslin, Mary Lou (b. 1944)
Mary Lou Breslin is the president and chair of the board of directors of the Disability Rights Education and Defense Fund (DREDF) and a nationally recognized leader of the disability rights movement. She represents a new generation of disability advocates: disabled persons who, while not attorneys, learned how to use the law to expand disability rights in the late 1970s and early 1980s. "Her example," according to Patrisha Wright, "sent a statement out to the grass-roots that we no longer had to rely on [nondisabled] people to advocate for us, that we could take care of ourselves." As its co-founder and executive director from 1988 to 1991, Breslin supervised DREDF's participation in a number of ground-breaking disability rights cases.

Breslin was born on 29 October 1944, in Louisville, Kentucky. A survivor of polio, she graduated from the University of Illinois at Urbana-Champaign with a B.A. in sociology in 1966. She pursued her graduate studies at Roosevelt College in Chicago and at the University of Oklahoma in Norman until 1971, then she worked as a psychiatric social worker, a peer counselor, and a tutor. In 1975, she became the coordinator of the Disabled Students Placement Program at the University of California at Berkeley. In October 1978, she co-founded DREDF, where she became director of the Section 504 Training and Technical Assistance Program, training people with disabilities and the parents of disabled children from 13 western and midwestern states in disability rights law and enforcement. This role made her an important catalyst in recruiting new activists, training them in advocacy skills and strategies, and establishing an advocacy network for future actions. When, for example, enforcement of Section 504 of the Rehabilitation Act was gutted by the Supreme Court in *Grove City College v. Bell* (1984), Breslin and others at DREDF were quickly able to pull together a group of disabled people to testify before Congress about discrimination they had experienced for which they now had no recourse. This testimony was crucial in passage of the Civil Rights Restoration Act of 1987.

In 1979, Breslin was named deputy director of DREDF, and then acting executive director in January 1987. She became the executive director one year later, responsible for plotting direction, strategy, and tactics for what is the nation's single most important disability rights legal advocacy organization.

Breslin has contributed articles to *Mainstream*, *Disability Rights Review*, the *Disability Rights Education and Defense Fund News*, and other publications. She is the author of "Doubly Disadvantaged Women—Disabled Women" in *The Women's Economic Justice Agenda: Ideas for States* (1987), and she has been a lecturer at San Francisco State and Stanford Universities.

See also Civil Rights Restoration Act of 1987; Disability Rights Education and Defense Fund.

Bristo, Marca (b. 1953)

Marca Bristo is the founder of Access Living, Chicago's first independent living program. She served on the Task Force on the Rights and Empowerment of Americans with Disabilities, co-founded and was president of the National Council on Independent Living (NCIL), and was appointed to chair the National Council on Disability by President Bill Clinton in May 1994.

Bristo was born on 23 June 1953 in Albany, New York. She received her B.A. in sociology from Beloit College in Wisconsin and a B.S. in nursing in 1976 from Rush University College of Nursing in Chicago. She founded Access Living in 1979 and has been its president and chief executive officer ever since. She co-founded the NCIL in 1982, served as its vice president from 1983 to 1984, and its president from 1986 to 1989. In March 1995, Bristo was part of the U.S. delegation to the UN World Summit on Social Development, the first person with a physical disability (Bristo is spinal cord injured) to participate in a UN Summit. Bristo has also remained active in the Chicago area as a board member of the Rehabilitation Institute in Chicago, the chair of the Illinois Public Action Council board from 1989 to 1994, and the co-chair for the Campaign for Better Health Care in Illinois beginning in 1990. Bristo was on the Executive Steering Committee of the UN International Decade of Disabled Persons, the Executive Committee of the President's Committee on Employment of People with Disabilities, and a member of the Clinton/Gore transition team in 1992.

Bristo has received numerous awards, including the Distinguished Service Award of the President of the United States in 1992 and the Henry B. Betts Award in 1993.

See also Americans with Disabilities Act of 1990; International Year, International Decade of Disabled Persons; National Council on Disability; National Council on Independent Living; Task Force on Rights and Empowerment of Americans with Disabilities.

Bronston, William (b. 1939)

William Bronston is best known for his advocacy on behalf of people with cognitive and developmental disabilities. He was the key figure in exposing the horrific conditions at the Willowbrook State School in Staten Island, New York, which was a pivotal event in the campaign for community services and deinstitutionalization. He has also been an impetus to passage of such disability rights legislation as the Civil Rights of Institutionalized Persons Act of 1980 (CRIPA).

Bronston was born in Los Angeles, California, on 18 March 1939. He was a Guest Fellow in Child Development at the Freud Hampstead Child Therapy Clinic in London in 1964 and received his M.D. at the University of Southern California School of Medicine in 1965. He was a resident in psychiatry at the Menninger School and the Topeka State Hospital in Kansas, but he was dismissed after helping to organize a sit-down strike by the hospital's direct care staff for higher wages and better working conditions. In 1968, Bronston moved to New York to work at a neighborhood mental health clinic in Manhattan. In 1970, he became a clinical physician at the Willowbrook State School.

Finding conditions at Willowbrook "unbelievably bad," Bronston filed complaints with the institution's administration, for which he was disciplined. When confronting the administration and attempting to organize institution staff and the residents' families did not work, Bronston and others took the story to the media. Local television reporter Geraldo Rivera's reports from Willowbrook shocked New York viewers and brought national attention. In March 1972, a group of disability rights attorneys, families of residents, and the New York Association of Retarded Citizens (ARC) filed suit in federal court. A consent decree was approved by the federal court in May 1975, and, by 1983, roughly half of the institution's residents were living in the community.

After leaving Willowbrook, Bronston moved to California, where he was appointed to a variety of positions in the state's Departments of Health and Rehabilitation. In 1981, Bronston became the director of Project Interdependence, a program to promote the full integration of high school youth with and without disabilities. In 1991, he founded the World Interdependence Fund, with Ed Roberts as secretary. In 1995, Bronston coordinated protests against the decision by California physicians to deny disability rights advocate Sandra Jensen a heart/lung transplant entirely on the basis of her disability.

See also Civil Rights of Institutionalized Persons Act of 1980; Deinstitutionalization; Jensen, Sandra; Willowbrook State School.

Buck v. Bell 274 U.S. 200 (1927)

The U.S. Supreme Court ruled, in *Buck v. Bell*, that the forced sterilization of people with disabilities who were wards of the state was not a violation of their constitutional rights. This was the first ever Supreme Court ruling concerning the civil rights of people with disabilities not charged with a criminal offense.

The case came out of the eugenics movement of the early twentieth century, a primary goal of which was to sterilize or otherwise prevent people with disabilities from having children. In March 1924, Virginia passed a law permitting the forced sterilization of "inmates of institutions supported by the State who shall be found to be afflicted with an hereditary form of insanity or imbecility." In September of that year 17-year-old Carrie Buck, a resident at the Virginia Colony for Epileptics and Feebleminded at Lynchburg, was ordered sterilized based on a diagnosis of "moral imbecility." Buck had given birth to a child shortly before being incarcerated at Lynchburg. Though eugenicists charged that Buck was a prostitute, her pregnancy was in fact the result of a rape committed by a member of her foster family. Buck appealed the order, asking for a court ruling. Without examining Buck or her mother, Harry Laughlin, head of the Eugenics Record Office, determined that the both of them belonged "to the shiftless, ignorant, and worthless class of anti-social whites of the South." Arthur Estrabrook, also of the Eugenics Record Office, examined Buck's daughter, Vivian, and testified that she too was "feeble-minded." The judge ordered the sterilization to proceed, and his ruling was upheld by the Virginia Supreme Court.

The case was brought before the U.S. Supreme Court on 22 April 1927. In an eight-to-one decision on 2 May 1927, the Court allowed the sterilization to proceed. Chief Justice Oliver Wendell Holmes wrote that "it is better for all the world, if instead of waiting to execute degenerate offspring for crime, or to let them starve for their imbecility, society can prevent those who are manifestly unfit from continuing their kind. . . . Three generations of imbeciles are enough." Ironically, Vivian Buck would go on to make the honor roll at her school in Charlottesville, excelling in all subjects except math, and there is serious doubt as to whether her mother was cognitively disabled at all.

Carrie Buck's sister Doris was also sterilized in 1928. In her case physicians told her they were performing an appendectomy, as it was the common practice of the time to deceive victims into having the operation.

See also Eugenics; Forced Sterilization; T-4.
References Trombley, Stephen, *The Right To Reproduce: A History of Coercive Sterilization* (1988).

Burgdorf, Robert L., Jr. (b. 1948)

Robert L. Burgdorf Jr. is the author of the original Americans with Disabilities Act, and thus a principal figure in the history of disability rights. He is the author, co-author, or editor of numerous major works on disability rights law.

Burgdorf was born on 27 July 1948, in Evansville, Indiana. As a young man and a polio survivor he was denied employment as an electrician's apprentice because he could not use his right arm. He graduated with his law degree from the University of Notre Dame in Indiana in 1973. He began

his involvement in disability rights litigation while still a law student, by helping to establish, and becoming a staff attorney at, the National Center for Law and the Handicapped. He left the center in 1976 to become the co-director and vice president of the Developmental Disabilities Law Project, Inc., at the University of Maryland Law School in Baltimore. From 1982 to 1985, he was an attorney advisor in the Office of the General Counsel of the U.S. Commission on Civil Rights, where he co-authored its report on discrimination against people with disabilities. The report demonstrated that there were serious gaps in the legal protections of people with disabilities, and it convinced Burgdorf of the need for a comprehensive federal disability rights law, modeled on the Civil Rights Act of 1964. In 1984, Burgdorf and his colleague Chris Bell published "Eliminating Discrimination against Physically and Mentally Handicapped Persons: A Statutory Blueprint," the first outline of such a law, in the *Mental and Physical Disability Law Reporter*.

It was as the attorney/research specialist for the National Council on the Handicapped, or NCH (since renamed the National Council on Disability, or NCD) that Burgdorf became instrumental in changing the face of disability rights law in the United States. In 1985, Burgdorf and council member Justin Dart Jr. began collaborating on an Americans with Disabilities Act (ADA). They prepared a report, *Toward Independence*, published by the National Council on the Handicapped in 1986, calling for an ADA. A draft of the legislation was introduced into Congress in 1988, but it had insufficient support for passage. Nevertheless, Burgdorf's draft legislation, although substantially rewritten, was passed as the Americans with Disabilities Act of 1990.

Burgdorf left the NCD in 1988, becoming vice president for Project ACTION (Accessible Community Transportation in Our Nation) at the National Easter Seal Society. In 1989, he became a professor of law at the District of Columbia School of

Law. He has also taught at the University of Maryland, and he gave a lecture series entitled "The Civil Rights of Handicapped Persons" at the University of Notre Dame School of Law as early as 1973.

Burgdorf's writing goes back to the mid-1970s, with "A History of Unequal Treatment: The Qualifications of Handicapped People as a 'Suspect Class' under the Equal Protection Clause" appearing in the *Santa Clara Lawyer* in 1975. Since then, he has written extensively on all aspects of disability law. His books include *Accommodating the Spectrum of Individual Abilities* (1983) and *The Legal Rights of Handicapped Persons: Cases, Materials, and Text* (1980), which at 1,126 pages was the first disability rights law school casebook. His 1,270-page *Disability Discrimination in Employment Law* was published in 1996. He has also written numerous articles and book chapters, including the foreword to *Sexuality, Law, and the Developmentally Disabled* (1981), and he is the editor of *One Nation Indivisible: The Civil Rights Challenge for the 1990s* (1989).

See also Americans with Disabilities Act of 1990; Dart, Justin, Jr.; National Council on Disability.

Burke, Christopher Joseph (b. 1965)

As the star of the television series "Life Goes On," Christopher Joseph Burke became a role model and spokesperson for people with cognitive disabilities. The show dramatized the challenges facing "Corky" Thatcher, an 18-year-old with Down syndrome, as he attempted to fit in at a mainstream high school. For millions of viewers, this was their first exposure to the idea that people with developmental disabilities were not alien or frightening. That Burke could become a television actor, memorizing dialogue and contributing ideas for scripts, also shattered many people's misconceptions about the capabilities of people with Down syndrome.

Burke was born on 26 August 1965, in New York City. His family doctor recommended that he be institutionalized, saying, "He'll probably never walk or talk. He won't amount to anything." Instead, Burke's parents raised him at home, insisting that he have a quality education. Even they, however, were skeptical about their son's ambition to become an actor. Their attitude changed after Burke's television debut, in the series pilot "Desperate," which aired in 1987. Although they rejected the series, ABC network producers were so impressed with Burke that they decided to design a series around him. *Life Goes On* premiered in September 1989, and the 23-year-old Burke went from being an elevator operator to a $250,000-a-year television star.

Burke has used his celebrity to advocate, through public speaking and television public service announcements, for greater employment opportunities for people with disabilities. After leaving television, Burke became an advocate and spokesperson for the National Down Syndrome Society and the editor of its quarterly *News and Views* newsletter.

References Burke, Chris, and Jo Beth McDaniel, *A Special Kind of Hero* (1991).

Burlington School Committee v. Department of Education
105 S. Ct. 1996 (1985)

In *Burlington School Committee v. Department of Education*, the U.S. Supreme Court answered several important questions regarding the rights and responsibilities of parents and school officials who disagree over what is an appropriate education for a disabled child under the Education for All Handicapped Children Act of 1975. Specifically, the Court ruled that the Burlington School Committee had to reimburse the parents of a disabled child for private schooling during the time they were in litigation to determine the most appropriate placement for that child.

The case began in June 1979, when the parents of third grader Michael Panico challenged the Burlington, Massachusetts, school system's plans for their son for the coming academic year. Michael had been experiencing difficulties in school since the first grade, and it had become evident that he had a learning disability. The school system proposed that Michael be sent to the Pine Glen School, where he would attend a highly structured class for children with emotional disabilities. However, a review by specialists at the Massachusetts General Hospital in Boston concluded that Michael's disability was primarily neurological, rather than psychological, and it recommended "a highly specialized setting for children with learning handicaps...such as the Carroll School," a state-approved private school in Lincoln, Massachusetts. The Panicos enrolled Michael at this school in September 1979, paying tuition and expenses out of their own pocket. Upon review of the public school's proposed Individualized Education Program (IEP), the Massachusetts Department of Education's Bureau of Special Education Appeals sided with the Panicos and ordered the Burlington School Committee to pay tuition and expenses and to reimburse the Panicos for bills already paid. The committee filed a federal suit to overturn this decision and, in the meantime, refused to pay tuition for Michael at the Carroll School or to reimburse the Panicos for bills already paid. The Department of Education decision was overturned by the U.S. District Court for the District of Massachusetts, which was itself overruled by the U.S. Court of Appeals. After further proceedings, the case was argued before the U.S. Supreme Court on 26 March 1985 and was decided on 29 April 1985.

In its ruling, the Court took up two issues: (1) whether financial relief to parents under the act includes reimbursement for private school tuition and expenses, if a court determines that a private school was the only way a child could receive "a free appropriate public education," and (2) whether the act bars such reimbursement to parents who place their child in a private school without official consent during proceedings to determine whether or not the proposed IEP is appropriate. Justice Rehnquist, writing for the majority, concluded that the act "authorizes such reimbursement." Secondly, the Court did not agree with the school committee that placing Michael in the Carroll School constituted "a waiver of reimbursement" because his parents had made the placement without the school committee's consent. To rule otherwise, wrote Justice Rehnquist, would force parents, during the years it might take to resolve a dispute, "to leave the child in what may turn out to be an inappropriate educational placement.... The Act was intended to give handicapped children both an appropriate education and a free one; it should not be interpreted to defeat one or the other of those objectives."

See also Education for All Handicapped Children Act of 1975.

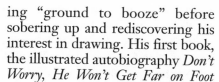

Callahan, John (b. 1951)

John Callahan is a cartoonist and humorist who uses his own life experience as a person with a disability as the primary source for his material. From two cowboys in wheelchairs, confronting each other on main street in the classic showdown pose ("This town isn't accessible enough for the both of us.") to a sketch of "The Hunchback Hiking Club Stops for Lunch" (none of its members can reach around far enough to undo their packs), Callahan's humor has delighted, and offended, people with and without disabilities. As Dave Barry says, "John Callahan is proof that a person can

"Don't worry, He won't get far on foot."

Cartoonist John Callahan, a quadriplegic, draws on his life experience to amuse and even offend people with and without disabilities. The cartoon, pictured here, appeared in John Callahan's first book, Don't Worry, He Won't Get Far on Foot, *an autobiography published in 1989.*

go through great adversity and pain and still—through a triumph of the human spirit—be really weird."

Callahan was born on 5 February 1951 in Portland, Oregon. Disabled in a car wreck at age 21, he spent several years los-

ing "ground to booze" before sobering up and rediscovering his interest in drawing. His first book, the illustrated autobiography *Don't Worry, He Won't Get Far on Foot* (1989), won acclaim for its realistic but often hilarious depiction of life as a quadriplegic.

Don't Worry was followed by *Do Not Disturb Any Further* (1989), *Digesting the Child Within* (1991), and *Do What He Says! He's Crazy!!!* (1992). In 1996, Callahan ran for Congress as a Republican, but dropped out before the election for health reasons.

References Callahan, John, *Do Not Disturb Any Further* (1989); ———, *Don't Worry, He Won't Get Far on Foot* (1989).

Callo, Tiffany Ann (b. 1967)

In the late 1980s, Tiffany Ann Callo lost custody of both her children to the Department of Social Services of Santa Clara County, California. She became a symbol of society's refusal to believe that people with disabilities can be loving, competent parents.

Callo was born on 21 April 1967 in San Jose, California, but her cerebral palsy was not evident until she was 18 months old. She was placed in foster care when she was 12 years old. Callo had an abortion at age 16, after being raped by a member of the staff of the group home where she was living. By age 19, she was living on her own, and in a relationship with Anthony Rios, also disabled, whom she eventually married. Their first son, David, was born on 3 March 1987. Within 24 hours, Santa Clara County social workers had separated David from his parents, refusing Callo and Rios permission to see their child. The county alleged that Callo suffered from "a physical disability rendering her incapable of providing appropriate nurturance, stimulation, and care to said infant minor." Callo's second son, Jesse, was also removed from his mother's custody almost immediately after his birth in January 1988, after which a story in the *San Jose Mercury News* about the county's actions was picked up by the national media.

One of the ironies of the case was that Santa Clara County was willing to spend more than a $1,000 a month to keep Callo's children in foster care, but unwilling to devote a cent to providing Callo with personal assistance services to help her with parenting. Instead, the county attempted to prove that Callo was incapable of being a good mother. A variety of "specialists"—none of whom had experience with people with disabilities—were brought in to "evaluate" Callo, labeling her paranoid, mentally retarded, and incapable of empathy for her children. When the county did bring in a consultant experienced with disabled parents, Megan Light Kirshbaum, she concluded that Callo was intelligent, quick to learn, eager to be a good parent, and highly empathetic. Kirshbaum's assessment was ignored. In June 1988, the Santa Clara County Juvenile Court heard arguments that Callo be allowed to regain custody of her children.

Disability rights advocates rallied to Callo's cause, and her attorney was willing to argue the case all the way to the U.S. Supreme Court. When he explained, however, that this could take as much as eight years and that losing would mean she would never see her children again, Callo decided to compromise. In return for the county allowing visitation rights and promising to keep her sons together, Callo agreed to relinquish her parental rights. The foster family in which they had been placed decided soon after that two new children was too great a burden, and Santa Clara County authorities, in violation of its agreement with Callo, separated the children.

In January 1989, Callo appeared on the *Phil Donahue* show to tell her story. A member of the audience asked her, "What are your plans if you do have another child?" She replied, "To have a whole lot of money and a good attorney."

See also Parenting and Disability; Personal Assistance Services (PAS).

Reference Mathews, Jay, *A Mother's Touch: The Tiffany Callo Story—The True Story of a Physically Disabled Mother's Fight for the Right To Keep Her Children* (1992).

Cannon, Dennis M. (b. 1943)

Dennis M. Cannon is a leading advocate and expert on transportation access, and he has been a transportation accessibility specialist for the U.S. Architectural and Transportation Barriers Compliance Board since 1981. A consumer of accessible public transit himself, he is the author and co-author of numerous articles, monographs, and books on access, including *Design Criteria for Transportation for Disabled Persons: A Test of Equivalence* (1976), *Full Mobility: Counting the Cost of the Alternatives* (1980), and *A Funny Thing Happened on the Way to the Bus Stop* (1980).

Cannon was born on 5 July 1943 in Los Angeles. He received a B.S. in physics in 1968 from the California State University at Northridge, where he also did graduate work in physics, mathematics, and computer sciences. He is the founder and past president of Synergy Systems, a consulting firm that helps to plan accessible mass transit systems; a past consultant for the U.S. Department of Transportation; and a member of numerous boards and committees related to transportation and telecommunications access.

See also Architectural and Transportation Barriers Compliance Board; Metropolitan Area Transit Authority (Metro) Access Campaign; Paratransit; Public Transportation.

Captioning/Closed Captioning

Captioning is the inclusion of printed text, appearing on the screen, to accompany movies or television programs. Captioning enables deaf and hard-of-hearing viewers to more fully understand the content of what they are watching.

Deaf viewers had no problem understanding movies when they first appeared in the late nineteenth and early twentieth centuries because all films were silent, and all films were subtitled. It was not until the advent of "talkies" that deaf people were excluded from full enjoyment of films. The development of television only intensified this alienation, with deaf viewers effectively shut out of a huge part of American popular culture.

Probably the first attempt to caption a talking movie for deaf viewers was made in the late 1940s by Emerson Romero, a deaf actor who had appeared in several silent films. The "talkies" brought an end to his movie career, though his cousin Caesar became a star. Romero bought copies of popular films, spliced captions between scenes, and then rented the films to deaf clubs and churches. This method was, however, expensive and awkward. In 1950, Edmund B. Boatner, headmaster of the American School for the Deaf, established Captioned Films for the Deaf, which acquired, captioned, and then rented popular films. The passage of Pub. Law 85-905 (an act to provide in the Department of Health, Education and Welfare for a loan service of captioned films for the deaf) in 1958 put the project under the aegis of the U.S. Department of Education. Only $78,000, however, was appropriated to provide captioned films for the entire U.S. deaf population, a sum clearly inadequate to the task. The program was expanded in the 1960s, and four regional media centers were established, with an early emphasis on educational films and documentaries for use in schools. By 1970, Captioned Films for the Deaf had an annual budget of $3 million.

Access to television for deaf and hard-of-hearing people began in late 1971, with the founding of the Caption Center at WGBH Public Television in Boston. The first television program to be captioned was Julia Child's "The French Chef" in 1972. Captions were "open," that is, visible to all television viewers. The Caption Center also began production of the *Captioned ABC News*, rebroadcast later in the evening by more than 190 PBS stations. For the first time, deaf and hard-of-hearing individuals had access to the daily television news. Commercial breaks were replaced with material of interest to deaf viewers.

Closed captions are television captions encoded so that they are visible only to viewers with the equipment necessary to decode them. This equipment can be built into the television or into a set-top decoder connected to a television without decoding capability. The Americans with Disabilities Act of 1990 requires that all public service announcements produced or funded in part or in whole by any agency of the federal government be closed captioned. The Television Decoder Circuitry Act of 1990 required that all televisions sold in the United States after July 1993 with screens 13 inches or larger must have built-in decoder circuitry. The Telecommunications Act of 1996 required that all "video programming first published or exhibited" after 18 months of the act's passage be closed captioned.

See also Communications Access.

References Gannon, Jack R., *Deaf Heritage: A Narrative History of Deaf America* (1981).

Carlin, John (1813–1891)

John Carlin was a poet, artist, writer, and activist. He was born on 15 June 1813 and deafened in infancy. The son of a cobbler, he wandered the streets of Philadelphia as a young boy, until he was taken in by David Seixas, a merchant who assisted deaf street children. Carlin received an education at Seixas's Mt. Airy School, later renamed the Pennsylvania Institution for the Deaf and Dumb. He left that school at age 12 to become a house painter. In the 1830s, he moved to New York to study art, then traveled to London and Paris to continue his studies. He returned to New York to found his own studio after three years as the student of French painter Hippolyte Paul Delaroche. Carlin also published a children's book, *The Scratchsides Family*, and a great deal of poetry, including autobiographical verse about his deafness.

Catlin, John H.

Carlin was an early advocate for the creation of the National College for the Deaf, which eventually became Gallaudet University in Washington, D.C. He gave a speech in American Sign Language (ASL) at the college's opening ceremony in 1864. Carlin, however, considered ASL a poor substitute for English. Although ambivalent about oralism and unable to either speak or lip-read, Carlin believed that fingerspelling and writing English were the best methods for teaching deaf children. He died on 23 April 1891.

See also Gallaudet University; Oral School, Oralism.

References Gannon, Jack R., *Deaf Heritage: A Narrative History of Deaf America* (1981); Moore, Matthew S., and Robert F. Panara, *Great Deaf Americans: The Second Edition* (1996).

Catlin, John H. (b. 1947)

John H. Catlin is nationally recognized as an advocate for and expert on the design of spaces and structures accessible to people with disabilities. The former director of Access Chicago, he was appointed by President Clinton to serve on the U.S. Architectural and Transportation Barriers Compliance Board in 1994, and he served as its chair from 1995 to 1996. He is an architect who specializes in barrier free design.

Catlin was born on 21 November 1947 in Ottawa, Illinois. He received a bachelor of arts in design from Southern Illinois University in Carbondale in 1974 and a master of architecture from the University of Illinois–Chicago in 1982. He was pivotal in the development of the Illinois Accessibility Standards of 1978 and the Illinois state Environmental Barriers Act of 1988. He has also been involved in drafting the Americans with Disabilities Act (ADA) Architectural Guidelines (ADAG) and in work under Title II of the ADA, mandating access in government facilities, most particularly the Chicago public schools. He has served and continues to serve on numerous boards and committees, and he lectures widely on access issues. He is a member of the American Institute of Architects and its Illinois Accessibility Task Force.

See also Architectural Access; Architectural and Transportation Barriers Compliance Board.

Center for Accessible Housing
See Center for Universal Design.

Center for Independent Living, Inc.

The Center for Independent Living, Inc. (or the CIL at Berkeley), the world's first community-based independent living center, was established in Berkeley, California, in March 1972. It was born out of the experience and advocacy of a group of disabled students at the University of California at Berkeley, most especially Edward V. Roberts and John Hessler.

Roberts began attending classes at U.C. Berkeley in the fall of 1962. He lived at the Student Health Service, located on campus at the Cowell Hospital, where he was joined in 1963 by Hessler. By 1967, Cowell was home to 12 severely disabled students, and, in 1968, it became a formal program managed by the California Department of Rehabilitation.

The Berkeley campus during the 1960s was a center of political activism, and the Cowell Residence Program students caught the excitement of the free speech movement, feminism, civil rights activism, black pride, and the students' antiwar movement. Inspired by what was happening around them, they began to define themselves in political terms, as an oppressed minority, instead of in medical terms as "patients" or "cases." They experienced a sense of community and of commonly shared obstacles, such as the lack of curb-cuts and ramps on campus and in the surrounding community. Calling themselves the "Rolling Quads" they protested the arbitrary restrictions imposed on them by the counselors of the Department of Rehabilitation. These conflicts came to a head when one counselor attempted to send two students into a nursing home, because she had determined they were "infeasible" and unlikely to get jobs after college. Roberts, Hessler, and other students insisted that the counselor be reassigned and that the students be reinstated in the program. When meetings with Department of Rehabilitation officials were unsuccessful (at one meeting a psychiatrist threatened the protesters with institutionalization), the Rolling Quads went to the local newspapers. The state backed down in the glare of the negative publicity, reassigning the counselor and reinstating both students.

The Rolling Quads now began to look for ways to leave Cowell entirely and to plan for what would happen after their graduation. In 1969, Roberts went to Washington, D.C., at the request of Jean Wirth, who had been his counselor at San Mateo College prior to his admission to Berkeley. Wirth had taken a position at the U.S. Department of Health, Education and Welfare (HEW) and had developed an innovative program of mentoring, peer counseling, and support services designed to reduce the drop-out rate of minority college students. She asked Roberts and the Rolling Quads to design a similar program for disabled students. The package they developed was the Physically Disabled Students' Program (PDSP). Included were provisions for personal assistance services (PAS), wheelchair repair, emergency attendant care, and help in obtaining whatever financial benefits were available under the various state and federal social service and rehabilitation programs.

The Cowell residents outlined three basic principles on which the PDSP would operate: (1) that the experts on disability are the people with the disabilities; (2) that the needs of people with disabilities can best be met by a comprehensive, or holistic, program, rather than by fragmented programs at different agencies and offices; and (3) that people with disabilities should be integrated into the community. These principles would become the heart of the independent living philosophy.

The PDSP was founded in July 1970 with $81,000 in HEW funding. It began full operation in September of that year. As word spread, many more disabled people began to apply for serices, even though they were not students. As a result, in May 1971, PDSP students began meeting with community residents with the goal of establishing a PDSP off campus. To a great extent, however, the impetus for a program independent from the university came from the students themselves. Without some new program to help them maintain their independence, reinstitutionalization seemed for many the only option. The Center for Independent Living, Inc., which came out of the PDSP meetings, was officially incorporated in 1972, receiving a one-year $50,000 grant from the federal Rehabilitation Services Administration.

The first years of the CIL were touch and go, with funding always a problem. Sonny Kleinfield, author of *The Hidden Minority* (1979) described the CIL's first "headquarters" as "a roach infested two-bedroom apartment." Roberts and others wrote grant proposals, approached the university and state and federal agencies, and held fund-raisers and benefit poker games to keep the CIL afloat. During this time, disability rights advocates from across the country became interested in what was happening at Berkeley. Judith Heumann, the founder of Disabled in Action in New York City, moved to California in September 1973, joining the CIL's board and eventually becoming its deputy director. Phil Draper, a disabled community activist and a CIL co-founder, became its second director after the departure of Roberts.

Central to the philosophy of the CIL was that it be an advocacy organization rather than a social service agency. To this end, in the late 1970s, the CIL founded the Disability Law Resource Center, which later became the independent Disability Rights Education and Defense Fund (DREDF). The CIL's definition of disability as a self-help, rather than a medical issue, was a defining breakthrough for many future disability rights activists. Besides Roberts, Hessler, and Heumann, national disability rights leaders who have worked at the CIL include Joan Leon,

Hale Zukas, Mary Jane Owen, Robert Funk, Don Galloway, Patrisha Wright, and Mary Lou Breslin.

As of 1995, more than 400 independent living centers had been founded worldwide. As of 1997, there were 367 centers and their satellites in the United States alone, all modeled to a greater or lesser extent on the first CIL at Berkeley, while the concept of PAS had become a major political issue for the disability rights movement in the United States. Today, the CIL at Berkeley provides services and advocacy, including peer counseling, and employment and housing referrals for thousands of people each year.

See also Breslin, Mary Lou; Disability Rights Education and Defense Fund; Funk, Robert J.; Independent Living, Independent Living Movement; Hessler, John; Heumann, Judith E.; Owen, Mary Jane; Personal Assistance Services; Roberts, Edward V.; Wright, Patrisha A.; Zukas, Hale.

References Laurie, Gini, *Housing and Home Services for the Disabled* (1977); Kleinfield, Sonny, *The Hidden Minority* (1979); Levy, Chava Willig, *A People's History of the Independent Living Movement* (1988); Shapiro, Joseph, *No Pity: People with Disabilities Forging a New Civil Rights Movement* (1993, 1994); Zukas, Hale, *CIL History* (1979).

Center for Universal Design

The Center for Universal Design (formerly the Center for Accessible Housing) at the North Carolina State University School of Design was founded in 1989 as an information clearinghouse and research center and to provide technical assistance for architects, builders, and consumers on accessible housing and universal design. It reviews plans by homeowners, designers, and developers for single and multifamily homes and for additions and modifications. The center assists with interpretation of the Fair Housing Act Accessibility Guidelines and publishes technical assistance booklets on accessible housing and universal design. It maintains a Design Advisory Network (DAN) of more than 1,300 people with disabilities, family members, or friends who provide feedback to the center. It also offers post–secondary level training on accessible design to people

with disabilities, disability advocates, and housing planners and providers. Among its publications are *Accessibility Standards for Children's Environments* (1992), *Financing Home Accessibility Modifications* (1993), and the *Accessible Stock House Plans Catalog* (1993).

See also Barrier Free Environments; Fair Housing Amendments Act of 1988; Housing; Mace, Ronald L.; Universal Design.

Center on Health and Disability
See Griss, Robert.

Center on Human Policy, Human Policy Press

The Center on Human Policy, established in 1971, is a research and advocacy organization based at Syracuse University in Syracuse, New York. It was founded by Burton Blatt, author of *Christmas in Purgatory* (1966), with the purpose of ending the warehousing of children with developmental disabilities. Through its investigations, community education, legal advocacy, and development of alternatives to institutionalization, the center has worked both locally and nationally for deinstitutionalization. Today, as the sponsor of the National Resource Center on Community Integration, it focuses on the integration of people with developmental disabilities into the community.

The center publishes a range of materials through its Human Policy Press from books such as *Ordinary Moments: The Disabled Experience* (1985) to works by Wolf Wolfensberger and texts by activists in People First and Self Advocates Becoming Empowered. The center also offers art reproductions by Eleanor Rubin and Mark Morris, whose poster "You Gave Us Your Dimes, Now We Want Our Rights" adorns the walls of disability rights activists across the country.

See also Christmas in Purgatory; Normalization; Ordinary Moments: The Disabled Experience; People First, People First International; Self Advocates Becoming Empowered.

Chamberlin, Judi (b. 1944)

Judi Chamberlin has worked on behalf of psychiatric survivors and people with mental disabilities since 1971. Her book *On Our Own: Patient-Controlled Alternatives to the Mental Health System*, published in 1978, is a basic text of the psychiatric survivor movement.

Chamberlin was born on 30 October 1944 in New York City. By 1965, she was married, employed as a secretary, and expecting her first child. After the child miscarried, she went into a period of mourning, which became a feeling of depression over the general course of her life. Seeing a psychiatrist, she was labeled a chronic schizophrenic. As she writes in *On Our Own*, she agreed to enter a mental hospital, where she "expected to find help and understanding; instead, I found that no one listened to me or took me seriously. Heavy doses of psychiatric drugs were the 'treatment.' When I protested that I didn't find them helpful, my opinions were simply dismissed. I soon found myself committed to a state hospital, where I remained for several months. It was the worst period of my life. My struggle to overcome the effects of this experience was what led me to become involved in the ex-patients' movement."

Like Clifford Beers' *A Mind That Found Itself* (1908), *On Our Own* recounts the abuse and neglect that are routine in the treatment of people with mental disabilities. Unlike Beers, Chamberlin and contemporaries such as Howard Geld dedicated themselves in the 1970s to starting a grassroots movement of patients and ex-patients. Chamberlin has been an important voice in defining the goals and strategies of this movement. In an article published in the *Disability Rag & Resource*, she defined its "overarching principles" as "challenging . . . commitment/involuntary treatment laws and practices," "challenging (or questioning) the medical model of mental illness," seeking "protection and expansion of legal rights," "dealing with issues around stigma and discrimination," and "meeting people's need through alternative non-psychiatric means." For Cham-

berlin, this means the establishment of patient-controlled crisis centers and cooperatives, several of which she describes in her book.

Chamberlin has been active in the Mental Patients' Liberation Front (MPLF) since 1975. In 1985, she was among the founders of the National Association of Psychiatric Survivors. She is a founder of the Ruby Rogers Center, a consumer-run mental health clinic in the Boston area, and she is a founder and member of the board of directors of the National Empowerment Center in Lawrence, Massachusetts. Chamberlin writes and lectures widely on the psychiatric survivor movement.

See also Beers, Clifford Whittingham; Mental Patients' Liberation Front; National Empowerment Center; Psychiatric Survivor Movement.

References Chamberlin, Judi, *On Our Own: Patient Controlled Alternatives to the Mental Health System* (1978); ———, "Psychiatric Survivors: Are We Part of the Disability Rights Movement?" *Disability Rag & Resource* (March/April 1995).

Chemical Restraint/ Chemical Straitjacket

The terms *chemical restraint* and *chemical straitjacket* refer to psychotropic medications that are used to make people with disabilities, particularly those defined as "mentally ill," compliant and docile. The terms came into wide use in regard to phenothiazines, a class of drugs developed in the 1890s and first used to treat mental illness in Paris in 1951. Soon thereafter, use of "antipsychotic" drugs such as Thorazine and Stelazine came to be seen by mental health professionals as a less violent form of coercion than straitjackets, cold packs, or four-point restraints. However, advocate Judi Chamberlin writes that "while it may appear far more humane to inject someone with a drug than it is to tie a person up, in actuality they are just two different ways of accomplishing the same thing." Chamberlin notes that the side efforts of Thorazine, for example, include "lethargy, drowsiness, pseudo-Parkinsonism, and the possibility of developing an irreversible brain syndrome called tardive dyskinesia (uncontrollable involuntary movements of the mouth, tongue, and jaw, and possibly the extremities)."

While not all psychiatric survivor groups condemn the use of antihallucinagens, tranquilizers, antidepressants, and other psychotropic drugs, most believe that they are vastly over prescribed. Some psychiatrists have also condemned the widespread use of chemical straitjackets.

See also Chamberlin, Judi; Psychiatric Survivor Movement.

References Chamberlin, Judi, *On Our Own: Patient-Controlled Alternatives to the Mental Health System* (1978); Brandt, Anthony, *Reality Police* (1975).

Chicago Center for Disability Research

Historically, most scholarly research on the experiences of people with disabilities has been conducted by people who are not disabled. The Chicago Center for Disability Research, originally called the Chicago Institute of Disability Research, was founded by disabled scholars and researchers to change this pattern and to research topics of importance to the disability rights movement. Established in 1991, the center conducts and publishes research on such topics as the school experience of people with disabilities, what medical schools teach about disabled women's health issues, and the content and impact of disability-related college and university courses. The center assists advocates for inclusive education, does extensive professional training, and publishes educational materials. Established as a nonprofit organization, the institute joined the University of Illinois–Chicago to become the Chicago Center for Disability Research in 1996.

Child Abuse Prevention and Treatment Act Amendments of 1984

The Child Abuse Prevention and Treatment Act Amendments of 1984 were passed in response to the growing number of reported cases, such as those of Baby Doe and Baby Jane Doe, of disabled infants in U.S. hospitals being denied medical care, food, and water. The amend-

ments broadened the definition of abuse in the original Child Abuse Prevention and Treatment Act of 1974 to include medical infanticide of disabled children. They also mandated that each state, in order to be eligible for federal funds for their child abuse programs, must establish a reporting system to alert the proper child care and law enforcement authorities whenever a disabled infant was suffering such abuse.

Life and death decisions about disabled infants have often been made out of fear and ignorance of disability. In the early 1980s, physicians at the University of Oklahoma Health Sciences Center in Oklahoma City went so far as to develop a formula to determine which disabled infants should live and which should die: QL (Quality of Life) = NE (the child's "Natural Endowment") x (H + S), where H is the contribution the child can expect from his or her family, and S is the contribution the child can be expected to make to society. Using this formula, doctors withheld medical treatment from selected infants with spina bifida, including surgery that could have minimized the extent of their disabilities, and allowed them to die of infection. The infants' parents were not told about the formula, nor of the possibility for successful intervention. They were only told that their children were too disabled to be allowed to live. Critics charged that the formula, with its emphasis on income (contribution from the child's family), virtually guaranteed that low-income and minority children were more likely to be denied treatment and care than middle-class or white children. In any event, despite this attempt to quantify it, "quality of life" remains an illusive and entirely subjective judgment.

See also Baby Doe Case; Baby Jane Doe Case; Eugenics; Euthanasia and Assisted Suicide.

Children of a Lesser God

Children of a Lesser God is both a play by Mark Medoff and a movie by Medoff and Hesper Anderson. The movie tells the story of a deaf woman who falls in love

Marlee Matlin and William Hurt communicate their emotions in the 1986 motion picture Children of a Lesser God. *Matlin won an Academy Award, the first for a deaf actor, for her performance.*

with a speech teacher at the deaf school where she works as a custodian. Released in 1986, it won praise for the fact that its producers employed a number of deaf actors, a break from the Hollywood tradition of "disability blackface" (that is, hiring nondisabled actors to portray characters with disabilities). Among these actors was Marlee Matlin, who won an Academy Award for her leading role (the first ever for a deaf actor) and went on to act in other movies and television programs.

Some Deaf viewers who were familiar with the play criticized the movie for eliminating a major subplot dealing with a lawsuit brought by a deaf activist against the school. Matthew Moore and Robert Panara wrote that this "blunted much of the play's political bite, reducing it to a conventional love story and sweetening it with a happy ending." Deaf critics also noted that few of the theaters where it screened offered captioning for deaf viewers.

See also American Sign Language; Disability Blackface; Matlin, Marlee; Oral School, Oralism.

References Moore, Matthew Scott, and Robert F. Panara, *Great Deaf Americans (1996)*; Norden, Martin F., *The Cinema of Isolation: A History of Physical Disability in the Movies* (1994).

Chilmark Community
See Martha's Vineyard Deaf Community

Christmas in Purgatory: A Photographic Essay on Mental Retardation

First published in August 1966, *Christmas in Purgatory: A Photographic Essay on Mental Retardation*, was a searing look inside U.S. institutions for people with developmental disabilities. The first edition of 1,000 copies was sent to prominent lawmakers, university professors, commissioners of mental health, and advocates in the mental retardation parents' movement.

The bulk of *Christmas in Purgatory* consists of photographs taken at five state institutions in four northeastern states visited in December 1965. Compiled by Burton

Blatt of Boston University, and freelance photographer Fred Kaplan, the purpose of the book was to "inspire constructive action among those in responsible positions . . . to shatter the shell of complacency born of ignorance." Kaplan took hundreds of photographs with a camera concealed in his belt. Blatt wrote in his introduction that "our pictures could not even begin to capture the total and overwhelming horror we saw, smelled, and felt. . . ." Blatt and Kaplan described "therapeutic isolation cells" where children were kept in solitary confinement without beds, water, or toilets. They remark, "We saw children with hands tied and legs bound," and after visiting institution day rooms, "we had to send our clothes to the dry cleaners to have the stench removed . . . in each day room is an attendant or two, whose main function seems to be to 'stand around' and, on occasion, hose down the floor 'driving' excretions into a sewer conveniently located in the center of the room." On other wards, they found hundreds of infants crowded in their cribs "without interaction with any adult, without playthings, without any apparent stimulation."

Blatt and Kaplan did not urge the end of state institutions, merely their reform. Nevertheless, *Christmas in Purgatory* was often cited by the advocates of deinstitutionalization in the 1970s and 1980s.

See also Deinstitutionalization.

Reference Blatt, Burton, and Fred Kaplan, *Christmas in Purgatory: A Photographic Essay on Mental Retardation* (1974).

City of Cleburne, Tex. v. Cleburne Living Center 105 S. Ct. 3249 (1985)

The U.S. Supreme Court decision of 1 July 1985, in *City of Cleburne, Tex. v. Cleburne Living Center* was a mixed victory for the advocates who filed suit. The unanimous Court struck down a decision by the Cleburne city government to prohibit the Cleburne Living Center from opening a group home for people with cognitive disabilities in a predominantly residential neighborhood. The Court, however, also rejected the argument that "the mentally retarded" constituted a "quasi-suspect classification," that is, a class of people with a history of oppression and discrimination that justifies "a more exacting standard of judicial review" of legislation alleged to deny this class equal protection under the law. This mixed decision, while it offered relief to the Cleburne Living Center, was of limited help to other group homes facing similar discrimination.

Justice Marshall, in a separate opinion, concurred with the majority ruling that "all retarded individuals cannot be grouped together as the 'feebleminded' and deemed presumptively unfit to live in the community." He did not agree, however, with the Court's ruling that laws concerning people with cognitive disabilities were not "quasi-suspect." Marshall traced the history of discrimination against those labeled mentally retarded, including the eugenics movement and the Court's own ruling in *Buck v. Bell* (1927), calling this period in American history "a regime of state-mandated segregation and degradation . . . that in its virulence and bigotry rivaled, and indeed paralleled, the worst excesses of Jim Crow." Marshall chided the majority for refusing to recognize that this history colored the way people with cognitive disabilities are treated today. "With respect to a liberty so valued as the right to establish a home in the community, and so likely to be denied on the basis of irrational fears and outright hostility, heightened scrutiny is surely appropriate."

See also Buck v. Bell; Eugenics.

Civil Rights of Institutionalized Persons Act of 1980 (CRIPA)

The Civil Rights of Institutionalized Persons Act of 1980 (CRIPA) authorized the U.S. Justice Department to file civil suits on behalf of residents of institutions, including psychiatric hospitals and facilities for people with developmental disabilities, whenever those persons are subject "to egregious or flagrant conditions which deprive such persons" of their constitutional rights. The law was passed after *Wyatt v. Stickney* (1974) and other litigation revealed to the public the horrendous conditions endured by the residents of state institutions. In response to these revelations, Sen. Lowell Weicker (R-CT), himself the parent of a disabled child, sent the Senate Subcommittee on the Handicapped to investigate conditions at various institutions, and he concluded that many particularly egregious cases of abuse required the intervention of the U.S. Justice Department. Because the Justice Department had never been given the explicit authority to "initiate or to intervene in litigation to enforce basic constitutional rights of institutionalized persons," however, such intervention had to wait for a judge's request or petitions from parties in whatever legal action had already been initiated. CRIPA was designed to remedy this problem, allowing the Justice Department to file suit whenever it receives evidence that an institution's residents are being denied their constitutional rights.

See also Wyatt v. Stickney.

Civil Rights Restoration Act of 1987

The purpose of the Civil Rights Restoration Act of 1987 was to overturn the U.S. Supreme Court decision in *Grove City College v. Bell* (1984). The Court's ruling in that case dramatically narrowed the federal government's ability to enforce each of the four major civil rights laws passed since 1964, including Section 504 of the Rehabilitation Act of 1973. Passage of the Civil Rights Restoration Act was a high priority for thousands of civil rights activists and organizations, including most of the national leadership of the disability rights movement.

In *Grove*, a woman alleged that she had been discriminated against by a department of her college on the basis of her gender. She brought suit under Title IX of the Education Amendments of 1972 prohibiting discrimination on the basis of gender in programs and activities receiving federal funds. The Court ruled that,

whether or not the discrimination actually occurred, the victim in this case was not protected because the particular department of the school discriminating against her did not receive federal funds. Title IX was modeled after Title VI of the Civil Rights Act of 1964, as were the Age Discrimination Act of 1975 and Section 504 of the Rehabilitation Act of 1973. Thus any Supreme Court decision affecting the government's ability to prohibit sex discrimination under Title IX would also affect efforts under the other acts to combat discrimination on the basis of race, age, and disability. Even so, efforts by nondisabled civil rights groups to address the problem at first focused exclusively on Title IX. It was not until Brad Reynolds, assistant attorney general for the Reagan administration, told the *New York Times* that he would apply *Grove* across the board that Section 504 was also addressed in the legislation. Ironically, Reynolds' statement helped to elevate disability rights activists to national prominence within the nondisabled civil rights movement and also rallied the disability community to protect Section 504.

Advocates soon encountered examples of discrimination against people with disabilities, which, because of *Grove*, they were powerless to address. In *Jacobson v. Delta Airlines* (1984) a policy of forcing disabled passengers to sign a statement before boarding, agreeing to be removed from the plane at any stop for unspecified reasons, was allowed to stand, even though the practice was blatantly discriminatory and even though Delta Airlines received considerable and varied types of federal assistance. In *Russell v. Salve Regina College* (1986), a Section 504 complaint against a nursing school was dismissed because the school only received federal funds through financial aid to its students and not directly through any school programs. Jerry Kicklighter of Bellville, Georgia, testifying before the Senate Committee on Labor and Human Resources, described how he lost his job as a botany/biology teacher at a community college after his superiors learned he had petit mal epilepsy: "Mr. Chairman, at worst, I had only two seizures a week—lasting a total of 40 seconds each, maximum. . . . The College even had a letter from my doctor stating that . . . [I] . . . in no way posed any hazard to my students." Nevertheless, Kicklighter was fired without any chance to argue his case. "I lost my job because of 80 seconds a week." Because of *Grove*, Kicklighter had no legal recourse.

An early version of the Civil Rights Restoration Act was first introduced into the 99th Congress in February 1985. It was not until March 1988, however, when Congress overrode President Reagan's veto, that a substantially rewritten bill was passed into law. In the meantime, national disability rights activists had joined in a broad coalition of advocates and organizations, representing the African Americans', women's, and elderly people's civil rights movements. This exposure of disability issues to a larger constituency and the personal and political relationships forged during this time were to have a major impact on future disability rights activism.

The Civil Rights Restoration Act explicitly explains what is meant by "program or activity" under the various civil rights titles. A part of the law labeled "Rehabilitation Act Amendment" specifically defines Section 504 to include virtually all of the activities and programs of any entity receiving federal funding. Under the provisions of the new act, the fact that one university department received federal funding or that some of the students or professors or programs did, meant that the entire college was covered by federal antidiscrimination law.

See also Section 504 of the Rehabilitation Act of 1973.

Clay, Julie Anna (b. 1958)

Julie Anna Clay is a leader in the Native American disability rights movement. She is a research specialist at the American Indian Rehabilitation Research and Training Center (AIRRTC) at Northern Arizona University in Flagstaff and a member of the Disability Issues Committee of the National Congress of American Indians. She was a member of the Task Force on the Rights and Empowerment of Americans with Disabilities and an advocate on behalf of passage of the Americans with Disabilities Act of 1990.

Clay was born on 2 November 1958 in Flandreau, South Dakota. She received her undergraduate degree in business administration and management from the University of Oklahoma in Norman in 1982 and a masters in public health from the University of Oklahoma in Oklahoma City in 1984. She has been a National Policy Fellow with the National Council on Disability and a project manager and program analyst at the Research and Training Center on Rural Rehabilitation at the University of Montana in Missoula. In 1993, she became the principal investigator at the Montana University Affiliated Rural Institute on Disabilities, before accepting her position at the AIRRTC in 1994. Among her publications are "Native American Independent Living," in *Rural Special Education Quarterly* (1992), and *Prevention of Disabilities, Meeting the Unique Needs of Minorities with Disabilities: A Report to the President and the Congress*, published by the National Council on Disability in 1993. She is a member of the Administration on Developmental Disabilities Multicultural Committee and a member of the American Indian Disability Legislation Project Advisory Committee.

See also American Indian Disability Legislation Project; Multicultural Issues, Minority Persons with Disabilities; Rural Institute on Disability.

Cleland, Max (b. 1942)

Max Cleland's appointment by President Jimmy Carter as director of the U.S. Veterans Administration (VA) in 1977 marked the first time that someone with a severe disability had been named to fill that position. Cleland was also the first Vietnam veteran, and at age 35 the youngest individual ever, to administer that agency.

Max Cleland, pictured here in 1978, was the first severely disabled person to head up the U.S. Veterans Administration when he was appointed in 1977.

Cleland was born on 24 August 1942 in Atlanta, Georgia. He graduated from Stetson College in Deland, Florida, in 1964. Inspired by President John Kennedy, Cleland became a congressional intern in 1965 while earning his masters degree in history. Upon graduating, Cleland volunteered for duty in the U.S. Army and received training in the Signal Corps and as a paratrooper. He arrived in Vietnam in May 1967 and was severely wounded during the Tet offensive in February 1968. His right arm and right leg were torn off by a grenade explosion, and his windpipe was severed. His left leg, also badly damaged, was later amputated.

Cleland spent more than a year recuperating in various VA hospitals, including eight months at Walter Reed Hospital in Washington, D.C. He would later recall how shocked he was at the conditions in facilities for wounded and disabled soldiers, telling an interviewer, "I guess that's what made me such a passionate head of the VA. I had been a patient, I had seen the system at the bottom. . . ." In his autobiography, *Strong at the Broken Places* (1980), Cleland described how the most helpful part of his treatment was the camaraderie he found among the other amputees on his ward. Cleland testified about conditions within the VA to the U.S. Senate Veterans' Affairs Committee in December 1969.

Returning to Georgia in 1970, Cleland entered state politics. That year, at age 28, he became the youngest person ever to be elected to the Georgia State Senate. During his campaign, he became friends with Jimmy Carter, then running for his first term as governor of Georgia. Once in office, the two men became political allies, attempting to reform state government over the objections of Lieutenant Governor Lester Maddox. Cleland was reelected to the state senate in 1972, but, in 1974, he lost in his bid to become lieutenant governor. Cleland moved to Washington, D.C., where in March 1975 he became an aide to Sen. Alan Cranston (D–CA), specializing in veterans' affairs. After his election to the presidency in 1976, Carter remembered his friend and political ally from Georgia, and, within the first hours of the new administration, Cleland became Carter's first appointee. Cleland was confirmed by the U.S. Senate and sworn into office on 2 March 1977.

Cleland left the VA in 1981. Returning to Georgia the following year, he was elected the youngest secretary of state in Georgia's history, subsequently winning reelection with wide margins. In November 1996, he won election to the U.S. Senate.

Cleland has been the recipient of numerous honors, including the Bronze Star for Meritorious Service, the Silver Star for Gallantry in Action, and several honorary doctorates.

Reference Cleland, Max, *Strong at the Broken Places* (1980).

Clerc, Louis Laurent Marie (1785–1869)

Louis Laurent Marie Clerc, together with Thomas Hopkins Gallaudet, is revered by the Deaf community as the founder of deaf education in the United States. As an educator, writer, advocate, and mentor, Clerc had an enormous influence on the development of both American Deaf culture and American Sign Language (ASL).

Clerc was born on 26 December 1785, in LaBalme les Grottes, Dauphine, France. He entered the Royal Institution for the Deaf in Paris when he was 12 years old, and became a teacher there under the supervision of Abbé Roch Ambroise Sicard. In July 1815, Sicard and Clerc went to London to deliver a series of demonstrations on the work of the institution. While there, they met Thomas Hopkins Gallaudet, who was in Europe studying methods of instruction for deaf people in preparation for founding a school for the deaf in the United States. Gallaudet was so impressed with Sicard and Clerc that he traveled to Paris in 1816 to study at the institution. Gallaudet asked Clerc to travel with him to the United States, and together they founded the American School for the Deaf in Hartford, Connecticut, in April 1817. Clerc learned to write English during the voyage, while Clerc tutored Gallaudet in sign language and teaching. One indication of Clerc's seminal role in the development of ASL is that, more than 150 years later, it is estimated that some 60 percent of American signs can be traced to a French origin.

Clerc was a highly visible advocate on behalf of the deaf community, lecturing and raising money for deaf education. In 1818, he became the first deaf person (perhaps the first person with any significant disability) to address the U.S. Congress. An acquaintance of such notables as Speaker of the U.S. House of Representatives Henry Clay and President James Monroe, Clerc was seen as living proof that deaf people could become accomplished writers, educators, and scholars. He became a teacher and mentor to two generations of deaf educators and activists, many of whom went on to found schools of their own.

In 1851, Clerc became president of an association to honor Thomas Gallaudet, which, in 1854, became the New England Gallaudet Association of the Deaf, the nation's first regional organization composed of and run by deaf people. Clerc retired from teaching in 1858, at age 73, but continued to be an influential and respected figure in the Deaf community. In 1864, he gave the keynote address at the founding of the National Deaf-Mute College, today's Gallaudet University.

Clerc died on 18 July 1869. He is buried in Spring Grove Cemetery, in Hartford, Connecticut. A monument to him at the American School in Hartford, erected in 1874, calls him "The Apostle to the Deaf-Mutes of the New World."

See also American School for the Deaf; American Sign Language; Gallaudet, Edward Miner; Gallaudet, Thomas Hopkins; Gallaudet University.

References Lane, Harlan, *When the Mind Hears: A History of the Deaf* (1984); Van Cleve, John V., and Barry A. Crouch, *A Place of Their Own: Creating the Deaf Community in America* (1989).

Client Assistance Projects/ Client Assistance Programs (CAPs)

The first 11 Client Assistance Projects (CAPs) were established in May 1974 to act as advocates for clients of state rehabilitation programs receiving federal funds through the Rehabilitation Act of 1973. They came out of 1972 Senate hearings, which demonstrated that rehabilitation clients often had difficulty actually receiving the services to which they were entitled. The number of projects, generally administered by state departments of rehabilitation, grew to a high of 42 in 1980, but decreased thereafter due to budget cuts. In 1984, Congress amended the Rehabilitation Act to make CAPs mandatory and independent of the rehabilitation commissions. Each state and territory, as a condition for receiving funds under Section 110 of the act, must have a client assistance program. CAPs are administered by the federal Rehabilitation Services Administration.

See also Rehabilitation Act of 1973.

Coalition of Provincial Organizations of the Handicapped (COPOH)
See Council of Canadians with Disabilities.

Cochlear Implants
In December 1985, the federal Food and Drug Administration approved a cochlear implant designed by the House Ear Institute and manufactured by the 3M Company. The device was designed to be surgically implanted into a person's cochlea as a form of "artificial ear." The mainstream press hailed it as a "cure" for deafness, and physicians began to discuss the desirability of performing the procedure on deaf children and even infants. *The Disability Rag & Resource*, however, labeled the implant "just the latest attempt to change Deaf people" and "the final putdown."

"The cochlear implant procedure may 'cure' deafness for a medically and financially eligible few," Scott Tenney, a student counselor at Southern Illinois University at Carbondale, told the *Disability Rag* in 1986, but the procedure is also "another disavowal of their worth as complete human beings," another signal from hearing society that deaf people are simply not good enough as they are. Other advocates for the Deaf community expressed the concern that the widespread use of cochlear implants would destroy Deaf culture and that "there'll be no more Deaf families."

The debate over technological "cures" for deafness continues. The September 1996 edition of *Silent News*, for example, contained an article attacking the development of "brain stem implants" with the question: ". . . why not take Deaf people out behind a building and shoot 'em all? What are they going to think up next, a new mouth to help us talk as 'hearing people?'" The same issue, however, featured another article with the headline "Deaf Man's Hearing Restored by Implant." The article describes how, ". . . for the first time in 20 years," Don Howard "knows what it sounds like to be part of a family. . . ."

See also American Sign Language; Audism; Deaf Culture; Oral School, Oralism.

References "Cochlear Implants: The Final Putdown?" *Disability Rag & Resource* (March/April 1986); "Deaf Man's Hearing Restored by Implant" and "Opinion," *Silent News* (September 1996); Van Cleve, John V., ed., *Gallaudet Encyclopedia of Deaf People and Deafness* (1987).

Coelho, Tony (b. 1942)

A former U.S. representative from California, Tony Coelho was the original congressional sponsor of the Americans with Disabilities Act and was instrumental in the early struggle for the bill's passage. In 1994, President Clinton appointed him chairman of the President's Committee on Employment of People with Disabilities.

Coelho was born in Los Banos, California, on 15 June 1942. His early ambitions were first to be a trial lawyer, then a priest. When he was 15, he began having grand mal seizures due to a truck accident, after which his parents sent him to faith healers. It was not until he had begun attending

Loyola University in Chicago, where he was president of the student body, that he was diagnosed as having epilepsy. The response of the seminary administration was to expel him: Catholic canon law forbade the ordination of those "who are or have been epileptics, insane or possessed by the devil." After Coelho's doctor reported his epilepsy to the authorities, his driver's license was revoked, and his health insurance canceled.

"Nothing about me had changed since taking that physical," Coelho wrote years later in an autobiographical article, "but suddenly I was an 'epileptic,' an outcast."

Shut out of the ministry, Coelho decided on a career in politics, running for Congress in 1978. Disability again became an issue when Coelho's opponent asked voters, "What would you think if Coelho went to the White House to argue a critical issue for you and had a seizure?" Despite this appeal to prejudice, Coelho won election as the representative from the central San Joaquin Valley. He became chairman of the Democratic Congressional Campaign Committee from 1981 to 1987. From 1986 to 1989, he was majority whip, third ranking member of the House Democratic Leadership. As such, he was ideally situated to introduce the first version of the Americans with Disabilities Act in the House in 1988, while Republican Sen. Lowell Weicker introduced the bill in the Senate.

Coelho left Congress in 1990 after a controversy involving his personal finances, but he enlisted his friend Maryland representative Steny Hoyer to take his place as principal advocate for the act. Hoyer was a member of what Coelho called "the hidden army" of the disabled: people with hidden disabilities such as epilepsy, or whose families or friends have disabilities. Hoyer's wife, like Coelho, has epilepsy.

In addition to serving as chairman of the President's Committee on Employment of People with Disabilities, Coelho is also a director of the National Foundation for Affordable Housing Solutions, and he serves on the boards of the National Organization on Disability, the National Rehabilitation Hospital, and Very Special Arts, a nonprofit organization dedicated to creating learning opportunities through the arts for people with disabilities.

See also Americans with Disabilities Act of 1990; National Organization on Disability; President's Committee on Employment of People with Disabilities.

References Coelho, Tony, "Epilepsy Gave Me a Mission," *Epilepsy Association of Greater Greensboro Newsletter* (November 1995); Shapiro, Joseph P., *No Pity: People with Disabilities Forging a New Civil Rights Movement* (1993); "Tony Coelho: The New Chairman of the President's Committee for the Employment of People with Disabilities," *Enabling Georgia* (Fall 1994).

Coleman, Diane (b. 1953)

Diane Coleman has been a state and national organizer with American Disabled for Attendant Programs Today (ADAPT) since 1987. Most recently, as a founding member of Not Dead Yet, she has organized demonstrations against practitioners of assisted suicide such as Jack Kevorkian.

Coleman was born on 11 August 1953 in Alpena, Michigan. Disabled since birth, she has used a wheelchair since she was 11 years old. She obtained both a law degree and a master's degree in business administration from the University of California at Los Angeles in 1981. She was an attorney for the State of California for seven years, also serving on the California Attorney General's Commission on Disability and on the Board of Directors of the Westside Center for Independent Living. She became the client assistance program coordinator for Tennessee's Protection and Advocacy agency, then moving on to become a co-director of the Technology Access Center and a policy and funding analyst for the Tennessee Technology Access Project. During this time, she also served on the State Advisory Committee to the U.S. Civil Rights Commission, the Statewide Independent Living Council, and on the boards of the Tennessee Health Care Campaign and the Center for Independent Living in Nashville.

Coleman is the author of numerous articles and papers on disability rights issues, particularly related to euthanasia and assisted suicide. These works include "The Problem of Euthanasia: A Disability Perspective" (presentation to the Fund for Southern Communities, 1993) and "Withdrawing Life-Sustaining Treatment from People with Severe Disabilities Who Request It: Equal Protection Considerations" (in *Issues in Law & Medicine*, Summer 1992).

Coleman is the executive director of the Progress Center for Independent Living in Oak Park, Illinois.

See also American Disabled for Attendant Programs Today; Euthanasia and Assisted Suicide.

Coming Home

Like the film *The Best Years of Our Lives* (1946), *Coming Home* (1978) chronicles the story of men returning from war, in this case the war in Vietnam. And like the earlier film, *Coming Home* focuses on the story of a disabled veteran, paraplegic Luke Martin, played by Jon Voigt. Unlike the earlier film, however, *Coming Home* explores social attitudes toward disability, showing uncaring VA hospital staff, the cold stares Martin gets when he shops, and the difficulty he has getting into and out of buildings without ramps. It takes a step backwards, though, in using a nondisabled actor to play the disabled lead.

Central to the story is Martin's relationship with Sally Hyde, played by Jane Fonda. Left alone when her husband is sent to Vietnam, Hyde volunteers at the local VA hospital, where she falls in love with Martin. The film won both acclaim and criticism for its portrayal of their relationship. It was the first time Hollywood attempted to depict the sexuality of someone with a disability as anything other than malevolent or kinky, or innocent and childlike. This realism was too provocative for some film critics, for instance Pauline Kael, who dismissed *Coming Home* as "porny romanticism" with "a morbid kick" and as "a movie about a woman who has her first orgasm when she goes to bed with a paraplegic." Roger Ebert, on the other hand, praised the film for its "emotional tenderness and subtlety."

The film, with its scenes of wheelchair basketball, of the camaraderie of disabled vets, and of Martin chaining himself to the hospital gate in protest of a friend's death, was generally praised by disability rights activists. For the first—and one of the only times—Hollywood portrayed a disabled character as competent, independent, and politically active. Nevertheless, the film premiered in inaccessible theaters, and activists across the country blockaded theater entrances in protest.

See also *The Best Years of Our Lives*; Media Images of People with Disabilities.

Reference Norden, Martin F., *The Cinema of Isolation: A History of Physical Disability in the Movies* (1994).

Committee of Ten Thousand (COTT)

The Committee of Ten Thousand was formed in 1990 by activists in the hemophilia community. It is the first national consumer organization of people with hemophilia and blood disorders, and it was founded specifically in response to the HIV/AIDS epidemic. Prior to its formation, people with hemophilia had never been represented on either the Blood Products Advisory Committee of the federal Food and Drug Administration or the board of directors of the National Hemophilia Foundation (NHF). One of COTT's principal goals has been to force these critical institutions to allow people with blood disorders into their deliberations.

There were approximately 20,000 Americans with hemophilia and related blood disorders at the beginning of the AIDS epidemic in 1980. These conditions, genetic disorders that prevent blood from clotting, are treated through the use of clotting elements (called factors). The manufacture of a single dose of factor requires the blood of thousands of donors, becoming a medium through which the HIV virus may be transmitted. Disability rights and AIDS activists charge that the

NHF and the manufacturers of these products were remiss in warning the hemophilia community about the risk of infection. Although researchers had expressed concerns about the danger of blood products as early as 1982, it was not until several years later that manufacturers began heat-treating their products to kill the virus. In the meantime, thousands of people had been infected, including the spouses and lovers of people with hemophilia and children conceived after their parents' exposure. The impact has been so devastating that advocates call what has happened to their community the "Hemophiliac Holocaust." As of 1996, an estimated 4,500 American hemophiliacs—almost a quarter of the community—had died, with two more individuals dying each day.

On 30 September 1993, activist Jonathan Wadleigh, as president of COTT, filed a class action suit against the major manufacturers of blood products and the NHF. On 19 April 1996, the defendants agreed to settle without admitting liability and, in August 1996, offered to pay $100,000 to each person infected by blood products between 1978 and 1985 and those infected by their exposure to people infected by blood products, including their children, spouses, and significant others.

Other COTT efforts include legislation changing the composition of the Blood Products Advisory Panel, the federal agency responsible for regulating the manufacture and sale of blood products, so that 25 percent of its members are blood product consumers. COTT has also been instrumental in forcing the federal government to remove individuals from regulatory boards and agencies that have a financial interest in the manufacture of blood products and thus an obvious conflict of interest. Other efforts include legislation introduced into Congress to force the federal government to acknowledge that it neglected to properly monitor blood product manufacture and to make restitution to the people who became ill as a result, or to their survivors.

See also HIV/AIDS and Disability.

References Gwin, Lucy, "Murder by Charity," *Mouth: The Voice of Disability Rights* (September/October 1993); Shilts, Randy, *And the Band Played On: Politics, People, and the AIDS Epidemic* (1987).

Communications Access

Just as buildings and homes have been constructed without physical access, our systems of communicating have been designed without addressing the needs of people with language, sensory, or cognitive disabilities. Courtroom proceedings conducted without a sign language interpreter discriminate against people who are deaf; telephones without a text option are of little use to people who cannot hear or speak; small print classroom materials shut out people who are blind. Legislation that addresses these issues includes Section 504 of the Rehabilitation Act of 1973 and its amendments, the Court Intepreter's Act of 1978 (which mandated sign language interpreters in the federal courts during litigation involving individuals who are deaf or hard of hearing), the Americans with Disabilities Act of 1990, and the Telecommunications Act of 1996.

See also Americans with Disabilities Act of 1990; Bowe, Frank G.; Captioning, Closed Captioning; Telecommunications Devices for the Deaf; Telecommunications for the Disabled Act of 1982.

Reference Van Cleve, John V., ed., *Gallaudet Encyclopedia of Deaf People and Deafness* (1987).

Community Assistance Services Act (CASA)
See Personal Assistance Services.

Computer Access

The development of adaptive hardware and software for use with personal computers has been of enormous benefit to people with disabilities. It has enabled people with severe disabilities to gain greater control of their environment through systems that use a computer to operate lights, heat, air conditioning, televisions, and other appliances. A variety of innovations ranging from mouthsticks and wrist splints

Bill Stillwater, pictured in 1996, displays the home page he created on the World Wide Web to provide resources for people with disabilities. Stillwater uses a breath activated device to operate his computer; other instruments that allow disabled people computer access include helmet mounted lasers, mouthsticks, and wrist splints.

to helmet-mounted lasers and voice-activated systems enable people with limited dexterity to have access to computers. The advent of the Information Superhighway has meant greater access to information, without having to deal with physically inaccessible libraries or archives. Computers, e-mail, and the Internet have enabled advocates such as Fred Fay to play an important role in the national disability rights movement, even though he is unable to travel because of his disability.

Developments in computer technology, however, can also threaten the ability of people with disabilities to participate in society. An example of this threat is the proliferation of systems that use Graphical User Interface (GUI), such as Microsoft Windows. GUI programs use a mouse and graphical images on the computer screen to enable users to input commands without typing lines of coded text. Such systems are convenient to sighted users, but present enormous obstacles for computer users who are visually disabled. The advent of GUI in the late 1980s caused many blind individuals to lose their jobs or promotions or prevented them from getting jobs for which they were otherwise qualified because they were unable to access office computers.

A variety of disability rights activists and organizations are working to ensure computer accessibility, including Commissioner Charles Crawford at the Massachusetts Commission for the Blind, Bonnie O'Day at the National Council on Disability, computer caucuses at the American Council of the Blind and the National Federation of the Blind, software researchers such as Gregg Vanderheiden at the Trace Research and Development Center at the University of Wisconsin, access advocates such as Deborah Kaplan and Judy Brewer, and the various state Technology Act projects across the country. Since the early 1990s, these advocates have waged an intensive campaign to convince Microsoft Corporation to develop software to make their Windows systems accessible. Although the Americans with Disabilities Act of 1990 has been of limited use in their efforts, advocates have been able to use other portions of disability rights law. Section 508 of the Rehabilitation Act Amendments of 1986 (extended in 1992 as Section 509), for example, requires that federal agencies must provide workers with and without disabilities equivalent access to electronic office equipment. Software inaccessibility, however, continues to be a major problem for blind computer users.

See also Assistive Technology; Fay, Frederick A.; Kaplan, Deborah; National Council on Disability; Technology-Related Assistance for Individuals with Disabilities Act of 1988.

Concrete Change

Concrete Change is a grassroots organization working for accessible housing. It operates out of organizer Eleanor Smith's home in Atlanta but has chapters all across the country. Founded in 1986, it advocates for the enforcement of existing housing access laws and stresses the concept of "visitability"—making all homes accessible, not only those currently occupied by people with disabilities. "Visiting others," Smith told *Mouth: The Voice of Disability Rights* in 1994, "is as important to disabled people as it is to non-disabled people. And finding the accessible house or apartment to rent or buy at the time it is needed is often impossible when only a small percentage has access." Concrete Change attacks the common myths about accessible housing: that it is expensive, unattractive, and hard to sell. Concrete Change drafted an Atlanta city ordinance, adopted in June 1992, requiring that all housing built with public funds, including single-family homes and duplexes, "be provided with design features to provide accessibility and usability for physically disabled people." In 1994, Concrete Change in Chicago organized teams to ensure that the builders of new apartment buildings complied with the Fair Housing Amendments Act of 1988.

Concrete Change publishes materials on housing access, including the videotape *Building Better Neighborhoods* (1994) and the book *Entryways* (1991).

See also Architectural Access; Fair Housing Amendments Act of 1988; Housing.

References Gwin, Lucy, "America, the Unvisitable: An Interview with Eleanor Smith of Concrete Change," *Mouth: The Voice of Disability Rights* (July/August 1994); Smith, Eleanor, "Visitability: A Revolution in Housing Development," *Mainstream* (August 1994).

Consolidated Rail Corporation v. Darrone 104 S. Ct. 1248 (1984)

In *Consolidated Rail Corporation v. Darrone*, the U.S. Supreme Court decided that Section 504 of the Rehabilitation Act of 1973 prohibited employment discrimination against otherwise qualified people with disabilities in agencies or organizations receiving federal funds, even if those funds were not specifically intended to promote employment. This case was the first that disability rights advocates had ever won before the U.S. Supreme Court.

The original suit was brought in 1979 by Thomas LeStrange, a railroad locomotive engineer who lost his left hand and forearm in a work-related accident in 1971. After the accident, LeStrange's employer, the Erie Lackawanna Railroad, refused to employ him, even though it could cite no reason why he was now unqualified for his job. The U.S. District Court for the Middle District of Pennsylvania dismissed the suit, saying LeStrange did not have "standing" to bring a private action under Section 504. The U.S. Court of Appeals for the Third Circuit reversed this decision, sending LeStrange's suit back to the district court for trial. Conrail, which by this time had acquired the Erie Lackawanna, appealed, and the U.S. Supreme Court heard the case on 29 November 1983, by which time LeStrange had died. For this reason, Conrail argued that the case was now moot. The suit, however, was continued by LeStrange's widow Lee Ann LeStrange Darrone.

On 28 February 1984, the Supreme Court declared, first, that LeStrange's death did not render the case moot. Secondly, the Court ruled that Section 504 covered all entities receiving federal funds, and not simply those agencies or organizations receiving money specifically to employ people or as part of a federal jobs program. Finally, the Court decided that LeStrange did indeed have "standing" to bring suit.

Arlene Mayerson, principal legal strategist in the case and consultant to the attorney of record, wrote later that *Consolidated Rail Corporation v. Darrone* "marked a significant victory for the disability rights community." She points out that the Court decision cited the Section 504 regulations issued by the U.S. Department of Health, Education, and Welfare, and that "these regulations, elevated by the Court in *Consolidated Rail Corporation* . . . formed the basis of the ADA." Disability advocates were concerned, however, when the Court also ruled that Section 504 should be interpreted as narrowly as the Court had interpreted Title IX of the Education Amendments of 1972 in *Grove City College v. Bell* (1984), decided that same day. In *Grove*, the Court ruled that only people working or studying in the specific part or office of a program receiving federal funds were protected from discrimination. In re-

sponse, disability rights activists joined a coalition of civil rights and women's groups seeking to overturn the *Grove* decision, leading to passage of the Civil Rights Restoration Act of 1987.

See also Civil Rights Restoration Act of 1987; Section 504 of the Rehabilitation Act of 1973.

Consortium for Citizens with Disabilities (CCD)

The Consortium for Citizens with Disabilities (CCD), based in Washington, D.C., is a national coalition of consumer, advocacy, provider, and professional organizations working for changes in national disability policy. It was established in 1973 as the Consortium for Citizens with Developmental Disabilities with 18 member organizations, primarily service providers, to promote passage of the Developmentally Disabled Assistance and Bill of Rights Act of 1975. Paul A. Marchand, director of the national Governmental Affairs Office of The Arc and a major figure in the parents' movement, has been chair of the CCD since its inception. Under his leadership, the CCD also played a major role in passage of the Education for All Handicapped Children Act of 1975.

In later years, as the CCD grew to include other disability groups, the focus broadened beyond services for people with developmental disabilities to include advocacy on a broad range of issues for a wider constituency. The CCD, for example, served as a central clearinghouse and coordinating forum during the campaign for passage of the Americans with Disabilities Act of 1990. As of 1996, there were more than 100 Washington-based member organizations, representing a vast range of disabled constituencies.

The work of the CCD is divided among task forces organized around topics such as housing, health care, and personal assistance services. Each task force collects data; publishes reports and position statements for use by disability rights activists; and lobbies for changes in legislation and regulation to enhance the civil rights, empowerment, and inclusion of children and adults with disabilities.

See also Americans with Disabilities Act of 1990; Developmentally Disabled Assistance and Bill of Rights Act of 1975; Education for All Handicapped Children Act of 1975.

Cook, Timothy M. (1953–1991)

Attorney Timothy M. Cook was involved in a wide variety of landmark disability rights cases, particularly in the struggle for accessible public transportation. His death at age 38 was a profound shock and a deep loss to the disability rights community.

Cook was born on 14 August 1953 in Pittsburgh, Pennsylvania. He received both his B.A. and M.A. from the University of Pennsylvania in 1975 and his J.D. from the University of Pennsylvania Law School in 1978. He spent the summer of 1977 in Washington, D.C., at the Department of Health, Education and Welfare's Office for Civil Rights, developing guidelines for enforcement of Section 504 of the Rehabilitation Act of 1973. Cook then moved to New York, where he established the Disability Rights Litigation Project at the Legal Aid Society of New York City, responsible for class action suits involving discrimination in employment and education. Cook represented the New York Mayor's Office for the Handicapped in *Southeastern Community College v. Davis* (1979), the landmark Section 504 case which first laid out the doctrine of "reasonable accommodation." After a federal judicial clerkship at the U.S. District Court for the Southern District of New York, Cook, in 1981, became an adjunct professor at the Antioch School of Law in Washington, D.C. From 1980 to 1983, he worked as a trial attorney at the Civil Rights Division of the U.S. Justice Department, where he was responsible for enforcement of the Civil Rights of Institutionalized Persons Act of 1980 and of Section 504 in a district covering 11 states. As a Department of Justice insider, Cook played a vital role informing disability advocates of pending moves by the Reagan

administration to curtail such crucial disability rights protections as the regulations for Section 504 and the Education for All Handicapped Children Act. In 1983, Cook became the director of the Western Law Center for the Handicapped (since renamed the Western Law Center for Disability Rights) in Los Angeles.

It was as an attorney at the Public Interest Law Center of Philadelphia from 1984 to 1988 that Cook litigated many of his most significant cases. Cook was counsel for the Spina Bifida Association in *Irving Independent School District v. Tatro* (1984), the U.S. Supreme Court's first decision concerning the related services requirements of the Education for All Handicapped Children Act. In 1985, he was counsel for the Association for Persons with Severe Handicaps (TASH) in *Alexander v. Choate* and for the Association for Retarded Citizens (ARC) in *City of Cleburne, Tex. v. Cleburne Living Center*, involving an attempt by city officials to prevent a group home for people with cognitive disabilities from opening in a residential area. In 1986, Cook played a major role in *Bowen v. American Hospital Association*, involving the right of disabled infants to medical care. In 1987, he was counsel for the American Diabetes Association et al. in *School Board of Nassau County, Florida v. Arline*, the landmark Supreme Court ruling delineating the rights of people with contagious diseases. That same year, he represented the class of people with mobility disabilities in *Disabled in Action of Pennsylvania v. Sykes*, arguing for accessible subway stations.

After working with the Democratic National Committee and the Dukakis presidential campaign in 1988, Cook returned to Washington to organize, and become executive director of, the National Disability Action Center, representing people with disabilities in cases involving discrimination in housing, education, and transportation. Cook represented ADAPT and 12 other disability rights groups in *ADAPT v. Skinner* (1989), which struck down the U.S. Department of Transportation rule allowing transit authorities to meet their access obligations by allocating only a small fraction of their budgets to "separate but equal" paratransit or "special needs" services. Through the 1980s, he was also ADAPT's "street attorney," attending the group's demonstrations and representing activists arrested during sit-ins and protests.

In addition to writing op. ed. pieces in the *Philadelphia Inquirer* and the *Washington Post*, Cook was the legal affairs columnist for *Mainstream* magazine and the author of the *Handbook on Access to Public Accommodations for Disabled People under Federal Access Laws* (1988) and "The Continued Viability of Deinstitutionalization Litigation," in *The Legal Rights of Citizens with Mental Retardation* (1989). His last published work was "The Americans with Disabilities Act: The Move to Integration," in the *Temple Law Review* (1991). Cook was the recipient of the 1989 Chairman's Award of the President's Committee on Employment of People with Disabilities, and, in July 1996, he posthumously received the Award for Transportation Advocacy, presented to his wife Geraldine Heneghan by Secretary of Transportation Frederico Peña.

Cook was infected with the AIDS virus as a result of using a blood product to treat his hemophilia. Disability rights advocates charge that his death, like thousands of others, was the result of negligence on the part of federal regulators, the manufacturers of blood products, and the National Hemophilia Foundation. Cook died on 22 October 1991.

See also ADAPT v. Skinner; Alexander v. Choate; Bowen v. American Hospital Association; Committee of Ten Thousand; Irving Independent School District v. Tatro; Public Transportation; School Board of Nassau County, Florida v. Arline; Southeastern Community College v. Davis.

Corbet, Barry (b. 1936)

Barry Corbet is an independent filmmaker who produces films on disability and rehabilitation. Since 1991, he has been the editor of *New Mobility*, a monthly magazine of disability lifestyle, politics, and culture.

Corbet was born on 25 August 1936 in Vancouver, British Columbia, and is a graduate of Dartmouth College in Hanover, New Hampshire. His film career began in 1963, as a member of the American Mount Everest (West Ridge) Expedition, which he filmed for the National Geographic Society. This expedition was followed by a 1966 journey to Antarctica, also filmed for National Geographic. He was spinal cord injured in a helicopter crash in 1968. Since 1978, he has been president of Educational Media, Inc., and Access, Inc.

Corbet has produced or co-produced approximately 125 films, including *Outside: Spinal Cord Injury and the Future* (1980), about life after discharge from a rehabilitation facility. Corbet is also the author of *Options: Spinal Cord Injury and the Future* (1980), and the editor of *The National Resource Directory: An Information Guide for Persons with Spinal Cord Injury and Other Physical Disabilities* (1985), as well as chapters in several books on disability and access.

See also New Mobility.

Reference Corbet, Barry, *Options: Spinal Cord Injury and the Future* (1980).

Council of Canadians with Disabilities (CCD)

In the early 1970s, Canadians with disabilities organized advocacy groups in Alberta, Saskatchewan, and Manitoba. In 1975, the Manitoba League of the Physically Handicapped sponsored a conference to pull all these groups together and to encourage the formation of disability rights organizations in the other provinces. Consequently, the Council of Canadians with Disabilities was founded as the Coalition of Provincial Organizations of the Handicapped (COPOH) in 1976, and, by the end of the decade, disability rights groups had been organized in most of the other provinces. COPOH sponsored a series of national forums to compare experiences, discuss issues, choose priorities, and pick strategies for winning civil rights for Canadians with disabilities.

The first forum was held in Winnipeg in 1978, and it passed a resolution calling employment a civil right. The 1979 COPOH Forum on Accessibility of Transportation for Disabled People was notable in that so many of the participants experienced discrimination simply trying to attend. One delegate was forced to ride in a baggage car because it was the only accessible carriage on his train (he was nevertheless required to pay full fare), dog-guides were separated from their users to be put in the baggage compartments of airplanes, and several wheelchair users were refused cab service to and from the airport. As a result, many COPOH delegates stayed in Winnipeg after the forum to demonstrate and testify at the Canadian Transportation Commission hearings held there a few days later.

COPOH was instrumental in the founding of Disabled Peoples' International in 1980. COPOH delegates, attending the 1980 conference of Rehabilitation International (an organization of rehabilitation professionals), published a daily newsletter to report on conference events from a disability rights perspective. When the conference rejected a resolution that people with disabilities be given a substantial voice in the organization, COPOH led the effort to found an independent group. In the mid-1980s, women members of COPOH were involved in founding the DisAbled Women's Network (DAWN) of Canada. From 1977 to 1983, COPOH lobbied for an amendment to the Canadian Human Rights Act to protect the civil rights of people with disabilities. COPOH called for two national protests, resulting in demonstrations across the country, including a march by nearly 100 people on Parliament Hill in Ottawa. The act was subsequently amended in March 1983. Since 1985, the renamed Council of Canadians with Disabilities (CCD) has pushed for a new amendment to the act requiring "a duty to accommodate."

Today the CCD, based in Winnipeg, continues to advocate for an end to employment discrimination and the growth of independent living options. COPOH advocacy has resulted in substantial improvements in the accessibility of Canadian mass transit, but access remains inadequate, and government budget cuts and administrative changes threaten what progress has been made. The CCD is also involved in the "right-to-die" issue and has intervened in cases of particular concern on this issue, such as those of Tracy Latimer and Ryan Wilkieson. In the Latimer case, the defense argued that the murder of Tracy by her father was a "mercy killing" justified by Tracy's disability, while Wilkieson was murdered by his mother, who then committed suicide, ostensibly because of Wilkieson's cerebral palsy. The CCD Human Rights Committee and local CCD affiliates sought "intervenor" status from the court so that they could present testimony and organized demonstrations and press events to bring a disability rights perspective into the public discussion of the cases. CCD committees have also been formed to address access in telecommunications and to the Information Superhighway.

See also Disabled Peoples International; Disabled Women's Network of Canada; Euthanasia and Assisted Suicide.

Covington, George A. (b. 1943)

George A. Covington is a photographer, attorney, journalist, educator, writer, and advocate for disability rights. As the former special assistant for disability policy to Vice President Dan Quayle, he was the first person to serve full-time as a White House aide on disability issues. Covington is also an advocate for universal design and a former co-chair of the Universal Design Task Force of the President's Committee on Employment of People with Disabilities. His work as a photographer has helped to dispell the common stereotypes about the abilities of people who are legally blind.

Covington was born on 2 November 1943 in Texarkana, Texas. He entered the University of Texas in 1964, earning a bachelor of journalism in 1967 and a doctorate of jurisprudence in 1973. It was during this time that Covington first took up photography. He explains, "I suddenly realized I could see great detail in these 4″ x 5″ pictures that I couldn't see in the real world." This interest was also a response to the prejudice he had experienced, "that horrible assumption that if you're half blind, you don't have an aesthetic, you couldn't have an appreciation of beauty, you definitely could not produce anything aesthetically pleasing."

From 1967 to 1973, Covington was editor and publisher of the *Austin Citizen* and then a staff writer at the University of Texas News and Information Service. In 1974, he accepted a position as assistant professor of journalism at West Virginia University in Morgantown, where he began to draw national attention for his photography. Covington has written that his work "demonstrates how photography can be used as an accessibility tool to art" by enlarging paintings for museum exhibition and by using it as a means of helping people with visual disabilities to explore their environment. Despite their utilitarian aspect, Covington's images, particularly his portraits, have been acclaimed for their artistry.

Covington has been involved in various aspects of the disability rights movement since the late 1970s. As an attorney, he wrote the regulations implementing Section 504 of the Rehabilitation Act of 1973 for the U.S. Department of the Interior. He worked as a consultant at the National Access Center in Washington, D.C., from 1981 to 1984 and then for the President's Committee on Employment of People with Disabilities, the National Institute on Disability and Rehabilitation Research, and the Office of the Speaker of the U.S. House of Representatives, on projects ranging from the use of technology as an employment tool for disabled workers to making Washington, D.C., accessible to disabled visitors. In January 1989, he became the special assistant for disability policy to Vice President Dan Quayle, writing speeches and advising the Vice President on disability issues. While working in this capacity, he also worked with the Executive Office of the President in developing an access plan for the White House. Covington has also been an accessibility specialist for the National Park Service since 1993.

Covington is the author of *Access by Design* (with Bruce Hannah, 1996), *Let Your Camera Do the Seeing: The World's First Photography Manual for the Legally Blind* (available free of charge in braille or on cassette from the National Library Service, Division of the Blind and Physically Handicapped), and *Crippling Images: White House Reflections* (work in progress). His many published articles include "Photography as a Museum Aid for the Visually Impaired" (monograph for the National Endowment of the Arts, July 1979), "Crippling Images, Educating the Vice President," (fall 1992 issue of *Ability Magazine*), and "Universal Design" (*Interiors Magazine*, August 1994). His videos include *Museum Accessibility for the Visually Impaired Visitor* (1982), *Faces I've Seen: The Photography of George Covington* (1986), and *Some of Your Visitors Are Disabled* (1987), a guide to universal access for museum administrators. Covington is a founding member of the National Council of Citizens with Low Vision, established in 1978 in Washington, D.C., as an affiliate of the American Council of the Blind.

See also Universal Design.

Cross-Disability Awareness/ Cross-Disability Sensitivity

Until the 1970s, most disability-related organizations focused on representing or providing services to persons with a specific disability. This was true both for consumer-controlled advocacy groups such as the American Council of the Blind or the National Association of the Deaf, for service organizations such as the National Multiple Sclerosis Society, and for parents' organizations such as United Cerebral Palsy Associations. This "ghettoization" made it difficult to work toward common goals. It meant that many disabled people shared the same stereotypes about people with differing disabilities as mainstream society. Furthermore, people with multiple disabilities, for instance blind wheelchair users, had difficulty obtaining services and participating in disability specific organizations.

In response, disability organizers fostered "cross-disability awareness and sensitivity." This concept encompassed everything from building organizations open to all disabled people to making sure that rallies for wheelchair access were sign-language interpreted for deaf participants. One major result of cross-disability awareness was the founding of the American Coalition of Citizens with Disabilities (ACCD) in 1974. It was the first ever cross-disability national advocacy coalition. The formation of the ACCD spurred the creation of cross-disability state coalitions, providing state and regional forums and offering many advocates and organizers the opportunity to meet their peers from other disability groups. Often, the first item on the agenda was breaking down fears and prejudices.

"In our early days," says Barbara Oswald, an organizer of the Massachusetts Coalition of Citizens with Disabilities, "we would sponsor conferences where we would deliberately room Deaf people with wheelchair users, or blind people with people with cognitive disabilities, just so we could begin to confront those issues of fear and ignorance head-on."

Another milestone in cross-disability awareness was the founding, in 1979, of the Disability Rights Education and Defense Fund (DREDF). Not only was DREDF a cross-disability organization, it was also cross-generational, representing disabled children and their parents as well as adults. The most successful example of the power of cross-disability organizing was the passage of the Americans with Disabilities Act in 1990, when virtually every major disability rights organization in the country united to assure its passage.

Cross-disability awareness continues to be a concern of many advocates, who acknowledge that there is still much work to be done in putting together a broad-based movement that includes all people with disabilities. Indeed, some disability advocates doubt that such a movement is possible. These critics of cross-disability organizing maintain that no amount of awareness and sensitivity can alter genuine differences in philosophy and agenda between the various constituencies in the disability community.

See also American Coalition of Citizens with Disabilities.

Curb-Cuts/Curb Ramps
Thomas Hopkins, a disability rights activist in Spencer, Massachusetts, has observed that, when it comes to access, "a couple of inches might as well be a couple of miles." Perhaps the best illustration of this can be seen in the need for curb-cuts (also curb ramps), or breaks in the curb that allow a wheelchair user to move from sidewalk to street and back again without assistance. Without curb-cuts, a street corner can become an impassable barrier, forcing a wheelchair user to backtrack until he or she can find a driveway or other entrance from or to the street.

Perhaps the first true curb-cuts in the United States specifically designed for wheelchair users were installed in Warm Springs, Georgia, after the founding of the polio rehabilitation center there in 1925. The first systematic installation of curb-cuts occurred at the Urbana-Champaign campus of the University of Illinois in the late 1940s, as the result of advocacy by Timothy Nugent and students at the school's disabled students' program. The city government of Minneapolis installed 9,000 curb-cuts between 1968 and 1974, under the direction of William B. Hopkins, director of public affairs of the Minnesota Society for Crippled Children and Adults, Inc. Since then, many, if not most,

Demonstrators in support of curb-cuts, which are vital to mobility for wheelchair users. Many states now require curb-cuts during construction or renovation of most streets.

states have required the installation of curb-cuts during the construction or renovation of most streets.

Curb-cuts are helpful, not only to wheelchair users, but to parents with baby carriages, bicyclists, and anyone else needing a smooth surface between the sidewalk and the street. Curb-cuts are, in fact, a good example of the benefits of universal design.

See also Architectural Access; Atlantis Community, Inc.; Federal-Aid Highway Act Amendments of 1974; Universal Design.

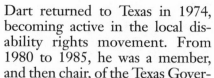

Dart, Justin, Jr. (b. 1930)

Justin Dart Jr. is one of the world's leading disability rights advocates. He is a principal architect of the Americans with Disabilities Act of 1990 (ADA) and has been an activist and organizer for more than two decades.

Dart was born on 29 August 1930 in Chicago, Illinois. His family was both wealthy and influential, and he would later describe how he grew up "with maids and a chauffeur." He contracted polio in 1948 and has used a wheelchair ever since. He earned his undergraduate degree in history and education in 1953 at the University of Houston, but officials withheld his teaching certificate, citing his disability. The University of Houston was, at that time, a segregated campus, and Dart organized its first student group opposed to racism and supporting integration. He earned a master's degree in history, also from the University of Houston, in 1954.

In 1963, Dart moved to Japan, where he founded three successful corporations, including Japan Tupperware, of which he was president until 1965. While in Japan, Dart also established what he called "a residential independent living program" for people with disabilities. In 1967, he traveled to Saigon, where he visited an institution filled with disabled children "with bloated bellies and matchstick arms and legs . . . lying in their own feces and urine and their bodies covered with flies." Dart, in Joseph Shapiro's *No Pity* (1993), describes how the experience "was like a branding iron burning . . . onto my soul." That same year, he abandoned his business career, and, after a long sojourn with his wife, Yoshiko, in a deserted farmhouse in Japan, he dedicated his life to the cause of civil rights for people with disabilities. He studied the writings of Martin Luther King Jr. and began corresponding with student activists at Berkeley and elsewhere.

Dart returned to Texas in 1974, becoming active in the local disability rights movement. From 1980 to 1985, he was a member, and then chair, of the Texas Governor's Committee for Persons with Disabilities; during the same time he was a member of the Texas Council on Disabilities. Dart was also chairman of the Governor's Long Range Planning Group for Texans with Disabilities from 1982 to 1983.

Dart was appointed vice-chair of the National Council on the Handicapped in 1982, remaining as vice-chair or member until 1986, and then again as a member from 1988 to 1989. He and others on the council became advocates for a single, all-encompassing federal civil rights act for people with disabilities—the Americans with Disabilities Act. As the co-chair of the Congressional Task Force on the Rights and Empowerment of Americans with Disabilities, Dart organized public forums in support of the bill in every state and in Puerto Rico, Guam, and the District of Columbia, attended by more than 30,000 people. In 1989, President Bush selected Dart to be chair of the President's Committee on Employment of the Handicapped (which Dart renamed the President's Committee on Employment of People with Disabilities), where he continued his advocacy for the ADA. Dart was one of the people on the dais when Bush signed the ADA into law in July 1990.

Dart was uncompromising in his commitment to disability rights. Appointed commissioner of the Rehabilitation Services Administration (RSA) by President Reagan in 1986, he soon ran into trouble with officials who opposed his efforts to appoint disabled people to positions of authority and who overruled his attempts to hold public hearings on administration proposals to change the Rehabilitation Act of 1973. The showdown came during a

Justin Dart Jr., a principal architect of the Americans with Disabilities Act, greets Jesse Jackson at the Capitol on 18 July 1989.

congressional hearing on 18 November 1987, when Dart abandoned the statement prepared for him, telling Congress instead that people with disabilities "are confronted by a vast, inflexible federal system which, like the society it represents, still contains a significant proportion of individuals who have not yet overcome obsolete, paternalistic attitudes about disability. . . . At issue here are . . . the civil and basic human rights of people with disabilities to have more than rubber-stamp figurehead representation in government." He was fired less than a month later.

Dart left the President's Committee on Employment of People with Disabilities in 1993. Despite his extensive ties to the Republican Party, he was critical of congressional Republicans such as Speaker of the House Newt Gingrich (R-GA) and House Majority Leader Dick Armey (R-TX) when they suggested weakening the ADA. In January 1993, Dart, together with Frederick Fay and Becky Ogle, founded Justice for All, an organization dedicated to defending the ADA, the Individuals with Disabilities Education Act, and other disability civil rights legislation from attacks by Congress and the media.

Dart's commitment to disability rights and independent living has been personal as well as political. Beginning in 1968, he and his wife have operated what they describe as their own "independent living program," and, in 20 years time, more than 70 disabled and nondisabled individuals have spent anywhere from six months to four years living in their home. He has been a generous donor to myriad disability organizations and publications, helping *Mouth: The Voice of Disability Rights* to publish and distribute *You Choose* (1995), its book on nursing homes and personal assistance services, and contributing the money to publish an insert in the *Washington Post* defending the ADA. In 1995, Dart was a principal organizer of a fifth year anniversary celebration of the ADA at the National Press Club in Washington, D.C. That same day, he presided over the official formation of the American Association of People with Disabilities, with its professed goal of having 2 million members by the year 2000.

Dart has traveled extensively, addressing meetings in Japan, Canada, Australia, Germany, and elsewhere. He was a major speaker at the 1992 and 1994 Congresses of Disabled Peoples' International. He has participated in countless demonstrations and has received dozens of citations and honorary degrees, including a doctorate from Gallaudet University in Washington, D.C. Indeed, there are now several awards that bear his name, including the Justin Dart Meritorious Public Service Award of the Coalition of Texans with Disabilities and the annual Justin Dart Award of the President's Committee on Employment of People with Disabilities.

Dart is also the editor of two books of poetry. He lives with his wife, Yoshiko Saji Dart, who is also active in the disability rights movement, in Houston, Texas, and in Washington D.C.

See also American Association of People with Disabilities; Americans with Disabilities Act of 1990; Fay, Frederick A.; Justice for All; National Council on Disability; President's Committee on Employment of People with Disabilities.

References Dart, Justin, Jr., "The ADA: A Promise To Be Kept," in Lawrence O. Gostin and Henry A. Beyer, eds., *Implementing the Americans with Disabilities Act* (1993); National Council on Disability, *Toward Independence* (1986); Shapiro, Joseph P., *No Pity: People with Disabilities Forging a New Civil Rights Movement* (1993).

Deaf Clubs and Organizations

Deaf clubs have served for nearly 200 years as places where deaf people can socialize without having to confront the prejudices of the hearing culture. They were among the first organizations run entirely by and for disabled people, helping to preserve American Sign Language when it was driven underground by oralism. Deaf clubs appear at least as far back as the 1820s, when alumni of the American School for the Deaf in Hartford, Connecticut, formed their own association. In addition to being organized for maintaining school ties, deaf clubs were organized around sports, amateur theatrics, and other activities. By the 1890s, each major city had its own deaf club or society, many of which are still in existence.

Deaf people have also founded a wide variety of professional, religious, and political organizations. Among these groups are the National Association of the Deaf (NAD), the Recreational Association of the Deaf (RAD), the International Catholic Deaf Association (ICDA), and the National Congress of Jewish Deaf (NCJD). Hartmut Teuber has remarked how "it is as if all (or most) facets of human culture are represented inside the 'Deaf World.' . . . Anyone entering the Deaf community, for example sign language interpreters or parents of deaf children, cannot help but memorize the alphabet soup of finger-spelled organization acronyms." Major deaf social service organizations, founded and managed by deaf people, include the Greater Los Angeles Council on Deafness, Inc. (GLAD) and the Developmental Evaluation and Adjustment Facilities (D.E.A.F. Inc.) in Boston.

See also Deaf Culture.

Reference Padden, Carol, and Tom Humphries, *Deaf in America: Voices from a Culture* (1988).

Deaf Culture

It was James Woodward who, in 1972, first proposed that a distinction be made between those who are "deaf"—people whose hearing was impaired—and "Deaf"—a particular group of people sharing a language (American Sign Language, or ASL) and a culture. Carol Padden and Tom Humphries, scholars who have written extensively on Deaf culture, describe Deaf people as those who "reside in the United States and Canada, have inherited their sign language, use it as a primary means of communication among themselves, and hold a set of beliefs about themselves and their connection to the larger society. We distinguish them from, for example, those who find themselves losing their hearing because of illness, trauma or age; although these people share the condition of not hearing, they do not have access to the knowledge, beliefs and practices that make up the culture of Deaf people."

Padden and Humphries stress, however, that the boundaries of Deaf culture are not always clear. "For example, consider deaf children from hearing families who encounter Deaf people and their culture outside the family." There is, as another instance, the case of hearing children of Deaf parents, who are fluent in sign, indeed ASL may be their first language. These individuals raise the intriguing question: Is it possible to be part of the Deaf culture without being deaf? Woodward, Padden, and Humphries sometimes extend the definition of Deaf culture to include Deaf communities in other countries, and in Quebec, which inherit a sign language other than ASL. "In fact, in nearly every nation in the world there are several distinct groups of Deaf people, their differences marked by political, historical, or geographical separation." Racial segregation in the United States, for example, has led to the development of a distinct, African-American form of ASL, used especially in some parts of the South.

Since the 1960s, the growing recognition of ASL as a distinctive language has produced an outpouring of Deaf theater and poetry. The use of videotape anthologies, such as Clayton Valli's *ASL Poetry: Selected Works* (1995), has expanded the audience for ASL poetry, while English memoirs, such as Raymond Luczak's *St. Michael's Fall* (1996), speak to both Deaf and hearing readers.

There are some in the Deaf community who reject the idea that an inability to hear constitutes a disability, maintaining instead that they are members of an ethnic and linguistic minority much like Haitian or Hispanic-Americans. "It is the hearing world," writes Ben Behan in his essay "Notes from a Seeing Person" (1989), "that tells us we are handicapped and disabled."

See also American Sign Language; Martha's Vineyard (Deaf Community); National Theatre of the Deaf; Oral School, Oralism.

References Padden, Carol, and Tom Humphries, *Deaf in America: Voices from a Culture* (1988); Wilcox, Sherman, ed., *American Deaf Culture: An Anthology* (1989).

Deaf Life

Deaf Life is a magazine that grew out of the half-hour open-captioned television news and lifestyle series *Deaf Magazine*, produced and directed by Matthew S. Moore in the summer of 1984, airing on WOKR-TV in Rochester, New York. The term *Deaf Life* is a gloss on an American Sign Language expression which, translated literally, means "the reality of being deaf." Although a critical success, Moore was unable to attract sponsors for a television news program aimed predominantly at deaf people, and the series ended. Moore turned his efforts to founding a magazine. He recruited a staff of volunteers, and the first "trial" issue of *Deaf Life* appeared in June 1987. It was not, however, until after the excitement generated by the Deaf President Now campaign at Gallaudet University in Washington, D.C., that *Deaf Life* began regular monthly publication in July 1988. I. King Jordan, Gallaudet's first deaf president, was featured on the cover of the first issue.

Deaf Life does not shy away from controversy, as when it published "Notes of a Gay Deaf Writer," by poet Raymond Luczak, in its March and April 1991 issues, and lost nearly 1,000 subscribers as a result. Among its regularly featured columns have been "The TTY Connection," by David Baquis, and "The Caption Report," by Stuart Gopen. Its question-and-answer columns, "For Hearing People Only," have been collected and published as a book (*For Hearing People Only: Answers to Some of the Most Commonly Asked Questions about the Deaf Community*, 1992). Other books available from the publishers of *Deaf Life* are *Great Deaf Americans* (1996), by Matthew S. Moore and Robert F. Panara, and *Victory Week*, a children's book on the Deaf President Now protest by Walter P. Kelley and Landon McGregor, scheduled for publication in 1997.

Deaf Life, published in Rochester, New York, has an estimated readership of 65,000, mostly in the United States and Canada.

See also Deaf Culture; Deaf President Now Campaign.

Reference "A Labor of Love: The (Not-So-Secret) History of Deaf Life," *Deaf Life* (July 1993).

Deaf Mutia

Deaf Mutia, also known as Gesturia, was to be the name of a new state in the United States populated entirely by deaf people. The plan was proposed in the 1850s by deaf activist John Flournoy, who believed that the attitudes of hearing people toward the deaf and hard of hearing were so oppressive that only complete separation would allow them some measure of freedom and fulfillment. His idea was for the Deaf community to approach Congress and ask that a tract of land unsettled by whites be set aside for the exclusive use of people who were deaf or hard of hearing. Flournoy was perhaps inspired by the example of the Mormons, who, when faced with religious persecution in the eastern United States, had transplanted their entire community to Utah.

The plan was vigorously debated in the *American Annals of the Deaf.* Some wrote objecting that any deaf commonwealth would inevitably dissipate over time as more and more hearing children were born. Others expressed concerns about leaving their hearing family and friends or about the scale of the undertaking. Deaf journalist William Chamberlain, one of the founders of the New England Gallaudet Association, proposed an alternative plan: the founding of a single township by an advance party of 200 to 300 deaf settlers. A friend of Chamberlain offered $5,000 toward the purchase of land and the outfitting of a party.

Deaf Mutia never went beyond the planning stage, but it can be seen today as an example of how oppressed many deaf people felt by the hearing culture around them. Similar ideas were also discussed in Europe.

See also Deaf Culture.
References Lane, Harlan, *When the Mind Hears: A History of the Deaf* (1984); Schein, Jerome D., *At Home among Strangers* (1989).

Deaf President Now Campaign

On the night of 6–7 March 1988, students at Gallaudet University in Washington, D.C., shut down their campus, declaring that it would remain closed until Gallaudet's board of trustees reversed its decision of the previous day to appoint a hearing person president of the world's only deaf liberal arts university. The week of marches and demonstrations that followed was a major watershed both for the Deaf community and for the disability rights movement in general.

The student uprising had its roots in six months of advocacy, begun soon after Jerry C. Lee announced his resignation as president of Gallaudet in September 1987. Gallaudet University Alumni Association President Gerald Burstein sent a telegram to the board of trustees announcing that "the choice is clear. It is time for a deaf president." The message was endorsed by other deaf organizations and leaders. When, in late February 1988, the board announced that two of the three final candidates were deaf, students, faculty, and alumni all hoped that, for the first time in its 124-year history, Gallaudet would have a deaf president.

Nevertheless, activists kept up the pressure, and the first Deaf President Now rally was held on campus on 1 March and was attended by an estimated 1,500 people. Among the speakers were Barbara Jean Wood, commissioner of the Massachusetts Commission for the Deaf and Hard of Hearing, and Jack Levesque, executive director of the Deaf Counseling, Advocacy and Referral Agency in California. At its conclusion, alumnus Jeff Rosen told the crowd, "People have died in the civil rights movement. People were jailed in protesting the Vietnam war. I stand here in 1988 asking: What do you believe in? What is your cause?" Rosen, along with students Jerry Covell, Bridgetta Bourne, and Greg Hlibok (president of the student body government, or SBG), were to emerge as the leadership of the student rebellion.

Late in the evening of Sunday, 6 March, the board of trustees issued a press release announcing that it had selected Elisabeth Ann Zinser, the only hearing finalist, to be the seventh president of Gallaudet University. Students were shocked and were angry that the announcement was made through a press release, rather than in person as expected. Copies of the press release were burned, and a large group of students marched—without a permit—through the streets of Washington to the Mayflower Hotel, where the board had been meeting. The trustees agreed to meet with a delegation of three: (1) SBG president Greg Hlibok, (2) past SBG president Tim Rarus, and (3) Jeff Rosen. At this meeting Trustee Chairwoman Jane Bassett Spilman was reported to have said, "Deaf people are not ready to function in a hearing world." Spilman insisted later that she had been misinterpreted, but, in the days that followed, the comment received wide circulation, further fueling the outrage felt by the deaf community.

By Monday morning, 7 March, Gallaudet students had occupied and shut down the entire main campus, denying entrance to all but fellow students. On Monday afternoon, at a meeting with Spilman, students leaders issued four nonnegotiable demands: (1) Zinser's resignation and the appointment of a deaf president, (2) Spilman's resignation from the board of trustees, (3) an increase in deaf representation on the board to 51 percent, and (4) no reprisals against the protesters. The trustees rejected all four demands, and students prepared for an indefinite strike. Deaf historian Jack R. Gannon, in *The Week the World Heard Gallaudet* (1989), describes how university "personnel returning to the campus Monday morning found all entrances . . . blocked by the students. Initially, only students and emergency personnel were permitted on campus. . . ." The Gallaudet provost, in response, closed the university. The protesters opened the gates on Tuesday, but students continued to boycott classes.

Hundreds of students block the entrance to Gallaudet University, forcing it to close on 7 March 1988. Students protested the appointment of a hearing president to the world's only liberal arts university for deaf people. The protests ended on 13 March, when the school's board of trustees agreed to all the students' demands, including the appointment of the university's first deaf president.

The dramatic events at Gallaudet drew national and then international attention. In part, this was due to Gallaudet's location, marching distance from the Capitol building, but more so to the unprecedented nature of the action: never before had a group of disabled students occupied a college campus. Telegrams and letters of support poured in, not only from the deaf community but also from civil rights activists, Congress, and the general public. The Reverend Jesse Jackson commented on how "the problem is not that the students do not hear. The problem is that the hearing world does not listen." *Newsweek* magazine stated that "for the first time in memory, deaf people as a group had spoken up and found . . . that the world would listen." Hlibok appeared on ABC's *Nightline*, along with Zinser and deaf actress Marlee Matlin. Newspaper editorials across the country took up the cry of "Deaf President Now!" Sen. Paul Simon (D-IL)

and Rep. Barney Frank (D-MA) declared their support from the floor of Congress.

Pivotal to the students' success was that both the alumni and the faculty declared their support for the strike. The students were also able to draw upon an extended network that included deaf business people such as John Yeh and David Birnbaum. Seventy volunteer interpreters agreed to interpret for the dozens of reporters now on campus. The American Postal Workers Union, with 4,000 deaf and hard-of-hearing members, marched in support and contributed $5,000 to the Deaf President Now Strike Fund, which had grown to more than $20,000 within days. This response, together with the faculty vote of 147 to 5 in support of the students, convinced Zinser that she could not hope to succeed as president of Gallaudet. She resigned on the evening of 10 March. As one student put it, "The era of hearing people deciding which is 'best' for deaf people has come to an end." Faced with a united front of students, faculty, alumni, and the larger deaf community, the board of trustees announced on 13 March that they agreed to the other student demands, and they appointed Irving King Jordan, dean of the College of Arts and Sciences, as president. It was a total victory for the students.

The Deaf President Now campaign put the issue of disability rights before the public, just as activists began to advocate for passage of the Americans with Disabilities Act (ADA). Patrisha Wright, coordinator of the campaign for passage of the ADA, notes that it was a "clear and easily understandable example of the absurdity" of ableism and of the patronizing and demeaning attitudes toward people with disabilities that the legislation was written to address. It also demonstrated the power of organization and united political action.

"The success of the week's protest," wrote Gannon, "sent a surge of elation through deaf people and their friends; it gave many a new self-image and renewed their pride in American Sign Language, deaf culture, and deaf history."

See also American Sign Language; Deaf Culture; Gallaudet University; Jordan, Irving King.

References Christiansen, John B. and Sharon N. Barnartt, *Deaf President Now! The 1988 Revolution at Gallaudet University* (1995); Gannon, Jack R., *The Week the World Heard Gallaudet* (1989); Schein, Jerome D., *At Home among Strangers* (1989).

Deaf Publications/Silent Press/ Little Paper Family

For much of the past century, printing and publishing offered deaf people employment opportunities generally unavailable in other professions or trades. The *Silent Press* was a term used earlier in the century to describe publications of and for the deaf—the first ever to be owned, edited, and written by people with disabilities. The term *Little Paper Family* (LPF) refers to the great variety of newspapers and journals published by students and teachers at deaf residential schools.

Beginning in the mid–nineteenth cen-

tury, a host of papers and journals, often connected with residential schools and their alumni, were founded by deaf people to report developments within the community. Historian Jack R. Gannon cites Levi S. Backus, editor of the New York *Canajoharie Radii* weekly newspaper beginning in 1837, as the nation's first deaf editor, while the monthly *Gallaudet Guide and Deaf-Mute's Companion*, founded in Boston in 1860, became the first publication aimed exclusively at a deaf readership. Other periodicals established during this time were the *Deaf Mute*, founded in 1849; *The Mute*, founded in 1868; and the *Deaf-Mute Advance*, founded in 1870. All of these publications were newsletters for residential schools. In 1875 in New York City, Henry C. Rider began publication of the *Deaf-Mute's Journal*, the nation's first deaf weekly newspaper. Edwin A. Hodgson became editor in 1876, and his editorials were influential in the founding of the National Association of the Deaf in 1880. Among the most politically radical of the Silent Press was the *Cavalier*, which, during the 1940s, had a circulation of more than 4,000 paid subscribers. Other periodicals of the late nineteenth and mid–twentieth centuries included *The National Exponent*, *The Silent Worker*, *The American Deaf Citizen*, and *The Modern Silents*.

Many of these papers had a short lifespan, some appearing for only a few years. The *Deaf-Mute's Journal* was one of the longest lived, lasting until 1951 under its new name, the *New York Journal of the Deaf*. The *Cavalier*, renamed *The National Observer*, ended publication in 1956, by which time most other periodicals had already ceased production. The end of the 1960s, however, brought the establishment of such publications as *The Deaf Spectrum*, *Deaf Life*, and *Silent News*. The Deaf press today continues to provide information of importance to the community, while many state associations also publish their own monthly or quarterly newsletters such as *Deaf Community News* in Massachusetts.

See also Deaf Life; National Association of the Deaf; *Silent News*.

References Gannon, Jack R., *Deaf Heritage: A Narrative History of the Deaf* (1981); Van Cleve, John Vickrey, and Barry A. Crouch, *A Place of Their Own: Creating the Deaf Community in America* (1989).

Deaf Sports
See Sports and Athletics.

Deaf Women United, Inc. (DWU)
Deaf Women United, Inc. (DWU) describes itself as a "non-profit national and international organization of, by, and for Deaf and hard of hearing women. Its mission is to promote the interests of Deaf and hard of hearing women in the United States and the world" and "to build a network of Deaf women."

The idea for the DWU was first floated in July 1985 at the First National Conference of Deaf Women in Santa Monica, California. The conference was sponsored and chaired by Marcella M. Meyer, chief executive officer at the Greater Los Angeles Council on Deafness, Inc. (GLAD). The Second National Conference of Deaf Women was held in Fairfax, Virginia, in July 1987, and the DWU became incorporated in the state of Maryland in November of that year. The DWU publishes its occasional *Newsletter* and a comprehensive booklist for deaf women, and it sponsors national conferences. It is currently based in East Hampton, Connecticut.

See also Women and Disability.

Deafpride, Inc.
Incorporated as a nonprofit organization in the District of Columbia in 1972, Deafpride, Inc., works "toward a society in which Deaf people are recognized as persons with their own language and culture and are allowed equal access to everything society has to offer." The organization is committed to diversity and to empowering the deaf community's most oppressed members. Deafpride, Inc., focuses on such issues as equal access to health care for deaf women, HIV/AIDS education in the deaf community, and outreach to deaf people who are drug or alcohol dependent.

In addition, Deafpride, Inc., plays an important role as resource and catalyst for other Deaf organizations. For example, it played a major role in the founding of National Black Deaf Advocates and Deaf Women United. Deafpride, Inc., also works with the National Association of the Deaf, the Washington, D.C., chapter of the Rainbow Alliance of the Deaf, and other local and national deaf organizations.

See also Deaf Culture; National Black Deaf Advocates; Rainbow Alliance of the Deaf.

Deinstitutionalization
The first institution for people with cognitive disabilities in the United States was established in 1848 by Samuel Gridley Howe in a wing of the Perkins Institution for the Blind in Boston. Howe's original purpose was to establish schools in or near the residents' town of origin to provide disabled children with a trade to enable them to live productively in the community. This ideal was abandoned, however, during the xenophobic, racist, and ableist hysteria generated by the eugenics movement. Mental disability had become equated with criminality and immorality and with the rise in immigration from Southern and Eastern Europe. Turn-of-the-century pamphlets such as *The Burden of Feeble-Mindedness* and *The Feeble-Minded; Or, The Hub to Our Wheel of Vice* argued that people with cognitive disabilities were a threat to society. By 1903, Walter Fernald, a leader of the Association of Medical Officers of American Institutions for Idiotic and Feeble-Minded Persons, was asking, "What is to be done with the feeble-minded progeny of the foreign hordes that have settled and are settling among us?"

In response, almost every state passed laws requiring doctors, nurses, teachers, even ministers to report disabled children to the authorities. Washington State went so far as to fine parents $200 for refusing to institutionalize their "feeble-minded" children. Simultaneously, efforts to alert the public to the "threat" of African Americans and immigrants resulted in "Jim Crow" laws passed throughout the states of the old Confederacy to restrict the rights of blacks and in legislation limiting Southern and Eastern European, Jewish, and Asian immigration into the United States.

Conditions within the "total institutions" subsequently built to house disabled persons were often appalling. Residents received little or no education, were exposed to abuse by staff and other residents, and subjected to medical experimentation by staff physicians. Many boys were castrated, and young women were often forcibly sterilized. At some institutions it was routine to extract children's teeth to keep them from biting. The situation was only marginally better for people with mental illness. For many, commitment to a state hospital for a "nervous breakdown" turned into lifelong incarceration, and Dorothea Dix's vision of enlightened treatment in humane institutions became a travesty.

Efforts to expose conditions in public mental hospitals began as early as 1908, with Clifford Beers' *A Mind That Found Itself*. It continued with *The Snake Pit* by M. J. Ward in 1946 and *The Shame of the States* by Albert Deutsch in 1948. Parents' organizations such as the National Association for Retarded Children (now The Arc) and United Cerebral Palsy Associations began in the 1950s to advocate for better conditions in institutions for developmentally disabled people. Erving Goffman's book *Asylums* (1961) demonstrated that the dysfunctional behavior of many institution residents (cited as a reason for keeping them locked away) often had less to do with their disability than with the harmful effects of the institutions themselves. *Christmas in Purgatory* (1966), by Burton Blatt and Fred Kaplan, provided photographic evidence of the inhumanity of total institutions. Despite all of the evidence, many thousands of Americans continued to be housed in such places. In 1967, there were some 228,500 people living in state "schools" or institutions.

In a series of landmark court cases, such as *Halderman v. Pennhurst State School and Hospital* (1978) and *New York ARC v. Rockefeller* (1973) (the Willowbrook case), federal judges ruled both that the conditions prevailing at institutions for people with developmental disabilities were so cruel as to be unconstitutional and that people with developmental disabilities had a right to a life in the community. In *O'Connor v. Donaldson* (1975), the U.S. Supreme Court ruled that people with psychiatric disabilities who were not dangerous to themselves or others could not be incarcerated against their will. Though the remedies imposed by the courts varied with the different cases, and relied on differing legal principles, the overall effect of these decisions was to make it both more difficult for the states to incarcerate people with disabilities and more expensive. No longer could people with disabilities be "warehoused"— kept in facilities that offered nothing in the way of education, rehabilitation, recreation, or safety.

Policy decisions by the federal government also provided an impetus for deinstitutionalization. The 1962 report by the President's Panel on Mental Retardation called for "the development of a wider range of diversified residential arrangements . . . [and] of group homes. . . ." That same year, the U.S. Department of Health, Education and Welfare first allowed state governments to use federal funds for public assistance to people with psychiatric disabilities living in the community. The Supplemental Security Income (SSI) program, beginning in 1974, made funds available to people with developmental disabilities living outside of institutions, providing a funding source for community living.

Finally, the acceptance of "normalization"—the concept that people with disabilities did best in environments that were as "normal" as possible—provided the intellectual rationale for deinstitutionalization. It could no longer be argued, as it had been from the 1850s into the 1960s, that institutions provided the best opportunity for children with developmental disabilities to be educated, or for people with mental illness to be rehabilitated. Indeed, the work of Erving Goffman and the radical psychiatrist Thomas Szasz indicated the opposite: that institutions prevented the very rehabilitation they were supposed to foster.

By the late 1960s, there was a move away from institutions and toward mainstreaming, normalization, and community placement. The creation of these community services, mandated by the courts, meant that massive institutions became unnecessary. During the course of the next two decades, most major state institutions for people with developmental disabilities were emptied. Many former institution residents were enrolled in group homes and community agencies. By 1989, there were some 38,657 such facilities, housing 148,000 people; by 1996, there were more than 50,000 community placements for people with developmental disabilities. By 1995, the census at institutions for people with developmental disabilities had fallen to below 70,000, and it continues to fall. Beginning in the 1970s, the population of public mental hospitals also declined. By the late 1980s, an estimated 300,000 to 400,000 people with psychiatric disabilities lived in "board and care" homes—small facilities where residents receive 24-hour, nonmedical supervision. Others were able to obtain jobs and blend into the community.

The prevailing public view is that deinstitionalization has led to homelessness, with disabled people "dumped" onto the street. In evaluating the success or failure of deinstitutionalization, a distinction must be made between the experiences of people with developmental disabilities and those of people with psychiatric disabilities. Although program quality varies and instances of abuse and neglect occur, it is well established that for persons with developmental disabilities community placements are generally far more humane than institutions such as Willowbrook or Pennhurst.

Deinstitutionalization has been less successful for people with psychiatric disabilities. In part, this has been due to a wide disparity between public spending on services for people with mental retardation and public spending on those with mental illness. For people with developmental disabilities, community services were usually mandated by the courts, and an advocacy infrastructure of parents' groups and other interested parties existed to monitor compliance. Often, no such safeguards existed for people with psychiatric disabilities. Ann Braden Johnson, writing in the *Encyclopedia of Social Work* (1995), notes that deinstitutionalization, "particularly of the mentally ill, never happened," with many residents of state hospitals, especially elderly people, simply transferred to "other custodial settings not run by the government," such as nursing homes. Irwin Garfinkel, in *Controversial Issues in Mental Health* (1994), sees deinstitutionalization "of the mentally ill" as a cause of homelessness. Previously, "the 200,000 to 250,000 severely mentally ill individuals who are now homeless would be involuntarily committed patients in large state mental hospitals." James D. Wright, taking the opposing view, argues that "the emphasis on mental illness as a causative factor [of homelessness] diverts attention from more basic issues of political economy" such as poverty, unemployment, and the lack of affordable housing. Advocates such as Judi Chamberlin note that simultaneous to deinstitutionalization came gentrification, the end of single room occupancy (SRO) boarding houses, and a massive cutback in the federal commitment to public housing.

See also Beers, Clifford Whittingham; *Christmas in Purgatory*; Eugenics; Normalization; *O'Connor v. Donaldson*; Parents' Movement; *Pennhurst State School & Hospital v. Halderman*; Supported Living; Willowbrook State School.

References Edwards, Richard L., ed., *Encyclopedia of Social Work: 19th Edition* (1995); Ferguson, Philip M., *Abandoned to Their Fate: Social Policy and Practice toward Severely Retarded People in America, 1820–1920* (1994); Kindred, Michael, et al., eds. *The Mentally Retarded Citizen and the Law* (1976); Kirk, Stuart A., and Susan D. Einbinder, eds., *Controversial Issues in Mental Health* (1994); Kugel, Robert B., and Wolf Wolfensberger, eds., *Changing Patterns in Residential Services for the Mentally Retarded* (1969);

Scheerenberger, R. C., *Deinstitutionalization and Institutional Reform* (1976); Trent, James W., Jr., *Inventing the Feeble Mind: A History of Mental Retardation in the United States* (1994).

Dendron

Dendron, a quarterly publication, describes itself as "an independent global non-profit information service promoting human rights, especially in psychiatry, and exploring humane, empowering options for emotional support." It has a circulation of 7,000 and an estimated readership of more than 18,000. Articles include accounts of psychiatric survivors fighting the use of electro-convulsive therapy (ECT), the abusive use of psychotropic medications, and protests by psychiatric survivors around the country. *Dendron* raises essential questions about the mental health system, such as: "Why, despite the efforts of so many well-intentioned workers, do the clients fail to improve? And why do so many clients die?"

See also Psychiatric Survivor Movement.

Developmental Disabilities

The term *developmental disabilities* was coined by Elizabeth Boggs, a parent advocate with the National Association for Retarded Children (now The Arc), and Ilse Helsel, a parent advocate with United Cerebral Palsy Associations. It put into one category people with cerebral palsy, epilepsy, and mental retardation, in an effort to increase their political clout and thus garner more funding for programs serving people with developmental disabilities. The term was incorporated into the Developmental Disabilities Services and Facilities Construction Amendments of 1970. The definition was amended by the Developmentally Disabled Assistance and Bill of Rights Act of 1975, which added autism and some forms of dyslexia to the original definition; subsequent amendments have added minimal brain injury and various aphasic disorders.

According to the Developmental Disabilities Assistance and Bill of Rights Act of 1990, "developmental disability means a severe, chronic disability of a person 5 years of age or older" that is "attributable to a mental or physical impairment or a combination of mental or physical impairments" and is "evident before the person attains age 22." It is "likely to continue indefinitely" and "results in substantial functional limitations in three or more" major life activities, such as self-care, language, learning, mobility, self-direction, capacity for independent living, and economic self-sufficiency. Rather than categorizing someone by medical diagnosis (cerebral palsy, autism, etc.), this definition emphasizes function and impact, and is considered to be less stigmatizing than labels such as "mentally retarded" or "epileptic."

The original 1970 Developmental Disabilities ("D.D.") Act provided federal funds for the creation of state Developmental Disabilities ("D.D.") Councils made up of representatives of the principal state and local agencies and nongovernmental groups serving or representing developmentally disabled people. The councils help to evaluate and plan state programs. Though their effectiveness has varied from state to state and in different administrations, the councils are credited with improving the quality of many state programs serving people with developmental disabilities.

See also Boggs, Elizabeth; Developmentally Disabled Assistance and Bill of Rights Act of 1975.

References Edwards, Richard L., ed., *Encyclopedia of Social Work: 19th Edition* (1995); Scheerenberger, R. C., *A History of Mental Retardation: A Quarter Century of Progress* (1987).

Developmentally Disabled Assistance and Bill of Rights Act of 1975

The Developmentally Disabled Assistance and Bill of Rights Act of 1975 obligated both federal and state governments to withhold funding from institutions for developmentally disabled people that did not "provide treatment, services, and habilitation which is appropriate to the needs" of their residents and to facilities that did not meet certain minimum standards for safety and habilitation, including "a nourishing, well-balanced daily diet," and "appropriate and sufficient medical and dental services." The act also prohibited the use of physical restraint "unless absolutely necessary," the use of restraint as "a punishment or as a substitute for a habilitation program," and the "excessive use of chemical restraints." The act also required institutions receiving state and federal funds to permit "close relatives" to visit residents "at reasonable hours without prior notice" and ordered compliance with "adequate fire and safety standards. . . ." Although sweeping in its intent, the bill of rights portion of the act as written was unenforceable, and the U.S. Supreme Court decisions in *Halderman v. Pennhurst* (1981, 1984) rendered this part of the legislation virtually useless to disability rights advocates.

The act also established a network of Protection and Advocacy (P&A) organizations to advocate for the rights of persons with developmental disabilities receiving state services. The governor of each state was required to designate an agency to serve as a P&A. In 1986, each designated P&A also became part of the Protection and Advocacy for Individuals with Mental Illness Program (PAIMI), funded and administered by the National Center for Mental Health Services. In 1994, the Native American P&A program was created, and the Technology Related Assistance for Individuals with Disabilities Act of 1988 was expanded to establish the Protection and Advocacy for Assistive Technology Program (PAAT) to help individuals with disabilities and their families gain access to assistive technology.

Disability rights advocates such as Patrisha Wright charge that many governors have hampered the P&A system by choosing agencies inadequate for the job. Indeed, for many years many P&As had no legal staff at all. Critics also maintain that some P&As "cream" only the most easily won cases, leaving the tougher ones for private disability rights advocates. The California P&A, for example, refused to support Rachel Holland, whose case was

won by parent advocate/attorney Diane Lipton at the Disability Rights Education and Defense Fund. The landmark lawsuit was brought after Rachel Holland's school district refused to allow her into a mainstream classroom.

See also Holland v. Sacramento City Unified School District; Halderman v. Pennhurst State School & Hospital.

Disability Blackface
Disability blackface refers to the tendency of the film and television industries to cast nondisabled actors in the roles of people with disabilities. Notable examples of this include Al Pacino as a blind man in *The Scent of a Woman* (1992), Mary McDonnell as a woman with quadriplegia in *Passion Fish* (1992), and Alan Arkin as a deaf man in *The Heart Is a Lonely Hunter* (1968). Disability activist Bill Bolte, in the March 1993 issue of *Mainstream* magazine, pointed out how such films generally feature the worst stereotypes about people with disabilities: that they are pathetic, miserable, bitter, and eager to die. This type of portrayal is not likely to change, writes Bolte, until people with disabilities "actively support our right to work [in the media] and . . . to be portrayed accurately. . . ." Until then, people with disabilities "will continue to have the unenviable choice between being held in contempt or being ignored."

See also Media Images of People with Disabilities.

References Bolte, Bill, "Hollywood's New Blackface: Just Spray 'em with Chrome," *Mainstream* (March 1993).

Disability Culture
Historian Paul K. Longmore calls disability culture "the second phase" of the disability rights movement. "The first phase," he wrote in a 1995 essay in *The Disability Rag & Resource*, "has been a quest for civil rights, for equal access and equal opportunity, for inclusion. The second phase is a quest for collective identity. Even as the unfinished work of the first

phase continues, the task in the second phase is to explore or to create a disability culture." Longmore sees this as a process of "redefining 'disability' from the inside."

Disability culture is created by people with disabilities, and it uses as its subject the experience of disability. Its artifacts include the novels of Jean Stewart and Lorenzo Milam, the short stories of Anne Finger, the plays of the National Theatre of the Deaf and Wry Crips, the poetry of Robert Williams, the performance art of Neil Marcus, the choreography of the AXIS Dance Troupe, and the songs of Johnny Crescendo. What these works and artists all have in common is a pride in who disabled people are and a commitment to their empowerment. "The pleasure we take in our own community," writes psychologist and disability rights advocate Carol Gill, and "the assertion of Disability pride and the celebration of our culture are a massive assault on ablecentric thinking. It really rocks people when we so clearly reject the superiority of nondisability." Performance artist Cheryl Marie Wade sees disability culture as a process of "finding a history, naming and claiming ancestors, heroes." Disability culture, says Wade, takes a figure such as Helen Keller and changes her from the child muttering "wah wah" in *The Miracle Worker* (1962) to a social activist, writer, world traveler, and political figure.

Disability culture presupposes a definition of disability, not as a medical problem to be treated by doctors and rehabilitation professionals and certainly not as a tragic "fate worse than death," but as a social/political reality. In this view, people with disabilities are members of a minority group. An essential step in achieving political and social equality is pride in one's roots and culture, without which minority peoples are inevitably defined and oppressed by the majority culture. "Without political action," writes activist Mark O'Brien, "there is no change. Without a culture, there is no identity, no feeling of 'us.'"

See also Deaf Culture; Disability Pride; Institute on Disability Culture; Lewis, Victoria Ann; Longmore, Paul K.; Marcus, Neil; Media Images of People with Disabilities; Milam, Lorenzo Wilson; Na-

tional Theatre of the Deaf; Stewart, Jean; Wade, Cheryl Marie; Wry Crips.

References Gill, Carol, "The pleasure we take in our community . . . ," *The Disability Rag & Resource* (September/October 1995); Longmore, Paul K., "The Second Phase: From Disability Rights to Disability Culture," *The Disability Rag & Resource* (September/October 1995); O'Brien, Mark, "Identity Squared," *The Disability Rag & Resource* (September/October 1995); Wade, Cheryl Marie, "Disability Culture Rap," *The Disability Rag & Resource* (September/October 1992).

Disability Pride

Meg Kocher, writing in *Ordinary Moments* (1985), muses about what it would be like in "a country in which everyone is disabled." Attending the 1977 White House Conference on Handicapped Individuals with 3,000 other disabled people, Kocher

saw every kind of disability imaginable, including combinations of disabilities; people in wheelchairs using respirators and portable iron lungs; short deaf people; and blind wheelchair users. . . . I was curious about our differences. . . . I was completely awed by the variety.

When the conference was over, I went to a restaurant with a friend. I couldn't believe how boring it was to be in a place with people who all walked the same, sat the same, talked the same. None of them used their hands to talk, none had canes or dogs or wheelchairs or respirators. . . . There was no wealth, no richness. I felt a loss.

Pride, writes Laura Hershey, is a feeling "that is not easy to come by in this segregated, inaccessible, often discriminatory world." People with disabilities are told, overtly and covertly, that they are defective and incompetent, and reactions from nondisabled friends, family, and strangers to the advent of a disability can range from pity to offers of help in committing suicide. The list of great disabled figures, however, seems endless: from composers such as Ludwig van Beethoven to writers such as John Milton and Flannery O'Connor and political leaders such as Julius Caesar and Franklin Delano Roosevelt. The point of disability pride is to proclaim that life with a disability is far from being necessarily tragic or pitiable. Furthermore, "without pride," writes Hershey, "our movement can never develop."

Disability leaders in several cities have organized annual Disability Pride Day marches, during which people with disabilities celebrate themselves and their community. The point made is similar to that of the Gay Pride marches on which they are modeled: disability is not something to be ashamed of or hidden away.

See also Deaf Culture; Disability Culture.
References Hershey, Laura, "Pride," *The Disability Rag & Resource* (July/August 1991). Kocher, Meg, "I Would Be This Way Forever," in Alan J. Brightman, ed., *Ordinary Moments: The Disabled Experience* (1985);

The Disability Rag & Resource

The Disability Rag & Resource has been described as the movement's *"Village Voice, Rolling Stone* and *Mother Jones* all rolled into one small powerfully written tabloid." Published six times a year in Louisville, Kentucky, *The Rag* (as it was known to its readers) featured articles from writers on the cutting edge of the disability rights movement, reporting on groups such as Jerry's Orphans and American Disabled for Attendant Programs Today (ADAPT), as well as containing critical analysis of disability rights organizations and their leadership. A regular feature—"We wish we wouldn't see . . ."—reprinted particularly egregious examples of patronizing or dehumanizing depictions of people with disabilities in the mass media, while its Letters to the Editor section offered discussion on everything from the use of the word *cripple* to sex and sexuality, the efficacy of civil disobedience, and nightmare experiences with social workers and rehabilitation counselors.

The Rag was founded by Mary Johnson and Cass Irvin, both disability rights activists from Louisville. Its first issue appeared in January 1980. In March of the following year, Johnson and Irvin incorporated The Advocado Press as a nonprofit company to publish *The Rag*. For a time *The Rag* also doubled as the newsletter for the Center for Accessible Living, the Louisville area's first independent living center.

Besides its reporting, *The Rag* served an important role as a place where writers with a disability rights perspective could be published for the first time. It was the first publication to use such phrases as *disconfirmation* and *disability chic*. Stories appearing in *The Rag* were quoted by mainstream publications such as *The Boston Globe, The Wall Street Journal,* and the *Dallas Times Herald*. In 1993, the last year of Johnson's editorship, *The Disability Rag* won the Utne Reader Alternative Press Award for Best Special Interest Publication.

The Advocado Press has also published a wide array of disability-related books and pamphlets, among them *The Ragged Edge: The Disability Experience from the Pages of the First Fifteen Years of* The Disability Rag (1995), considered an essential text of the disability rights movement.

The Rag often struggled financially, with from 3,000 to 4,300 paying subscribers and an estimated pass-along readership of 23,000. In early 1996, the Advocado Press Board of Directors announced that there would be "a hiatus, hopefully brief" in publication. In late 1996, *The Rag* was reborn as *The Ragged Edge*, with Mary Johnson back as editor.

See also Disconfirmation; Johnson, Mary; Media Images of People with Disabilities.
Reference Shaw, Barrett, ed., *The Ragged Edge: The Disability Experience from the Pages of the First Fifteen Years of* The Disability Rag. (1994).

Disability Rights Center (DRC)

The Disability Rights Center (DRC) was founded in Washington, D.C., in 1976 by Deborah Kaplan, with funding from Ralph Nader's Center for the Study of Responsive Law. It focused primarily on protecting the rights of consumers of wheelchairs and durable medical equipment, and on ensuring enforcement of the affirmative action provision of Section 501 of the Rehabilitation Act of 1973. Among the highlights of its decade of activism were a class action suit filed in conjunction with antitrust action taken by the U.S. Justice Department against Everest & Jennings (at that time the nation's largest producer of wheelchairs) and a review undertaken in 1977 of Section 501 compliance by federal agencies. The DRC was also a litigant in the Transbus case (*Disabled in Action of Pennsylvania, Inc. v. Coleman*, 1976), an effort to ensure that U.S. mass transit systems purchased only accessible buses. Kaplan left in 1980 to become an attorney for the Disability Rights Education and Defense Fund (DREDF), and, after a brief period, Evan Kemp Jr. became the DRC's new director. Under his leadership, the organization played an important role in attempts to convince the National Muscular Dystrophy Association to discontinue its Jerry Lewis Telethon, and in opposing efforts to gut the regulations implementing Section 504 of the Rehabilitation Act of 1973 and the Education for All Handicapped Children Act of 1975. The DRC ended operations soon after Kemp left to become a commissioner at the U.S. Equal Employment Opportunity Commission in 1987.

See also Kaplan, Deborah; Kemp, Evan, Jr.; Rehabilitation Act of 1973; Telethons; Transbus.

Disability Rights Education and Defense Fund (DREDF)

The Disability Rights Education and Defense Fund (DREDF) is a nonprofit national law and policy center dedicated to expanding the civil rights of all people with disabilities and their families. Its primary role is to serve as the disability community's national legal defense fund, analogous to the way the NAACP Legal Defense Fund works to defend and expand the civil rights of people of color. Founded in 1979, it has a home office in Berkeley, California, and a governmental affairs office in Washington, D.C.

DREDF grew out of the Berkeley Center for Independent Living (CIL) and its Disabled Paralegal Advocacy Program (DPAP). Founded in the mid-1970s, the DPAP was staffed mostly by volunteers. In 1978, when the CIL received grants from the federal Department of Health, Education and Welfare, the DPAP became the Disability Law Resource Center (DLRC), which in turn received funding from the Legal Services Corporation. The DLRC grew rapidly, from a staff of 8 volunteers to more than 45 paid employees. Its focus changed from local issues in Berkeley and in California to disability rights cases of national significance. Among the attorneys either working for or trained by the DLRC were Robert Funk, Deborah Kaplan, Diane J. Lipton, Linda D. Kilb, and Arlene B. Mayerson, all of whom became important disability rights advocates. The DREDF was founded by Patrisha A. Wright, Mary Lou Breslin, and Robert Funk, and incorporated on 1 October 1979, with Funk as its founder and first director.

DREDF has played a crucial role in developing and coordinating the legal strategy for much of the ground-breaking disability rights litigation of the 1980s and 1990s, including *Conrail v. Darrone* (1984), *Alexander v. Choate* (1985), and *School Board v. Arline* (1987). Sometimes DREDF attorneys directly represent disabled plaintiffs, as in *Holland v. Sacramento City Unified School District* (1994), or they act as resources for the attorneys of record, articulating principles of disability rights law so that the civil rights of people with disabilities are protected or expanded. Much of the language in the *Arline* decision, for example, is quoted directly from the brief drafted by DREDF attorney Arlene Mayerson.

Staff at DREDF were the key organizers in the campaign in the early 1980s to thwart attempts by the Reagan administration to curtail or rescind the regulations implementing Section 504 of the Rehabilitation Act of 1973 and the Education for All Handicapped Children Act of 1975. DREDF ran an extensive series of workshops in the West and Midwest after passage of the Rehabilitation Act of 1973, training disability advocates in the use of

Section 504 as a way to secure their civil rights. These workshops provided the framework for much of the disability rights advocacy that followed.

DREDF was integrally involved in the drafting and passage of the Americans with Disabilities Act of 1990. By 1996, DREDF staff had trained more than 50,000 people in how to secure their rights or the rights of their clients under the new law. DREDF has received contracts from many federal agencies, including the Department of Justice, to provide technical assistance and consultation. Critical also in passage of the Civil Rights Restoration Act of 1987 and the Fair Housing Amendments Act of 1988, DREDF now has an international presence, working with governments and advocates drafting their own disability rights law.

See also *Alexander v. Choate*; Americans with Disabilities Act of 1990; Breslin, Mary Lou; Civil Rights Restoration Act of 1987; *Consolidated Rail Corporation v. Darrone*; Fair Housing Amendments Act of 1988; Funk, Robert; Golden, Marilyn; *Holland v. the Sacramento City Unified School District*; Mayerson, Arlene B.; *School Board of Nassau County, Florida v. Arline*; Section 504 of the Rehabilitation Act of 1973; Wright, Patrisha A.

Disability Studies Quarterly

Disability Studies Quarterly (DSQ) is a scholarly journal on the social and political aspects of disability. It was founded in 1982 by Irving Zola, who remained its editor until his death in 1994. Topics explored in *DSQ* have included technology, women and gender-related issues, media depictions of disability, the "Baby Doe" case and neonatal issues, self help and independent living, and history. In 1996, responsibility for publishing *DSQ* was assumed by the Society for Disability Studies.

See also Society for Disability Studies; Zola, Irving Kenneth.

Disabled American Veterans (DAV)

Disabled American Veterans (DAV) was established in the aftermath of World War I, in which more than 300,000 American soldiers were disabled. American society,

disillusioned by the war, sought a "return to normalcy," and successive administrations and Congresses refused to adequately fund programs for disabled veterans. In response, disabled veterans organized their own local self-help groups, many of which came together in 1920 as DAV. DAV was founded in Cincinnati, but soon opened a Washington, D.C., office. Among its first priorities was the creation of a centralized federal Veterans Bureau, the forerunner of today's Department of Veterans Affairs. In 1935, DAV began stationing its own representatives at Veterans Bureau claims offices and hospitals to ensure that veterans with disabilities received appropriate services and benefits. After World War II, specially trained DAV counselors became mentors for disabled veterans returning from that conflict.

DAV was chartered by Congress in 1932 as the official representative of American soldiers disabled as a result of their service; however, DAV is not a government agency and receives no government funds. Membership is open to any American veteran disabled in the military during wartime, or during duty in conditions similar to war. As of 1997, veterans disabled during the Vietnam War made up roughly one third of its membership. DAV runs more than 60 offices across the country, where veterans and their families, whether they are members or not, receive information and support free of charge. Its national legislative program fights for funding for veterans programs, while the DAV employment program fights discrimination directed against disabled veterans on the job.

Disabled Children's Computer Group (DCCG)

See Alliance for Technology Access.

Disabled in Action (DIA)

Disabled in Action (DIA) was founded in New York City in 1970 by Judith Heumann as a grassroots, direct action disability rights group. It has chapters today in New York City, Syracuse, Philadelphia, and Baltimore. Determinedly grassroots and nonprofessional, DIA has no national organization, no office, and no paid staff.

Among DIA's early actions were demonstrations to protest President Nixon's 1972 veto of what would become the Rehabilitation Act of 1973. These protests included a demonstration at the Lincoln Memorial and the take-over, in conjunction with a group of disabled Vietnam veterans, of the Nixon reelection campaign's New York City headquarters. In 1976 and 1977, DIA picketed the United Cerebral Palsy Associations' telethon, becoming perhaps the first disability group to publicly protest telethons as a way to raise money for disability services. During the mid-1970s, DIA was also involved in the fight for Transbus, with the Philadelphia chapter filing a lawsuit (*Disabled in Action of Pennsylvania, Inc. v. Coleman*, 1976), in conjunction with the Public Interest Law Center of Philadelphia, to mandate the purchase of wheelchair accessible buses by the nation's mass transit systems. In 1984, the New York City DIA, through a series of demonstrations and lawsuits, was successful in forcing the Metropolitan Transit Authority to agree that all new vehicles purchased and all new subway stations constructed would be accessible. In the late 1980s, each of the DIA chapters pushed for passage of the Americans with Disabilities Act of 1990, with members traveling to Washington on several occasions to participate in actions such as the Wheels of Justice protests organized by the American Disabled for Attendant Programs Today (ADAPT).

In January 1992, the New York City DIA filed the first ever lawsuit under Title III of the Americans with Disabilities Act, forcing the owners of the Empire State Building to ramp its observation tower. More recently, the group has launched its One Step Campaign to convince businesses with single-step entrances to ramp them for wheelchair access. The group has advocated for accessible taxicabs, for increased registration of disabled voters, and

for accommodations to make the New York subway system safer for blind and visually disabled riders. In this last effort, DIA aligned itself with the local chapter of the American Council of the Blind. Other efforts have it working with the Eastern Paralyzed Veterans of America. DIA's major focus in the 1990s has been on issues of health care reform, managed care, and personal assistance services, and it has protested proposed changes in Medicaid that would compromise the health and independence of people with disabilities.

DIA in New York has an estimated 300 members. It receives funding through progressive foundations such as the Funding Exchange and through its own musical group, the Disabled in Action Singers. Chapters in other cities are smaller.

See also Heumann, Judith E.; Rehabilitation Act of 1973; Transbus; Wheels of Justice.

Disabled in Action of Pennsylvania, Inc. v. Coleman.
See Transbus.

Disabled Peoples' International (DPI)

Disabled Peoples' International (DPI) is a cross-disability network of some 110 organizations, more than half of which are in Latin America, Africa, and Asia. To be a member of DPI, an organization must be national in scope and run by people with disabilities. DPI is nonprofit and nongovernmental, and it helps connect U.S. disability rights organizers with activists all around the world.

According to a World Health Organization study published in 1980, there are more than half a billion people with disabilities worldwide, the majority of whom live in developing nations. In many societies, disability within a family is regarded as a source of shame, and the disabled member is hidden away. According to a study cited by Diane Driedger in *The Last Civil Rights Movement* (1989), only 2 percent of people with disabilities in Asia and the Pacific Rim receive any rehabilitation services at all. Even such basic necessities as crutches, wheelchairs, and guide canes are in short supply, and people with disabilities are often forced to beg in order to avoid starvation.

The catalyst for DPI's formation was a series of world conferences convened by Rehabilitation International (RI), an organization of rehabilitation agency administrators and specialists. There had been complaints from the disabled delegates, who were often themselves rehabilitation professionals, that the 1976 RI conference in Tel Aviv was held in an inaccessible site, with little provision for accessible accommodations or transportation. As a result, people with disabilities found themselves marginalized at a conference whose stated purpose was to help bring them into the mainstream. RI's 1980 conference was held in Winnipeg, Canada, the headquarters of the Coalition of Provincial Organizations of the Handicapped (COPOH), Canada's national cross-disability rights organization. COPOH, together with disability rights leaders from Sweden and elsewhere, formed the Ad Hoc Committee on Participation of Disabled People and Their Organizations and drafted a resolution calling for half of RI's governing council to be people with disabilities. When their resolution was defeated, the disabled delegates decided to form an independent organization—DPI.

DPI was officially founded in Singapore in late November/early December 1981 at a conference attended by 400 disabled people from 51 nations. The conference adopted a "Plan of Action" for setting up the organization and a manifesto: "We maintain that all people are of equal value. This conviction implies that disabled people have the right to participate in every sphere of society. . . . We therefore reject all forms of segregation and we refuse to accept lifetime isolation in special institutions." It listed for all people with disabilities everywhere rights to education, rehabilitation, employment, independent living, and income security. Finally, it stated that "organizations of the disabled must be given decisive influence in regard to all measures taken on their behalf." The "Singapore Declaration" approved by the conference also condemned violence and war as "policies perpetuating disability" (Driedger 1989).

Over the next 15 years, DPI, headquartered in Winnipeg, provided logistical support and training to grassroots disability rights groups around the world. Joshua Malinga, a participant at the RI conference in 1980 and later a DPI chairperson, was struck by DPI's civil rights philosophy, which he took back to his own organization in Zimbabwe. "It was at that meeting," Malinga recalled in 1989, "that most of us from Africa first understood what was meant by a 'disabled rights movement.' We had never thought about disabled rights as a cause, or the disabled community as a community. . . . It was a shift from looking at disability as a health issue, to looking at it as a human rights issue" (Pelka 1989).

Today, DPI sponsors workshops for disability organizers, focusing especially on low-income, rural, and women's issues. It also presents a disability rights perspective at international forums and has advisory status with the United Nations (UN) and the International Labor Organization. DPI played a role in developing the UN's Decade of Disabled Persons, 1983–1992. DPI assists local disability groups with fund-raising and helps monitor and evaluate disability-related programs and projects. It has a research clearinghouse for information on disability and people with disabilities and publishes a quarterly newsletter, *Vox Nostra*, and a quarterly journal, *Disability International*. Archbishop Desmond Tutu delivered the keynote speech at the DPI World Assembly in Australia in December 1994, telling delegates that the oppression of people with disabilities "is as much a moral issue as the struggle against apartheid . . . and we must all take it up as a matter of religious and political conviction."

See also Council of Canadians with Disabilities; International Year, International Decade of Disabled Persons; World Institute on Disability.

References Driedger, Diane, *The Last Civil Rights Movement: Disabled Peoples' International* (1989); Pelka, Fred, "Disability Rights in Zimbabwe," *Mainstream* (October 1989).

Disabled Sports USA (DS/USA)

Disabled Sports USA (DS/USA), formerly National Handicapped Sports, was founded in 1967 by a group of disabled Vietnam veterans interested in resuming their participation in team and individual sports. By 1996, it had grown into a national nonprofit organization with 87 chapters in 40 states, with a mission to "ensure that disabled people have access to sports, recreation and physical education programs, from preschool through college, to elite sports levels." Its chapters offer opportunities for participation in a wide variety of athletic activities, including skiing, hiking, and sailing. DS/USA is a member of the U.S. Olympic Committee and an official advisor to the President's Council on Physical Fitness and Sports. It is based in Rockville, Maryland.

See also Paralympics, Paralympic Movement; Sports and Athletics.

Disabled Student Services/ Higher Education

Gallaudet College, founded in 1864, was the first U.S. institution of higher learning to accommodate students with disabilities, in this case students who were deaf. The first concerted efforts to make college campuses accessible to people with mobility disabilities began in the mid-1940s, with the return to civilian life of veterans disabled during World War II. In 1947, Professor Tim Nugent, at the University of Illinois at Urbana-Champaign, began an extensive program to provide accessibility to physically disabled students. Other campuses, among them the University of California at Los Angeles, Wayne State in Detroit, Wright State in Dayton, Ohio, the University of Missouri, and Earlham College in Indiana, admitted disabled students and made efforts to provide access during the 1950s and 1960s, though none of the

programs were as large or successful as that at the University of Illinois. The University of California campuses at Berkeley, Riverside, and Stanford, as well as a number of community colleges in that state, also admitted disabled students during the same period. The founding of the National Technical Institute for the Deaf in 1965 provided an opportunity for deaf students wanting a college education in the sciences, enabling many to go on to do post-graduate work at other institutions.

Passage of the Rehabilitation Act of 1973, with its Section 504 prohibiting discrimination against people with disabilities by entities receiving federal funds, brought a tremendous increase in efforts to open campuses to disabled students. Besides architectural access for physically disabled students and communication access for students who are blind or deaf, campuses were now required to provide programmatic access for students with learning disabilities, for example, by providing more time for testing. The Higher Education and the Handicapped (HEATH) Project was organized by the American Council on Education in 1977, as a response to Section 504, to collect and disseminate information on disability, access, and higher education.

Since 1984, HEATH has been funded by the U.S. Department of Education. There are also a number of federally sponsored databases providing information on access to college administrators, teachers, and students. Among these are the Educational Resources Information Center (ERIC) and the National Rehabilitation Information Center (NARIC).

With the growth in the numbers of disabled college students came an increase in disability rights organizing on the nation's campuses. Among the disability rights student groups organized in the 1960s and early 1970s were the Rolling Quads at the University of California at Berkeley and the Student Organization for Every Disability United For Progress (SO FED UP) in New York City. Campus activism in turn played a role in further expanding opportunities for people with disabilities seeking a higher education. Groups pressed for architectural access on campus and in the surrounding communities and for the expansion of existing disabled student services, enabling thousands of other students to matriculate in the following decades.

See also Nugent, Timothy J.; Office of Special Education and Rehabilitative Services (OSERS).

DisAbled Women's Network of Canada (DAWN)

The DisAbled Women's Network of Canada (DAWN), based in Vancouver, is the largest disability rights group in North America with a distinctly feminist orientation. Funded by the Canadian federal government, it researches issues of importance to women with disabilities in areas of employment equity, violence, mothering, self-image, health, and sexuality.

DAWN was officially founded in Winnipeg, Canada, in 1987. Its roots go back to a national disabled women's conference in Ottawa in 1985, when women with disabilities from across Canada came together for the first time to discuss issues of mutual interest. Among DAWN's principal founders were longtime disability rights and feminist activists Pat Israel, Pat Danforth, and Paula Keirstead. Joan Meister, another co-founder, was the first chair of DAWN's board of directors. Following the first conference, local DAWN chapters were established throughout Canada, with British Columbia and Ontario the first to organize. Today, DAWN chapters exist in most provinces and in several foreign countries such as Trinidad and Tobago.

Among DAWN's significant contributions is its research into the prevalence of sexual and physical violence against women with disabilities and the link between this abuse and low self-esteem and suicide. When DAWN began its research, most battered women's shelters and rape crisis centers in North America were inaccessible to the majority of women with disabilities. In response to this inaccessibility, DAWN published *Meeting Our Needs* (1990), a manual on how to make shelters and rape crisis centers accessible. It has become a standard text for shelters and centers across Canada and the United States.

The 2,000-member DAWN defines itself as a cross-disability group that is pro-choice and feminist. Meister explains, "We're autonomous because otherwise our issues wouldn't be addressed" by disability rights groups without a feminist perspective. She cites the need for accessible womens' health services and the concerns of mothers with disabilities as examples of such issues. Most recently, DAWN has become involved in the issues of new reproductive technologies, suicide, and euthanasia.

See also Abortion and Reproductive Rights; Euthanasia and Assisted Suicide; Council of Canadians with Disabilities; Rape/Sexual and Domestic Violence.

Disconfirmation

Two people, one of them walking, the other using a wheelchair, enter a restaurant. After leading them to a table, the waiter asks the nondisabled diner what she would like to eat. After taking the order, he then asks that same diner, "And what would your friend like?"

Disconfirmation is what happens when nondisabled people pretend that people with disabilities do not exist or that they are incapable of thinking, speaking, deciding, or acting for themselves. The term came into use after publication of an article titled "Discomfirmation" by Billy Golfus in the November/December 1989 issue of *The Disability Rag & Resource*. As an example of disconfirmation, Golfus pointed out how his friends cut him out of their lives after his head injury. "Some people have walked by me on the street and pretended they didn't recognize me." This is a common experience for newly disabled people, who often report that their old friends act as though they had never existed.

See also Golfus, Billy.

References Golfus, Billy, "Disconfirmation," in Barrett Shaw, ed., *The Ragged Edge: The Disability Experience from the Pages of the First Fifteen Years of* The Disability Rag (1994).

Disincentives

The term *disincentives* refers to social service regulations that discourage people with disabilities from working, marrying, or otherwise leading more independent lives. As an example, a disabled person who gets a job might, by making more money than the Medicaid program allows, end up losing the Medicaid-funded personal assistance services (PAS) that enable the individual to work in the first place. Similar Catch-22s are built into the workers' compensation and Social Security programs, with the result that many people with disabilities must remain in poverty, even if they can work, in order to remain eligible for otherwise prohibitively expensive health insurance and home care services. Such disincentives can also discourage disabled people from marrying, since, under government programs such as the Supplemental Security Income (SSI) program, the incomes of both spouses are counted, making the disabled recipient ineligible.

Douglas Martin, in a 1994 article in *Mainstream* magazine, describes how disincentives arise from "assumptions made at the inception of these programs" that people fall into two categories, "those who can work and therefore are not disabled, and those who cannot work and therefore are disabled—and eligible for disability benefits." Advances in technology, he points out, have made it possible for even the most severely disabled people to work, provided they have support services such as PAS. Martin was the principal author of the Employment Opportunities for Disabled Americans Act of 1986, which was intended to remove work disincentives from the Social Security disability programs.

Federal and state governments, eager to cut costs, have in recent years exacerbated the problem of disincentives. For example, in the mid-1990s the Social Security Administration imposed a moratorium on the Plan for Achieving Self Support (PASS) program. PASS allows disabled Social Security recipients to set aside money they earn for the purchase of equipment, for example, a lift-equipped van or a modified computer, that will enable them to become more independent. Joe Ehman, in a 1996 article in *Mouth: The Voice of Disability Rights*, noted that "even at its height in 1994, PASS plans cost taxpayers [nationwide] less than $30 million. (The new Milwaukee Brewers stadium cost taxpayers $160 million)." Nevertheless, after lifting the moratorium, Social Security administrators rewrote the PASS rules to make the program even more difficult for disabled recipients to use.

See also Employment Opportunities for Disabled Americans Act of 1986; Health Care Reform; Martin, Douglas A.; Personal Assistance Services (PAS); Social Security, Social Security Disability Insurance (SSDI), Supplemental Security Income (SSI); Waxman, Barbara Faye.

References Ehman, Joe, "Social Security's New Follies," *Mouth: The Voice of Disability Rights* (May/June 1996); Martin, Douglas A., "A Call for Reform," *Mainstream* (February 1994).

Dix, Dorothea Lynde (1802–1887)

A tireless investigator, writer, and lobbyist, Dorothea Lynde Dix is remembered today for her advocacy for the humane treatment of persons with mental illness and mental retardation.

Dix was born on 4 April 1802 in Hampden, Maine, and moved to Boston at age 12. She opened a school for the daughters of well-to-do families in 1821, as well as a charity school for poor children. Because of her poor health, however, Dix was forced to give up most of her teaching, and instead she became a writer. She produced a science textbook, *Conversations on Common Things* (1824), edited an anthology of children's poetry, *Hymns for Children* (1825), and wrote several books of meditations on religion and the natural world: *Evening Hours* (1825), *Meditations for Private Hours* (1828), and *The Garland of Flora* (1829). For a time her health recovered sufficiently for her to teach again. In 1836, however, she was diagnosed with tuberculosis and once more forced to retire. Her doctor recommended that she leave Boston, and so she traveled to England, staying for two years.

American reformer Dorothea Dix.

While there, she was befriended by a circle of social reformers, and she began to hear about the inhumane treatment of people with mental disabilities.

It was not until March 1841, when Dix was asked to teach a Sunday school class for the women inmates of the East Cambridge jail, north of Boston, that she began her own career of public advocacy. At that time, Americans with mental illness or mental retardation were incarcerated in prisons, jails, and poorhouses. Others were turned over to private individuals who would provide food and accommodations for a fee. In almost all cases the treatment ranged from callous neglect to outright physical and sexual torture. The treatment was made worse by the common myths of the time that mental illness and mental retardation were God's punishment for sin and that people who were mentally disabled were impervious to pain, cold, and hunger.

Dix learned that the disabled women in the East Cambridge jail were often kept naked in dark cells, chained to the walls, and frequently beaten and abused by the guards and other inmates. She began a campaign to expose these conditions, resulting in some small improvements at the jail. She then began a survey of all the jails, prisons, almshouses, and private contractors housing mentally ill and mentally retarded people in Massachusetts. It was a massive undertaking, the first of its kind, and Dix was hindered by the sexism and ableism of New England society, which believed such work either demeaning or too demanding for a woman in fragile health.

Dix's notebooks provide a clear picture of the way mid–nineteenth century America treated those with mental disabilities:

"Newton almshouse, a cold morning in October . . . the furniture was a wooden box or bunk containing straw. . . .protruding from the box was—it could not be feet! Yet from these stumps were swinging chains, fastened to the side of the building. . . . A few winters since, being kept in an out-house, the people 'did not reckon how cold it was,' and so his feet froze. 'Are chains necessary now?' I asked. 'He cannot run.' 'No, but he might crawl forth, and in his frenzy do some damage.'"

"Barnstable. Four females in pens and stalls. . . ."

"Westford. Young woman fastened to the wall with a chain. . . ." and so on.

Dix took the results of her survey to the state legislature, an accomplishment in itself since at that time women were generally not permitted to speak at the Massachusetts State House. She campaigned for the end of the jailing of people with mental disabilities and called for a system of state hospitals. Dix played a role in the founding of 32 state mental institutions in the United States, the number of which, as a result of her campaign, grew from 13 in 1843 to 123 by 1880. In 1854, she convinced Congress to pass legislation providing federal lands for the establishment of institutions to care for "the indigent insane"—as well as people who were deaf, mute, or blind—but the bill was vetoed by

President Franklin Pierce, who regarded it as a dangerous expansion of the federal government.

In September 1854, still struggling with her health, Dix again left for Europe, where she inspected asylums, jails, and poorhouses in Scotland, France, Turkey, Russia, and Italy. Shocked at the treatment of residents in institutions in Rome, she secured a personal audience with Pope Pius IX to urge him to make reforms. She returned to the United States in September 1856, and, by 1860 was recommending vocational and remedial education for children with mental disabilities. In 1861, Dix was appointed superintendent of Union army nurses, bringing needed reforms to the management of army hospitals during the Civil War. In 1866, she resumed her work on behalf of people with emotional and developmental disabilities.

In 1881, Dix became a resident in the New Jersey Hospital, which she had founded years before in Trenton. She died there on 18 July 1887. Ironically, Dix's achievement in fostering the creation of institutions led to many of the same abuses she campaigned to end: the incarceration of people with disabilities in (now massive) facilities where they were often neglected and abused. Even so, Dix can still be regarded as an early champion of disability rights.

See also Deinstitutionalization.

Reference Wilson, Dorothy Clarke, *Stranger and Traveler: The Story of Dorothea Dix, American Reformer* (1975).

Dole, Robert Joseph (b. 1923)

Robert Joseph Dole, as U.S. senator, Senate majority leader, vice-presidential and then presidential candidate, has been one of the most visible and influential disabled people in America. He was born on 22 July 1923, in Russell, Kansas, and was a student at the University of Kansas from 1941 to 1943, when he entered the U.S. Army. A platoon leader in Italy, he was wounded on 14 April 1945 while leading an assault on a German machine-gun nest. His wounds

left him almost completely paralyzed. After three major operations and three years in hospitals, Dole recovered his ability to walk and the partial use of his left hand, but his right arm and hand remained paralyzed.

Dole returned to college, earning his B.A. and L.L.B. from Washburn University of Topeka in 1952. He had by this time entered politics, winning election to the Kansas state legislature in 1951, then serving several terms as Russell County prosecutor. He entered the U.S. Congress in 1960 and was elected to the Senate in 1968. He was the vice-presidential candidate during President Gerald Ford's unsuccessful 1976 bid for reelection and then campaigned unsuccessfully for the Republican presidential nomination in 1980 and in 1988.

Dole founded the Dole Foundation in 1984 as the only national foundation in the United States focusing solely on competitive employment for people with disabilities. When the U.S. Supreme Court, in *Department of Transportation v. Paralyzed Veterans of America* (1986), ruled that private airlines could refuse to sell tickets to people with disabilities, Dole headed a bipartisan coalition to pass the Air Carrier Access Act of 1986, reversing the effects of that decision. He received the Republican Party's nomination for president in 1996, resigning from the Senate to focus on the campaign. In November 1996, he was defeated by President Bill Clinton.

See also Air Carrier Access Act of 1986.

Donaldson v. O'Connor

See O'Connor v. Donaldson.

Dybwad, Gunnar (b. 1909)

Born on 12 July 1909 in Leipzig, Germany, Gunnar Dybwad for more than 40 years has been at the forefront of efforts to secure the civil rights of people with cognitive disabilities. Dybwad brought a lawyer's skills and sensibility to his work, and he is credited with being one of the first in the world to frame mental disability as an issue of civil rights, rather than as a medical or social work problem. "It was Gunnar," recalls Thomas K. Gilhool, "who first said that when you improve the world for people with disabilities, you improve it for everyone."

Dybwad received his J.D. from the Faculty of Laws at the University of Halle, in Germany, in 1934. His specialty was penal reform, and he had studied prisons in Germany, Great Britain, and Italy. After marrying in the United States, the Dybwads returned to Germany in 1935 so that Rosemary could finish her doctorate in sociology at the University of Hamburg, completing her degree in 1936. Unwilling to live under Nazism, the two left Germany shortly thereafter. In 1938, while studying at the New York School of Social Work, Dybwad did his field work at the Letchworth Village Institution, a residential facility for people with mental disabilities in New York. He would later describe his experience there as one of "culture shock."

"On one adult ward I saw incontinent 'untidy' men lying in boxes of sawdust." Children were housed in "dormitories with 100 beds and 125 children in those beds." "Only a small number of children went to a school program—the rest of them marched every morning and afternoon with hoes and other farm implements for a full day of slave labor on the institutional farm. . . . Here was my first object lesson that persons committed to a mental deficiency institution were denied the protection of the law, a lesson I would have to face time and again in subsequent years."

Dybwad received his graduate degree in social work in 1939, and he then worked at prisons and in institutions for juvenile offenders in Indiana, New Jersey, New York, and Michigan. From 1943 to 1951, he was the supervisor of the Children's Division of the Michigan State Department of Social Welfare. In 1951, he became the executive director of the Child Study Association of America. Through this period, he maintained his interest in people, particularly children, with mental disabilities.

In 1957, Dybwad was named executive director of the Association for Retarded Children (ARC, now called The Arc), a parents' advocacy group founded in 1950. Some of his colleagues were concerned that he was throwing away his social services career by accepting a position with a nonprofessional, parents' organization. Dybwad, however, saw ARC as having a potential to affect powerful change in the status of people with mental disabilities. To this end he pursued a strategy of grassroots organizing, insisting that it be the parents themselves, rather than social service professionals, who led ARC and set its agenda. His wife, Rosemary, volunteered at ARC, where she founded its International Relations Committee newsletter in 1959, becoming its editor. Rosemary Dybwad was instrumental in establishing the European and then the International League of Societies for Persons with Mental Handicap, of which she served as senior vice president from 1974 to 1978. (Gunnar was president of the league from 1978 to 1982).

Dybwad left his position at ARC in 1963, becoming a consultant to President Kennedy's Special Assistant on Mental Retardation. In 1964, he and Rosemary moved to Geneva, Switzerland, where they co-directed the Mental Retardation Project of the International Union for Child Welfare. The couple visited more than 30 countries, encouraging the parents of mentally retarded children to organize and serving as catalysts to the worldwide parents' movement.

Returning to the United States in 1967, Dybwad became a mentor and consultant to the national ARC and its chapters, advocating a strategy of litigation that became a model for the larger disability rights movement. Drawing an explicit analogy to the black civil rights movement, particularly its victory in *Brown v. Board of Education* (1954), Dybwad was instrumental in convincing the leadership of the Pennsylvania ARC to look to the courts to help improve the lives of their children. The resulting case, *PARC v. Pennsylvania* (1972), established, for the first time, the right of children with disabilities to receive a public education, and it sparked an explosion of disability rights litigation. Dybwad himself was directly involved in some 15 federal lawsuits relating to the civil rights of people with mental disabilities, including two that were argued before the U.S. Supreme Court. From 1968 to 1969, he was also a consultant to the newly formed President's Committee on Mental Retardation.

In 1967, Dybwad became a professor of human development at Brandeis University in Waltham, Massachusetts, the acting dean of the university's Florence Heller Graduate School for Advanced Studies in Social Welfare in 1971, and professor emeritus in 1977. He has been involved in a host of organizations, for example, as a member of the Commission on the Mentally Disabled of the American Bar Association from 1973 to 1979, the Governor's Commission on the Legal and Civil Rights of the Developmentally Disabled in Massachusetts from 1974 to 1976, and the president and then the chair of the Board of the Epilepsy Society of Massachusetts from 1976 to 1981. Dybwad continues to serve on the boards of such organizations as the Boston Self Help Center and the Boston Center for Blind Children. He is the author and editor of numerous articles and books, including the recent *New Voices: Self-Advocacy by People with Disabilities* (with Hank Bersani Jr., 1996).

Parents and self-advocates alike consider Dybwad "the grandfather" of the rights to education and community service. Well into his eighties, he continues to advise the national disability rights movement. He is the recipient of numerous honors, including honorary doctorates from Temple University in Philadelphia and the University of Maryland.

Dybwad currently resides in Wellesley, Massachusetts. Rosemary Dybwad, who was born on 10 May 1910 in Howe, Indiana, died on 4 November 1992. She is fondly remembered as a pioneer and mentor of the international parents' movement.

See also The Arc; Boston Self Help Center; Parents' Movement; *Pennhurst State School & Hospital v. Halderman; Pennsylvania Association for Retarded Children et al. v. Pennsylvania*; People First, People First International.

References Dybwad, Gunnar, and Hank Bersani Jr., eds., *New Voices: Self-Advocacy by People with Disabilities* (1996); Trent, James W., Jr., *Inventing the Feeble Mind: A History of Mental Retardation in the United States* (1994).

Dykes, Disability & Stuff

Dykes, Disability & Stuff is a project of the Disabled Women's Educational Project (DWEP). The DWEP was founded in 1987 in Boston, Massachusetts, to address issues of concern to women, particularly lesbians, with disabilities. *Dykes, Disability & Stuff* is published primarily for "Disabled lesbians and/or their partners and/or allies of diz lez's." Its editor, Catherine O'Dette, describes it as "a reader's forum quarterly publication of the newsletter variety." It is published in Madison, Wisconsin.

Education for All Handicapped Children Act of 1975 (Pub. Law 94-142)

Until passage of the Education for All Handicapped Children Act of 1975, it was perfectly legal for a public school system to deny a child an education solely because of that child's disability. During deliberations leading to passage of the act, Congress found that, in the mid-1970s, fully 1 million children in the United States were being excluded from the public schools solely because of their disabilities. Furthermore, more than "half of the handicapped children in the United States do not receive appropriate educational services which would enable them to have full equality of opportunity." The Education for All Handicapped Children Act was designed to change this state of affairs by guaranteeing to disabled children their right to a public education. Together with the Rehabilitation Act of 1973 and the Americans with Disabilities Act of 1990, it is one of the three main pillars of civil rights protection for people with disabilities. In the two decades since its passage, the act has had a profound impact on the lives of millions of people.

Historically, many children with disabilities received no schooling at all, or they were educated in special facilities such as the Perkins School for the Blind in Boston and the American School for the Deaf in Hartford, Connecticut. While their goal was to educate disabled people so that they could live independently in the community, these schools were nonetheless segregated, while residential schools for developmentally disabled children, established in the latter half of the nineteenth century and the first decades of the twentieth century, soon devolved into massive custodial institutions. There were no attempts to teach deaf children in the public schools until the 1860s, and the first attempts to provide a public school education to children labeled mentally retarded did not occur until 1900.

By the 1960s, a larger number of disabled children were being permitted to attend the public schools, a direct result of the advocacy of the parents' movement. These students, however, were generally shunted into "health conservation" or "special education" classrooms, often located in the school basement, boiler room, or some similar setting. They were excluded from gym, science labs, music, and other programs, and from after-school activities. Academic programs were generally substandard, with school officials regarding special education as little more than day care. Added to the substandard education was the stigma of being segregated, affecting not only students' ability to learn but also their ability to develop friendships and social skills. Special education classes were often used to segregate minority and immigrant children, who were disproportionately and inappropriately classified as "retarded" or "disturbed." Finally, whatever education did occur was available only at the whim of local school boards or individual teachers or "experts." Parents of disabled children had little or no recourse when any of these people decided that their children were "uneducatable."

Congress was prompted to act by two landmark disability rights lawsuits: *Mills v. Board of Education* (1972) and, most especially, *PARC v. Pennsylvania* (1972). In both cases, the Court issued what was in essence a wake-up call to American educators, ruling that segregating disabled children was no more constitutional than segregating children of color. *PARC v. Pennsylvania* galvanized disability advocates, particularly parent groups such as the Association for Retarded Children (now The Arc), who then played a pivotal role in passing the legislation. The Education for All Handicapped Children Act (also called Pub. Law 94-142 or EAHCA) was passed by the U.S. House of Representatives on 18 November 1975 by a vote of 404 to 7, and by the Senate on the following day with an equally lopsided margin. It was signed by President Gerald Ford on 29 November 1975, to take effect at the beginning of 1978.

The Education for All Handicapped Children Act mandates that children with disabilities are entitled to a "free, appropriate public education." The law established a "zero-reject" principle, meaning that no child can be denied a publicly funded education, no matter what his or her disability. This education must be appropriate, that is, reasonably calculated to yield real educational benefits. It must be integrated, meaning that public schools can no longer segregate disabled children from nondisabled children, unless it is clearly impossible to educate them in a mainstream classroom, even with appropriate accommodations and assistance. The act also requires school districts to make available to teachers the latest information on educational practices regarding disability, so they can adapt them where appropriate. Finally, it lays out a series of procedural requirements, most notably the Individualized Education Program (IEP), to ensure that the purposes of the law are fulfilled and giving parents a central role in planning for their disabled children's education.

Under the act, appropriate special services must be provided at public expense, and states are required to identify and evaluate students in need of such services. States are offered federal funds to help provide whatever additional services are required, including speech therapy, audiological services, counseling, occupational and physical therapy, and accessible transportation. After a child has been identified as having a disability, an IEP must be drawn up by the child's teachers and parents or guardians, with input from special education experts as needed. There must

be a face-to-face meeting between educators and parents, and parents have the right to contest aspects of the IEP with which they disagree. The IEP must be explicit, with clear goals and cogent steps for reaching those goals. Listed within the IEP are whatever special services the child might require to reach the goals agreed upon by educators and parents. The IEP is then reviewed and, if need be, revised each year.

The act recognizes that school districts have limited resources. For this reason there is no requirement that they provide the *best possible* education, but rather one that provides opportunities for education roughly equivalent to those provided nondisabled children. Necessary services cannot, however, be arbitrarily denied, and the act sets out an appeal process for parents who feel that their children, because of their disability, are receiving a less adequate education than their nondisabled peers.

The federal courts have affirmed the central aspects of the law, particularly the zero-reject provision, ensuring that it continues to be an Education for *All* Handicapped Children Act. For instance, a federal court of appeals in 1989 ruled, in *Timothy W. v. Rochester, N.H., School District*, that, under the law, the Rochester School District could not deny services to a child whose disabilities included cerebral palsy, mental retardation, and quadriplegia. The court ruled that, in the event necessary services cannot be provided in the usual school setting, the district is required to seek and purchase alternative services. Disability rights advocates such as Thomas K. Gilhool contend, however, that portions of the implementing regulations adapted after passage of the act undercut the integration and "promising methods" portion of the legislation, aiming instead for an education for disabled children in "the least restrictive environment"—a phrase widely used in conjunction with the act, but which appears nowhere in its language. It was also perhaps inevitable that educators have tended to focus on the IEP as an end unto itself, an annual exercise in meeting the letter of the law, rather than a means of ensuring that the larger purposes of the act are met.

Even so, the act has been the major impetus in the mainstreaming of children with disabilities, allowing them the opportunity to attend classes with children not identified as being disabled. Although the experiences of many mainstreamed children have been difficult, especially those in the first wave in the late 1970s and early 1980s, this drive toward integration has been important in making disability and people with disabilities better known to the general public. It has also demonstrably improved the educational opportunities available to disabled children.

Not everyone in the disability community was entirely happy the act. Some advocates in the Deaf community have expressed concerns that the push to mainstream children with disabilities would mean that deaf children would again be forced to learn lip-reading and speech, as opposed to being given an education in American Sign Language (ASL). In an important demonstration of cross-disability solidarity, the American Coalition of Citizens with Disabilities, although in strong support of the act, supported the Deaf community's right to ASL, and as a result the act requires that sign language interpreters be considered an appropriate special service. Even so, Deaf advocates such as Ben Bahan have labeled mainstreaming a "mistake" for deaf children, noting that many hearing teachers who claim to know ASL are in fact barely conversant with the language. Bahan and others instead argue for all-deaf schools taught by Deaf teachers.

The act was amended in 1986 to extend protections to disabled children ages 3 to 5 and to establish a state grant program to benefit disabled infants and toddlers (birth through age 2). Early services must include a written Individualized Family Service Program (IFSP), similar to the IEP except that the plan must address the needs of both child and family. In 1990, the act was renamed the Individuals with Disabilities Education Act (IDEA). Among other changes were additions to the list of mandated services. Autism and traumatic brain injury were added to the definition of the phrase *children with disabilities*, and emphasis was placed on education of children with more severe disabilities.

The act has been criticized by some as imposing too expensive a burden on schools. These critics contend that an increasing number of children have been classified as disabled and thus entitled to special services. Disability advocates respond by saying that society has often grossly underestimated the number of people with disabilities, including children, and that the benefits of the act outweigh whatever increased costs it has imposed. Aside from the moral and civil rights arguments, integration and quality education are always less expensive, in the long run, than segregation and ignorance.

See also Burlington School Committee v. Department of Education; Holland v. Sacramento City Unified School District; Honig v. Doe; Inclusive Education; Irving Independent School District v. Tatro; Mills v. Board of Education of the District of Columbia; Pennsylvania Association for Retarded Children v. Commonwealth of Pennsylvania (PARC v. Pennsylvania).

References Bahan, Ben, "Who's Itching To Get into Mainstreaming?" in Sherman Wilcox, *American Deaf Culture* (1989); Goldman, Charles D., *Disability Rights Guide* (1991); Kreunen, Warren L., "The Law and the Handicapped Student," in M. A. McGhehey, ed., *School Law for a New Decade* (1981); Levine, Ervin L., and Elizabeth M. Wexler, *PL 94–142: An Act of Congress* (1981).

Employment Opportunities for Disabled Americans Act of 1986

The Employment Opportunities for Disabled Americans Act of 1986 was designed to address the disincentives faced by people receiving Social Security Disability Insurance (SSDI) or Supplemental Security Income (SSI) benefits. Before passage of the act, people in these programs were faced with the total loss of benefits, including health insurance provided under Medicaid or Medicare, if they became gainfully employed. For those collecting SSDI, any employment at all meant the total loss of benefits, since the program defined eligibility as the complete inability to work. SSI recipients also faced an earning threshold, at that time $300 a month, over which they would lose their benefits.

The act was primarily the result of the advocacy of Douglas Martin and the Westside Center for Independent Living in Los Angeles, together with the national leadership of the Paralyzed Veterans of America, United Cerebral Palsy Associations, and independent living centers across the country. Their work received an added impetus when Lynn Thompson, an SSI recipient, committed suicide because she had lost her Medicaid benefits after taking a part-time job. Thompson's death brought the attention of the national media, in particular the CBS program *60 Minutes*, which, in 1978, ran a segment on work disincentives and the efforts of Martin and others to change the system. As a result, section 1619 of the Social Security Disability Amendments of 1980 contained provisions allowing SSDI and SSI recipients to retain their health coverage and a portion of their cash benefits after they had begun or resumed working. The more an individual made, the less money he or she collected from SSI or SSDI, with medical insurance remaining until the individual made enough to offset medical and personal assistance services (PAS) expenses. Section 1619 was a three-year pilot program, which was then extended for another three years.

The 1986 act made the provisions of Section 1619 permanent. By the mid-1990s, approximately 50,000 people a year were participating. Advocates such as Martin believe far more would take advantage of the program if it were better publicized, and if more Social Security workers were themselves aware of its existence.

See also Disincentives; Martin, Douglas A.; Social Security, Social Security Disability Insurance (SSDI), Supplemental Security Income (SSI); Westside Center for Independent Living.

Environmental Illness
See Multiple Chemical Sensitivity.

Equal Employment Opportunity Commission
See Americans with Disabilities Act of 1990.

Eugenics
The word *eugenics* was coined by British mathematician Sir Francis Galton in 1883. He defined it as the "science of improving the stock." The eugenics movement, he said, would be dedicated to allowing "the more suitable races or strains of blood a better chance of prevailing speedily over the less suitable." The American eugenics movement had its heyday from the 1890s to the 1940s, and it caused enormous suffering to hundreds of thousands of people with disabilities. It led to the passage of laws forbidding many to marry and caused the forced sterilization of thousands of people with mental illness and cognitive disability. The American eugenics movement inspired the German Nazis to pass their own eugenics legislation in the 1930s, which eventually led to the murder by poisonous gas and lethal injection of several hundred thousand disabled Europeans.

Eugenicists believed that white, heterosexual, temporarily able-bodied Protestants of northern European descent were at the apex of human evolution. All others: southern Europeans, Jews, people of color, homosexuals, and most especially people with disabilities, were inferior. "Herein lies . . . the great biological menace to the future of civilization," wrote Margaret Sanger in 1922 in *The Pivot of Civilization*. Sanger, hailed as a pioneer of women's rights, was concerned about "the gradual but certain attack upon the stocks of intelligence and racial health by the sinister forces of the hordes of irresponsibility and imbecility." Eugenicists believed that poverty, illiteracy, criminality, and character traits such as honesty, thrift, laziness and greed were all tied to heredity. Henry H. Goddard, in *The Kallikak Family* (1912), purported to trace the "moral degeneracy" of one family back to colonial times and concluded that the solution to the "menace of the feeble minded" was institutionalization and

THE FEEBLE-MINDED

OR THE

HUB TO OUR WHEEL OF VICE, CRIME AND PAUPERISM

Cover of The Feeble-Minded, *a pamphlet distributed by the Juvenile Protective Association of Cincinnati in 1915. Eugenicists, a white supremacy movement, believed disabled people to be inferior and sponsored such publications as the one pictured here, which states that the "feeble-minded" are "the hub to our wheel of vice, crime, and pauperism."*

forced sterilization of people with cognitive and developmental disabilities. His book was the runaway best-seller of 1913.

Eugenicists opposed social programs for people who were poor and disabled, believing such programs aided the unworthy in the struggle for survival. They opposed trade unions, unemployment insurance, and the minimum wage for the same reason, and they supported restricting immigration to white northern Europeans. They favored legislation punishing interracial marriages. Eugenicists had the support of scientists such as Alexander Graham Bell, politicians such as Theodore Roosevelt and Herbert Hoover, and industrialists such as Andrew Carnegie. By the 1940s, the majority of states had passed laws allowing the forcible sterilization of people, especially women, who were mentally ill, epileptic, or mentally retarded. In 1927, the U.S. Supreme Court, citing eugenicist arguments, ruled that the forced sterilization of people with disabilities was constitutional.

American eugenicists developed close links with eugenicists in other countries, especially those in Nazi Germany. Until 1941, American eugenicists distributed Nazi propaganda, in one case sending flyers for the Nazi film *Erbkrank* (Hereditary Defective) to biology teachers at 3,000 American high schools. The film described people with disabilities as "weeds" who needed to be cut away in order that the healthy might thrive.

By the 1940s, it was apparent that eugenics was not only racist, ableist, and anti-Semitic but also bad science. Acquired characteristics such as thrift and laziness could not be passed down in "the blood." Mental retardation and mental illness, epilepsy, homosexuality, and physical disability could not be prevented by forced sterilization. The Great Depression demonstrated that even those of "pure blood" could lose their jobs and become poor. Finally, American eugenicists lost public support because of their close identification with German Nazism.

Eugenics made somewhat of a comeback in the 1990s. Organizations such as the Pioneer Fund provide financial support to scientists who claim to have discovered new "evidence" linking race and ethnicity with intelligence and character. As recently as the spring of 1995 the Mensa newsletter in Los Angeles published articles favoring the extermination of people who are homeless, elderly, mentally retarded or "infirm." Some disability rights advocates see the development and unquestioning use of genetic in-utero testing (allowing doctors to identify some disabilities before birth and then urging that the "defective" fetus be aborted) as a new phase in the effort to "purify" society by eliminating people with disabilities.

See also Abortion and Reproductive Rights; *Buck v. Bell;* Euthanasia and Assisted Suicide; Forced Sterilization; T-4.

References Bajema, Carl J., ed., *Eugenics: Then and Now* (1976); Blumberg, Lisa, "Eugenics and Reproductive Choice," in *The Ragged Edge: The Disability Experience from the Pages of the First Fifteen Years of*

The Disability Rag (1994); Gallagher, Hugh Gregory, *By Trust Betrayed: Patients, Physicians, and the License To Kill in the Third Reich* (1990); Trombley, Stephen, *The Right To Reproduce: A History of Coercive Sterilization* (1988).

Euthanasia and Assisted Suicide

Euthanasia means "easy death." In classical Greece, where the term was coined, disabled infants born in the city-state of Sparta were routinely abandoned and left to die. Since then, the murder of people with disabilities in the name of "easing their misery" has been practiced in a wide variety of societies, including the United States. In 1991, for example, newspapers in Wisconsin reported that a young mother, despondent over her child's cerebral palsy, starved him to death. Though she admitted her action to the police, no charges were brought against her.

"Severely disabled people," writes psychologist Carol Gill, "are an affront to those who cannot handle any bumps in the human landscape. Many people fear our needs and worry that they may someday share our fate." While generally not advocating that people with disabilities be killed outright, the assumption of many in the right-to-die movement seems to be that life with a disability is not worth living. This is a prejudice that Gill and others see as a deadly threat.

Moreover, in many instances when disabled people become suicidal, it is not so much in response to their disability, but because they are denied essential services, kept in nursing homes, or forced to live lives of stultifying isolation. Larry McAfee is a case in point. In 1989, a Georgia court ruled (in *State of Georgia v. McAfee*) that McAfee had "the right" to be given a sedative and removed from his respirator. McAfee had petitioned the court because, he said, he was despondent at being disabled. McAfee changed his mind, however, when disability rights activists met with him, offering options other than death or institutionalization. Elizabeth Bouvia checked into a California hospital in 1983, requesting that physicians give her pain

Members of the Not Dead Yet group take part in an anti-euthanasia march on the Michigan State University campus in June 1996.

medication while she starved herself to death. The media, the American Civil Liberties Union, and the right-to-die movement all saw her request as a reasonable response to disability, in her case quadriplegia resulting from cerebral palsy. In fact, Bouvia had suffered a series of traumatic losses, including the death of her brother by drowning, financial problems, a miscarriage, the breakup of her marriage, and discrimination at college, all in the two years before her request. Eventually she changed her mind, and at last report was living independently in California.

In the 1990s, the most famous advocate of assisted suicide in the United States has been Jack Kevorkian, who has been the defendant in a series of highly publicized trials for assisting in the suicides of more than 40 people with disabilities or chronic illness. Disability advocates insist that at least some of Kevorkian's patients were depressed over their lack of options rather than their disability or illness; others may not have been seriously physically disabled at all. Echoing the eugenicist argument in favor of sterilizing, and the Nazi argument in favor of killing people with disabilities, Kevorkian has written that "the voluntary self-elimination of . . . mortally diseased or crippled lives taken collectively can only *enhance* the preservation of public health and welfare." In response to Kevorkian's notoriety, Diane Coleman, Carol Gill, and others in 1996 formed Not Dead Yet, which has organized demonstrations in Michigan, Massachusetts, and elsewhere. They and others worry that a "right to die" will eventually become "an obligation" to die, as society moves to ration health care, and as people with disabilities and elders are seen as a burden to the nondisabled and young. Advocates report instances of disabled people or their families being pressured by health care providers to sign "Do Not Resuscitate" (DNR) orders as an example of cost-driven pressure on people with disabilities to die. On 26 June 1997, in *Washington v. Glucksberg* and *Vacco v. Quill*, the Supreme Court ruled that there is no constitutional "right to die," but left open to states the option of legalizing physician-assisted suicide.

This is not to say that all disability activists oppose suicide in all cases. Julie Reiskin, writing in *The Disability Rag & Resource* (March/April 1991), tried to find a middle ground between "self-righteous crips" who "angrily denounce people with disabilities who are suicidal" and "crips who choose public suicide . . . appearing on national television to demand their right to die, with assistance if need be." "In the final analysis," writes Mary Johnson, "everyone's decision is his own." Disability rights advocates, however, insist that decisions about suicide, just like decisions about aborting a disabled fetus, should not be made based on stereotypes about the quality of life with a disability. Rather than fight for their right to die, they instead prefer to fight for their right to live with dignity and independence.

See also Abortion and Reproductive Rights; Coleman, Diane; Eugenics; Gill, Carol J.; National Legal Center for the Medically Dependent and Disabled; T-4.

References Gallagher, Hugh Gregory, *By Trust Betrayed: Patients, Physicians, and the License To Kill in the Third Reich* (1990); Longmore, Paul K., "Elizabeth Bouvia, Assisted Suicide and Social Prejudice," *Issues in Law & Medicine* (Fall 1987); Shaw, Barrett, ed., *The Ragged Edge: The Disability Experience from the Pages of the First Fifteen Years of* The Disability Rag (1994).

Everest & Jennings
See Wheelchairs.

Facilitated Communication

Some people with disabilities have tremendous difficulty communicating. People with severe cerebral palsy, autism, and certain neuromotor disorders may be unable to speak, write, use a letterboard, or even control their eye movements. Facilitated communication was designed to help these individuals by having another person, trained in the technique, assist them by supporting or supplying mild restraint on their arm, wrist, or hand as they type or point to letters or pictures on a keyboard. The best-known American proponent of facilitated communication is Douglas Biklen, director of the Facilitated Communication Institute at the Syracuse University School of Education, who studied its use in Australia in the 1980s. His book on the subject, *Communication Unbound*, was published in 1993.

Biklen's work brought facilitated communication to national attention, and there was a great increase in its use. It was heralded as a "key that has unlocked the imposed silence" of people with communication disabilities. It also generated what Michele Molnar called "a firestorm of controversy," with many critics questioning whether the words being typed or spelled out were those of the ostensible communicator, or of the (generally) nondisabled facilitator. The situation was greatly complicated by the proliferation of charges made by those using facilitated communication of sexual and physical abuse by caretakers and parents. A number of these cases resulted in criminal investigations, in which some of the accused were charged and convicted. In some cases, those cleared of accusations sued the facilitator for the damages caused by the accusation.

Supporters of facilitated communication point to those cases where independent evidence corroborated the charges, and they advocate judicial acceptance of the technique. Critics point to those cases where the accused were cleared, or where there was insufficient evidence to proceed with criminal proceedings. They also cite a large number of studies (disputed by Biklen) that apparently demonstrate that facilitated communication does not reflect the thoughts of those who are supposed to be communicating. Among the harshest critics of the widespread use of facilitated communication has been Bernard Rimland, a research psychologist and editor of *Autism Research Review* and the parent of an individual with autism. He argues that "everyone loses as the result of ill-advised use of . . . facilitated communication. The accused families suffer the most. But there are other losers," including individuals who can use the technique but might never get the chance "if F/C is discredited . . . by repeated charges that it is a hoax."

See also Rape/Sexual and Domestic Violence.

References Biklen, Douglas, *Communication Unbound* (1993); Molnar, Michele, "Whose Words Are They Anyway?" *Mainstream* (November 1993).

Fair Housing Amendments Act of 1988 (FHAA)

The Fair Housing Amendments Act of 1988 (FHAA) added people with disabilities to the list of groups protected from housing discrimination under the Civil Rights Act of 1968, marking the first time that people with disabilities were included under the provisions of a law intended to ban discrimination against other groups. (The Civil Rights Restoration Act of 1987, which also included people with disabilities, was passed after the FHAA.)

It is illegal under the FHAA for a landlord or homeowner to refuse to rent, lease, or sell housing to someone because of their disability. It is also illegal to charge a higher rent, lease, or sales price, or to ask for a larger security deposit from a disabled tenant or buyer than from a nondisabled tenant or buyer. Landlords are barred from enforcing a "no pets" policy against assistance animals, such as dog-guides for blind tenants or hearing-dogs for deaf tenants. The FHAA limits a municipality's ability to zone group homes and other disability-specific housing out of residential neighborhoods, and it also prohibits a municipality from restricting people with disabilities to only such housing. The protections of the FHAA extend to people who are associated with people with disabilities, so that, for example, a landlord cannot refuse to rent to someone because his or her spouse or child has a disability.

The FHAA also requires that all multi-family housing with four or more units have an accessible entrance, if first occupancy was after 13 March 1991. Common areas, such as the lobbies and public restrooms, must also be accessible. The units must be easily adaptable for access, so that, for example, power switches and electrical outlets are in accessible locations, and bathrooms allow for the installation of grab bars if needed. Doorways must be wide enough to accommodate a wheelchair. Builders are encouraged to use accessibility specifications developed by the American National Standards Institute (ANSI) or the Uniform Federal Accessibility Standard (UFAS).

Finally, under the FHAA, owners must allow tenants to make reasonable modifications to their apartments, at the tenant's expense, "if such modifications may be necessary to afford such person full enjoyment of the premises." Tenants are not required to undo these modifications when they move, unless they will affect enjoyment of the premises by future tenants.

Language against housing discrimination was included in the original draft of the Americans with Disabilities Act (ADA) when it was first considered by Congress in 1988, but disability activists decided to address the issue under the FHAA, which seemed more certain to pass that year.

Thus, these specific provisions on housing were subsequently dropped from future versions of the ADA.

See also Architectural Access; Housing; Mace, Ronald L.

References Bazelon Center for Mental Health Law, *What Does Fair Housing Mean to People with Disabilities?* (1991, 1994); Goldman, Charles D., *Disability Rights Guide: Practical Solutions to Problems Affecting People with Disabilities* (1991).

Fair Labor Standards Act of 1938
See Sheltered Workshops.

Fay, Frederick A. (b. 1944)
Frederick A. Fay has had a profound impact on both public policy toward people with disabilities and grassroots organizing and advocacy in the national disability rights movement. Considered a mentor and "behind the scenes wizard" by disability rights leaders nationwide, he is a pioneer in the independent living movement and an innovator in the development of computer technology for use by people with disabilities. Fay has also been outspoken about the oppression of people with disabilities on an international level, drawing particular attention to the condition of disabled people in the former Soviet Union.

Fay was born in Washington, D.C., on 12 September 1944 and disabled with quadriplegia after a spinal cord injury in 1961. Within a year of his accident he and his mother, Janet Carolyn Wright Fay, had co-founded Opening Doors, a counseling and information service for people with disabilities in the Washington area. (One Opening Doors member, Paul O'Donnell, a paraplegic who helped start the organization, later convinced Hertz to become the first car rental company to provide hand controls for paraplegic drivers).

Fay received his bachelor's degree in psychology in 1967 from the University of Illinois at Urbana-Champaign. Inspired by Tim Nugent's revolutionary program for disabled students, Fay and his mother founded the Washington Architectural

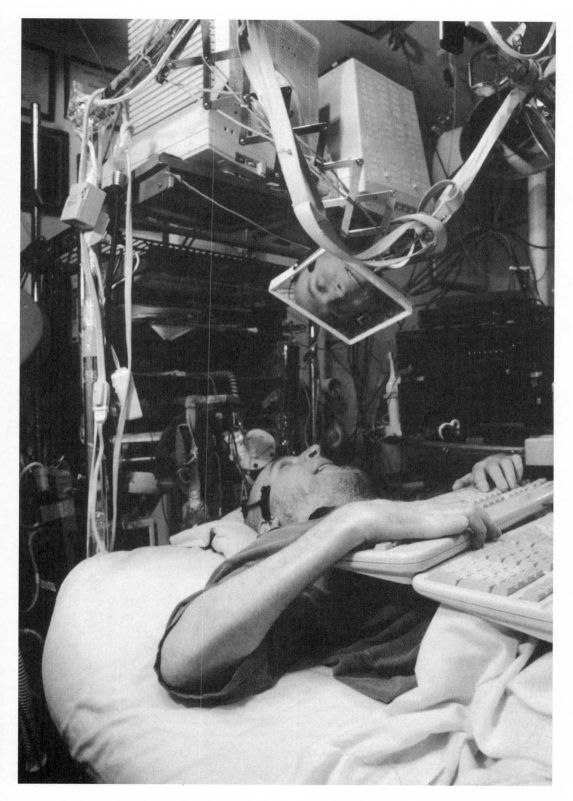

Surrounded by an array of electronic gear, Fred Fay connects to the world, 1995.

Barriers Project that same year. The project spearheaded the successful campaign to make the multibillion dollar Washington, D.C., Metro accessible, and it sponsored the first meeting in American history between people with disabilities and transit officials to talk about accessible public transit. In 1967, Fay and his mother also founded the Washington chapter of the National Spinal Cord Injury Association (then called the National Paraplegia Foundation) with Fay serving as its first president.

Fay received his doctorate in educational psychology in 1972, also from the University of Illinois. In 1975, he served as senior research associate for the Urban Institute in Washington, D.C., in the Comprehensive Needs Study of Individuals with Most Severe Handicap, which laid the foundation for federal funding of independent living centers. In 1977, Fay was appointed director of research at Tufts New England Medical Center in Boston, moving to Massachusetts to supervise disability-related projects ranging from bioengineering to computerized data management to independent living and consumer involvement in rehabilitation. His numerous published writings from this period include such articles as "Heat Intolerance in Quadriplegia" in the *International Journal of Biometeorology* (1972) and *A Guide to Accessible Housing and Transportation*, a booklet published in 1974 by the New England Spinal Cord Injury Foundation in Boston.

Fay was a prime mover in the passage of sections 503 and 504 of the Rehabilitation Act of 1973. In 1974, he co-founded the Boston Center for Independent Living, one of the first independent living centers in the nation. In the early 1970s, Fay brought together advocates for the first meetings of what was to become the American Coalition of Citizens with Disabilities (ACCD). He then helped draft the ACCD's bylaws. On a local level, Fay was a leader in consumer organizations such as the Massachusetts Association of Paraplegics and the Massachusetts Council of Organizations of the Handicapped, the forerunner of the Massachusetts Coalition of Citizens with Disabilities.

Fay pioneered the use of assistive technologies to enable people with severe disabilities to manage their physical environment. He invented sophisticated computer systems that enable people to control lights and thermostats, and he modified phones and computer keyboards for people to use from their beds or wheelchairs. He put these devices to personal use after a spinal tumor exacerbated his quadriplegia and left him unable to travel. Using a fax modem he was able to do extensive lobbying for passage of the Americans with Disabilities Act of 1990 (ADA).

In early 1995, Fay, together with Justin Dart Jr. and Becky Ogle, founded Justice for All to address attacks on the ADA and other disability rights legislation by the Republican-controlled Congress elected in November 1994. As the Justice for All e-mail coordinator, Fay pulled together a national network of advocates. He was also a co-founder in 1995 of the American Association of People with Disabilities.

Fay has been at the forefront in urging people with disabilities to be involved in electoral politics. He is an advisor to the National Democratic Party, as well as to Senator Edward Kennedy (D–MA), and other national public figures. In 1996, Fay was the chair of Americans with Disabilities for Clinton/Gore, and he coordinated efforts by disability activists seeking the election of congressional candidates supporting the disability rights agenda.

Fay has received numerous awards, including being named one of the U.S. Jaycees 10 Outstanding Young Men of America in 1978 (previous winners included John F. Kennedy and Elvis Presley) and a Distinguished Service Award from President Bush in 1992.

See also American Association of People with Disabilities; American Coalition of Citizens with Disabilities; Americans with Disabilities Act of 1990; Boston Center for Independent Living; Justice for All; Metropolitan Area Transit Authority Access Campaign; Rehabilitation Act of 1973; Section 504 of the Rehabilitation Act of 1973.

Federal-Aid Highway Act Amendments of 1974

The Federal-Aid Highway Act of 1973 offered federal financial assistance to states repairing or constructing highways. The act was amended in 1974 to require that all highway projects funded under its provisions be "planned, designed, constructed, and operated to allow effective utilization by elderly or handicapped persons. . . ." While this sounded impressive, in actuality the legislation's impact has been limited. Only highway projects directly funded under the Federal-Aid Highway Program were covered, and even these in some cases were exempted by the federal courts from full architectural and operational access.

Another 1974 amendment prevented the secretary of transportation from approving any state highway safety program for funding under the act that did not "provide adequate and reasonable access for the safe and convenient movement of physically handicapped persons, including those in wheelchairs, across curbs constructed or replaced on or after July 1, 1976, at all pedestrian crosswalks throughout the State." In 1980, disability law scholar Robert L. Burgdorf Jr. described this amendment as "the closest thing we have to a federal curb-cut law."

See also Curb-Cuts/Curb Ramps.
Reference Burgdorf, Robert L., Jr., *The Legal Rights of Handicapped Persons: Cases, Materials, and Text* (1980).

Fiesta Educativa, Inc.

Journalist Gisselle Acevedo-Franco writes that "if the Latino population is politically oppressed, the Latino Handicapped community is twice as oppressed." Since almost all social services for people with disabilities are provided in an English-only setting, Latino families with developmentally disabled children are less likely to obtain the services to which they are legally entitled. The preparation of an Individualized Education Program (IEP), due process hearings at the public schools, and opportunities for vocational rehabilitation, all come with added obstacles for Spanish-speaking families and their children.

Fiesta Educativa is an organization of Spanish-speaking parents of children with developmental disabilities, as well as concerned professionals and service providers, formed in Los Angeles in 1978 to address these problems. Its principal founders were Irene Martinez and Herman Fogata, together with Amalia Guerrero, Alfonzo Perez, and Victor Franco. The name *Fiesta Educativa* was coined by Theresa Saming Bolette, keynote speaker at the organization's first annual conference, who had been running community workshops under the same name on issues related to Latino families and developmental disabilities.

Fiesta Educativa, a nonprofit organization, holds an annual conference for parents, advocates, and interested professionals. Recent conferences have included workshops on family-centered services, multisensory reading programs, health care reform and its impact on persons with disabilities, human sexuality, personal assistance services, and advocacy to fight changes in the federal Supplemental Security Income (SSI) program.

See also Multicultural Issues, Minority Persons with Disabilities; Parents' Movement.
Reference Rueda, Robert, and Irene Martinez, "Fiesta Educativa: One Community's Approach to Parent Training in Developmental Disabilities for Latino Families," *Journal of the Association for Persons with Severe Handicaps* (1992).

Fiorito, Eunice K. (b. 1930)

Eunice K. Fiorito is one of the founders of the American Coalition of Citizens with Disabilities (ACCD), and she was its first president. She was an early and prominent advocate of cross-disability awareness and organizing.

Fiorito, born on 1 October 1930, in Chicago, Illinois, has been blind since age 16. In the 1950s, she worked in a sheltered workshop for ten cents an hour. Her rehabilitation counselor discouraged her from going to college, saying she would only drop out. Instead, Fiorito pursued her degree and graduated cum laude with a B.S.

Eunice Fiorito (right, seated), joined by Deborah Kaplan (left, seated) and Judy Heumann (center, seated), leads an HEW rally at Lafayette Park, Washington, D.C., in 1977.

in education from Loyola University in Chicago in 1954, completing the four-year program in only three years. She began her work as a rehabilitation teacher/caseworker with the Illinois Department of Public Welfare, before moving to New York City and obtaining a master's degree in psychiatric social work from Columbia University in 1960. Despite her excellent record and credentials (she graduated fourth in her class at Columbia), she was turned down by more than 60 prospective employers before being offered a position as a social worker at the Jewish Guild for the Blind in New York City, where she established the nation's first out-patient psychiatric clinic for blind, multiply disabled children. From 1964 to 1972, she worked at the Bellevue Medical Center at New York University, beginning as a senior psychiatric social worker and ending as the di-

rector for Psychiatric Social Work and Rehabilitation Services. In 1970, she became coordinator for the Mayor's Advisory Committee on the Handicapped, convincing New York Mayor John V. Lindsay to expand that office into the nation's first Mayor's Office for the Handicapped in 1971, and serving as its director until 1978.

Fiorito's work at the Mayor's Office for the Handicapped confirmed for her the need for a national, cross-disability, advocacy organization. She recognized that "if people with disabilities worked together their numbers would bring them real political power." Together with activist Fred Fay, she announced the formation of the ACCD at the 1974 annual meeting of the President's Committee on Employment of the Handicapped. The ACCD was officially launched in April 1975. Two years later, Fiorito organized the occupation of the federal Health, Education and Welfare (HEW) offices in Washington, D.C., as part of a nationwide effort by disability rights activists to force HEW Secretary Joseph Califano to issue regulations implementing Section 504 of the Rehabilitation Act of 1973.

Fiorito became a member of Disabled Peoples' International in 1981, a Regional Council and World Council member of that organization in 1985, and then treasurer for a three-year term beginning in 1986. She was also the founder of the League of Disabled Voters in 1978, and its first president until 1980. She currently serves in a variety of capacities in numerous other organizations, including the National Organization of Women, the American Council of the Blind, the World Blind Union, and the League of Women Voters. She has been a member of the Executive Committee of the President's Committee on Employment of People with Disabilities since 1974.

Fiorito works as the special assistant to the commissioner of Rehabilitation Services in the U.S. Department of Education, a position she has held since 1978. She is the co-author, with Allen Spiegel, of *Rehabilitating People with Disabilities into the Mainstream of Society*, published in 1980. She has written numerous articles on disability rights and rehabilitation and has won a variety of awards and honors, including the National Rehabilitation Association Leadership Award in 1972 and a commission as a Kentucky colonel in 1975.

See also American Coalition of Citizens with Disabilities; Cross-Disability Awareness/Cross-Disability Sensitivity; HEW Demonstrations.

Fischer, Angeline A. Fuller (1841–1925)

Angeline A. Fuller Fischer, a deaf feminist activist and writer, was born in Savannah, Illinois, on 11 August 1841, but she was raised in Omaha, Nebraska. Deafened during her childhood, she attended the Illinois School for the Deaf at Jacksonville until 1869. In the late 1870s, she began a cam-

paign to force Gallaudet College in Washington, D.C., to admit women students, going so far as to call for the founding of a separate college—as far from the men's college as possible—if the administrators of Gallaudet did not end their discriminatory policy. The Gallaudet board of directors voted to admit women in January 1887. In 1880, Fischer attended the National Convention of the Deaf, where the National Association of the Deaf was founded.

Fischer was also a poet, publishing her book *The Venture* in 1883 and contributing poems to numerous newspapers and magazines.

See also Gallaudet University; National Association of the Deaf.

References Braddock, Guilbert C., *Notable Deaf Persons* (1975); Holcomb, Mabs, and Sharon Wood, *Deaf Women: A Parade through the Decades* (1989).

Fleming, G. Andrew (b. 1952)

G. Andrew Fleming was born on 25 October 1952, in Oakland, California. He became a double leg amputee at age 24 as the result of being run over by a train. An athlete before his disability, Fleming became a wheelchair athlete and an advocate for disabled sports and for accessibility in general sports and athletic programs.

"Historically," he told an interviewer in 1995, "sports have always been a vehicle for changing society's attitudes. Look back to the 1950s when black athletes broke the color barrier in baseball and other sports. If people with disabilities can gain the recognition they deserve through athletic competition, then they can break through other barriers too."

Fleming became a star wheelchair athlete in Santa Barbara, California, but discovered that much of the city's recreational programs and facilities were inaccessible. In 1979, he convinced the city's recreation department to hire him as director of adaptive recreation. In 1982, he became the first executive director of the National Wheelchair Athletic Association and a member of the U.S. Olympic Subcommittee on Programs for Athletes with Disabilities. He was also an advisor to the Los Angeles Olympic Organizing Committee in 1984. During this time, he was also an all-star wheelchair basketball player, winning medals in international competitions in track and swimming. From 1983 to 1987, he was chairman of the Committee on Athletics for the Disabled, a part of the Athletics Congress of the U.S.A., and, in 1990, he became president and CEO of the Atlanta Paralympic Organizing Committee, in charge of organizing the 1996 Atlanta Paralympic Games.

See also Paralympics (Paralympic Movement); Sports and Athletics.

Forced Sterilization

A major goal of the eugenics movement was the forced sterilization of people with disabilities deemed "unfit" to have children. People with developmental disabilities or mental retardation, mental illness, and epilepsy were particular targets of this campaign.

The earliest form of forced sterilization was castration. In the 1880s and 1890s, physicians such as Issac Newton Karlin, superintendent of the Pennsylvania Training School for Feeble-Minded Children at Elwin, and F. Hoyt Pilcher, supervising physician at the Kansas Asylum for Idiotic and Imbecilic Youth, castrated dozens of boys under their care. At the turn of the century, Edwin Kehrer in Germany and Albert J. Ochsner in Chicago developed the technique of "tying" the fallopian tubes of women and the vas deferens of men. These procedures were considered minor surgery with no ill after-effects. (In fact, forced sterilization almost always has severe psychological and often physical sequelae, including depression and infection). Perhaps more importantly, they were much cheaper than previous methods, and several American physicians were soon using these techniques to sterilize large numbers of institutionalized people. One of these physicians, Harry C. Sharp, the chief physician at an Indiana mental institution, experimented on disabled men to perfect the vasectomy. In ten years, he completed 236 vasectomies on the disabled residents entrusted to his care. Sharp became a crusader for forced sterilization. In 1907, as a result of the efforts of proponents like Sharp, Indiana passed the first forced sterilization law permitting the procedure on "confirmed idiots, imbeciles, and rapists."

Eugenicists were soon pushing for legislation in other states to allow the forced sterilization of those people with disabilities possessed of "moral imbecility," "moral idiocy," "moral degeneracy," or "imbecility with criminal instincts." These terms all arose out of the common belief that people with mental disabilities were depraved and sexually dangerous. "Some exponents of sterilization," according to Donald K. Pickens in *Eugenics and the Progressives* (1968), "thought of the mentally incompetent as half-people whose chief characteristics were 'astonishing fecundity,' and a general irresponsibility creating increased demands on charity." Forced sterilization was made easier by the mass institutionalization of people with disabilities during the late nineteenth and early twentieth centuries. In California alone, 6,000 operations were performed between 1909 and 1929.

Any legal constraints on this campaign were removed by the U.S. Supreme Court's 1927 decision in *Buck v. Bell*, in which the Court decided that forced sterilization was not a violation of the constitutional rights of people with disabilities. In all, 32 states passed laws permitting the sterilization of people with disabilities, and, according to reporter Mary Bishop, an estimated "60,000 Americans were rounded up, judged genetically inferior, held in government asylums and sterilized against their wills."

Disability activists and civil libertarians successfully challenged the laws permitting forced sterilization in the 1970s, when a number of public scandals highlighted the abusive nature of these procedures. The Virginia Sterilization Law, under which Carrie Buck was sterilized, was finally repealed in 1974. The forced sterilization of people with disabilities, however, has never specifically been ruled unconstitutional.

See also Abortion and Reproductive Rights; *Buck v. Bell*; Eugenics; Parenting and Disability.

References Friedman, Ina, *The Other Victim* (1990); Pickens, Donald K., *Eugenics and the Progressives* (1968); Trombley, Stephen, *The Right To Reproduce: A History of Coercive Sterilization* (1988).

Fowler, LaDonna G. (Kirkaldie) (b. 1954)

LaDonna G. Fowler is a leading advocate in the American Indian disability rights movement. Of Assiniboine, Sioux, and Turtle Mountain Chippewa descent, she is the project director and co-principal investigator of the American Indian Disability Legislation Project (AIDL) at the Rural Institute on Disabilities at Montana University in Missoula.

Fowler was born on 22 July 1954. She was a peer advisor with the Handicapped Student Support Services at Salish Kootenai College, in Pablo, Montana, beginning in 1988. She worked at the college in various capacities until 1994, when she joined the staff of the Rural Institute. She has represented AIDL at the National Congress of American Indians (NCAI), and she revitalized the NCAI Disability Caucus. She is a member of the National Council on Independent Living Multi-Cultural Committee and of the Personal Assistant Services Advisory Council of the World Institute on Disability. She received an associate of applied sciences in secretarial/data processing from Kootenai College in 1988 and is a self-employed artist and craftsperson.

See also American Indian Disability Legislation Project; Rural Institute on Disability.

"Freaks" as Sideshow Performers

For centuries, people with disabilities were displayed as "sideshow freaks" at carnivals, circuses, exhibitions, and fairs. The Catholic Church, during the Middle Ages in Europe, sponsored traveling exhibitions of disabled people, while families exhibited their disabled members for a fee or sold them to royalty for exhibition at court. By Victorian times, these forms of "entertainment" had evolved into the carnival sideshow or "dime museum," where the public paid to see "armless and legless wonders," "giants," "dwarfs," "seal boys," "living skeletons," and "pinheads." Such exhibitions were particularly popular in small town America, although impresarios such as P. T. Barnum took their "acts"— disabled individuals such as "Tom Thumb" or the "Siamese Twins"—to New York, Chicago, London, and Paris.

The life of a sideshow freak was often filled with brutality and exploitation. "Performers" were the virtual prisoners of carnival owners, working for subsistence wages. Leslie Fiedler described them as "fellow humans more marginal than the poorest sharecroppers or black convicts on a Mississippi chain gang." Often, such "freaks" were not in fact functionally disabled; they could see and hear, walk and talk, and were physically capable of caring for themselves and living independent lives. Rather, people such as "Jo Jo the dog-faced boy," "Lionel, the lion-faced man," and the numerous "half man-half woman" hermaphrodites were "freaks" because their physical appearance alone made them outcasts from mainstream society. Fiedler points out that the very terms used to describe the sideshow "freak" "call into question our [society's] conviction that the line separating us from all other beasts is unpassable. The legless dwarf Samuel D. Parks, for instance, was known as 'Hopp the Frog Boy.' . . . and Prince Randian, an armless and legless native of New Guinea . . . was known not just as the 'Living Torso,' but also as the 'Snake Man' and the 'Caterpillar Man.'" Randian in fact was a husband and father of five children and described by his contemporaries as "a kindly fellow."

Freak shows became less popular in the 1950s and 1960s, their audience pulled away by television and a growing uneasiness among the public with this sort of "entertainment." Nevertheless, as late as

Barnum and Bailey "freaks" George Anger the circus giant and Pygmie Klik-Ko. Circus mogul P. T. Barnum displayed unusual looking disabled people, such as Tom Thumb and the Siamese Twins, as sideshow "freaks."

the 1960s, they were attended by some 75 million Americans a year. Some states attempted to ban freak shows, but were challenged not only by carnival owners but also by some "freaks" themselves, who argued that the sideshow offered their only hope for employment. In October 1972, the Florida Supreme Court ruled the law prohibiting freak shows in that state was unconstitutional. In 1996, the Chicago radio station WRCX sponsored "The Mancow Freak Show," featuring such "attractions" as "The Man Who Lost Half His Face to Cancer" and "The Armless, Legless Torso."

See also Media Images of People with Disabilities.

References Bogdan, Robert, *Freak Show: Presenting Human Oddities for Amusement and Profit* (1988); Drimmer, Frederick, *Very Special People: The Struggles, Loves and Triumphs of Human Oddities* (1973); Fiedler, Leslie, *Freaks: Myths and Images of the Secret Self* (1978).

Frieden, Lex (b. 1949)

Lex Frieden was an early pioneer of the independent living movement in the 1970s and a major player in the drafting and passage of the Americans with Disabilities Act of 1990 (ADA). Considered a pivotal figure in the national disability rights movement, he is also an internationally recognized authority on independent living and rehabilitation. He has been involved in numerous local and national disability rights organizations, some of which he was instrumental in founding.

Frieden was born on 5 March 1949, in Alva, Oklahoma. His undergraduate education at Oklahoma State University was interrupted in 1967 by an automobile accident resulting in quadriplegia. He graduated with a B.S. in psychology from the University of Tulsa in 1971, and he received his M.A. in social psychology from the University of Houston in 1979. Frieden began working in the independent living movement in the early 1970s, founding Wheelchair Independence Now in Tulsa in 1971. He was a co-founder in 1975 of the Houston Coalition for Barrier Free Living, and the group's director until 1977. He was the national secretary of the American Coalition of Citizens with Disabilities from 1975 to 1976 and a cofounder of the Coalition of Texans with Disabilities in 1978. Professionally, Frieden held many positions, among them director of the National Commission on Rehabilitation Counselor Certification from 1976 to 1987 and the legislative ambassador of the American Congress of Rehabilitation Medicine from 1982 to 1984. He also worked as a research instructor at the Department of Rehabilitation at the Baylor College of Medicine in Houston, Texas, from 1978 to 1980 and as an assistant professor at Baylor from 1980 to 1991.

In 1984, President Reagan appointed Frieden to be executive director of the National Council on the Handicapped. He was one of the principal contributors to the council's ground-breaking report *Toward Independence* (1986), calling for national civil rights legislation to end discrimination against people with disabilities, what was to become the Americans with Disabilities Act of 1990 (ADA). In 1988, Frieden was named coordinator of the congressionally created Task Force on the Rights and Empowerment of Americans with Disabilities, which for two years held public forums across the country and provided information to members of Congress and the Bush administration on the need for federal disability rights legislation. The task force was crucial in winning support for the ADA.

Frieden left the council in 1988 to become the executive director of the Institute for Rehabilitation and Research (TIRR) in Houston, Texas, becoming senior vice president there in 1991. In 1990, he became assistant national secretary of the U.S. Council on International Rehabilitation and, in 1993, a clinical associate professor at the Department of Community Medicine at Baylor. Frieden has been a member of numerous other boards and committees, including the Board of Directors of the President's Committee on Employment of People with Disabilities, beginning in 1989, and of the editorial or advisory boards of various publications, including *Rural Special Education Quarterly* (1986–1994), *Journal of Disability Policy Studies* (1989–present), and *Rehabilitation Education* (1987–present). He is the winner of two Presidential Citations, as well as numerous other awards.

See also American Coalition of Citizens with Disabilities; Americans with Disabilities Act of 1990; Houston Cooperative Living Residential Project; National Council on Disability; Task Force on the Rights and Empowerment of Americans with Disabilities.

Funk, Robert J. (b. 1944)

Robert J. Funk was one of the founders and the first executive director of the Disability Rights Education and Defense Fund (DREDF). He is considered one of the founding philosophers of disability integration, arguing that, in order to gain their civil rights, people with disabilities must be considered as a legal class, analogous to racial, religious, ethnic, and gender classes. This theory has been described as moving people with disabilities "from caste to class," and Funk is credited with being a major architect of the disability civil rights agenda.

Funk was born on 18 December 1944. He was a Peace Corps volunteer in Nigeria from 1964 to 1966, earned a B.A. from the University of Michigan in Ann Arbor in 1972, and a law degree from the University of California at Davis in 1976. In 1977, Funk became the deputy director of the Center for Independent Living in Berkeley (CIL), where he founded and directed the Disability Law Resource Center (DLRC), a community-based legal advocacy and training center within the CIL. DREDF was founded when it became ap-

parent to Funk and others that there needed to be a national legal advocacy organization with the goal of expanding the civil rights of people with disabilities. During his term as executive director, DREDF filed amicus briefs in such crucial disability rights cases as *Consolidated Rail Corporation v. Darrone* (1984), *Paralyzed Veterans of America v. William French Smith* (1986), and *Southeastern Community College v. Davis* (1979), all of which were argued before the U.S. Supreme Court.

Funk left DREDF in 1986 to become the policy research and project officer at the National Institute on Disability and Rehabilitation Research, an office in the U.S. Department of Education, where he conducted research on issues such as personal assistance services (PAS), computer-based networking systems for independent living centers, and health insurance issues for people with disabilities. From January to December 1987, Funk was also a consultant for the National Council on the Handicapped and for the President's Committee on Employment of the Handicapped. In March 1990, Funk was appointed chief of staff of the U.S. Equal Employment Opportunity Commission, a position he held for three years before leaving to become a partner with Evan Kemp Associates, Inc., a Washington, D.C., consulting firm specializing in disability rights issues.

Funk is also the author of numerous articles and book chapters on disability civil rights litigation and legislation, including "From Caste to Class: The Humanization of Disabled People" in *Law Reform in Disability Rights: Articles and Concept Papers* (1981).

See also Disability Rights Education and Defense Fund.

Gallagher, Hugh Gregory (b. 1932)

Hugh Gregory Gallagher's research and writing on such topics as the Nazi campaign of extermination against people with disabilities and the influence of disability in the life and presidency of Franklin Roosevelt have played an important role in providing the disability rights movement with a historical context. Gallagher is also the principal author of the Architectural Barriers Act of 1968.

Gallagher was born on 18 October 1932, in Palo Alto, California, and became a polio quadriplegic in 1952. He was a member (along with novelist Lorenzo Milam) of the Warm Springs Polio Rehabilitation Center in Georgia "class of '53." His experience there sparked his interest in Franklin Roosevelt (co-founder of the center) and the president's relationship with polio. Gallagher received his B.A. in 1956 from Claremont College (then known as the Claremont Men's College) in California and a B.A. and M.A. from Oxford University in 1959. In 1959, he became a legislative assistant to Sen. John A. Carroll (D–CO), and then an administrative assistant to Sen. E. L. Bartlett (D-AK). Gallagher was the Alaska coordinator for Lyndon Johnson's 1964 presidential campaign and the manager of Bartlett's reelection campaign in 1966. He worked in the White House from 1967 to 1968, writing Johnson's legislative signing and veto messages.

As the person who conceived and wrote the Architectural Barriers Act of 1968, Gallagher played a pivotal role in the evolution of disability rights law and the disability rights movement. The act was the first ever federal disability rights legislation, allowing advocates to frame access as a legal and civil rights issue. Activists in Washington, D.C., cited the law in their litigation with the D.C. Metro beginning in 1972, scoring a significant victory in the struggle for accessible public transportation.

Gallagher's first book, *Advise and Obstruct: The Role of the United States Senate in Foreign Policy Decisions* (1969), was a Pulitzer Prize nominee. This book was followed in 1974 by *Etok: A Story of Eskimo Power*. Gallagher's best-known historical work, *FDR's Splendid Deception*, was published in 1985. It chronicles the role Roosevelt's post-polio paraplegia played in his personal and political life and exposes the collaboration between Roosevelt and the press to downplay his disability. *By Trust Betrayed: Patients, Physicians, and the License To Kill in the Third Reich* was published in 1990, with a revised edition appearing in 1995. The book details the Nazi campaign of extermination against people with disabilities, and it was hailed by the American Library Association *Booklist* as "a valuable contribution . . . to the literature on the struggle for the rights of the disabled." Gallagher is a consultant at the Library of Congress and the United States Holocaust Museum in Washington, D.C.

Gallagher has received numerous awards, including the Henry B. Betts Award in 1995 for lifetime career achievement in improving the quality of life for people with disabilities. He is on the board of directors of the International Polio Institute, a member of the National Committee of Roosevelt Historians, and a member of the Society for Disability Studies. He was the subject of the PBS documentary *Coming to Terms*, first broadcast in August 1991.

See also Architectural Barriers Act of 1968; Roosevelt, Franklin Delano; T-4; Warm Springs.

References Gallagher, Hugh Gregory, *FDR's Splendid Deception* (1985); ———, *By Trust Betrayed: Patients, Physicians, and the License To Kill in the Third Reich* (1990).

Gallaudet, Edward Miner (1837–1917)

Edward Miner Gallaudet was the principal founder and first president of what is now Gallaudet University in Washington, D.C. Born on 5 February 1837 in Hartford, Connecticut, he was the son of Thomas Hopkins Gallaudet, founder of the American School for the Deaf. His mother, born Sophia Fowler, was herself deaf, and deeply involved with his work. Indeed, Sophia Gallaudet has been revered as "Mother Gallaudet" and "Queen of the Deaf Community."

Fluent in sign, Gallaudet accepted a teaching position at the American School for the Deaf starting in December 1855. He was called at age 20 to become the superintendent of the Columbia Institution for the Deaf and Dumb and Blind, a residential school for disabled boys in Washington, D.C., founded by philanthropist Amos Kendall and funded by the U.S. Congress. Early in 1864, Gallaudet drew up a bill for the expansion of the Columbia Institution into a full-fledged college, with the ability to confer degrees in the arts and sciences. Gallaudet was named president of the new college and of its corporation and board. He devoted the rest of his life to expanding "The National College for the Deaf," lobbying Congress, fund-raising, and recruiting teachers and students. The Gallaudet University of today is his enduring legacy to the Deaf community.

After 1867, Gallaudet became a proponent of what he termed the "Combined Method" of deaf education, meaning the use of sign language, lip-reading, and speech. He organized a conference in May 1868 to discuss "the articulation controversy." The conference revived the *American Annals of the Deaf* and the Convention of American Instructors of the Deaf, both of which had been suspended during the Civil War. The conference report endorsed the Combined Method, and more radical proponents of oralism, such as Alexander Graham Bell, criticized Gallaudet for continuing to advocate the use of sign language. Bell and Gallaudet locked horns on a number of occasions, as when Bell lobbied Congress to prevent Gallaudet from founding a school within the National College to train teachers of deaf students. Bell feared that those trained there would be deaf themselves and thus not disposed to use "the oral method." Gallaudet had by this time become the nation's most prominent defender of the use and value of American Sign Language.

Gallaudet expressed an interest in his pupils long after they graduated, visiting them and on occasion providing money or other support when needed. In 1895, he began work on his memoir, the *History of the College for the Deaf 1857–1907*. He moved back to New Haven, Connecticut, after his retirement in 1910. He died on 26 September 1917.

See also Bell, Alexander Graham; Gallaudet, Thomas Hopkins; Gallaudet University; Oral School, Oralism.

References Boatner, Maxine Tull, *Voice of the Deaf: A Biography of Edward Miner Gallaudet* (1959); Gallaudet, Edward Miner, *History of the College for the Deaf 1857–1907* (1983); Winefield, Richard, *Never the Twain Shall Meet: Bell, Gallaudet, and the Communications Debate* (1987).

Gallaudet, Thomas Hopkins (1787–1851)

Thomas Hopkins Gallaudet was a pioneer of deaf education in the United States. He co-founded the American School for the Deaf in Hartford, Connecticut, and through his writings and lectures inspired the founding of other schools for deaf people across the country. He was also an early supporter of colleges for women, public high schools, and other social and educational innovations.

Thomas Hopkins Gallaudet was born on 10 December 1787, in Philadelphia. Often ill as a child, he nevertheless entered Yale University at age 14, graduating in 1805 at the top of his class. He returned in 1808 to earn his master of arts degree, which he received in 1810. Deciding to be a minister, he enrolled at the Andover Theological Seminary in Massachusetts in 1812. Although he graduated with a preacher's license in 1814, ill health prevented him from accepting a position as a full-time minister. Uncertain what to do, Gallaudet went to Europe at the urging of physician Mason Cogswell, a neighbor whose daughter Alice was deaf. Eager to have her educated, Cogswell solicited the support of Hartford's wealthier citizens to enable Gallaudet to travel to Europe to study methods of deaf instruction.

The British approach, as practiced by the Braidwood family in Scotland, was a form of oralism, that is, the attempt to teach deaf people to speak and lip-read. Gallaudet was unimpressed with the results and put off by the Braidwoods' desire to keep their methods secret. Gallaudet was more impressed by the work of Abbé Sicard, director of the Royal Institution for the Deaf in Paris, and with his use of sign language. Gallaudet convinced Laurent Clerc, a deaf instructor at the institution, to return with him in 1816 to Hartford, where they founded the American School for the Deaf the following year. Gallaudet was principal of the school until 1830, by which time five more schools for the deaf had been founded in various other states. One of the first graduates of the American School for the Deaf was Sophia Fowler, Gallaudet's wife. His son, Edward Miner Gallaudet, became the principal founder and first president of the National College of the Deaf in Washington, D.C., which was renamed Gallaudet College in 1894 (in honor of Thomas Hopkins Gallaudet).

Gallaudet was an avid defender of the use of sign language in the education of deaf people. In 1847, he wrote an essay for the newly established *American Annals of the Deaf*, refuting the contention that European oralism was superior to American Sign Language. Gallaudet died on 10 September 1851.

See also American School for the Deaf; American Sign Language; Clerc, Laurent; Gallaudet, Edward Miner.

References Lane, Harlan, *When the Mind Hears: A History of the Deaf* (1984); Van Cleve, John V., *Gallaudet Encyclopedia of Deaf People and Deafness* (1987).

Gallaudet Demonstrations
See Deaf President Now Campaign.

Gallaudet University

Gallaudet University is the first and only liberal arts university in the world for deaf and hard-of-hearing people. A center for Deaf culture and scholarship, its students and alumni are often at the forefront of Deaf politics, as demonstrated by the Deaf President Now campaign of 1988. Originally known as the National College for the Deaf, it was renamed Gallaudet College in 1894, in honor of Thomas Hopkins Gallaudet, who with Laurent Clerc had founded the first school for deaf children in the Western Hemisphere. Congress conferred university status in 1986, and the school has since been known as Gallaudet University. In the fall of 1993, it had an enrollment of 1,762 undergraduate and 439 graduate students, attending classes on two campuses located in Washington, D.C.

The idea of a college for deaf people had been suggested as early as the 1850s. John Carlin, writing in the *American Annals of the Deaf* in April 1854, lamented how as a deaf person he could not receive a college education anywhere in the world. He called for the creation of a "National College" to meet the needs of deaf people seeking higher education.

The Columbia Institution for the Deaf and Dumb and Blind, the seed of what was to become Gallaudet University, was founded in 1857 by philanthropists concerned about the exploitation of indigent disabled children in Washington, D.C. James C. McGuire, one of the boarding school's co-founders, described how "a despicable wretch [named Platt H. Skinner] . . . got possession of a building . . . and fenced it in like a sort of prison. . . . He then hunted up all the deaf and dumb children in the community . . . and took them to his building, pretending to call it a school for them. He would then take them about the city and exhibit them for money." McGuire learned about the situation from one of his servants, whose son was deaf. McGuire and his friend Amos Kendall, forcing their way into the building, found several children so weak from starvation and illness that they could not move. Kendall went to court to remove the children from Skinner's "school" and assumed custody of some of them himself. Moving them into his home, he and McGuire founded their own school, calling together a board of notable citizens and applying to Congress for a charter and funding. Their choice for the school's first president was 20-year-old Edward Miner Gallaudet, son of the co-founder of the American School for the Deaf in Hartford, Connecticut. Gallaudet accepted the position on the condition that the institution would eventually grow into a full-fledged college under his tutelage.

It was not until early 1864 that Gallaudet and his board felt able to approach Congress for a new charter and funding. Funding was required since many, if not most, deaf people could not afford to pay their own tuition. The debate in Congress reflected the attitudes of the general public toward deaf people. Some objected to the notion of a college for "the deaf and dumb" being able to "confer degrees in the arts and sciences the same as Harvard University and Yale." Rep. Henry Bowen Anthony of Rhode Island believed the idea "ridiculous" and urged that the school only be allowed to confer a special degree "appropriate to the institution upon the deaf and dumb." Others suggested that such degrees would hardly matter anyway. "Is anybody going to employ a deaf-mute or a man who has not the power of utterance and give him any greater confidence because he has a diploma from this deaf and dumb asylum than they would if he had not one?" Still others questioned the constitutionality of the federal government appropriating money to set up a school to benefit one segment of the population. Gallaudet responded to this argument by noting that people who were deaf (or for that matter disabled in most any manner) were excluded from attending any of the colleges receiving grants under federal

programs of the time. A college for deaf students would, in some measure, redress this injustice.

The bill authorizing the formation and funding of the college as part of the Columbia Institution passed both houses of Congress, and it was signed by President Abraham Lincoln on 8 April 1864. The school's original campus was on land donated by Kendall, along with 13 adjacent acres purchased later that year. Its first instructor was James Denison, a deaf man from Vermont, and its first matriculated student was Melville Ballard, from Maine. An act of Congress passed on 23 February 1865 authorized the abolition of the Columbia Institution's department for the blind, and seven blind students were transferred to a school in Maryland. After that time, the National College for the Deaf (as it then became known) was devoted entirely to people who were deaf or hard-of-hearing.

By June 1866, there were 25 students enrolled at the college, two of them women. They were soon joined by two other women, but none completed the full course of study in "the higher class," and thus never graduated. After their departure, the college adopted a policy of accepting men only. Deaf feminist Angeline A. Fuller Fischer waged a campaign to convince the board of directors to change this policy, going so far as to publicly threaten to form her own college just for women and to locate it as far from the National College as possible. The board voted to accept women in January 1887. In its early years, the college also accepted "colored deaf-mutes"—housing them in segregated dorms. In 1905, Congress passed legislation making what was by then Gallaudet College a whites-only institution, which was not to change until the early 1950s. Until then, deaf people of color were denied any opportunity for a liberal arts college education.

The National College demonstrated early on that people who were deaf were not, as was widely assumed, the intellectual inferiors of the hearing. "It had been abundantly proved by experience," wrote Joseph Henry, the head of the Smithsonian Institution and an early supporter of the college, "that as a class [the deaf] have excellent mental capacities and [they] are susceptible of high mental and moral development." Nevertheless, opposition continued. Rep. Elihu B. Washburne (R-IL), acting chairman of the House Appropriations Committee, was a staunch adversary of the college who waged a several-year battle to end its funding, believing that "higher education of the deaf is a useless extravagance." Rep. Benjamin Butler of Massachusetts made a speech on the House floor saying it would be better to give the funds to "those who had all their faculties" and that a "deaf-mute" would never be more than "half a man." In response, National College student Joseph G. Parkinson sent Butler a card, saying, "Half a man desires to see the Beast"—a reference to when Butler, a general in the Union army in command of the occupation troops at New Orleans, was called "Beast Butler" by the white citizens of that city. As far as is known, Butler never agreed to meet with Parkinson.

The National College for the Deaf graduated its first class in 1869, with Melville Ballard the first to receive his diploma, a bachelor's degree in science. By this time, oralism, the teaching of speech and lip-reading coupled with the suppression of sign language, was becoming increasingly popular with hearing educators of deaf children. Though Gallaudet saw some merit to teaching deaf people to lipread and speak, he did not believe in the suppression of sign language, preferring instead the "Combined Method" using both oralism and sign. For this reason, both Gallaudet and the college were attacked, particularly by Alexander Graham Bell and his followers.

Edward Gallaudet retired as president of the college in 1910, and he was succeeded by Percival Hall, who held the position until 1945. In 1988, the board of trustees appointed I. King Jordan, the university's dean of the College of Arts and Sciences, as Gallaudet's first deaf president. This appointment came after a week of demonstrations by campus activists opposed to the board's first choice of a hearing woman, Elisabeth Ann Zinser, to succeed retiring president Jerry C. Lee.

Today, the university is home to the International Center on Deafness, the Gallaudet Research Institute, and the National Information Center on Deafness, as well as the Kendall Demonstration Elementary School and the Model Secondary School for the Deaf.

See also Deaf President Now Campaign; Fischer, Angeline A. Fuller; Gallaudet, Edward Miner; Gallaudet, Thomas Hopkins; Jordan, I. King; Oral School, Oralism.

References Boatner, Maxine Tull, *Voice of the Deaf: A Biography of Edward Miner Gallaudet* (1959); Gallaudet, Edward Miner, *History of the College for the Deaf 1857–1907* (1983).

Galloway, Donald (b. 1938)

Donald Galloway is a leader in efforts to include African Americans in the national disability rights movement and to found a national, cross-disability organization of African Americans. He was vice president of the National Association of Minorities with Disabilities, based in Milwaukee, Wisconsin, from the group's founding in 1981 until it dissolved in 1985. He founded the Multi-Cultural Committee of the National Council on Independent Living (NCIL) in 1986, and he is a member of the NCIL executive board.

Galloway was born on 21 March 1938 in Washington, D.C. He received his B.A. in sociology from California State University in Los Angeles in 1967 and his master of social work from California State University in San Diego in 1969. He worked at the Center for Independent Living in Berkeley from 1974 to 1977, developing a peer counseling program that would serve as a model for independent living centers across the country, and then as the executive director of the Colorado Governor's Council on the Handicapped from 1977 to 1978. From 1978 to 1980, he was the director of Peace Corps programs in Jamaica, returning to the United States in 1980 to coordinate Peace Corps programs worldwide in conjunction with the United Nation's International Year of Disabled Persons. From 1982 to 1986, he was director of the District of Columbia Center for Independent Living. In 1987, he accepted his current position at the District of Columbia Department of Housing and Community Development.

Galloway was a member of the Task Force on the Rights and Empowerment of Americans with Disabilities, advocating for passage of the Americans with Disabilities Act of 1990. He was also the founder and director of Visually Impaired Persons of Color from 1987 to its dissolution in 1991, when its members joined the National Federation of the Blind (NFB). He is a leader of the NFB and the independent living movement in the Washington, D.C., area.

See also Multi-Cultural Issues, Minority Persons with Disabilities; National Council on Independent Living; National Federation of the Blind; Task Force on the Rights and Empowerment of Americans with Disabilities.

Gannon, Jack Randle (b. 1936)

Jack Randle Gannon is a preeminent historian of Deaf America. His *Deaf Heritage: A Narrative History of Deaf America* (1981) is an essential text on Deaf history and culture, covering the period from colonial times to the early 1980s. Another of his works, *The Week the World Heard Gallaudet* (1989), offers a day-by-day illustrated account of the Deaf President Now campaign.

Gannon was born on 23 November 1936 in West Plains, Missouri, and deafened at age eight by spinal meningitis. He graduated from the Missouri School for the Deaf in 1954 and from Gallaudet College in 1959 with a B.S. in education, later becoming Gallaudet's director of alumni affairs and editor of the quarterly *Gallaudet Today*. Among other achievements, Gannon is the co-founder and past editor of *The Deaf Nebraskan*, past chair of the International Relations Committee of the National Association of the Deaf (1984–

1986), and co-founder and co-chair of the Deaf History International Organizing Committee (1991–1995). In 1995, he became co-curator of *DEAF: A Community of Signers*, a joint project of Gallaudet University and the Smithsonian Institution.

In 1988, Gannon was awarded an honorary degree of doctor of humane letters from Gallaudet University for his service to the Deaf community. He retired in 1996 as special assistant to the president for advocacy at Gallaudet University.

See also Deaf Culture; Deaf President Now Campaign; Gallaudet University.
Reference Gannon, Jack R., *Deaf Heritage: A Narrative History of Deaf America* (1981).

Gazette International Networking Institute (G.I.N.I.)
See Laurie, Virginia Grace.

Geld, Howard ("Howie the Harp") (1952–1995)

Howard Geld was one of the foremost organizers of the psychiatric survivor liberation movement in the United States. Born in 1952 in New York City's Lower East Side, by age 13 he was an inmate in a psychiatric hospital, where he was taught to play the harmonica by one of the night attendants. "When you cry out loud in a mental hospital you get medicated. When I was sad, I could cry through my harmonica." Geld ran away from the institution when he was 17 years old. Homeless on the streets of New York, Geld played the harmonica for money, earning the nickname "Howie the Harp" (or "Howie T. Harp" as he is identified in Judi Chamberlin's 1978 book *On Our Own*).

Geld moved to the West Coast in 1970, where he and his sister Helen joined one of the earliest mental patients' civil rights groups, the Insane Liberation Front in Portland, Oregon. The two moved back to New York City in 1971 and founded the Mental Patients' Liberation Project. Among the organization's founding principles was the belief that every person with a psychiatric disability was "a human being . . . entitled to be treated as such." The project advocated for the rights of mental patients to have access to their records; to refuse medication, insulin, and electric shock treatments; to receive decent medical care when needed; and to refuse to work inside hospitals unless compensated. "You have a right not to be treated like a criminal. . . . You have a right to decent living conditions. . . . You have a right to refuse to be a guinea pig for experimental drugs and treatments."

In 1975, Geld co-founded Project Release, the first client-run residence for people with psychiatric disabilities in the country. The project was a radical departure from traditional treatments of "the mentally ill." People were free to come and go, and treatment consisted of peer support and counseling. Indeed, one of the tenets of the mental patients' liberation movement that Geld helped to articulate was that people with psychiatric disabilities are their own best resource, better able to help each other than nondisabled psychiatrists, nurses, or social workers.

By 1981, Geld had moved back to the West Coast, settling in Berkeley, California. He worked at the Center for Independent Living, trying to integrate psychiatric survivors into the general disability rights movement. In 1983, Geld was a founding member of the Alameda County Network of Mental Health Clients, made up of self-help and political advocacy groups. In 1986, he helped start the Oakland Independence Support Center (OISC), which he called "an alternative to the mental-health system that truly helps people, that doesn't violate their rights, that supports their independence and quality of life, that encourages decent housing, jobs, and good attitudes about oneself, and that is run by and empowering of us." Geld worked with the OISC until 1992. He was also active in the Oakland Union of the Homeless, chair of the board of the Henry Robinson Multi-Service Center, and on the boards of numerous other homeless advocacy organizations.

Geld returned once more to New York City in 1993 to work as the director of advocacy at Community Access, providing housing and support services to people in poverty. During this time, he founded the New York City Recipients' Coalition, a network of 25 client-run organizations advocating for the rights of individuals receiving mental services.

Geld was known throughout the psychiatric survivor movement for "his generosity, magnanimous spirit, and humor." He was also a writer and editor, overseeing the publication of two books on the movement, *Reaching Across: Mental Health Clients Helping Each Other* (1987, with Sally Zinman and Sue Budd) and *Reaching Across II: Maintaining Our Roots/The Challenges of Growth* (1992, also with Zinman and Budd), as well as a founding member of Altered States of the Arts, a national organization to encourage "mad art" by psychiatric survivors. Geld is remembered as a unifying force in the often contentious disability rights movement. "To this end," recalls activist Sally Zinman, "when two national organizations were formed, in contradistinction to each other, he joined both." Howie the Harp died in his home in New York City on 5 February 1995.

See also Altered States of the Arts; National Empowerment Center; Psychiatric Survivor Movement.

References Chamberlin, Judi, *On Our Own: Patient-Controlled Alternatives to the Mental Health System* (1978); Intergalactic Network of Crazy Folks, "Mad Memoria: Howie the Harp Is Gone," *Dendron* (Spring 1995); Zinman, Sally, "The Legacy of Howie the Harp Lives On," *National Empowerment Center Newsletter* (Spring/Summer 1995).

Gilhool, Thomas K. (b. 1938)

Thomas K. Gilhool is the attorney most responsible for the rise of community services for people with developmental disabilities, allowing for their deinstitutionalization beginning in the 1970s. His work was pivotal in establishing the constitutional right of children with disabilities to a public education and a major impetus toward passage of Section 504 of the Rehabilitation Act of 1973 and the Education for All Handicapped Children Act of 1975.

Born on 10 September 1938 in Ardmore, Pennsylvania, Gilhool received a B.A. in international relations from Lehigh University in Bethlehem, Pennsylvania, in 1960 and both a masters in political science and a J.D. from Yale University in 1964. As an attorney with Community Legal Services, Inc., in Philadelphia from 1966 to 1969, Gilhool litigated a number of important poverty law cases.

From 1969 to 1972, Gilhool represented the Pennsylvania Association for Retarded Children (PARC) in *PARC v. Pennsylvania* (1972), the nation's first "right-to-education" case, leading to a consent decree that opened the Pennsylvania public schools to disabled children. The case became a precedent for all subsequent right-to-education litigation and a milestone in the struggle to open the public schools to children with disabilities. Parallel to *PARC* was *Halderman v. Pennhurst State School and Hospital* (1978), with Gilhool again representing PARC, institution residents, and their families. Gilhool had a personal tie to Pennhurst; his younger brother, who was cognitively disabled, had been sent to live there as a 10-year-old. The case, eventually argued before the U.S. Supreme Court on two occasions, resulted in the closing of Pennhurst in 1986, with the community placement of all its 1,500 residents and almost 1,000 people on the institution waiting list. Like *PARC*, this victory triggered similar suits in other states, a number of them with Gilhool as counsel or consultant to the plaintiffs. Among these were *Connecticut ARC v. Thorne* (1982), resulting in community services for 1,300 institutionalized people, and *Homeward Bound, Inc. v. The Hissom Memorial Center* (1986), in which the plaintiffs won a court order replacing an Oklahoma institution with community services and schooling for 2,000 people. As a result of these and similar suits, the resident population at state institutions nationwide fell from more than 220,000 in 1967 to less than 70,000 in 1996, with the number continuing to drop.

The Pennsylvania cases complemented each other and established important precedents. By opening up the public schools, Gilhool created options for parents with disabled children other than institutionalization. By shutting down the institutions, Gilhool forced the public schools to develop strategies for effectively educating children they had previously excluded. The impact on the lives of people with disabilities and their families cannot be overstated.

PARC, and the suits that followed, led to three years of congressional hearings on discrimination against disabled children, culminating in passage of the Education for All Handicapped Children Act of 1975 (Pub. Law 94–142, now the Individuals with Disabilities Education Act, or IDEA). The act opened up the public schools nationwide for millions of disabled children. The *PARC* decision of 1972 also influenced the authors of Section 504 of the Rehabilitation Act of 1973, another landmark in disability rights law.

From 1975 to 1987, Gilhool was the chief counsel at the Public Interest Law Center of Philadelphia. Among the cases he argued were *Lloyd v. Regional Transportation Authority* (1977), establishing the "right of action" of individuals under Section 504 of the Rehabilitation Act, and *City of Cleburne, Tex. v. Cleburne Living Center* (1985), which barred the exclusion of family-scaled residences of cognitively disabled people by city zoning ordinances, in essence adding "a right to community living" to *PARC*'s "right to education." Gilhool was also a major player in the Transbus campaign of the late 1970s. In 1987, he was appointed Pennsylvania's secretary of education, leaving that position in 1989 to teach junior high school in Philadelphia and education law and policy at the University of Pennsylvania Law School. In 1990, he returned to the Public Interest Law Center of Philadelphia, where he continues his work as a disability rights attorney.

Gilhool has lectured and consulted widely and is the author of numerous articles, reports, and book chapters. He has served on a wide variety of boards and organizations, including the National Center for Law and the Handicapped (1971–1977) and the Western Center on Law and the Handicapped (1973–1977).

See also The ARC; *City of Cleburne, Tex. v. Cleburne Living Center;* Deinstitutionalization; Dybwad, Gunnar; Education for All Handicapped Children Act of 1975; *Halderman v. Pennhurst State School & Hospital; Lloyd v. Regional Transportation Authority; Pennsylvania Association for Retarded Children v. Pennsylvania;* Transbus.

References Burt, Robert A., "Pennhurst: A Parable," in Mnookin, Robert H., *In the Interest of Children: Advocacy, Law Reform, and Public Policy* (1985); Gilhool, Thomas K., "The Right to Community Services," in Michael Kindred et al., eds., *The Mentally Retarded Citizen and the Law* (1976).

Gill, Carol J. (b. 1949)

Carol J. Gill is a widely published writer on disability issues, particularly as they relate to disabled women, and an activist and writer on the issue of assisted suicide. She is the president and director of Psychological Research at the Chicago Center for Disability Research.

Gill was born on 16 June 1949. She earned her B.A. in psychology from Saint Xavier College in Chicago and her M.A. and Ph.D. from the University of Illinois–Chicago. She has served on numerous boards and committees, including the Advisory Board of the Research Project on Sexual Harassment of Girls with Disabilities (1994 to the present); the advisory board of Project LEEDS, a national leadership training program for post-secondary students with disabilities (1994 to the present); the board of directors of the Westside Center for Independent Living in Los Angeles (1986–1987); and as a project consultant to the Assault Prevention Project for Women with Disabilities at the Los Angeles Commission on Assaults Against Women (1986–1987). Among her many published writings are chapters in *Feminist Parenting* (D. Taylor, ed., 1994) and *Reframing Women's Health* (A. J. Dan,

ed., 1994), as well as regular columns in *Mainstream* magazine and the disability rights newspaper *One Step Ahead.*

Gill, who uses a motorized wheelchair for mobility and a nighttime ventilator, has been particularly outspoken about the danger to people with disabilities of the right-to-die movement. In 1996, she testified before Congress with disability rights activist Diane Coleman, stressing that, "as long as people with disabilities are disenfranchised and treated as unwelcome and costly burdens on society, assisted suicide is forced 'choice.'" In 1996, Gill, Coleman, and others founded Not Dead Yet, a grassroots organization opposing assisted suicide and the "right to die."

Gill's professional positions have included director of Rehabilitation Psychology at Glendale Adventist Medical Center, acting director of the Program on Disability and Society at the University of Southern California, and commissioner on Mental Health for the Los Angeles County Commission on Disabilities. She is currently an adjunct professor of physical medicine and rehabilitation at Northwestern University Medical School in Chicago and research chair of the Health Resource Center for Women with Disabilities at the Rehabilitation Institute of Chicago.

See also Chicago Center for Disability Research; Euthanasia and Assisted Suicide; Rape/Sexual and Domestic Violence; Women with Disabilities.

Glen Ridge Case

On 1 March 1989, a 17-year-old woman described in press accounts as "mildly retarded" was raped in a basement recreation room in suburban Glen Ridge, New Jersey. At one point, there were 13 to 14 young men in the room with her, participating in or watching the assaults. All of the youths were known to the victim.

The Glen Ridge rape, and the trial that followed, raised concerns about the vulnerability of people with disabilities to sexual assault and exploitation. It highlighted what some see as the laxity of the authorities toward those who assault people with disabilities. People with cognitive disabilities were also concerned that the case would lead to calls for limits to their independence, in the name of protecting them.

It took four years for the Glen Ridge case to come to trial. The defense argued that the victim had provoked and enjoyed the assault, describing her as a "Lolita" who "craved euphoria because her brain functioned that way." Advocates feared that stereotypes about the cognitively disabled—specifically, that they are "oversexed"—would be reinforced by such an argument. The prosecution argued, in part, that because of her disability the young woman was incapable of giving informed consent, despite the fact that she had been in apparently consensual sexual relationships prior to the rape. Again, disability advocates were concerned this argument would reinforce popular misconceptions of the disabled as being childlike and sexless.

Finally, for many people, Glen Ridge was a reminder of the depth of hatred faced by people with disabilities, particularly those labeled mentally retarded. It was explained at the trial that the defendants had for years publicly taunted and abused the victim, with tacit approval from the community. Barbara Faye Waxman, a writer on issues of disability, sexuality, and violence against people with disabilities, labeled what happened at Glen Ridge "a hate crime."

One of the points repeatedly made by the mainstream press was the apparent "acquiescence" of the victim, who agreed to accompany the youths to the basement, and who, at the trial, seemed eager to please both the defense and prosecution attorneys. Many seemed to believe that this acquiescence was an inevitable consequence of being mentally disabled. In fact, according to researchers such as Dick Sobsey at the University of Alberta Abuse and Disability Project, people with cognitive disabilities are often trained to be compliant, so they can be more easily managed by caretakers or institutional staff. This training can then render them more vulnerable to sexual abuse and rape.

In March 1993, three of the assailants were convicted of sexual assault and conspiracy; a fourth was convicted of conspiracy. In May 1997, a New Jersey state appeals court overturned a part of the convictions of three of the defendants, ruling that there was insufficient evidence that the victim had been coerced. It let stand their convictions for having sex with "a mentally defective person."

See also Hate Crimes against People with Disabilities; Media Images of People with Disabilities; Rape/Sexual and Domestic Violence.

Reference Sobsey, Dick, *Violence and Abuse in the Lives of People with Disabilities* (1994).

Gold, Stephen F. (b. 1942)

Stephen F. Gold is a leading "movement lawyer"—an attorney who specializes in disability rights law. Born on 20 September 1942, he received a B.A. in political science from La Salle College in Philadelphia in 1964 and his J.D. from the University of Pennsylvania in Philadelphia in 1971. He has litigated or participated in such nationally significant disability rights cases as *Helen L. v. Snider* (1995) and *ADAPT v. Skinner* (1989), as well as in numerous cases of local and regional importance. He has trained disability rights groups in San Francisco, Nashville, and Washington, D.C., and he has taught at Duke University in Durham, North Carolina, the University of Pennsylvania Law School in Philadelphia, and Temple University School of Law in Philadelphia.

See also American Disabled for Accessible Public Transit v. Skinner (ADAPT v. Skinner). Personal Assistance Services.

Golden, Marilyn (b. 1954)

Marilyn Golden is a senior policy analyst at the Disability Rights Education and Defense Fund (DREDF) in Berkeley, California. Born on 22 March 1954 in San Antonio, Texas, she was a key organizer and advocate in passage of the Americans with Disabilities Act of 1990 (ADA). Golden set up a nationwide system of 25

ADA regional contact persons to organize grassroots disability rights groups in their regions. The same strategy was employed after passage, when the network turned its attention to ADA enforcement.

Golden has a B.A. in sociology from Brandeis University in Waltham, Massachusetts. She was the social action director of the Coalition for Barrier Free Living in Houston, Texas, in 1977 and a founder of the Coalition of Texans with Disabilities in 1978. That same year, she moved to California and became a consultant at the Center for Independent Living in Berkeley, joining DREDF in 1988.

In 1987, Golden was the principal organizer of the American Disabled for Accessible Public Transit (ADAPT) demonstrations in San Francisco. These demonstrations were notable in that they marked one of the first times that the mainstream press reported on transportation access as a civil rights issue.

Golden specializes in the areas of public accommodations, architectural accessibility, transportation, and employment. She was appointed by President Clinton to the Architectural and Transportation Barriers Compliance Board in 1994.

See also Disability Rights Education and Defense Fund.

Golfus, Billy (b. 1944)

Billy Golfus is a writer and filmmaker, as well as a co-producer of *When Billy Broke His Head . . . and Other Tales of Wonder* (1995), a film about disability and the disability rights movement. He was born on 10 August 1944 in Minneapolis, Minnesota. After receiving his B.A. in the humanities and journalism from the University of Minnesota in 1971, he became a television and radio journalist in Minneapolis. His work won the Corporation for Public Broadcasting Excellence in Radio Award (in 1981) and the Northwest Broadcast News Association Award (in 1984), among others.

After he was brain-injured in a motorcycle accident, Golfus discovered that, de-spite these credentials, none of his former employers were interested in his new work. He started writing for the disability press and became known for his acerbic wit and his insight into the experience of disability oppression. Among his most influential articles are "Disconfirmation" (1989) and "The Do Gooder" (1990), both in *The Disability Rag & Resource*, while his "Sex and the Single Gimp" (1994) was among the more controversial articles printed in the *Mouth: The Voice of Disability Rights*.

When Billy Broke His Head was first nationally broadcast on PBS on 23 May 1995 and has since been shown at numerous film festivals and disability cultural events. It won the 1996 Columbia University Award for Excellence in Broadcast Journalism, First Place in the National Educational Media Competition, Best Documentary at the Atlanta Film and Video Festival, and other awards. It was nominated for an Emmy in 1996. Golfus did not receive the award, but he was named ABC's Person of the Week.

See also Disconfirmation.

Reference Corbet, Barry, "Billy Golfus' Righteous Surprise," *New Mobility* (January/February 1995).

Grandin, Temple (b. 1947)

Temple Grandin is the author of *Thinking in Pictures and Other Reports from My Life with Autism* (1995) and the principal subject of Oliver Sacks's *An Anthropologist on Mars* (1995).

Born on 29 August 1947 in Boston, Grandin describes the difficulties of growing up different and the realization that her mode of thinking was fundamentally dissimilar from that of people around her. She believes it is this difference, which she characterizes as "thinking in pictures," that leads to the behavior of people with autism that others see as bizarre. Grandin discovered that she felt more comfortable with animals than with people, because they seemed more closely to approximate her way of thinking and feeling. It was while watching the calming effect of squeeze chutes (narrow corridors between holding pens) on cattle that she came up with the idea for her "squeeze machine," now recognized as having a therapeutic effect for people with autism.

Grandin earned her B.A. in psychology from Franklin Pierce College in Rindge, New Hampshire, in 1970, her M.S. in animal science from Arizona State University in Tempe 1975, and her doctorate in animal science from the University of Illinois in 1989. She lectures on livestock handling and is the editor of, and the author of four chapters in, *Livestock Handling and Transport* (1993). She has also written dozens of articles in scientific journals and popular magazines on animal behavior. Grandin lectures on autism and has appeared on ABC's *20/20* and the Discovery Channel's *Series on the Brain*. She was also profiled on the PBS series *People in Motion*.

Grandin is an assistant professor at the Department of Animal Sciences at Colorado State University in Fort Collins.

See also Autism Society of America.

Reference Grandin, Temple, *Thinking in Pictures and Other Reports from My Life with Autism* (1995).

Gray, David B. (b. 1944)

David B. Gray has developed federal initiatives to research access to housing and electronic equipment, communications links, health insurance, and other areas of importance to people with disabilities. He was the first person with a physical disability to reach a position where he could direct and initiate federal rehabilitation research programs. Previously, such research had often been ableist in its assumptions and largely irrelevant to the day-to-day lives of people with disabilities. As a health scientist administrator at the National Institutes of Health (NIH) in 1982, he developed the first national research program in the area of learning disabilities.

Gray was born on 7 February 1944 in Grand Rapids, Michigan. He has a B.A. in psychology from Lawrence University in Appleton, Wisconsin, and he received his doctorate in psychology and genetics from the University of Minnesota at Minneapolis in 1974. From 1974 to 1977, he was the supervisor of behavior modification at the Mental Retardation Institute in Valhalla, New York, then director of Institute Programs for the Mentally Retarded at the Rochester State Hospital in Minnesota, where he worked to integrate institution residents into the community. Gray was spinal cord injured in July 1977, becoming quadriplegic after falling from the roof of his house. Mary Jane Owen, in her 1986 profile of Gray for *Mainstream* magazine, describes how the experience taught him "about rehabilitation from the other side of the treatment mirror." This new perspective made him "question the superior stance which is sometimes applied to abstract knowledge about what disability is really like."

Gray left clinical work to pursue a career in rehabilitation research. From 1981 to 1986, he was a health scientist administrator at the National Institute on Child Health and Development at the NIH. The first person with a disability to become the director of the National Institute on Disability and Rehabilitation Research (NIDRR) at the U.S. Department of Education (1986–1987), he tightened its review process and initiated research projects in traumatic brain injury, employment of disabled persons, and computer-based communications systems. He returned to the NIH in 1987. From 1991 through 1995, he was the acting deputy director and then deputy director of the National Center for Medical Rehabilitation Research, again at the Institute for Child Health and Human Development at the NIH. In 1995, Gray became a professor of health sciences and the associate director for research at the Program in Occupational Therapy at the Washington University School of Medicine in St. Louis, Missouri.

Gray publishes and lectures extensively. Among his recent publications are *Using, Designing and Assessing Assistive Technology* (editor, with L. A. Quantrano and M. L. Lieberman, 1997) and *Reproductive Issues for Persons with Physical Disabilities* (editor, with F. Haseltine and S. Cole, 1993).

Reference Owen, Mary Jane, "David Gray, Ph.D.: Disability Leadership at the Top," *Mainstream* (May 1986).

Griss, Robert (b. 1945)

Robert Griss is the nation's foremost expert on health care finance as it relates to people with disabilities. He was born on 29 May 1945 and graduated from Princeton University with a B.A. in Public and International Affairs in 1967 and from the University of Wisconsin with a master's in sociology in 1969. He worked for the Wisconsin Department of Health and Human Services from 1979 to 1986 and with the Wisconsin Coalition for Advocacy in 1981. From 1986 to 1990, he worked with a variety of organizations, including the Center for the Study of Social Policy, the National Institute on Disability and Rehabilitation Research, and the World Institute on Disability, where he analyzed the problems of financing access to adequate and affordable health care for persons with disabilities or chronic illness and authored a series of health policy bulletins called *Access to Health Care*. From 1990 to 1993, he was the senior health policy researcher for United Cerebral Palsy Associations in Washington, D.C., providing information and leadership to the national disability community during the debate on President Clinton's proposed health care finance reform legislation. During this time, Griss also co-chaired the Health Task Force of the Consortium for Citizens with Disabilities and provided a disability rights perspective on various health care issues for the Robert Wood Johnson Foundation (a role he still plays) and the National Council on Disability.

Griss has been an outspoken critic of efforts to "ration" health care, such as Oregon's 1991–1992 proposal for "reforming" its Medicaid system. In 1994, he founded the Center on Disability and Health, a Washington, D.C., think tank and advocacy organization. "My goal," Griss writes, "is to build support for publicly accountable health care by linking together civil rights, public health, and health care as a public utility."

See also Consortium for Citizens with Disabilities; Health Care Access.

Grove City College v. Bell
See Civil Rights Restoration Act of 1987.

Halderman v. Pennhurst State School & Hospital 446 F. Supp. 1295 (1978)

Commonly known as the Pennhurst decision, *Halderman v. Pennhurst State School & Hospital* was a landmark case on the rights of people with disabilities to receive community services. Federal District Judge Raymond J. Broderick ruled that institutionalization was inherently damaging to people with developmental disabilities, and he ordered that Pennhurst be closed. Although this decision was scaled back by subsequent proceedings, it set a crucial precedent and was an important victory for advocates of deinstitutionalization.

The case began when the mother of Terri Lee Halderman, a cognitively disabled resident of Pennhurst, brought suit in May 1974 against the facility's administration and officials of Pennsylvania. Halderman was joined in her suit by the parents of seven other Pennhurst residents, as well as the Parents and Family Association of Pennhurst, representing another 200 parents. In November 1974, the United States Justice Department joined the suit on the side of the plaintiffs. Additional residents, families, and the Pennsylvania Association for Retarded Citizens (PARC) joined in June 1975.

Pennhurst had been founded in 1908 as part of the national movement to identify and incarcerate people with developmental disabilities. The Pennsylvania legislature in 1913 enacted a law devoting the institution "to the segregation . . . of epileptic, idiotic, imbecile or feeble-minded persons." Robert Smilovitz's *A Brief History of Pennhurst 1908–1926* (1974) notes how critics early on complained of the institution's "few staff, crowded buildings, inadequate facilities...[and] inappropriate placements." If anything, these problems grew worse over time. The lawsuit exposed the same hellish conditions that existed in other state institutions such as Willowbrook in Staten Island, New York, and Partlow in Tuscaloosa, Alabama. In January 1976, PARC, represented by Thomas K. Gilhool and Frank Laski, asked that the court shut down the institution entirely and require the state to provide community services for its residents.

On 23 December 1977, Broderick ruled that conditions at Pennhurst violated residents' rights under Section 504 of the Rehabilitation Act of 1973, Pennsylvania law, Title XIX of the Social Security Act prohibiting unnecessary institutionalization, and most especially the Equal Protection Clause of the Fourteenth Amendment. The court, in its "Factual Findings," described "urine and excrement on the ward floors. Infectious diseases are common. . . . Serious injuries inflicted by staff members, including sexual assaults, have occurred. Physical restraints . . . have caused injuries and at least one death. . . . " Testimony revealed, for example, that one female resident, during the month of August 1976, had been in physical restraints for a total of 720 hours. Broderick held that "the mentally retarded have a federal statutory right to nondiscriminatory habilitation . . . and federal constitutional rights . . . to freedom from harm, and adequate treatment by the least restrictive means." On 17 March 1978, he ruled that adequate treatment could not be provided in an institution, and he ordered that Pennhurst "be closed and suitable community living arrangements and necessary support services provided for all Pennhurst residents," numbering at that time some 1,230 people.

In December 1979, the U.S. Court of Appeals for the Third Circuit affirmed most of this ruling, but it based its decision on entirely new grounds. While it came to no conclusion about its residents' constitutional rights, it held that conditions at Pennhurst, and the failure to provide community services, violated the federal Developmentally Disabled Assistance and Bill of Rights Act of 1975. It also removed the requirement that the institution be closed, but its ruling, for all intents and purposes, had the same effect. This decision was also appealed, and the case was argued before the U.S. Supreme Court on 8 December 1980.

On 20 April 1981, the Court ruled that the Developmentally Disabled Bill of Rights Act "did not create in favor of the mentally retarded any substantive [that is, enforceable] rights to 'appropriate treatment' in the 'least restrictive' environment." Since the appeals court had been silent on the other bases of Broderick's decision, the Supreme Court too took no position. Instead, it reversed the appeals court ruling and remanded the case back for further deliberation. The appeals court then reaffirmed its original decision but this time cited Pennsylvania state law as its justification. The Supreme Court, on 23 January 1984, again reversed the appeals court ruling. In this second decision, the Court ruled that the Eleventh Amendment "prohibited federal district court from ordering state officials to conform their conduct to state law with respect to conditions of confinement" at Pennhurst.

The case returned once more to the court of appeals, which finally began to consider the other grounds for Broderick's original decision. State officials, realizing that a third appeals court decision would also go against them, agreed to a settlement on 13 July 1984, under which Pennhurst would be closed by 1 July 1986 and its residents provided with community services. This goal was met not only for Pennhurst residents but also for the 925 persons on the institution's waiting list.

The Pennhurst case served as a model and impetus for similar deinstitutionalization litigation across the country. Since *Pennhurst*, every major residential institution has seen its population drastically reduced; many have closed entirely, with the

concommitant provision of community services.

See also The Arc; Developmentally Disabled Assistance and Bill of Rights Act of 1975; Deinstitutionalization; Gilhool, Thomas K.; Willowbrook State School.

Reference Mnookin, Robert H., *In the Interest of Children: Advocacy, Law Reform, and Public Policy* (1985).

Hamilton, Marilyn
See Wheelchairs.

Handicapped Children's Protection Act of 1986
See Smith v. Robinson.

Handicapped Organized Women, Inc. (HOW)

Handicapped Organized Women Inc. (HOW) was founded in 1979 by Deborah Crouch McKeithan in Charlotte, North Carolina, as a peer support group for disabled women. By 1988, there were more than 120 chapters in 36 states. Among the issues HOW addressed were work disincentives for women receiving Social Security Disability Insurance and/or Supplemental Security Income benefits, access to obstetric and gynecological care, and sexism within the disability rights movement. "When I became involved nationally," McKeithan told an interviewer in 1988, "my biggest disappointment was that my battle was not my disability. It was my womanhood."

Most of HOW's work was done on a local level, for example, efforts by the Minnesota chapter in the campaign to free Sharon Kowalski, a disabled lesbian kept in a nursing home against her will for eight years because of her disability and sexual orientation. In 1988, McKeithan changed the focus of the national office, renaming it Learning How, Inc., which now serves as an employment agency for people with disabilities—women and men—in the Charlotte area. Some local HOW chapters continue to be active, though they no longer are part of any formal, national network.

See also Kowalski, Sharon and Karen Thompson; Women with Disabilities.

References Brown, Dale, "Leadership: Some Views and Perspectives from the Top," *Mainstream* (May 1988); Traustadottir, Rannveig, *Women with Disabilities: Issues, Resources, Connections* (1990).

Hate Crimes against People with Disabilities

In 1994, the New York City Police Department became the first government agency in the United States to track the incidence of hate crimes against people with disabilities. Though the concept is new to law enforcement and government officials, disability rights activists such as Barbara Faye Waxman have for years documented attacks on people with disabilities, which can best be labeled as hate crimes. Among these crimes are the vandalizing and firebombing of community-based group homes of developmentally disabled adults, attacks by groups of adolescents on people with mental disabilities, and vandalizing or theft of wheelchair lift–equipped vans. Waxman notes these crimes are often treated by police authorities as "isolated incidents" or "pranks gone wrong."

See also Rape/Sexual and Domestic Violence; Waxman, Barbara Faye.

References Sobsey, Dick, *Violence and Abuse in the Lives of People with Disabilities* (1994); Waxman, Barbara Faye, "Hatred: The Unacknowledged Dimension in Violence Against Disabled People," *Journal of Sexuality and Disability* (October/November 1991).

Health Care Access

It is a paradox of the American medical system that people with disabilities and chronic illness are among those least likely to have health insurance, and most likely to have difficulty receiving the care they need. Despite the fact that the United States spends more money per capita on health care than any other nation on earth, more than 40 million Americans are uninsured or under-insured, most because they are unable to afford health insurance premiums.

A number of factors contribute to the inaccessibility of health care: pre-existing conditions, inadequate coverage, employment-based coverage, managed care, lifetime caps and annual limits, rationing, and expense.

Pre-Existing Conditions. The very disability or chronic illness for which some people need care has been used by health insurers as a reason to deny them coverage. Even when coverage is not entirely denied, most policies will not cover a previously existing condition for anywhere from six months to a year. The Health Insurance Portability and Accountability Act of 1996, taking effect in July 1997, was an attempt to address part of this problem. It prohibits insurers from imposing pre-existing conditions clauses of more than a year on individuals *already insured* who lose or change their jobs.

Inadequate Coverage. Health insurance policies often do not cover essential services, or they have exorbitant deductibles. Health finance analyst Sara D. Watson cites the example of a woman with multiple sclerosis forced to spend $8,000 a year on uncovered health care related expenses, on an annual income of $20,000. Often, health insurance companies will categorically refuse to pay for such essential items as power wheelchairs—which can run from $8,000 to $12,000—respirators, catheter supplies, and certain medications.

Employment-Based Insurance. Most people who have private health insurance receive their coverage through their job or through the job of a family member. People with disabilities have the highest unemployment rate of any minority group in the United States, and are thus disproportionately represented among the under-insured. Those in poverty, however, are generally covered by Medicaid and Medicare, mitigating to some extent the impact of unemployment.

Managed Care. Health maintenance organizations (HMOs), preferred provider organizations (PPOs), and other forms of managed care employ primary caregivers to minimize patient use of more expensive specialists. Such "gatekeepers" often have little experience treating people with disabilities or chronic illness and may be a barrier to needed care. HMOs and PPOs require pre-authorization for certain treatments, prescriptions, or supplies, and they often delay or deny payment for those not considered "medically necessary." If an appropriate specialist is not in the managed care network, there may be difficulty getting a referral from the managed care plan to pay for the appropriate care.

Lifetime Caps and Annual Limits. According to United Cerebral Palsy Associations, Inc., 79 percent of employer-sponsored plans in 1989 had lifetime maximums, meaning they would not spend more than a set amount on any one patient no matter what the need. These lifetime caps range from $1 million to as low as $100,000. By way of contrast, a spinal cord injury might well require more than $1 million in treatment over the course of an individual's lifetime. Most plans also had annual limits, for example, 60 days per year in a rehabilitation program, $500 for durable medical equipment, $500 for mental health counseling, etc. Given the exorbitant expense of health care, these caps often represent only a small fraction of the care that might actually be medically necessary for an individual.

Rationing. Proposals to ration health care necessarily discriminate against people with disabilities or chronic illness. An example of rationing would be the Medicaid "reform" proposed by the state of Oregon in 1991/1992. Under the Oregon plan, medical procedures were listed top to bottom according to their "medical effectiveness" and cost. The proposed cut-off point, below which the state would deny payment for particular procedures, fluctuated each year depending on budget priorities, so that infants born with spina bifida, for example, might in some years be denied the surgery they needed to live and be independent. "Oregon claims that its prioritization process was designed to eliminate ineffective medical treatments," health care reform advocate Robert Griss wrote in *Word from Washington* (1992),

"but the prioritization list actually represents subjective judgements about how various treatments are expected to affect the 'quality of life' of a person with a particular illness or disability." Among the methods Oregon used to determine which conditions were not worth treating was a telephone survey of 1,001 Oregonians, who were asked to rate various illnesses and conditions on a scale from zero ("as bad as death") to 100 ("good health"). Not surprisingly, average Oregonians, reflecting society's ableism, rated such conditions as spina bifida and quadriplegia "as bad as death." The Bush administration rejected the Oregon Medicaid waiver on the grounds that it violated the Americans with Disabilities Act of 1990 (ADA), citing the subjective "quality of life" criteria. The Clinton administration approved the waiver in 1993, after changes were made to avoid violating the ADA.

Expense. The greatest single barrier to health care insurance is its excessive cost. People on fixed or low incomes and many self-employed people or small business owners simply cannot afford to purchase health insurance. Again, since people with disabilities are disproportionately poor or on fixed incomes, they are disproportionately represented among the uninsured.

Disability advocates such as Griss believe that only a radical restructuring of the health care financing system, and not various "reforms" around the edges, will ensure that people with disabilities or chronic illness have access to the care they need. Indeed, some cost-saving "reforms," such as medical savings accounts, undermine the interests of people with disabilities by encouraging healthy, nondisabled people to self-insure with a high deductible, thus driving up the per capita insurance costs of low-deductible insurance for everyone else. Griss has called on the disability rights movement "as the most logical consumer group" to advocate for comprehensive changes in the health care system, defining access to health care as a civil rights issue.

See also Griss, Robert.

References Byron, Peg, "The Health Insurance Conspiracy," *Ms.* (September/October 1992); Consortium for Citizens with Disabilities Health Task Force, "Principles for Health Care Reform from a Disability Perspective" (1992); Griss, Robert, "UCPA's Comments to EEOC on Health Insurance," *Word from Washington* (March/April 1991); ———, "Health Insurance at Risk," *Word from Washington* (May/June 1991); ———, "HHS Rejects Oregon Medicaid Rationing Plan: Violates ADA," *Word from Washington* (August/September 1992); Pelka, Fred, "Trauma Time: Disability Issues Must Be a Litmus Test for Evaluating the Validity of Any Proposal for Health Care Reform," *Mainstream* (March 1993); Skelley, Richard V., *Insuring Health Care for People with Disabilities* (1990); Watson, Sara D., "Alliance at Risk: The Disability Movement and Health Care Reform," *American Prospect* (1993).

Hearing Aid Compatability Act of 1988
See Telecommunications for the Disabled Act of 1982.

Hearne, Paul G. (b. 1949)
Paul G. Hearne's career as a disability rights advocate began when he was president of the student government at Hofstra University in Hempstead, New York, in 1971, working to make that school's dormitories accessible. As director of the National Council on Disability from July 1988 to August 1989, he played a pivotal role in the drafting and passage of the Americans with Disabilities Act of 1990 (ADA).

Hearne was born on 27 November 1949. He earned a B.A. in political science from Hofstra in 1971 and a J.D. from the Hofstra Law School in 1974. He worked as an attorney for poor people through the Reginald Heber Smith Community Lawyer Fellowship (affiliated with Howard University in Washington, D.C.) from 1974 to 1977, providing legal council to individuals below the poverty line in New York City. From 1976 to 1979, he was executive director of the Handicapped Persons Legal Support Unit, an organization he founded in New York City in 1976. From 1979 to 1989, he was the executive director of Just One Break, Inc., the job placement agency founded in 1947 by Howard Rusk and Henry Viscardi, Jr.

In 1980, Hearne wrote *Legal Advocacy for the Disabled*, the first national training manual for attorneys working in disability rights, published by the Legal Services Corporation in Washington, D.C. He is the author of numerous articles and book chapters on disability rights, including a chapter on employment rights of people with disabilities for the American Civil Liberties Union's *Legal Rights of the Physically Handicapped* (1980). An advisor on disability issues to corporate America, he served, for example, as a member and past chair of the AT&T Consumer Advisory Group and the I.B.M. Diversity Task Force. Since 1989, Hearne has been president of the Dole Foundation on Employment of People with Disabilities, one of the first persons with a disability to direct a large, national foundation. Born with osteogenesis imperfecta, an inherited, connective tissue disorder, Hearne was a board member of the Osteogenesis Imperfecta Foundation, Inc., from 1991 to 1994.

See also Americans with Disabilities Act of 1990; National Council on Disability.

Helen L., Beverly D., Florence H., Ilene F., Idell S., and American Disabled for Attendant Programs Today (ADAPT) v. Karen F. Snider 46 F. 3rd 325 (1995)
See Personal Assistance Services

Hemophiliac Holocaust
See Committee of Ten Thousand; HIV/AIDS and Disability.

Hershey, Laura (b. 1962)
Laura Hershey is an activist, public speaker, poet, and writer. She has written on disability issues for *Ms.* magazine, *The Progressive*, *Women and Therapy*, and other publications, and she writes a monthly column for *The Denver Post*. She is a contributing editor to *One Step Ahead*.

Hershey was born on 11 August 1962 in Denver, Colorado. As a teenager, she was a poster child for the Muscular Dystrophy

Laura Hershey and friend Laurilene Gery in Alaska, 1994.

Association (MDA), but as an adult she has organized demonstrations against MDA's Jerry Lewis Telethon. She graduated from Colorado College in Colorado Springs with a B.A. in history in 1983 and received a Thomas Watson Fellowship in 1984 to study the disability rights movement in Great Britain. Hershey was a co-founder in 1985 of the Denver chapter of Handicapped Organized Women and the Domestic Violence Initiative for Women with Disabilities. She was director of the Denver Commission for People with Disabilities from 1989 to 1990. Since 1990, she has been the owner and manager of Access*Plus* Consulting, providing advice to businesses, agencies, and persons seeking to enhance the independence and empowerment of people with disabilities.

See also Handicapped Organized Women; *One Step Ahead*; Telethons.

Hessler, John (1940–1993)

John Hessler was co-founder and first director of the Physically Disabled Students' Program at the University of California at Berkeley. He was also a co-founder of the Center for Independent Living, a member of the Rolling Quads, and an early advocate for independent living.

Hessler was born on 11 December 1940 in St. Louis, Missouri. His family moved first to Alameda and then to Antioch, California. Hessler became quadriplegic after a swimming accident in May 1957. He spent the next six years at the Contra Costa County Hospital in Martinez, California, where he was told to expect a lifetime in the hospital or in a nursing home. During his hospitalization, he earned first his high school diploma, and then he attended Diablo Valley College in Pleasant Hill, California, for four years, majoring in French and German. "I didn't always think I would succeed, especially after living in a county hospital for six years," he told reporter Lynn Kidder in 1982. "After a while, you think that it's going to be your life." Patients were treated like children, and punishment for breaking the rules was

loss of their wheelchairs. Amazingly, even on a unit for people with severe disabilities, much of the facility was inaccessible. Hessler began his advocacy in the hospital, organizing patients to argue for accessible bathrooms so they could roll into toilet stalls and showers without assistance.

Hessler decided to leave the hospital in 1963. Although his grades were excellent, his first 20 college and university applications were rejected. He finally won acceptance to the German studies program at the University of California at Berkeley, becoming, after Ed Roberts, the school's second severely disabled student. "We were called 'The Experiment.' Ed and I had to prove you could make it academically. Once we'd done that, it really opened the door to other people." In 1966, they were joined by several other disabled students, and, by 1969, there were more than a dozen living and studying on campus. Together they organized the advocacy group Rolling Quads, and then, in July 1970, the Physically Disabled Students' Program, with Hessler as its first director. In the meantime, Hessler finished his master's degree in French. By the time the program held its twentieth anniversary reunion, 130 severely disabled students had lived and studied on campus. In 1972, Hessler, together with Ed Roberts and Phil Draper, founded the Center for Independent Living in Berkeley.

Joseph Shapiro, in *No Pity* (1993), describes Hessler as a "lanky six-foot-seven-inch quadriplegic" who would astonish his fellow students by driving his own specially modified van. In 1975, Hessler went with Roberts to Sacramento to be his assistant, after Governor Jerry Brown appointed Roberts director of the California Department of Rehabilitation. While there, the two oversaw the creation of independent living centers all across California, sparking the independent living movement nationwide. In 1978, Hessler became chief of the state Department of Health's Policy and Operations division, supervising and funding county health programs. He later took a position at the California Department of

Health Services, becoming chief of expanded access to primary care programs. Reflecting on the progress of the disability rights movement he did so much to advance, Hessler told an interviewer in 1982, "We have gone from the equivalent of the Dark Ages or worse to almost being the equals of other people in American society." Hessler died in Sacramento on 10 May 1993.

See also Center for Independent Living, Inc.; Independent Living, Independent Living Movement; Roberts, Edward V.

References Kidder, Lynn, "They Fought Disabilities and Won," *Antioch Daily Ledger* (2 May 1982); Shapiro, Joseph, *No Pity: People with Disabilities Forging a New Civil Rights Movement* (1993).

Heumann, Judith E. (b. 1947)

Judith E. Heumann is a pioneer in the independent living movement and an internationally known advocate for disability rights.

"I'm part of a survivor family," Heumann once told an interviewer. "We're Jewish and lost a number of relatives in the Holocaust. When my parents immigrated to the United States, they thought if you followed the American dream you could get whatever you wanted. But I learned very early that my disability would prevent me from taking my rightful place in society."

Judith E. Heumann was born on 18 December 1947. Disabled by polio at 18 months, Heumann was kept out of her neighborhood public elementary school in Brooklyn, New York, because the principal considered her wheelchair "a fire hazard." After more than three years of home instruction she was bused to a special "health conservation" class, where she and other disabled children were taught in the school basement. Discrimination followed her to college. Admitted to Long Island University, Heumann had to take her case all the way to the university president before she was allowed to live on campus. While there, Heumann and other students fought for the establishment of a Disabled Students' Program at the university. Heumann graduated with a B.A. in speech

and theater in 1969. After passing her licensure test for a teaching certificate, she was denied employment with the New York City Public Schools because of her inability to walk (this time it was the Board of Education that deemed her a fire hazard). In 1970, she won one of the earliest, if not the first, disability-based employment discrimination lawsuits in the nation, and she took a job as the first wheelchair-using teacher in the history of the New York City Public Schools.

That same year, Heumann founded Disabled In Action (DIA), a cross-disability group committed to political agitation. Among its many actions, DIA organized demonstrations after President Richard M. Nixon vetoed the Rehabilitation Act of 1972 and conducted sit-ins at his reelection campaign headquarters in New York City. The group's philosophy, Heumann later said, was that "we needed to be looking not just at isolated issues, but at changing society." The group's purpose, according to Heumann, was "to address our problems in a forthright, political way, to show that we were not helpless and disempowered."

Heumann moved to Berkeley, California, in 1973, at the behest of Ed Roberts, to become a member of the Center for Independent Living's board of directors. During this time, she also earned her master's degree in public health administration and planning from the University of California. Beginning in 1974, she was a legislative assistant to Sen. Harrison Williams (D-NJ), chair of the Senate Labor and Public Welfare Committee. In this position she worked on the Education for All Handicapped Children Act of 1975 and assisted in drafting the original regulations promulgated under Section 504 of the Rehabilitation Act of 1973. Heumann was also a co-founder of the American Coalition of Citizens with Disabilities and a member of its board.

From 1975 to 1982, Heumann was the deputy director of the Center for Independent Living in Berkeley. While there, she helped to draft both the California and then the federal legislation that became the basis for the founding of independent living centers nationwide. Heumann was a principal organizer of the occupation of federal offices in San Francisco in 1977 to protest the refusal of the Carter administration to issue regulations for Section 504 of the Rehabilitation Act. This action electrified the disability community all across the country. At the end of the decade, *Ms.* magazine picked her as one of the 80 women to watch for in the 1980s. Two years later, she was appointed by Governor Jerry Brown to be special assistant of community affairs to the director of the California Department of Rehabilitation.

In 1983, Heumann, along with Ed Roberts and Joan Leon, founded the World Institute on Disability (WID), serving as WID's vice president and director of the Research and Training Center on Policy in Independent Living. In 1990 she was the first winner of the Prince Charitable Trusts' Henry B. Betts Award, presented to individuals who have improved the quality of life for people with disabilities.

Heumann has served on a wide variety of boards, including the National Council on Independent Living, the U.S. Council on International Rehabilitation, Disabled Peoples' International, and the Over-60s Health Center Project. In 1993, she was appointed by President Clinton to her current position as the assistant secretary for Special Education and Rehabilitative Services at the U.S. Department of Education, responsible for ensuring access to education and rehabilitation for all Americans with disabilities. In 1994, she served a one-year term as chair of the Architectural and Transportation Barriers Compliance Board.

See also Center for Independent Living in Berkeley; Disabled in Action; Education for All Handicapped Children Act of 1975; HEW Demonstrations; Independent Living, Independent Living Movement; Section 504 of the Rehabilitation Act of 1973; World Institute on Disability.

References Levy, Chava Willeg, *A People's History of the Independent Living Movement* (1988); Maddox, Sam, *Spinal Network: The Total Resource for the Wheelchair Community* (1987).

HEW Demonstrations

On 5 April 1977, disability rights activists in ten cities staged sit-ins and demonstrations at the offices of the federal department of Health, Education, and Welfare (HEW). Their purpose was to force the Carter administration, represented by HEW secretary Joseph Califano, to issue regulations implementing Section 504 of the Rehabilitation Act of 1973. Demonstrators in Washington, D.C., and other cities were able to maintain their sit-ins for a day or more, while those in San Francisco occupied federal offices for almost a month. The sit-ins attracted national attention and forged a new sense of solidarity and pride in the disability rights community.

Section 504 of the Rehabilitation Act mandated that no program receiving funds from the federal government could deny access, services, or employment to someone solely on the basis of their disability. This was the most sweeping disability rights measure up to that time, since tens of thousands of public and private institutions receive federal funds. Without regulations and some sort of enforcement mechanism, however, Section 504 would remain little more than a fine sentiment. Frank Bowe wrote in *Changing the Rules* (1986), "that [Section 504] held the key for opportunity for handicapped people in our country. . . . But I knew, too, that there was an unwritten rule in Washington: any provision of law that has not been implemented within three years of its enactment is, for all practical purposes, dead." Time was thus running out for Section 504. "Joseph Califano...was the one person whose signature could transform the lives of tens of millions of disabled Americans."

Action on the regulations at HEW had already been spurred by a lawsuit brought by James L. Cherry and a group in Louisville, Kentucky, called the Action League for Physically Handicapped Adults. In July 1976, the Federal District Court for the District of Columbia ruled that Congress had intended that 504 be enforced, and it ordered that regulations

People cheer at a rally in Lafayette Park, Washington, D.C., as part of the HEW demonstrations of April 1977. In San Francisco, more than 120 protesters occupied the HEW offices for 25 days, the longest occupation of a federal building in U.S. history. The sit-in, and other demonstrations across the country, ended when HEW Secretary Joseph Califano agreed to sign regulations implementing Section 504 of the Rehabilitation Act of 1973, which prohibited programs receiving federal funds from discriminating on the basis of disability.

be issued "with no further unreasonable delays." John Wodatch and Ann Beckman, staff attorneys at the Office for Civil Rights within HEW, drafted a 185-page set of regulations setting out the responsibilities under Section 504 of the recipients of federal funds. These draft regulations had the support of the American Coalition of Citizens with Disabilities (ACCD). David Mathews, secretary of HEW under the Ford administration, however, delayed issuing them, and with the election of Jimmy Carter in 1976, disability rights advocates had to deal with new leadership at HEW.

The ACCD adopted promulgation of the 504 regulations as its number one priority. ACCD representatives met in early 1977 with officials of the Carter administration, urging that they issue the regulations as written. Califano, by his own admission, knew little of disability issues and

nothing about Section 504 until his appointment. Still, disability rights advocates Eunice Fiorito and David Moss had worked on Carter's campaign. Carter himself had specifically mentioned 504 in a speech at Warm Springs, Georgia, noting that it was "fine in theory" but would "mean very little until an administration...stands behind the law." Nevertheless, the first inclination of the newly elected Carter administration was to delay issuing Wodatch and Beckman's regulations.

Negotiations with Califano stalled, so ACCD sent a letter to President Carter on 18 March 1977, threatening that, unless the regulations were issued by 4 April, the "ACCD would mount a massive sit-in demonstration in every HEW office coast to coast." Portions of the letter were reprinted in the media, most notably in Jack Anderson's syndicated column. The

ACCD and the disability rights community were thus committed.

Negotiations failed, and, on 5 April, demonstrations began at HEW offices in Washington, D.C., New York, Boston, Atlanta, San Francisco, Denver, and elsewhere. Among the leaders and supporters of the various actions was a virtual who's who of the disability rights movement of the 1970s: Judy Heumann and Mary Jane Owen in California; attorneys Thomas K. Gilhool, James Raggio, and Frank Laski for Disabled in Action in Philadelphia; Fred Fay, Andrea Schein, and the Massachusetts Coalition of Citizens with Disabilities in Boston; and Fred Schreiber, Terrence J. O'Rourke, and Eunice Fiorito in Washington. In Denver, demonstrators spilled out into the street, blocking rush-hour traffic with their wheelchairs.

The more than 300 Washington demonstrators were denied food, water, life-sustaining medications, and all contact with the outside world. They departed Califano's office after 28 hours. By contrast, demonstrators in San Francisco received support both from state officials and the general community. Ed Roberts, appointed by Governor Jerry Brown as director of California's Department of Rehabilitation, visited the demonstrators at the HEW office on the sixth floor of the United Nations Plaza on several occasions, urging them "to keep up the pressure." The more than 120 demonstrators (the number grew at times to as many as 400) also received support from San Francisco Mayor George Moscone, who brought air mattresses and hoses with showerheads, prompting HEW regional director Jose Maldonado to complain, "We're not running a hotel here." Food for the demonstrators was donated by Safeway, MacDonald's, and local labor unions, and it was prepared and delivered by members of the Black Panther Party. Even HEW employees offered their (surreptitious) support, saying they would warn the demonstrators ahead of time should the decision be made to arrest them. Nevertheless, the most severely disabled demonstrators, those who used catheters and ventilators, were putting their health and even their lives at risk. Said Mary Jane Owen, "It didn't matter if you were mentally retarded, blind, or deaf. Everybody who came out felt: 'We are beautiful, we are powerful, we are strong, we are important.'" Meanwhile, activists in other cities kept up the pressure. In Washington, delegates from around the country met with Califano's staff. A delegation from San Francisco flew to Washington, where they slept in a church basement and were provided food by the International Association of Machinists, which also arranged transportation for wheelchair users in the form of a rented U-Haul delivery truck. A candlelight vigil was held outside Califano's home. Demonstrators followed President Jimmy Carter to church.

On 28 April 1977, Frank Bowe received a call from HEW, telling him that Secretary Califano had scheduled a press conference for that afternoon, when he would announce that he had signed the 504 regulations that morning. Disability activists in San Francisco ended their occupation, and the disability rights community across the country celebrated one of its most significant victories to date. The regulations were published in the *Federal Register* on 4 May 1977.

See also American Coalition of Citizens with Disabilities; Bowe, Frank; Disabled in Action; Fay, Frederick A.; Fiorito, Eunice; Heumann, Judith E.; O'Rourke, Terrence James; Owen, Mary Jane; Rehabilitation Act of 1973; Roberts, Edward V.; Section 504 of the Rehabilitation Act of 1973: Wright, Patricia A.

References Bowe, Frank G., *Changing the Rules* (1986); Scotch, Richard K., *From Good Will to Civil Rights* (1984); Shapiro, Joseph P., *No Pity: People with Disabilities Forging a New Civil Rights Movement* (1993); Treanor, Richard Bryant, *We Overcame: The Story of Civil Rights for Disabled People* (1993).

Hidden Disabilities

Hidden disabilities are those disabilities not apparent to a casual or uninformed observer. Such disabilities can range from head injury to fibromyalgia; multiple chemical sensitivity; chronic fatigue syndrome; and the early stages of multiple sclerosis (MS), lupus, or acquired immune deficiency syndrome (AIDS). These conditions are in contrast to disabilities that are generally apparent to an outside observer, for example, quadriplegia or paraplegia resulting from polio or spinal cord injury. People with hidden disabilities are often derided as impostors, particularly by nondisabled people, as when someone with MS, who fatigues easily but does not use a wheelchair, parks in a space reserved for drivers with disabilities, or when people with learning disabilities request reasonable modifications in academic programs.

HIV/AIDS and Disability

It is a truism of the disability rights movement that everyone is just one accident or infection away from having a disability. For this reason, people with disabilities are said to belong to an "open" minority, meaning that anyone, no matter what their race, ethnicity, gender, religion, or class, can join. The HIV/AIDS (human immunodeficiency virus/acquired immune deficiency syndrome) epidemic is the most recent and notable example of this reality.

People with HIV/AIDS share many of the concerns and problems of people with other disabilities, particularly as treatments for the disease have extended the life expectancy of those who are HIV positive. AIDS has become a chronic condition resembling in some ways multiple sclerosis, muscular dystrophy, or other degenerative, and as yet incurable, disabling diseases. In 1988, the British Columbia Coalition of the Disabled published *Common Barriers: Toward an Understanding of AIDS and Disability*, exploring the commonalties between the two communities. Jim Sands, the study's author, described how "access to employment and housing and the right to financial support, services and treatments are among the day-to-day issues that both groups are confronted with. Human rights issues are also an important area of common interest."

The Supreme Court, in *School Board of Nassau County, Florida v. Arline* (1987),

ruled that Section 504 of the Rehabilitation Act of 1973 covered people with infectious diseases. This precedent was used by advocates to press for civil rights protection for people with HIV/AIDS, who were recognized by the Americans with Disabilities Act of 1990 as being disabled. Disability rights and AIDS activists successfully opposed efforts by some members of Congress to delete portions of this protection during deliberations on the bill.

In some cases, people with disabilities are especially at risk for HIV infection. The devastating impact of AIDS among those with hemophilia and other blood disorders has been called the "Hemophiliac Holocaust," and the disease has killed or infected a majority of the approximately 20,000 people with hemophilia living in United States prior to the epidemic, as well as having infected their spouses, lovers, and children conceived after their parents' exposure. The Deaf community has also been hard hit. According to *Time* magazine reporter David Van Biema, as late as 1994, the lack of American Sign Language interpreters at hospitals and clinics and the paucity of funding for AIDS awareness programs in the deaf community had lead to a situation where "13 years into the epidemic, the average deaf person may—just recently—have learned AIDS exists." AIDS awareness programs among disabled people in general have lagged, because of the prevailing stereotypes that people with disabilities are asexual, and unlikely to use intravenous (IV) drugs.

HIV/AIDS has also had a devastating effect on those people with IV drug dependency. Social stereotypes and prejudice have impeded efforts that might lessen the epidemic's impact, such as needle exchange programs, while funding for drug treatment programs has remained constricted and inadequate.

See also Americans with Disabilities Act of 1990; Committee of Ten Thousand; *School Board of Nassau County, Florida v. Arline.*

References Sands, Jim, *Common Barriers: Toward an Understanding of AIDS and Disability* (1988); Van Biema, David, "AIDS: In One Community, Silence Equals Death," *Time* (4 April 1994).

Hlibok, Greg
See Deaf President Now Campaign.

Hockenberry, John (b. 1956)
John Hockenberry is the winner of two Peabody Awards and one Emmy for journalism for his reporting from the Middle East, Romania, Somalia, and elsewhere. He was born in June 1956, in Dayton, Ohio. A car accident in February 1976 left him paraplegic, and his autobiography, *Moving Violations* (1995), recounts his injury and rehabilitation, his life as a journalist, and his family's response to its disabled members: himself, his grandfather, and his uncle.

Hockenberry offers an insider's critique of media portrayals of disability. "Today the only sure way to get an editor interested in disability is to work Dr. Kevorkian into the lead; otherwise, forget it." Hockenberry, though, is skeptical of the idea of a "disability beat," writing how the "assumption that disability...is some separate category independent of other news, or that disability rights stories, by themselves, reveal anything of the people they claim to be about, are two equal and opposite fallacies. They would have us believe that the experiences of the disabled are not universal, and that people with disabilities have little or no life outside their struggles and strangeness."

Hockenberry started his career in journalism at the National Public Radio (NPR) station in Eugene, Oregon, in 1980. The explosion of nearby Mt. St. Helens gave national exposure to his reporting. In November 1981, he moved to Washington, D.C., to work as the newscaster/writer for *All Things Considered* on NPR. From there he went to the NPR bureau in Chicago, where, in 1986, he applied to become the first journalist in space, becoming a finalist along with Walter Cronkite. (NASA cancelled the civilian-in-space program after the shuttle *Challenger* exploded shortly after lift-off in January 1986). In the spring of 1988, Hockenberry traveled to Israel to become NPR's Middle East correspondent.

"In the three short years I was in Jerusalem," Hockenberry writes in *Moving Violations*, "I confronted most of my theories and assumptions about independence, disability, journalism, and America. The Middle East was where I learned how to keep a wheelchair moving regardless of weather, geography, and national politics." Hockenberry found that people's reaction to his disability provided him an entree that other journalists did not have. He returned to Israel to cover the 1991 Gulf War. In 1992, as a reporter for ABC News, Hockenberry reported on the famine in Somalia.

Hockenberry has also been an activist, filing a lawsuit against a New York theater for refusing him admittance and speaking at rallies and other events. He is profiled in the PBS series *People in Motion*.

See also Media Images of People with Disabilities.

Reference Hockenberry, John, *Moving Violations: War Zones, Wheelchairs, and Declarations of Independence* (1995).

Holland v. Sacramento City Unified School District 14 F. 3d 1398 (1994)
On 24 January 1994, the U.S. Court of Appeals for the Ninth Circuit affirmed a federal court decision requiring that the Sacramento City Unified School District place Rachel Holland in classes with nondisabled children. On 13 June 1994, the U.S. Supreme Court refused to hear the district's appeal, ending five years of litigation. "At a time when school districts are crying for money," commented Patrisha Wright, "this district was willing to spend enormous sums to keep Rachel out of its classrooms." Wright saw this as "an indication of the depth of hostility toward disabled children."

The case began when the Sacramento California School District insisted that Rachel Holland, at that time 11 years old and labeled mentally retarded, be segregated in a special education classroom. An administrative hearing, however, upheld her right to an education in a mainstream

John Hockenberry (seated) and Henry Holden served as masters of ceremonies for the Disability Independence Day March in New York, 1993.

first-grade classroom. The school district appealed this decision, and the case went to federal court.

In 1992, U.S. District Court Judge David Levi amended the administrative hearing decision, ruling that Rachel would best benefit from "full inclusion"—regular classroom instruction coupled with an aide and a special education consultant to assist her classroom teacher on a part-time basis. The district insisted that these services would be prohibitively expensive, but the court found its claim "hyperbolic and exaggerated." The appeals court upheld Levi's ruling.

Rachel and her parents were represented by Disability Rights Education and Defense Fund (DREDF) attorneys who framed the case as an extension of *Brown v. Board of Education* (1954), the landmark U.S. Supreme Court ruling that declared "separate but equal" education for African Americans to be unconstitutional. The *Holland* decision, said DREDF attorney Diane Lipton, "signals the end to a system that automatically excludes children with disabilities from the public school classroom."

See also Disability Rights Education and Defense Fund; Education for All Handicapped Children Act of 1975; Inclusive Education.

Reference "Victory in Landmark 'Full Inclusion Case,'" *Disability Rights Education and Defense Fund News* (September 1994).

Honig v. Doe 108 S. Ct. 592 (1988)

The U.S. Supreme Court, in *Bill Honig, California Superintendent of Public Instruction v. John Doe and Jack Smith*, affirmed the "stay put rule," established under the Education for All Handicapped Children Act of 1975. Under this rule, school officials cannot unilaterally exclude disabled children from the classroom for dangerous or disruptive conduct growing out of their disabilities without a hearing to review whether such removal is necessary. The case was filed on behalf of two emotionally disturbed children, "John Doe" and "Jack Smith," after officials at the San Francisco Unified School District attempted to expel them indefinitely for violent and disruptive conduct directly related to their disabilities.

The U.S. District Court for the Northern District of California ruled that the indefinite suspensions and proposed expulsions violated the right of John Doe and Jack Smith to a free appropriate education, as defined in the Education for All Handicapped Children Act, and permanently enjoined school officials from taking such summary action against other disabled children. The state was also prohibited from making unilateral changes in the placement of disabled children, without parental consent, before completion of a due process hearing. The U.S. Court of Appeals for the Ninth Circuit upheld this ruling and went further by declaring invalid California laws allowing the indefinite suspension or expulsion of disabled children for misconduct arising from their disabilities. The state of California appealed, and the case was argued before the U.S. Supreme Court on 9 November 1987.

On 20 January 1988, the Court affirmed the court of appeals decision, declaring that the language of the Education for All Handicapped Children Act was "unequivocal." Justice Brennan, writing for the majority, pointed out that Congress passed the EAHCA after hearing evidence "that school systems across the country had excluded one out of every eight disabled children from classes" and "used disciplinary measures to bar children from the classroom," without providing any alternative education, or even notice to their parents.

School officials could still use "normal procedures for dealing with children who are endangering themselves or others...the use of study carrels, timeouts, detention, or the restriction of privileges." Schools can suspend students for up to ten days. "And in those cases in which the parents of a truly dangerous child adamantly refuse to permit any change in placement, the 10-day respite gives school officials an opportunity to invoke the aid of the courts . . . ," which can "enjoin a dangerous disabled child from attending school." The burden of proof, however, is on the schools to demonstrate that such a student is dangerous and that no alternative remains but to bar that child from school.

See also Education for All Handicapped Children Act of 1975.

Hotchkiss, Ralf David (b. 1947)

Ralf David Hotchkiss is an inventor whose innovations have revolutionized wheelchair design in developing countries. He is the "technical genius" (to use Thomas K. Gilhool's phrase) of the disability rights movement, making his expertise available, for example, to the Transbus Coalition of the late 1970s. Hotchkiss has traveled throughout the developing world, helping to establish local programs owned and managed by people with disabilities to manufacture high-quality, low-cost "wheeled mobility devices." Since it is difficult to get an education, work, or do political organizing if you cannot leave your home, Hotchkiss' work has been a catalyst for disability rights activism internationally.

Hotchkiss was born on 6 December 1947 in Rockford, Illinois. Paralyzed in a motorcycle accident in 1966, Hotchkiss quickly learned what thousands of disabled people had discovered before him: that the only wheelchairs available were unwieldy, prone to breakdowns, and prohibitively expensive. Years later, in an article for *The Sciences* (1993), Hotchkiss recalled how "thousands of miles of rough rural roads never inflicted the kind of damage to my bicycle that an ordinary week on paved roads and sidewalks took out of a top-of-the-line wheelchair." Hotchkiss, a machinist and engineer, was soon customizing his wheelchairs. In 1966, he invented wraparound wheelchair armrests, in 1967, a stairclimbing electric wheelchair, then a standing chair (which raises a user into a standing position) in 1972. In 1971, he became director of the Center for Concerned Engineering in Washington, D.C.

In 1980, Hotchkiss traveled to Nicaragua to work with advocates at the Independent Living Center in Managua. He and other disabled designers from Nicaragua, the Philippines, Malawi, Siberia, Zimbabwe, and elsewhere developed the "Whirlwind"—"the most effective wheelchair of which we know in the rough urban and rural conditions of developing countries"—each costing only $150. By 1993, more than 30 shops, owned and operated by people with disabilities, had turned out more than 10,000 chairs for use in 25 countries. The Wheeled Mobility Center was founded in San Francisco in 1989, with Hotchkiss as technical director, to coordinate the efforts of "the Whirlwind Network." That same year, Hotchkiss received a MacArthur Foundation "Genius Award" Fellowship.

Hotchkiss was a member of the board of directors of the American Coalition of Citizens with Disabilities from 1974 to 1975. From 1976 to 1980, he worked at the Disability Rights Center in Washington, D.C., which filed a class action suit against the Everest & Jennings Company for its virtual monopoly of the wheelchair market. Hotchkiss was also a co-founder, in 1985, of the Rehabilitation Engineering Program at San Francisco State University. He is the author of *The Lemon Book* (with Ralph Nader and Lowell Dodge, 1971), *Independence through Mobility* (1985), and *Manual Wheelchairs: A Guide* (1986), as well as numerous articles on wheelchair manufacture.

See also Disability Rights Center; Transbus; Wheelchairs.

References Hotchkiss, Ralf D., "Ground Swell on Wheels," *The Sciences* (July/August 1993).

Housing

The vast majority of America's private housing stock is inaccessible to people with mobility disabilities. Most homes can only be entered using stairs, and they have doorways too narrow to accommodate a wheelchair. Few homes have stoves and kitchen surfaces accessible to people in wheelchairs, grab bars in the bathroom, or roll-in showers. Although the Fair Housing

Inventor Ralph Hotchkiss reaches for a tool while working in his workshop in 1989. Hotchkiss, whose wheelchair innovations revolutionized wheelchair design in developing countries, has helped to establish more than 30 shops that have produced 10,000 chairs for use in 25 countries since 1980.

Amendments Act of 1988 requires improved access in multifamily housing, and the Architectural Barriers Act of 1968 and the Americans with Disabilities Act of 1990 require access in public housing and accommodations, no federal law compels access in privately owned single-family dwellings. As a result, people with mobility disabilities are shut out of entire neighborhoods, unless they can afford the considerable added expense of remodeling an inaccessible structure. Even then, the lack of access everywhere else means people with disabilities are often unable to visit neighbors, friends, and family.

"Without adequate housing," wrote Ronald Mace in 1995, "a person—regardless of ability—is deprived of independence, self-determination, and personal security. . . . In too many cases people with disabilities must turn to special, more institutional housing programs . . . when a more accessible home may be all they need to achieve self-reliance."

The Housing and Community Development Act of 1974 authorized federal funds for specialized public housing "for the elderly and handicapped," and, in 1977, the U.S. Department of Housing and Urban Development (HUD) announced that it would make 5 percent of all new publicly funded family-unit housing accessible. The result, where the policy was implemented, was the development of "elderly/handicapped" public housing ghettos, as opposed to community-wide integration. Draconian cuts in federal funds for public housing in the 1980s resulted in a virtual halt in construction, while differences in age and lifestyle between the physically disabled minority and the elder majority led to tension between the two groups, exacerbated when passage of the Fair Housing Amendments Act of 1988 admitted people with psychiatric disabilities, AIDS, and substance abuse histories into elderly/disabled projects.

Mace describes how local "[a]ccessible housing laws almost always require a small percentage of rental units (usually 5%) to be wheelchair-accessible, but little or noth-

ing else." Little provision is generally made under such laws for other forms of access, for example, fire alarm warning lights for deaf people. In addition, "some accessibility specifications have resulted in unpopular, ugly, and obtrusive features such as stainless steel grab bars and lengthy outdoor ramping. These unpopular units in some locations have been made less desirable by owners who adapted only small, one-bedroom units, precluding their use by families and those who need live-in companions."

Rather than seeking to rebuild existing structures, accessible housing advocacy organizations, such as Barrier Free Environments (founded by Mace) in Raleigh, North Carolina , Concrete Change in Atlanta, and the Adaptive Environments Center in Boston, have focused on the concepts of universal design and adaptable housing. Housing that meets universal design standards is built for easier use by everyone. Adaptable housing, while not immediately accessible, is built so that it can be made accessible with little additional cost or effort, incorporating features such as lowered light switches, wider doorways, and level entrances and minimizing the need for long ramps and other features to which nondisabled homeowners or renters might object. Accessible housing advocates such as Mace and Eleanor Smith have attempted to educate architects and builders to the advantages of universal design and adaptable housing and to provide expertise and resources for those wishing to incorporate access into their designs.

The need for accessible housing will grow as America's population ages, with growing numbers of people faced with having to enter a nursing home or retirement community only because their housing is inaccessible and difficult to adapt.

See also Adaptive Environments Center; Architectural Access; Barrier Free Environments; Center for Universal Design; Concrete Change; Fair Housing Amendments Act of 1988; Mace, Ronald L; Universal Design.

References Barrier Free Environments, *The Accessible Housing Design File* (1991); Lebovich, William L., *Design for Dignity: Accessible Environments for Peo-*

ple with Disabilities (1993); Mace, Ronald L., "Housing," in Arthur E. Dell Orto and Robert P. Marinelli, eds., *Encyclopedia of Disability and Rehabilitation* (1995).

Houston Cooperative Living Residential Project

Beginning in 1972, a group of people with disabilities in the Houston area began a series of experiments that placed them in the vanguard of the independent living movement. The first of these, the Houston Cooperative Living Residential Project, was established by David D. Stock at the Texas Institute for Rehabilitation and Research (TIRR) and managed by Rodney Shaw, himself quadriplegic. The project was housed in a barrier-free, dormitory-style building near downtown Houston, where residents hired and managed their own personal assistance providers. Forty people passed through the project during its three-year existence, most graduating to community living arrangements, finding jobs, or entering school. Project alumni formed a series of organizations to continue the mutual support they had received: Independent Lifestyles, Free Lives, and Cluster Living and Shared Providers (CLASP). Living arrangements ranged from a group of condominiums, owned and developed by the disabled residents of Independent Lifestyles, to the "cluster housing" arrangement of Free Lives, whose residents lived in a separate wing of a federal housing project for elderly and disabled people. The Coalition for Barrier Free Living (CBFL) was organized by project alumni to advocate for greater access and more options for independent living in the Houston area. The project itself evolved into the New Options program, an independent living skills training program directed by Lex Frieden, while the CBFL founded the Houston Center for Independent Living in 1980.

The "Houston experience" (as Frieden called it) demonstrated "that well conceived and well managed service programs can provide the support required for most severely disabled people to live independently." It became a model, along with the Center for Independent Living in Berkeley, California, for the advocates who founded the Boston Center for Independent Living in 1974 and other centers across the country.

See also Frieden, Lex; Independent Living, Independent Living Movement; Personal Assistance Services.

References Frieden, Lex, "IL: Movement and Programs," *American Rehabilitation* (July/August 1978); Frieden, Lex, and Joyce Frieden, "Organized Consumerism at the Local Level," *American Rehabilitation* (September/October 1979); Laurie, Gini, *Housing and Home Services for the Disabled* (1977).

Howe, Samuel Gridley (1801–1876)

Samuel Gridley Howe is best remembered for his work at the Perkins School for the Blind (now located in Watertown, Massachusetts). Unlike most of his contemporaries, he did not believe blindness to be an insurmountable obstacle to a productive life. Nevertheless, Howe also held opinions that could only be described as "ableist," warning for example against marriage or sexual relations between disabled people, believing these would lead to a class of social misfits. He was also an oralist and a key figure in the nineteenth-century move to institutionalize people with developmental disabilities.

Howe was born on 10 November 1801 in Boston. He graduated from Harvard Medical School in 1824. In 1831, Howe was approached by John Dix Fisher, the founder in Boston of what was then called the New England Asylum for the Blind (later, Perkins), and asked to become the school's director. For a time, classes were held in Howe's own home, but they were soon moved to the home of businessman and philanthropist Thomas Handasyd Perkins.

Howe advanced the radical notions that people who were blind could be educated and were entitled to an education as good as that of sighted children. He took his students on a tour of 15 states, becoming the impetus for the founding of schools for blind students in Ohio, Tennessee, Kentucky, and Virginia. He developed a method of embossed printing called the Howe Type, or the Boston Line Type, which was used at Perkins until superseded by braille. In 1837, Howe met Laura Bridgman, born in 1829, who had become deaf and blind after an attack of scarlet fever at age two. Howe taught her to sign, read, and write. Bridgman's success brought the two of them, and Perkins, international recognition, proving that those who were both deaf and blind could be educated.

Howe founded the Massachusetts School for Idiotic and Feeble Minded Children (originally housed at Perkins), the nation's first public institution for children with cognitive disabilities, in 1848.

An early supporter of Dorothea Dix, Howe, at first, opposed permanent institutionalization, believing that the residents of the new asylums and state schools could be re-integrated into the community. He eventually modified this view, declaring in 1857, "Do all that we may, we cannot make out of a *real idiot* a reasoning and self-guiding man." Nevertheless, he still opposed the trend toward massive institutions, favoring instead smaller facilities close to the resident's community and family. Howe died on 4 January 1876.

See also Deinstitutionalization; Dix, Dorothea Lynde; Perkins School for the Blind.

References Lane, Harlan, *The Wild Boy of Aeyron* (1976); ———, *When the Mind Hears* (1984); Richards, Laura, *Samuel Gridley Howe* (1935).

Inclusive Education

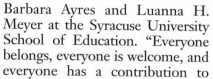

The term *inclusive education* denotes the complete integration of disabled children into all aspects of public school education. Whereas *mainstreaming* implies the notion of a "mainstream" that is "normal" and to which disabled children must adjust, inclusive education strives for classrooms flexible enough to accommodate all learning styles and students, whatever their abilities, language, gender, race, or class background. It was developed in response to the perception that mainstreaming and integration, widely undertaken after passage of the Education for All Handicapped Children Act of 1975, had failed large numbers of disabled students. In 1986, the U.S. Department of Education called upon special educators to work with general educators to develop ways to teach more effectively students with disabilities, leading to the concept of inclusive education.

Inclusive education, according to its proponents, "does not require students to possess any particular set of skills or abilities," again in contrast to mainstreaming, in which a skills threshold, or "readiness model," is used to determine which students are eligible for general education. In addition, mainstreamed students are often sent for much of the school day out of the general classroom to special clinics or skills classes, which some advocates argue defeats the purpose of integration and stigmatizes the students. In inclusive classrooms, specialists come to the disabled student to work with him or her in the general environment. Inclusive classrooms operate on the assumption that all students have unique abilities and disabilities, and students are encouraged to help each other to maximize their abilities and accommodate their differences.

"Inclusion has no conditions and makes no differential value judgements," write Barbara Ayres and Luanna H. Meyer at the Syracuse University School of Education. "Everyone belongs, everyone is welcome, and everyone has a contribution to make." Proponents argue that the advantages for disabled children range from improved language, communication, and social skills to the building of friendships with disabled and nondisabled children alike.

Some advocates, while not disagreeing with the general principle of inclusion, are concerned about the content of inclusive education. Some in the Deaf community, for example, worry that an inclusive classroom with only one or two deaf pupils might not provide them with an adequate understanding of Deaf culture, which is analogous to other minority cultures whose history and traditions have been slighted or overwhelmed by the mainstream. They are also concerned that hearing teachers may not be proficient enough in American Sign Language (ASL) to teach it and that signing students in a nonsigning environment will be cut off from classroom and social activities. The Learning Disabilities Association of America has expressed the concern that children with learning disabilities in an inclusive classroom may fall behind. Proponents of inclusion acknowledge these concerns but believe that inclusion can provide a grounding in both ASL and Deaf culture, as well as adequate assistance to students with learning disabilities.

See also Education for All Handicapped Children Act of 1975.

References Duncan, Janet, and Kathy Hulgin, *Resources on Inclusive Education* (1993); Villa, R. A., and J. S. Thousands, *Creating an Inclusive School* (1995).

Independent Living, Independent Living Movement

"Independent living," Lex Frieden wrote in 1979, "means participating in day-today life and making decisions that lead to self-determination. For disabled people, this implies living in the community, away from custodial institutions, and being responsible for one's own affairs." Independent living centers (IL centers) are nonprofit organizations established to enable people with disabilities to live independently in the community of their choice. Independent living and the independent living movement have played a major role in the general disability rights movement.

A 1953 survey conducted by Los Angeles County revealed that respiratory quadriplegics (most often polio survivors) could get comparable or better personal care in the community for less than a third of the money it cost to keep them in hospitals or nursing homes. Until 1959, when the program was discontinued, the National March of Dimes provided monthly stipends of $300 to polio survivors to enable them to live at home. A program at the University of Illinois at Urbana-Champaign, established in 1948 to accommodate disabled students, offered many of the features of independent living, though its services were limited to university students. The National Rehabilitation Association passed a resolution supporting the independent living concept in 1956, while early independent living legislation was introduced in Congress in 1957 and 1961, with neither bill generating much support.

Edward V. Roberts, often called the "father of the independent living movement," was a political science student who entered the University of California at Berkeley in September 1962. Because the dormitories were inaccessible and could not accommodate his iron lung, Roberts had to live at the university's Cowell Hospital, while his older brother, also a Berkeley student, helped with his personal needs. Roberts' enrollment brought a good deal of attention, and there were more than a dozen other severely disabled students enrolled at the college by the mid-1960s, including John Hessler and Hale Zukas. They formed the Rolling Quads, a political action group, and in 1970 started the Physi-

cally Disabled Students' Program (PDSP). In 1972, they founded the Center for Independent Living in Berkeley, and Roberts became the center's first executive director. By the time he left in 1976 to become the director of the California State Department of Rehabilitation, the center had drawn the attention of other disability activists around the country. In his new position, Roberts founded IL centers across California, proving that the model could be replicated. By this time, independent living–type programs had also been established in Houston, Denver, and Boston. By 1985, the Independent Living Research Utilization Project (ILRU) in Texas listed 298 independent living programs throughout the United States, with at least one in every state. By 1995, there were more than 400 centers worldwide.

Independent living centers have become forums for people with disabilities and centers for political organizing. For example, in 1981, the Brooklyn center, together with the Eastern Paralyzed Veterans of America, protested the use of inaccessible buses by the New York City Transit Authority. In 1985, the Boston Center for Independent Living's (BCIL) Transportation Committee took over the board room of the Massachusetts Bay Transit Authority to protest inadequate paratransit and mainline service, and, in the early 1990s, BCIL was a prime sponsor of Boston's Disability Pride rallies. Advocates at the Westside Independent Living Center in Los Angeles drafted and lobbied for legislation to end Social Security work disincentives. In Denver, the Atlantis Community, Inc., organized a civil disobedience campaign beginning in 1978 to protest the city's inaccessible mass transit, the forerunner to the national actions organized by American Disabled for Accessible Public Transit (ADAPT), which was founded in the Atlantis offices in 1983. IL centers brought together people with different disabilities, although, until the mid-1990s, they were staffed and run predominantly by wheelchair users.

IL centers focus on enabling people with disabilities to obtain access to personal assistance services (PAS). Some act as direct conduits for PAS funding, passing money along from the state to the individual. All IL centers offer peer counseling and skills training. The 1978 amendments to the Rehabilitation Act of 1973 authorized federal funding for IL centers, and the National Council on Independent Living (NCIL) was organized in 1982 to represent the interests of IL centers on a national level.

The progress of the independent movement has stalled at times, and PAS remains unavailable to the vast majority of disabled Americans, especially those in rural areas. By the mid-1980s, some disability rights activists were charging that the independent living movement had lost its edge. The movement was accused of catering to a disability elite of articulate, mostly white, wheelchair users, while neglecting issues involving people with cognitive, sensory, or psychiatric disabilities and disabled people of color. Advocates of direct action and civil disobedience, such as Wade Blank and ADAPT, complained that the independent living movement had backed away from confrontation, afraid of alienating the public officials, federal and state rehabilitation agencies, and private foundations that provided the major portion of IL center funding.

Independent living remains, however, a powerful and empowering concept. The independent living philosophy continues to take root around the world, embraced by advocates as the best alternative to lives spent languishing in nursing homes or institutions.

See also Atlantis Community, Inc.; Boston Center for Independent Living; Center for Independent Living at Berkeley; Fay, Frederick A.; Hessler, John; Houston Cooperative Living Resident Project; Laurie, Virginia Grace; National Council on Independent Living; Nugent, Timothy J.; Personal Assistance Services; Roberts, Edward V.; Switzer, Mary; Zukas, Hale.

References Crewe, Nancy M., and Irving Kenneth Zola and Associates, *Independent Living for Physically Disabled People* (1987); Laurie, Gini, *Housing and Home Services for the Disabled* (1977); Levy, Chava Willig, *A People's History of the Independent Living Movement* (1988).

Individualized Education Program (IEP)

See Education for All Handicapped Children Act of 1975.

Individuals with Disabilities Education Act (IDEA)

See Education for All Handicapped Children Act of 1975.

Information Services

People with disabilities have often been isolated from one another and cut off from information relevant to their lives. In response, advocates and rehabilitation specialists have established a growing network of information services to connect people with disabilities, their families, and professionals to the information they need. The advent of personal computers has been of particular use in this regard.

Disability information providers include the Rehabilitation Research and Training Centers and Rehabilitation Engineering Research Centers at various colleges, universities, and nonprofit organizations. There are also ten Disability and Business Technical Assistance Centers (DBTACs), which are resources for information on employment, the Americans with Disabilities Act of 1990, public services, and communication. The National Rehabilitation Information Center (NARIC) is a library devoted to rehabilitation and disability. ABLEDATA is a national database on assistive technology, while the Job Accommodation Network (JAN), sponsored by the President's Committee on Employment of People with Disabilities, provides information on workplace accommodations. The Directory of National Information Sources on Disabilities (NIS), published by NARIC, is a resource "for professional and consumer organizations" that expedites "searching for appropriate information resources."

The advent of the Internet and the World Wide Web have given disability advocates access to an international forum.

Disabled People South Africa (DPSA), the Intellectual Disability Network of Australia (SAIDIE), and Web sites in the Czech Republic, Finland, the Pacific Rim, and Canada tie home computer users to a wealth of information and resources. In addition, many disability rights groups, such as the Council of Canadians with Disabilities, and institutions such as Gallaudet University, have their own Web sites, while "Gopher" (or information retrieval) sites, such as the Trace Research and Development Center at the University of Wisconsin and the Adaptive Environments Universal Design Education Project, give disability advocates the opportunity to search out and download information. *Blind News Digest*, *ADA-LAW*, *DEAF* (a Deaf online magazine), and online mailing lists have been set up to offer users up-to-the-minute information on topics of concern.

Institute on Disability Culture

The Institute on Disability Culture was founded in 1993 by Lillian Gonzales Brown and Steven E. Brown. (Lillian helped to develop the first independent living skills curriculum taught through the Center for Independent Living in Berkeley. Steven is an author, lecturer, and disability rights organizer.) The institute offers speakers and materials on disability history and culture, including *Independent Living: Theory and Practice* (1994) and *Investigating a Culture of Disability* (1994), both by Steven Brown. The institute is a nonprofit organization based in Las Cruces, New Mexico.

See also Disability Culture.

International Association of Assistance Dog Partners

See Assistance Animals.

International Congress of Educators of the Deaf

See Oral School, Oralism.

International Year, International Decade of Disabled Persons

The General Assembly of the United Nations (UN) in 1976 voted to proclaim 1981 the International Year of Disabled Persons. It was intended to publicize the UN's 1975 Declaration on the Rights of the Disabled, a proclamation by the world body that people with disabilities are entitled to the same political rights as other human beings. It was also intended to encourage governments and international organizations to bring attention and resources to bear on the needs of the world's half-billion people with disabilities. Subsequent to the naming of the Year, national committees on disability were established in 127 countries, and ongoing programs were started in 90, with the goal of "Full Participation and Equality" for all people with disabilities. The Decade of the Disabled, 1983 to 1992, was declared in 1982 as a follow-up to the Year of the Disabled. A United Nations Educational, Scientific and Cultural Organization (UNESCO) paper issued in 1987 reported that one tangible result of the these efforts was the integration of disabled young people of many countries into general education.

Invalid Corps

See Veterans Reserve Corps.

Irving Independent School District v. Tatro 104 S. Ct. 3371 (1984)

The U.S. Supreme Court, in 1984, ruled in *Irving Independent School District v. Tatro*, that the district was required, under the Education for All Handicapped Children Act of 1975, to provide intermittent catheterization to a disabled student, since without this "related service" the student would not be able to continue in a mainstream school setting. The Court distinguished between essential personal care assistance that could be provided by a school nurse or aide, such as catheterization, and medical procedures requiring the attention of a physician. Medical services, the Court ruled, were not required under the act. This distinction allowed access to education for a broad range of children with disabilities who had previously been excluded from public schools.

In *Tatro*, however, the Court also reaffirmed limits it had earlier imposed on ways in which parents of disabled children could seek relief when confronted by discrimination in the public schools. Most significantly, the majority held that parents of disabled children who sued a school district under the Education for All Handicapped Children Act could not recover attorneys' fees as they might under a Section 504 (of the Rehabilitation Act of 1973) lawsuit, even if they prevailed. The exception to this rule came in cases where there was also an issue involving Section 504 separate from that covered under the Education Act. The net effect of this section of the *Tatro* ruling, according to disability rights attorney Robert Funk, was to "severely limit access to the courts for all but wealthy parents on issues concerning their disabled child's right to a public education."

See also Education for All Handicapped Children Act; Section 504 of the Rehabilitation Act of 1973; *Smith v. Robinson*.

Irwin, Robert Benjamin (1883–1951)

Robert Benjamin Irwin was an early advocate in the blindness community and a leader of the American Foundation for the Blind. He was the nation's first statewide supervisor of education for blind children, and he opposed the institutionalization of blind and visually disabled children.

Irwin was born on 2 June 1883 in Rockford, Iowa, but grew up in what was then the Washington Territory. Blinded at age five by fever, at age seven he was sent to live at the State School for Defective Youth (later renamed the Washington State School for the Blind) in Vancouver. This early experience of isolation from his family was an important influence on his later advocacy. He left school in 1901, matriculating at the University of Washington in Seattle where he earned his A.B. in

1906. He then spent a year at Harvard, earning a master's degree in history, and a further two years doing post-graduate research on the administration of schools for the blind. In 1909, Irwin was hired by the Cleveland Board of Education to organize the city's first classes for blind children. Irwin spent 14 years at this post, introducing a number of innovations, including the first use of large-print textbooks for children with low vision, and founding the Howe Publishing Company to produce braille books for adults. In 1922, Irwin was named director of research at the newly formed American Foundation for the Blind (AFB), becoming the executive director in June 1929. In this role, Irwin had a major impact on the final resolution of the debate over which form of braille should become the standard ("the war of the dots"), on the development of federal rehabilitation programs for blinded veterans and civilians, and on the education of blind and visually disabled students. Irwin also lobbied to have blind children and workers included in the Social Security Act of 1935. During this period, Irwin was also president of the American Association of Workers for the Blind (AAWB).

Irwin held many controversial opinions and was not shy about publicly opposing other blind advocates. He was against special scholarships or stipends for blind college students, believing them a form of patronization. He wrote in the January 1909 issue of *Outlook for the Blind* how "all that is needed by a blind man who has fight and ability enough to succeed in competition with his sighted brothers is sufficient pecuniary aid to enable him to employ all the reading he needs. He can then attend with very little handicap, any college he chooses. Any handicap which still remains is that which is his lot as a blind man. This he must face throughout his life and the sooner he faces it the better it will be for him." Irwin also opposed the foundation of a separate college for blind people, but perhaps his most unpopular position was his opposition to automatic state pensions or welfare for blind people, a position that earned Irwin and the AFB much ill will in the blind community.

Irwin retired as director of the AFB in September 1949, moving back to Washington. He died on 12 December 1951. His autobiography and history of the blindness civil rights movement, *As I Saw It*, was published posthumously by the AFB in 1955.

See also American Foundation for the Blind; Braille.

References Irwin, Robert B., *As I Saw It* (1955); Koestler, Frances A., *The Unseen Minority: A Social History of Blindness in the United States* (1976).

It's Okay!: Adults with a Disability Write about Living and Loving

The publishers of *It's Okay!: Adults with*

Disability Write about Living and Loving describe it as the world's only "international, consumer-written, self-help quarterly magazine" about sexuality and disability. Published by Sureen Publishing in St. Catharines, Ontario, it was founded in 1993 by Linda Crabtree. Issues covered by *It's Okay!* include the paucity of positive depictions in the mainstream media of gays and lesbians with disabilities, the need for more research on women with disabilities, profiles of disability rights activists and artists such as singer/songwriter Jane Field, along with poetry, personal essays, and book and product reviews. *It's Okay!* also provides practical advice on accessing social services.

See also Sexuality and Disability.

Jensen, Sandra (1960–1997)

In January 1996, Sandra Jensen became the first person with Down syndrome to receive a heart/lung transplant. Though she was a prime candidate for the procedure, without which she would have died, several California hospitals had refused to treat her because of her disability. Jensen's fight for a place on the transplant waiting list became a national cause and a symbol of discrimination by the medical profession against people with disabilities.

Jensen was born on 6 December 1960. Like many people with Down syndrome, she had congenital heart problems, which went untreated as a child on the advice of her family's doctor. These problems became life threatening in March 1995, with her only option being a heart/lung transplant. Jensen was denied treatment at the Stanford University School of Medicine, its physicians maintaining that people with Down syndrome are unable to understand the complicated after-care regimen. Disability rights advocates pointed out that Stanford did not deny treatment to nondisabled children, who presumably would also have difficulty understanding the regimen, while Stanford's own neuropsychological report had declared that Jensen "has an atypically good prognosis to understand and comply with the required rehabilitation regime." Among the activists working on Jensen's behalf were William Bronston, Justin and Yoshiko Dart, Janine Bertram, Cyndi Jones, and Fred Fay. The California State Office for Civil Rights intervened on her behalf, and, in January 1996, Stanford reversed its decision. A suitable donor became available within a week, allaying fears that Jensen would die due to the delay. Jensen's difficulties led to an effort by disability advocates in California to pass legislation prohibiting discrimination against people with disabilities in need of organ transplants.

Jensen was an activist with People First and appeared on California radio and television to urge that babies born with Down syndrome not be denied medical treatment. She was the president of Capitol People First and a member of the staff at the World Interdependence Fund in Sacramento, California.

Sandra Jensen died on 23 May 1997 due to side effects of the medications she was taking to control her body's rejection of the donated organs, a common cause of death among transplant recipients.

See also People First, People First International.

Sandra Jensen, pictured here in 1995, was the first person with Down syndrome to receive a heart/lung transplant.

Jernigan, Kenneth (b. 1926)

Kenneth Jernigan was the president of the National Federation of the Blind (NFB) from 1968 until July of 1986, serving con-

171

tinuously except for the period of 1977 to 1978. As the executive director since 1986, he has remained an influential voice within the NFB, the nation's largest advocacy organization of blind people.

Jernigan was born on 13 November 1926 in Detroit. He grew up on a farm in central Tennessee and attended the Tennessee School for the Blind in Nashville. He earned a bachelor's degree in social work at the Tennessee Technological University in Cookeville in 1948, and a master's in English from the George Peabody College for Teachers in Nashville in 1949. In the early 1950s, Jernigan became active in the Tennessee Association of the Blind (TAB), the NFB state affiliate. He was elected TAB's president in 1951, becoming a member of the NFB Board of Directors for the first time in 1952. In 1958, Jernigan was appointed director of the Iowa State Commission for the Blind, where he oversaw reforms of that agency's rehabilitation services. Floyd Matson, historian of the NFB, writes that, during Jernigan's tenure, Iowa went from having "possibly the worst rehabilitation agency [for blind people] in the nation . . . to arguably the best." Jernigan's work in Iowa was the subject of a Special Citation by President Lyndon Johnson in 1968, and many of the graduates of the Iowa program would go on to assume leadership positions in the NFB.

Jernigan became president of the NFB after the death of the organization's founder and first president, Jacobus tenBroek. He continued the expansion of the NFB membership begun under tenBroek, and he supervised the construction of the organization's national headquarters in Baltimore. He became the executive director of the American Action Fund for Blind Children and Adults in 1978 and the president of the North American/Caribbean region for the World Blind Union in 1987.

Jernigan has appeared before the National Press Club and on *Today* and *Larry King Live* shows. The winner of numerous awards, including several honorary doctorates and a Distinguished Service Award from President Bush in 1990, he has been a member of the National Advisory Committee on Services for the Blind and Physically Handicapped, an advisor to the Smithsonian Institution, and a special advisor to the White House Conference on Library and Information Services.

Kenneth Jernigan lives in Baltimore with his wife, Mary Ellen, who is also active in the NFB.

See also National Federation of the Blind; tenBroek, Jacobus.

Reference Matson, Floyd, *Walking Alone and Marching Together: A History of the Organized Blind Movement in the United States, 1940–1990* (1990).

Jerry's Orphans
See Telethons.

Johnson, Mark (b. 1951)
Mark Johnson is a founder of, and organizer for, American Disabled for Attendant Programs Today (ADAPT). He was born on 11 June 1951 and became spinal cord injured in a diving accident in 1971 at age 19. He earned a B.A. in psychology in 1975 and a master's in guidance and counseling in 1977 from the University of North Carolina at Charlotte. He was a founder of the Metrolina chapter of the National Paraplegia Foundation in 1977, chair of the Handicapped Advisory Committee for Charlotte, North Carolina, from 1979 to 1981, chair of the Colorado Coalition of Persons with Disabilities from 1983 to 1985, and accessibility coordinator for the Democratic National Convention in Atlanta, Georgia, in 1988. Johnson also worked as the assistant director (from 1983 to 1985) of Holistic Approaches to Independent Living (HAIL) in Denver, and then as an independent living specialist for the Colorado Division of Rehabilitation. He is currently the coordinator of advocacy and community support at the Shepherd Spinal Center in Atlanta.

Johnson has been an organizer and participant in every national action undertaken by ADAPT since its founding in 1983, including the first demonstrations at the annual meeting of the American Public

Transit Association (APTA) in Denver that year. In 1984, he and other ADAPT members followed APTA to Washington, D.C., and demonstrated at every APTA annual meeting until 1989. In 1990, Johnson and ADAPT returned to Washington to press for passage of the Americans with Disabilities Act of 1990, where he was arrested for sitting in at the Capitol rotunda as part of the Wheels of Justice demonstrations.

Johnson has also been active in opposing the right-to-die movement. He was a founder, together with Eleanor Smith, of Life Worthy of Life, formed in response to the 1989 Larry McAfee decision (in *State of Georgia v. McAfee*), in which an Atlanta judge ruled that McAfee, because he was disabled, had a right to assisted suicide. Johnson and others pointed out that McAfee's decision to die had more to do with state policies that kept him a prisoner in hospitals and nursing homes than with his disability as such. Johnson and two dozen demonstrators occupied the office of Georgia's Medicaid director to protest Medicaid's refusal to pay for McAfee's community care.

Johnson is also a wheelchair athlete and was a member of the Disability Advisory Council for the 1996 Paralympics in Atlanta.

See also American Disabled for Attendant Programs Today (ADAPT); Euthanasia and Assisted Suicide; Paralympics (Paralympic Movement); Wheels of Justice.

Johnson, Mary (b. 1948)

Mary Johnson was a founder and first editor of the *Disability Rag & Resource*, the radical disability rights bimonthly. She was born on 31 July 1948 in Louisville, Kentucky. She graduated from Spalding University in Louisville, Kentucky, with an A.B. in English literature in 1970. In 1975, she became president of the Action League for Physically Handicapped Adults, Inc., the Louisville disability rights group that supported a lawsuit (*Cherry v. Johnson* 1976) by member James Cherry against the federal government over its failure to issue regulations to implement Section 504

of the Rehabilitation Act of 1973. In 1978, Johnson founded and became the first president of Prime Movers, Inc., a research and development group in Louisville. In this capacity Johnson supervised the development of the Center for Accessible Living, Louisville's first independent living center, which opened in 1981.

In 1980, Johnson, together with Cass Irvin, founded the Advocado Press and the *Disability Rag* (later, the *Disability Rag & Resource*), first published in 1981. As the principal editor at Advocado, Johnson edited books and publications such as *Reporting on Disability: Approaches and Issues* (1989), *Strange People with Books* (by Nancy Gall-Clayton, 1990), and *Media Savvy: A Self-Training Curriculum* (1991).

Johnson left the *Disability Rag & Resource* in 1993, but she continued to write. Her articles on disability issues appeared in the *Progressive*, the *New York Times*, the *Nation*, the *Christian Science Monitor*, and elsewhere. In 1996, she returned to the Advocado Press to help with publication of the *Ragged Edge*, the successor magazine to the *Disability Rag & Resource*.

See also The Disability Rag & Resource.

Jones, Cynthia A. (b. 1951)

Cynthia A. Jones is the publisher of *Mainstream: Magazine of the Able-Disabled*, a national disability rights monthly based in San Diego. She started at *Mainstream* in 1976 as the production manager and became editor in 1982. In 1984, she became president of Exploding Myths, Inc., the company that owns *Mainstream*. She is a nationally recognized grassroots advocate, turning *Mainstream* from a small, local publication into one with a national readership. Jones and *Mainstream* serve as a bridge between manufacturers of disability products, advocates, consumers, and rehabilitation researchers.

Jones was born on 1 October 1951 in Terre Haute, Indiana. Disabled by polio, she was the West Coast coordinator of the Episcopal Women's Caucus, 1974–1976; the president of the California Association

Surrounded by students, Irving King Jordan raises his hands to celebrate his appointment on 13 March 1988 as the first deaf president of Gallaudet University in Washington D.C.

of Persons with Handicaps, San Diego, in 1982; a founding member of Disabled Women's Opportunity Week in San Diego in 1985; and the public relations manager of the American Disabled for Accessible Public Transit (ADAPT) San Francisco demonstrations. In 1983, she successfully campaigned to put George Murray (first wheelchair winner of the Boston Marathon) on the cover of Wheaties cereal boxes. In 1995, she was a principal advocate on behalf of Sandra Jensen, who was initially denied a heart/lung transplant because of her disability.

Jones has a bachelor of arts degree in biology from the University of California at San Diego.

See also Jensen, Sandra; *Mainstream: Magazine of the Able-Disabled.*

Jordan, Irving King (b. 1943)

Irving King Jordan became the first deaf president of Gallaudet University in Washington, D.C., in March 1988. Born on 16 June 1943 in Glen Riddle, Pennsylvania, Jordan became deaf after sustaining a head injury in a motorcycle accident when he was 21 years old. He earned a B.A. in psychology from (what was then) Gallaudet College in 1970 and a master's (1971) and a doctorate (1973) in psychology, both from the University of Tennessee.

Jordan became an assistant professor of psychology at Gallaudet in 1973. In 1983, was named chair of the Department of Psychology, and, in 1986, he became dean of the College of Arts and Sciences. He helped establish a special interest group on deafness as part of the American Educational Research Association, and he chaired the special interest group on education within the Convention of American Instructors of the Deaf.

In late February 1988, Jordan was one of three finalists for the position of president of Gallaudet University, along with Harvey J. Corson and Elisabeth A. Zinser. Both King and Corson were deaf; Zinser was not, and a student uprising erupted when Zinser was selected. After a week-long student strike and demonstrations at the Gallaudet campus, the board of trustees appointed Jordan the eighth president of Gallaudet University. A statement he made during the student campaign, "Deaf people can do anything hearing people can—except hear," has become a rallying cry of Deaf rights activists.

See also Deaf President Now Campaign; Gallaudet University.

Reference Moore, Matthew S., and Robert F. Panara, *Great Deaf Americans: The Second Edition* (1996).

Judge David L. Bazelon Center for Mental Health Law

The Judge David L. Bazelon Center for Mental Health Law (formerly the Mental Health Law Project, and often abbreviated to the Bazelon Center), located in Washington, D.C., was founded in 1972 by attorneys Charles Halpern and Bruce Ennis as a nonprofit advocacy organization specializing in defending the legal rights of people with mental illness. The center provides training and technical assistance to lawyers and programs, and it publishes materials pertaining to federal civil rights laws and regulations.

The Bazelon Center attorneys have litigated, or been involved in, many significant cases involving the civil rights of people with mental disabilities, among them *O'Connor v. Donaldson* (1975) and *New York ARC v. Rockefeller* (1973). The center advocates for full coverage of mental health care by health insurers, community living alternatives to institutional or nursing home care, expanded housing and employment opportunities for people with mental disabilities, and full implementation of the Americans with Disabilities Act of 1990.

See also O'Connor v. Donaldson; Psychiatric Survivor Movement; Willowbrook State School.

Just One Break (JOB)

See Viscardi, Henry, Jr.

Justice for All

Justice for All was founded on 6 January 1995 by Justin Dart Jr., Fred Fay, and Becky Ogle in response to the Republican victory in the congressional elections of 1994. It provides updates via e-mail and fax to disability activists on the status of disability rights legislation and programs of concern to people with disabilities. Justice for All "Truth Teams," organized in all 50 states, respond to misinformation in the media concerning the Americans with Disabilities Act of 1990, the Individuals with Disabilities Education Act, and other disability rights legislation.

See also Dart, Justin Jr.; Fay, Frederick A.

Kafka, Robert (b. 1946)

Robert Kafka is a national organizer for the group American Disabled for Attendant Programs Today (ADAPT). He was born on 24 February 1946 in the Bronx, New York, and served in the U.S. Army in Vietnam from 1966 to 1967. He earned both his bachelor of business administration in economics in 1971 and his M.Ed. in special education in 1973 from the University of Houston. His involvement in the disability rights movement began in the 1970s when he served on the board of Houston's Coalition for Barrier Free Living, becoming president of the group in 1979. From 1974 to 1980, he was also the director of disabled students services at the University of Houston. He was a volunteer for Volunteers in Service to America (VISTA) from 1981 to 1983, worked with the Coalition of Texans with Disabilities (as president from 1984 to 1987), and became co-director of the Institute for Disability Access in 1984. He was also active in the American Coalition of Citizens with Disabilities, serving on its board of directors in 1981.

Kafka founded the Texas chapter of ADAPT in 1984 and has been an organizer with both the Texas and the national ADAPT since. He has also been president of the Texas Paralyzed Veterans Association (1987 to 1991), founder and president of the Southwest Wheelchair Athletic Association (1981 to 1991), and chairperson of the Coalition of Texans with Disabilities Personal Attendant Services Task Force (1988 to 1993).

See also American Disabled for Attendant Programs Today (ADAPT).

Kaleidoscope

Kaleidoscope is an international magazine of literature, fine arts, and disability published by United Disability Services in Akron, Ohio. First produced in 1979 as part of a creative writing class for adults with physical disabilities, *Kaleidoscope* has featured first-time publication of some of the most respected writers on disability issues in the United States, including Troy Reeves, Laura Hershey, Irving Zola, and MacArthur Award winner Andre Dubus.

See also Disability Culture; Hershey, Laura; Zola, Irving Kenneth.

Kaleidoscope: The Health & DisAbility Channel

Kaleidoscope: The Health & DisAbility Channel was founded in 1990 as the nation's first fully accessible cable television 24-hour network. It offers an option for people with disabilities and parents of disabled children who want to avoid the ableist programming offered on mainstream television, and it features educational and entertainment programming by and for people with disabilities. Based in San Antonio, Texas, Kaleidoscope airs movies with captions for deaf people and audio descriptions for blind and visually disabled viewers. Original programming includes *Kim's World*, featuring deaf/blind actress Kim Powers; *Very Special Arts*; and *KTV News*.

See also Media Images of People with Disabilities.

Kaplan, Deborah (b. 1950)

Deborah Kaplan is an attorney who has been involved in a wide range of disability rights litigation and activism. She was born on 17 January 1950 in Cleveland, Ohio, and received her B.A. in religious studies from the University of California in Santa Cruz in 1971 and her J.D. from the University of California at Berkeley in 1976. That same year, Kaplan moved to Washington, D.C., to found the Disability Rights Center (DRC). (At the time, she was probably the only disability lobbyist working in the nation's capital who was herself a person with a disability.) The DRC focused on federal employment discrimination legislation and consumer protection legislation for the users of medical devices and equipment. Kaplan served as the DRC executive director until June 1979. In April 1980, after working with the Public Interest Law Center of Philadelphia and the National Organization of Women Legal Defense and Education Fund, she became a staff attorney at the Disability Rights Education and Defense Fund (DREDF). She worked with DREDF until January 1985, when she became a private consultant on disability law, and then became an associate attorney in private practice.

Kaplan joined the World Institute on Disability (WID) in Oakland, California, in the late 1980s. A pioneer in the issues of technology and communication access, Kaplan became vice president and director of WID's Division on Technology Policy. In 1996, she left WID to work for Issue Dynamics, a private consulting firm for corporate clients in public affairs and the communications industry.

See also Bowe, Frank; Disability Rights Center; World Institute on Disability.

Keller, Helen Adams (1880–1968)

Helen Keller is the world's best-known advocate for disability rights. Deaf and blind in an era when persons with either disability were judged inferior and incompetent, she graduated summa cum laude from Radcliffe College in Cambridge, Massachusetts, and wrote hundreds of articles and several critically and commercially successful books. She advocated for an end to the oppression of people with disabilities as well as an end to racism and sexism.

Keller was born on 27 June 1880 in Tus-cumbia, Alabama. Her father, Arthur, was a Confederate veteran turned newspaper editor and U.S. marshall. Her mother, a "Memphis Belle" whose father had been a Confederate general, is described by Keller's biographer, Joseph Lash, as having "a lively intelligence" and as "widely read with an excellent memory." A precocious child, Keller began to talk at 6 months and to walk at age 1. At 19 months she contracted an illness described as "acute congestion of the stomach and brain," which left her unable to see or hear. At that time, there were almost no educators working with deaf-blind children, certainly none in rural Alabama.

When Helen was 6 years old, her father took her to see Alexander Graham Bell. Bell recommended that Captain Keller contact the Perkins School for the Blind in Boston, where Samuel Gridley Howe had gained international recognition for his work with a deaf-blind woman named Laura Bridgman. Although Howe had died in 1876, his successor, Michael Anagnos, recommended that Anne Sullivan (later Anne Sullivan Macy), a recent graduate of Perkins, travel to Alabama to work with Helen.

Sullivan, herself partially sighted, turned out to be an excellent choice as Helen's educator and mentor. She was born of Irish immigrant parents on 14 April 1866 in Feeding Hills, Massachusetts. Sullivan, together with her younger brother Jimmie, also disabled, was committed to the state poorhouse in Tewksbury in 1876, soon after the death of their mother. Both children suffered abuse and neglect, and Jimmie died during their confinement. Sullivan spent six years in the poorhouse. "Very much of what I remember about Tewksbury is indecent, cruel, melancholy," she told her biographer Nella Braddy Henney years later. "I doubt if life or for that matter eternity is long enough to erase the terrors and ugly blots scored upon my mind during those dismal years from 8 to 14." In 1880, a visiting inspector arranged for Sullivan's transfer to the Perkins School for the Blind, where

Helen Keller

she had difficulty making up for 14 years of virtually no education. She adapted an attitude of belligerence toward authority that would last her entire life, and she was dubbed "Miss Spitfire" by her teachers and classmates.

Sullivan's distrust of authority and regimentation turned out to be one of her great strengths as a teacher, while Keller proved to be a brilliant student. Sullivan traveled to Alabama to live with the Kellers, where she met Helen on 3 March 1887. Within months, Keller was carrying on conversations through finger-spelling and lip-reading with her fingers, and she was writing both braille and print English. Keller's letters to Michael Anagnos and the children at Perkins, to her parents and family, to Bell, and to a widening circle of admirers and literati fascinated by her story were later reprinted as an appendix to her autobiography, *The Story of My Life* (1903).

Early on, Keller began to advocate for the interests of people with disabilities. Her first effort, when she was 11 years old, was to solicit funds so that Tommy Stringer, another deaf-blind child, could be educated at Perkins. Keller entered the Wright-Humason School in New York City in 1894; in 1896, she enrolled in the Gilman School for Young Ladies in Cambridge, Massachusetts, determined to be educated with "normal" children. She became the first deaf-blind person ever to enter college, matriculating at Radcliffe in 1900 and graduating in 1904. Through it all, Sullivan remained her "teacher" and closest friend.

After graduation, Keller became an advocate for the education and employment of blind persons. Unafraid of controversy and unwilling to cater to Victorian prudishness, she wrote articles and delivered lectures describing the link between syphilis in mothers and blindness in newborns, pointing out that a third of all blindness in the United States could be prevented by the use of nitrated silver eye drops. In an article she titled "The Vultures That Prey on My Kind," written in 1908, Keller condemned the sellers of quack cures and patent medicines and criticized the presidential candidates of both major parties in the election that year for being associated with those who exploited disabled persons. The *Ladies' Home Journal* printed a heavily censored version of the article in 1909, retitling it "I Must Speak."

Keller's first book, *The Story of My Life*, first appeared in serial form in the *Ladies' Home Journal* in 1902, and then as a book in March 1903. Still an undergraduate at Radcliffe, she had written what was immediately hailed as a classic autobiography. Sullivan's letters to her friends and her reports to Perkins, which comprise the last third of the book, are remarkable for their insights on the acquisition of language by children.

Despite their fame, Keller and Sullivan often lived in near poverty. At one point, struggling for money, they went on tour with a vaudeville troupe, going on stage between jugglers, magicians, clowns, and comedians to tell the story of Keller's "miracle" and then answer questions from the audience. Joseph P. Lash, in his 1980 biography, *Helen and Teacher*, wrote how "the two women were determined . . . to run their own lives and to make it on their own," although they were at times the beneficiaries of various endowments and trust funds.

Keller was often a controversial figure. She was a feminist and ardent supporter of women's suffrage and a critic of Theodore Roosevelt's interventionist foreign policy. She opposed the U.S. entry into World War I, and, after the Russian Revolution, she proclaimed herself a Bolshevik and a supporter of the militant International Workers of the World. For a time, she devoted herself almost exclusively to socialist politics, believing in the need for revolutionary economic and political change. In the 1930s, she lent her name to efforts to raise funds for the anti-Franco forces in the Spanish Civil War and to rescue Jews from Nazi Germany. She was also a critic of American racism and segregation in her native Alabama. Told that her outspoken politics might lead her into trouble, even among liberals, she replied, "I don't give a damn about semi-radicals."

After 1924, however, Keller and Sullivan devoted most of their energy to fund-raising and lobbying on behalf of the American Foundation for the Blind. Their work was instrumental in forcing the inclusion of provisions for blind persons in the Social Security Act of 1935. The two toured Europe, Latin America, and Asia, speaking out everywhere against the marginalization and oppression of people with disabilities. Keller also continued to write books and essays, including *The World I Live In* (1908), *Out of the Dark* (an anthology of socialist essays, 1913), *Midstream: My Later Life* (1929), and *Helen Keller's Journal* (1938). Her last book, *Teacher* (1955), was a biography of Sullivan, who died on 20 October 1936.

In recent years, there has been a re-examination of Keller's near-symbiotic relationship with Anne Sullivan. Some of their biographers, most notably Joseph Lash, see Sullivan fostering in Keller an unnecessary dependence. Keller herself recounted incidents during her childhood education that can only be termed abuse, as when Sullivan would tie her hands behind her back, thus cutting off her only method of communication. Keller's personal assistant after Sullivan's death, Polly Thomson, has also been accused of unnecessarily restricting her freedom, for instance, dictating her choices of food. Keller was limited further by her mother, who forbade Keller at age 36 to marry, believing her daughter too disabled to keep the affection of any man. Personally, Keller was sometimes plagued by self-doubt. She gave up her attempts at fiction after age 12 when she was accused of plagiarism. As an adult, she became frustrated when urged to write or speak about herself, and she commented angrily on how no one seemed interested in her opinions about anything other than disability.

A documentary of her life entitled *The Unconquered* was released to critical acclaim in 1953. A play based on her first months with Sullivan, *The Miracle Worker*, appeared on Broadway in 1957. It was then turned into a successful motion picture in 1962.

Keller retired from public life after a stroke in 1961. She died on 1 June 1968. In 1996, it was reported that the F.B.I. had kept a file on her, much of which is still classified.

See also American Foundation for the Blind; Perkins School for the Blind.

References Keller, Helen Adams, *The Story of My Life* (1954); Lash, Joseph P., *Helen and Teacher: The Story of Helen Keller and Anne Sullivan Macy* (1980).

Kemp, Evan, Jr. (b. 1937)

A self-described "insider" and a friend and advisor to Vice President and then President George Bush, Evan Kemp played a pivotal role in advancing the disability rights agenda of the 1980s, and in educating Bush on disability issues to the point where the president was willing, in 1990, to sign the Americans with Disabilities Act (ADA).

Kemp was born on 5 May 1937 in New York City and became disabled at age 12 with Kugel-Welander syndrome, a form of muscular dystrophy. He earned his bachelor's degree from Washington and Lee University in Lexington, Virginia, in 1959 and his law degree from the University of Virginia in Charlottesville in 1964. Despite graduating near the top of his class, Kemp, because of his disability, was turned down by 39 national firms before his uncle Drew Pearson helped him to find a position at the U.S. Internal Revenue Service. In 1967, Kemp joined the U.S. Securities and Exchange Commission (SEC), where he was subject to another form of discrimination. For his first seven years as an SEC attorney, Kemp was able to move without a wheelchair and received steady raises. The raises stopped as soon as Kemp stopped walking and were not to resume for six years, when he filed and won an antidiscrimination lawsuit against the federal government.

In 1980, Kemp became the director of the Disability Rights Center, a national advocacy organization co-founded by Deborah Kaplan and consumer activist Ralph Nader. In 1981, Kemp criticized the National Muscular Dystrophy Association's Jerry Lewis Telethon, writing in an op. ed. piece in the *New York Times* that the annual Labor Day Weekend fund-raiser played on the public's fear of disability. This was the beginning of a 15-year public feud between Kemp and Jerry Lewis.

Kemp has been described as "a bridge" to the White House for disability activists during the Reagan and Bush administrations. His role as a friend and advisor to C. Boyden Gray, Bush's legal counsel, was particularly significant. In 1981, the newly elected Reagan administration targeted the regulations implementing both Section 504 of the Rehabilitation Act and the Education for All Handicapped Children Act as part of their drive to "get government off the people's backs." The disability rights community responded with a massive letter-writing and telephone campaign, coordinated by Patrisha Wright and the Disability Rights Education and Defense Fund. Kemp, with his Republican Party connections, was perfectly placed to represent the community "on the inside," seeking to dissuade Bush, who had been put in charge of the deregulation effort, from gutting federal disability rights protections. Kemp was also able to arrange meetings between advocates and high-level administration officials. This combination of grassroots pressure and Kemp's inside advocacy led, in March 1983, to an announcement that the administration had abandoned its effort to rescind or alter the regulations. "Pat [Wright] and I worked day and night for a couple of years," Kemp said later. "It was an important fight for the disability rights movement, because it got us together. It's when we started really organizing." The campaign to save the regulations also educated Gray and Bush, setting the stage for their support of the ADA in 1990.

Kemp was nominated by President Reagan as a commissioner on the U.S. Equal Employment Opportunity Commission (EEOC) on 10 March 1987, and he was unanimously confirmed by the Senate on 19 June 1987. By this time, Kemp had become a Bush advisor, helping to draft the vice president's speeches on disability issues. When Bush accepted the presidential nomination at the 1988 Republican National Convention, he included in his speech a commitment to work toward bringing people with disabilities into the American mainstream. This was the first time disability rights had been mentioned by the presidential candidate of either major party in so public a forum, a direct result of Kemp's influence. President Bush appointed Kemp to succeed Clarence Thomas as chair of the EEOC on 8 March 1990. As the chief enforcer of federal employment discrimination law, Kemp was ideally placed to argue the need for an ADA, both to the public and within the administration.

Kemp's tenure as EEOC chairman was praised for what the *National Journal* called "an aggressive crackdown on workplace discrimination." *National Journal* reporter W. John Moore in 1991 described how "many civil rights activists favorably compared Kemp's chairmanship with that of his controversial predecessor." Disability rights activists came to Kemp's defense when Jerry Lewis urged that the president fire him for his continuing public criticism of the Muscular Dystrophy Association's telethon. Bush refused to do so.

Kemp stepped down as EEOC chair in 1992. He has continued to play a leading role in the disability rights movement, founding and directing Evan Kemp Associates, a lobbying and consulting firm that also publishes *One Step Ahead—The Resource for Active, Healthy, Independent Living* (formerly, *One Step Ahead—The Disability Resource*), a monthly newspaper reporting on issues of concern to people with disabilities. In late 1996, he joined Justin Dart Jr. in urging that the Supreme Court reject arguments favoring the right to die.

See also Disability Rights Center; *One Step Ahead—The Resource for Active, Healthy, Independent Living;* Section 504 of the Rehabilitation Act of 1973; Telethons; Wright, Patrisha A.

Kemp, John D. (b. 1949)

John D. Kemp has gone from being a National Easter Seals Society poster child at age 10 to serving as the organization's general counsel and vice president for development. The former executive director of United Cerebral Palsy Associations Inc., Kemp is today the president and chief executive officer of Very Special Arts.

John Kemp was born on 10 October 1949 in Waterloo, Iowa. He graduated from Georgetown University in 1971 and earned his J.D. from the Washburn University Law School in Topeka, Kansas, in 1974. He worked in the legal department of the U.S. Environmental Protection Agency in Kansas City, Missouri, and then as a consultant in consumer advocacy for the National Easter Seal Society in Chicago from 1976 to 1977. Kemp became the director of human resources for the society in 1982 and its general counsel and vice president in 1986. In 1990, he left the society to become executive director of United Cerebral Palsy Associations, Inc., in Washington, D.C., a position he held until 1995, when he was appointed president and CEO of Very Special Arts, an affiliate of the John F. Kennedy Center for the Performing Arts in Washington, D.C.

Kemp's advocacy for disability rights goes back more than two decades. He testified before the U.S. Senate Select Subcommittee on Education and the Subcommittee on the Handicapped, in support of passage of the Rehabilitation Act of 1973. In 1986, he appeared before the U.S. Commission on Civil Rights to decry discrimination against disabled infants needing medical treatment and, in 1991, before the U.S. Department of Justice to testify about proposed regulations for the Americans with Disabilities Act of 1990.

Kemp is a member of the advisory board of the Amputee Coalition of America and of the panel of experts at the International Disability Exchange and Studies (IDEAS) program at the World Institute on Disability. He has given numerous radio and television interviews and written for publications such as *The Exceptional Parent* and *American Rehabilitation*. Kemp was appointed to the National Council on Disability by President Clinton in 1995.

See also United Cerebral Palsy Associations, Inc.

Kowalski, Sharon (b. 1956), and Karen Thompson (b. 1947)

In November 1983, the car Sharon Kowalski was driving was struck head-on by a drunk driver near Onamia, Minnesota. Kowalski, 27 years old, emerged from a coma unable to speak and with much of her body paralyzed. Her lover of four years, Karen Thompson, wanted Kowalski to return to the home they had shared, a wish also communicated by Kowalski after regaining consciousness. Kowalski's parents, however, wanted her to remain in a nursing home. The ensuing legal struggle between Thompson and Kowalski's parents, which lasted more than eight years and cost Thompson some $300,000, came to represent the unwillingness of society to allow people with disabilities their right to live where they want and love whom they choose.

Prior to the accident, Kowalski and Thompson had not publicly declared their relationship, believing this revelation might threaten Thompson's position as an assistant professor of physical education at St. Cloud State University. In January 1985, Kowalski typed out to the staff at the St. Cloud Handicap Services that she was gay and that Thompson was her lover. In June, Kowalski asked that the Minnesota Civil Liberties Union represent her. Nevertheless, on 23 July 1985, the court awarded full guardianship to her father, who promptly forbade Kowalski to see Thompson, many of her friends, her court-appointed attorney, members of the Civil Liberties Union, and any representatives of the gay/lesbian or disability rights movements. Within 48 hours, Kowalski was moved to a nursing home in Hibbing, Minnesota, many hours distant from Thompson and other friends and advocates. While there, Kowalski was denied access to physical therapy and other rehabilitation, so that her condition, once improving, now began to deteriorate.

For the next three and a half years, Kowalski and Thompson were prevented from seeing each other. During that time, Thompson took her story to the lesbian and disability rights communities. Speaking at rallies and giving interviews to the disability and gay rights press, Thompson enlisted the support of hundreds of people across the country in an attempt to pressure the court to reverse its decision.

The mainstream media at first repeated all the usual stereotypes, both about people with disabilities and lesbians. Kowalski was described as having "a six-year-old's mentality," despite testimony by experts that such a characterization was inaccurate and demeaning. She was seen as "the eerily silent daughter" "trapped in her twisted body," even though she was able to communicate using a letterboard or typewriter. Thompson was described as obsessed, greedy, and eager to exploit Kowalski's disability for financial, political, and sexual reasons. "It seemed," Thompson wrote in *Why Can't Sharon Kowalski Come Home?* (1988), "as though we were suffering more from society's homophobia and handicapism, than from the accident itself."

In November 1988, a competency hearing determined that Kowalski could indeed communicate, and it recommended that she be moved from a nursing home to a rehabilitation center. In January 1989, Kowalski was moved to a rehabilitation center in Duluth, where she again told staff that she wanted to see Thompson. In February 1989, the couple were at last reunited. Thompson filed once more for guardianship. Although the Kowalski family had withdrawn their guardianship, the court would still not allow Thompson to take Kowalski home with her. Thompson appealed, and finally, in August 1992, Thompson was awarded guardianship. By this time, Kowalski's physical condition had deteriorated to such an extent that it was not until April 1993 that she was able to move back home.

"They say it was a victory," says Thompson, "but certainly it was a loss. Sharon didn't get the rehabilitation at the time she needed it, and as a result she's lost some things for life. But at least now we've got the opportunity to get on with our lives."

Kowalski was born on 8 August 1956, in Grand Rapids, Minnesota. Thompson was born on 24 July 1947, in Belpre, West Virginia. The two continue to live together in St. Cloud and have remained politically active, occasionally attending women's, lesbian, and disability rights events. Thompson also leads anti-ableism workshops.

See also Boston Self Help Center; Handicapped Organized Women; Panzarino, Connie.

Reference Thompson, Karen, and Julie Andrzejewski, *Why Can't Sharon Kowalski Come Home?* (1988).

Kriegel, Leonard (b. 1933)

Leonard Kriegel's intention in *The Long Walk Home*, published in 1964, was "to write a book free of the sentimentality and cant and papier-maché religiosity usually found" in books about disability. In it, he recounts his experience with polio, which he contracted when he was 11 years old. In his essays "Uncle Tom and Tiny Tim: Some Reflections on the Cripple as Negro" and "Claiming the Self: The Cripple as American Man," Kriegel examines the interplay between disability, society's expectations, and the self-image of people with disabilities. In "The Wolf in the Pit in the Zoo," he examines "the cripple in American literature."

"Our condition is intense, our isolation massive. Society views us as both pariah and victim. We are pitied, shunned, labelled, classified, analyzed, and categorized. . . ."

Born on 25 May 1933 in the Bronx, New York, Kriegel received his B.A. from Hunter College in New York City in 1955 and his Ph.D. from New York University in 1960. He has been an assistant professor at Long Island University; an assistant and then full professor of English at the City College of the City University of New

York; and a Fulbright lecturer at the University of Leiden, University of Groningen, and the University of Paris. Kriegel's other books include *Edmund Wilson* (1971), *Working Through: An Autobiographical Journey in the Urban University* (1973), *Notes for the Two Dollar Window* (1976), and *Of Mice and Manhood* (1979). His recent essays on disability are collected in *Falling into Life* (1991).

References Kriegel, Leonard, *The Long Walk Home* (1964); ———, *Falling Into Life* (1991).

Labor Day Telethon
See Telethons.

LaFollette-Barden Act of 1943
The LaFollette-Barden Act of 1943, also known as the Vocational Rehabilitation Amendments Act of 1943, provided people with disabilities who were 15 years old or older with government services intended to enhance their ability to find and keep a job. Passed as a wartime measure with an eye both toward maximizing available manpower on the home front and toward aiding veterans disabled in their nation's service, it expanded the services offered under the civilian Vocational Rehabilitation Act of 1920, and it established the federal Office of Vocational Rehabilitation. The act also included provisions for medical, surgical, and mental health services as well as physical rehabilitation for adults with disabilities, all under the bureaucratic umbrella of the newly organized Federal Security Agency, later the federal department of Health, Education and Welfare. The LaFollette-Barden Act is credited with helping to bring unprecedented numbers of disabled people into the work force.

See also Vocational Rehabilitation and Vocational Rehabilitation Acts and Amendments.

References Groce, Nora, *The U.S. Role in International Disability Activities: A History and a Look towards the Future* (1992); Rothstein, Laura F., *Disabilities and the Law* (1992).

Lane, Harlan (b. 1936)
Harlan Lane is a specialist in the psychology of language, and in deafness and the history of American Sign Language (ASL) and Deaf culture. The author of *The Mask of Benevolence: Disabling the Deaf Community* (1992), *When the Mind Hears: A History of the Deaf* (1984), *The Wild Boy of Aveyron* (1976), and *Deaf and Hearing Children*

(1976), Lane lectures at the Harvard Medical School and is a research associate at the Massachusetts Institute of Technology and a distinguished professor at Northeastern University in Boston.

Lane was born on 19 August 1936, in New York City. He received his master's degree from Columbia University in 1958, his doctorate in psychology from Harvard University in 1960, and a state doctorate in linguistics from the University of Paris (the Sorbonne) in 1973. He became chair of the psychology department at Northeastern in 1974, founding its program of instruction in ASL and sponsoring research on ASL, the Deaf community, and deafness. Among his other works are *A Journey into the Deaf World* (1996), *Deaf People in Society: Education and Access* (which he edited in 1994), *Looking Back: A Reader on the History of Deaf Communities and Their Sign Languages* (edited with R. Fischer, 1993), and *Diary of a Deaf Boy: The Youth of Laurent Clerc* (edited with Cathryn Carroll, 1991).

See also American Sign Language; Deaf Culture.

References Lane, Harlan, *The Wild Boy of Aveyron* (1976); ———, *When the Mind Hears: A History of the Deaf* (1984, 1988); ———, *The Mask of Benevolence: Disabling the Deaf Community* (1993).

Language and Disability
Language can be a powerful tool for both oppression and liberation. Members of ethnic, religious, and racial minorities have always objected to certain demeaning words and expressions when used to describe them. Similar objections have long been raised by disability rights advocates, who reject words and phrases such as *hopelessly crippled, deformed, twisted, afflicted by, stricken with, invalid, misshapen,* and others. Such language, they argue, objectifies and diminishes them, and contributes to their second-class citizenship. Euphemisms

such as *physically challenged, differently abled,* and *hearing impaired,* coined by social service and medical professionals, are also generally rejected by disability advocates.

"The language of disability," writes historian Paul Longmore, "indicates that persons with disabilities are usually perceived exclusively in terms of their disabilities, that they are confined to a 'handicapped role' in which they are seen primarily as recipients of medical treatment, and that this role also includes ascribed traits of helplessness, dependency, abnormality of appearance and mode of functioning, pervasive incapacitation of every aspect of personhood, and ultimately subhumanness." Longmore points out that "the most common terms used to identify persons with disabilities"—such as "'the handicapped,' 'the disabled,' 'the deaf,' 'the blind,' 'the mentally retarded,'"—are used as "abstract nouns," lumping people together on the basis of "the most visible or apparent characteristic of the person" ("A Note on Language and the Social Identity of Disabled People" 1985).

Disability rights activists have attempted, with some success, to change the way society uses language to describe disabilities and the people who have them. The very phrase *person with a disability* is a product of the disability rights movement, as is the phrase *disability rights.* In "person with a disability," the person comes first in the phrase as he or she does in life: one is a human being before one is either disabled or not. Agreement on its use is not universal, however, and Leonard Kriegel has written that "to be 'disabled' or 'handicapped' is to deny oneself the rage, anger, and pride of having managed to survive as a cripple in America."

Like other minority communities, disability communities have developed their own expressions and slang. For example, people without disabilities are sometimes described as "TABs" (temporarily able-bodied people). Sometimes the old, stigmatizing labels are reclaimed, as in a slogan such as "Crip is hip," or a theater group calling itself "Wry Crips." Disability

rights activists have coined the terms *ableism* and *handicappism* to describe the attitudes that impede equal rights for people with disabilities, while *disability cool* and *disability chic* demonstrate the sense of pride people with disabilities have for themselves and their community. Some activists believe that the next step is eliminating the use of disability terms to describe negative behaviors or characteristics, for example, replacing *he turned a deaf ear* to *he ignored,* or *they were blind to the implications* to *they were oblivious.*

References Gartner, Alan, and Tom Joe, eds. *Images of the Disabled, Disabling Images* (1987); Kriegel, Leonard, *Falling into Life* (1991); Longmore, Paul K., "A Note on Language and the Social Identity of Disabled People," *American Behavioral Scientist* (January/February 1985).

Laski, Frank J. (b. 1943)

Frank J. Laski is a disability rights attorney who uses litigation to effect change in the treatment of people with disabilities. "The use of the courts for systems reform is not a one shot process," he wrote in *American Rehabilitation* in 1976, "nor is it a solitary strategy. . . . Legal action on all levels will . . . lead to a revolution which will change our lives and our relationships with the handicapped."

Frank Laski was born on 27 April 1943. He received a B.A. in government from the University of Massachusetts at Amherst in 1964 and his J.D. from Harvard Law School in 1967. Since 1976, Laski has been a member of the faculty at the Institute on Disabilities at Temple University in Philadelphia and the director of disability projects at the Public Interest Law Center of Philadelphia. He has worked at the National Center for Law and the Handicapped in South Bend, Indiana (1973–1974), the Center on Human Policy (1987), the National Institute of Handicapped Research (NIHR) (1986–1987), and elsewhere. Laski has litigated cases involving architectural access, the right of disabled infants to medical care, and the right of children with autism to quality education. He has been involved in such groundbreaking cases as *Halderman v. Pennhurst* (1978), *Timothy W. v. Rochester, N.H., School District* (1989), and *ADAPT v. Skinner* (1989). He opposes the use of "aversives" and has written and lectured extensively on such topics as disability rights law, deinstitutionalization, community housing, and employment.

See also *ADAPT v. Skinner*; Aversives; *Halderman v. Pennhurst State School & Hospital*.

Laurie, Virginia Grace Wilson "Gini" (1913–1989)

Virginia Grace Wilson Laurie, or "Gini," has been called, along with Mary Switzer, one of the "grandmothers" of the independent living movement. Laurie was the editor and guiding force behind the *Rehabilitation Gazette: International Journal of Independent Living by and for Persons with a Disability*. Although its circulation has never exceeded 12,000, the *Gazette* has had a tremendous impact on the disability community in the United States and abroad. By the time of Laurie's death in 1989, it had readers in 83 countries and was being translated into several foreign languages.

Laurie was born on 10 June 1913 in St. Louis, Missouri. A year before her birth, an epidemic of poliomyelitis caused the deaths of two of her sisters (for whom she was named) and left an older brother severely disabled. Laurie attended Randolph Macon Women's College in Lynchburg, Virginia, majoring in biology and Latin. Unable to become a physician because of the sexism of the time, she married Joseph Scott Laurie III when she was 25. They moved to Cleveland, where Virginia became a Red Cross volunteer at the Toomey Pavilion rehabilitation center during the 1949 polio epidemic. Laurie visited patients, read to them, provided personal assistance, and was accepted as part of the polio community.

Polio survivors in the 1940s could expect to be hospitalized for two years or more after the onset of their illness. During this time, they formed intense personal bonds. In an effort to keep in touch after leaving the center, staff and residents founded the *Toomeyville Gazette*, a mimeographed newsletter pulled together by volunteers and mailed out to Toomey alumni. Laurie took the (unpaid) job of editor in 1958. Together with other volunteers, she "gathered news from patients, staff, volunteers and keyholes" and sent the information to everyone listed on the Toomey Christmas card list. The renamed *Toomey j. Gazette* was incorporated in 1959 under the name Iron Lung Polio Assistance, Inc., a nonprofit organization. As a "leisurely quarterly" it offered tips on how best to turn the pages of the *Wall Street Journal* with a mouthstick and designs for a cheek-operated telephone and an "over-bed typewriter mount." "Our aim," wrote Laurie in 1960, is "to reach and advance respiratory polios all over the world and to share the problems, experiences, thoughts and adventures that would be of value." Among the *Gazette's* readers were future leaders of the disability rights movement such as Ed Roberts and Hugh Gallagher.

Under Laurie's direction, the *Gazette* published articles on legislation, activism, and what would come to be called the independent living philosophy. As early as 1963, Laurie wrote how "morally, institutionalizing young people with so many potentialities for service is wrong." The *Gazette* protested the ending of attendant funding by the National March of Dimes in 1959, and praised the passage of the Vocational Rehabilitation Amendments of 1965. The *Toomey j. Gazette* was renamed the *Rehabilitation Gazette* in 1970. "Of first importance," Laurie wrote in a 1977 *Rehabilitation Gazette* editorial, "is the right to freedom of choice to live as normal a life as possible within the community. . . . Segregation is unnormal."

Laurie was a proponent of cross-disability organizing, and she ran articles on the founding of the American Coalition of Citizens with Disabilities, becoming the only nondisabled member of its board of directors. She was a leader in calling for greater research into "post-polio syndrome"—a variety of health problems endemic to polio survivors as they age. Discerning a pattern to the complaints she was hearing from her older readers, Laurie, in 1981, organized the first international conference on post-polio problems. She founded the International Polio Network in 1985, which publishes *Polio Network News*, to disseminate information about post-polio and, in 1987, the International Ventilator Users Network, which publishes *I.V.U.N. News*. Both publications followed in the tradition of the *Gazette*, mixing first-person accounts, medical and rehabilitation advice, and news and editorials on political and social issues.

Together with Frederick M. Maynard, D. Armin Fischer, and Judy Raymond, Laurie edited and published the *Handbook on the Late Effects of Poliomyelitis for Physicians and Survivors* (1984), "the bible on post-polio problems." She wrote *Housing and Home Services for the Disabled: Guidelines and Experiences in Independent Living* (1977), a landmark exposition of the independent living philosophy. In it, she reported how "four severely disabled individuals can live at home for the cost of maintaining one in a nursing home. For both economic and humane reasons, the rules of government must be amended to make independent living as feasible as nursing home subsistence." In 1983, Laurie founded the Gazette International Networking Institute (G.I.N.I.) as an umbrella organization for the variety of networks and publications she had established. Today, both G.I.N.I. and the *Rehabilitation Gazette* are based in St. Louis, Missouri.

In her later years, Laurie became what Nora Groce called "an elder statesperson" for the disability rights movement, "staying above the fray and upon occasion quietly mediating disputes." She also became its de facto archivist, pulling together one of the world's largest collections of books, articles, letters, and documents on disability, rehabilitation, and independent living. Laurie and her husband, who shared much of her work, were awarded the President's Distinguished Service Award in 1979.

Joseph Scott Laurie died in 1985. Virginia Grace Laurie died of cancer in her native St. Louis on 28 June 1989.

See also American Coalition of Citizens with Disabilities; Personal Assistance Services.

References Groce, Nora, *The U.S. Role in International Disability Activities: A History and a Look towards the Future* (1992); Laurie, Gini, *Housing and Home Services for the Disabled: Guidelines and Experiences in Independent Living* (1977); Laurie, Virginia, "Glimpses of Gini and G.I.N.I.," *Rehabilitation Gazette* (1990).

League of the Physically Handicapped

Organized in New York City in 1935, the League of the Physically Handicapped was a direct action disability rights group foreshadowing later groups such as Disabled in Action and American Disabled for Attendant Programs Today (ADAPT). Drawing its inspiration from the labor movement, the league organized sit-ins and picket lines to protest discrimination against people with disabilities in employment and in New Deal social welfare programs. The history of the league was uncovered by historian Paul Longmore, who has interviewed several members. "They were all young adults, and they all had a physical disability. Most of them had had polio as children," although the group also included people with cerebral palsy, amputees, disabled veterans, and people with tuberculosis. Among the group's half dozen founders was Sylvia Flexer (later Sylvia Flexer Bassoff), Florence Haskell, and Hyman Abramowitz.

The league began in May 1935, when six disabled people went to the office of the Emergency Relief Bureau (ERB) in New York City to protest the fact that the ERB refused to refer people with disabilities for jobs with the federal Works Progress Administration (WPA). The six decided to hold a sit-in when the director of the ERB refused to meet with them. Abramowitz's wife, denied entrance to the office the next morning by a guard, went to speak at a rally nearby, and, within hours, several hundred people had gathered outside the ERB office to demonstrate their support for the protesters. Three of the six disabled protesters sat in for nine days, while some of the disabled picketers were arrested, attracting considerable press attention. The participants in these actions decided to form an organization that became the League of the Physically Handicapped.

At its height, the league had several hundred members. Among its actions were a three-week picket of the WPA's New York headquarters at the New York Port Authority, pickets and demonstrations at other government offices, and two trips to Washington, D.C., to meet with officials of the Roosevelt administration. Members of the group spoke at labor union meetings and leftist rallies, trying to raise awareness of the oppression of people with disabilities. The league was able to get WPA jobs for some 500 disabled New Yorkers, though it was unsuccessful in changing overall federal policy.

The league was also a precursor of disability pride. Longmore describes how "many members had been taught to be ashamed of how they looked, and so getting on a picket line was very difficult, emotionally." It sponsored social gatherings, and there were marriages within the group. After a meeting with presidential advisor Harry Hopkins in the summer of 1936, the result of another sit-in, members of the group wrote their *Thesis on Conditions of Handicaps*. This landmark report chronicled job discrimination in both the private and public sectors, and it criticized the paternalism of relief agencies, the vocational rehabilitation system, and New Deal welfare policies as they affected people with disabilities.

By the late 1930s, many of its leaders, now working and married with children, became less active politically. The group was also torn by ideological divisions and red-baiting. It dissolved sometime before 1940, but many members remained friends, and some continued their advocacy. Florence Haskell, for example, was still involved in disability rights work in the 1980s as a member of Disabled in Action.

"In the process of their activism," says Longmore, "they also became a community. Many had been socially isolated, and their activism helped to reshape their sense of themselves as people with disabilities."

See also Disability Pride; Longmore, Paul K.

Learning Disabilities Association of America (LDA)

The Learning Disabilities Association of America (LDA) is a nonprofit volunteer organization of more than 60,000 members, organized into approximately 600 state and local chapters, advocating on behalf of people with learning disabilities. Founded in 1964, its membership is composed of individuals with learning disabilities, their families, and concerned professionals. The LDA was active in passage of the Elementary and Secondary Education Amendments Act of 1969, the Education for All Handicapped Children Act of 1975, and other legislation of concern to learning disabled people and their families.

The LDA provides information to its members and to the general public, encourages research, pushes for enforcement of relevant civil rights and education law, and lobbies federal and state governments. It offers a wide range of publications including *Representing Learning Disabled Children: A Manual for Attorneys* (1987), *So You're Going to a Hearing: Preparing for a PL 94-142 Due Process Hearing* (1980), *Attention Deficit Disorder and the Law: A Guide for Advocates* (1992), and *Self-Advocacy Resources for Persons with Learning Disabilities* (1990). The LDA, based in Pittsburgh, also sponsors conferences and symposia on learning disability and publishes *LDA Newsbriefs*, a bimonthly newsletter, and the biannual *Learning Disabilities: A Multidisciplinary Journal*.

See also Education for All Handicapped Children Act of 1975.

Legal Action Center

The Legal Action Center, founded in 1972, is the only public interest law firm in the United States that specializes in legal and policy issues involving alcohol, drugs, and HIV/AIDS. It was the principal litigator on behalf of people with disabilities in *Traynor v. Turnage* (1988), *Beazer v. New York City Transit Authority* (1977), and *Mary Doe v. New York City Department of Social Services and the New York City Police Department* (settled out of court in 1995). *Beazer* prohibited New York City civil service employers from discriminating against people receiving substance abuse treatment, while *Mary Doe* involved the confidentiality of a minor who was HIV positive. The center played a major role in ensuring that the Americans with Disabilities Act of 1990 protected people with histories of alcoholism, drug dependence, and HIV/AIDS. More recently, the center (with offices in Washington, D.C., and New York City) has fought efforts to exclude people with histories of alcoholism and drug dependence from public housing, and from receiving Supplemental Security Income and Social Security Disability Insurance benefits.

See also Alcoholism, Drug Dependence; *Traynor v. Turnage* and *McKelvey v. Turnage*.

Lewis, Victoria Ann (b. 1946)

Victoria Ann Lewis is the founder and director of the Other Voices Workshop at the Los Angeles Mark Taper Forum. She describes her work as "developing strategies to translate complex social ideas into theater." She was one of the first physically disabled actors to appear in a regular role on prime-time television (as Peggy on *Knots Landing*), and she has directed a series of plays about the disability experience, including two television specials for Embassy Television: "Tell Them I'm a Mermaid" (1983) and "Who Parks in Those Spaces?" (1985). Other works she has directed and produced include "Ph*reaks: The Hidden Story of Disability" (1993), "The Greatest Stories Never Told" (1987), and "Teenage Ninja Mothers" (1991).

Lewis was born on 7 January 1946, in Kansas City, Kansas. Initially denied admission to drama school because of her disability (due to polio), Lewis went on to receive her M.A. from Columbia University and to win awards for her acting, writing, and directing. Prior to 1981, she was a writer and editor at the *Independent*, a quarterly published by the Center for Independent Living in Berkeley, and co-author (with Ann Cupolo Carrilo and Katherine Corbett) of *No More Stares*, a chronicle of women with disabilities, published by the Disability Rights Education and Defense Fund in 1982. Her work has also appeared in *Ms.* magazine, *Spare Rib*, and the *Disability Rag & Resource*, as well as various anthologies. She is currently pursuing her doctorate in theater at the University of California in Los Angeles. Since 1995, she has also been performing *Stuck*, a solo performance work she created about her experiences at an American Disabled for Attendant Programs Today (ADAPT) demonstration in Nashville.

See also Disability Culture.

"Little Paper Family" (LPF)
See Deaf Publications.

Little People of America, Inc. (LPA)

Little People of America, Inc. (LPA) is a nonprofit organization headquartered in Washington, D.C., that provides support and information to people of short stature and their families. Membership is offered to people no more than 4'10" in height, whose short stature is caused by any of 200 medical conditions known collectively as "dwarfism" and to their relatives and interested professionals.

LPA was founded in 1957. Actor William Barty issued a public appeal for little people to join him for a national meeting in Reno, Nevada, after which Barty and 20 others announced the formation of the new organization. One of the primary purposes of LPA was to combat stereotypes of little people as circus performers and objects of amusement or derision. It undertook to inform the public that most people with dwarfism have an average lifespan and intelligence and that, despite intense job discrimination, little people have become physicians, lawyers, ministers, teachers, welders, and artists. Within two years of its founding, LPA had more than 200 members, with organizers looking for new members in hospitals, fraternal groups, schools, and even jails. Barty and other founding members such as Launa Shelton Turner, Dan Turner, and Anna Dixon appeared on television programs such as "This Is Your Life" to publicize the new organization.

One issue of concern to LPA was the sudden popularity, in the late 1980s, of "sports" such as dwarf-tossing and dwarf-bowling. LPA organized efforts to convince state legislators and the general public that these exhibitions were both dangerous and demeaning. Aside from the medical issues, such as the risk of spinal cord and brain injury, LPA was concerned that the practices perpetuated "the myth that little people still belong in the side shows as objects of ridicule. . . . We are not playthings of society and we want to be taken seriously." LPA won a series of victories, beginning in Florida in June 1989, where the state legislature passed legislation banning the activities. Similar ordinances were approved later that same year by city councils in New York, New Jersey, and Michigan.

After the gene for achondroplasia—the most common type of dwarfism—was discovered in 1994, LPA expressed concern about the possible eugenic use of new discoveries in genetics. While some LPA members are excited about discoveries that lead to a better understanding of their conditions, others fear that genetic tests developed to detect dwarfism before birth might lead to the routine abortion of all dwarf fetuses. In its *Position Statement on Genetic Discoveries in Dwarfism* (1996), LPA stressed, "We as short statured individuals are productive members of society who must inform the world that, though we face challenges, most of them are environmental . . . and we value the opportunity to contribute a unique perspective to the diversity of our society."

See also Abortion and Reproductive Rights; Eugenics; "Freaks" as Circus Performers; Media Images of People with Disabilities.

Lloyd v. Regional Transportation Authority 548 F.2d 1277 (1977)

George A. Lloyd, quadriplegic since 1953, and Janet B. Wolfe, mobility-disabled because of a chronic pulmonary dysfunction, filed a class action suit on behalf of all mobility-disabled people living in northeastern Illinois against the Regional Transportation Authority (RTA) of that area and the Chicago Transit Authority. They argued that the inaccessibility of the mass transit system was a violation of Section 504 of the Rehabilitation Act of 1973 and other disability rights law. They asked the court to prohibit the RTA from purchasing or putting into operation any new federally funded facilities, unless these were accessible, and to require that the existing system be made accessible. The district court dismissed the suit, saying that the laws in question did not confer "a private right of action," that is, the ability of individual citizens to sue for enforcement. The plaintiffs appealed, and the case was argued before the U.S. Court of Appeals for the Seventh Circuit on 1 December 1976.

The court ruled on 18 January 1977 that Section 504 did in fact give plaintiffs the right to sue for its enforcement. It cited the similarity between Section 504 and Section 601 of the Civil Rights Act of 1964, which the federal courts had long maintained provided a private right of action. The case was remanded to the district court, which ruled that not providing access in mass transit (for example, wheelchair lifts on buses) discriminated against people with disabilities. By contrast, the U.S. Court of Appeals for the Fifth Circuit upheld a ruling, in *Snowden v. Birmingham-Jefferson County Transit Authority* (1977), that transit companies operating buses without lifts did not discriminate against wheelchair users, provided they did nothing to prevent them from attempting to drag their wheelchairs onto the bus. These two decisions did little to settle the controversy over the access obligations of public transit providers.

See also Public Transportation; Section 504 of the Rehabilitation Act of 1973.

Local Option
See Americans Disabled for Accessible Public Transit v. Skinner (ADAPT v. Skinner).

Longmore, Paul K. (b. 1946)
Paul K. Longmore, along with Hugh Gregory Gallagher and Jack R. Gannon, is one of the first historians to "uncover the hidden history of people with disabilities." His writings provide an important conceptual framework for disability rights activism.

"Only recently," Longmore writes in his article "Elizabeth Bouvia, Assisted Suicide and Social Prejudice" (1987), "have historians begun to reconstruct the social history of persons with disabilities and the ideological history of 'disability.' . . . Historical research is substantiating that, whatever the social setting and whatever the disability, people with disabilities have been, and are, subjected to a common set of prejudicial values and attitudes and share a common experience of social oppression."

Longmore was born on 10 July 1946 in Mount Holly, New Jersey, contracting polio in 1953. He received his B.A. in history from Occidental College in Los Angeles in 1968 and his doctorate from Claremont Graduate School in California in 1984. His dissertation, "The Invention of George Washington," became the basis for his book of the same title, published in 1988. He was administrator of the Program in Disability and Society at the University of Southern California in Los Angeles from 1983 to 1986, visiting assistant professor of history at Stanford University from 1990 to 1993, and assistant professor

of history at San Francisco State University beginning in 1992, receiving his tenure there as an associate professor in 1995.

Longmore is an articulate chronicler of the development of disability rights theory. "Social scientists studying the disability experience have increasingly turned to a minority group model, defining 'disability' . . . as a socially constructed identity and role triggered by a stigmatized biological trait." In his essay on Elizabeth Bouvia, Longmore examines the prejudices of those arguing for the assisted suicide of people with disabilities, noting "their persistent use of intensely stigmatizing language: disabled people are defective, damaged, debilitated, deformed. . . . Apparently, to live with disability is to 'suffer' and to suffer because of disability. There is no recognition that the greatest suffering of people with disabilities is the socially stigmatized identity inflected upon them." This "stigmatized identity" is reflected in our mass media. Longmore's essay "Screening Stereotypes" (1987) examines the prevalence of disabled villains, from the malevolent dwarf in the *Wild Wild West* television series to the one-armed man in the *Fugitive*, to movie depictions of disability as pathos in *Whose Life Is It, Anyway?* and the television movie "An Act of Love," which recounts the murder of someone with a disability.

Longmore is a member of the editorial board of *Disability Studies Quarterly*, the advisory board of the Chicago Center for Disability Research, the Organization of American Historians, the Society for Disability Studies, and a variety of other boards and organizations.

See also League of the Physically Handicapped; Media Images of Disability.

References Longmore, Paul K., "Screening Stereotypes: Images of Disabled People in Television and Motion Pictures," in *Images of the Disabled, Disabling Images* (1987); ———, "Uncovering the Hidden History of People with Disabilities," *Reviews in American History* (September 1987); ———, "Elizabeth Bouvia, Assisted Suicide and Social Prejudice," *Issues in Law & Medicine* (December 1987).

McDaniel, Durward K. (1915–1994)

Durward K. McDaniel was one of the principal founders of the American Council of the Blind (ACB) and a leader of that organization through its first two decades. A distinguished civil rights attorney, McDaniel was instrumental in fashioning the ACB into a large and active disability rights group.

McDaniel was born on 25 November 1915. An activist with the National Federation of the Blind, he and others broke with that group in the late 1950s, establishing the ACB in 1961. For many years, he was the ACB's only Washington representative. He was also the legal counsel for the Randolph-Sheppard Vendors of America (RSVA) and advocated for passage of the Randolph-Sheppard Amendments of 1974. (The amendments, among other changes, gave blind operators priority in operating vending stands in all buildings leased or owned by the federal government.) A pioneer in cross-disability activism, McDaniel was an early organizer of the American Coalition of Citizens with Disabilities.

McDaniel received the Distinguished Service Award from President Clinton on 21 March 1993. He died on 6 September 1994.

See also American Council of the Blind; Randolph-Sheppard Act of 1936 and its Amendments.

Mace, Ronald L. (b. 1941)

Ronald L. Mace is an architect, a product designer, and an advocate for accessible architecture. He is the founder and director of the Center for Universal Design at North Carolina State University in Raleigh, the founder and president of Barrier Free Environments, and a member of the faculty at Fayetteville Technical Institute in North Carolina. Mace has been instrumental in the evolution of access and *universal design*—a phrase he coined to denote designing products and buildings for accessibility to everyone.

Mace was born on 3 August 1941 in Jersey City, New Jersey. A wheelchair user since contracting polio at age 9, he has always tried, he says, "to redesign my whole environment—particularly since we lived in some pretty lousily designed houses when I was a kid." He graduated from North Carolina State University in Raleigh with a B.A. in architecture in 1966. He was soon trying to convincing the firms he worked for to include access in their designs, with limited success. Frustrated, he left the profession to teach, and was then inducted into an effort by rehabilitation professionals to draft an access code for North Carolina. As both an architect and a person with a disability, Mace served as an intermediary between the two communities. Mace ended up drafting the Handicapped Section of the North Carolina Building Code. The code was published as a book, illustrated and easy to read, and it was an effective introduction for architects and laypeople to the concept of architectural access. In 1974, the code became law. It was the most far-reaching standard of the time, serving as a model for subsequent legislation in other states. Mace himself was a consultant on the development of access codes in Washington, Georgia, Illinois, New Jersey, Florida, and elsewhere. He has also been an access consultant for government agencies, public institutions, and private businesses, including the U.S. Department of Housing and Urban Development, the Washington National Airport, and the Hyatt Hotels Corporation. In 1976, he was a consultant for accessibility renovations in the U.S. Capitol Building. He has also been integrally involved with the update of access standards by the American National Standards Institute (ANSI).

In the 1980s, Mace developed the concept of "adaptability"—designing dwellings with features such as lower light switches and reinforced bathroom beams for grab bars for increased accessibility. This concept was crucial to passage of the Fair Housing Amendments Act of 1988, offering a compromise between no access at all and government-mandated access in private dwellings. Mace frequently testifies before Congress, and he provides his expertise to advocates when they lobby for disability rights legislation.

Mace is the author of articles, brochures, and books on accessible design, including the *Fair Housing Act Accessibility Guideline Design Manual* (1995), *Universal Design: Housing for the Lifespan of All People* (1988), and *Adaptable Housing* (1987, with J. A. Bostrom and M. G. B. Long). Among other honors, he received the President's Distinguished Service Award in 1992.

See also Architectural Access; Barrier Free Environments; Center for Universal Design; Housing; Universal Design.

Reference Johnson, Mary, "Universal Man: Architect Ron Mace Leads the Way to Design That Includes Everybody," *Mainstream* (August 1994).

Madness Network News
See Psychiatric Survivor Movement.

Mainstream: Magazine for the Able-Disabled

Mainstream: Magazine for the Able-Disabled was founded in 1975 as a news monthly focused on "trying to bring Section 504 of the Rehab Act into implementation," along with the Education for All Handicapped Children Act. Since then, it has featured articles on important developments in legislation, litigation, demonstrations, mass media, and disability culture and lifestyles. *Mainstream* has been a pioneer in exploring issues of sexuality, racism, universal design, the international disability rights movement, parenting, do-

mestic violence, and sexual abuse. It also provides coverage of wheelchair athletics and athletes.

Mainstream was the brainchild of Jim Hammitt. Born with cerebral palsy, Hammitt fought his way through "the vagaries of special education," and then through community college, where he first conceived of a magazine published by and for people with disabilities. In 1975, he established Able-Disabled Advocacy, Inc., a nonprofit program for people with disabilities who wanted to learn marketable skills and obtain work experience. *Mainstream* was an outgrowth of Able-Disabled Advocacy. When Able-Disabled Advocacy ran out of funds in 1982, *Mainstream* was sold to Exploding Myths, Inc., a for-profit corporation entirely owned by people with disabilities, and Cyndi Jones became publisher and editor.

Mainstream, edited by William G. Strothers, has a circulation of 21,000, with an estimated readership of 94,000. It is based in San Diego, California.

See also Jones, Cyndi.

Mainstreaming
See Education for All Handicapped Children Act of 1975.

Marcus, Neil (b. 1954)
Neil Marcus is a performance artist, an actor, and the author of *Storm Reading* (1988, written with Rod Laithim and Roger Marcus and produced by Access Theatre), *My Sexual History* (1992), *The Art of Human Being* (1994), and other works. "You stare at me in fear," Marcus tells his audience, "without realizing you have just come one step closer to liberation." Part of this liberation comes by recasting the language used to describe disability. In one scene from "Storm Reading," Marcus recounts how the Dystonia Medical Foundation describes his disability (Dystonia Musculoram Deformans, with which he was diagnosed at age 8) as "the most severe and painful form of

the disorder, denying him the ability to speak, stand, walk and/or control sudden and sometimes bizarre movements." Marcus changes this description to "flourishing dystonia—a neurological condition that allows me to leap and soar and twist and turn constantly in public . . . making me very interesting to sit next to at lunch time." *Storm Reading* has been performed at the World Theatre (St. Paul, Minnesota), the James A. Doolittle Theatre (Hollywood, California), Ford's Theatre and the Kennedy Center for the Performing Arts (both in Washington, D.C.), and elsewhere. *Storm Reading* was filmed in its entirety, and it was broadcast on Kaleidoscope: The Health and Disability Channel in September 1996.

Marcus was born on 3 January 1954 in White Plains, New York, and raised in Ojai, California. Like many disabled children, he grew up isolated from disability culture and community, until he became involved in the disabled student organization at Solano Community College in northern California. Marcus' writing has appeared in *Toward Solomon's Mountain* (1986), an anthology of disabled poets, and he is the founder (in 1979) and editor of the disability counseling journal *Complete Elegance*. He is also the author of the children's book *The Princess and the Dragon: A Disabled Fable* (1988). Marcus' work was awarded the Medal of Honor by the United Nations Society of Writers in 1992. He is featured in the 1990 film documentary *Speaking through the Walls* and in the NBC-TV special "From the Heart" (1989).

Martha's Vineyard Deaf Community

Martha's Vineyard is an island off the southeastern coast of Massachusetts. Today, it is known as a resort community, but for more than a century it was a whaling and shipping center and one of the busiest seaports in the United States. For more than two centuries, Martha's Vineyard was also the site of a thriving community of deaf people. Nora Ellen Groce, in her book *Everyone Here Spoke Sign: Heredi-*

tary Deafness on Martha's Vineyard (1985), documents how deaf people were accepted as equal citizens, and hearing people learned sign language almost as commonly as they learned to read and write English. Deafness, according to one of Groce's informants, "was pretty much taken for granted. . . . It was as if somebody had brown eyes and somebody else had blue . . . as if . . . somebody was lame and somebody had trouble with his wrist." "One of the strongest indications that the deaf were completely integrated into all aspects of society," writes Groce, "is that in all the interviews I conducted, deaf Islanders were never thought of or referred to as a group or 'the deaf.' Every one of the deaf people who is remembered today is thought of as a unique individual."

The result of this acceptance of disability was that deaf people on Martha's Vineyard married, were employed, owned homes and businesses, and were integrated into the community at far higher rates than their deaf compatriots on the mainland. Eighty percent of deaf people graduated from high school—the same percentage as hearing islanders. Ninety percent of deaf people married, as compared to 92 percent of hearing islanders. Income levels were similar, as were family size and types of occupation. Ironically, all of this was accomplished through the use of sign language, which oralists believed to be inherently limiting and isolating.

The deaf community on Martha's Vineyard (also referred to as the Chilmark Community) began to dissipate beginning in the 1860s, when deaf children were sent "off-island" to be educated at residential schools. Many remained "off-island," marrying and pursuing their lives on the mainland.

See also Deaf Culture.

Reference Groce, Nora Ellen, *Everyone Here Spoke Sign: Hereditary Deafness on Martha's Vineyard* (1985).

Martin, Douglas A. (b. 1947)

Douglas A. Martin has been a nationally known disability rights advocate since the

1970s. A co-founder of, and the first executive director of, the Westside Center for Independent Living, Inc., in Los Angeles, Martin has advocated for the elimination of work disincentives under the Social Security Disability Insurance (SSDI) and Supplemental Security Income (SSI) programs and has been at the forefront of every major reform of both programs for the past two decades.

Martin was born on 8 May 1947 in rural Nebraska. He contracted polio at the age of 5 and spent several years at Children's Hospital in Omaha. When he returned home in 1956, he was denied access to his local public school system, and he instead received minimal home schooling. Even so, he did well enough on a statewide exam to win a college scholarship. Officials at the University of Nebraska in Lincoln decided that Martin, a respiratory quadriplegic, was "too disabled to attend college." Martin was accepted instead at the University of California in Los Angeles, where he earned his undergraduate degree in urban geography and urban planning summa cum laude and Phi Beta Kappa in 1973, concurrently completing his master's degree in the same subjects and becoming the first significantly disabled person to receive the UCLA Chancellor's Fellowship. Martin remained at UCLA and received his doctorate in urban studies in 1975.

That same year, Martin co-founded the Westside Center for Independent Living, Inc. He served as its executive director (without pay) for the next three years. In the late 1970s, he was the chair of the Southern California branch of Californians for Strong Access and was an advocate for the issuing and implementation of the Section 504 (of the Rehabilitation Act of 1973) regulations. In 1978, he consulted with the producers of CBS's *60 Minutes* on "Help Wanted," a segment highlighting the injustice of SSI work disincentives. At that time himself a recipient of SSI benefits, Martin began a campaign to convince Congress to reform Social Security law that culminated in the passage in 1986 of the Employment Opportunities for Dis-

abled Americans Act. As a result of Martin's advocacy, an estimated 550,000 disabled SSI recipients have been able to obtain work. As an added benefit, it is estimated that, from 1986 to 1996, Martin's reforms saved the Social Security system more than $110 million. Martin, as chair of the National Council on Independent Living's Social Security Subcommittee (1986 to 1991) and as a fellow at the World Institute on Disability (1985 to present), also spearheaded the development and enactment of reforms in Medicare for SSDI beneficiaries.

Among other positions, Martin has been the Disability Services coordinator for Culver City, California (1983–1989), a member of the Advisory Committee for the National Council on Disability Study of Health Insurance and Health Related Services for Persons with Disabilities (1990–1992), and a founding member, in 1987, of the Society for Disability Studies. Martin is currently the special assistant to the chancellor/ADA and Section 504 compliance officer at UCLA, a position he has held since 1989.

See also Disincentives; Employment Opportunities for Disabled Americans Act of 1986; Social Security; Social Security Disability Insurance; Supplemental Security Income.

Matlin, Marlee (b. 1965)

Marlee Matlin was born on 24 August 1965 in Morton Grove, Illinois, and attended William Rainey Harper College in Palatine. She is an actor and representative of deaf culture, best known for her role as Sarah Norman in the movie version of *Children of a Lesser God* (1986), for which she won an Academy Award. Her other films include *Walker* (1987) and *Bridge to Silence* (1989). In 1991, she appeared as a regular character in the television series *Reasonable Doubts*. She is also the host of *People in Motion*, a documentary series appearing on PBS on the lives of people with disabilities.

See also Children of a Lesser God.

Maurer, Marc (b. 1951)

Marc Maurer, president of the National Federation of the Blind (NFB), is one of the nation's leading authorities on laws, litigation, and administrative rulings concerning the civil rights of people who are blind.

Maurer was born on 3 June 1951 in Boone, Iowa. Like tens of thousands of American infants born prematurely from the late 1940s to the mid-1950s, Maurer became blind as a result of overexposure to oxygen while in an incubator. He attended the residential Iowa Braille and Sight Saving School in Vinton until the fifth grade, when he returned to Boone to attend parochial schools. He graduated from high school in 1969 and enrolled as a student at the Orientation and Adjustment Center of the Iowa Commission for the Blind (now the Iowa Department for the Blind) in Des Moines. He met Kenneth Jernigan, at that time the director of the Iowa Commission as well as president of the NFB. Maurer joined the NFB, and in 1971 was elected president of its Student Division, then re-elected in 1973 and 1975. He graduated from the University of Notre Dame in South Bend, Indiana, in 1974 and received his J.D. from the University of Indiana School of Law in 1977. He moved to Toledo, Ohio, to accept a position as the director of the Senior Legal Assistance Project of Advocates for Basic Legal Equality (ABLE).

Maurer moved to Washington, D.C., in 1978 to become an attorney with the Civil Aeronautics Board, and then to Baltimore in 1981 to go into private practice. He specialized in civil rights litigation, representing blind individuals and a variety of blindness organizations. Maurer became president of the Maryland chapter of the NFB in 1984. He was elected president of the NFB in 1986 and has served in that capacity since.

See also National Federation of the Blind.

Mayerson, Arlene B. (b. 1949)

Arlene B. Mayerson is one of the nation's leading experts and theoreticians in disability rights law, "the secret weapon" (as disability rights advocate Patrisha Wright calls her) for disability rights. Since 1981, she has been the directing attorney for the Disability Rights Education and Defense Fund (DREDF), overseeing that organization's groundbreaking work in litigation and national policy development.

Mayerson was born on 11 November 1949 in Cincinnati, Ohio. She received her B.S. in political science and secondary education from Boston University in 1971, her J.D. from the Boalt Hall School of Law at the University of California at Berkeley in 1977, and her L.L.M. from the Georgetown University Law Center in Washington, D.C., in 1978. She was a graduate law fellow at the Institute for Public Interest Representation at the Georgetown Law Center in 1978. In 1979, she became a staff attorney at the Disability Law Resource Center at the Center for Independent Living in Berkeley (the predecessor to DREDF), where she represented people with disabilities and parents of children with disabilities in discrimination claims. In a first-of-its-kind victory, she successfully represented parents of disabled children who sought to halt federal Department of Health, Education and Welfare funding to the state of California for failing to implement the Education for All Handicapped Children Act of 1975, the first time this strategy had been used to compel compliance with federal disability rights law.

Mayerson has served as a key advisor to Congress, federal agencies, several presidential administrations, and the disability community on the development and implementation of such major disability rights law as the Handicapped Children's Protection Act, the Civil Rights Restoration Act, the Fair Housing Amendments Act, and the Americans with Disabilities Act (ADA). She has represented clients, consulted with attorneys, and coordinated amicus strategies for all of the major disability rights cases argued before the Supreme Court, including *Alexander v. Choate* (1984), *Consolidated Rail Corp. v.*

Darrone (1984), and *School Board of Nassau County v. Arline* (1987). In the tradition of Louis D. Brandeis, Mayerson has championed the use of briefs to educate the Court about the oppression of people with disabilities, specializing in amicus briefs on behalf of members of Congress.

In the early 1980s, Mayerson developed the legal analysis used to challenge the Reagan administration's attempt to deregulate Section 504 of the Rehabilitation Act and the Education for All Handicapped Children Act. She represented the disability community on the Leadership Conference on Civil Rights team that drafted the Civil Rights Restoration Act of 1987. Mayerson served as expert outside counsel during deliberations by congressional committees on how to overturn the Supreme Court decision in *Smith v. Robinson* (1984), which limited due process rights in education for parents of disabled children. Arguing that parents of disabled children should have the same civil rights protection afforded other groups, she authored a paper analyzing the impact on minority children of unequal due process protections. Her analysis was instrumental in securing the Congressional Black Caucus endorsement of the Handicapped Children's Protection Act of 1986.

Mayerson also served as outside counsel during enactment of the Americans with Disabilities Act to Senators Edward M. Kennedy (D–MA) and Thomas Harkin (D–IA), prime sponsors of the ADA. She monitored the ADA drafting process, crafting revisions and coordinating proposed legislative language with national organizations and advocates. Her legal analysis is found throughout the legislative history of the ADA and its implementing regulations. Mayerson also provided expert testimony during hearings on the ADA, and she coordinated the testimony of others.

As DREDF directing attorney, Mayerson emphasizes cases that set a federal, law-reforming precedent in disability rights. One innovation she developed is the use of the ADA to break down barriers to the participation of disabled children in day care. Mayerson won a nationwide case against KinderCare, the nation's largest day care provider, which had barred children with juvenile diabetes, who required a finger prick blood test during the day, from participating in their day care programs.

Mayerson is the author of numerous publications, including the three-volume *Americans with Disabilities Act Annotated* (1994), "The History of the ADA: A Movement Perspective," in *Implementing the Americans with Disabilities Act* (Gostin and Beyers 1993), and "Smashing Icons: Disabled Women and the Disability and Women's Movement," in *Women with Disabilities: Essays in Psychology, Culture, and Politics* (Asch and Fine 1988).

Mayerson is an adjunct professor in disability rights law at the University of California Boalt Hall School of Law and Stanford Law School.

See also Americans with Disabilities Act of 1990; Civil Rights Restoration Act of 1987; Disability Rights Education and Defense Fund; *Holland v. Sacramento City Unified School District.*

Media Images of People with Disabilities

Leye J. Chrzanowski, editor-in-chief of *One Step Ahead—The Resource for Active, Healthy, Independent Living*, writes, "Every time we start breaking down stereotypes, we're slapped back into the 'helpless cripple' role by a *Love Affair* or a *Passion Fish*." Adding "insult to injury, someone without a disability acting out this delusion is usually either an Oscar nominee or winner."

Until very recently, most mass media depictions of people with disabilities played in one way or another to these "helpless cripple" stereotypes. If not pathetic and childlike, disabled characters were portrayed as embittered by their disability, even setting out to wreak vengeance on the nondisabled world. For these fictional characters, outward physical disability was a manifestation of an inner, spiritual evil. Alternatively, the disabled characters were players in what historian Paul Longmore calls "dramas of adjustment," stories in

English physicist Stephen Hawking, in a cameo appearance on Star Trek: The Next Generation. *The popular television series featured a regular character, Geordi LaForge, who defied the "helpless cripple" media stereotype through his sense of pride in his identity as a disabled person.*

porting their own rights; few face problems of physical accessibility."

People with mental or psychiatric disabilities, meanwhile, have almost always been depicted as weird, dangerous "nuts." From Alfred Hitchcock's main character in *Psycho* (1960) to the "lethal schizophrenic" of *Serial Mom* (1994), popular culture rarely acknowledges the reality that people with mental disabilities are far more likely to be victims of violence than they are to be violent offenders.

Perhaps most insidious are those depictions generated by nondisabled writers, producers, and entertainers with the goal of "helping the helpless" or drawing "inspiration" from their "courage." Newspaper and magazine stories about disabled people using headlines such as "No Longer a Human Wreck" or "Bilateral Amputee Is a Lesson in Courage" serve to reassure nondisabled readers that "overcoming" disability is a matter of personal courage, having nothing to do with access or social attitudes. They also depict disability in an entirely negative light, as if no person could ever be comfortable at being disabled. In these depictions, people with disabilities are seen as doing extraordinary things to "conquer" or deny their disability: the blind mountain climber, the paralyzed skydiver, the "supercrip" who never complains about his or her lot in life. Says George Covington, "We're seen as 'inspirational,' and inspiration sells like hotcakes. My disability isn't a burden; having to be so damned inspirational is."

In response, people with disabilities have created their own disability counterculture. Filmmakers such as Neal Jimenez and Billy Golfus, writers such as Cheryl Marie Wade and Anne Finger, and actors such as Marlee Matlin and Ellen Stohl all present their own version of the realities of life with a disability. At the same time, the disability rights movement has had an impact on the mainstream media. While much children's programming still parlays images of people with disabilities as evil or bizarre, programs such as *Sesame Street* feature disabled characters (played by disabled actors)

which characters come to terms with their disabilities, but only through the intercession of a nondisabled friend. In these accounts, people with disabilities were either (again) embittered and self-isolated, as in films such as *Passion Fish* (1992) and *Whose Life Is This Anyway?* (1981), or saintlike and inspiring. Even the more sympathetic of these dramas, such as *The Best Years of Our Lives* (1946), depicted disabled people as oppressed, not by ableist attitudes or lack of access, but by their own stubbornness and self-loathing.

"In looking at some 100 cases of [spinal] cord-injured characters, it is interesting to note that few are shown as parents, either pre-or-post injury, . . ." says Lauri Klobas, in *Spinal Network: The Total Resource for the Wheelchair Community* (1988). "[F]ew are illustrated as being politically active in supas individuals like anyone else, and a series as popular as *Star Trek: The Next Generation* has portrayed a person with a disability, in this case blindness, as a full member of the crew, not only competent at his job but also actually comfortable with and proud of his identity as a disabled person. (It should be noted, however, that this character, Geordi LaForge, was nevertheless played by a nondisabled actor). By the mid-1980s, major corporations were using people with disabilities in their television and print advertising. As in media depictions of women and people of color, these changes have been the result of the growing political and social clout of those who had been previously unorganized and unrepresented.

See also Ableism; *The Best Years of Our Lives; Children of a Lesser God; Coming Home*; Disability Blackface; National Stigma Clearinghouse.

References Gartner, Alan, and Tom Joe, eds., *Images of the Disabled, Disabling Images* (1987); Norden, Martin F., *The Cinema of Isolation: A History of Physical Disability in the Movies* (1994); Zinn, Harlan, *Media Stereotypes of Mental Illnesses* (1995).

Mental Health Law Project
See Judge David L. Bazelon Center for Mental Health Law.

Mental Patients' Liberation Front (MPLF)

The Mental Patients' Liberation Front (MPLF) was founded in Boston in 1971 by two former mental patients meeting at the offices of the journal *Radical Therapist*. Its purpose is to secure the civil rights of people who are hospitalized because of a psychiatric disability. Among its first projects was the publication of *Your Rights as a Mental Patient* (1975), a 56-page booklet dealing with issues such as voluntary versus involuntary commitment, the rights of ex-patients in child custody cases, government and personal access to psychiatric records, job discrimination, and discrimination when filing for a driver's license or applying to college. Members of the group distributed copies of *Your Rights* to in-pa-

tients at Boston State Hospital, ran weekly current events groups inside that institution, and helped patients at other institutions to form their own advocacy groups. The MPLF was incorporated in 1974.

In April 1975, seven members of the group, patients at Boston State Hospital, filed the landmark patients' rights case *Rogers v. Okrin*, in which they challenged the hospital's practice of secluding and medicating patients against their will. The U.S. District Court for the District of Massachusetts ruled in 1979 that mental patients have a constitutional right to refuse treatment in nonemergency situations. The ruling was appealed and eventually was heard by the U.S. Court of Appeals for the First Circuit (*Rogers v. Commissioner of Mental Health* 1983), which affirmed the right of Massachusetts patients to refuse treatment, specifically psychiatric drugs, concluding that "a mental patient has the right to make treatment decisions and does not lose that right until the patient is adjudicated incompetent by a judge through incompetence proceedings." The court also ruled, however, that "the police power of the Commonwealth permits forcible medication as a chemical restraint . . . in an emergency," and "forcible treatment with antipsychotic drugs may be given to a patient to prevent the immediate, substantial, and irreversible deterioration of a serious mental illness." The result of the decision, therefore, has been mixed, and patients' rights advocates complain that judges often "rubber stamp" the requests of doctors to treat patients against their will. Similar cases were brought in New York (*Rivers v. Katz* 1986) and California (*Reise v. St. Mary's Hospital* 1987) with similar results.

In the early 1980s, the MPLF organized demonstrations against electro-convulsive therapy (ECT) and psychosurgery, picketing the Massachusetts General Hospital in Boston. In 1985, the MPLF founded the Ruby Rogers Center, named after an MPLF activist and a principal litigant in *Rogers*. It is one of the only client-run mental health facilities in the nation, with the MPLF as its parent corporation.

See also Psychiatric Survivor Movement.

Reference Chamberlin, Judi, "The Ex-Patients' Movement: Where We'e Been and Where We're Going," *Journal of Mind and Behavior* (Summer/Autumn 1990).

Metropolitan Area Transit Authority ("METRO") Access Campaign

In the early 1960s, the Washington Metropolitan Area Transit Authority (WMATA) began plans for an all-new subway and rail system to serve the nation's capital. Access advocates in the Washington Architectural Barrier Project met with WMATA officials as early as 1964 to explain the need for accessibility. As disability rights activist Richard Heddinger explained, "Without elevators hundreds of thousands of elderly and handicapped persons in the Washington area would be barred from using the METRO system. If elevators were not available, many . . . who are now users of the public bus system would literally be stranded when many future bus routes end at METRO stations. And millions across the nation would be denied the use of METRO when visiting the Nation's Capitol."

What followed was a 12-year battle between WMATA officials and disability rights advocates. Officials at first claimed that funds were not available even to *study* access, let alone implement it, and so disability advocates conducted their own study under the auspices of the President's Committee on Employment of the Handicapped. This study, "Barrier Free Rapid Transit," by architect E. H. Noakes, was finished in 1969. In the meantime, Congress had enacted the Architectural Barriers Act of 1968, mandating access in federally funded construction projects such as the METRO. Nonetheless, METRO officials ignored the study, disregarded the law, and announced plans for construction of an entirely inaccessible, 87-station system. In March 1970, Pub. Law 91-205 was passed by Congress, amending the Architectural Barriers Act specifically to require that the METRO be accessible. WMATA ignored this law as well.

On 19 April 1972, frustrated by WMATA's intransigence, the Paralyzed Veterans of America, the National Paraplegia Foundation, and Richard Heddinger filed suit in federal court, seeking an injunction to prevent "construction which would make the provision of elevators more costly." This initial injunction was denied; however, on 29 June 1972, the court ruled that the METRO was required to be accessible and warned that stations would not be permitted to open without elevators. In August 1973, Congress appropriated the estimated $65 million it would cost to make the system accessible (out of a total budget that eventually reached $2.5 billion). WMATA continued to balk, however, refusing to commit to having elevators ready in stations as they opened. On 23 October 1973, the District Court of the District of Columbia issued a permanent injunction prohibiting stations without elevators from opening. In November 1973, the WMATA board of directors finally voted to install elevators. "It was not until the middle of 1974," Heddinger noted, "4 years after METRO construction began, that actual work began on the elevator shafts at the first station!"

The battle, however, was not yet over. Plans indicated that "in at least a dozen of the 87 stations, WMATA was not providing 'ready access' as required by law." In some stations elevators were to be located as much as a third of a mile away from where the trains would come in, the length, as Heddinger points out, "of well over five football fields." Advocates again brought their concerns to WMATA officials, who again ignored them. Instead, in 1975, WMATA returned to court, requesting that three of the first six stations to be finished be allowed to open without elevators. Disability activists agreed that two of the three need not have elevators, but they would not concede the centrally located stop at Gallery Place. WMATA asked the court to exempt this station from immediate access, but it refused. Accessible METRO stations were allowed to open, but trains had to pass by the otherwise finished Gallery Place without stopping. This marked the first time ever that a public facility was ordered not to open because of lack of access. WMATA was able to circumvent the injunction, however, by obtaining a waiver from the General Accounting Office, which was charged with enforcing the Architectural Barriers Act. Finally, six months after the rest of the system opened in 1976, the Gallery Place elevator was installed.

This accomplishment was a significant, if long delayed, victory for disability rights advocates. Richard Bryant Treanor, in *We Overcame: The Story of Civil Rights for Disabled People* (1993), writes that the District of Columbia subway is today "a model for accessible subways in other cities, not only in America but throughout the world."

See also Architectural Barriers Act of 1968; Public Transportation.

References Heddinger, Richard W., "The Twelve Year Battle for a Barrier Free METRO," *American Rehabilitation* (March/April 1976); Treanor, Richard Bryant, *We Overcame: The Story of Civil Rights for Disabled People* (1993).

Milam, Lorenzo Wilson (b. 1933)

Lorenzo Wilson Milam is an author, media consultant, critic, and observer of the disability community and experience. Among his best-known works are *The Cripple Liberation Front Marching Band Blues* (1984) and *Crip Zen: A Manual for Survival* (1993). They are written, Milam says, "as an antidote to the Life-Is-Great-No-Matter-What-Happens message that has plagued us since the advent of the good Dr. Norman Vincent Peale."

Milam was born on 2 August 1933 in Jacksonville, Florida. He was disabled by polio in 1952, while studying at Yale University. He received his B.A. in English literature from Haverford College in Pennsylvania in 1957 and his M.A. also in English literature from the University of California at Berkeley in 1959. His work in radio began in 1958. Throughout the 1960s, he founded or co-founded a number of noncommercial, community radio stations. From the mid-1960s into the

mid-1970s, he was co-owner of stations in California and St. Louis and a consultant for radio and television stations in Miami, New Orleans, and elsewhere. One result of this work in radio was *Sex & Broadcasting: A Handbook on Building a Station for the Community* (1974), cited as an essential book on "do-it-yourself media." Milam has written two other books on broadcasting, *The Petition against God, the Full Story Behind the Milam-Lansman Petition* (1976) and *The Radio Papers* (1990), as well as *Under a Bed of Poses* (1959), *The Myrkin Papers* (1969), *The Blob That Ate Oaxaca and Other Travel Tales* (1992), and *Gringolandia* (1996, with Jon Gallant). His travel articles have appeared in *New Mobility*, *Mainstream*, the *Washington Post*, and elsewhere.

Among other activities, Milam has been an instructor in literature at the Monroe State Reformatory in Washington State, an adjunct professor of English, broadcasting, and journalism at the University of San Diego, the editor of the *Fessenden Review* in San Diego, and a book reviewer for the San Diego *Tribune*. In 1973, he was one of the twelve founding members of the National Foundation of Community Broadcasters. He is secretary treasurer of the Reginald A. Fessenden Educational Fund, Inc., a nonprofit organization that sponsors the *Fessenden Review* and the publishing company Mho & Mho Works.

References Milam, Lorenzo W., *The Cripple Liberation Front Marching Band Blues* (1984); ———, *Crip Zen: A Manual for Survival* (1993).

Miller, Oral O. (b. 1933)

Oral O. Miller has been executive director of the American Council of the Blind (ACB) since 1981. Born on 7 April 1933 in Sophie, Kentucky, he attended the Kentucky School for the Blind in Louisville and the Louisville Male High School, and he earned an A.B. from Princeton University and a J.D. from the Chicago Law School.

Miller was a member in 1986 of the committee that wrote *Toward Independence*, the National Council on Disability report that led to the drafting of the Americans with Disabilities Act of 1990, and he was a member of the Task Force on the Rights and Empowerment of Americans with Disabilities. He was ACB's representative in the discussions and advocacy that led to the passage of other landmark disability rights legislation such as the Air Carrier Access Act of 1986, the Fair Housing Amendments Act of 1988, and the Civil Rights Restoration Act of 1987, testifying before Congress on numerous occasions. In 1995, he was a member of the Disability Advisory Committee of the White House Conference on Aging. Miller has also been active in the International Blind Sports Association, the American Blind Lawyers Association (of which he is past president), and other organizations.

Miller received the Distinguished Service Award from President Bush in 1992 for "promoting the dignity, equality, independence and employment of people with disabilities."

See also American Council of the Blind; Task Force on Rights and Empowerment of People with Disabilities.

Miller, Paul Steven (b. 1961)

On 29 September 1994, Paul Steven Miller was unanimously confirmed by the U.S. Senate as a commissioner at the U.S. Equal Employment Opportunity Commission (EEOC). This confirmation was a triumph for Miller and for the disability rights movement, since as a dwarf, or little person, Miller for a long time had been unable to find work as an attorney, even though he graduated near the top of his class at Harvard Law School.

Miller was born in New York City on 4 May 1961. He received his undergraduate degree cum laude from the University of Pennsylvania in Philadelphia in 1983 and his J.D. from Harvard Law School in 1986, where he was a member of the *Harvard Civil Rights-Civil Liberties Law Review*. After his graduation, Miller was rejected by more than 40 law firms, because, as one attorney told him, their clients might

"think we're running some kind of circus freak show." Miller moved to Los Angeles to become the director of litigation for the Western Law Center for Disability Rights, where he litigated cases involving employment, education, transportation, and access discrimination. He litigated a defamation suit filed with the Federal Communications Commission on behalf of Bree Walker Lampley, a disabled television news anchor in Los Angeles who was attacked on talk radio for wanting to have children. Miller was also an adjunct professor at Loyola Law School in Chicago, a visiting professor of law at the University of California in Los Angeles, and a Parson Visiting Scholar at the University of Sydney in Australia. Moving to Washington, D.C., prior to his appointment to the EEOC, Miller served as the deputy director of the U.S. Office of Consumer Affairs and as the White House liaison to the disability community.

Miller is the author of numerous articles, including "Coming Up Short: Employment Discrimination against Little People" (*Harvard Civil Rights-Civil Liberties Law Review*, Winter 1987) and "The Impact of Assisted Suicide on Persons with Disabilities" (*Issues in Law & Medicine*, Summer 1993). He is a frequent speaker on disability rights law and, in 1996, was a guest on *Nightline* to discuss the implications of genetic screening for little people who want to have children. One of the five current commissioners, Miller is the co-chair of the commission-wide task force to develop an alternative dispute resolution program for the EEOC.

See also Little People of America.

Mills v. Board of Education of the District of Columbia 348 F. Supp. 866 (1972)

Mills v. Board of Education of the District of Columbia was brought in September 1971 on behalf of seven disabled children who had been excluded from the District of Columbia's public schools. They were not alone. Expert witnesses called by the plaintiffs estimated that there were "22,000 retarded, emotionally disturbed, blind, deaf, and speech or learning disabled children [in the District], and perhaps as many as 18,000 of these children are not being furnished with programs of specialized education." All of the children in the *Mills* case were African American, but "the class they represent is not limited by their race. They sue on behalf of" all disabled children who were residents of the District and were being denied publicly supported education.

The court ruled on 1 August 1972 that the district could not exclude disabled children from a publicly funded education, no matter what type or how severe their disability. The judge wrote that "requiring parents to [send their children to] school under pain of criminal penalties presupposes that an educational opportunity will be available to the children. The Board of Education is required to make such opportunity available." The court also ruled that lack of money could not be used as an excuse to deny children with disabilities their right to an education. "If sufficient funds are not available to finance all of the services and programs that are needed and desirable in the system, then the available funds must be expended suitably in such a manner that no child is entirely excluded from a publicly supported education consistent with his needs and ability to benefit therefrom." Furthermore, if placement in a mainstream setting was indeed not in the child's best interest, then the district must provide "adequate alternative educational services suited to the child's needs which may include special education or tuition grants" for a placement outside the public school, but only after "a constitutionally adequate prior hearing and periodic review of the child's status."

Mills, together with *Pennsylvania Association for Retarded Children (PARC) v. Pennsylvania* (1972), established the principle that children could not be denied a public education because of their disability. Their successful conclusion led to a firestorm of education litigation on behalf of disabled children. *Mills* and *PARC* were precursors to the Education for All Handicapped Children Act of 1975 (Pub. Law 94-142), and were cited by the act's congressional sponsors.

See also Education for All Handicapped Children Act of 1975; *Pennsylvania Association for Retarded Children (PARC) v. Pennsylvania.*

References Bowe, Frank G., *Handicapping America: Barriers to Disabled People* (1978); Rothstein, Laura F., *Disabilities and the Law.* (formerly, *Rights of Physically Handicapped Persons* (1992).

Mobility International USA (MIUSA)

Mobility International USA (MIUSA), based in Eugene, Oregon, was founded by Susan Sygall and Barbara Williams in 1981 as a nonprofit organization to advocate for equal opportunities for persons with disabilities in international educational exchange, leadership development, travel, and community service. The first organization of its kind in the world, MIUSA offers exchange programs for disability rights activists from the United States and abroad, and it sponsors training programs in cross-cultural issues and in how to organize and work for disability rights. These exhanges have been an important catalyst for the development of disability rights organizations and independent living centers in other countries. MIUSA publishes materials related to accessibility, travel, and the legal rights of disabled travelers as well as a quarterly newsletter, *Over the Rainbow*. MIUSA, as one of five partner organizations in the International Disabilities Exchanges and Studies (IDEAS) Project 2000, organized and coordinated the International Symposium on Issues of Women with Disabilities in Beijing, China, in August 1995. (Other participating organizations included Disabled Peoples' International, the World Blind Union, Inclusion International, and the World Institute on Disability.)

Mothers From Hell

Mothers From Hell was founded in 1992 in Eugene, Oregon, "to affirm the value and improve the quality of lives and education of people with developmental and other disabilities . . . [and] to ensure the implementation and continuation of special education and other services." Its use of demonstrations, press conferences, complaint procedures, and litigation has been reported in the disability press and *U.S. News and World Report*, and it has served as an example to other local, grassroots parents' groups. Mothers From Hell publishes a newsletter, the *Brimstone Bulletin*, which is read nationwide and in several countries outside the United States.

See also Parents' Movement.

Mouth: The Voice of Disability Rights

Lucy Gwin woke from a coma in 1989 after being hit by a drunk driver and suffering a severe head injury. "I was being admitted to a New Medico brain injury 'community re-entry center.' I couldn't yet remember my name but I knew my civil rights. My first words out of the coma were, 'I want a copy of your patients' rights document.' 'Oh, you won't need one of those here,' the admitting clerk said."

Six months later, Gwin began publishing *Mouth*, or, as it was first called, *This Brain Has a Mouth*. The bimonthly magazine features investigative journalism, news, and interviews with disability rights activists, reserving some of its harshest criticism for the "helping professions." Sometimes *Mouth* simply juxtaposes figures, for example the salary of a sheltered workshop CEO ($115,000 in 1992) as compared to one of its average workers ($662.28 a year). Other times, it reproduces documents, as in a series called "The Peanut Butter Papers"— "interoffice communications" to and from the deputy commissioner of the New Jersey Department of Human Services debating whether or not clients with disabilities housed in state-funded institutions should be allowed to eat peanut butter. *Mouth* also publishes poetry, essays, and illustrations. "We think of most every page as a poster," writes Gwin. "In short, we are *visual*. We use great photographs and wild drawings in abundance."

In 1995, *Mouth*, in conjunction with American Disabled for Attendant Programs Today (ADAPT), published *You Choose*, a 32-page packet of information making the argument for personal assistance services for people with disabilities, as opposed to incarceration in nursing homes. *Mouth* has also been active in fighting the right-to-die movement. In 1996, *Mouth* rejected the *Utne Reader* "Special Interest" publication award, citing that magazine's lack of coverage of disability rights issues and the name of the award. "Since when," wrote Gwin in an editorial about the award, "are anyone's civil rights special?"

See also Personal Assistance Services.

Reference Gwin, Lucy, et al., *You Choose: Long Term Care Policy* (1995).

Multicultural Issues, Minority Persons with Disabilities

According to a 1992 report by the National Council on Disability (NCD), individuals with disabilities who are members of ethnic, racial, or cultural minority groups "frequently experience discrimination disproportionately in comparison to their White or European counterparts. The combination of disability and ethnicity, race and or cultural background often results in a double form of discrimination." African Americans, Hispanic Americans, Asian Americans, and Native Americans are all at risk for this multiple oppression, facing ableism in their own communities, ableism and racism in society at large, and racism in the general disability rights movement. The report, of a conference co-sponsored by Jackson State University in Mississippi, also found that "persons of minority backgrounds with disabilities . . . have less personal and family resources, have less knowledge and understanding of externally available resources, and fare less well socio-economically than minorities without disabilities." As an example, in 1992, the unemployment rate among disabled blacks was a crushing 82 percent.

Minority group members are also less likely to receive rehabilitation and social services than whites with disabilities, even though minority people are more likely to be disabled and are a disproportionate percentage of the disabled population. Studies cited in the same NCD/Jackson State report indicated that, in the mid-1980s, blacks and Hispanics comprised almost half of the total disabled population in New York State, while more than three quarters of that state's Office of Vocational Rehabilitation clients were white. When minority group members do receive rehabilitation and medical services, they are often treated differently than whites. A 1980 study reported that the most prevalent reason for ending vocational rehabilitation services to nonwhites was "failure to cooperate," an indication that the almost entirely white vocational rehabilitation establishment had difficulty relating to nonwhites. Similarly, minority children with disabilities are less likely to receive quality education than majority whites.

The leadership of the disability rights movement is itself less diverse than the general disability community. The leadership of the independent living movement, for example, was until recently almost entirely white (and disproportionately male). Few of the major national disability rights organizations have had a representative number of people of color in either their leadership or their membership, leaving minority group members unheard and disempowered.

This history of exclusion is ironic, given the enormous influence that the black civil rights movement has had on the philosophy and tactics of the disability rights movement. *PARC v. Pennsylvania* (1972) and the right to education lawsuits that followed were prompted by the success of *Brown v. Board of Education* (1954). Disability rights leaders such as Justin Dart Jr., the Reverend Wade Blank, Edward V. Roberts, and Mark Johnson have repeatedly cited the life and writings of the Reverend Martin Luther King Jr. as an inspiration, while the "Black is Beautiful" movement of the 1960s is seen as the inspiration of Disability Pride. Black civil

rights activists have, at pivotal moments, provided direct support to the disability rights movement, as when the Black Panther Party delivered food to the demonstrators sitting in at the San Francisco Health, Education and Welfare offices in 1977, or when the Reverend Jesse Jackson publicly supported the Deaf President Now campaign at Gallaudet University in Washington, D.C.

A variety of national and local organizations have arisen to advocate for minority persons with disabilities. Fiesta Educativa in Los Angeles addresses issues of importance to Hispanic parents of disabled children, while local organizations such as African Americans with Disabilities in Pittsburgh, the Harlem Independent Living Center in New York, Insight Enterprises in Hampton, Virginia, and Access Now in Boston address issues of concern to disabled African Americans. In the Deaf community, black Deaf citizens of Washington, D.C., in the 1940s organized their own Washington Silent Society (the forerunner of today's Capital City Association of the Deaf, or CCAD), since they were excluded from the whites-only District of Columbia Association of the Deaf (forerunner of today's Metropolitan Washington Association of the Deaf, or MWAD). Advocates Ernest Hairston and Linwood Smith point out that even in the 1980s the CCAD remained a predominantly black organization, while the MWAD remained predominantly white. Similarly, until the 1960s, many Deaf schools, churches, and institutions were segregated by race, particularly in the South, and so Deaf African Americans formed their own independent churches and business associations. In 1981, black Deaf activists came together at Howard University in Washington, D.C., and, in 1982, founded National Black Deaf Advocates, which today has chapters all across the country. The National Hispanic Council for the Deaf and Hard of Hearing focuses on advocating on behalf of members of the Hispanic deaf community.

As African-American disability activist Ralph Shelman has pointed out, the disability community is in many ways a microcosm of American society in general, where life and politics continue to be divided along the fault lines of race and ethnicity. Racism, therefore, continues to be a problem within the disability rights movement, one that must be addressed if the movement is to be successful in empowering all people with disabilities to achieve their full civil and human rights.

See also American Indian Disability Legislation Project; Batiste, Gerald; Fiesta Educativa, Inc.; National Black Deaf Advocates; Walker, Sylvia.

References Hairston, Ernest, and Linwood Smith, *Black and Deaf in America: Are We That Different?* (1983); Lopez, John R., "Hispanic Americans: Roots of Oppression and Seeds of Change," in Gary W. Olsen, ed., *Kaleidoscope of Deaf America* (1984); Wright, Tennyson J., and Paul Leung, *The Unique Needs of Minorities with Disabilities: Setting an Agenda for the Future* (1992).

Multiple Chemical Sensitivity (MCS)

In the past half-century, there has been an exponential increase in the number and prevalence of artificial chemicals present in the environment. Multiple Chemical Sensitivity (MCS) is a newly recognized disability, believed to result from exposure to these chemicals; however, because the existence of MCS has been so recently recognized, people with MCS are commonly denied access to the social and rehabilitation services available to people with other disabilities.

According to Mary Lamielle, president of the National Center for Environmental Health Strategies, people with MCS "find themselves in desperate situations. Loss of health and livelihood along with lack of validation of the symptom complex are significant burdens." People with MCS, sensitive to chemicals that are found in common detergents, paints, carpets, air conditioning and ventilation systems, perfumes, etc., become virtual social outcasts, unable to work or travel, sometimes even to live in their own homes or to be near family members. According to a report prepared in 1995 by the Minnesota chapter of the National Association of Social Workers, the problem is especially preva-

lent among poor and minority communities, which "are disproportionately exposed to toxic dumps, smokestack emissions, agricultural pesticide applications and other pollution sources." Health insurers are reluctant to pay for treatment of MCS, while private corporations and public entities such as the U.S. Department of Defense, which produce huge quantities of toxic materials, have attempted to minimize the seriousness of the problem. Workers with MCS have been denied reasonable accommodation, even though MCS has been recognized by several federal agencies and in a number of federal court rulings as being covered by the Americans with Disabilities Act of 1990.

The inclusion of people with MCS in the larger disability rights movement has also been a slow process, with some activists sharing the skepticism of the mainstream medical establishment toward MCS. Nevertheless, groups such as the Boston Self Help Center are attempting to work with persons with MCS and to advocate for their civil rights.

See also Boston Self Help Center.

Reference Martin, Rosemary M., "People with Multiple Chemical Sensitivity: A New Social Policy for NASW" (1995).

Murphy, Robert F. (b. 1924)

Robert F. Murphy is the author of *The Body Silent*, published in 1987. Murphy, a professor of anthropology at Columbia University in New York City, describes the impact of his own progressive disability, following an inoperable spinal tumor that renders him quadriplegic. Murphy examines the consequences to his self-image, his marriage, and his academic career. He places quadriplegia in a social context, describing both the economic and attitudinal oppression faced by those with disabilities and the fear and ambivalence felt by many nondisabled people. Murphy concludes that "the disabled are indisputably the quintessential American anti-heros," challenging by their very existence the Calvinist obsession with rugged self-reliance and the American belief that hard work and a positive attitude will triumph over any adversity. "Disablement is at one and the same time a condition of body and an aspect of social identity—a process set in motion by somatic causes but given definition and meaning by society."

Murphy's other books include *The Dialectics of Social Life: Alarms and Excursions in Anthropological Theory* (1971) and *Cultural and Social Anthropology: An Overture* (2d edition, 1986).

Reference Murphy, Robert F., *The Body Silent* (1987).

NARC
See The Arc

National Alliance for the Mentally Ill (NAMI)

The National Alliance for the Mentally Ill (NAMI) was founded in 1979 by two mothers of mentally ill persons in Madison, Wisconsin. By 1995, NAMI had expanded to 1,100 chapters with 140,000 members in all 50 states. NAMI, headquartered in Arlington, Virginia, describes itself as "a national network of people working to improve the lives of all of us affected by serious mental illnesses. . . . Our goal is to enable each individual who has one of these illnesses to live the best life possible." NAMI advocated for the inclusion of people with psychiatric disabilities under the protections of the Americans with Disabilities Act of 1990.

NAMI offers family support groups, advocacy, and information referrals for people seeking local services. It also tries to counter the negative stereotypes about people with mental illness so often encountered in the mass media and in public life. For example, when Rep. Chuck Douglas (R-NH) took his concerns about "Berserkers: Time Bombs in the Workplace" (the title of his speech) to the floor of the U.S. Congress in 1995, the New Hampshire NAMI organized a press conference and letter-writing campaign to counter Douglas' misconceptions about people with mental illness seeking employment. NAMI also publishes a bimonthly newsletter, the *NAMI Advocate*, with a circulation of approximately 180,000, and sponsors an annual conference where researchers, service providers, and consumers and their families meet to share their experiences and insights. Some psychiatric survivor advocates (for example, Rae Unzicker) have criticized NAMI for representing the interests of the parents and families of people with mental illness, as opposed to disabled people themselves. For this reason, given its roots and make-up, NAMI is perhaps best classified as part of the disability parents' movement.

See also Parents' Movement; Psychiatric Survivor Movement.

National Alliance of Blind Students
See American Council of the Blind.

National Association for Rights, Protection and Advocacy (NARPA)

The National Association for Rights, Protection and Advocacy (NARPA) was founded in 1980 by advocates for people with psychiatric disabilities to support local advocacy efforts across the country. Based in St. Paul, Minnesota, it believes that the "recipients of mental health services are capable of and entitled to make their own choices and that they are, above all, equal citizens under the law. . . . NARPA's fundamental mission is to help empower people who have been labelled mentally disabled so that they may learn to independently exercise their legal rights."

NARPA's membership includes people who are consumers of mental health services, family of persons with psychiatric disabilities, service providers, disability rights attorneys, and others. Board members have included nationally known advocates such as Judi Chamberlin and Rae Unzicker, and, at any given time, more than half the board are people with psychiatric disabilities. NARPA lobbied for the reauthorization of the Protection and Advocacy Act for Mentally Ill Individuals of 1986. It publishes a quarterly newsletter, *The Rights Tenet*, with articles ranging from reports on efforts in Texas to ban electro-convulsive therapy (ECT) to coverage of psychiatric disability issues in the mainstream press and updates on the activities of NARPA.

See also Chamberlin, Judi; Protection and Advocacy for Mentally Ill Individuals Act of 1986; Psychiatric Survivor Movement; Unzicker, Rae.

National Association of Psychiatric Survivors
See Psychiatric Survivor Movement.

National Association of the Deaf (NAD)

The National Association of the Deaf (NAD) was founded in 1880 and is the oldest national disability rights organization in the United States that is still active today. Originally called the National Convention of Deaf-Mutes, the name was changed before its third national convention in 1889. The first meeting of the NAD in Cincinnati, Ohio, was attended by 143 people from 21 states. The organization's goal, as stated in its charter, was "to bring the deaf of the different sections of the United States in close contact and to deliberate on the needs of the deaf as a class. We have interests peculiar to ourselves which can only be taken care of by ourselves."

Edwin Allan Hodgson, publisher of *The Deaf-Mutes' Journal*, is generally credited with being the main impetus behind the founding of the NAD, along with Edmund Booth and Robert P. McGregor. McGregor, a writer who was the founder and first principal of the Cincinnati Day School for the Deaf, was elected the NAD's first president. Hodgson succeeded McGregor in 1883 to become the NAD's second president. By 1890, state associations of the deaf, affiliated with the NAD, had been established in Iowa, Pennsylvania, Virginia, Minnesota, Texas, Michigan, and Arkansas.

From its inception, NAD was committed to defending American Sign Language and the right of deaf people to become teachers of deaf students. Early milestones include a successful campaign in 1908 for the right of deaf people to be employed as federal civil servants and to be included in the Civilian Conservation Corps in the 1930s (and in the Job Corps in the 1960s). Throughout the first decades of the twentieth century, the NAD fought against public ignorance of deafness, as manifested in state laws that prevented deaf people from obtaining drivers' licenses. In the late 1940s, NAD started a campaign to discourage deaf people from begging on the street. In the next decade, it argued against special tax exemptions for deaf people, urging instead an end to employment discrimination. The NAD also fought to expose quacks and scam artists who preyed on the community by selling various pills, lotions, and devices as "cures" for deafness.

The NAD experienced tremendous growth in membership and influence in the 1960s and 1970s, due largely to the work of Frederick C. Schreiber. Schreiber had already demonstrated his organizing skills as the president of the Hebrew Association of the Deaf in New York City in the 1950s. He was elected NAD secretary-treasurer in 1964. Two years later, he became the organization's first executive secretary (later renamed executive director). At Schreiber's prompting, the NAD moved its headquarters in 1965 from Berkeley, California, to Washington, D.C. In 1966, the NAD began publishing books on deafness and Deaf history. Three years later, it received federal money to conduct the first ever National Census of the Deaf Population. Schreiber and others with the NAD were among the first organizers of the American Coalition of Citizens with Disabilities. In 1975, the NAD, a member of the World Federation of the Deaf, hosted the World Congress of the Deaf in Washington, D.C. By 1980, the NAD had an annual budget of $2 million, as compared to $25,000 in 1964.

Today, the NAD, with its headquarters in Silver Spring, Maryland, consists of 51 affiliate state associations (including the District of Columbia), which hold a national convention every two years. The NAD publishes a monthly newsletter, the

Broadcaster, as well as dozens of books. It maintains the NAD Law Center to advise deaf and hard-of-hearing people on their legal rights and represents them in civil rights cases before the federal courts. It also intervenes when judges refuse to provide interpreter services in the courtroom or when medical providers refuse to provide interpreters in hospitals, clinics, or health education classes. The NAD sponsors a yearly Miss Deaf America competition, and there is also a Junior NAD (JNAD) for high school students. Many of the leaders of the 1988 Gallaudet University Deaf President Now campaign were alumni of the JNAD.

NAD has an estimated membership of 30,000.

See also American Coalition of Citizens with Disabilities; American Sign Language; Deaf President Now Campaign; Oralism, Oral School; Schreiber, Frederick Carl.

References Gannon, Jack R., *Deaf Heritage: A Narrative History of Deaf America* (1981); Schein, Jerome D., *At Home among Strangers* (1989).

National Association of the Physically Handicapped, Inc. (NAPH)

The National Association of the Physically Handicapped (NAPH) was formed in May 1958 at the conference dissolving the American Federation of the Physically Handicapped (AFPH). It is a nonprofit organization that "seeks to help improve the social, economic and physical welfare of the physically handicapped . . . a voluntary, independent, self-help action group." The NAPH has approximately 800 members organized into state and local chapters in Michigan, Indiana, Ohio, New Hampshire, and North Carolina. Although membership is open to nondisabled people, 60 percent of the members of the governing body of any chapter must have a physical disability. Local chapters offer members a chance to socialize as well as to engage in political activities such as working to pass local and national disability rights legislation.

The NAPH assisted in the development of the architectural access standards published by the American National Standards Institute (ANSI) in 1961, which became the basis for subsequent architectural standards incorporated into federal law and regulation. Several NAPH chapters were members of the American Coalition of Citizens with Disabilities, and the NAPH was a supporter of the Americans with Disabilities Act of 1990. It publishes the quarterly *NAPH National Newsletter (NNN)* and has a business office in Cincinnati, Ohio. Its current president, Clarence Averill, has been involved with the organization since its inception and was a leader in the AFPH.

See also American Federation of the Physically Handicapped (AFPH).

National Black Deaf Advocates (NBDA)

National Black Deaf Advocates (NBDA) was formed in 1982 by Deaf African Americans who felt that their issues were not being addressed by the already existing, mostly white Deaf organizations. Organizers also wanted to educate the hearing African-American community about the experience and potential of black people who are deaf. As of 1996, there were 17 NBDA chapters with more than 700 members across the country.

Charles Williams, an NBDA cofounder, had begun voicing his concern about the lack of black representation in the National Association of the Deaf (NAD) as early as 1980, when he attended the NAD annual conference in Cincinnati. Although there are an estimated 240,000 black deaf Americans, and blacks represent about 5 percent of all deaf Americans, there are disproportionately few black teachers at schools for the deaf, and few African-American organizations provide interpreters at meetings and events. Barbara Morris Hunt, a member of the National Alliance of Black Interpreters (NAOBI), described to journalist Victoria Valentine how black deaf Americans often feel isolated, both as blacks among deaf whites and as deaf people among hearing

African Americans: "At Gallaudet [University] you can be deaf; but you can't be Black. At Howard [University] you can be Black, but it's hard being deaf."

The beginnings of NBDA can be traced to the First Black Deaf Conference at Howard University in Washington, D.C., in June 1981. The following year, nearly 300 participants met in Cleveland, and an executive secretary was elected to coordinate the organization of a national group. NBDA's major goal, according to Ernest Hairston and Linwood Smith, "is to prepare Black deaf people for leadership roles—to train them in the art of planning, organizing, and implementing programs and goals—and to provide them with the opportunity to function as leaders or to interact with role models."

See also Multicultural Issues, Minority Persons with Disabilities.

References Hairston, Ernest, and Linwood Smith, *Black and Deaf in America: Are We That Different?* (1983); Valentine, Victoria, "Being Black and Deaf: Coping in Both Communities," *Emerge: Black America's Newsmagazine* (December/January 1996).

National Center for Law and the Handicapped

The National Center for Law and the Handicapped, founded in 1971, was the first national legal advocacy center for persons with disabilities in the United States. It was established by faculty and students at the University of Notre Dame School of Law in South Bend, Indiana, under the sponsorship of the Association for Retarded Citizens (ARC, now The Arc). Attorneys at the center argued several early disability rights cases, principal among them *In re G. H.* (1974), argued before the Supreme Court of North Dakota. In this right-to-education case, the court ruled that, even though "a great many handicapped children in this State have had no education at all[,] . . . we are satisfied that all children in North Dakota have the right, under the State constitution, to a public school education. . . . Handicapped children are certainly entitled to no less than unhandicapped chil-

dren under the explicit provisions of the [state] Constitution."

Several notable disability rights attorneys were involved in the center. Thomas K. Gilhool was on its advisory board from 1971 to 1977. Frank Laski was a staff attorney from 1973 to 1974, as was Robert Burgdorf from 1973 to 1976. The center ceased operations by 1980.

See also Burgdorf, Robert L., Jr.; Gilhool, Thomas K.; Laski, Frank J.

National Council on Disability

The National Council on Disability (formerly the National Council on the Handicapped) was originally established within the U.S. Department of Education by the 1978 amendments to the Rehabilitation Act of 1973. It was charged with reviewing and evaluating federal policies related to disability. The 1984 amendments to the Rehabilitation Act made it an independent federal agency, headed by a 15-member panel appointed by the president and confirmed by the U.S. Senate. The council is mandated to make recommendations to the president, Congress, the National Institute on Disability and Rehabilitation Research, and other federal officials and agencies regarding ways to promote equal opportunity, economic self-sufficiency, independent living and integration into society for Americans with disabilities.

The council is best known for its leadership in calling for federal civil rights protection for people with disabilities. Its 1986 report *Toward Independence* led to the drafting by its attorney Robert L. Burgdorf Jr. of the first version of the Americans with Disabilities Act (ADA), introduced into Congress in April 1988. The council and individual council members then provided technical assistance for passage of the ADA, which was signed into law in July 1990. Its ADA Watch Project collects data and monitors compliance both by government and the private sector.

The council acts as a conduit of information about the status, needs, and concerns of Americans with disabilities. Council members use their access to Congress, the administration, and the national media to bring attention to significant issues. One example would be its work advocating on behalf of blind computer users for the development of accessible Graphical User Interface software, particularly by the Microsoft Corporation. In 1992, it co-sponsored a major conference on "Meeting the Unique Needs of Minorities"; in 1990, it conducted a "Wilderness Accessibility Forum"; in 1989, it held forums on education and long-term health care; and so on. The council maintains connections with disability activists and agencies in other nations; for example, it co-sponsored an Eastern European Conference on Disabilities in Prague in 1992. The council also commissions national surveys on topics of importance to people with disabilities. Under the Clinton administration, for the first time the majority of council members were people with disabilities.

See also Americans with Disabilities Act of 1990; Computer Access; Dart, Justin, Jr.; Parrino, Sandra Swift.

National Council on Independent Living (NCIL)

The National Council on Independent Living (NCIL) is an association of independent living centers based in Washington, D.C. It advocates on behalf of the centers and the independent living movement, and it provides technical assistance to centers and other groups in the disability community.

The NCIL was founded in 1982 as an all-volunteer, nonprofit organization. It has pushed for changes in federal law to provide funding and greater consumer control over federal rehabilitation services and independent living centers. It played a role in passage of the Civil Rights Restoration Act of 1987, the Fair Housing Amendments Act of 1988, and the Americans with Disabilities Act of 1990 (ADA). In 1989, for example, the NCIL organized a march in support of the ADA from the Rayburn building on Capitol Hill to the White House, where approximately 175 disabled people kept a candlelight vigil. It has worked with attorneys, activists, and federal agencies on implementation of disability rights law, and it advocates on issues such as health care finance reform, personal assistance services, and the Social Security Disability Insurance and Supplemental Security Income programs. The NCIL sponsors national conferences, administers an ADA Peer Training Project, and publishes the quarterly *NCIL Newsletter*. It receives funding through membership dues, private donations, and grants. There are 22 people on its governing board, 20 of whom have disabilities.

See also Independent Living and Independent Living Movement.

National Empowerment Center

The National Empowerment Center in Lawrence, Massachusetts, describes itself as "an organization of people who are mental health consumers and psychiatric survivors, who have come together to build a national voice for consumer/survivors and to offer technical assistance to individuals and groups, in an effort to promote recovery, empowerment, hope and healing." Founded in 1992, the center offers a national directory of mutual support groups and consumer-controlled drop-in centers and statewide organizations, as well as literature and audiotapes on the legal rights of people subject to forced treatment, the youth movement against psychiatric abuse, and organizing self-help and political advocacy groups. It publishes a biannual newsletter (the *National Empowerment Center Newsletter*, circulation 6,000) with articles on the psychiatric self-help and civil rights movements in the United States and abroad.

See also Psychiatric Survivor Movement.

National Federation of the Blind (NFB)

The National Federation of the Blind (NFB), founded in 1940, is one of America's oldest disability advocacy organizations.

Unlike previous blindness organizations, which for the most part were organized and led by sighted professionals, the NFB is an organization of blind people themselves, with blind and visually disabled people in all leadership positions.

Blind people at the time of the NFB's founding were subject to widespread discrimination. Some were able to go to residential, segregated schools; others were denied any education at all. Generally prevented by discrimination from gainful employment, some blind people worked in sheltered workshops for subminimum wages under demeaning and exploitive conditions. "Vocational training" meant learning to weave baskets or make mops, while many blind people lived off family or public charity. Prominent physicians and psychologists argued that "the blind" were mentally and emotionally impaired, and blind people were routinely denied service in restaurants and hotels, kept off public transportation and out of theaters, excluded from juries, and even denied membership in the YMCA, solely because of their disability.

The NFB was organized at a meeting in Wilkes-Barre, Pennsylvania, in November 1940. Sixteen delegates representing seven states drafted a constitution and announced that "the purpose of the National Federation of the Blind is to promote the economic and social welfare of the blind." The principal founder and first president of the NFB was Jacobus tenBroek, a historian and professor of political science. TenBroek was to be the NFB's guiding force throughout the 1940s and 1950s.

TenBroek and others looked to the labor movement as a model. The NFB fought exemptions in the Fair Labor Standards Act of 1938 that allowed employers to pay blind people less than minimum wage, and it protested the exclusion of blind people from the federal and state civil service. In 1948, the annual convention in Baltimore issued "A Bill of Rights for the Blind," which included the right to work at a real job for a real wage and the right to rehabilitation services that would enable blind

Marc Maurer, president of the National Federation of the Blind.

people to do so. TenBroek wrote that year how "too often the blind are virtually made wards under social worker guardianship," and he called for the NFB to work for "Security, Equality, and Opportunity" for all blind people in the United States.

NFB membership grew steadily. By 1960, there were affiliates in 47 states sending 900 delegates to its twentieth anniversary convention in Miami. The NFB made a major effort to organize workers in the country's sheltered workshops and at state commissions for the blind and rehabilitation agencies. While some agencies were open to blind people organizing their own federation, others harassed employees they suspected of NFB involvement. These employers put so much pressure on their employees and clients that Sen. John F. Kennedy (D-MA) introduced federal legislation safeguarding blind people's right to organize. (The bill was not passed).

The NFB became known both for its

militancy and its sense of community. Meetings and demonstrations featured sing-alongs of NFB songs, such as "I've been Workin' in the Workshop." The NFB instilled in its members feelings of pride and collective power, and it stressed the concept that blindness was less a physical handicap than a problem of social attitudes and political disempowerment.

Toward the end of the 1950s, ideological and personal rifts erupted into what the NFB's official history terms "a civil war." A group of dissidents charged that the NFB "was not truly democratic" and criticized what they saw as the lack of local input into its national policies. The struggle began at the 1958 annual convention, and it culminated at the 1960 convention with the rewriting of the constitution and the suspension of six state affiliates for "activities destructive of the Federation." By 1961, the number of suspended chapters had grown to 15, including all those that had originally founded the NFB in 1940. Many of the dissidents, having resigned or been suspended, formed the nucleus of the American Council of the Blind. TenBroek stepped down from the presidency in 1961, but he was reelected in 1966. When he died in 1968, Kenneth Jernigan became the new NFB president.

The NFB under Jernigan carried out campaigns against the rehabilitation establishment and the U.S. airline industry. A particular target was the National Accreditation Council for Agencies Serving the Blind and Visually Handicapped (NAC). The NFB set out "to reform or retire" NAC, staging demonstrations at NAC meetings, calling for greater participation in its proceedings by "the organized blind." The NFB exposed abuses within agencies for the blind and deaf/blind, agencies often accredited by NAC. It attacked airlines for refusing to seat blind passengers in seats next to emergency exists, labeling the policy condescending and discriminatory. The NFB also advocated that braille be made available to all blind people, stressing the importance of braille literacy as a crucial step toward independence. Jernigan con-

tinued an initiative begun under tenBroek, the passage of state "white cane laws," requiring drivers to exercise caution when they saw someone using a cane, along with opening public spaces to dog-guide users, legislation that historian Paul Longmore has described as "in effect, the first equal access statutes."

Jernigan was sometimes a controversial figure, both within the blindness community and within the larger disability rights movement. Under his leadership, the NFB began to operate its own rehabilitation centers in Minnesota, Louisiana, and Colorado, prompting one critic to ask, "Where do clients of Federation operated agencies turn if they are dissatisfied with its services?" The NFB initially took no position regarding the Americans with Disabilities Act of 1990 (ADA), and then it publicly threatened to oppose it unless the bill was amended to prohibit businesses from forcing accommodations on disabled people. Sponsors of the ADA agreed to the change, but some were disturbed that the NFB waited until so late in the process to make their objections known, and did so in such a confrontational manner.

Nevertheless, with 50,000 members representing fully one-tenth of all blind Americans, the NFB is the nation's largest political organization of blind people. Its monthly publication, the *Braille Monitor*, covers NFB news and issues. Its Job Opportunities for the Blind (JOB) program, in cooperation with the U.S. Department of Labor, assists blind people in finding employment, while the NFB offers scholarships to students, legal aid to victims of discrimination, and legal and advocacy training to young activists.

Jernigan stepped down in 1986, and Marc Maurer became president of the NFB, which is headquartered in Baltimore, Maryland. Its purpose remains "the complete integration of the blind into society on a basis of equality."

See also American Council of the Blind; Jernigan, Kenneth; Sheltered Workshops; tenBroek, Jacobus.

Reference Matson, Floyd, *Walking Alone and Marching Together: A History of the Organized Blind Movement in the United States, 1940–1990* (1990).

National Fraternal Society of the Deaf/Deaf Insurance

Insurance companies in the early 1900s rarely offered life, disability, or automobile insurance to deaf people, and they charged exorbitant premiums when they did. Deaf people were deemed to be higher risks, though the insurance industry had no evidence to support this claim. In response, a group of young deaf men at a 1901 class reunion at the Michigan School for the Deaf in Flint made plans to form a "mutual benefit organization." The National Fraternal Society of the Deaf (NFSD) was incorporated on 12 August of that year, offering its members financial support in times of need. In 1907, the NFSD was officially incorporated as a "legal reserve society" in Illinois, and, by 1945, membership exceeded 10,000. Although membership was originally open only to men, women's auxiliaries were formed in 1937, and women were granted full membership in 1951. As a result of NFSD advocacy in the 1960s, insurance companies no longer discriminate against deaf drivers, and deaf people today experience less difficulty obtaining other forms of insurance.

The NFSD remains the world's only fraternal life insurance company managed primarily by deaf persons. It also advocates for legislation of benefit to the Deaf community, particularly on the state level. It sponsors social and cultural activities, does charitable work, and publishes a bimonthly newsletter, the *Frat*. The NFSD has its headquarters in Mt. Prospect, Illinois.

National Legal Center for the Medically Dependent and Disabled

The National Legal Center for the Medically Dependent and Disabled was founded in 1984 in response to the Baby Doe case in Bloomington, Indiana. The nonprofit center focuses on defending the rights of vulnerable persons threatened by infanticide, euthanasia, assisted suicide, nonvoluntary withdrawal or withholding of essential medical treatment and care, and discrimination in health care financing.

The center was established as a national support center of the Legal Services Corporation, but it became an independent entity when Congress defunded all national support centers in 1996. It has been involved in "right-to-die" litigation, for example, *Quill v. Vacco*, decided by the U.S. Court of Appeals in the Second Circuit in 1996, and *Washington v. Glucksberg*, decided by the U.S. Court of Appeals in the Ninth Circuit, both of which were to be argued before the U.S. Supreme Court (as *Vacco v. Quill* and *Washington v. Glucksberg*) in 1997. The center argues that efforts to ensure a right to die discriminate against people with disabilities. In their amici curiae to the Supreme Court, center attorneys maintained that "assisted suicide cannot be regarded as a special accommodation or benefit for those with terminal disabilities under the ADA any more than a race-based exception to assisted suicide law would be permissible under constitutional law."

The center is based in Indianapolis and publishes the quarterly *Issues in Law and Medicine*.

See also Baby Doe Case; Baby Jane Doe Case; Euthanasia and Assisted Suicide.

National Mental Health Foundation

During World War II, many conscientious objectors were sent to work as attendants in the nation's public mental hospitals. This was the first time that such a large number of "nonprofessionals" were exposed to the way state mental patients were treated, and they were shocked at what they encountered. Leonard Edelstein, Phil Steer, Harold Barton, and Willard Hetzel, working at the Philadelphia State Hospital, began during the war to gather information from other conscientious objector attendants around the country. In 1946, they founded the National Mental Health Foundation, headquartered at the American Friends School in Philadelphia. The foundation published a periodical entitled *Psychiatric Aide* and a series of pamphlets such as *Toward Mental Health*. Hetzel, an attorney, did a survey of state laws concerning institutionalization, the first of its kind.

The leaders of the foundation hoped that by gathering and disseminating information they could convince state legislators to change conditions at the institutions. Their first and greatest success in this regard came in May 1946, even before the foundation's official founding, with an exposé in *Life* magazine. The pressure of public opinion, along with advocacy by the foundation, brought increases in the per-patient funding of state institutions, making them increasingly more expensive to operate. This increase in expense, together with the public reaction to the revelations of abuse within the institutions, contributed to the push for community mental health services in the 1960s and the deinstitutionalization of mental patients in the 1970s.

The National Mental Health Foundation disappeared in the fall of 1951, when it merged with the National Committee for Mental Hygiene and the Psychiatric Foundation to form the National Association for Mental Health, now called the National Mental Health Association (NMHA). Based in Alexandria, Virginia, the NMHA furnishes information to the general public about mental illness, and it has a referral service for people seeking treatment options in their community.

See also Deinstitutionalization; Psychiatric Survivor Movement.

National Organization on Disability (NOD)

The nonprofit National Organization on Disability was founded in 1982 to bring disability-related issues to nondisability organizations, particularly business and civic groups. Through its National Organization Partnership Program, it encourages nondisability organizations to solicit the participation of people with disabilities through their national, state, and local chapters and affiliates. Member organizations include the Boys and Girls Clubs of America, the General Federation of Women's Clubs, the Hispanic Association of Colleges and Universities, and the American Association of Homes and Services for the Aging. More than 3,500 town, city, and county governments are involved in NOD's Community Partnership Program. Its World Committee on Disability offers direct aid to people with disabilities in other countries.

NOD encourages participating groups to employ people with disabilities as members of their staff, particularly at management and leadership levels; to form disability committees to make their communities more accessible; and to ensure that people with disabilities are included in local government, both in paid positions and on voluntary boards and commissions. James Brady, former White House press secretary for President Reagan, is a principal spokesperson. NOD actively supported passage of the Americans with Disabilities Act of 1990.

National Paraplegia Foundation
See National Spinal Cord Injury Association.

National Spinal Cord Injury Association (NSCIA)

In July 1948, several members of Paralyzed Veterans of America (PVA), led by Robert Moss, founded the National Paraplegia Foundation (NPF) to address the needs of civilians with spinal cord injury. NPF's state and local chapters were often the first disability rights organizations in their areas and participated in such crucial campaigns as the struggle to make the Washington METRO subway system accessible. It became the National Spinal Cord Injury Foundation in 1979 after merging with the New England Spinal Cord Injury Foundation. The focus shifted at that time from political activism to providing direct services through a network of local chapters and to advocating for research toward a cure for spinal cord injury. A few years later, the name was changed to the National Spinal Cord Injury Association (NSCIA).

In 1996, the NSCIA consisted of 30 chapters, 25 developing chapters, and 5 support groups. They are each dedicated to "the three C's" of improving standards of quality and availability of health *Care*, funding research for a *Cure*, and helping individuals *Cope* with the realities of life with a spinal cord injury. The NSCIA, based in Silver Spring, Maryland, is a nonprofit organization that operates the National Spinal Cord Injury Resource Center (NSCIRC) and publishes a range of materials including the magazine *SCI Life*.

See also Paralyzed Veterans of America; Metropolitan Area Transit Authority (METRO) Access Campaign.

National Stigma Clearinghouse

The National Stigma Clearinghouse was founded in New York City in 1990 to combat damaging stereotypes in the mass media about people with mental illness. Television, movies, and other popular arts often depict people with mental illness as strange, evil, and dangerous. An all-volunteer group, the clearinghouse issues reports and organizes letter-writing campaigns and other actions to exert pressure on the purveyors of such harmful images. Among its targets have been DC Comics, for its depiction in *Superman* of a dangerous and evil "lunatic" escaped from an "interplanetary insane asylum," and the sponsors of a business seminar titled "How To Avoid Hiring Lemons, Nuts, and Flakes."

See also Media Images of People with Disabilities; Psychiatric Survivor Movement.

National Technical Institute for the Deaf (NTID)

The National Technical Institute for the Deaf (NTID), located on the campus of the Rochester Institute of Technology in Rochester, New York, was founded by Congress in 1965 to provide technical and professional training at a college and post-graduate level to deaf and hard-of-hearing students. Beginning in September 1968, with a class of 71 students, the NTID had a total enrollment of more than 1,000 by 1994. The NTID offers degrees in applied science and technology, business, engineering, the imaging arts and sciences, liberal arts, and science. It is a center of Deaf politics and culture.

National Theatre of the Deaf (NTD)

Skits, mime shows, and signed songs and poems have long been an integral part of Deaf culture, generally performed by amateurs during weekend gatherings at the numerous Deaf clubs and conventions across the United States and Canada. In New York City alone, by the late 1950s, there were three major Deaf theater groups: the Metropolitan Theatre Guild of the Deaf, the New York Hebrew Association of the Deaf, and the New York Theatre Guild of the Deaf. Other groups staged regular performances in Chicago, San Francisco, and Washington, D.C., where Gallaudet University began offering classes in drama in 1961. The Gallaudet Drama Club was formed as early as 1892.

The idea of a national, professional troupe of Deaf actors, performing their repertoire in American Sign Language (ASL), was first conceived by Edna S. Levine, a psychologist and author of *The Psychology of Deafness* (1960). She enlisted actress Anne Bancroft, who had studied ASL for her part as Anne Sullivan in the Broadway and movie versions of *The Miracle Worker*. Levine, Bancroft, and set designer David Hays, together with Broadway producer Arthur Penn, first approached Mary Switzer and Boyce R. Williams at the Office of Vocational Rehabilitation in 1959, looking for seed money for their project. It was not until 1967 that Levine, Hays, Switzer, and Williams were able to procure a grant from the Vocational Rehabilitation Administration for $16,500 to launch the National Theatre of the Deaf, selling it as a program to expand vocational opportunities for deaf people.

A deaf actor concentrates as a pair of hands perform sign language during a beginner's workshop at the National Theatre of the Deaf center in Chester, Connecticut, 1991.

Among the first performances of the NTD were ASL translations of classics by Puccini, Shloime Ansky, Moliere, and Dylan Thomas. Hays, the NTD's artistic director, stressed, "Our theatre is for everyone. It is a mistake to assume that deaf talent has no place in the world of entertainment." This commitment to bringing deaf theater and ASL to the hearing world was both lauded and criticized by members of the deaf community. Some felt that the NTD went too far in catering performances to a hearing audience. Actor Bernard Bragg responded "that deaf audiences are simply too small a minority to sustain a thriving deaf professional theatre. To survive, plays about the deaf must be geared to hearing audiences by focusing on universal experiences and conflicts between the hearing and deaf worlds." Beginning in 1971, with its first original play, *My Third Eye*, the NTD offered hearing audiences a glimpse into these conflicts, for example, the experiences of deaf children denied access to ASL.

The NTD, based in Chester, Connecticut, became a hothouse for developing deaf actors, directors, set designers, and playwrights. Between 1977 and 1982, the NTD commissioned 17 new plays by deaf writers and held conferences and workshops for aspiring playwrights. During its tours, the NTD provided technical assistance to deaf artists, writers, and performers in Europe, Africa, and Asia. It has had a major impact both in exposing hearing audiences to ASL and in fostering pride and cultural awareness in the American Deaf community. Many NTD alumni, such as Linda Bove, Andree Norton, Phyllis Frelich, Marlee Matlin, Julia Fields, and Tim Scanlon, have moved on to award-winning careers in mainstream media.

See also American Sign Language; Deaf Culture.

References Baldwin, Stephen C., *Pictures in the Air: The Story of the National Theatre of the Deaf* (1993).

Neas, Ralph G., Jr. (b. 1946)

Ralph Graham Neas Jr. was for 14 years the executive director of the Leadership Conference on Civil Rights (LCCR), a coalition of some 180 national organizations representing minorities, women, persons with disabilities, older Americans, labor, and major religious institutions. He was born on 17 May 1946, in Brookline, Massachusetts. Neas earned a B.A. from the University of Notre Dame in South Bend, Indiana, in 1968 and his J.D. from the University of Chicago Law School in 1971. He became a legislative attorney on Civil Rights at the Congressional Research Office of the Library of Congress in 1971 and legislative assistant and then chief legislative assistant to Sen. Edward W. Brooke (R-MA) from 1973 to 1978. He began work as chief legislative assistant to Sen. Dave Durenberger (R-MN) in January 1979, but he took a leave of absence that year after contracting Guillain-Barré syndrome (GBS). During this eight-month sabbatical, he helped to found the Guillain-Barré Syndrome Foundation, which has since become the Guillain-Barré Syndrome Foundation International, with 15,000 members and 130 chapters worldwide. He became the LCCR's first full-time executive director in 1981 and became executive director of the Leadership Conference Education Fund in 1983.

Neas oversaw a vast expansion of the LCCR and its involvement in health care reform, family and medical leave, gay and lesbian rights, and immigration and disability rights issues. Because of his own experience with disability, Neas was open to moving a disability rights agenda within LCCR. During passage of the Americans with Disabilities Act of 1990, he was a crucial link to members of Congress sympathetic to other, more established civil rights constituencies.

Neas left the LCCR in 1995 to become visiting professor of law at the Georgetown University Law Center in Washington, D.C., and president and CEO of the Neas Group, a legal consulting firm.

See also Americans with Disabilities Act of 1990; Civil Rights Restoration Act of 1987; Fair Housing Amendments Act of 1988.

New England Gallaudet Association of the Deaf

The New England Gallaudet Association of the Deaf was the first formal regional deaf organization in the United States. It was originally composed of alumni of the American School for the Deaf and grew out of efforts to honor that school's founder, Thomas Hopkins Gallaudet, after his death in 1851. The association was the brainchild of William M. Chamberlain, a deaf journalist and editor of the *Gallaudet Guide and Deaf Mute's Companion*, and Thomas Brown, a deaf farmer from Henniker, New Hampshire, where deaf people had settled and formed a community much as they had in Martha's Vineyard, Massachusetts. The association first officially convened in Montpelier, Vermont, in March 1854. Over the next three decades, it was on the cutting edge of advocacy for deaf people. Some of its officials and members were among the original founders of the National Association of the Deaf in 1880.

See also American School for the Deaf; Gallaudet, Thomas Hopkins; National Association of the Deaf.

Reference Lane, Harlan, *When the Mind Hears: A History of the Deaf* (1989).

New Mobility

Founded in 1989, *New Mobility* is a monthly magazine of "disability lifestyles, culture and resources." It features profiles of well-known people with disabilities, such as Christopher Reeve and Andre Dubus, and articles on topics such as childhood experiences of disability, parenting, wheelchair athletics, and consumer guides to wheelchairs and other products. It is published in Malibu, California, by Miramar Communications, Inc., and Sam Maddox, and it is edited by Barry Corbet. *New Mobility* and Miramar also publish *Spinal Network: The Total Resource for the Wheelchair Community* (1988, by Sam Maddox). In 1995, *New Mobility* had a circulation of 30,000, and a readership of 110,000.

See also Corbet, Barry.

No Pity

Subtitled *People with Disabilities Forging a New Civil Rights Movement, No Pity* is one of the first serious journalistic accounts of the history of the disability rights movement in the United States. Written by Joseph P. Shapiro, a writer on social policy issues for *U.S. News & World Report*, and published in 1993, *No Pity* traces the history of Americans with disabilities from the 1700s down to the present, focusing in particular on the emergence of the disability rights movement starting in the late 1950s. It profiles several prominent disability rights activists, including Judith Heumann, Edward V. Roberts, Justin Dart Jr., Cyndi Jones, and Evan Kemp Jr.; describes the activities of groups such as American Disabled for Attendant Programs Today (ADAPT) and Disabled in Action; and traces the struggle for the passage of the Americans with Disabilities Act of 1990. It is considered an essential text for those interested in learning about the disability rights movement.

Reference Shapiro, Joseph P., *No Pity: People with Disabilities Forging a New Civil Rights Movement* (1993).

Normalization

The concept of normalization originated in Denmark in the late 1950s as a new principle governing the education and treatment of people with cognitive disabilities. The basic idea was to make their lives as "normal" as possible. This meant that parents would be encouraged to raise their mentally disabled children at home, with their siblings, as opposed to institutionalizing them, and that disabled children would go to school with their nondisabled peers. Adults with cognitive disabilities would live in the community, independent of their parents or families, much as any other adult. This approach was a radical departure from the way people with mental disabilities, and indeed most disabilities, were treated in the United States at that time. The prevailing notion was that mental retardation was a pathological condition best "treated" by doctors and psychiatrists in massive residential institutions, where people with mental disabilities were kept isolated from society. Normalization took most cognitive disability out of this segregated, medical context, making it the province of educators and sociologists, and ultimately, of disability rights advocates.

Normalization was brought to the United States in 1969, when Niels Erk Bank-Mikkelsen, director of the Danish Service for the Mentally Retarded, and Bengt Nirje, secretary general of the Swedish Parents' Association for Mentally Retarded Children, spoke at a conference organized by the President's Committee on Mental Retardation. Initially, their presentation was met with skepticism, and many institution superintendents rejected normalization outright. The idea, however, gathered support throughout the 1970s, largely through the work of Wolf Wolfensberger, a psychologist and researcher at the Nebraska Psychiatric Institute in Omaha and the leading American proponent of normalization.

Wolfensberger broadened the concept beyond education or living accommodations to include all spheres of human experience. His book *The Principle of Normalization in Human Services* (co-authored with Nirje, Simon Olshansky, Robert Perske, and Philip Roos, 1972) was an exposition of this more general theory. In it,

Brock Holloway (right) helps 10-year-old Chris Laboy with food identification and motor skills at a New York school kitchen in 1990. Normalization has played a central role in the deinstitutionalization of many thousands of people with disabilities.

Wolfensberger concluded that "ultimately, integration is only meaningful if it is social integration, i.e., if it involves social interaction and acceptance, and not merely physical presence."

While normalization called for community integration, its emphasis on "normal" or "normative" behavior and appearance has made some disability rights advocates uneasy. Wolfensberger called for the "utilization of means which are as culturally normal as possible, in order to establish and maintain personal behaviors and characteristics which are as culturally normative as possible." Normalization in this light was seen by its critics to discourage people with cognitive disabilities from socializing amongst themselves and from forming self-help and political groups. People First criticized normalization for

not adequately meeting "the social needs of the consumer. Consumers find special and important meaning in their relationships with each other. They . . . need a group identity. They need a culture, a history and their own heroes." Normalization, it was argued, did not lead to political or social empowerment for people with disabilities, because it still used nondisabled people as the measure of what was "normal" and desirable.

These criticisms aside, normalization played a central role in the deinstitutionalization of many thousands of people with disabilities. By insisting that people with disabilities be integrated into the community, it helped provide the intellectual framework for disability rights landmarks such as Section 504 of the Rehabilitation Act of 1973, the Education for All Handicapped Children Act of 1975, and the Americans with Disabilities Act of 1990.

See also Deinstitutionalization, People First, People First International.

References Kugel, Robert B., and Wolf Wolfensberger, eds., *Changing Patterns in Residential Services for the Mentally Retarded* (1969); Wolfensberger, Wolf, *The Principle of Normalization in Human Services* (1972).

Not Dead Yet
See Euthanasia and Assisted Suicide.

Nugent, Timothy J. (b. 1923)
Timothy J. Nugent is the founder and former director of the world's first disabled students' program. He is a visionary in the fields of rehabilitation, architectural access, and wheelchair athletics. "Long before advocacy became a buzzword and accessibility became the law," rehabilitation specialist Paul Corcoran wrote in 1994, "Tim Nugent was defining these concepts by action."

Nugent was born on 10 January 1923 in Pittsburgh, Pennsylvania. He holds degrees in pre-medicine and health and physical education from the University of Wisconsin at La Crosse (B.S. in 1947, M.S. in 1948), and he served in the Army Medical Corps, the Army Corps of Engineers, and the infantry during World War II. Nugent's involvement with disability began with his family: his younger sister was blind, his father was both visually and hearing disabled, and a family servant had cerebral palsy. Nugent himself has a heart murmur, and the common wisdom during his young adulthood required him to limit his physical activity. He told an interviewer, "I came to appreciate what a hidden disability meant."

In 1947, Nugent began a program for disabled students at the Galesburg campus of the University of Illinois, which was then officially established in September 1948. The Galesburg program was the first effort ever to accommodate people with severe disabilities in the totality of campus life, including housing, academics, sports and recreation, and social activities. When the state closed the campus in 1949, Nugent was notified that his program would be terminated. In April, he and 28 paraplegics traveled to Springfield to meet with the governor, who refused to see them. They then drove to the capitol building to meet with legislators. Their efforts received front-page coverage in the *Chicago Tribune*, which drew the attention of Disabled American Veterans, the American Legion, and other veterans' organizations. Nugent and his students then went to the main campus at Urbana-Champaign. Using painters' scaffolding planks, they built a makeshift ramp over the steps leading into the campus' main building to demonstrate how students using wheelchairs could attend classes. Because of the publicity, and the pressure from veterans' groups, university officials granted Nugent's program permission to come to the campus at Urbana-Champaign "as an experiment." The program received no university or state funding for its first seven to nine years, relying instead on grants from the American Legion, other veteran's groups, the U.S. Veterans Administration, and the Department of Vocational Rehabilitation.

Disabled students lived on campus and off, individually or in groups. At Tanbrier, an old, three-story house just off campus, quadriplegic students lived on the ground floor, their personal assistants upstairs. Nugent and his students pioneered self-care techniques for people with spinal cord injury, demonstrating that it was possible for them to live outside a hospital or medical setting. Where adaptive equipment did not exist, they invented it: bathroom and toilet hardware, pneumatic tires for wheelchairs, power-assist doors, urinary appliances. Nugent and his team created the nation's first hydraulic lift–equipped buses, pressed for the construction of an accessible student services building, and urged that all other campus buildings be accessible. They encouraged local merchants to ramp their stores and convinced the city government to install curb-cuts during street repairs, also the first effort of its kind. By 1958, the program had graduated 102 students, all of whom were employed. By 1960, Urbana-Champaign was the world's most accessible campus, with more than 150 disabled students, 100 or more using wheelchairs.

Nugent was also an early advocate of wheelchair sports. In 1949, he founded the National Wheelchair Basketball Association; he was its commissioner for 25 years. In 1948, he founded Delta Sigma Omicron, a national rehabilitation service fraternity, serving as its secretary for four decades.

In 1959, Nugent became the first director of research and development of the American National Standards Institute (ANSI) Project A117. The project's groundbreaking *Making Buildings and Facilities Accessible to, and Usable by, the Physically Disabled* (October 1961) became the basis upon which all subsequent architectural access legislation and regulation was written. Nugent remained director of research until 1974 and from 1976 to 1983 he was chairman of Project A117.1.

Nugent was also instrumental in the growth of the National Paraplegia Foundation, founded after World War II as a civilian offshoot of the Paralyzed Veterans of America. He served four terms as its president and helped with its early fund-raising.

Nugent has been a consultant to myriad organizations, businesses, and government agencies, and he is the author of dozens of articles, book chapters, and encyclopedia entries on all aspects of rehabilitation. One measure of his impact can be seen in the fact that, as of 1994, graduates of his program were directors of disabled student services at more than 20 campuses and of dozens of programs for accessible recreation, rehabilitation, and independent living. Many current leaders of the disability rights movement, for example Fred Fay, Curtis Cone, and Mary Lou Breslin, are graduates of Urbana-Champaign.

Nugent retired as professor of rehabilitation education and as director of the Rehabilitation Education Center and the Division of Rehabilitation Education Services at Urbana-Champaign in 1986. He has received dozens of prestigious awards, including the Public Personnel Award from President Eisenhower and the President's Committee on Employment of the Physically Handicapped in 1958 and the Distinguished Service Award from President Clinton in 1993.

See also Architectural Access; Disabled Student Services; Independent Living, Independent Living Movement; National Spinal Cord Injury Association; Sports and Athletics.

O'Connor v. Donaldson
95 S. Ct. 2486 (1975)

"May the state fence in the harmless mentally ill solely to save its citizens from exposure to those whose ways are different?" So asked U.S. Supreme Court Justice Stewart, writing for the unanimous majority in *O'Connor v. Donaldson*. In that decision, handed down on 26 June 1975, the Court ruled that it was unconstitutional for individuals who were not charged with any crime, and who were a threat to neither themselves nor others, to be institutionalized against their will.

William Kenneth Donaldson had been incarcerated in the Florida State Hospital at Chattahoochee for more than 15 years, beginning in 1957. During his incarceration, Donaldson filed numerous writs of habeas corpus, wrote to newspapers, and attempted to interest civil liberties advocates in his case. All rejected his pleas, which were seen by the institution doctors as further evidence of Donaldson's "delusions of persecution." Compounding Donaldson's problems were numerous errors in his medical record (for instance, that he had served three years in jail prior to his institutionalization). Donaldson was not permitted to review his records, and, when errors did come to his attention, institution staff refused to acknowledge them. Donaldson received no therapy or treatment, other than the offer of psychotropic medication, which he refused because of his Christian Science beliefs.

"What is significant about the decision in Donaldson's case," wrote Judge David L. Bazelon, chief judge of the U.S. Court of Appeals for the Fourth Circuit in Washington, D.C., "is not that the court ruled for Donaldson. In view of the extreme facts of the case, how could it have done otherwise? Donaldson was incarcerated for fifteen years even though he was an articulate, white, essentially middle class, educated man with no history of violating the law." The case, as Bazelon and patient advocates saw it, was significant in demonstrating how the mere *label* of a mental disability was enough to deprive Donaldson of his liberty for a significant portion of his life, requiring a Supreme Court decision to set him free.

O'Connor v. Donaldson helped to lay the legal grounds for the wave of deinstitutionalization of mental patients during the late 1970s and early 1980s. Donaldson himself, after his release, wrote a book about his experience, *Insanity Inside Out* (1976). Born on 22 May 1908, Donaldson died on 5 January 1995.

See also Deinstitutionalization; Psychiatric Survivor Movement.

Reference Donaldson, Kenneth, *Insanity Inside Out* (1976).

Office of Special Education and Rehabilitative Services (OSERS)

The Office of Special Education and Rehabilitative Services (OSERS) is the federal agency, housed within the U.S. Department of Education, responsible for ensuring access to education and rehabilitation for people with disabilities. It is divided into three parts: (1) the Office of Special Education Programs (OSEP); (2) the Rehabilitation Services Administration (RSA); and (3) the National Institute on Disability and Rehabilitation Research (NIDRR). The OSEP has major responsibility for programs relating to the free appropriate public education of children and youth with disabilities; the RSA administers programs related to employment and independent living (what used to be called vocational rehabilitation); and the NIDRR sponsors and oversees research related to disability and rehabilitation.

OSERS directors have included parent advocate Madeleine C. Will, deaf educator Robert Davila, and disability rights activist Judith Heumann (appointed by President Clinton as the first mobility disabled person to head the agency). *American Rehabilitation*, the official publication of the RSA, began publication as the *Rehabilitation Record* in January 1960 and as *American Rehabilitation* in September 1975. It published some of the first articles on independent living and disability rights by activists such as Lex Frieden and John Hessler. A bimonthly until 1983, *American Rehabilitation* today is a quarterly publication.

Office of Vocational Rehabilitation (OVR)
See Vocational Rehabilitation.

One Step Ahead—The Resource for Active, Healthy, Independent Living
One Step Ahead—The Resource for Active, Healthy, Independent Living (formerly, *One Step Ahead—The Disability Resource*) is a monthly newspaper published in Capitol Heights, Maryland, by Evan Kemp Associates. It is mailed to approximately 65,000 households. A typical issue features articles on topics such as financial planning for parents with disabled children, consumers replacing the leadership at an independent living center, the Americans with Disabilities Act, and health care for women with disabilities. Among its regular writers are Mike Ervin (a senior editor) and Carol Gill.

The first issue of *One Step Ahead* was published in Washington, D.C., on 12 January 1994. Executive Director Leye J. Chrzanowski describes its mission as providing readers "with reliable unbiased information about products, resources and services that will enable them to live healthy independent lives as educated consumers and politically savvy voters."

Oral School, Oralism
Oralism is a technique of educating deaf children with emphasis on speech and lip-reading to the exclusion of sign language. It was the predominant method in use in this country through the last half of the nineteenth century and the first half of the twentieth, despite the wishes of many deaf people, who considered it an attack on their language and culture. Its best-known proponent was the inventor Alexander Graham Bell, and its best-known critic was Edward Miner Gallaudet, founder and first president of what is now Gallaudet University.

The first "pure oral school" in the United States was founded by Bernard Engelsman, who had learned the technique as a teacher at Deutsch's Jewish School (for the Deaf) in Vienna. Within a month of his arrival in New York City in 1864, Engelsman began using what was known as the "German Method" with his first deaf pupil. In 1867, he founded the New York Institution for the Improved Instruction of Deaf Mutes. After moving to Lexington Avenue the New York Institution was renamed the Lexington School, by which time it had expanded to more than 100 students.

Up until this point, American schools for the deaf had taught and used sign language, and educators were soon divided into opposing camps: oralism versus "the manual" or sign language approach. Oralism received a significant boost from millionaire philanthropists such as Gardiner Greene Hubbard, who established the Clarke School for the Deaf in Northampton, Massachusetts, and Samuel Gridley Howe, the educator of blind and deaf-blind students at the Perkins School in Boston. Schools began to compete for funding and for pupils. What made the debate especially vituperative was the insistence by oralists that sign language inhibited the development of spoken language and lip-reading among deaf children. Though there was in fact no evidence to support this contention, oralists such as Hubbard pressured their state legislatures to ban the use of sign language at all publicly funded schools. Several states adopted such bans.

In 1867, Edward Miner Gallaudet traveled to Europe with deaf educators Lewis

Hard-of-hearing and deaf students try a new device, the radioear teaching set, which supposedly determined the degree of "latent hearing" in each student and amplified the voice of the teacher accordingly. The California School for the Deaf, pictured here in 1930, subscribed to the oral school, a teaching philosophy that emphasized speech and lip-reading and excluded sign language.

Weld and I. L. Peet to study oralism at its origin. They wrote a report calling for the introduction of lip-reading and speech training at all schools. The report also noted that most oralist students still could not speak intelligibly, and it recommended that the use of sign language be continued. Gallaudet labeled this use of speech, sign language, and lip-reading the "Combined Method." His report did much to legitimize oralism but did not satisfy proponents such as Bell, who called for the absolute suppression of sign language.

In 1880, the International Congress of Educators of the Deaf adopted a resolution at their conference in Milan declaring oralism the only acceptable method of deaf education. Out of 164 participants at the Milan conference, only one was deaf. Many American schools that had not already embraced oralism did so at this time. Deaf children were discouraged from associating with deaf adults who might use sign language to communicate. Schools that

switched from the manual to the oral method fired their deaf teachers and went to extraordinary lengths to keep their students from signing, including corporal punishment and tying their hands. American Sign Language (ASL) became, for most deaf children, an "underground" language.

Oralists claimed that any deaf child could learn to lip-read and speak. Bell, in part, based his opinion on the experience of his wife, Mabel Hubbard, who became deaf at age 5. In fact, according to some accounts, Mabel Hubbard Bell was never a good speaker or lip-reader, although others claimed she was an "amazing success story," able to lip-read German as well as English. In any case, oralists, even when they were able to maintain a sign-free environment, were never successful with more than a minority of their students, and generally those who, like Mabel Hubbard, had already learned some language before becoming deaf. Even when successful, the focus on lip-reading and speech was often at the expense of neglecting the rest of the child's education. Since almost all deaf students first went through years of oral instruction, they were often in their teens before those classified as "oral failures" were turned over to a manual school. As a result, an enormous percentage of deaf people reached maturity with a substandard education, often barely able to read or write.

Historian Jack Gannon described how "the controversy split families, broke up marriages, and led to divorces. It embittered deaf children and adults alike, leaving lifelong scars on the lives of many." Gannon called oralism an "attempt to make a 'hearing' person out of a deaf child. . . . They are, in effect, saying that it is wrong to be deaf" (1981). Others labeled oralism a social policy as opposed to a teaching method. "Is it not ironic," Gannon wrote, "that deaf people are rarely, if ever, asked what they believe is best for them?" In the early 1900s, George William Veditz, at that time president of the National Association of the Deaf, declared oralists to be "enemies of the true welfare of the deaf."

Despite its suppression, all through the years of oralism deaf people continued to use and to cherish ASL. Deaf children residing in oral schools taught each other signs at night in the dorms, and when outside the sight of their teachers and parents. Even Bell acknowledged that ASL was expressive and beautiful, indeed so much so that he condemned its power to seduce deaf people away from the more difficult path of oralism.

It was not until the 1960s that ASL began, as Gannon puts it, "to come out of the closet." In the mid-1950s, William C. Stokoe Jr., chair of the English Department at Gallaudet College in Washington, D.C., began to study ASL as a language in its own right, as opposed to a signed form of "pidgin English." In 1965, Stokoe, together with his colleagues Carl Croneberg and Dorothy Casterline, published *A Dictionary of American Sign Language on Linguistic Principles*. In California the parents and teachers of deaf children, unhappy

with the results of oralism, began to experiment with "total communication"—a revisit of Gallaudet's Combined Method. Meanwhile, the debate between oralists and proponents of the Combined Method continued. Richard Winefield, in his book *Never the Twain Shall Meet: Bell, Gallaudet, and the Communications Debate* (1987), estimates that in 1915 approximately 65 percent of classes for deaf students were oral, and 35 were combined. By the mid-1970s that ratio had been reversed.

Passage of the Education for All Handicapped Children Act in 1975 added a new dimension to the debate over the education of deaf children. Some Deaf advocates, for example, Nancy Becker in *Ordinary Moments* (1985), expressed concern that the emphasis on "mainstreaming" and "inclusive education" was a newer form of oralism, leaving many deaf children isolated again from ASL and Deaf culture. Oralism remains the preferred method of many hearing educators of deaf children, for example, at the Clarke School for the Deaf in Northampton, Massachusetts.

See also American Education for All Handicapped Children Act of 1975; American Sign Language; Inclusive Education; Bell, Alexander Graham; Deaf Culture; Gallaudet, Edward Miner; Total Communication.

References Gannon, Jack R., *Deaf Heritage: A Narrative History of Deaf America* (1981); Neisser, Arden, *The Other Side of Silence: Sign Language and the Deaf Community in America* (1983); Winefield, Richard, *Never the Twain Shall Meet: Bell, Gallaudet, and the Communications Debate* (1987).

Ordinary Lives
See Zola, Irving Kenneth.

Ordinary Moments: The Disabled Experience

Published in 1984, *Ordinary Moments: The Disabled Experience* is a collection of autobiographical essays by eight people with disabilities. Edited by Alan J. Brightman, the stories describe life in "a society largely ignorant of the disabled experience, a society that continues to view . . . disabled people as poster children." Ed Long writes about trying to use the New York subway in a wheelchair. Marsha Saxton recounts being hospitalized as a child with spina bifida during the 1950s for multiple operations to "correct" her walk. Stephen Spinetto fights to regain his driver's license, revoked after his leg was severed in a boating accident.

Ordinary Moments began as a photo exhibit honoring the International Year of Disabled Persons in 1981, with captions written by the people in Brightman's photographs. Originally published by University Park Press in Baltimore, the book was reissued by Human Policy Press in 1985.

See also International Year, International Decade of Disabled Persons; Saxton, Marsha.

Reference Brightman, Alan J., *Ordinary Moments: The Disabled Experience* (1985).

Oregon Medicaid Rationing Plan

See Health Care Access.

O'Rourke, Terrence James (T. J.) (1932–1992)

Terrence James (T. J.) O'Rourke, deaf publisher and writer, was a proponent of captioning and American Sign Language (ASL) and a leader of the American Coalition of Citizens with Disabilities (ACCD) and the National Association of the Deaf (NAD). He was born on 17 April 1932 in Bellingham, Washington, and attended the California School for the Deaf at Berkeley, Gallaudet College in Washington, D.C., Catholic University of America in Washington, D.C., and the University of Maryland at College Park. He was a high school teacher at the North Dakota School for the Deaf at Devil's Lake (1953–1956) and the North Carolina School for the Deaf at Morgantown (1956–1960), and an instructor at the Kendall School at Gallaudet (1960–1962). He was a professor of English at Gallaudet from 1962 until 1968.

From 1968 to 1978, O'Rourke was the national director of the Communication Skills Program of the NAD, helping to establish ASL programs in schools, colleges, and agencies across the country. In 1972, he wrote and edited *A Basic Course in Man-ual Communication*, published by the NAD, which sold more than 3 million copies to become the nation's best selling sign language text. In 1975, he founded the Sign Language Instructors Guidance Network (SIGN) and, in 1977, helped to organize the first National Symposium on Sign Language Research and Teaching. He founded his own publishing company, T. J. Publishers, Inc., in 1978 to publish books and materials on deafness and deaf culture. Among its publications is *A Basic Course in American Sign Language* (1980), which he co-authored with Tom Humphries and Carol Padden. He was also a leader with Friends of Libraries for Deaf Action (FOLDA), which works to improve library access for deaf people. In 1983, he founded the Caption Club, an advocacy group to convince television producers to caption their programs. By 1984, more than 14,000 persons and organizations had joined, and the club had provided partial funding for captioning some 170 television series. By 1989, because of the club's efforts, all prime-time network programs were captioned.

O'Rourke was a believer in cross-disability activism. He was an organizer of the Health, Education and Welfare (HEW) demonstrations of 1977 and participated in the sit-in in Washington, D.C. He was both a vice president (1977–1978) and president (1978–1982) of the ACCD and a member of the executive committee of the President's Committee on Employment of the Handicapped (1978–1980). Terence James O'Rourke died on 10 January 1992.

See also American Coalition of Citizens with Disabilities; American Sign Language; Captioning/Closed Captioning; HEW Demonstrations.

Reference Moore, Matthew Scott, and Robert F. Panara, *Great Deaf Americans* (1996).

Owen, Mary Jane

The thinking and activism of Mary Jane Owen have had a profound impact on the disability rights movement. An early activist at the Center for Independent Living in Berkeley in 1972 and an organizer and participant in the Health, Education and

Mary Jane Owen speaks to reporters at a protest against euthanasia in 1996.

Welfare (HEW) occupation in San Francisco in 1977, Owen is also a mentor to younger disability activists, particularly women, and the author of more than 600 published articles on disability rights.

Owen's political activism preceded her disability. Raised in "a family of pacifists," she was a student of Gandhism at the New School for Social Research in New York City. As a young woman in the 1940s, she was a member of the Congress of Racial Equality (CORE) and later helped to found the CORE chapter in Albuquerque, New Mexico. She recalls how, in Los Angeles, she "was slammed with fire hoses through a plate glass window when we tried desegregating a swimming pool," while her refusal to pay taxes in protest of the Vietnam War made her liable for fines and imprisonment. She received her bachelor's degree in fine arts from the University of New Mexico in Albuquerque in the early 1960s and her master's degree in social work from the University of California at Berkeley in 1966. In the following years,

she was an artist and designer in Greenwich Village, a social worker in Phoenix, a psychiatric social worker at Arizona State Hospital in Phoenix, a program supervisor at the Lincoln Child Center in Oakland, California, and an assistant professor and administrative officer at the San Francisco State University Department of Social Work Education.

Owen became disabled in the late 1960s, losing her eyesight and then, over the years, much of her hearing and ability to walk. Her work in the disability rights movement began in 1972, when she became a paralegal at the CIL's Disability Rights Center, precursor to the Disability Rights Education and Defense Fund (DREDF). In 1977, she was one of the principal organizers of the sit-in at the San Francisco HEW offices, part of a national effort to force HEW Secretary Califano to issue regulations implementing Section 504 of the Rehabilitation Act of 1973. When word came that the Washington, D.C., occupation had ended because police had denied food and medicine to the demonstrators, Owen went on a hunger strike. A dozen or so of the more than 100 activists sitting in at the HEW offices joined her, refusing to eat until the Carter administration acceded to their demands. Owen's influence as an educator was evident when several of her students and former students convinced Mayor George Moscone and Congressman Philip Burton (D-CA) to express publicly their support of the demonstrators. Owen moved to Washington, D.C., in 1978 to become special assistant to the director of ACTION/Peace Corps, where she worked to remove the medical requirements for Peace Corps volunteers. She also cultivated a growing cadre of young women with disabilities, arranging for grants and scholarships to school them for leadership in the movement.

Owen was congressional liaison for the President's Committee on Employment of People with Disabilities from 1981 to 1986. In 1984, she became the executive director and president of Disability Focus, Inc., a position she holds today. For five years, she was a member of the Grey Panthers Task Force on Disability. At a panel discussion in 1983, she first broached the idea of defining disability, not as something unusual or abnormal, but rather as "the natural outcome of the risks, stresses and strains of the living process itself; therefore disabilities become less an individual tragedy than an expected event in any community."

In 1990, Owen became a Mary Switzer Research Fellow at the U.S. Department of Education, participating in the production of the video *Living History: The 1977 "504" Sit-In as a Catalyst in the Disability Rights Movement.* That same year, Owen received her theological certification from Georgetown University and converted to Catholicism, and today she is the executive director of the National Catholic Office for Persons with Disabilities.

Owen was born in Evanston, Illinois, and refuses to disclose her age or date of birth. "The last time I was in the hospital for surgery, it was decided I wasn't going to be allowed any rehabilitation because I was too old. Well, I'm not too old. I may be blind, I may be partially hearing, I may be in a wheelchair, and I may be mature, but when they put all those elements together and decide I'm 'not worth' rehabilitating, that scares me." Owen was one of the first to speak out against Jack Kevorkian and assisted suicide, warning that people with disabilities are being prompted by society to choose death as a way of cutting health care costs. "The legal precedents being established over the past few years," she wrote in the June 1996 issue of *Horizons*, "are not going to go away as quickly as they have come upon us." Owen warns that health insurers, physicians, and right-to-die activists are all making it easier for people with disabilities to be denied the care they need to live.

See also Center for Independent Living; Euthanasia and Assisted Suicide; HEW Demonstrations; Religion.

PAIL or Personal Assistance for Independent Living Legislation
See Personal Assistance Services.

Panzarino, Concetta (Connie) (b. 1947)

Concetta (Connie) Panzarino is the author of *The Me in the Mirror* (1994), which describes her life as a woman, lesbian, and person with a disability. She is also an artist, art therapist, lecturer, and disability and lesbian rights advocate. "When you are disabled," she writes in her introduction, "some people look to you for wisdom, others look at you in fear; most of the world doesn't notice you or tries not to. And in the midst of all their conceptions of you, you exist."

Panzarino was born on 26 November 1947 in Brooklyn, New York. Early in her childhood she developed the symptoms of a progressive neuro-muscular disease that today allows her movement only in her right thumb and facial muscles. She was denied the right to attend public school, receiving several hours of home teaching each week. She received her B.A. in English and the humanities in 1969 and her M.A. in art and psychology in 1978, both from the New College of Hofstra in Hempstead, New York. In 1983, she received her M.A. in art therapy from New York University.

Panzarino has worked extensively with women and men survivors of physical and sexual abuse. She lectures nationwide on the subjects of disability, homophobia, sexism, and the ethics of genetic engineering. She was the director of the Beechtree, an independent living program for disabled women in Forestberg, New York, from 1980 to 1985 and executive director of the Boston Self Help Center from 1986 to 1989. Panzarino was an activist in the campaign to free Sharon Kowalski, a disabled lesbian kept in a nursing home against her will for eight years, and is a member of the board of directors of the Project on Women and Disability and the Boston Disability Law Center.

In addition to *The Me in the Mirror*, Panzarino is the author of *Follow Your Dreams* (1995) and co-author of *Rebecca Finds a New Way (1994)*, both distributed by the National Spinal Cord Injury Association for children with spinal cord injuries and diseases. Her most recent project, *Tell It Like It Is*, is a similar book for teenagers and is scheduled for publication in 1997.

See also Boston Self Help Center; Kowalski, Sharon, and Karen Thompson.

Reference Panzarino, Connie, *The Me in the Mirror* (1994).

Paralympics (Paralympic Movement)

The idea for an international competition of the world's best disabled athletes was first advanced by English neurosurgeon Sir Ludwig Guttman, who organized the first International Wheelchair Games in 1948 at the Stoke-Mandeville Hospital in Aylesbury, England, to coincide with the London Olympics. The Paralympic Games in Rome in 1960, the first to be recognized by the International Olympic Committee, drew 400 athletes from 23 countries. At first, only wheelchair users participated, but athletes with other disabilities were soon competing. The International Coordinating Committee of World Sports Organizations for the Disabled was founded in 1982 to accommodate this interest, and it was organized into four separate federations: (1) the Cerebral Palsy International Sports and Recreation Association (CP-ISRA); (2) the International Blind Sports Association (IBSA); (3) the International Stoke-Mandeville Wheelchair Sports Federation (ISMWSF); and (4) the International

Mark Weeks of New Zealand competes in the men's Super-G at the fifth Paralympics Winter Games in Tignes, France, 1992.

Sports Organization for the Disabled (ISOD), which includes athletes with a wide variety of disabilities, including amputees and dwarves. In 1992, the International Coordinating Committee was renamed the International Paralympic Committee, the Paralympics' governing body, with athletes still organized into the same four basic federations.

The Paralympic Games are among the world's largest sporting events. They are held to coincide with the Olympics, occurring immediately afterwards and always in the same venue. The 1996 Paralympic Games in Atlanta drew 3,500 athletes from 120 nations, participating in 700 events for ten days of competition. The 17 full medal sports included archery, basketball, cycling, fencing, judo, powerlifting, soccer, swimming, and tennis. The Paralympic Committee also runs a variety of youth education programs, a Paralympic Youth Camp, and a mentor program.

The Paralympics are an occasion for dis-ability rights activists to share their concerns and insights. The 1996 games, for example, featured presentations by American activists such as Justin Dart Jr. and Marca Bristo, along with international activists, such as Joshua T. Malinga from Zimbabwe.

See also Sports and Athletics.

Paralyzed Veterans of America (PVA)

The end of World War II saw an unprecedented number of disabled veterans returning home. An estimated 2,500 had spinal cord injuries, many of them patients at the Birmingham Hospital in Van Nuys, California. Apart from their physical disabilities, attitudinal and architectural barriers effectively shut them off from the American mainstream. In response, disabled veterans organized to become the vanguard of the disability rights movement of the 1940s and 1950s.

One of the first disabled veterans groups, the Bilateral Leg Amputee Club of

America (BLACA), was founded before the end of the war at the Bushnell Hospital in Utah. Disability rights historian Richard Bryant Treanor described their activities as touring "the country selling savings bonds and generally creating drunken brawls." BLACA, however, served as the model for a more serious group organized at the Birmingham Hospital, which Treanor identifies as "the precursor" of the Paralyzed Veterans of America (PVA). The PVA was founded on 7 February 1947 by delegates from this group and other Veterans Association hospitals across the country. In 1948, the PVA sponsored the founding of the National Paraplegia Foundation (since renamed the National Spinal Cord Injury Association) as its civilian offshoot.

PVA chapters were involved in some of the earliest experiments in independent living. The national organization was an original member of the American Coalition of Citizens with Disabilities and one of the founders of the 1981 International Year of Disabled Persons. The PVA has been integral in passage of such landmark legislation as the Civil Rights Restoration Act of 1987, the Fair Housing Amendments Act of 1988, and the Americans with Disabilities Act of 1990 (ADA). The Air Carrier Access Act of 1986 was the direct result of a PVA lawsuit filed against the U.S. Department of Transportation and then appealed to the U.S. Supreme Court as *Department of Transportation v. Paralyzed Veterans of America* (1986). The PVA pushed to ensure that the Vietnam Veterans Memorial in Washington, D.C., was accessible, and it has participated in every major effort to draft building codes for architectural access. It has also been involved in such landmark lawsuits as *American Disabled for Accessible Public Transit (ADAPT) v. Skinner* (1989) and in litigation (together with Disabled in Action) in New York City from 1981 to 1984 to gain access to that city's mass transit system. More recently, in 1996, it filed suit against the owners of the MCI Center Sports Arena for building a stadium for the Washington Bullets in violation of ADA access standards.

The PVA today consists of more than 34 chapters and subchapters nationwide, and it operates 59 service offices to assist veterans seeking claims and benefits through the U.S. Department of Veterans Affairs. It sponsors research in the treatment of spinal cord injury and disease and administers a Spinal Cord Injury Education and Training Foundation (ETF) to assist and educate people with spinal cord injury, their families, and health care professionals. PVA publications include *The Economic Consequences of Traumatic Spinal Cord Injury* (1992), *Yes You Can: A Guide to Self Care for Persons with Spinal Cord Injury* (1989, updated in 1996), *Inform Yourself: Alcohol, Drugs, and Spinal Cord Injury* (1990), *Sexuality Reborn* (1993), and *A Guide to Wheelchair Sports and Recreation* (2d edition, 1996). The PVA also publishes *Sports 'n Spokes*, a bimonthly magazine covering wheelchair competitive sports and recreation and the monthly *PN/Paraplegia News*.

The PVA, with headquarters in Washington, D.C., today represents some 17,000 veterans with spinal cord injury.

See also Air Carrier Access Act; *American Disabled for Accessible Public Transit v. Skinner*; National Spinal Cord Injury Association.

Reference Treanor, Richard Bryant, *We Overcame: The Story of Civil Rights for Disabled People* (1993).

Paraquad
See Starkloff, Max J.

Paratransit Systems
Paratransit systems are designed to transport people for whom mainline mass transit systems, that is, buses and subways, are inaccessible. Paratransit systems generally involve the use of lift- or ramp-equipped vans, taxis, and buses to take people who are elderly and/or disabled directly from their homes to their destination and back: so-called door-to-door service. Paratransit rides generally must be reserved at least one day in advance and are available only

to those people deemed eligible by the transit authority.

The development of paratransit systems, beginning in the 1970s, was both controversial and problematic, and paratransit evolved as a generally separate but hardly equal system of public transportation. Scheduled vans were often late, and trips could take up to six times longer because of ride-sharing (stacking people with different destinations on the same van) than the same trip on mainline transit. Sometimes vans simply did not arrive at all. Paratransit users in Boston in the mid-1980s reported that, because of the unreliability of the local "Ride," they might be late for work four out of five mornings a week, and on some mornings unable to get to work at all. The same uncertainty prevailed during the ride home, with some disabled passengers stranded at work when a "Ride" van failed to arrive. Furthermore, paratransit operators would take upon themselves the task of deciding which rides were a priority; thus, people wishing to worship, or visit a friend, or see a movie, were sometimes "bumped" for people traveling to medical appointments. In Boston, the paratransit system refused to provide service on weekend nights, until local activists in the mid-1980s forced an expansion of service hours.

The segregated nature of paratransit allowed people without disabilities to see the system as adequate compensation for the inaccessibility of mainline transit. Philip K. Howard, in *The Death of Common Sense* (1994), described paratransit as "front of the bus service" and castigated disability rights advocates for wanting mainline access. Apparently unaware of the inadequacy and inequity of paratransit, Howard labeled the inconvenience of temporarily able-bodied riders forced to wait a few extra minutes for a disabled rider to be loaded onto a mainline, lift-equipped bus as an affront to "common sense."

Paratransit was also, in the long run, far more expensive for transit operators than providing accessible mainline bus and subway service. Nevertheless, for individuals whose disability prevents them from traveling to a subway or bus stop or from waiting for the arrival of a train or bus, or for those who are otherwise unable to negotiate mainline transit, paratransit is a necessary option, even if mainline subways, trains, and buses are made completely accessible. For this reason, most disability rights activists see a need for both mainline access and some form of paratransit service.

Title II of the Americans with Disabilities Act of 1990 (ADA) recognizes this dual need. It stipulates that it is "discrimination . . . for a public [transit system] . . . to fail to provide . . . paratransit and other special transportation services." Under the ADA, paratransit services must be extended to the same area, and during the same hours of service, as mainline services available to nondisabled riders, to the extent that providing such service is not "an undue financial burden." The process and criteria for establishing "undue financial burden" are detailed in the U.S. Department of Transportation's ADA regulations.

See also *American Disabled for Accessible Public Transit (ADAPT) v. Skinner*; American Disabled for Attendant Programs Today; Public Transportation; Undue Hardship/Undue Burden.

Parenting and Disability

Most people would be outraged if the government, the medical establishment, private charitable organizations, or religious institutions attempted to tell them that they could not have children. The right to have a family is so fundamental that most take it for granted. And yet, until recently, people with severe disabilities were routinely denied any hope for family life. Through the second half of the nineteenth and much of the twentieth centuries, institutionalization, segregation by gender, and even forced sterilization all were used to keep people with disabilities from becoming parents. In many states, laws were passed prohibiting people with certain disabilities, for example epilepsy, from marrying. And when disabled people did have children, the government, as in the case of

Blind father Julio Perez reads a story to his sighted daughter Hannah in 1993 by using a book overlaid with braille.

Tiffany Callo, took them away, as if anyone with a disability was by definition incapable of being a good parent. The courts, in divorce proceedings, have routinely awarded custody to the nondisabled parent, despite all other factors. Furthermore, disabled people wishing to adopt have been told, more often than not, that agencies do not award children to individuals with disabilities.

As late as the 1980s, the prevailing view among nondisabled psychologists was that having one or both parents with a disability damaged a child's mental health, despite the fact that very little research had been done to test this assertion, and what evidence existed contradicted it. In her 1980 paper *The Influence of Parental Disability on Children*, Frances Buck at the University of Arizona described a study in which psychological tests were conducted with children from more than 50 families with spinal cord injured fathers, and the results were then compared with test results of children from families where parents were not disabled. Buck concluded, "The children [of spinal cord injured fathers] appeared generally well adjusted and functioning adequately, and none of the predicted specific adverse affects (psychological maladjustment, inappropriate sex role orientation, poor or distorted body images, failure to develop interest in physical activities and athletics, etc.) was confirmed." Buck went on to say that the disabled fathers "were perceived as warm, affectionate, and helpful. Their children showed no difference in social skills or friendship and dating patterns from the children of non-disabled fathers."

Since then, a variety of studies have confirmed Buck's results for families with disabled fathers and disabled mothers. Stanley Ducharme, a psychologist who has worked with hundreds of families in which one or both parents are disabled, contends that "what makes a good parent is not necessarily who changes the diapers or plays ball with the kid. It's who is emotionally available to the child." In this view, as long as provision is made for personal assistance services (PAS), including help with the more physical aspects of parenting, even the most severely disabled individuals can in fact be excellent parents.

Many health professionals, however, continue to believe the old stereotypes, and state social service agencies often continue to view disabled parents with suspicion. Other obstacles faced by disabled parents include inaccessible day care centers, recreational programs, church clubs, and parent-teacher groups. Finally, the general lack of access in our schools, stores, mass transit systems, workplaces, etc., all exacerbate the difficulties of being a parent with a disability.

See also Callo, Tiffany Ann; Eugenics; Forced Sterilization; Sexuality and Disability.

References Mathews, Jay, *A Mother's Touch: The Tiffany Callo Story: The True Story of a Physically Disabled Mother's Fight for the Right To Keep Her Children* (1992); National Institute of Handicapped Research, Office of Special Education and Rehabilitative Services, "The Influence of Parental Disability on Children," *Rehab Brief* (January 1982).

Parents' Movement

Beginning in the 1930s, parents of children with disabilities, particularly children with cerebral palsy and mental retardation, began to organize themselves into small, local groups meeting for support and to discuss issues of mutual interest. This process accelerated in the 1940s, in large part due to the participation of returning veterans. It led, in 1949, to the founding of United Cerebral Palsy Associations, and, in 1950, of the National Association for Retarded Children (later the National Association for Retarded Citizens and then The Arc). Later parents' groups included the Autism Society of America, the National Alliance for the Mentally Ill, and Fiesta Educativa, Inc.

The parents' movement was instrumental in forcing the creation and expansion of federal, state, and local programs for children with disabilities. The creation of recreational programs and summer camps for disabled children and the first paratransit systems were all due to the advocacy of parents' organizations. In 1972, *PARC v. Pennsylvania* and *Mills v. Board of Education* established the right of disabled children to receive a public school education. Parents' organizations followed up these victories by lobbying for passage of the Education for All Handicapped Children Act of 1975, enabling subsequent generations of children with disabilities to be educated. Lawsuits such as *Halderman v. Pennhurst* (1978) and *New York ARC v. Carey* (1973) forced the deinstitutionalization of thousands of children and adults with disabilities and established their right to community services. The ARC and United Cerebral Palsy Associations then established community programs for those who were deinstitutionalized. Parents' organizations also provided pivotal support for passage of bills from the Rehabilitation Act of 1973 to the Americans with Disabilities Act of 1990.

These successes have had an enormous impact on American society, people with disabilities, and the parents' movement itself. Martha Ziegler, founder of the Federation for Children with Special Needs in Boston, Massachusetts, writes how passage of the Education for All Handicapped Children Act of 1975 "brought a profound change in parents, a change that has been internalized and cannot be undone. . . . No longer did they need to be grateful for every crumb; they could actually make demands on behalf of their children and expect reasonable responses to those demands." The act has also fostered cross-disability cooperation among parents, since "the process of developing an IEP [Individualized Education Program] was the same whether the child had Down syndrome or dyslexia." Since 1975, a network of Parent Training and Information (PTI) Centers, federally funded but managed by local advocacy groups, has been established as a resource for parent advocates. The National Parent Network on

Disabilities was formally established in December 1988 as an umbrella organization for these centers.

As the children of the parents' movement have grown into adulthood, there has been some tension between the now well-established parents' organizations and the organizations of advocates who are themselves disabled. People First, founded in 1974, criticized the ARC on a variety of issues, including the use of the word *retarded* in its title (a dispute that eventually led to the renaming of the organization). The move by parents' organizations into the management of day programs and group homes has at times led them into an adversarial relationship with disabled consumers. The use of telethons and poster children has also been a sore point, with many advocates believing that these fundraising techniques are inherently damaging to disability rights. Psychiatric survivor advocates have been critical of positions taken by the National Alliance for the Mentally Ill, including its support of involuntary commitment laws. "Its very name," survivor Rae Unzicker writes, "is stigmatizing; we do not call people with cancer, for example, the cancerous."

National parents' groups, with their large budgets and memberships, continue to play an important role in advocating on issues such as health care reform, education, and access to rehabilitation services and adaptive technology. Publications such as *Exceptional Parent*, an independent magazine founded by Stanley D. Klein and Maxwell J. Schleifer in 1971, provide information on disability rights issues to tens of thousands of readers. Smaller, grassroots groups such as Mothers From Hell advocate for their children on a more local level, providing a new, more radical edge to the movement.

See also The Arc; Developmental Disabilities Assistance and Bill of Rights Act of 1975; Dybwad, Gunnar; Education for All Handicapped Children Act of 1975; Fiesta Educativa; *Halderman v. Pennhurst State School & Hospital; Holland v. Sacramento City Unified School District; Mills v. Board of Education;* Mothers From Hell; National Alliance for the Mentally Ill; People First, People First Interna-

tional; *Pennsylvania ARC v. Pennsylvania*; Telethons; United Cerebral Palsy Associations, Inc.

References Dybwad, Gunnar, and Hank Bersani Jr., eds., *New Voices: Self-Advocacy by People with Disabilities* (1996); Turnbull, H. Rutherford, III, and Ann P. Turnbull, *Parents Speak Out: Then and Now* (1985, 1978).

Parrino, Sandra Swift (b. 1934)

Sandra Swift Parrino was chair of the National Council on Disability from 1983 to 1993. She was born on 22 June 1934 in New Haven, Connecticut. The parent of a physically disabled son, her first disability-related work was with the Office for the Disabled in Ossining/Briarcliff Manor, New York, where she was director from 1979 to 1982. She was appointed to the National Council on Disability in 1982, at which time it was a part of the U.S. Department of Education. Parrino insisted that the council become an independent agency and lobbied for passage of the Rehabilitation Act Amendments of 1984 to make it so. The newly independent council then called for changes in federal law culminating in the drafting and passage of the Americans with Disabilities Act of 1990. During Parrino's tenure, the council cosponsored a conference with Jackson State University (Jackson, Mississippi) on minority people with disabilities. It also sponsored hearings, research, and forums on such topics as education, infants at risk, employment, and personal assistance services.

Parrino left the council in 1994, after founding and becoming president of the Alliance for International Development, based in Scarborough, New York, in 1993. The alliance provides assistance to governmental and nongovernmental organizations related to disability. In addition to her advocacy for disabled individuals, Parrino has also worked to aid incarcerated women and their children.

See also National Council on Disability; Parents' Movement.

PAS

See Personal Assistance Services.

Peer Counseling

Marsha Saxton defines peer counseling as "a process by which one person is helped by another person who has had similar or related experiences." For people with disabilities, who have so often been abused, exploited, or patronized by nondisabled "helping professionals," peer counseling is not only an alternative resource for working out life's problems but often the *only* method with any chance of success.

Peer counseling can occur in groups or between individuals. It can be in a strictly counseling context, or it can come as part of "skills training," where newly disabled people are shown the ropes by someone with more experience managing their disability. It can also serve much the same function as the women's consciousness-raising groups of the 1960s and 1970s, where people learn to recognize their shared oppression and to explore ways to achieve social and political change. With passage of the Rehabilitation Act Amendments of 1978, peer counseling became a recognized, and federally funded, part of the services at independent living centers.

See also Boston Self Help Center; Saxton, Marsha.

Reference Saxton, Marsha, "A Peer Counseling Training Program for Disabled Women: A Tool for Social and Individual Change," in Mary Jo Deegan and Nancy A. Brooks, eds., *Women and Disability: The Double Handicap* (1985).

Pennhurst Decision

See Halderman v. Pennhurst State School & Hospital.

Pennsylvania Association for Retarded Children v. Commonwealth of Pennsylvania (PARC v. Pennsylvania) 343 F. Supp. 279 (1972)

PARC v. Pennsylvania was the nation's first right-to-education case argued on behalf of children with disabilities. The consent decree reached by the parties guaranteed for the first time in American history the right of disabled children to receive a public education. The case was pivotal in the passage of the Education for All Handicapped Children Act three years later and

the precursor to such central concepts of disability rights education law as the zero-reject principle, the requirement of a free, appropriate public education for every child, the intergration mandate, and the requirement to know and to adopt promising education practices.

Prior to the case, school officials in Pennsylvania districts had used state laws to deny disabled children a public education. The state's own 1965 Pennsylvania Mental Retardation Plan estimated that between 70,000 and 80,000 Pennsylvania children with developmental disabilities were denied access to any public education, or to services at home, day care, or community facilities. The only other option—institutionalization—was also often unavailable, since the state "schools" were already vastly over crowded. Furthermore, of 4,159 school-age children institutionalized in Pennsylvania, only 100 were receiving anything even remotely comparable to a full public education, while more than 3,000 received no education at all. Children who were poor, members of a minority group, or non–English speaking were often incorrectly classified as mentally retarded and thus also denied an education.

The class action lawsuit was brought by the parents of 13 children classified as mentally retarded, all of whom had been excluded from public education. It named as plaintiffs all mentally retarded persons between ages 6 and 21, and it named as defendants every school district in Pennsylvania. The plaintiffs, represented by Thomas K. Gilhool, presented testimony that children were excluded often on the judgment of a single school official, with no opportunity for parents to appeal or even question the decision. Plaintiffs maintained that this exclusion was a violation of their children's right to equal protection under the law and to due process, and of the Pennsylvania state constitution, which ensured to all children the right to a public education. They urged that the court prohibit the state from denying disabled students a publicly funded education. In cases where school officials sought to exclude a child from a mainstream classroom, the plaintiffs asked that the court require that school administrators first meet with parents whose child was to be excluded; that the meeting had to take place in the presence of a special hearing officer; and that parents be allowed to bring an attorney, to examine their children's records, to present evidence to contest the school's decision, and to cross-examine witnesses, such as school psychologists, who were offering evidence in support of exclusion. Even before the trial began, the state of Pennsylvania conceded the strength of the parents' case by entering into a preliminary agreement, approved by the court, which stipulated all of their proposals.

The final consent agreement concluded in May 1972 that, "[e]very retarded person between the ages of six and twenty-one shall be provided access to a free public program of education and training appropriate to his capacities as soon as possible but in no event later than September 1, 1972." If a child could not attend a regular public school or mainstream classes, the school district would pay for alternatives such as home or private schooling.

PARC established a number of important precedents. Gilhool based his case on what Robert L. Burgdorf called "the two-barreled (due process and equal protection) attack," which "has become standard fare in subsequent lawsuits. . . . The impact of Gilhool's initial legal insights are difficult to overestimate." The decree also acknowledged the role of social stereotypes in stunting the lives of children with disabilities, a strategy of education and persuasion that Gilhool was to repeat when arguing *City of Cleburne, Tex. v. Cleburne Living Center* (1985).

PARC generated enormous publicity, inspired similar lawsuits all across the country, and was a major impetus for passage of the Education for All Handicapped Children Act. Finally, and perhaps most significantly, it served as a catalyst for the disability rights movement in general, much as *Brown v. Board of Education* (1954) catalyzed the black civil rights movement.

See also The Arc; Dybwad, Gunnar; Education for All Handicapped Children Act of 1975; Gilhool, Thomas K.
References Burgdorf, Robert L., Jr., *The Legal Rights of Handicapped Persons: Cases, Materials and Text* (1980); Lippman, Leopold D., *Right to Education: Anatomy of the Pennsylvania Case and Its Implications for Exceptional Children* (1973).

People First, People First International

People First, founded in Salem, Oregon, in 1974, is the nation's largest self-advocacy organization made up of and run by people with cognitive disabilities. The group has chapters throughout the United States and in more than 30 other countries, but the main office remains in Salem.

The origins of People First go back to November 1973, when three residents and two staff members of Oregon's Fairview Hospital and Training Center in Salem attended the "First Convention for the Mentally Handicapped in North America" in Victoria Island, British Columbia. The five returned to Oregon inspired with the idea of founding an organization of and for people with cognitive disabilities, as distinct from groups such as The Arc (made up of parents and family members) or the American Association on Mental Retardation (AAMR)(made up of physicians, educators, social workers and administrators). "We wanted to let those in authority know that we were just like them and would like to be treated in the same way," Valerie Schaaf, first president of the new group, wrote years later. "We wanted to speak for ourselves."

On 8 January 1974, eight Fairview residents and former residents met, agreeing to hold an organizing convention for the following October. The name *People First* was adopted in May, as a way of emphasizing that people with cognitive disabilities are *people* first and foremost. The organizers visited all the residential programs, sheltered workshops, day programs, and activity centers in the counties surrounding Salem, and more than 500 people with disabilities attended the organization's first convention on 12–13 October 1974.

Steady expansion followed, with more than 900 people attending the 1976 convention, and more than 1,000 the 1978 convention in Portland, Oregon.

People First chapters were soon organizing, first in the Pacific Northwest, then in the Midwest and beyond. These groups were held together less by any central organization than a philosophy of self-advocacy and self-empowerment. Among the principles around which they organized were the need for people with developmental disabilities to have decent jobs with living wages and their right to make their own decisions about where they live, with whom they associate, whether or not to enter into intimate relationships, and whether or not to have families. Among the first issues tackled was the label "mentally retarded." People First activists attended state and national meetings of the ARC, which at that time was an acronym for the Association for Retarded Citizens, and over time convinced the ARC to eliminate the word *retarded* from its name (the organization is known today as The Arc). People First members pressed for representation on boards and committees of the state and nonprofit organizations that held power over their lives. Chapters protested poor work conditions at sheltered workshops and participated in lawsuits designed to free people with developmental disabilities from warehousing in residential institutions.

In 1982, an international coalition of groups, including the Campaign for Mentally Handicapped People of London; the Massachusetts Coalition of Citizens with Disabilities; People First chapters in Oregon, Washington State, and Nebraska; and the Australian Union of Intellectually Disadvantaged Citizens, began planning an international conference for 1984 in Tacoma, Washington. Other self-advocates, inspired by People First, founded groups such as Speaking for Ourselves in Philadelphia. The First North American People First Conference was held in 1990 in Estes Park, Colorado, where the national umbrella group Self Advocates Becoming Empowered was incorporated.

In 1984, activists in California People First conducted an extensive investigation of the California service system for persons with developmental disabilities. Their report, *Surviving in the System: Mental Retardation and the Retarding Environment* (1984), was a devastating portrayal of the way a paternalist social service system harms the people it is intended to serve. Other publications include *We Can Speak for Ourselves* (1983), by Paul Williams of England and Bonnie Shoultz of the United States, *Speaking Up and Speaking Out* (1985), by People First of Washington State, and *No More BS! A Realistic Survival Guide for Disability Rights Activists* (1992), by Victoria Medgyesi, also published by People First of Washington.

In the 1990s, People First of Tennessee filed a series of lawsuits on behalf of institution residents. The proposed 1996 settlement not only restructured Tennessee's services to people with developmental disabilities but also marked the first time that former institution residents themselves designed, filed, and successfully concluded a class action lawsuit.

See also The Arc; *Christmas in Purgatory;* Developmentally Disabled Assistance and Bill of Rights Act of 1975; Dybwad, Gunnar; *Halderman v. Pennhurst State School & Hospital;* Jensen, Sandra; *Pennsylvania Association for Retarded Children v. Commonwealth of Pennsylvania;* Self Advocates Becoming Empowered; Supported Employment; Willowbrook State School; *Wyatt v. Stickney.*

References Dybwad, Gunnar, and Hank Bersani, Jr., eds., *New Voices: Self-Advocacy by People with Disabilities* (1996); Medgyesi, Victoria, *No More B.S: A Realistic Survival Guide for Disability Rights Activists* (1992).

Perkins School for the Blind

The Perkins School for the Blind, originally called the New England Asylum for the Blind and then the Perkins Institution, was chartered by the Commonwealth of Massachusetts on 2 March 1829 and opened in July 1832. Its first director was Samuel Gridley Howe, and the school was originally housed in his father's house on Pleasant Street in Boston. The school opened with two students, the sisters

Sophia and Abbey Carter, and two teachers, Emile Trencheri and John Pringle, both of whom were also blind. Trencheri had been an instructor at the National Institution for Blind Youth in Paris, while Pringle had taught in Edinburgh, Scotland. Within a month, student enrollment had grown to six, and a third teacher, Lowell Mason, was hired to teach music. The school then moved to the home of Colonel Thomas Handasyd Perkins, for whom it would eventually be named.

The school was modeled on the National Institution and other schools for visually disabled children that Howe had visited during a trip to Europe. Howe felt, however, that the European institutions did not go far enough in teaching independence, and he felt it crucial that his students be prepared "to go out in the world, not to eat the bread of charity, but to earn a livelihood by honest work." By 1839, the school had grown to 65 students and moved out of the Perkins residence and into the Mount Washington House hotel. In 1837, Laura Bridgman was accepted as the school's first deaf-blind student, and her work with Howe earned them both international recognition. Charles Dickens, on his trip to America, wrote about Howe's work with Bridgman in *American Notes* (1842).

Howe died in 1876 and was succeeded as director by his son-in-law Michael Anagnos. Anagnos established the Perkins Research Library and Museum, and he founded the nation's first kindergarten for blind children. Anagnos was succeeded as director by Edward E. Allen, who moved the school to its present site in Watertown, Massachusetts. As director Allen oversaw the development of the Hayes-Binet standardized test for the blind, which, for the first time, demonstrated that the average intelligence of people with blindness does not differ from that of the sighted population.

With the advent of the disability rights movement and the acceptance of students who are blind and visually disabled into mainstream public school classrooms,

Perkins underwent profound changes. By the 1970s, its student population was increasingly multiply-disabled, and the school was offering a wide range of services to children and young adults not living on campus, and to educators of children with multiple disabilities at other schools. Perkins continues to play a role in the blind community, for example, through the Howe Press, one of the world's largest braille printing houses, and through the production of the Perkins Brailler, a portable braille typewriter of which more than 180,000 have been manufactured.

See also Howe, Samuel Gridley; Keller, Helen Adams.

References Lash, Joseph P., *Helen and Teacher: The Story of Helen Keller and Anne Sullivan Lacy* (1980); *Perkins School for the Blind: Annual Report 1987* (1988).

Perske, Robert (b. 1927)

Robert Perske documents and then intervenes in circumstances where people with cognitive or mental disabilities are abused by the criminal justice system. His 1991 book *Unequal Justice?* lays out several such cases. Perske attends trials, visits prisons, and rallies support for defendants and their families.

Robert Perske was born on 16 October 1927 in Denver, Colorado. He became a freelance writer after working in institutions and community services for people with developmental disabilities. In 1968, he received the Rosemary Dybwad International Award that enabled him to study attitudes toward people with developmental disabilities in Sweden and Denmark. He returned to the United States and began writing about and advocating for normalization and community living. His first book, *Hope for the Families: New Directions for Parents of Persons with Retardation and Other Disabilities* (1974), was followed by *Mealtimes for Persons with Severe Handicaps* (1978), the young adult novels *Show Me No Mercy* (1984) and *Don't Stop the Music* (1986), and *Circle of Friends: How People with Disabilities and Their Friends Enrich the Lives of One Another* (1988). *Deadly*

Innocence? (1995) recounts the story of Joe Arridy, a mentally disabled man executed in the early 1900s for a murder even his jailers acknowledged he did not commit. In this book, Perske recounts the history of the eugenics movement and the neglect and prejudice that led to Arridy's murder by gas chamber.

Perske's work was featured in the 1995 PBS documentary "A Passion for Justice." The Emmy Award–winning program describes his founding of "The Friends of Richard Lapointe"—a group of activists dedicated to winning the release of Lapointe from a Connecticut prison. Lapointe, brain injured and disabled by Dandy Walker syndrome, was convicted for murder solely on the basis of a coerced confession. Journalist Tom Condon, who also studied the case, concluded in his article "Reasonable Doubt" that "Lapointe didn't get a fair shake." During the nine-hour police interrogation, Lapointe "had no lawyer, his statements weren't taped and his family wasn't allowed to call or visit . . . Police subjected him to lies, tricks and intimidation to obtain his confession." Lapointe later said that he signed the confession so his interrogators would let him use the bathroom.

Martha Perske, Robert's wife, is an artist who does the illustrations for his books.

See also Stewart, Jean.

References Condon, Tom, "Reasonable Doubt," *Hartford Courant Northeast* (February 1993); Perske, Robert, *Unequal Justice? What Can Happen When Persons with Retardation or Other Developmental Disabilities Encounter the Criminal Justice System* (1991); ———, *Deadly Innocence?* (1995).

Personal Assistance Services (PAS)

The World Institute on Disability (WID) has defined personal assistance services (PAS) "as the assistance of another person with those tasks which individuals would normally do for themselves if they did not have a disability." This is, however, a broader definition than that of most government agencies administering PAS, and of some disability rights advocates. These groups tend to restrict their definition to assistance with basic personal maintenance, hygiene, and light household tasks, provided to persons with severe physical disabilities.

Estimates of the number of Americans requiring PAS range from 7.7 million to 9.6 million. Of these, roughly 1.9 million are in institutions or nursing homes, most of whom could live in the community if they had assistance. Government-funded PAS programs exist in every state, but they provide services to only a small fraction of those who need them. Access to publicly funded PAS is generally restricted to people with low incomes, sometimes below the federal poverty level, and those with the most severe physical disabilities. The number of hours of care provided is often capped at an arbitrary level. In addition, PAS programs usually preclude individuals living with nondisabled family members, and some require recipients to live in cluster or semi-institutional housing arrangements. They also count the income of a spouse or reduce services to disabled married couples. These conditions act as disincentives: people receiving PAS may, for example, be unable to marry or take a job without jeopardizing their eligibility.

PAS has emerged as a priority issue for the disability rights movement. A Harris poll of noninstitutionalized disabled adults showed that 56 percent of those whose activities were limited reported that the limitation was due to lack of PAS. WID, in October 1991, declared PAS to be "critical to the exercise of our full human and civil rights." American Disabled for Accessible Public Transit (ADAPT), after passage of the Americans with Disabilities Act of 1990 (ADA), changed its name to American Disabled for Attendant Programs Today and made expansion of publicly funded PAS its number one priority.

PAS programs, where they exist, vary widely in how they are structured. On one end of the spectrum are programs where PAS is seen as a traditional medical service, with heavy involvement of physicians, nurses, and nurse's aides. These programs tend to be more expensive, allowing their recipients less personal autonomy. At the other end of the spectrum are programs in which PAS funds are channeled to individual consumers who hire, train, and supervise their own PAS providers: college students, working mothers, and unemployed or underemployed workers. These systems are generally less expensive per consumer. They also give consumers greater independence in their day-to-day lives, allowing them, for example, to decide what time during the day the assistance will be provided and thus when they will wake up, eat, shower, etc. In fact, most advocates do not define PAS as a medical service at all, pointing out that even catheter and ventilator care can be provided by nonmedical assistants trained by the PAS recipient.

Providing PAS is a cheaper alternative to nursing home or institutional care. According to figures published in 1995 by *Mouth: The Voice of Disability Rights*, the national average annual cost to the taxpayers of housing one aging or disabled person in a nursing home in 1994 was $40,784. The average cost of providing Medicaid-funded PAS to the same individual would be $9,692. This figure includes people who require 24-hour support as well as people who require fewer services. Additional savings occur when a PAS consumer is employed and pays taxes, a virtual impossibility for someone living in a nursing home or institution. Mary Johnson has written that, "simply recognizing that personal care is not medical and can be managed at home could save this country untold billions of dollars."

The Consortium for Citizens with Disabilities advocated for including PAS in the Clinton health care reform legislation of 1993. Prior to that, disability rights groups had drafted the Personal Assistance for Independent Living (PAIL) legislation, introduced in Congress beginning in 1988, but neither of these efforts was successful. Several court cases, most notably *Helen L. v. Karen F. Snider* (1995) and *People First of Tennessee v. The Arlington Developmental Center* (1992), have won judgments that public programs denying PAS (and the

community living it allows) and keeping disabled people instead in nursing homes are a violation of the ADA.

Some disability rights advocates, such as Marca Bristo at the National Council on Disability, want to extend PAS to include readers for blind and visually disabled persons, sign language interpreters, and assisted-living prompters for people with cognitive and mental disabilities. Others, such as Bob Kafka at ADAPT, want to keep PAS more narrowly defined as basic services, such as dressing, toileting, etc., required by people with severe physical disabilities. ADAPT's own PAS bill, the Community Attendant Service Act (CASA), reflects this narrower definition.

See also American Disabled for Attendant Programs Today; Center for Independent Living; Consortium for Citizens with Disabilities; Health Care Access; Independent Living, Independent Living Movement; World Institute on Disability.

References Crewe, Nancy M., and Irving Kenneth Zola, *Independent Living for Physically Disabled People* (1987); Johnson, Mary, "The Nursing Home Rip-Off," *New York Times* (2 June 1991): Op. Ed. page; "You Choose," *Mouth: The Voice of Disability Rights*. (1995).

Pfeiffer, David (b. 1934)

David Pfeiffer has been instrumental in elevating disability studies to serious academic attention. In 1993, his department at Suffolk University in Boston was the first masters of public administration (MPA) program in the nation to offer a disability studies concentration.

Pfeiffer was born on 13 May 1934 in Dallas, Texas. Diagnosed with polio at age 9, Pfeiffer received his B.A. in philosophy from the University of Texas at Austin in 1956 and his Ph.D. in political science from the University of Rochester in 1975. From 1977 to 1980, he was chair of the Council of State Directors for the White House Conference on Handicapped Individuals and a leader in the disability rights movement in New England. He was a cofounder of the Massachusetts Coalition of Citizens with Disabilities and served on the early boards of the Boston Self Help Center, the Boston Center for Independent

Living, and the Adaptive Environments Center. He proposed an amendment to the Massachusetts Constitution banning discrimination against people with disabilities, which was passed by voters in November 1980. The author of more than 140 articles on disability policy, Pfeiffer helped to establish the Society for Disability Studies (SDS) in 1986, and he became editor of *Disability Studies Quarterly* in 1995.

Pfeiffer joined the teaching staff of Suffolk University in 1975, became a professor at its Department of Public Management in 1981, and was promoted to department chairperson and MPA program director in 1990.

Physically Disabled Students' Program (PDSP)

See Center for Independent Living, Inc.

Postsecondary Education

See Disabled Student Services

President's Committee on Employment of People with Disabilities

The President's Committee on Employment of People with Disabilities (formerly, President's Committee on Employment of the Handicapped) is a federal agency, the chair and vice chairs of which are appointed by the president. Its mission is "to facilitate the communication, coordination and promotion of public and private efforts to enhance the employment of people with disabilities."

The committee's roots go back to World War II, when millions of nondisabled young men were inducted into the military. The resulting "manpower shortage" provided unprecedented employment opportunities for women, people of color, and people with disabilities. In 1942, Paul A. Strachan, president of the American Federation of the Physically Handicapped, asked Congress to pass a joint resolution designating the first week in October "National Employ the Physically Handicapped Week." Strachan was concerned that, with the end of the war, newly employed disabled workers would be displaced by returning, nondisabled veterans. He and others, such as Millard Rice, legislative representative of Disabled American Veterans, were also concerned about the great numbers of newly disabled veterans who would be looking for employment. The joint resolution passed the House on 4 June 1945 and the Senate on 1 August 1945. A permanent committee to coordinate the yearly campaign held its first meeting on 12 September 1947. This President's Committee on National Employ the Physically Handicapped Week was renamed the President's Committee on Employment of the Physically Handicapped by President Harry Truman in 1952.

The committee's first years were spent publicizing National Employ the Physically Handicapped Week. Task groups bringing together representatives of government, rehabilitation medicine, and business were formed on the state, city, and local levels. These groups used movie trailers, billboards, radio and television public interest spots, floats in parades, skywriting, and blimps to advertise their message: "It's good business to hire the handicapped." The campaign was notable in that it did not use pity or urge businesses to hire disabled workers out of charity. Rather, the committee used research conducted by the Bureau of Labor Statistics to demonstrate that disabled employees rated high in efficiency, productivity, and safety and low in absenteeism, often outscoring their nondisabled co-workers. The committee's first chair, Admiral Ross T. McIntyre, was replaced in 1954 by retired Marine General Melvin Maas. Maas, himself disabled, broadened the committee's scope, lobbying for changes in rehabilitation legislation and for architectural access. Among other innovations, the committee suggested the use of a symbol to designate which structures or facilities were accessible; this symbol (a stick figure profile of a person in a wheelchair) became the international symbol of access. In the mid-1950s, the committee, together with the National Society for Crippled Children and Adults, sponsored the development of architectural access standards, leading to the standards published by the American National Standards Institute (ANSI) in 1961.

The committee dropped the word *Physically* from its title in 1962, becoming the President's Committee on Employment of the Handicapped. This change reflected a desire to advocate on behalf of those who had mental or emotional disabilities, and it had the approval of President Kennedy, whose sister Rosemary was mentally disabled. In 1964, Harold Russell replaced Maas as chair of the committee. During the late 1960s and 1970s, under the leadership of transportation subcommittee chair Henry Viscardi, the committee advocated for the rights of disabled people to ride on national airlines. It urged the Urban Mass Transit Administration to require local transit authorities to purchase lift-equipped buses with their federal grants, and, when the District of Columbia began planning a subway system, the committee was adamant that access be included. The committee also sponsored meetings and conferences that acted as catalysts for disability rights organizing. The founders of the American Coalition of Citizens with Disabilities, for example, used the annual meeting of the committee in 1974 as a forum to announce their organization. The committee took part in efforts to enforce the employment provisions of the Rehabilitation Act of 1973, particularly Section 503 with its affirmative action mandate for employers under federal contract. The Job Accommodation Network (JAN), an information clearinghouse on workplace access, was founded by the committee in 1983. Justin Dart Jr., named committee chair by President Bush in 1989, renamed it the President's Committee on Employment of People with Disabilities. Tony Coelho became committee chair in 1994.

The committee, based in Washington, D.C., continues its work on what has now become the National Disability Employment Awareness Month. It tracks legislation and research concerning the employment of people with disabilities and administers the JAN. In 1995, it had a staff of 37, along with some 300 volunteer members working with governor's committees in all 50 states, Puerto Rico, and Guam, and with more than 600 mayor's committees and some 6,000 disability community activists comprising the Disability Communications Network.

See also American Coalition of Citizens with Disabilities; American Federation of the Physically Handicapped; Architectural Access; Architectural Barriers Act of 1968; Coelho, Tony; Dart, Justin Jr.; Disabled American Veterans; Metropolitan Area Transit Authority ("METRO") Access Campaign; Russell, Harold.

President's Panel, President's Committee on Mental Retardation (PCMR)

The election of John F. Kennedy as president of the United States in November 1960 marked a turning point in the treatment of people with mental retardation. Eunice Kennedy Shriver, sister to the president, publicly discussed the family's experience with her disabled sister Rosemary, providing what disability historian Nora Groce called "a quantum leap in attention to the needs of people with intellectual impairment." On 11 October 1961, Kennedy appointed a special President's Panel on Mental Retardation. The panel brought together the recognized experts in the field of retardation: physicians, educators, and psychologists. Also included was Elizabeth M. Boggs, a founder of the National Association for Retarded Children, who brought the perspective of the parents' movement to the panel's deliberations. The panel undertook a survey of existing programs and treatments and conducted a series of public hearings and fact-finding visits to Europe. Its report, *A Proposed Program for National Action To Combat Mental Retardation* (1962), contained 112 recommendations under eight broad headings, including strengthened educational programs, more comprehensive and improved clinical and social services, and the development of a new legal and social concept of the retarded.

In a speech to Congress on 5 February 1963 summarizing the report, Kennedy urged the nation "to reduce, over a number of years, and by hundreds of thousands, the persons confined to . . . institutions; to retain in and return to the community the mentally ill and mentally retarded, and there to restore and revitalize their lives through better health programs and strengthened educational and rehabilitation services. . . ." This was, in essence, a call for mainstreamed education, community services, and deinstitutionalization.

As a result of the panel's work, Congress passed the Maternal and Child Health and Mental Retardation Planning Amendments and the Mental Retardation Facilities and Community Mental Health Centers Construction Act in 1963. These landmark acts provided research into the causes and prevention of mental retardation, grants to the states to survey the need for and to assist in designing comprehensive community services, and funds for research or demonstration projects for the education of children with mental retardation. The acts led to a tremendous expansion in research and programming for people with mental retardation, providing a foundation for the normalization and deinstitutionalization movements that followed.

The panel disbanded after releasing its report, but on 11 May 1966, President Lyndon Johnson established the President's Committee on Mental Retardation (PCMR) to continue and expand the work it had begun. The original PCMR was made up of 21 citizen members appointed by the president. In 1974, President Nixon expanded it to include 6 public members, including the secretary of Health and Human Services, the secretary of Housing and Urban Development, and the attorney general. Through the 1960s and 1970s, the PCMR played a crucial role in monitoring progress toward community services and deinstitutionalization. In 1969, it issued its

groundbreaking *Changing Patterns in Residential Services for the Mentally Retarded*, the printed proceedings of the conference that introduced "normalization" to the United States. Another pivotal publication of the PCMR came in 1976: *The Mentally Retarded Citizen and the Law*, which explored the legal and social changes necessary to ensure full citizenship for people with mental retardation. This volume came out of another conference, convened by the PCMR, that brought together the key players in the struggle for community services and deinstitutionalization.

Today, the PCMR continues to conduct forums and publish papers and reports addressing the field of mental retardation and the needs, concerns, and quality of life experienced by Americans with cognitive disabilities.

See also Boggs, Elizabeth Monroe; Deinstitutionalization; Developmentally Disabled Assistance and Bill of Rights Act of 1975; Normalization.

References Kugel, Robert B., and Wolf Wolfensberger, eds., *Changing Patterns in Residential Services for the Mentally Retarded* (1969); Scheerenberger, R. C., *A History of Mental Retardation: A Quarter Century of Promise* (1987).

Project on Women and Disability

The Project on Women and Disability was founded in Boston in 1987. It is composed of and led by women with disabilities, chronic illness, and deafness. Its members learn self-advocacy, political organizing, and lobbying. Among the issues addressed by the project have been reproductive health care, the impact of genetic research and technology, sexism and discrimination against women with disabilities, and sexuality and disability. Marsha Saxton, a writer and disability rights activist, was among the project's principal founders. It sponsors the Women and Disability Think Tank, which meets monthly to develop theory and social policy, and it publishes *WILDA*, a quarterly journal for Women in Leadership/Disability Activists. The project also acts as an information clearinghouse and referral service on issues relating to women and disability.

See also Abortion and Reproductive Rights; Saxton, Marsha; Women with Disabilities.

Protection and Advocacy for Mentally Ill Individuals Act of 1986

The Protection and Advocacy for Mentally Ill Individuals Act of 1986 authorized federal grants to the states to establish and operate protection and advocacy systems for people who are in-patients or residents of mental health facilities. These systems are modeled on the protection and advocacy systems (P&As) established under the Developmentally Disabled Assistance and Bill of Rights Act of 1975. They are empowered to "investigate incidents of abuse and neglect of mentally ill individuals" and to "pursue administrative, legal, and other appropriate remedies."

The act also contains a section outlining a bill of rights for consumers of mental health services, adopted from the Mental Health Systems Act of 1980. Included is the right "to appropriate treatment" under conditions that are "most supportive of . . . personal liberty." Consumers have the right to an "individualized, written treatment or service plan" to ensure "ongoing participation, in a manner appropriate to such person's capabilities" in planning their treatment, and they have the right "not to receive a mode or course of treatment . . . in the absence of . . . informed, voluntary, written consent" except "during an emergency situation." Patients have the right not to participate in medical experiments without their informed consent and the right to be free from "restraint or seclusion" except "during an emergency situation . . . pursuant to or documented contemporaneously by a written order of a responsible mental health professional." Patients have the right to "a humane treatment environment that affords reasonable protection from harm and appropriate privacy," the right to converse with others privately, and the right to convenient access to telephones, mail, and visitors, unless denial of such rights is necessary to their treatment.

The act was amended in 1988 so that the death of a consumer was also considered a form of abuse, and so that a protection and advocacy agency could investigate instances of abuse or neglect where the whereabouts of the patient were unknown or where the abuse or neglect occurred while a patient was being transported to or from a facility. The act was further amended in 1991 so that the term *facilities* would include, "but need not be limited to, hospitals, nursing homes, community facilities for individuals with mental illness, board and care homes, homeless shelters, and jails and prisons."

See also Developmentally Disabled Assistance and Bill of Rights Act of 1975; Psychiatric Survivor Movement.

Protection and Advocacy for Persons with Developmental Disabilities Program (PADD or P&As)

See Developmentally Disabled Assistance and Bill of Rights Act of 1975.

Psychiatric Survivor Movement

Individuals identified as "mentally ill," "insane," or "lunatic" are among the most oppressed people on earth. Throughout history, and in almost every culture, people with mental disabilities have been (and continue to be) seen as violent, dangerous, and strange. Furthermore, many of the "treatments" developed to "cure" mental illness resemble physical and psychological torture. These include four-point restraints (tying a person hand and foot to the bed); solitary confinement, sometimes for weeks or months on end; cold packs (wrapping a person in freezing wet sheets or blankets, *then* tying them to the bed); insulin shock and electroshock "therapy"; straitjackets and the use of drugs as "chemical straitjackets"; even surgical mutilation such as lobotomy. Until the advent of deinstitutionalization in the 1970s, hundreds of thousands of Americans with mental illness were incarcerated in massive state "hospitals" where neglect, and physical and sexual abuse, were rife. Many abusive "treatments" continue to be used. For example, psychiatric survivor Anne C. Woodlen, in her essay "Mind Control" (*Beyond Bedlam*, 1995), reports that, in the mid-1990s, four-point restraint is "not a remnant of prehistoric history, it is state of the art. . . ." Dorothy Washburn Dundas, in "The Shocking Truth" (also in *Beyond Bedlam*), notes that modern for-profit psychiatric hospitals are often no better than the old state mental institutions. "The 'nice' places were an illusion where more drugging and sexual and physical abuse happened to me than anywhere else."

Judi Chamberlin (1978) cited as the basic principle of the psychiatric survivor movement the belief that "all laws and practices which induce discrimination toward individuals who have been labelled 'mentally ill' need to be changed, so that a psychiatric diagnosis has no more impact on a person's citizenship rights and responsibilities than does a diagnosis of diabetes or heart disease." She describes the movement as focused primarily on self-help and empowerment. Some activists in this movement call themselves ex–mental patients, others psychiatric survivors or psychiatric inmates. Still others prefer to call themselves mad or insane, hoping to strip these words of their power to frighten and ostracize.

Early antecedents to the psychiatric survivor movement include Elizabeth Packard, who founded the short-lived Anti-Insane Asylum Society in the 1860s and published several books and pamphlets describing how her husband had her committed against her will at the Jacksonville (Illinois) Insane Asylum. Elizabeth Stone, another forerunner to the movement, was a Massachusetts woman, also committed by her husband, who tried at about the same time to stop the arbitrary and unjust incarceration of those deemed to be "insane."

In the twentieth century, one of the first long-lasting psychiatric groups was We Are Not Alone (WANA), a peer support group started in 1948 by patients and ex-patients at Rockland State Hospital in New York. Beginning in the early 1970s, activists on the East and West Coasts came together to deal with what was more and more coming to be recognized as their political and social oppression. The Insane Liberation Front in Portland, Oregon, was organized in 1970. The Mental Patients' Liberation Front in Boston and the Mental Patients' Liberation Project in New York City were both founded in 1971. The Network Against Psychiatric Assault was founded in San Francisco in 1972. *Madness Network News*, established in 1972 as a San Francisco newsletter, later evolved into a national forum for activists across the United States and Canada. The first national Conference on Human Rights and Psychiatric Oppression was held in 1973 at the University of Detroit. "Groups were united," wrote Chamberlin in 1990, "by certain rules and principles: mental health terminology was considered suspect; attitudes that limited opportunities for mental patients were to be discouraged and changed; and members' feelings—particularly feelings of anger toward the mental health system—were considered real and legitimate, not 'symptoms of illness.'"

All of these groups were independently organized and followed different agendas. Some ran drop-in or crisis intervention centers for people with mental disabilities who wanted to avoid traditional, medical-based care. Some groups pursued entirely political agendas, trying to change legislation or bringing litigation. The plaintiffs in cases such as *Rogers v. Commissioner of Mental Health* (1983) tried to establish a right to refuse treatment for people involved in the mental health system, so that they could not be drugged, incarcerated, or experimented or operated upon against their will. Some groups called for the abolition of procedures such as electro-shock and lobotomy and for the abandonment, or at least the curtailing, of the use of psychotropic drugs. Indeed, some activists believe that the entire medical model of "mental illness" is flawed and that rather than search for a "cure" that means the suppression of "symptoms," treatment should involve examining the circumstances and life problems faced by an individual in their social, racial, class, gender, and political context. Advocates confronted "the experts"—psychiatrists, psychologists, hospital administrators—at forums such as the President's Commission on Mental Health, demanding that funds be switched from coercive medical "treatment" into patient-run self-help alternatives.

The National Association of Psychiatric Survivors (NAPS) was founded in 1985 to provide a national voice for the movement, and as a response to what was seen as the co-opting of earlier radicalism by "consumer-oriented" but medically based self-help programs funded by the mental health establishment. Local activists kept in touch through NAPS, while the annual Human Rights Conferences were discontinued after 1985. More recently, there have been attempts by survivor activists to establish links with other constituencies in the general disability rights movement. In the 1990s, the publication *Dendron* has played the role of *Madness Network News*, which ceased publication in 1986, while NAPS is no longer active. Nevertheless, many local groups continue to function, and survivor issues have of late received greater coverage in the general disability rights press.

See also Beers, Clifford; Chamberlin, Judi; *Dendron*; Geld, Howard; National Empowerment Center; Unzicker, Rae.

References Chamberlin, Judi, *On Our Own: Patient-Controlled Alternatives to the Mental Health System* (1978); ———, "The Ex-Patients' Movement: Where We've Been and Where We're Going," *Journal of Mind and Behavior* (Summer/Autumn 1990); Glenn, M., ed., *Voices from the Asylum* (1974); Grobe, Jeanine, ed., *Beyond Bedlam: Contemporary Women Psychiatric Survivors Speak Out* (1995).

Public Transportation

The struggle for accessible public transportation has been a major focus of the American disability rights movement. Without accessible mass transit, many people with disabilities, who either cannot drive or cannot afford their own adapted car or van, are unable to travel to work or school, to socialize, to worship, or to attend cultural events. Activists find themselves in a Catch 22, where the lack of accessible transportation makes it difficult to bring people together to organize for accessible transportation. A 1986 Harris poll revealed that more than half the disabled people surveyed indicated that transportation was a major problem and that three out of ten disabled people without jobs said that lack of accessible transportation was a major reason they remained unemployed. "Accessible transportation," says advocate Denise Karuth, "can make the difference between living in the community or being imprisoned there."

Establishing a legal right to accessible public transit has been a slow and frustrating process. The Architectural Barriers Act of 1968, the first federal access law, theoretically included under its provisions train and subway stations, but advocates found the act virtually unenforceable. Of greater value was Section 504 of the Rehabilitation Act of 1973, which mandated access in federally funded services and programs. The Department of Transportation regulations that were issued for its implementation, however, left the provision of accessible transportation in the hands of local transit authorities, which, in almost every case, chose to meet their obligations through separate paratransit services, often contracted out to social service agencies. Such services almost always required users to book their rides several days in advance, provided each user with a limited number of rides per month during limited hours of service, and generally served only a fraction of the area covered by mainline transit. In many cities those who wished to use paratransit were placed on a long waiting list, in the meantime receiving no service at all. Those who did receive service complained that it was so unreliable that they were unable to hold a job or pursue an education. In 1979, the Carter administration, under pressure from advocates, drafted new regulations requiring that all new buses purchased with federal funds meet accessible "Transbus" specifications,

Gregory Manfield is assisted onto a wheelchair accessible city bus in 1982. Accessible public transportation has been one of the biggest struggles of the disability rights movement. Although the Americans with Disabilities Act of 1990 outlined provisions for accessible transit, advocates claim that disabled travelers continue to find poorly designed buses, inadequate operator training, and occasional defiance of the law.

thus ensuring eventual 100 percent bus access. The American Public Transit Association (APTA) filed suit, and the regulations were struck down by the federal courts. By the mid-1980s, little progress had been made in making America's transit systems accessible.

This lack of progress spurred further activism by groups such as the American Coalition of Citizens with Disabilities and Disabled in Action (DIA), together with many local grassroots organizations. In Washington, D.C., Paralyzed Veterans of America, the National Paraplegia Foundation, and activist Richard W. Heddinger filed suit in 1972 against that city's METRO system and, after a long and bitterly contested case, forced the system to provide elevators and other acess features. American Disabled for Attendant Programs Today (ADAPT) was originally founded as American Disabled for Accessible Public Transit. For most of the 1980s, it targeted APTA annual meetings for public demonstrations and civil disobedience.

The issue of accessible transit—the right to ride the bus and subway like everyone else—was easily understood by the general public and proved a valuable organizing tool for groups such as ADAPT and DIA. In addition, cuts in federal funding to public transit brought home to authorities the cost of running separate paratransit systems, making mainline access more attractive. Disability advocates, when drafting the Americans with Disabilities Act of 1990 (ADA), included provisions mandating accessible mainline transit as well as paratransit services for those disabled people unable to use buses and subways. The act also expanded requirements for audible and visual signs and announcements in transit systems and detectable warnings at the edge of transit platforms. This combination of financial and legal incentive began to have an impact, and a 1993 APTA survey found that some 53 percent of America's fixed route public transit buses were accessible. Advocates report, however, that the commitment to access by public authorities is often lukewarm, and disabled travelers continue to encounter poor design and maintenance, inadequate operator training, and occasional outright defiance of the law.

Access to intercity buses, operated by companies such as Greyhound and Trailways, has also been a problem. The provision in the ADA mandating eventual access in "over the road coaches" has been resisted by the bus lines, and most intercity service remains inaccessible to wheelchair users. An exception to this inaccessibility is Massachusetts, where the Intercity Bus Capital Assistance Program (IBCAP) used state bonds to purchase lift-equipped buses for lease and sale to private Massachusetts bus companies at greatly reduced cost. The success of the program, established in 1985, was cited in testimony that led to the intercity access provisions of the ADA.

See also American Coalition of Citizens with Disabilities; *American Disabled for Accessible Public Transit v. Skinner*; American Disabled for Attendant Programs Today (ADAPT); Americans with Disabilities Act of 1990; Architectural Barriers Act of 1968; *Lloyd v. Regional Transit Authority*; Paratransit; Section 504 of the Rehabilitation Act of 1973; Transbus.

References Capozzi, David M., and Dennis J. Cannon, "Transportation Accessibility," in Arthur E. Dell Orto and Robert P. Marinelli, eds., *Encyclopedia of Disability and Rehabilitation* (1995); Golden, Marilyn, "Title II–Public Services, Subtitle B: Public Transportation," in Lawrence O. Gostin and Henry A. Beyer, eds., *Implementing the Americans with Disabilities Act: Rights and Responsibilities of All Americans* (1993).

**Quickie Wheelchairs,
Quickie Designs, Inc.**
See Wheelchairs.

Rainbow Alliance of the Deaf (RAD)

The Rainbow Alliance of the Deaf (RAD) was founded in 1977 to promote the educational, economic, and social welfare of deaf gays and lesbians. It is a nonprofit organization with approximately 20 chapters in the United States and Canada. There are also affiliated chapters in Australia, Germany, and Great Britain. Membership of the U.S. and Canadian chapters is estimated to be between 1,000 and 1,500.

In its own words, RAD's mission is "to foster fellowship, to defend our rights, and advance our interests as Deaf Gay and Lesbian citizens concerning social justice; to build up an organization in which all worthy members may participate in the discussion of practical problems and solutions related to their social welfare." Alliance policy is set at biennial conferences and by an executive board between conferences, and it is reported in the RAD newsletter, *Tattler.*

Reference Luczak, Raymond, *Eyes of Desire: A Deaf Gay and Lesbian Reader* (1993).

Randolph-Sheppard Act of 1936 and its Amendments

The Randoph-Sheppard Act of 1936 was designed to provide "blind persons with remunerative employment, enlarging the opportunities of the blind, and stimulating the blind to greater efforts in striving to make themselves self-supporting." The act led to the creation of vending stands selling fruit, newspapers, coffee, and such, staffed by blind people, in the lobbies of government buildings. Vendors were required to be blind or significantly visually disabled U.S. citizens, aged 21 or older, and they were to be certified by a local vocational rehabilitation agency as qualified to operate a vending stand. Startup, stock, and equipment costs were paid for by the government or managing agencies, which then collected a percentage of each stand's income. The overall program was initially managed by the federal Office of Education, but responsibility shifted in 1946 to the Office of Vocational Rehabilitation. Twenty years after passage of the act, there were 1,804 vending stands with gross sales of more than $20 million annually. In 1955, Randolph-Sheppard stands employed 1,721 blind operators and 310 blind assistants.

The act represented one of the first federal efforts to foster economic independence for people with disabilities. This effort was limited, however, when a regulation issued in 1941 prohibited blind workers from purchasing these businesses. The Randolph-Sheppard programs were also marred by a paternalistic attitude toward blind operators, who were believed to need close supervision and "discipline." Management decisions were almost always made by sighted government or agency workers.

Among other changes, the 1954 amendments to the act entitled a vendor to a hearing for complaints about the administration of their stand. The National Federation of the Blind (NFB) successfully lobbied for language in the amendments that expanded the ability of blind vendors to manage and purchase their stands. There was still considerable opposition from sighted rehabilitation professionals, however, to the idea of blind people actually owning and running their own stands, and such organizations as the American Association of Workers for the Blind and the American Foundation for the Blind continued to insist that there be close government or agency "supervision of the operation of each individual stand." "In this way," wrote Jacobus tenBroek, a founder of the NFB, "spokesmen for the agencies for the blind made explicit their opposition to any plan which would give blind vending-stand operators the opportunity to manage their own affairs." The 1974 amendments were drafted in part to address this issue, and they greatly strengthened the position of the vendors. In 1994, the average salary of a Randolph-Sheppard vendor was $25,832.

The Randolph-Sheppard Vendors of America (RSVA), a chapter of the American Council of the Blind, was founded in 1969 to advocate on behalf of vendors.

See also American Council of the Blind; National Federation of the Blind; Vocational Rehabilitation.

Reference TenBroek, Jacobus, and Floyd W. Matson, *Hope Deferred: Public Welfare and the Blind* (1959).

Rape/Sexual and Domestic Violence

According to studies conducted by the DisAbled Women's Network (DAWN) of Canada, women with disabilities are twice as likely to be raped or sexually assaulted as women without disabilities. These figures confirm the impression of clinicians and members of disability self-help groups, who report a high incidence of sexual violence against their disabled clients, both female and male. This violence cuts across all disabilities, but is particularly prevalent among people with mental and cognitive disabilities. Researcher Dick Sobsey at the University of Alberta reports that "studies from many countries (e.g., U.S., U.K., Australia) suggest that child abuse, beatings, and rape are common occurrences in the lives of many, probably most, people with developmental disabilities" (1994).

Little provision has been made to provide services to disabled survivors of sexual or domestic violence. DAWN took as one of its first priorities changing the fact that, in the mid-1980s, there was not a single rape crisis center or battered women's shelter in Canada that was accessible to people with mobility disabilities or those who were deaf. The same situation prevailed in the United States.

There are numerous reasons why abusers might target people with disabilities, placing them at higher risk. Some people with disabilities may be more physically vulnerable. They are often shut out of the mainstream and unable to get the help they might need to escape abuse where it is being committed by a caretaker or family member. Disabled children and adults are also exposed to far more caretakers—paratransit drivers, special education teachers, physicians, physical therapists, etc.—who are in a position to abuse their relative power. Furthermore, many people with disabilities, especially those who are or have been institutionalized, are encouraged to be compliant to caretakers and authority figures, who then have an even greater opportunity to abuse with impunity. Some advocates, for example, Barbara Faye Waxman, believe that rape and sexual violence are expressions of hate and contempt, which many nondisabled people feel toward people with disabilities.

One traditional theory, rejected by disability advocates, is the so-called stress-dependency model, which holds that disabled people are abused by their caretakers because of the stress related to providing them care. According to Sobsey, "there has never been any research to support that idea. The stress-dependency explanation doesn't reflect anything but an enormous underlying bias we've had to blame the victim for the problem" (1994).

Disabled feminists have criticized the disability rights movement for its lack of attention to the issues of rape, sexual violence, and domestic abuse. Rape crisis centers, hospitals, battered women shelters, and other such public accommodations are covered under the Americans with Disabilities Act of 1990.

See also DisaAbled Women's Network (DAWN) of Canada; Glen Ridge Case; Hate Crimes against People with Disability; Waxman, Barbara Faye.

Reference Sobsey, Dick, *Violence and Abuse in the Lives of People with Disabilities: The End of Silent Acceptance?* (1994).

Rarus, Tim

See Deaf President Now Campaign.

Reasonable Accommodation/ Reasonable Modification

The concepts of "reasonable accommodation" and "reasonable modification" were introduced into disability rights law after passage of the Rehabilitation Act of 1973. Under Section 504 of that act, entities receiving federal funds were prohibited from discriminating against people with disabilities. The U.S. Supreme Court ruled, in *Southeastern Community College v. Davis* (1979), that covered entities had to make "reasonable modifications" to avoid such discrimination. By "reasonable," the Court meant that these modifications could not impose "undue financial and administrative burdens."

This concept of reasonable accommodation is generally applied to employment and employers. It was incorporated into the Americans with Disabilities Act of 1990 (ADA), where it is defined as including: "(A) making existing facilities used by employees readily accessible to and usable by individuals with disabilities"; and "(B) job restructuring, part-time, or modified work schedules, reassignment to a vacant position, acquisition or modification of equipment or devices, appropriate adjustment or modifications of examinations, training materials or policies, the provision of qualified readers or interpreters, and other similar accommodations for individuals with disabilities."

Reasonable accommodation is determined on a case-by-case basis, and it is limited by the corollary concept of "undue burden"—that is, employers are not required to make accommodations that would seriously impinge upon their ability to do business. A law firm, for example, would not have to risk bankruptcy making its 100-year-old office building wheelchair accessible. It would, however, have to make arrangements to meet with wheelchair-using clients or attorneys in an accessible space outside the office.

The concept of reasonable modification was incorporated into the regulations implementing Titles II and III of the ADA. In Title II, which prohibits discrimination on the basis of disability in the provision of services by public entities (that is, state and local governments), the regulations require that "a public entity shall make reasonable modifications in policies, practices or procedures when the modifications are necessary to avoid discrimination on the basis of disability, unless the public entity can demonstrate that making the modifications would fundamentally alter the nature of the service, program, or activity." In Title III, which prohibits discrimination on the basis of disability in public accommodations (that is, places of lodging, restaurants, theaters, stores, museums, etc.), the regulations require public accommodations to make "reasonable modifications in policies, practices or procedures," which provide an individual with a disability the opportunity to "obtain the benefits of or access to goods, services, facilities, privileges, or accommodations." Public accommodations are not required to make modifications that would "fundamentally alter the nature of such goods, services, facilities, privileges, or accommodations." Although similar in scope and intent to the concept of reasonable accommodation, reasonable modification sets a higher standard because proving that a "fundamental alteration" is required to accommodate an individual is more difficult than proving "undue burden" with regard to the employment of an individual with a disability.

See also Americans with Disabilities Act of 1990; Section 504 of the Rehabilitation Act of 1973; *Southeastern Community College v. Davis*; Undue Hardship/Undue Burden.

Reference Gostin, Lawrence O., and Henry A. Beyer, *Implementing the Americans with Disabilities Act: Rights and Responsibilities of All Americans* (1993).

Reeve, Christopher (b. 1952)

Christopher Reeve is best known as the star of *Superman* (1978) and its sequels. Spinal cord injured in 1995, he has become an advocate for increased funding to research a cure for spinal cord injury.

Reeve was born on 25 September 1952, in New York City. He received his B.A.

Christopher Reeve and his wife, Dana, 9 November 1995.

from Cornell University in Ithaca, New York, in 1974 was a student at the Juilliard School in New York City, and began his movie career in 1978. His injury, which happened while horseback riding at a charity event in 1995, drew international attention. He spoke at the Democratic National Convention in Chicago on 16 August 1996—a speech that was carried by all the major television networks. Although Reeve mentioned the need for enforcement of the Americans with Disabilities Act, the majority of the speech dealt with his desire for increased funding for finding a cure for spinal cord injury.

It is this emphasis on finding a cure that has made Reeve's sudden acclaim as a spokesperson for the community so controversial among disability rights advocates. "The public," wrote Carol Gill in *Mainstream* magazine soon after Reeve's convention speech, "wants to believe disability is a personal tragedy that requires only individual fixing. Reeve agrees with them, letting them off the hook for changing their attitudes and public policies. Why work hard to make the world acces-

sible and inclusive when we can just wait for people to be cured?" Others have defended Reeve. Anthony Tusler in the same issue of *Mainstream* remarked, "I also wish he would have shown more enthusiasm when he talked about fighting discrimination, but to have the concept mentioned [at all] in prime time, by the Democrats, is a major victory for our community."

See also Media Images of People with Disability.

Reference Brown, Steven E., "Super Duper? The (Unfortunate) Ascendancy of Christopher Reeve and the Cure-All for the 1990s," *Mainstream* (October 1996).

Rehabilitation Act of 1973

Congress, in passing the Rehabilitation Act of 1973, stated that its purpose was "to develop and implement, through research, training, services, and the guarantee of equal opportunity, comprehensive and coordinated programs of vocational rehabilitation and independent living." The act amended the vocational rehabilitation acts of the previous 50 years, but it went far beyond them in safeguarding the civil rights of people with disabilities, particularly in Title V and most particularly in Section 504. The Rehabilitation Act of 1973 is in fact America's first major comprehensive civil rights law for people with disabilities.

A version of the bill was first passed in 1972, but President Richard Nixon refused to sign it, using his "pocket veto." Disability rights activists Eunice Fiorito, Judith Heumann, and members of Disabled in Action demonstrated at the Lincoln Monument, and 150 disabled activists marched down Washington's Connecticut Avenue. Congress reconsidered the bill at the beginning of the 1973 session. John Nagle, director of the National Federation of the Blind's Washington office, testified that the act, particularly Section 504, "brings the disabled within the law when they have been so long outside the law. It establishes that because a man is blind or deaf or without legs, he is not less a citizen. . . ." Congress again passed the act, and President Nixon again vetoed it, saying that it created too many new programs and went too far in requiring the participation of people with disabilities in designing and administering rehabilitation services. The bill was rewritten to meet his concerns, and this third version was signed by President Nixon on 26 September 1973.

Testimony before Congress had brought to light the failure of traditional vocational rehabilitation services to meet the needs of people with disabilities. Because vocational rehabilitation was defined as preparing someone for a job, and because agencies were judged by their success in placing disabled clients in the work force, rehabilitation agencies often refused to provide services to people with more severe disabilities, judging them unable or unlikely to work. Many of the most severely disabled people were institutionalized, had no specific vocational goals, and were thus ineligible for federal rehabilitation services. During the Nixon administration there had also been "a diminution of emphasis at the Federal level on research and training of personnel in rehabilitation problems. . . ." The testimony revealed that there was no action to combat "employment discrimination, lack of housing and transportation services and architectural and transportation barriers." The 1973 act broadened the definition of rehabilitation and required the federal government for the first time to address societal discrimination against people with disabilities.

Title I of the act authorized federal grants to state vocational rehabilitation programs meeting minimum federal criteria. Such programs had to be open to any disabled individual who might become employable after receiving services. State agencies were required to prepare a written rehabilitation program plan for each client, including long-range goals, details of the services to be provided, and methods of evaluating whether those goals were being met. Agencies and programs were required to solicit the client's direct input into their plan. Title I also included provisions for "Innovation and Expansion Grants" to be used by "a public or non-profit organization or agency . . . to expand vocational rehabilitation services . . . to individuals with the most severe handicaps." Edward Roberts, newly appointed director of the California Department of Rehabilitation, used these funds to establish independent living centers throughout California, catalyzing the national independent living movement.

Title II provided for funds for research and for pilot programs in rehabilitation, under the direction of the National Institute of Handicapped Research.

Title III provided federal funding for up to 90 percent of the cost of providing vocational rehabilitation services to eligible people with disabilities by public or private nonprofit rehabilitation facilities. It required that special emphasis be placed on meeting the rehabilitation needs of people with the most severe disabilities. It allowed the secretary of Health, Education and Welfare (HEW) to make grants and to guarantee the mortgages of newly constructed public or nonprofit rehabilitation facilities. Title III also appropriated funds "for the purpose of establishing and operating a National Center for Deaf-Blind Youths and Adults."

Title IV authorized the secretary of HEW "to conduct studies, investigations, and evaluation of the programs authorized by this Act. . . ."

Title V of the Act, labeled "Miscellaneous," has been called a "Bill of Rights" for Americans with Disabilities. The federal government, under Section 501, was committed to providing equal opportunity at all agencies and departments to qualified workers with disabilities. These executive departments and agencies, including the U.S. Post Office, were required to submit affirmative action plans aimed at increasing the numbers and standing of federal employees with disabilities.

Section 502 established the Architectural and Transportation Barriers Compliance Board (ATBCB) to enforce the Architectural Barriers Act of 1968. The ATBCB was empowered to "conduct investigations, hold public hearings, and issue such orders as it deems necessary to insure compliance" with the Architectural Barriers Act.

Section 503 required affirmative action by federal contractors with contracts of more than $2,500 in the hiring, placement, and promotion of qualified people with disabilities. This requirement could be waived by the president "when he determines that special circumstances in the national interest so require."

In terms of disability rights, it is Section 504 that became the most significant part of the Rehabilitation Act of 1973, and implementation of Section 504 became a priority of national disability rights organizations during the 1970s. Attempts by the Reagan administration to repeal or diminish the various Section 504 regulations and restrictive interpretations of its language by the U.S. Supreme Court were the focus of much of the disability rights activism of the 1980s.

The Rehabilitation Act of 1973 was amended for the first time in December 1974 and has been amended on several occasions since. The 1974 amendments clarified the act's definition of a handicapped individual as "any person who (A) has a physical or mental impairment which substantially limits one or more of such person's major life activities, (B) has a record of such impairment, or (C) is regarded as having such an impairment." The 1978 amendments authorized federal funding for independent living centers. They also established the National Council on the Handicapped (since renamed the National Council on Disability) and extended Section 504 to include the executive branch of the federal government, and all programs conducted by the government. The 1986 amendments extended federal authority to make grants to tribal authorities to pay up to 90 percent of the costs of vocational rehabilitation services on Indian reservations. The 1986 amendments also required federal agencies to provide their workers with and without disabilities equivalent access to electronic office equipment, and they included a "formula grant" program for supported employment to provide peo-

ple with cognitive and mental disabilities assistance in obtaining and keeping employment. The 1992 amendments required every state rehabilitation agency participating in the public rehabilitation program to establish an advisory council with a majority of membership comprised of people with disabilities.

Together with the Education for All Handicapped Children Act of 1975 and the Americans with Disabilities Act of 1990 (ADA), the Rehabilitation Act remains one of the most important protections of the civil rights of Americans with disabilities. Much of the language of the act (for example, its definition of a disabled individual) and concepts developed under the act, such as reasonable accommodation and undue burden, are used in the ADA.

See also American Coalition of Citizens with Disabilities; Americans with Disabilities Act of 1990; Architectural and Transportation Barriers Compliance Board; Architectural Barriers Act of 1968; Disabled in Action; Fiorito, Eunice K.; Heumann, Judith E.; HEW Demonstrations; National Council on Disability; National Federation of the Blind; Section 504 of the Rehabilitation Act of 1973; Reasonable Accommodation/Reasonable Modification; Roberts, Edward V; Vocational Rehabilitation; Undue Hardship/Undue Burden.

References Burgdorf, Robert L., Jr., *The Legal Rights of Handicapped Persons: Cases, Materials, and Text* (1980); Gostin, Lawrence O., and Henry A. Beyer, eds., *Implementing the Americans with Disabilities Act: Rights and Responsibilities of All Americans* (1993); Scotch, Richard K., *From Good Will to Civil Rights: Transforming Federal Disability Policy* (1984).

Rehabilitation Gazette
See Laurie, Virginia Grace Wilson "Gini."

Religion
Theologian Nancy L. Eiesland has written that the "persistent thread within the Christian tradition has been that disability denotes an unusual relationship with God and that the person with disabilities is either divinely blessed or damned: the defiled evildoer or the spiritual superhero" (1994). Christianity is not alone in drawing these characterizations. James I. Charleton, in "Religion and Disability: A World

View" in the *Disability Rag & Resource* (September/October 1993), quotes disability rights activists from Zimbabwe, Malaysia, and Indonesia as saying that their religious traditions regard disability as a form of "divine punishment" for alleged sinfulness. William Blair and Dana Davidson in the *Encyclopedia of Disability and Rehabilitation* (1995) observe that "fear of those who are different has hindered acceptance and inclusion of persons with disabilities as equal participants in religious observance. Persons with disabilities may be seen as threats to others, capable of 'infecting,' or unable to practice self–care and therefore 'dirty.'" Disability rights advocates Tony Coelho and Henry Viscardi Jr., for example, were both told as young adults that they could not enter the priesthood because they were disabled. Some priests continue to refuse to perform marriages of disabled people, arguing that the marriage will never be consumated. The number of ministers, priests, rabbis, and employees of religious institutions who have disabilities remains small, and seminaries and theological programs are often inaccessible. Few churches, temples, or mosques have wheelchair ramps; fewer still offer such basics to accessibility as bulletins and hymnals in formats accessible to people who are blind. When people with disabilities *are* included in religious observance, it is often as objects of pity or charity or as part of a "healing" ministry that sees disability as a test of faith or an obstacle to be overcome. "There are many in the Church," writes the Reverend Nancy J. Lane in the *Disability Rag & Resource* (September/October 1993), "who have an obsession with wanting disabled bodies to be 'healed,' meaning fixed, turned into something society defines as 'normal.' Disability is seen as a basic flaw rather than a human variation."

Such views are hardly conducive to people with disabilities taking their place as full members of society. Nevertheless, through the ages, many people with disabilities have been able to find some measure of satisfaction in their religious traditions. Helen R. Betenbaugh (1996) notes that "the same Bible which pronounces Levitical laws excluding persons with a lame foot from approaching the alter also commands us to act in compassion and with radical inclusiveness toward persons with disabilities." Religious organizations have been particularly significant to the deaf community, with Sister M. Alverna Hollis noting in her entry on religion in the *Gallaudet Encyclopedia of Deaf People and Deafness* (1987) that, "without church programs for deaf people in the past, the present status of deaf education might have been delayed for another hundred years." And while religious groups lobbied to be excluded from meeting various requirements of the Americans with Disabilities Act of 1990, many denominations have established offices on disability and have made efforts to reach out to their disabled parishioners. In recent years, a number of theologians such as Betenbaugh and Eiesland have attempted to reconcile religious thought with the experiences of disabled people. This may reflect the growing influence of the disability rights movement, or the fact that the number of ordained persons with disabilities is slowly rising, with the result that disability issues have become a larger part of the agenda of mainstream denominations. It may also be attributed to the work of disability rights activists such as Mary Jane Owen at the National Catholic Office for Persons with Disabilities, the Reverend Harold Wilke at the Caring Congregation in Claremont, California, and Ginny Thornburgh at the National Organization on Disability, who are all working toward the goal of ending ableism in their denominations.

See also Owen, Mary Jane; Thornburgh, Ginny; Wilke, Harold.

References Betenbaugh, Helen R., "ADA and the Religious Community: The Moral Case," *Journal of Religion in Disability & Rehabilitation* (1996); Blair, William, and Dana Davidson, "Religion," in Arthur E. Dell Orto and Robert P. Marinelli, eds., *Encyclopedia of Disability and Rehabilitation* (1995); Charleton, James I., "Religion and Disability: A World View," *Disability Rag & Resource* (September/October 1992); Eiesland, Nancy L., *The Disabled God: Toward a Liberatory Theology of Disability* (1994); Hollis, M. Alverna, " Religion, Catholic," in John V. Van Cleve, ed., *Gallaudet Encyclopedia of Deaf People and Deafness* (1987); Wolfe, Kathi, "The Bible and Disabilities," *Disability Rag & Resource* (September/October 1993).

Roberts, Edward V. (1939–1995)

Edward V. Roberts has been called the "the father of the independent living movement." He was co-founder and first executive director of the world's first community-based independent living center, which became the model for more than 400 centers worldwide, many of them established with Roberts' direct input. He was mentor to an entire generation of disability rights activists and active in every major disability rights struggle from the early 1970s to the time of his death.

Roberts was born on 23 January 1939 in San Mateo, California. Contracting polio when he was 14 years old, Roberts became "a respiratory quadriplegic"—paralyzed and unable to breathe without a respirator during the day and an iron lung at night. Roberts remembered overhearing a doctor at that time telling his mother that it would be best to let him die, as he would be "a vegetable" for the rest of his life. "I absorbed all the stereotypes: I would never marry, have a job, or be a whole person. I tried to starve myself, the only way to commit suicide." Years later he would joke that, if he had to be a vegetable, he preferred being an artichoke, "a little prickly on the outside [but] with a big heart. . . . I'd like to call on all the vegetables of the world to unite."

Roberts was an honor student, but his high school principal at first refused to allow him to graduate because he had not taken gym courses or drivers' education. He spent two years at San Mateo Community College, doing well enough to win encouragement from his academic advisor to continue his studies at the University of California at Berkeley. Unable to afford the tuition, Roberts applied for assistance from the state Department of Vocational Rehabilitation, which rejected him, labeling him an "infeasible" client and unlikely ever to work. His vocational rehabilitation

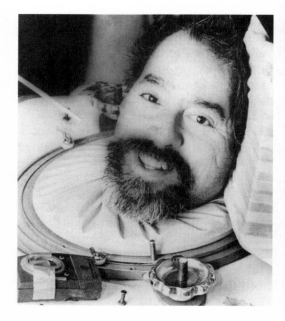

Ed Roberts, 1981.

case manager also claimed that he was not "college material," despite two years of good grades at the community college. Roberts, along with his supporters at San Mateo College, went to the local press, winning the intervention of a rehabilitation official who approved the needed assistance. Officials at Berkeley were also reluctant to allow Roberts on campus, citing concerns about his health and the lack of access. One administrator reportedly told him, "We've tried cripples and it didn't work." Roberts convinced them that he could handle the challenge and began classes in the fall of 1962.

In an era before independent living services, Roberts had to rely on his brother Ron, also a student at U.C. Berkeley, to provide personal assistance. Because none of the dormitories were accessible (and none could accommodate his iron lung), Roberts lived on campus at the Cowell Hospital. A newspaper article about his acceptance at Berkeley, with the headline "Helpless Cripple Attends U.C. Classes," made him something of a celebrity, and, within a few years, a dozen other students with severe disabilities had matriculated at the school. They formed the Rolling Quads, dedicated to making the campus and surrounding community accessible. One result of their advocacy was the formation of the Physically Disabled Students' Program. With its provision for personal assistance services (PAS), community living, and advocacy, it became a prototype for independent living centers and a forerunner of the independent living movement. Roberts, in the meantime, had completed his M.A. in political science in 1966. He continued his education at the school, working toward a doctorate in political science, eventually completing all the requirements except his thesis.

The Center for Independent Living (CIL) was founded in March 1972, with Roberts as its first executive director. In its first years, the CIL struggled to accommodate the growing number of people in the San Francisco area applying for services. So successful was Roberts as CIL director that, by the time he left, the organization's budget had grown from $40,000 to more than $1 million a year.

In 1975, Roberts was named by California Governor Jerry Brown to be the director of that state's Department of Vocational Rehabilitation—the same department that had once described him as too disabled to work. Attitudes had changed little in the intervening 13 years, and his mother, Zona Roberts, recalls that some of the staff balked at having "one of their former clients be their boss. They were used to being the big saviors of disabled people, and here this cripple was telling them what to do."

Roberts dedicated himself to furthering the concept of independent living. The new federal Innovation and Expansion Grants, available under Title I of the Rehabilitation Act of 1973, gave Roberts the capital he needed to found nine new independent living centers, each staffed and managed by people with disabilities. The federal government challenged this use of its funds, claiming that independent living centers were not "rehabilitation." Roberts' victory in this argument was a crucial moment in the history of the incipient independent living movement. "I don't think you could have sold the concept of independent living on the basis of one CIL," said Joan Leon, his co-worker at the CIL and the Department of Rehabilitation. "But by [showing that the concept worked in ten centers] he started something that was absolutely unstoppable."

Roberts was also one of the principal organizers of Disabled Peoples' International (DPI), and he was instrumental in pulling together DPI's founding conference at the Singapore World Congress in November/December 1981. DPI, like the CIL, became a catalyst, helping newly born disability rights movements all over the world.

Roberts left the California Department of Vocational Rehabilitation in 1983 and spent the rest of his life proselytizing for independent living. Roberts was named a MacArthur fellow from 1985 to 1989 and used the prize money to fund the World Institute on Disability (WID), which he had founded in 1983 along with Judith Heumann and Joan Leon. WID became a forum and conduit for information on disability rights issues and movements internationally, helping to found independent living centers in Eastern Europe, Russia, and Central America, often with Roberts' direct involvement. Altogether, Roberts traveled more than 1 million miles to spread the message of disability rights and independent living, addressing disability rights groups and granting interviews to the disability and mainstream press.

Roberts died in California on 14 March 1995. He was eulogized throughout the disability and mainstream press, and his loss was mourned by advocates all around the world.

See also Center for Independent Living, Inc.; Disabled Peoples' International; Independent Living; Independent Living Movement; World Institute on Disability.

References Driedger, Diane, *The Last Civil Rights Movement* (1989); Levy, Chava Willig, *A People's History of the Independent Living Movement* (1988); Pelka, Fred, "Ed Roberts, 1939–1995: Father of Independent Living," *Mainstream* (May 1995); Shapiro, Joseph, *No Pity: People with Disabilities Forging a New*

Civil Rights Movement (1993); Treanor, Richard Bryant, *We Overcame: The Story of Civil Rights for Disabled People* (1993).

Rochlin, Jay F. (1932–1996)

Jay F. Rochlin was the executive director of the President's Committee on Employment of People with Disabilities from 1987 to 1990, the committee's acting executive director from November 1985 to 1987, and the executive assistant to the committee's chair from January to October 1985. He helped to change the committee's message from the volunteerism of "Hire the Handicapped" to one of civil rights for people with disabilities. He was involved in passage of the Americans with Disabilities Act of 1990, telling Senate Republicans that "fifty years of volunteerism has not worked." He was also instrumental in helping to write and pass the Technology Related Assistance for Individuals with Disabilities Act of 1988.

Rochlin was born on 27 August 1932 in White Plains, New York. He graduated from the Newark College of Engineering in 1970 and from the Rutgers University Advanced Management Program in New Brunswick, New Jersey, in 1972. He was a member or advisor to numerous organizations, including the World Institute on Disability and Gallaudet University. Rochlin was also a member of the National Council on Independent Living (1988 to 1990) and the Rehabilitation Services Administration's Task Force on Rehabilitation of People with Mental Illness. Among his publications are: "Working with Disabilities: Problems, Progress and Promise" in *Washington Jobline* (November/December 1989), "Employment: The Key to Independence" in *Employment Relations Today* (Summer 1988), and "Employment of Persons with Disabilities: A Changing Perspective" in *International Forum: Leisure, Sports, Cultural Arts and Employment for People with Disability* (published by the National Council on the Handicapped in 1985).

Rochlin died on 6 April 1996, in Mt. Hood, Oregon.

See also President's Committee on Employment of People with Disabilities; Technology Related Assistance for Individuals with Disabilities Act of 1988.

Rolling Quads

See Center for Independent Living, Inc.; Roberts, Edward V.

Roosevelt, Franklin Delano (1882–1945)

"Franklin Delano Roosevelt," according to historian Hugh Gallagher, "was the only person in the recorded history of mankind who was chosen as a leader by his people even though he could not walk or stand without help. Roosevelt dominated his times from a wheelchair; yet he was simply not perceived as being in any major sense disabled."

Roosevelt was born on 30 January 1882 in Hyde Park, New York, into a wealthy and influential family. He was appointed assistant secretary of the Navy by President Wilson during World War I. After the war, Roosevelt was a New York state senator and, in 1920, the vice-presidential candidate of the Democratic Party. One year later, he was stricken with poliomyelitis, which left him paralyzed and a wheelchair user.

Roosevelt's first reaction to his disability was to attempt to end it. Moving to Warm Springs, Georgia, he began a rigorous program of physical rehabilitation. A co-founder of the Warm Springs Foundation, Roosevelt organized an innovative program that was a forerunner of today's peer counseling and disability self-help groups. He was, however, unsuccessful in his attempts to regain his ability to walk unassisted. Roosevelt resumed his political career in 1928, running for governor of New York. The campaign was arduous, not because he was disabled, but because so few places were accessible to someone using a wheelchair. Wherever he went, ramps had to be specially built, or else the candidate was forced to use service elevators or to be carried up steps and fire escapes to enter

Franklin D. Roosevelt and Ruthie Bye, with dog Fala, 1941. Very few pictures show Roosevelt in his wheelchair.

the halls where he would speak. All these special efforts were made in secrecy, the common wisdom being that no wheelchair user could ever be a successful political leader. Despite rumors that he was "an invalid," Roosevelt won the election, and he was reelected by a wide margin in 1930.

In his first annual message to the New York state Legislature, Roosevelt declared it "the duty of the State to give the same care to removing the physical handicaps of its citizens as it now gives to their mental development. Universal education of the mind is, after all, a modern conception. We have reached the time now when we must recognize the same obligation of the State to restore to useful activity those children and adults who have the misfortune to be crippled. . . . As a matter of good business, it would pay the State to help in restoring these cripples to useful citizenship." Gallagher (1985) points out that this "call for universal care and treatment of the physically disabled was a radical proposal for 1929. Some fifty years later, it is still a radical proposal."

After two, two-year terms as governor of New York, Roosevelt was elected president of the United States, the only person with an obvious physical disability ever to hold that office. Roosevelt, however, felt compelled to conceal the extent of his disability, engaging in what Gallagher calls his "splendid deception." Of the more than 35,000 still photographs of Roosevelt at his presidential library, only two show him using his wheelchair.

Roosevelt is, of course, best remembered for the New Deal and for his leadership during World War II, but he also participated in many disability organizations, though always, as Nora Groce (1992) points out, "in the guise of an influential benefactor, rather than as an individual who was disabled." Early in his first term, he helped to start a charitable organization, the National March of Dimes, to raise funds for rehabilitation, education, and adaptive equipment for polio survivors, and to fund research. Roosevelt's sponsorship of the March of Dimes was a prime factor in the eventual development of the polio vaccine. Throughout his life, Roosevelt would return to the community in Warm Springs, maintaining close connections with disabled people across the country. His more than twelve years as president saw important gains for people with disabilities, including the establishment of Social Security in 1935, the passage of the LaFollette-Barden Act of 1943, and the development of physical rehabilitation medicine.

Roosevelt died at Warm Springs on 12 April 1945. Fifty years after his death, controversy erupted over proposals to erect a Roosevelt memorial in Washington, D.C. The FDR Memorial Commission chose to "honor the fact that FDR himself chose to guard his condition closely and not reveal the extent of his disability to the public," and so the commission decided to depict Roosevelt without cane or leg braces, certainly without his wheelchair. Disability rights advocates saw this portrayal as pandering to ableism and as an attempt to hide the fact that one of the most revered American presidents was a person with a physical disability.

See also Gallagher, Hugh Gregory; LaFollette-Barden Act of 1943; Social Security, Social Security Disability Insurance, Supplemental Security Income; Warm Springs, Georgia.

References Gallagher, Hugh Gregory, *FDR's Splendid Deception* (1985); Groce, Nora Ellen, *The U.S. Role in International Disability Activities: A History and a Look toward the Future* (1992).

Rousso, Harilyn (b. 1946)

Harilyn Rousso is an educator, social worker, psychotherapist, and disability rights advocate who has done landmark work in the area of women and girls with disabilities. She is best known as the founder (in 1984) of the Networking Project for Disabled Women and Girls of the Young Women's Christian Association of New York City, a unique mentoring and counseling program for adolescent girls with disabilities.

Rousso was born on 21 May 1946 in Brooklyn, New York. She received her B.A.

in economics from Brandeis University in Waltham, Massachusetts, in 1968 and her master's in education from Boston University in 1972. In 1984, Rousso received her certificate in psychoanalytic psychotherapy from the New York School for Psychoanalytic Psychotherapy in New York City.

In addition to her work with the Networking Project for Disabled Women and Girls, Rousso has been a commissioner with the New York City Commission on Human Rights (1988–1993), a consultant on mainstreaming youth with disabilities at the Girls Incorporated National Headquarters in New York (1991–1994), and an adjunct lecturer in the Women's Studies Program at Hunter College, also in New York. She is currently the executive director of Disabilities Unlimited Consulting Services, which offers counseling and advocacy services to people with disabilities and their families. Disabilities Unlimited was founded by Rousso in 1979.

Rousso is the author of numerous publications, including "Disabled People Are Sexual Too!" (*Exceptional Parent* magazine, 1981), "Therapists with Disabilities: Theoretical and Clinical Issues" (with Adrienne Asch, in *Psychiatry*, 1985), *Disabled, Female and Proud! Stories of Ten Women with Disabilities* (with S. O'Malley and M. Severance, 1988), and "Affirming Adolescent Women's Sexuality" (in the *Western Journal of Medicine*, 1991). From 1990 to 1992, she was a member of the board of directors of the Brooklyn Center for Independence of the Disabled, and she is today a member of the boards of the Ms. Foundation for Women and the Society for Disability Studies.

See also Women with Disabilities.

Rural Institute on Disabilities

Based at the University of Montana in Missoula, and funded by the federal Administration on Developmental Disabilities, the Rural Institute on Disabilities was founded in 1979 to advocate for the full participation in community life by Americans with disabilities living in rural areas. Among its projects are annual national rural disability conferences, a rural early intervention training program, a Vietnam Veterans' Children's Assistance Program, and the American Indian Disability Legislation Project. The institute sponsors the Rural Disability Information Service and the Rural Disabilities Info-Net. It publishes the monthly newsletters the *Rural Exchange* and *Rural Facts*, as well as the *Montana Respite Training Resource Service Newsletter*. Recent issues of *Rural Facts* have included articles on starting small businesses, accessible rural housing, and the demographics of rural disabilities.

See also Administration on Developmental Disabilities; American Indian Disability Legislation Project.

Rusk, Howard (1901–1989)

Howard Rusk, a pioneer in the field of rehabilitation, was born on 9 April 1901 in Brookfield, Missouri. Rusk believed that any individual, no matter how severely disabled, could learn techniques and use adaptive technology to regain some measure of independence. "To believe in rehabilitation," Rusk wrote in his 1972 autobiography *A World To Care For*, "is to believe in humanity."

Rusk, one of the country's first specialists in internal medicine, entered the Army Air Force during World War II and was assigned to the hospital at Jefferson Barracks, Missouri. At this time, disabled soldiers, once their wounds healed, were virtually abandoned by the medical profession. People with spinal cord injury were literally left in their beds until they died of sores or pneumonia, usually within six months to a year of their injuries. In *A World To Care For*, Rusk describes how one time he came across a disabled soldier weeping, because an orderly had swept away the spider weaving its web above his bed, his only distraction in all the weeks he had been in the hospital. Rusk realized "that there was no precedent for rehabilitation programs on a large scale in the military. And as far as I knew, there were no extensive civilian programs either."

Rusk started a program of physical therapy and exercise. He brought in teachers to offer his patients courses in math, languages, and American history. Patients were encouraged to socialize with each other, to become each others' mentors and teachers. Rusk's innovations brought him considerable attention. In early 1944, he was assigned to open a convalescent center in Pawling, New York. Results were again dramatic, and Rusk was asked to found rehabilitation programs at a dozen other Air Force hospitals. Toward the end of the war, President Roosevelt ordered that rehabilitation programs based on Rusk's work be started for all the armed forces.

Leaving the military, Rusk established the country's first municipal rehabilitation center at Bellvue Hospital in New York City. There, he and his team scored several significant firsts, among them the first rehabilitation ever attempted of someone with spina bifida. In January 1951, he opened the Institute of Rehabilitation Medicine at New York University Medical Center. A large portion of his patients were members of the United Mine Workers Union, disabled at work. Again, Rusk and his staff broke the rules, improvising solutions. Because wheelchairs at the time were inadequate, Rusk's team designed new ones. Electric typewriters (first developed by IBM as a way to enable disabled people to write), mouthsticks, and improved prosthetic limbs all were developed or refined by Rusk's team.

While at the medical center, Rusk worked to interest the medical establishment in rehabilitation medicine. It was a hard sell. "Rehab" was not glamorous, and funding was scarce. It was considered by many doctors to be unmedical and unprofessional. Rusk's reliance on people with disabilities themselves to staff his facilities and do the training was unprecedented, and rehabilitation medicine was dubbed "Rusk's folly."

Even so, Rusk's reputation grew. His patients often came to him after a lifetime of deprivation; nevertheless, graduates of his program became nurses, lawyers, artists, teachers, and entrepreneurs. When his patients encountered discrimination in the workplace or at school, Rusk sometimes personally intervened. He wrote a weekly column in the *New York Times*, where he outlined the benefits of rehabilitation and urged businesses to hire disabled workers.

In 1955, Rusk co-founded and became the first president of the World Rehabilitation Foundation, travelng extensively to lecture on rehabilitation medicine. Over the course of more than twenty years, rehabilitation medicine was gradually accepted, and Rusk's role as an innovator recognized. Rusk died on 4 November 1989 in New York City.

See also Assistive Technology; Viscardi, Henry, Jr.
Reference Rusk, Howard A., *A World To Care For: The Autobiography of Howard A. Rusk, M.D.* (1972).

Russell, Harold (b. 1914)

Harold Russell was born on 14 January 1914 in Nova Scotia, Canada, and raised in Cambridge, Massachusetts. A meat cutter before the war, Russell became a paratrooper during World War II. He lost both his arms up to the elbows in a hand grenade explosion on 6 June 1944, while serving as a demolitions instructor at Camp Mackall, North Carolina. He was fitted with prosthetic hands and appeared in a U.S. Army documentary, *The Diary of a Sergeant* (1945). Hollywood director William Wyler, himself disabled, saw the film and decided to cast Russell as one of the characters in *The Best Years of Our Lives* (1946), a film depicting the struggles of veterans returning home from the war. Russell in the meantime had begun classes at Boston University. When the call came from Samuel Goldwyn's studio asking if he could come to Hollywood to star in a movie, Russell hung up, thinking it was a prank.

The film was an enormous success, due in large part to Russell's unique portrayal of a person with a disability who was neither evil nor superhumanly courageous. Though obviously not a professional actor, Russell brought an authenticity to the role that garnered him two Academy Awards in

1947, one for best supporting actor and one—a special award—"for bringing hope and courage to his fellow veterans."

Russell was asked by President Truman to become a member of the President's Committee on Employment of the Handicapped in October 1948. The next year, he published his autobiography, *Victory in My Hands*. President Lyndon Johnson appointed Russell chair of the committee in 1964. In this capacity he testified before Congress for the inclusion of strong, antidiscriminatory language in the Rehabilitation Act of 1973 and its regulations. During this time, Russell was also a consultant on access and employment both for the federal government and for private firms such as ITT.

Russell stepped down from the committee in 1989. He is currently retired, but he continues to work on behalf of homeless and disabled Vietnam veterans.

See also *Best Years of Our Lives;* Media Images of People with Disabilities; President's Committee on Employment of People with Disabilities.

Reference Russell, Harold, *Victory in My Hands* (1949).

Ryan White Comprehensive AIDS Resources Emergency (CARE) Act of 1990

The Ryan White Comprehensive AIDS Resources Emergency (CARE) Act of 1990 was sponsored by Senators Edward M. Kennedy (D-MA) and Orrin G. Hatch (R-UT). It was named after and is dedicated to Ryan White, a young hemophiliac who died on 8 April 1990, after a six-year battle with AIDS.

Work on the bill started in January 1987, when the Senate Committee on Labor and Human Resources began its investigation of the health care needs of individuals and families with AIDS and HIV. That month, Senator Kennedy declared the epidemic "a health disaster," the severity of which had the potential to surpass "any disease in history." The committee learned that the epidemic was overwhelming the resources of localities such as New York City and San Francisco. By March 1990, approximately 128,000 AIDS cases had been reported to the Centers for Disease Control, with more than 78,000 deaths, almost as many Americans as had died in the Korean and Vietnam Wars combined. A congressional report concluded that "nearly 1 million Americans are already infected, most of whom, in the absence of medical intervention, will progress to full blown AIDS." This "tidal-wave of health care needs" will "present an enormous challenge to our health care system in the decade to come."

To meet this challenge, the Ryan White CARE Act, under Title I, offers emergency relief in the form of federal funding to localities disproportionately affected by the epidemic. Title II provides for federal grants for "comprehensive care programs" to pay for home care, transportation, counseling, hospice care, and other support services. States are also encouraged to establish a program of financial assistance for low-income individuals trying to maintain their health insurance. Title III provides funding for early intervention services, including HIV testing, counseling, referrals, and "other clinical and diagnostic services with respect to HIV disease." Title IV provides for periodic evaluation of the effectiveness of programs funded under the other titles. The act also contains provisions for the protection of the confidentiality of people who test positive for HIV and for informing individuals at risk through blood transfusion. It prohibits funding to states that do not have laws to protect the intentional infection of one person by another with HIV/AIDS.

The act was extended by Congress and President Clinton in 1996, by which time more than 300,000 people had received care under its provisions. Some $738 million was allocated under the act in fiscal year 1996. AIDS activists pointed out, however, that even this enormous sum was inadequate to the task of meeting the health care needs of all those affected by, or at risk because of, the continuing epidemic.

See also HIV/AIDS and Disability.

Savage, Elizabeth (b. 1955)

Elizabeth Savage, as assistant director of government affairs for the Epilepsy Foundation of America, worked closely with Patrisha Wright at the Disability Rights Education and Defense Fund (DREDF) in the campaign to pass the Americans with Disabilities Act of 1990 (ADA). She was born on 7 May 1955 in Norwich, Connecticut. She earned a B.A. in political science from Tufts University in Medford, Massachusetts, in 1977 and received her law degree from the University of California Hastings College of Law in San Francisco in 1982. She worked in the Carter White House from 1977 to 1979, as a private attorney until 1984, and as a deputy scheduler in the Mondale-Ferraro presidential campaign in 1984. In 1985 she joined the Epilepsy Foundation of America, where she supervised its national grassroots advocacy and legislative efforts.

Savage used her presidential campaign experience to coordinate the efforts of a coalition of 75 disability, civil rights, religious, and civic organizations pushing for passage of the ADA. She was also a member of the Congressional Task Force on the Rights and Empowerment of Americans with Disabilities. In 1991, she became the national training director for DREDF. Today, Elizabeth Savage is a special assistant attorney general for civil rights, the first person with a disability to hold so high a position within the U.S. Department of Justice, specializing in ADA policy and enforcement. She was appointed to this position in 1993.

See also Americans with Disabilities Act of 1990; Disability Rights Education and Defense Fund; Task Force on the Rights and Empowerment of Americans with Disabilities; Wright, Patrisha A.

Saxton, Marsha (b. 1951)

Marsha Saxton is a women's health and disability rights activist and writer. She is the founder and director of the Project on Women and Disability in Boston, the former director of services at the Boston Self Help Center, and a former contributing editor and board member of the Boston Women's Health Book Collective, the publisher of *The New Our Bodies, Ourselves* (1984).

Saxton was born on 23 May 1951 in Oakland, California. She completed her bachelor's degree in psycholinguistics from the University of California in 1973, her master's in speech and language pathology from Boston University in 1977, and her doctorate in feminist bio-ethics from the Union Institute in Cincinnati in 1996. Among her many publications are "That Something That Happened before I Was Born" in *Ordinary Moments* (1984), "Born and Unborn: Implications of the Reproductive Technologies for People with Disabilities" in *Test Tube Women: What Future for Motherhood?* (1984), and "Peer Counseling" in *Independent Living for Physically Disabled People* (1983). She is the co-editor, with Florence Howe, of *With Wings: An Anthology of Literature by and about Women with Disabilities* (1987) and the author of more than 100 articles on disability, women's health, genetic screening, and peer counseling.

Saxton's commitment to the issues of women's health and disability rights comes out of her own experience as a person with spina bifida. In her chapter in *Ordinary Moments* she recounts how, as a small child, she endured numerous surgeries to "fix" her body. "All those people trying so hard to help me. . . . They never asked me what I wanted for myself. They never asked me if I wanted their help."

Saxton held teaching positions at the

Kennedy School of Government at Harvard University, the University of Massachusetts at Boston, and Suffolk University, also in Boston. She serves on the Council for Responsible Genetics and as a Working Group member on the National Institutes of Health (NIH) Ethical, Legal, Social Implications Branch of the Human Genome Initiative.

See also Abortion and Reproductive Rights; Baby Doe Case; Baby Jane Doe Case; Boston Self Help Center; *Bowen v. American Hospital Association*; *Ordinary Moments*; Project on Women and Disability.

Reference Saxton, Marsha, and Florence Howe, eds., *With Wings: An Anthology of Literature by and about Women with Disabilities* (1987).

School Board of Nassau County, Florida v. Arline 107 S. Ct. 1123 (1987)

In *School Board of Nassau County, Florida v. Arline*, the U.S. Supreme Court ruled that a public school teacher with a history of tuberculosis was a "handicapped individual" within the meaning of the Rehabilitation Act of 1973 and could not be dismissed from her job simply because of her medical history.

Gene H. Arline was hospitalized with tuberculosis in 1957, but she recovered. Her illness remained in remission for 20 years. During that time, Arline taught elementary school in Nassau County, Florida, from 1966 until 1979, when she was dismissed after suffering a third relapse of tuberculosis within two years. Arline went through the state administrative process, which refused to reinstate her. She then filed federal suit, claiming that her dismissal was a violation of Section 504 of the Rehabilitation Act of 1973, which prohibits entities receiving federal funds from discriminating against "otherwise qualified handicapped individuals."

On 3 March 1987, the Court decided first that Arline was in fact a "handicapped individual" as defined by the Rehabilitation Act, and thus protected by Section 504. The Court dismissed the school board's argument that Arline was terminated not because of her disability but because of the threat of contagion and that

therefore she was not "otherwise qualified." "The fact that a person with a record of impairment [such as tuberculosis] is also contagious," the Court ruled, "does not remove that person from Section 504 protection."

The Court did not prohibit an entity receiving federal funds from terminating an employee if there was a genuine threat to the safety of co-workers or students. Rather, it mandated that such decisions be made "based on reasonable medical judgements given the state of medical knowledge about (a) the nature of the risk (*e.g.*, how the disease is transmitted), (b) the duration of the risk (how long is the carrier infectious), (c) the severity of the risk (what is the potential harm to third parties), and (d) the probabilities the disease will be transmitted and will cause varying degrees of harm." Finally, "in light of these findings," the employer had to determine whether "reasonable accommodation" could be made to minimize the risk of contagion while allowing the handicapped individual to continue working. Such a process, the Court felt, was necessary "to ensure that handicapped individuals are not denied jobs or other benefits because of the prejudiced attitudes or ignorance of others."

Arline became a legal precedent for people who are HIV positive and a basis for ties between the disability and HIV civil rights communities. Given that the current "reasonable medical judgement" is that HIV can only be transmitted through exposure to blood or semen, it would seem that the Supreme Court decision can be cited to protect school teachers, for example, from being dismissed simply because they are HIV positive.

See also HIV/AIDS and Disability; Reasonable Accommodation/Reasonable Modification; Section 504 of the Rehabilitation Act of 1973.

Schreiber, Frederick C. (1922–1979)

Frederick C. Schreiber was the first executive director of the National Association of the Deaf (NAD), and as such he was primarily responsible for turning the NAD from a small organization of little relevance on the national disability scene into the major voice representing the Deaf community. A printer by profession, he founded and edited several influential Deaf journals. He was also an advocate of cross-disability activism.

Schreiber was born on 1 February 1922 in Brooklyn, New York. He became deaf at age 6 after four attacks of spinal meningitis. He graduated from Gallaudet College in Washington, D.C., with a B.S. in chemistry in 1942, and he worked in a defense plant in Akron, Ohio, until 1945. Following the end of World War II, Schreiber taught briefly at the Texas School for the Deaf in Austin, and tutored deaf clients for the Office of Vocational Rehabilitation in New York City. He moved to Washington, D.C., in the early 1950s to become a linotypist, first for the *Washington Star* and then for the U.S. Government Printing Office.

From the mid-1950s to 1966, Schreiber volunteered with a number of deaf advocacy and self-help organizations. In 1960, he founded and became the first editor of *Dee Cee Eyes*, the official publication of the Metropolitan Washington Association of the Deaf. Though he stepped down as editor in 1966, Schreiber would continue to contribute articles to *Dee Cee Eyes* for the next 12 years.

Schreiber was elected secretary treasurer of the NAD's board of directors in 1964. Two years later, he was named the NAD executive secretary (later the position was renamed executive director). Although the NAD had existed for more than 80 years, at the time Schreiber took charge the NAD had no home office, little central organization, few members, and a minimal budget. Under Schreiber's leadership, the NAD experienced rapid growth and assumed a growing role in advocating for the rights of deaf people. Among Schreiber's accomplishments was the founding of programs for deaf youth, the establishment of a nationwide communications skills program, and the rapid growth of NAD state affiliates. He was instrumental in founding self-help organizations such as D.E.A.F. Inc. in Boston, Massachusetts, the state's first multiservice deaf community agency, also known as the Frederick C. Schreiber Center. Reflecting Schreiber's interest in printing and publishing, the NAD also opened its own publishing house. In 1979, Schreiber founded the *NAD Broadcaster*, the NAD's first tabloid paper. So successful was Schreiber's fund-raising that the NAD was able to purchase a home office building in Silver Spring, Maryland, and open a branch office in Indianapolis. With a budget of just $51,000 in 1966, the NAD, by the time of Schreiber's death in 1979, had an annual budget of $2 million and a paid staff of 40 people.

Schreiber's tenure saw the NAD taking a much more active role in Washington, lobbying, for example, for the establishment of the National Technical Institute for the Deaf. Perhaps the most significant change during Schreiber's administration was the acceptance of American Sign Language (ASL) at deaf institutions and in mainstream American life (and the subsequent growth of Deaf Pride and Deaf Culture). The NAD, with its long history of opposition to oralism, was seen as being vindicated in its decades of championing of ASL.

Schreiber was a founder of the American Coalition of Citizens with Disabilities (ACCD) and its first vice president. He was a participant in the occupation of the Washington headquarters of the Health, Education and Welfare (HEW) offices in April 1977, as part of the nationwide effort by ACCD to force the Carter administration to issue the first set of regulations implementing Section 504 of the Rehabilitation Act of 1973. Schreiber died in New York City on 5 September 1979.

See also American Coalition of Citizens with Disabilities; Cross-Disability Awareness/Cross-Disability Sensitivity; HEW Demonstrations; National Association of the Deaf.

References Moore, Matthew Scott, and Robert F. Panara, *Great Deaf Americans: The Second Edition* (1996); Schein, Jerome D., *A Rose for Tomorrow: Biography of Frederick C. Schreiber* (1981).

Section 504 of the Rehabilitation Act of 1973

Section 504 of the Rehabilitation Act of 1973 is the most significant disability rights legislation prior to passage of the Americans with Disabilities Act of 1990 (ADA). The regulations promulgated for its enforcement opened up unprecedented opportunities for disabled individuals and introduced the concept of disability rights to American society. Getting those regulations signed and enforced were major priorities of the disability rights movement of the 1970s and 1980s. "Section 504," writes Frank Bowe, "is historic in its scope and depth." Jane West, describing the evolution of disability rights legislation, calls it "the most significant building block" of the ADA.

For all its importance, Section 504 is a single sentence at the very end of the Rehabilitation Act: "No otherwise qualified handicapped individual in the United States, as defined in section 7(6), shall, solely by reason of his handicap, be excluded from participation in, be denied the benefits of, or be subjected to discrimination under any program or activity receiving Federal financial assistance." Defense contractors, public universities, public school districts, courts, hospitals, nursing homes, museums, airports, *any* entity receiving federal funding would be covered by Section 504.

Several states, at the instigation of disability rights activists, had already passed legislation intended to prohibit discrimination against people with disabilities. The models for Section 504, however, were Title VI of the Civil Rights Act of 1964 and Title IX of the Education Amendments of 1972, outlawing discrimination against racial minorities and women. Section 504 was added to the Rehabilitation Act at a meeting of Senate staff working on the bill in August 1972. Richard K. Scotch, in *From Good Will to Civil Rights* (1984), recounts how participants "were concerned that, when disabled individuals completed their training in the VR [vocational rehabilitation] system and were ready to enter the

workplace, many employers appeared to be reluctant to hire them." Section 504 was intended to help end this discrimination.

Disability activists seized upon Section 504 as a potent tool, and groups such as Disabled in Action and the American Coalition of Citizens with Disabilities made the signing of the 504 regulations a major focus of their efforts. The first regulations were signed by Department of Health, Education and Welfare (HEW) secretary Joseph A. Califano on 28 April 1977. These regulations required that all new facilities built with federal money be accessible to people with disabilities and that all existing facilities had to be made accessible within two months, although an extension of three years could be granted where major alterations, such as the addition of ramps or elevators, were necessary. All public schools receiving federal funds were required to admit and educate children with disabilities and to make the necessary accommodations to do so. The regulations also required colleges and universities receiving federal funds to provide interpreters, readers, and other accommodations for disabled students, and they prevented employers from discriminating against qualified employees solely because of their disability. Section 504 regulations issued by other federal departments were modeled, to a greater or lesser extent, on the HEW regulations, while authority to ensure compliance was given to the U.S. Department of Justice.

The signing of the regulations led to "504 workshops" to train advocates in how to use them. These workshops were coordinated by the Disability Rights Education and Defense Fund (DREDF) in the West and the Midwest, Barrier Free Environments in the Southeast, and the Public Interest Law Center of Philadelphia in the North. Grassroots organizations sprang up to force compliance through lobbying, litigation, or direct action. When Brad Reynolds, assistant attorney general for civil rights under the newly elected Reagan administration, threatened in 1981 to rescind the 504 regulations, along with regulations implementing the Education for All Handicapped Children Act of 1975, the White House received some 40,000 cards and letters from disability activists across the country. One of the outcomes of this campaign was the sensitizing of Vice President George Bush and his counsel Boyden Gray to disability issues and to the emerging clout of the disability rights movement. The importance of this education would be seen in 1990, when President Bush was faced with the choice of accepting, or rejecting, the ADA.

Two central concepts arose out of the implementation of Section 504: "reasonable accommodation" and "reasonable modification." Litigation, including several U.S. Supreme Court decisions, focused on definitions of "undue burden" and "otherwise qualified," also concepts developed in response to Section 504. In turn, Section 504 was affected by litigation involving other civil rights law, as when the Supreme Court, in *Grove City College v. Bell* (1984), ruled that only those programs *directly* receiving federal monies (for instance, a single university department or program, rather than the entire university) need comply with Title IX of the Education Amendments of 1972. Section 504 was amended by the Civil Rights Restoration Act of 1987 to undo the effects of this decision.

Within ten years of the signing of the Section 504 regulations, people with disabilities constituted fully 7 percent of all college freshmen. New buildings by institutions or agencies funded, even partially, by the federal government were built with ramps, elevators, braille signage and curb-cuts. Older buildings, when renovated, were required to aim for accessibilty. There was also important progress in employment of people with disabilities after Section 504.

Section 504 was limited, however, most importantly in that it did nothing about entities not receiving federal money. Enforcement of 504 was spotty at best, and federal court decisions about its requirements were often confused and contradic-

tory, tending to limit its effectiveness. As a result, entire aspects of American public life, for example, mass transit and housing, continued to be inaccessible to people with disabilities. Clearly, more far-reaching legislation was needed, and, by 1983, the National Council on Disability had begun to advocate for a national civil rights law that would become the ADA.

See also Civil Rights Restoration Act of 1987; HEW Demonstrations; Reasonable Accommodation/Reasonable Modification; Rehabilitation Act of 1973; *Southeastern Community College v. Davis*; Undue Hardship/Undue Burden.

References Bowe, Frank G., *Changing the Rules* (1986); Rothstein, Laura F., *Disabilities and the Law* (formerly, *Rights of Physically Handicapped Persons*) (1992); Scotch, Richard, *From Good Will to Civil Rights: Transforming Federal Disability Policy* (1984); West, Jane, "The Evolution of Disability Rights," in Lawrence O. Gostin and Henry A. Beyer, eds., *Implementing the Americans with Disabilities Act: Rights and Responsibilities of All Americans* (1993).

Self-Advocacy

One of the tenets of the disability rights movement is that people with disabilities are themselves their own best advocates. This may seem an almost absurdly obvious principle, but throughout history nondisabled family, educators, physicians, philanthropists, and most recently social service and rehabilitation professionals have taken upon themselves the task of speaking on behalf of people with disabilities. That disabled people should decide for themselves how they would live was until relatively recently a radical proposition.

Self-advocacy became an especially important concept among people with developmental and cognitive disabilities beginning in the early 1970s, when great numbers previously consigned to institutions began to enter the community. Many banded together in loosely organized but determined groups to educate and advocate for each other. There was a progression from small steps made in advocating for oneself and one's friends on purely personal issues, such as the right to decide when to sleep and when to eat in a group home, to political actions taken to effect major changes in society. Self-advocacy has been adopted by groups in Great Britain, Sweden, Canada, Australia, and elsewhere, while David Braddock, at the Institute on Disability and Human Development at the University of Illinois in Chicago, estimated that, as of 1996, there were more than 700 self-advocacy groups formed by people with cognitive disabilities in the United States, with an estimated membership in excess of 17,000.

See also People First, People First International; Self Advocates Becoming Empowered.

Reference Dybwad, Gunnar, and Hank Bersani Jr., *New Voices: Self-Advocacy by People with Disabilities* (1996).

Self Advocates Becoming Empowered

Self Advocates Becoming Empowered was founded during the Second North American People First Conference in Nashville, Tennessee, on 2 August 1991. Among its goals are to promote legislation at state and national levels to protect the rights of people with disabilities, to support local and state self-advocacy groups, to close institutions, to ensure opportunities for people with disabilities to work for fair wages, and to work with the criminal justice system and people with disabilities regarding their rights. Among the issues its organizers feel are most important are choices for people with cognitive disabilities in friendships and relationships, affordable and accessible transportation, quality education, community living, choices in sexual expression, and the prevention of physical, sexual, and emotional abuse. Since its formation, the group has completed its first position paper, *Taking Our Place: Standing Up and Speaking Out about Living in Our Communities*, met with President Clinton, and filed a federal suit on behalf of institutionalized people.

Self Advocates Becoming Empowered is based in Nashville, Tennessee. Representatives of its nine regions meet four times a year.

See also People First, People First International; Personal Assistance Services.

Self Help for Hard of Hearing People, Inc. (SHHH)

Self Help for Hard of Hearing People, Inc. (SHHH) was founded in 1979 and today is "the largest international consumer organization dedicated to the well-being of people who do not hear well." Its members state that its primary purpose is "to educate ourselves, our relatives and friends about the causes, nature, and complications of hearing loss—and what can be done about it."

SHHH was founded by Howard E. "Rocky" Stone, who was also the group's first executive director. Stone, who had been deafened in an explosion during World War II, had a 25-year career in the Central Intelligence Agency before founding SHHH. Its first elected president was William Cutler, who also played an instrumental role in building the organization. By the mid-1990s, SHHH had a membership of 40,000, including hard-of-hearing people, their families, parents of hard-of-hearing children, and friends, organized into more than 280 local groups and chapters. Although predominantly a self-help and educational group, SHHH also advocates for communication access and for enforcement of the Americans with Disabilities Act of 1990. During the health care finance reform debate of 1993, it lobbied for inclusion of insurance coverage for hearing aids, aural rehabilitation, and cochlear implants. That year, it also, in conjunction with the American Association of Retired Persons (AARP), sponsored a program to identify barriers faced by people with hearing loss in the workplace. SHHH has a policy of encouraging its members, trustees, and staff to be active in the government boards and agencies that set policy on hearing loss, communication access, and other issues relevant to hard-of-hearing people.

SHHH, headquartered in Bethesda, Maryland, publishes the *SHHH Journal* and a variety of books and materials.

See also Cochlear Implants.

Sexuality and Disability

One of the most damaging misconceptions about people with disabilities is that they are unable or uninterested in having sexual relationships. The one exception to this stereotype concerns people with cognitive or emotional disabilities—those labeled mentally ill or mentally retarded—who are commonly held to be oversexed or sexually dangerous. Many nondisabled people (and some people with disabilities) see disability as sexually repulsive; conversely, people with disabilities are harassed by those who find disability inherently erotic. This denial of disabled people's genuine sexuality has been especially prevalent in institutions and nursing homes, but, even for people living in the community, the advent of a disability can mean the end to their marriage or long-term sexual relationship.

"Living under the shadow of sexual exclusion," according to Edward John Hudak, writing in the April 1992 issue of *Mainstream* magazine, "has its price in terms of self-image and viability. Some of the worst offenders are the professionals responsible for the rehabilitation of people who become disabled. Many with spinal cord injuries are told by their doctors not to expect a return of their sexual capacity. . . . Unfortunately, there might be a reluctance to act on [sexual feelings] . . . because the way people are perceived often becomes the way they perceive themselves." The fact is that, while some disabilities may adversely impact certain expressions of sexuality, sexuality remains a component of everyone's life, and people with disabilities are no exception.

The notion that disability precluded sexual feelings and expression was first publicly challenged in the 1960s by advocates such as Fred Fay and the National Paraplegia Foundation and, in the 1970s, by the publication of books such as *Not Made of Stone* (1974) and movies such as *Coming Home* (1978). Subsequent explorations of disability and sexuality include the British film *The Skin Horse* (1986) and the resource book *The Sensuous Wheeler*, by Barry Rabin. Yvonne Duffy, in *All Things Are Possible*

(1981), interviewed women with disabilities about their sexual education, fantasies, and relationships. "Sex was never, but never talked about," said one woman. "Only, 'Don't get pregnant, you're a cripple now.'" In May 1994, *Mouth: The Voice of Disability Rights* devoted an entire issue to sexuality, and *It's Okay!*, a Canadian quarterly, features articles on sex written by and for people with disabilities. Mainstream and feminist publications, such as *The New Our Bodies, Ourselves* (1984), have also begun to take notice of sexuality as it relates to people with disabilities.

Sam Maddox, in *Spinal Network* (1987), writes that "sexuality need not be defined by technique, but by expression and emotion; sex is not something to be performed, it is something to be shared." A redefinition of what is sexual and sexy is one of the ways in which the disability rights movement is broadening the acknowledged range of human experience for everyone.

See also *It's Okay: Adults with a Disability Write about Living and Loving.*

Reference Brown, Susan, Debra Connors, and Nancy Stern, eds., *With the Power of Each Breath: A Disabled Women's Anthology* (1985); Duffy, Yvonne, *All Things Are Possible* (1981); Maddox, Sam, *Spinal Network: The Total Resource for the Wheelchair Community* (1987).

Shapiro, Joseph P.
See No Pity.

Sheltered Workshops

"Sheltered Workshops," write Stephen Murphy and Patricia Rogan in *Closing the Shop: Conversion from Sheltered to Integrated Work* (1995), "are one of the last bastions of therapeutic paternalism facing people with disabilities." In 1989, the Association for Persons with Severe Handicaps (TASH) called for their "permanent and rapid replacement" by "individualized and integrated employment for all people with severe disabilities."

What might properly be called the first sheltered workshop in the United States was founded in 1838 by Samuel Gridley Howe at the Perkins School for the Blind in Boston. His plan was to provide vocational training so that blind students could acquire jobs in the community, but Howe abandoned this idea after employers refused to hire blind workers, no matter how well qualified. The training program, now separate from Perkins, became a sheltered workshop. This pattern was to be repeated over the next 150 years, with "transitional" programs turning into permanent, segregated workplaces. Blind or otherwise disabled workers were paid low wages to turn out goods, the sale of which subsidized the continued operation of the workshop and the salaries of nondisabled owners and managers. These workshops were often run by charitable institutions, for instance Goodwill Industries, formally established in Brooklyn, New York, in 1918.

The passage of the Fair Labor Standards Act of 1938 brought an enormous expansion of the sheltered workshop system. The act pertained to workshops employing blind workers; it was amended in 1971 to include people with other disabilities. It gave sheltered workshops—where 75 percent or more of the labor force have a severe disability—exclusive bidding rights on federal contracts for various goods and services, and it waived minimum wage and other federal labor regulations. The purpose of the law was to provide people with disabilities an opportunity to learn the skills they needed to move into the general work force. Instead, by providing workshop managers with a guaranteed market, the law encouraged workshops to employ only the most productive, often least disabled workers, and to hang on to them as long as possible. By the early 1970s, there were some 1,500 sheltered workshops with approximately 160,000 disabled workers. With deinstitutionalization, the number of workers had grown to more than 650,000 by the mid-1980s. By this time, the majority of workshop employees were people with cognitive disabilities.

Among the earliest critics of sheltered workshops was Jacobus tenBroek, founder of the National Federation of the Blind. In *Hope Deferred: Public Welfare and the Blind*

A disabled woman uses a pair of tweezers to place black chips into a white pan at a sheltered workshop for adults in this undated photograph.

(written with Floyd W. Matson and published in 1959), he described how the subminimum wages covered "only a fraction of the cost of living" and how workers lacked "pension plans, paid vacations, security of employment, or systematic and free relations with management." Workers were often forced, either by poverty or workshop policy, to live in dormitories (often in the same building where they worked), where they were segregated by gender, and where every aspect of an employee's life was monitored and controlled. TenBroek and Matson described how workers were "harassed and intimidated to spur production," "making goods for nonblind salesmen who capitalize on public sympathy for 'blind-made' products."

These complaints have intensified with the growth of the disability rights movement and the success of alternatives such as supported employment. A 1992 survey conducted for the federal agency that oversees the sheltered workshop industry (the Committee for Purchase from People Who Are Blind or Severely Disabled), found that 22.9 percent of blind employees and 48.3 percent of employees with other disabilities of sheltered workshops nationwide were paid less than minimum wage. Added to the charges of demeaning conditions and economic exploitation is the contention that segregating people with disabilities, for whatever reason, contributes to the perception that they are different from and inferior to nondisabled people, and it is thus inherently oppressive.

Some defend the sheltered workshop system as offering the only possible employment for people with severe or multiple disabilities. They point out that many "workshop" employees in fact work in the community, for example, as janitors or cafeteria workers, fulfilling service contracts between private nonprofits and state agencies. According to this viewpoint, some people are so disabled they are incapable of working at competitive jobs, while private employers simply will not hire people with severe disabilities, particularly cognitive or psychiatric disabilities, who are perceived as incompetent or even dangerous.

Disability rights activists reject these arguments. They point out that the experience of the past 20 years has shown that people with even the most severe physical, emotional, and cognitive disabilities can be gainfully employed in the community, given the necessary accommodations. The solution to workplace discrimination, they argue, is not a system of segregated or second-class employment but the enforcement of disability rights laws.

See also Association for People with Severe Handicaps; Howe, Samuel Gridley; National Federation of the Blind; Supported Employment; Ten-Broek, Jacobus.

References Ervin, Mike, "Have Sheltered Workshops Outlived Their Usefulness?" *One Step Ahead—The Resource for Active, Healthy, Independent Living* (August 1996); Murphy, Stephen T., and Patricia M. Rogan, *Closing the Shop: Conversion from Sheltered to Integrated Work* (1995); Nelson, Nathan, *Workshops for the Handicapped in the United States: An Historical and Developmental Perspective* (1971); Ten-

Broek, Jacobus, and Floyd W. Matson, *Hope Deferred: Public Welfare and the Blind* (1959).

Silent News: **World's Most Popular Newspaper of the Deaf**

Julius Wiggins first had the idea of publishing a newspaper by and for deaf people during a trip to Las Vegas for a Deaf convention in 1968. He and his wife, Harriet, had been frustrated by the fact that developments in the Deaf community spread through "the grapevine." Wiggins and his wife raised the capital for their venture from friends and family, and by rendering services in kind, as when Julius, a furrier by trade, offered to custom-make a mink coat for the wife of a press owner, in exchange for one year's worth of printing. *Silent News* was founded in 1969, and it was incorporated as a nonprofit in 1975.

Silent News reaches a diverse audience, from deaf teenagers and elders to hearing professionals in the field of deaf education. Published monthly, *Silent News* covers stories that rarely, if ever, get space in the mainstream press. A sample issue included a front-page story on a deaf man shot dead by police ("second deaf man to be killed by Illinois police in three weeks") together with an editorial ("Why can't police remember deaf people exist?"), efforts to bring "hidden captioning" (captioning not apparent to hearing viewers that appears to deaf people using a special device) to mainstream movie theaters, and a front-page obituary for deaf actor Alan Barwiolek. Editor Tom Willard defines the role of *Silent News:* "to report the news clearly, fairly, and accurately, and then just let our readers do with the knowledge what they will."

Silent News has a circulation of approximately 7,000, with an estimated readership of more than 30,000. It is based in Mount Laurel, New Jersey.

See also Deaf Publications.

"Silent Press"
See Deaf Publications.

Smith v. Robinson
104 S. Ct. 3457 (1984)

The U.S. Supreme Court, in *Smith v. Robinson*, refused to award attorneys' fees to the parents of a disabled child after they had prevailed in a lawsuit against their local school authorities, arguing that Congress had made no provision for such awards through the Education for All Handicapped Children Act of 1975.

Thomas F. Smith III was 8 years old in November 1976, when his parents were told that the Cumberland School Committee would no longer fund his day program in East Providence, Rhode Island. Smith had cerebral palsy "and a variety of physical and emotional handicaps." Citing these "emotional handicaps," the school superintendent determined that Smith's education was not the district's responsibility, but rather that of the Rhode Island State Division of Mental Health, Retardation, and Hospitals. Smith's parents sued, claiming that failure to educate Thomas was a violation of state law, the Education for All Handicapped Children Act of 1975, Section 504 of the Rehabilitation Act of 1973, and the Equal Protection Clause of the Fourteenth Amendment. The U.S. District Court for the District of Rhode Island held that Smith was entitled to a free and appropriate education to be paid for by the local school committee, but the Court of Appeals for the First Circuit denied his parents' award of attorneys' fees.

The Supreme Court ruled on 5 July 1984 that the Smiths were not entitled to legal fees, since Congress had not inserted language allowing such awards into the Education for All Handicapped Children Act. The Court dismissed the Smiths' assertion that they were entitled to attorneys' fees under the regulations for enforcement of Section 504, arguing that "Congress intended the EHA [Education for All Handicapped Children Act of 1975] to be the exclusive avenue through which such a claim can be pursued."

Advocates worried that this decision made the courts inaccessible to low-income families of disabled children, since attorneys were unlikely to take cases without hope of payment. In response, the Handicapped Children's Protection Act of 1986 was enacted to allow the use of Section 504 regulations, with their provision for the award of the prevailing attorneys' fees, in cases of educational discrimination.

See also Education for All Handicapped Children Act of 1975; Section 504 of the Rehabilitation Act of 1973.

Social Security Disability Reform Act of 1984

Congressional concern about the growth of the Social Security Disability Insurance (SSDI) program led to passage of the Social Security Disability Amendments of 1980. The amendments called for a periodic reevaluation of recipients' eligibility, but they did not specify what criteria were to be used to determine whether or not a disabled recipient was able to return to work. Beginning in 1981 under the newly elected Reagan administration, the Social Security Administration (SSA) began a massive review of those receiving SSDI, with almost 500,000 cases reviewed in fiscal year 1982 alone. Almost half of all reviewed cases were "terminated," some 470,000 people in less than three years. In many cases, people with severe and permanent disabilities were informed through the mail that a review board had ruled them completely recovered, without any medical examination or even a personal meeting.

By the end of 1983, more than 90 percent of those terminated had requested a review of the decision, with two-thirds of these winning upon appeal; however, winning an appeal often took more than a year, during which time the disabled individual received no income and was without health insurance. Critics charged that the administration was slashing the disability rolls, regardless of the needs of those receiving benefits, in order to trim the budget. Congressional hearings revealed "an alarming pattern of questionable terminations . . . often without much warning, and in many instances without much evidence that the individual was not disabled." When the federal courts, in several cases, ordered the SSA to cease terminations unless the individual's medical condition had improved, the Reagan administration refused to comply, claiming that "the federal courts do not rule SSA's programs." The media carried stories of severely disabled individuals unjustly terminated by SSA, some of whom, in desperation, committed suicide. A nationwide campaign by disability rights groups, including the Alliance of Social Security Disability Recipients, the Ad Hoc Committee on Social Security Disability, and the Disability Rights Center, urged Congress to address the crisis, while terminated recipients and their families contacted their elected representatives. Disability rights attorneys filed class action lawsuits on behalf of those terminated, while an estimated 40,000 individual lawsuits were filed in the federal courts.

Congress responded with the Social Security Disability Reform Act of 1984. The law requires the SSA to continue benefits to terminated recipients until their appeals are exhausted (if the recipient loses, she or he must then reimburse SSA for money received after termination). Furthermore, decisions about terminations must be made on the "basis of the weight of the evidence" and "without any preconception or presumption as to whether the individual is or is not disabled."

The Social Security Disability Reform Act was approved by Congress on 19 September 1984, with the House voting 402 to 0 and the Senate voting 99 to 0. President Ronald Reagan signed the bill into law on 9 October 1984.

See also Social Security, Social Security Disability Insurance, Supplemental Security Income.

Reference Mezey, Susan Gluck, *No Longer Disabled: The Federal Courts and the Politics of Social Security Disability* (1988).

Social Security, Social Security Disability Insurance (SSDI), Supplemental Security Income (SSI)

The Social Security Act of 1935 created a federal safety net for elderly workers, indigent dependent children, and people who are blind. Although there was discussion of also creating an insurance program for citizens with disabilities other than blindness, at the time such a step was considered too radical. It was not until 1956 that congressional liberals, under the direction of Senate Majority Leader Lyndon B. Johnson (D-TX), were able to pass through Congress a Social Security Disability Insurance (SSDI) system, enlarging the safety net to include workers who become disabled. The measure was opposed by the National Association of Manufacturers, the American Medical Association, and large segments of the insurance industry, who argued it would be too expensive and lead to socialized medicine. As a compromise, legislation was drafted that limited SSDI to those 50 years and older and gave the states authority to determine eligibility. The age threshold was repealed in 1960.

As with both the workers' compensation and vocational rehabilitation programs, disability under SSDI was defined as the inability "to engage in any kind of substantial gainful work." Eligible individuals received a monthly payment dependent on how long they had worked and how much they had contributed in Social Security taxes. Applicants were required to have worked a minimum number of quarters and to have paid into the Social Security trust fund during this time. Those rejected for benefits could appeal to a specially constituted system of federal administrative law judges (ALJs), and ultimately, to the federal courts.

Congress created the Supplemental Security Income (SSI) program in 1972 to extend coverage to those disabled before age 22, who had never been able to work. Unlike Social Security old age insurance or SSDI, SSI applicants were subject to a "needs test," meaning their income and assets had to be below a certain level in order for them to be eligible for benefits. The 1972 amendments also made SSDI recipients eligible for federal Medicare coverage after receiving SSDI benefits for 2 years, while SSI was tied to state-administered

Medicaid programs. SSI took effect on 1 January 1974, and it replaced previous federally subsidized state programs of aid to blind and mentally disabled persons of low income.

SSI contained some provision for people with disabilities seeking to enter the work force and get off the system. A recipient could file a Plan to Achieve Self Support (PASS), allowing them to accumulate more in cash assets than allowed under SSI ($2,000 as of 1996), with the goal of using this money to purchase adaptive equipment that would enable them to work, such as a computer or a wheelchair lift on a van. Many, if not most, recipients, however, remain unwilling to risk losing their medical benefits by attempting to return to or to begin to work, particularly since private health insurers have generally refused to insure people with disabilities or to provide personal assistance services as a part of their coverage (while very few people would be able to earn, through their own efforts, enough money to pay for medical and personal care out of pocket). Attempts have been made to mitigate these disincentives, for example, the Employment Opportunities for Disabled Americans Act of 1986, but these attempts have been of limited success. There have also been periodic revisions of the PASS program, but disability rights advocates charge that such revisions have had more to do with achieving short-term savings and lowering the federal budget deficit than with fostering the financial independence of people with disabilities.

By December 1995, 4,984,467 Americans were receiving total SSI benefits of $2,334,664,000 a month, while 4,185,263 were receiving SSDI benefits totaling $2,853,365,000 a month. Under SSI, as of January 1996, the maximum federal monthly benefit was $470, with a number of states contributing additional benefits. Payments are lower if the recipient has access to other income. Nationwide, in December 1995, the average total SSI benefit, federal and state combined, was $389.47 a month.

In 1996, Congress made several substantial changes in the SSI program, tightening requirements for assistance, despite warnings from advocates that this would end benefits for more than 100,000 disabled children. The new legislation also ended benefits to people with disabilities related to drug and alcohol dependence, and it ended SSI eligibility for legal immigrants. (Legislation passed that year also eliminated the federal guarantee of aid to families with dependent children, included in the original Social Security Act of 1935.)

See also Disincentives; Employment Opportunities for Disabled Americans Act of 1986.

References Berkowitz, Edward D., *Disabled Policy: America's Programs for the Handicapped* (1987); Mezey, Susan Gluck, *No Longer Disabled: The Federal Courts and the Politics of Social Security Disability* (1988).

Society for Disability Studies (SDS)

The Society for Disability Studies (SDS) is a nonprofit scientific and educational organization concerned with the problems of people with disabilities in society. Founded in 1986, it is composed of social scientists, scholars, and disability rights advocates. Its annual meeting is generally held in June, and it features panels and discussions on topics such as history, culture, politics, sexuality, cross-cultural studies, and activism. Among its notable members are Gunnar Dybwad, Paul Longmore, Adrienne Asch, David Pfeiffer, and Hugh Gregory Gallagher. In June 1996, SDS, based at Suffolk University in Boston, assumed responsibility for publishing *Disability Studies Quarterly*, formerly published by sociologist and disability scholar Irving Zola at Brandeis University.

See also Disability Studies Quarterly.

Southeastern Community College v. Davis 99 S. Ct. 2361 (1979)

Southeastern Community College v. Davis was the first U.S. Supreme Court decision regarding Section 504 of the Rehabilitation Act of 1973. The Court ruled on 11 June 1979 that Southeastern Community

College in Whiteville, North Carolina, did not violate the law by refusing to admit Frances B. Davis, a "hearing impaired" woman, into its nursing program. The Court did, however, stipulate that "situations may arise where a refusal to modify an existing program might become unreasonable and discriminatory."

Davis was already a licensed practical nurse (LPN) when she sought to enter the program at Southeastern to become a registered nurse (RN). The school contended that Davis' reliance on lip-reading would prevent her from completing the program and place her patients at risk; therefore, she did not fit the Rehabilitation Act's definition of an "otherwise qualified" person with a disability. The school also stated that Davis would have difficulty finding work even if she did complete the program, though her former employer had expressed willingness to rehire her after her graduation.

In its opinion, the Court rejected the idea that Section 504 required or implied affirmative action for people with disabilities. It ruled that, in order to be covered by the Rehabilitation Act, an individual must meet the program's basic requirements despite their disability and that a program or institution need not make fundamental alterations to facilitate the participation of people with disabilities if these would substantially alter the program's basic character or involve undue financial and administrative burdens. A school could also consider legitimate physical requirements during its admission process. Conversely, it implied that a failure to make reasonable modifications could constitute discrimination and leave the offending institution liable to legal sanction.

The ruling was widely criticized by disability rights activists, not only for its limited conception of Section 504 but also because it was seen as unclear and subject to a wide range of interpretation. Some considered it a major setback. In retrospect, writes Stephen L. Percy (1989), the "decision was reached primarily on the basis of the specific elements of the Southeastern nursing program," and thus it was not as damaging as was first thought. Instead, the concepts it generated—reasonable modification, reasonable accommodation, undue burden—have since become central in disability rights legislation and litigation, including the Americans with Disabilities Act of 1990.

See also Reasonable Accommodation/Reasonable Modification; Section 504 of the Rehabilitation Act of 1973; Undue Hardship/Undue Burden.

References Liachowitz, Claire H., *Disability as a Social Construct: Legislative Roots* (1988); Percy, Stephen L., *Disability, Civil Rights, and Public Policy* (1989); Shrauder, Betsy, and Jeannine Villing, eds., *Proceedings of the Supreme Court Davis Decision: Implications for Higher Education and Physically Disabled Students* (1979).

Special Education
See Education for All Handicapped Children Act of 1975.

Special Olympics
See Sports and Athletics.

Sports and Athletics
Sports and athletic competitions have played an important role in the disability rights movement and have spurred the creation of some of America's largest disability organizations. As well as offering individuals the opportunity to excel, they present to society, and to people with disabilities themselves, an image of disabled people as competitors, achievers, and winners.

Organized sports have been a favorite pastime among deaf people going back at least to the nineteenth century, particularly since many auditorily based activities (music, radio, lectures, plays, movies) are often inaccessible to them. The hand signals that umpires use in baseball and the football huddle originated in the Deaf community. Today, regional and national championships in softball and basketball are organized annually in the United States by the American Athletic Association of the Deaf (AAAD) and its regional affiliates. The AAAD sponsors a national

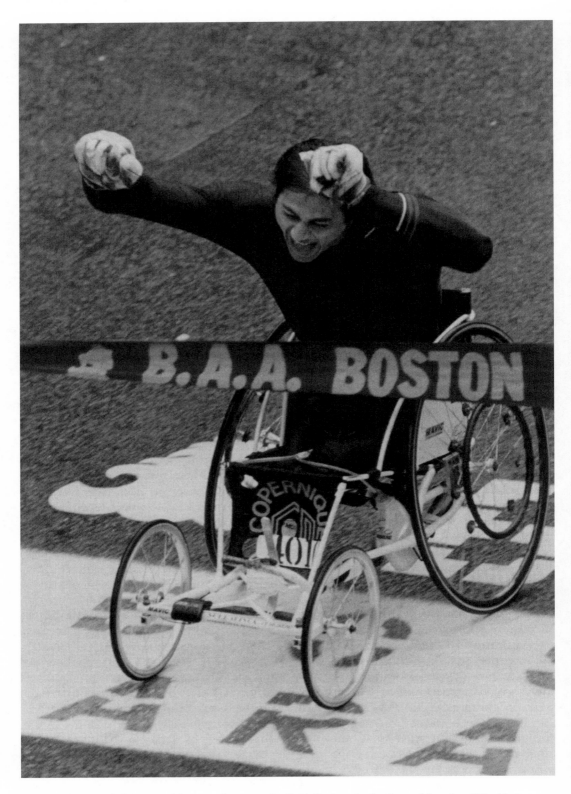

Moussetapha Badid of France celebrates as he crosses the finish line to win the Boston Marathon Wheelchair division.

team of top deaf athletes to compete in the international Silent Games (called colo-quially the Deaf Olympics), held every four years since 1924. Summer and winter competitions include track and field, wrestling, swimming, skiing, skating, etc., and are sponsored by the *Comité Interna-tionale Sports Silencieux* (CISS). National and International chess tournaments are held under the aegis of the International Committee on Deaf Chess.

Athletics for wheelchair users and peo-ple with physical disabilities were first de-veloped as a form of physical and psycho-logical rehabilitation. A U.S. Army film shows disabled veterans, in this case single-leg amputees, playing baseball soon after the end of World War I. Wheelchair archery, table tennis, and javelin throwing were practiced at the Spinal Injuries Cen-tre at the Stoke Mandeville Hospital in England, where wheelchair polo was played as early as 1944. The earliest re-ported wheelchair team sport in the United States was wheelchair basketball, and, depending on the source, the first re-ported game was played by veterans at the Corona Naval Station in California in 1945, or at Cushing Hospital in Framing-ham, Massachusetts, in 1946. Most of these first wheelchair basketball players were veterans, with the Paralyzed Veterans of America (PVA) sponsoring annual tour-naments and the formation of teams in several major cities. The National Wheel-chair Basketball Association was founded by Timothy Nugent at Illinois University in 1949. The National Wheelchair Games in 1957 drew 63 competing teams. Wheel-chair athletes began to compete in other sports, and, in 1956, the National Wheel-chair Athletic Association was founded in New York City, encompassing six federa-tions: (1) air guns; (2) track and field; (3) weightlifting; (4) swimming; (5) table ten-nis; and (6) archery. The first Women's U.S. National Wheelchair Basketball Tournament was held in 1974, as was the first National Wheelchair Marathon.

The next two decades saw an enormous increase in interest in wheelchair and dis-ability sports and athletics. In 1978, George Murray became the first person in a wheelchair to beat the nondisabled win-ner in the Boston Marathon and the first wheelchair athlete to appear on the Wheaties cereal box (after a campaign by Cyndi Jones and other disability rights ac-tivists). David Kiley and his Casa Colina Condors dominated wheelchair basketball in the 1980s, winning five national cham-pionships in seven years. Kiley was not only "the King" of basketball but also a fierce competitor in tennis and racquetball. Susan Hagel in archery; Rick Hansen, Jean Driscoll, Candace Cable-Brooks, George Murray, and Jim Knaub in marathon; Bradley Parks (founder of the National Foundation of Wheelchair Tennis) and Randy Snow in tennis; and Max Rhodes in track and field, all became celebrities.

Athletic competitions bring together people with disabilities from around the world. The 1996 Paralympics Games in Atlanta attracted some 3,500 competitors from 120 nations, along with thousands of spectators, making them among the largest ever gatherings of people with dis-abilities. Competing athletes are not only wheelchair users, but also amputees, dwarfs, and people with sensory disabili-ties. People with cognitive disabilities compete in the Special Olympics, first or-ganized in 1968. In 1991, the Special Olympics introduced the concept of Uni-fied Sports—a program that places ath-letes with mental retardation and their peers without mental retardation on the same team for training and competition—as a way to break down stereotypes about people with cognitive disabilities.

A variety of businesses, some owned and managed by people with disabilities, have grown up around disability sports. These businesses range from the manufacturers of lightweight wheelchairs to publications such as *Sports 'n Spokes* and *Disabled Out-doors*.

The increasing popularity of disability sports has brought an increased competi-tiveness and commercialization. In August 1996, *New Mobility* published allegations of the use of performance-enhancing drugs by athletes at the Atlanta Paralympics. Some criticism has arisen too. Hugh Gallagher has described the paralympics as "the return of the poster kids," while others worry that the focus on star athletes is another form of "super crip." Even so, the numbers of young people in competition continue to grow, with junior programs added to the National Wheelchair Basketball Association and the National Foundation of Wheelchair Tennis. In 1996, the U.S. Cerebral Palsy Athletic Association held its first ever CP Junior Nationals competition.

See also Disabled Sports USA; Fleming, G. Andrew; Jones, Cyndi; Nugent, Timothy J; Paralympics, Paralympic Movement; Paralyzed Veterans of America; Supercrip.

References Maddox, Sam, *Spinal Network: The Total Resource for the Wheelchair Community* (1987); Strohkendl, Horst, *The 50th Anniversary of Wheelchair Basketball* (1996).

Starkloff, Max J. (b. 1937)

Max J. Starkloff became a disability rights activist in 1970, while still a resident of a nursing home. Starting as a single advocate for accessible housing in St. Louis, Starkloff became the founder and president of Paraquad, Inc., and a national leader in the independent living movement.

Starkloff was born on 18 September 1937 in St. Louis, Missouri. He was attending St. Louis University in 1959 when he became quadriplegic as the result of a car accident. Given minimal rehabilitation, Starkloff was sent home to a community without curb-cuts, accessible housing, workplaces, or transportation. Independent living and personal assistance services did not exist. The physical, emotional, and financial burden on his family proved overwhelming, and Starkloff entered a nursing home in 1963. He was 25 years old, confronting, in his own words, "the probability that I'd spend the rest of my life there. . . . The average age at this place was 82 years."

Starkloff soon ran into trouble with the nursing home administration. He learned to paint with a mouthstick, but staff protested that the art books stacked in his window looked messy to people passing by on the street. When Starkloff protested about the food—"meatloaf and mashed potatoes floating in this watery tomato sauce"—he was told he had no right to complain. When he left the facility on a date, he was told he would need "a legal guardian." He was by this time 30 years old.

Starkloff started Paraquad, Inc., a self-help group, in 1970 in an effort to move out of the nursing home. He began by attempting to locate accessible housing and transportation. Finding none, he called meetings of disabled people to discuss the problem. His efforts came to the attention of Morton D. ("Buster") May, a local department store magnate who contributed $5,000 to Starkloff's fledgling organization. Starkloff's efforts resulted, in 1972, in St. Louis' first curb-cuts. In 1971, Starkloff established the St. Louis chapter of the National Paraplegia Foundation, serving as its president from 1971 to 1977.

In 1975, Starkloff married Colleen Kelly, and at the age of 38 he moved out of the nursing home. The two of them dedicated themselves to Paraquad, struggling to keep the organization going with little funding and no paid staff. In 1977, Starkloff was elected to the board of directors of the American Coalition of Citizens with Disabilities and two years later became coordinator of the Missouri Section 504 Conference, at which disabled people were trained in how to obtain their legal rights under the Rehabilitation Act of 1973. In 1979, Paraquad became one of the first ten independent living centers in the country to receive federal funds under Title VII of the Rehabilitation Act; Starkloff served as president and his wife as director of independent living services. Starkloff and Paraquad were largely responsible for St. Louis's purchasing its first lift-equipped buses in 1977. Twenty years later, some 80 percent of the city's buses were accessible to people in wheelchairs. By 1995, Paraquad had more than 20 full-time staff and a budget of $1.2 million, providing independent living services and advocating for enforcement of the Americans with Disabilities Act of 1990.

In 1983, Starkloff was elected president of the National Council on Independent Living, serving three one-year terms. In 1984, he was appointed an official advisor to the National Council on the Handicapped and elected to the board of directors of the Gazette International Networking Institute (G.I.N.I.), the umbrella organization founded by Gini Laurie in St. Louis, Missouri, to disseminate information on independent living and other topics. Starkloff and Paraquad worked with Sen. Thomas Eagleton (D–MO) to reinstate federal funds for independent living centers after they had been cut by the Reagan administration. Starkloff became a member of the board of directors of the World Institute on Disability (WID) in 1990, serving on the institutes's blue ribbon panel on the National Project for Telecommunications Policy. He became co-director of the Institute for Disability Studies, a group he co-founded, in 1995. That year, he was also appointed to the Disability Advisory Council of the Democratic National Committee in Washington, D.C., and elected to the board of directors of the American Association of People with Disabilities.

Starkloff has been the recipient of numerous awards, most notably a 1981 Human Rights Award from the United Nations Association and a 1991 Distinguished Service Award from President George Bush. He lectures widely and is the subject of the 1995 film documentary *Max and the Magic Pill.*

See also American Association of People with Disabilities; American Coalition of Citizens with Disabilities; Independent Living, Independent Living Movement.

Stewart, Jean (b. 1947)

Jean Stewart is the author of *The Body's Memory* (1989), described as "the first real novel for a disability rights movement," and an advocate for disability and human rights. Born on 3 September 1947 in Morristown, New Jersey, Stewart graduated with a B.A. in botany from Drew University in Madison, New Jersey, in 1968. She became disabled after surgeries performed from 1975 to 1978 to remove a tumor from her hip muscle, thought to have been caused by exposure to dioxin-related compounds during her work for a pharmaceutical firm in the late 1960s.

Stewart, already active in the women's and antiwar movements and in farm worker and tenant organizing, began her involvement in the disability rights movement in 1980. In 1981, she edited a special issue of *Sing Out!* magazine on the folk music and culture of people with disabilities, and she was program coordinator for the Clearwater's Great Hudson River Revival, which became an international model for accessible cultural events. In 1984, Stewart founded an independent living center in Poughkeepsie, New York, becoming its first executive director. Stewart's writing has appeared in numerous magazines, literary journals, and newspapers and has been anthologized in several collections: *With Wings: An Anthology of Literature by and about Women with Disabilities* (1987), *Beyond Crisis: Confronting Health Care in the United States* (1984), and *Staring Back: An Anthology of Writers with Disabilities* (1997).

The Body's Memory uses journal entries, letters, poems, and inner monologues, as well as more traditional narrative, to tell the story of the fictional character "Jen's" disability experience. Along the way, the narrator explores everything from how disability changes self-image to the struggles inherent in living independently to faith healers and friends who admonish, "If you convince yourself that you can do it, you'll be off those crutches in six months." Stewart has a keen insight into how their discomfort with disability can alter the behavior of nondisabled people. "With the advent of my wheelchair, much has changed. Many of the men who would have stared when I was using crutches now avert their eyes."

Stewart is the founder of the Disabled Prisoners' Justice Fund, which promotes the rights of prisoners with disabilities. Her work with the fund is chronicled in her most recent book in progress, *Inside Abuse: Disability Oppression Behind Bars*.

See also Deaf Culture; Disability Culture; Perske, Robert.

Reference Stewart, Jean, *The Body's Memory* (1989).

Stokoe, William C.
See American Sign Language; Oral School, Oralism.

Stothers, William G.
See Mainstream: Magazine of the Able-Disabled.

Strachan, Paul A.
See American Federation of the Physically Handicapped; President's Committee on Employment of People with Disabilities.

Sullivan, Anne
See Keller, Helen Adams.

Super Crip
"*Super crip* has been around since the penny newspaper," writes George Covington, who has himself been the subject of several super crip stories. "*Super crip* is a character, usually struck down in the prime of life who fights to overcome insurmountable odds to succeed as a meaningful member of society. Through strength of will, perseverance and hard work, the disabled individual achieves a *normal* life. . . . Too often, the news media treats an individual with disabilities who has attained success in his field or profession as though they were one-of-a-kind. While this one-of-a-kind aspect might make for a better story angle, it perpetuates in the mind of the general public how rare it is for the citizen with disabilities to succeed" (1994).

Another damaging aspect of super crip stories is that they focus entirely on individual effort and willpower, as opposed to group effort and political action. The implicit and sometimes spoken assumption is "If they can do it, why can't you?" and super crip becomes the standard by which all disabled people are judged. Super crip stories rarely describe the architectural, attitudinal, or other barriers put up against people with disabilities in terms of civil or human rights, nor do they acknowledge the need for a disability rights movement to remove those barriers. The disability rights movement eliminates the need for super crip and for disabled people to pretend that they are not disabled.

See also Media Images of People with Disabilities.

Reference Covington, George, "Shattering the Myth of Super Crip," *Home Health Dealer* (March/April 1994).

Supported Employment
Supported employment enables people with disabilities to adapt to the demands of the workplace through the use of a "job coach," who works with the disabled employee and his or her co-workers and employer. Supported employment is almost always funded through the various state offices of vocational rehabilitation, and it is usually, but not always, geared toward people with brain injury and/or cognitive or psychiatric disabilities.

Historically, great numbers of people with such disabilities have always been employed. Prior to the twentieth century, many Americans with disabilities living at home worked in the family business or workshop or on the family farm. Those in state institutions or asylums often worked, without pay, in the gardens and kitchens, in the fields tending livestock, or in workshops weaving fabric and making clothing or other products, which were sold to help support the institution. This all changed in the twentieth century, when the urbanization of American life meant the end of most family farms and when court rulings prohibiting unpaid labor brought an end to the state-institution-for-profit system.

Supported employment was developed in the late 1980s as a response to the evident shortcomings of traditional vocational rehabilitation programs, sheltered workshops in particular. Beginning in the 1970s, the principle of "normalization" led to calls for a movement away from sheltered workshops and toward training for jobs in the real world. One of the first steps in this process was the development of "work crews" or "work stations in industry," where groups of disabled people worked in a mainstream factory or business office with supervisory staff from a state or nonprofit agency. This setup evolved into the placement of disabled people into individual work sites, with a job coach or employment specialist who analyzed the requirements of the job, broke it down into its component tasks, and then trained the person with the disability to do those tasks.

Supported employment and job coaching produced results that came as a surprise to many social service providers. According to supported employment specialists David Hagner and Dale Dileo, human service agencies learned that "their beliefs about the limitations of people with severe disabilities and their need for ongoing professional 'care' and human service supervision have been artificially created." Furthermore, "these beliefs have been fostered by the way services were designed rather than real inherent characteristics of the people being served" (1993). Even supported employment, however, can end up fostering these beliefs about people's limitations. One study, for instance, demonstrated that the more time a work coach spent at a job with a particular client, the more trouble that client would have becoming adjusted to his or her job.

The Rehabilitation Act of 1973 was amended in 1986 so that supported employment could be funded as a "legitimate rehabilitation outcome."

See also Sheltered Workshops; Vocational Rehabilitation.

Reference Hagner, David, and Dale Dileo, *Working Together: Workplace Culture, Supported Employment, and Persons with Disabilities* (1993).

Supported Living

John O'Brien, at Responsive Systems Associates in Lithonia, Georgia, defines supported living as when "a person with a disability who requires long term, publicly funded, organized assistance allies with an agency whose role is to arrange or provide whatever assistance is necessary for the person to live in a decent and secure home of the person's own. . . . Supported living focuses at the scale of individual lives, where there is the best chance of understanding the problems and complexities in each person's situation" (1993).

According to Dennis Heath, co-founder of People First of Oregon, supported living began to catch on in the mid-1980s as the next step in the progression from institutionalization to congregate care to group homes. Supported living stands in contrast to institutionalization and is in many ways its antithesis. Where institutionalization categorizes people by disability, supported living seeks to treat them as individuals. Where institutionalization stresses the incapacity of people with cognitive and developmental disabilities and the need for nondisabled people to control them, supported living assumes that people with disabilities are competent to manage their own lives and to decide how and when they need assistance. Supported living is not living in a group home owned by a social service agency, nor is it living in an agency-controlled apartment. The individuals with the disability control the circumstances of their lives, with assistance as needed from supported living workers.

An important factor in the success of supported living has been people with developmental disabilities organizing to assist each other. People First chapters, for example, have set up People First Welcome Wagons to help individuals in their transition into the community from an institution or nursing or group home.

See also Deinstitutionalization; People First, People First International.

Reference O'Brien, John, *Supported Living: What's the Difference?* (1993).

Mary Switzer, newly appointed administrator of social and rehabilitation service at the Department of Health, Education and Welfare, poses with President Johnson at the White House on 15 August 1967.

Switzer, Mary Elizabeth (1900–1971)

Frank Bowe, in *Handicapping America* (1978), describes Mary Elizabeth Switzer as the one woman who, from 1950 to 1969, "exerted more influence in upgrading the quality of life in America for disabled persons than anyone else in public life." As director of the federal Office of Vocational Rehabilitation (OVR) in Washington, D.C., she oversaw a radical expansion of its programs for people with disabilities. So profound was her influence that OVR became known as "Switzerland," and Switzer has been called one of the "grandmothers" of the independent living movement.

Switzer was born on 16 February 1900 in Newton Falls, Massachusetts. She began working at the federal Treasury Department in 1921, the year she graduated from Radcliffe in Cambridge, Massachusetts. While at the Treasury Department, she

became friends with Tracy Copp, an administrator for the newly established Vocational Rehabilitation program. During this time, Switzer also served as executive secretary of the Women's International League for Peace and Freedom. In 1934, she was appointed assistant to the assistant secretary of the treasury in charge of public service. In 1939, she moved to the Federal Security Agency (forerunner of the Department of Health, Education and Welfare, or HEW). In 1950, she was named the director of the OVR.

Switzer was primarily interested in funding OVR programs that helped people with disabilities become economically self-sufficient. Switzer, along with rehabilitation pioneer Howard Rusk, lobbied Congress for passage of the Vocational Rehabilitation Amendments of 1954, which broadened already existing state/federal programs. The legislation also authorized federal funding to help establish nonprofit and public rehabilitation services. "In one fell swoop," writes Nora Groce, "Mary Switzer was now empowered to fund, in effect, whatever she chose within the field of rehabilitation."

Switzer put this authority to wide use. During the 17 years she headed OVR, she sponsored more than 100 university-based rehabilitation-related training programs serving tens of thousands of people. The OVR budget during this period increased by some 4,000 percent. Among OVR's new clients were people with mental retardation and mental illness, who had previously been all but ignored. In 1967, Switzer became the administrator of the Social and Rehabilitation Service at HEW, making her the highest ranking woman in the federal bureaucracy of the time, ad-ministering an annual budget of approximately $6 billion.

Among many other achievements, Switzer helped write the legislation and then develop the guidelines for establishing the National Technical Institute for the Deaf in Rochester, New York, and was instrumental in the founding of the National Theatre of the Deaf. Switzer won numerous awards for her work and at least 16 honorary degrees, including one from Gallaudet College in Washington, D.C. Switzer retired in 1970, and she died on 17 October 1971.

See also Vocational Rehabilitation.

References Groce, Nora, *The U.S. Role in International Disability Activities: A History and a Look toward the Future* (1992); Walker, Martha Lentz, *Beyond Bureaucracy: Mary Elizabeth Switzer and Rehabilitation* (1985).

T-4

"T-4" was the code name for the Nazi program of extermination of physically and mentally disabled adults in Germany during the early 1940s. It was the culmination of the Nazi notion of *lebunsunwertes Leben*, or "life unworthy of life"—people that Adolf Hitler termed "useless eaters."

An early step in the destruction of Germany's disabled population was the demonization, followed by the forced sterilization, of people with disabilities. A German children's arithmetic text of the time asked "normal" school children to determine how much money could be doled out to healthy newlyweds from the money spent on "the crippled, the criminal, and the insane." Funding for schools and hospitals for people with disabilities was cut, and disabled children were registered with the government. Eventually, more than 30 institutions within Germany, Poland, and Austria became killing centers for disabled children. Estimates of the number of children murdered under this program start at 5,000, but the figure could be much higher. Some of the children were drugged to death, others were starved.

T-4 began in October 1939 with the "Fuhrer decree" granting physicians the authority to administer a "mercy death" to adults with disabilities. According to Robert Jay Lifton, the T-4 program "involved virtually the entire German psychiatric community and related portions of the general medical community" (1986). (The name *T-4* referred to the operation's headquarters address—*Tiergarten* 4, in Berlin.) The murders were carried out by doctors at designated killing centers, most often psychiatric hospitals or nursing homes. Most of the victims were gassed. In one two-week period in 1940, 1,558 mental patients from the German province of East Prussia were murdered in this way. Disabled people and others were also murdered in the concentration camps under another program code named "14f13." It is difficult to determine exactly how many people with disabilities were murdered under the various "euthanasia" programs. The figure often cited is between 90,000 and 100,000, but psychiatrist Frederic Wertham puts the figure at 275,000 for Germany and Austria alone.

T-4 is significant to modern American disability rights activists for a number of reasons. First, much of the "justification" for the program was based on the premises of the British and American eugenics movements. Second, the extermination of people with disabilities was carried out by health care professionals: physicians, nurses, nurses' aides, and most especially psychiatrists and psychiatric social workers. Disability activists see this as a compelling reason for empowering people with disabilities to make decisions about their own lives. Finally, there are still those who call for "mercy killings." Some advocates in the assisted-suicide and right-to-die movements make many of the same assumptions about people with disabilities as the proponents of T-4: that disability is suffering and people with disabilities often need to be "put out of their misery." Of particular concern to writers such as Mary Johnson, Julie Reiskin, Lisa Blumberg, and Steve Mendelsohn is the concept of "wrongful birth"—the notion that existence with a disability is so loathsome as to be not worth living, and thus a physician can be sued for delivering a disabled child. Some disability activists see this as a throwback to *lebunsunwertes Leben*.

See also Ableism; Baby Doe Case; Baby Jane Doe Case; Eugenics; Euthanasia and Assisted Suicide; Forced Sterilization.

References Friedman, Ina, *The Other Victim* (1990); Gallagher, Hugh Gregory, *By Trust Betrayed: Patients, Physicians, and the License To Kill in the Third Reich* (1990); Kuhl, Stefan, *The Nazi Connection: Eugenics, American Racism, and German National Socialism* (1994); Lifton, Robert Jay, *The Nazi Doctors* (1986).

TASH

See Association of Persons with Severe Handicaps.

Task Force on the Rights and Empowerment of Americans with Disabilities

The Task Force on the Rights and Empowerment of Americans with Disabilities was created in May 1988 by Congressman Major R. Owens (D-NY), chair of the House Subcommittee on Select Education, to assist the Congress in its consideration of the Americans with Disabilities Act (ADA). The task force played a crucial role in passage of the ADA. It was chaired by Justin Dart Jr. and co-chaired by Elizabeth M. Boggs, with Lex Frieden as its coordinator. Among its members were the Reverend Wade Blank, Frank Bowe, Donald Galloway, I. King Jordan, Sylvia Walker, and other prominent disability rights activists.

Receiving no public funds, the task force conducted 63 public forums in all 50 states, the District of Columbia, Guam, and Puerto Rico. These and other events were attended by more than 30,000 people with disabilities and their advocates, who provided feedback on the need for an ADA. The task force also organized public hearings before Congress, where people with disabilities testified about their experiences of discrimination and oppression. It collected more than 5,000 documents and tapes detailing the experiences of disabled people, which were also delivered to Congress. The task force met extensively with congressional members and staff, as well as with President Bush, Vice President Quayle, and members of their cabinet.

In its final report, submitted to Congress on 12 October 1990, the task force found that "millions of our citizens with disabilities suffer unconscionable infringement of their human rights." It recommended that the president "provide strong leadership to implement" the recently passed ADA, that "appropriate ADA regulations" be drafted and enforced, and that legislation be passed to negate Supreme Court decisions limiting the rights of people with disabilities, among other recommendations.

See also Americans with Disabilities Act of 1990; Dart, Justin, Jr.

Reference Task Force on the Rights and Empowerment of Americans with Disabilities, *From ADA to Empowerment: The Report of the Task Force on the Rights and Empowerment of Americans with Disabilities* (October 1990).

TDD/TTY

See Telecommunications Devices for the Deaf, Teletypewriters, Text Telephones.

Technology Related Assistance for Individuals with Disabilities Act of 1988 (Tech Act)

The Technology Related Assistance for Individuals with Disabilities Act of 1988 (Tech Act) was signed into law in August 1988 as Pub. Law 100-407. It was then reauthorized in March 1994 as Pub. Law 103-218. It makes federal funds available to the states, territories, and the District of Columbia to assist in developing programs to make assistive technology available to people with disabilities. The Tech Act was passed in response to the fact that many people with disabilities were either unaware of or unable to afford assistive technology that would make them more independent. In addition, there was an apparent widespread lack of cooperation and coordination between the various agencies that funded the development and acquisition of assistive technology.

Some Tech Act programs focus on raising public awareness, others have developed referral systems for people who need information on appropriate technology, still others advise state governments on how they can help to make assistive technology more available to their citizens. All of these programs are required to be "consumer responsive" (the first time this phrase occurs in federal legislation), meaning they must provide a way for people who actually use the technology to have some say in what the programs do.

States must provide assurance to the federal government that they are in compliance with Section 508 of the Rehabilitation Act of 1973 in order to qualify for Tech Act money. Under Section 508 (later revised by Section 509), government offices and subcontractors are required to support accessibility whenever possible when they purchase computers, software, or other information technology.

See also Assistive Technology; Rehabilitation Act of 1973.

Telability Media

Telability Media is a monthly newsletter for people with disabilities who work, want to work, or are interested in mass media. It is published by the National Telability Media Center in Columbia, Missouri. *Telability Media* features articles on such topics as the publication of books by disabled writers, lists of new disability-oriented publications, and announcements of conferences or other events of interest. Founded in 1992 by Charles Winston, the center also publishes *America's Telability Media*, a directory listing magazines, newspapers, newsletters, and professional organizations, as well as journalists, writers, and film and television producers who have disabilities or who focus on disability issues.

See also Media Images of People with Disabilities.

Telecommunications Devices for the Deaf (TDDs), Teletypewriters (TTYs), Text Telephones (TTs)

The invention of the telephone by Alexander Graham Bell in 1876 placed the world's deaf people at a distinct disadvantage. Employment and social opportunities for deaf people, already constrained by

discrimination and language barriers, became even more limited because of the inaccessibility of this widely used means of communication. It was not until the 1960s that advances in technology began to ease this disadvantage.

The inventor of modern telephone systems for deaf people was deaf physicist Robert H. Weitbrecht. During World War II, Weitbrecht had worked on the Manhattan Project to develop the atomic bomb; after the war he designed radar systems for the U.S. Navy and the WWV Radio Time Signal, still in use today. In 1964, he unveiled a device to enable teletypewriter (TTY) messages to be sent over the regular telephone lines. Prior to this invention, teletypewriter messages could only be sent over the vastly more expensive teletypewriter exchange (TWX) system, used by companies such as the Associated Press and the Stock Exchange. Weitbrecht's "acoustic coupler," the forerunner of the computer modem, led to an explosion of telephone use by deaf people, as AT&T agreed to release surplus TTYs to deaf customers through the nonprofit Teletypewriters for the Deaf Distribution Committee, founded by the leaders of the Alexander Graham Bell Association for the Deaf and the National Association of the Deaf. (The organization changed its name to Teletypewriters for the Deaf (TDI) in 1969 and then Telecommunications for the Deaf, Inc., in 1979). These TTYs were bulky, expensive to purchase and install, and could be used only if the other party also had one. Since messages took longer to type than to speak, long distance or toll calls were still prohibitively expensive.

The telecommunications or telephone device for the deaf (TDD) came into use in the 1970s. A TDD produces an electronic readout of the message. It has the advantages of being cheaper and also much more portable than a TTY. A variety of programs came into being to make TDDs more available, allowing for rental and donations of devices, lower toll rates for eligible phone customers, and a change in the federal tax code in 1971 to allow

A telephone receiver rests on top of a TDD. A message appears on a small screen above the keyboard. The ADA has resulted in wider availability of such devices.

their deduction as a medical expense. By 1984, approximately 150,000 TTY and TDD devices were in use throughout the United States, as opposed to a mere 25 TTY stations in 1968. Nevertheless, availability continued to be a problem, and most businesses, and even most hospitals and police stations, did not have TDD or TTY service. The Telecommunications for the Disabled Act of 1982 and the Americans with Disabilities Act of 1990 (ADA) both included requirements for telephone access at important public places. The ADA, in particular, has led to rapid growth in the use of TDDs.

Another response to the problem of telephone access was the development of relay networks, in which a deaf TDD/ TTY user calls a hearing TDD/TTY user, who then relays a message intended for a party at a non-TDD/TTY phone. Deaf communities in many cities established such net-

works. Title IV of the ADA requires that companies providing telephone service make relay services available to TDD/TTY users. Electronic mail (e-mail) offers another avenue of telecommunications access, while the proliferation of facsimile, or "fax," machines has also expanded the ability of deaf people to communicate via the mainstream phone network.

Recently, the use of the term *TTY* has become the norm, and *TDD* has slipped from usage, even though the devices currently in use bear little resemblance to the original teletypewriters. *TDD* is misleading, since not all users are deaf (many can hear but have speech disabilities), while *TTY* is felt to be a more elegant acronym, in both American Sign Language and English, than the more correct alternative *TT* (for text telephone, another name for TDD). A 1995 consumer poll by Telecommunications for the Deaf, Inc., found *TTY* to be the overwhelming favorite.

See also Americans with Disabilities Act of 1990; Telecommunications for the Disabled Act of 1982.

References Moore, Matthew S., and Robert F. Panara, *Great Deaf Americans: The Second Edition* (1996); Van Cleve, John V., ed., *Gallaudet Encyclopedia of Deaf People and Deafness* (1987).

Telecommunications for the Disabled Act of 1982

The Telecommunications for the Disabled Act of 1982, signed into law on 3 January 1983, was written to resolve some of the problems that people who are deaf, hard of hearing, or speech impaired have in using telephones. The act required that the Federal Communications Commission (FCC) establish regulations to ensure reasonable access to the telephone network, and it required that certain telephones considered "essential" be hearing aid–compatible. Essential phones were defined by Congress as pay phones, emergency telephones, and telephones often used by people who are deaf or hard of hearing.

The regulations implemented by the FCC mandated that all coin-operated phones, existing and new, had to be hearing aid–compatible by 1 January 1985.

Credit card phones were also covered by the regulations, unless a hearing aid–compatible coin phone was nearby. New phones in businesses, emergency phones in isolated areas, and phones installed after 1 January 1985 in hospitals, convalescent and nursing homes, prisons, and other public or quasi-public facilities were also required to be hearing aid–accessible, along with 10 percent of all new phones in hotels and motels. Congress also made provision in the act for state subsidies to individuals who needed compatible phones but could not afford them. These subsidies were to be financed from the revenues generated by other telephone services.

The act also addressed the needs of individuals whose disability requires them to use a telecommunications device for the deaf (TDD, but commonly referred to as a TTY). According to a congressional report issued in 1982, an estimated 1.2 million Americans fell into this category. The act and resulting regulations allowed for state subsidization of the production and distribution of such devices, which are much more expensive than standard voice-operated phones.

The act also covered assistive devices for persons who could hear but could not speak. These devices included phones compatible with artificial larynxes and breath activated-telephones, which were to be made available to disabled persons in the same way as TTYs. Also included under the act were telebraille machines for people who are deaf-blind.

The Hearing Aid Compatibility Act of 1988 required that virtually all telephones used in the United States be compatible with hearing aids.

See also Telecommunications Devices for the Deaf (TDDs), Teletypewriters (TTYs), Text Telephones (TT).

Telethons

"I know the courage it takes to get on the court with other cripples and play wheelchair basketball," wrote Jerry Lewis in "If I Had Muscular Dystrophy," published in the 2 September 1990 issue of *Parade* magazine. In an effort to publicize his Muscular Dystrophy Association (MDA) Telethon, Lewis pretended to be writing from the point of view of someone with a disability. "I'd like to play basketball like normal, healthy, vital and energetic people. . . . When I sit back and think more rationally, I realize my life is half, so I must learn to do things halfway. I just have to learn to try to be good at being half a person."

This article infuriated disability rights activists, and it epitomized what they found offensive about telethons. Designed to raise money, telethons play on the audiences' heartstrings, presenting people with disabilities as pathetic, helpless, perpetual children, "Jerry's kids," whose only goal in life is to be cured. People with disabilities, in this vision, are primarily the objects of charity, or, as Jerry Lewis has said on another occasion, "My kids aren't going to the workplace. There's nothing they can do."

"Telethons undermine everything the disability rights movement is trying to accomplish," says Mike Ervin, a former poster child for MDA. He and his sister Cris Matthews, another former poster child, are the founders of Jerry's Orphans, a loosely organized association of activists opposed to the Jerry Lewis MDA Telethon.

The use of poster children to represent various charities began in the 1930s; telethons began in the early 1950s. Historian Hugh Gregory Gallagher, writing in the September 1996 issue of *New Mobility*, describes how, "when it came time to raise funds, the various societies—Crippled Children, Cerebral Palsy, Muscular Dystrophy, Polio—would each choose a child . . . to feature on their posters. . . . It was the job of the poster kids to arouse both love and pity." Over the years, telethons became enormous enterprises, with the Jerry Lewis MDA Telethon, for example, pulling in tens of millions of dollars. Some of the money, audiences were told, was spent on services, but primarily it went to research a cure for the disease or disability in question.

Protests against telethons and the use of poster children began in the 1970s. In

Entertainer Jerry Lewis on the set of his annual muscular dystrophy campaign for cash in 1977. Disability rights activists oppose Lewis's campaigns for presenting disabled people as helpless children in need of charity.

1976 and 1977, Disabled in Action picketed the United Cerebral Palsy Associations telethons in New York, calling them "demeaning and paternalistic shows which celebrate and encourage pity." "The very human desire for cure . . . ," wrote Evan Kemp Jr. in a 1981 editorial in the *New York Times* attacking the Jerry Lewis MDA Telethon, "can never justify a television show that reinforces a stigma against disabled people." Lewis struck back with a public campaign to convince President Bush to fire Kemp from his position as chair of the federal Equal Employment Opportunity Commission. Bush refused.

Ervin sees other problems with telethons, besides their defamatory depictions of people with disabilities. "They give the public the idea that everything is taken care of, that there's no need to worry about discrimination or civil rights or social services, because 'those people' have 'their charities' to take care of them. We've never had a national discussion about who

should be providing services, who should be funding research." Telethons and charities in fact provide only a small fraction of the services delivered to people with disabilities, and much of the money that is raised, according to Ervin and others, goes not into research or services, but into further fund-raising and administration.

Jerry's Orphans, founded in response to the *Parade* article, held its first antitelethon demonstration in 1991. Every Labor Day Weekend since then, activists have picketed the Jerry Lewis MDA Telethon and local stations carrying the program.

See also Kemp, Evan, Jr.

Reference Kemp, Evan, "Aiding the Disabled: No Pity Please," *New York Times* (3 September 1981); Lewis, Jerry, "If I Had Muscular Dystrophy," *Parade* (2 September 1990); Shaw, Barrett, ed., *The Ragged Edge: The Disability Experience from the Pages of the First Fifteen Years of* The Disability Rag (1994).

Television Decoder Circuitry Act of 1990

See Captioning/Closed Captioning.

TenBroek, Jacobus (1911–1968)

Jacobus tenBroek was the principal founder of the National Federation of the Blind (NFB) and president for most of its first 28 years. His espousal of self-determination for blind people remains an important influence on the contemporary blindness and disability rights movements. He was one of the first to frame the disability experience as a civil rights issue, drawing an analogy between discrimination against people with disabilities and oppressed workers and minorities.

TenBroek was born on 6 July 1911 in Alberta, Canada. As a child, he lost the sight of one eye at age 7, his vision in the other eye deteriorated until he was totally blind by age 14. His family moved to the United States in 1919 and then to Berkeley so tenBroek could attend the California School for the Blind. TenBroek received an A.B. in 1934, an M.A. in 1935, an LL.B. in 1938, and a doctorate in law in 1940, all from the University of California at Berkeley. In 1940, he was also a Brandeis Research Fellow at the Harvard Law School and a member of the faculty at the University of Chicago Law School. He returned to Berkeley in 1942 to teach at the University of California, becoming a full professor in 1953 and the chair of the speech department two years later. His book *Prejudice, War, and the Constitution* (with Floyd W. Matson) received the American Political Science Association's Woodrow Wilson Award as the best book published in 1955 on government and democracy. His other books include *The Antislavery Origins of the Fourteenth Amendment* (1951, reprinted ten years later as *Equal Under Law*), *Hope Deferred: Public Welfare and the Blind* (also with Matson, 1959), and *California's Dual System of Family Law* (1964). In 1963, he became a professor of political science at Berkeley. TenBroek was also the author of scores of articles on political science, government, law, blindness, and the rights of blind people in the United States, and he was a fellow at both the Center for Advanced Study in the Behavioral Sciences and the Guggenheim Foundation. He was appointed in 1950 to the California State Board of Social Welfare and was its chair from 1960 until 1963. He became a member of the President's Committee on Employment of the Physically Handicapped in 1950.

By 1934, tenBroek had co-founded the California Council of the Blind, which later became the National Federation of the Blind of California. In 1940, tenBroek, his wife, Hazel, and a small group of others founded the NFB at a meeting in Wilkes-Barre, Pennsylvania. Over the next two and a half decades, tenBroek, as president, leader, and then "elder-statesman," was instrumental in building the NFB into the largest national political organization in the United States made up of people who are blind and visually disabled. TenBroek was president of the NFB from 1940 to 1961 and from 1966 to 1968.

In his books, essays, and speeches, tenBroek debunked the common stereotypes that blind people are intellectually, psychologically, or morally inferior to people with sight. (That this notion is still prevalent can be seen as recently as 1995, when a writer for the *American Spectator* magazine protested the absurdity of allowing blind people to serve on juries). The blind as a group, tenBroek insisted, "are mentally competent, psychologically stable, and socially adaptable. . . . Their needs are therefore those of ordinary people, of normal men and women, caught at a physical and social disadvantage. This proposition implies that the blind, like other persons, have a need for shelter but not a need to be sheltered: a need for adjustment and acceptance but not a need for toleration and patronage. More specifically, it affirms the capacity of the blind for self-reliance and self-determination—for full participation in the affairs of society and active competition in the regular channels of economic opportunity" (TenBroek and Matson 1959).

TenBroek died on 27 March 1968 in California and was eulogized as the "leader, mentor, spokesman, and philosopher" of America's organized blind community.

See also National Federation of the Blind; Sheltered Workshops; Vocational Rehabilitation.

References Matson, Floyd W., *Walking Alone and Marching Together: A History of the Organized Blind Movement in the United States, 1940–1990* (1990); TenBroek, Jacobus, and Floyd W. Matson, *Hope Deferred: Public Welfare and the Blind* (1959).

Thomas, Stephanie K. (b. 1957)

Stephanie K. Thomas is a founding member of American Disabled for Attendant Programs Today (ADAPT) of Texas, an organizer or participant in every national ADAPT action since 1985, and an editor of *Incitement*, the national ADAPT newsletter. She was an advocate for passage of the Americans with Disabilities Act of 1990 (ADA), working to ensure that it included a firm and timely commitment to accessible mainline bus service.

Thomas was born on 21 August 1957 in New York City, and she received her B.A. in folklore and anthropology from Harvard-Radcliffe College in Cambridge, Massachusetts, in 1980. She became a peer counselor and housing rights advocate at the Endependence Center of Northern Virginia in 1982, the independent living coordinator at the El Paso Center for the Handicapped (now the Disability Awareness Resource Environment) from 1982 to 1983, and the community outreach coordinator at the Austin Center for Independent Living from 1983 to 1985. In 1984, she co-founded the E-Z-J Ranch in Nacogdoches, Texas, for children with disabilities and was a counselor there until 1987. From 1985 to 1988 she was executive director of the Coalition of Texans with Disabilities. Since 1989, she has been self-employed as a consultant on disability rights.

Thomas' most visible work has been with ADAPT. Consistent with ADAPT's philosophy, Thomas favors the use of civil disobedience and public demonstrations, as well as outreach to the poorest and most oppressed in the disability community, particularly those incarcerated in nursing homes. Thomas was a member of the National Lawyer's Guild Disability Rights Task Force (1989–1990) and a board member of Central Texas Legal Services (1990–1996, and board chair 1993–1994). She has participated in numerous other organizations, including the Austin Mayor's Committee for Disabled Persons (1983–1985) and the Texas Transition Task Force (1986–1988, 1990–present). Since 1984, she has been an associate member of the Texas Paralyzed Veterans Association.

See also American Disabled for Attendant Programs Today; Public Transportation.

Thompson, Karen

See Kowalski, Sharon, and Karen Thompson.

Thornburgh, Ginny (b. 1940), and Richard Thornburgh (b. 1932)

Ginny Thornburgh is the director of the Religion and Disability Program of the National Organization on Disability in Washington, D.C. She is the co-author of *That All May Worship* (1992), a guide to breaking down architectural, communication, and attitudinal barriers in churches and synagogues. She is the author of *From Barriers to Bridges* (1996), a guide to community action, and editor of *Loving Justice: The ADA and the Religious Community* (1994). She was born on 7 January 1940 in New York City. She has an undergraduate degree in philosophy and religion from Wheaton College in Norton, Massachusetts, and a masters in education from Harvard. Thornburgh began her advocacy in the 1960s on behalf of her son Peter, brain injured in a car accident, and as a member of the Pennsylvania Association for Retarded Citizens. She was the coordinator of programs for persons with disabilities at Harvard University from 1988 to 1989. In 1992, she and her husband, former U.S. Attorney General Richard Thornburgh, were featured speakers at the Vatican Conference on Disability and at the Eastern European Conference on Disabilities, held in Prague.

Richard Thornburgh was born on 16 July 1932 in Rosslyn Farms, Pennsylvania. He graduated from Yale University with a degree in engineering in 1954 and from the University of Pennsylvania School of Law in 1957. He served two terms as governor of Pennsylvania (1978–1986), and he was appointed U.S. attorney general by President Ronald Reagan in 1988. Thornburgh's appointment meant that the nation's highest law enforcement official, and a member of the cabinet, was the parent of a disabled child and the husband of a disability rights advocate, and he had personal experience with the oppression faced by people with disabilities. Thornburgh thus played a key role in passage of the ADA, along with other highly placed disability rights allies such as Madeleine C. Will and Boyden Gray.

See also Americans with Disabilities Act of 1990; The Arc; National Organization on Disability; Religion and Disability.

Tiny Tim

To call someone with a disability a "Tiny Tim" is roughly equivalent to calling an African American an "Uncle Tom." The connotation is of someone who is eager to please the nondisabled people in his or her life, or mainstream society in general, by ignoring slights to his or her rights and dignity and acting the part of the cheerful "handicapped" person, grateful for any crumbs. The term comes from the Charles Dickens story *A Christmas Carol* (1843), in which Tiny Tim is a saintlike, but pathetic, disabled child who asks God to "bless us, everyone." Billy Golfus quotes this story in his documentary *When Billy Broke His Head and Other Tales of Wonder* (1995), and the term has been used in the *Disability Rag & Resource* and elsewhere.

See also Media Images of People with Disabilities.

Total Communication

Historian Jack R. Gannon (1981) cites Margaret S. Kent's definition of Total Communication as "the right of every deaf child to learn to use all forms of communication so that he may have full opportunity to develop language competence at the earliest possible age." Kent was principal of the Maryland School for the Deaf in Frederick in the early 1970s, when that school became probably the first residential school to adapt Total Communication as its official teaching method. First popularized when oralism—the teaching of speech and lip-reading to the exclusion of signing—was still the predominant method of deaf education, Total Communication represented an important step toward the reacceptance of sign language as a way to instruct deaf and hard-of-hearing people.

Dorothy Shifflett, a public school teacher in California, developed what she called the "Total Approach" after becoming dissatisfied with her own daughter's experience with oralism. Beginning in the early 1960s, she persuaded the parents and teachers of deaf students in the Anaheim Union High School District to learn and teach sign and fingerspelling, as well as speech and lip-reading, in what was a reversion to Edward Miner Gallaudet's "Combined Method" of the 1860s. In addition, deaf students were integrated with hearing children during recess, gym, lunch, and occasional classes. Shifflett also urged hiring a deaf teacher to teach deaf students at a public day school.

The phrase *Total Communication* was coined by Roy Holcomb, supervisor of the program for deaf students at the James Madison Elementary School in Santa Ana, California. By 1968, the school's Total Communication program included 34 deaf children ages 3 to 12. Holcomb, deaf himself, was impressed with his students' progress, and he began publicizing his results. His efforts earned him the reputation as "the Father of Total Communication," as well as a letter from the California State Credentials Department threatening to revoke his teacher's license because of his disability. Holcomb, however, kept his teacher's license, lectured widely on Total Communication, and received numerous awards for his work educating deaf children.

More recently, some Deaf activists have criticized the way Total Communication has been implemented. Ben Bahan, for example, labels "TC" a compromise that "usually means talking and signing at the same time," leading to confusion among deaf students. Instead, Bahan and others advocate "bilingualism," where American Sign Language is used as the classroom's spoken language, while reading and writing are used to teach students English.

See also American Sign Language; Oral School, Oralism.

References Bahan, Ben, "Total Communication: A Total Farce," in Sherman Wilcox, ed., *American Deaf Culture* (1989); Gannon, Jack R., *Deaf Heritage: A Narrative History of Deaf America* (1981).

Transbus

The Transbus was a revolutionary concept in U.S. mass transit: a bus designed with a wide body, low floor, and retractable ramp and touted as easy to maintain, energy efficient, and accessible to people with disabilities. The project was designed by engineers in the private sector, with $27 million in grants from the federal government. By 1973, there were three prototypes for Transbus, created by General Motors (GM), the Flxible Company, and AM General. Although federal funding for the project was terminated in 1976, disability activists hoped that the prototype developed by GM would soon be ready for mass production.

On 17 June 1976, a coalition called the Transbus Group, led by Disabled in Action (DIA) of Pennsylvania and represented by the Public Interest Law Center of Philadelphia, filed a class action suit in federal court on behalf of all disabled Americans denied access to mass transit systems receiving federal funds. Among the organizations in the group were the American Coalition of Citizens with Disabilities (ACCD), United Cerebral Palsy Associations, the National Association of the Deaf, and both the American Council of the Blind and the National Federation of the Blind. The lawsuit, *Disabled in Action of Pennsylvania, Inc. v. Coleman* (1978), asserted that various federal laws, including Section 504 of the Rehabilitation Act of 1973, required that mass transit systems be accessible. The group asked that the court order the secretary of transportation under the Ford administration, William T. Coleman Jr., to require transit authorities to purchase only buses built to Transbus specifications as they retired their older, inaccessible models. Coleman was replaced in 1977 by Brock Adams under the newly elected Carter administration. In May of that year, Adams mandated that all future public bus purchases meet Transbus specifications. Although the federal court therefore dismissed the DIA lawsuit as moot, the secretary's decision was seen as a major victory for advocates of accessible mass transit.

GM soon announced, however, that it would not go forward with production of the new bus, nor would any of the other major manufacturers. They cited the expense of retooling their factories and problems with the Transbus rear aisle design. Frank Bowe, with the ACCD, then convinced the DeLorean Motor Company to manufacture Transbus, and DeLorean representatives demonstrated their prototype to Congress and the American Public Transit Association (APTA). The DeLorean Company, however, for reasons unrelated to the project, declared bankruptcy a short time later, and transit authorities, reluctant to comply with the new mandate, protested that they could not buy vehicles that manufacturers refused to produce.

"Without Transbus," wrote Bowe (1986), "the guts of the regulation [requiring accessible mass transit] were gone." Furthermore, the loss of Transbus seemed to embolden opponents of accessible transportation. APTA filed suit on behalf of transit operators against the Department of Transportation (DOT), arguing that the agency had overstepped its authority by requiring that mass transit be made accessible. In 1981, a federal appeals court ruled in APTA's favor, and the DOT scaled back its regulations so as to require only that transit authorities make "special efforts" to be accessible.

Title II of the Americans with Disabilities Act of 1990 prohibits discrimination in public mass transit, and transit authorities are now required to purchase wheelchair accessible vehicles when they order new buses. American bus manufacturers, abandoning the Transbus design, have begun producing old-style buses with mechanical lifts added during manufacture. Consumers complain that these lifts, as opposed to the Transbus ramps, are prone to breakdowns and remain difficult for many people to use.

See also American Coalition of Citizens with Disabilities; Disabled in Action; Public Transportation.

References Bowe, Frank G., *Handicapping America: Barriers to Disabled People* (1978); Burgdorf, Robert L., Jr., *The Legal Rights of Handicapped Persons: Cases, Materials, and Text* (1980).

Traynor v. Turnage (1988) and *McKelvey v. Turnage* 108 S. Ct. 1372 (1988)

The U.S. Supreme Court, in *Traynor v. Turnage* and in *McKelvey v. Turnage*, upheld a Veterans Administration regulation defining primary alcoholism as, in all cases, caused by an individual's "willful misconduct." It ruled that veterans with alcoholism not caused by an underlying psychological disability were not protected under Section 504 of the Rehabilitation Act of 1973.

Eugene Traynor began drinking as a child; James P. McKelvey was alcohol dependent by the time he was 13. Both men entered the U.S. military and received honorable discharges, McKelvey in 1966, Traynor in 1969 after serving in Vietnam. After being discharged, both men were hospitalized on several occasions for alcoholism or alcoholism-related illness. Both men stopped drinking and decided to resume their college educations. They applied for assistance under the Veterans' Readjustment Benefit Act (or G.I. Bill) of 1966, only to learn that veterans were ineligible for benefits ten years after their discharge, a limit both Traynor and McKelvey had passed. There was, however, an exception for veterans who could not avail themselves of assistance within the required time because of a disability. Traynor and McKelvey applied for this extension, arguing that their alcoholism was a disability. Their applications were denied. Both men filed suit. Both prevailed at the federal district court level, and both claims were rejected at the appellate level. The two cases were combined and argued before the U.S. Supreme Court on 7 December 1987.

The Supreme Court decided, on 20 April 1988, that the Veterans Administration ruling did not violate Section 504 of the Rehabilitation Act. Justice White, writing for the majority, found that there "is no inconsistency between Section 504 and a conclusive presumption that alcoholism not motivated by mental illness is necessarily 'willful.'" The decision was a major setback for people with alcoholism hoping to avail themselves of protection under Section 504.

See also Section 504 of the Rehabilitation Act of 1973.

Twitch and Shout

Tourette syndrome (TS) is a genetic disorder characterized by involuntary, often bizarre movements, uncontrolled and sometimes obscene vocalizations, and a variety of compulsions. People with TS not only have to contend with their disorder, but they also have to deal with the reactions of people around them, who often conclude that they are drunk, on drugs, or emotionally disabled.

Produced and directed by Laurel Chiten, and narrated by Lowell Handler, *Twitch and Shout* offers a look at the day-to-day lives of people with Tourette syndrome. Among those profiled are a professional basketball player, an artist, an actress, and a Mennonite lumberjack. The film was completed in 1994 and broadcast nationally on the PBS series "Point of View" in 1995. It received awards at the 1995 San Francisco International Film Festival and the New England Film and Video Festival. It also received the CINE Golden Eagle and other awards.

Undue Hardship
Undue Burden

Under the Americans with Disabilities Act of 1990 (ADA), employers are required to make "reasonable accommodation" in order to enable people with disabilities to gain or continue their jobs, presuming they are otherwise qualified. An accommodation, however, is not considered reasonable if it creates an "undue hardship" for the employer. Undue hardship is determined by the employer on a case-by-case basis. It is defined by the act as "an action requiring significant difficulty or expense, when considered in light of the factors set forth. . . ." Among these factors are the nature and net cost of the accommodation, the number of persons employed, the overall financial resources of the employer, and the type of operation or operations of the employer. An accommodation that is an undue hardship for one employer may not be an undue hardship for another, or even for that same employer at another time. For example, if a medium-sized computer company employs a deaf computer programmer, it may not be an undue hardship for it to hire a sign language interpreter to assist the programmer in conversations with co-workers; however, if a deaf individual applies for a job at a small restaurant, a full-time sign language interpreter might well be an undue hardship. Disagreements over what constitutes a reasonable accommodation or an undue hardship, along with other complaints by disabled employees or potential employees, are handled by the federal Equal Employment Opportunity Commission (EEOC). Suits can also be filed in the federal courts.

Undue burden is defined in terms almost identical to undue hardship, but relates to public accommodations and services as opposed to employment. It is defined in Department of Justice regulations as an action requiring "significant difficulty or expense."

See also Americans with Disabilities Act of 1990; Reasonable Accommodation/ Reasonable Modification; Section 504 of the Rehabilitation Act of 1973.

Reference Golden, Marilyn, Linda Kilb, and Arlene Mayerson, *The Americans with Disabilities Act: An Implementation Guide* (1991).

Unified Sports
See Sports and Athletics.

United Cerebral Palsy Associations, Inc. (UCPA)

The beginnings of United Cerebral Palsy Associations, Inc. (UCPA) can be traced to New York City in January 1946, when a group of parents met to discuss their experiences raising children with cerebral palsy (CP). Among their first actions was to place an ad in the *New York Herald Tribune*, hoping to hear from other parents who shared their situation. The ad drew some 350 responses, and it led to the formation of the Cerebral Palsy Society of New York City on 13 September 1946. Other parents' groups sprang up across the state, and these groups joined together in June 1946 to form the New York State Association for Cerebral Palsy. The New York City group (renamed United Cerebral Palsy of New York City in 1952) spearheaded an effort to form a national organization, and the National Foundation for Cerebral Palsy was chartered on 12 August 1949. In 1950, the name was changed to United Cerebral Palsy Associations, Inc. Today, UCPA describes itself as "the country's number one voluntary health organization for people with disabilities."

The situation for people with CP in the 1940s resembled that of people with cognitive disabilities. Indeed, physicians routinely misdiagnosed CP as a form of mental retardation. Little research had been done on what CP was or how it might be treated. Marie Killilea, in her memoir *Karen* (1952), describes how after the birth of her daughter the family pediatrician said, "I don't believe that cerebral palsy children have any mentality." Physicians uniformly recommended that children with CP be institutionalized in massive, inhumane state "schools," while society encouraged parents to view their disabled children as a source of shame. Doctors and dentists often refused to treat children with CP. Those children who were not institutionalized were often denied access to public schools.

Among UCPA's first priorities then were medical care and education. UCPA also undertook to educate the public, began a campaign for legislation to establish and fund programs such as respite care and special education, and tried to stimulate research into the causes, treatment, and prevention of CP. In 1950, it held its first telethon, called Celebrity Pride, in Chicago, both to raise money and to promote public awareness. Killilea's *Karen* was published in 1952, becoming a best-seller and bringing CP and UCPA to the attention of millions. The United Cerebral Palsy Research and Educational Foundation was established in 1955, and, in 1956, UCPA spearheaded the planning of a Joint National Conference on Vocational Guidance of the Neurologically Disabled.

By 1964, there were some 324 UCPA affiliates across the country. In 1969, research funded by UCPA led to the development of a vaccine for the rubella (German measles) virus. That same year, *Word from Washington* was created to inform affiliates of developments in Congress. This national newsletter would serve as an important source of information for advocates on the progress of the Rehabilitation Act of 1973 and the Education for All Handicapped Children Act of 1975. Perhaps inspired by the successes of the Association for Retarded Children (ARC) in cases such as *PARC v. Pennsylvania* (1972), UCPA reversed its long-standing policy of avoiding litigation and established a Legal Advocacy Committee in 1975. It also became involved in the issue of housing, co-sponsoring, with the federal Department of Housing and Urban Development, a 1983 workshop for architects on accessible design. Also in the 1980s, UCPA worked with the Consortium for Citizens with Disabilities and other organizations to pass the Americans with Disabilities Act of 1990.

UCPA has been a leader in advocating for disability rights legislation. Through *Word from Washington* and other publications, and its lobbying at the federal level, UCPA continues to push for greater access for people with disabilities to telecommunications and education technology, housing, supported living, inclusive education, and medical care. UCPA has also opposed damaging changes in the children's Supplemental Security Income program and other federal and state programs that serve people with disabilities and their families.

UCPA is a nonprofit organization, with headquarters in Washington, D.C.

See also The Arc; Kemp, John D.; Parents' Movement; Telethons.

Reference Killilea, Marie, *Karen* (1952).

Universal Design

Universal design is a phrase coined by architect Ronald L. Mace, a longtime advocate of architectural and product accessibility. Using universal design, architects plan buildings and designers design products that work for everyone, whatever their abilities. This is in contrast to retrofitting buildings for access, or designing special products for use only by people with disabilities.

Examples of universal product design would be large-button phones or lamps that can be turned on and off simply by touching the base, rather than twisting a knob or flicking a switch. Such design is more convenient for everyone, including children, elderly people, and people with disabilities. Another example would be the use of door lever handles, rather than door knobs. Lever handles are more easily used by people in wheelchairs and by people with limited use of their hands, whether caused by a disability or by carrying a bag of groceries. In Europe, lever handles are not considered a special accommodation, but are used universally. Similarly, level entries into homes and offices make it easier to enter and exit and to move furniture, equipment, and appliances for everyone, not just people in wheelchairs. If all houses and apartments were built using universal design, people would be less likely to be forced into nursing homes or institutions once they become older or acquire a disability.

Proponents of universal design maintain it is, in general, only minimally more expensive than the inaccessible building and product designs that are in standard use today. Eleanor Smith, an architect with Concrete Change in Atlanta, uses the term *visitability* to describe homes where people with disabilities can at least visit their nondisabled friends. Smith estimates that the additional cost of building a new home so that it is "visitable" ranges from "zero up to $200." Visitability is important in that, if the only homes that are accessible are those where people with disabilities actually live, then disabled people are still shut out of the rest of the community. Smith calls this "segregation imposed by architecture."

Mace, Smith, and other advocates have had some success convincing mainstream architects, builders, and manufacturers to adopt universal design. Nevertheless, the vast majority of structures and products are still designed as if everyone using them will always be young, agile, and nondisabled.

See also Architectural Access; Barrier Free Environments; Center for Universal Design; Concrete Change; Housing; Mace, Ronald L.

University of Illinois at Urbana-Champaign
See Nugent, Timothy J.

Unzicker, Rae E. (b. 1948)
Rae E. Unzicker is a leading activist in the psychiatric survivor movement. A princi-

pal organizer of the National Association of Psychiatric Survivors, she is the first "out of the closet psychiatric survivor" to be appointed to the National Council on Disability.

"To be a mental patient," she once said, "is to have everyone controlling your life but you."

Unzicker was born on 20 August 1948 in Monett, Maryland, but she spent her childhood in Kansas. At age 7, she "went into an altered state of consciousness," brought on, she believes, by her chaotic and abusive home life. Her first experience with the mental health system came when, at age 14, she was diagnosed as schizophrenic and catatonic. Her doctor recommended that she be institutionalized. She spent the next 12 years in the mental health system, including time in at least five mental hospitals and treatment by 19 psychiatrists. "I was subjected to every type of drug, every type of treatment, except for shock therapy," including weeks in "seclusion."

Her political education began in 1978, when she read Judi Chamberlin's book *On Our Own* (1978) and her first copies of *Madness Network News*. Living by this time in Sioux Falls, South Dakota, Unzicker began attending conferences on alternatives to the mental health system. After appearing as "an ex-mental patient" on the "Phil Donahue" show, Unzicker received hundreds of phone calls from other psychiatric survivors. Together with Chamberlin and others, she organized the National Association of Psychiatric Survivors in 1985, serving as its national coordinator until 1993. In the 1970s and 1980s, she and her husband provided emergency shelter to hundreds of mentally ill people in Sioux Falls, letting them stay in their home during times of crisis.

In April 1995, the U.S. Senate confirmed her appointment by President Clinton to the National Council on Disability. Her appointment was delayed when, because of her status as "an ex-mental patient," the F.B.I. was required to do an extensive background check, costing the government some $25,000. "My FBI agent and I wound up being good buddies, and I passed with no problems, but it caused them a lot of work."

Unzicker earned a journalism degree in 1967 from the University of Kansas in Lawrence and has worked as the general manager of a family-owned film company and in advertising. In 1982, she founded her own consulting firm, based in Sioux Falls.

See also Chamberlin, Judi; Psychiatric Survivor Movement.

References Chamberlin, Judi, *On Our Own* (1978); Grobe, Jeanine, ed., *Beyond Bedlam: Contemporary Women Psychiatric Survivors Speak Out* (1995).

Urban Mass Transportation Assistance Act of 1970

The Urban Mass Transportation Assistance Act of 1970 declared it "a national policy that elderly and handicapped persons have the same right as other persons to utilize mass transportation facilities and services." The act amended the Urban Mass Transportation Act of 1964 and required that "special efforts shall be made in the planning and design" of mass transit systems so that "the availability to elderly and handicapped persons of mass transportation which they can effectively utilize will be assured; and that all Federal pro-

grams offering assistance in the field of mass transportation . . . should contain provisions implementing this policy."

Passage of the law had, however, little impact in terms of increasing access to mass transit. Disability law scholar Robert Burgdorf Jr. noted how its vagueness, "coupled with the lack of specific enforcement mechanism, has generated a great deal of confusion among the courts that have attempted to apply it to specific fact situations." In *Snowden v. Birmingham-Jefferson County Transit Authority* (1977), for example, transit officials were deemed to have met the requirements of the law by providing "features such as stanchions, grab-rails, step-well lighting, power-assisted doors, etc., to aid handicapped persons *other than those confined to wheelchairs* in boarding and alighting from its buses" (emphasis added). In July 1989, the U.S. Court of Appeals for the Third District in *ADAPT v. Skinner* (1989) rejected the argument that the Urban Mass Transportation Assistance Act required the use of wheelchair accessible vehicles throughout a transit system.

See also ADAPT v. Skinner; Paratransit; Public Transportation.

Reference Burgdorf, Robert L., Jr., ed., *The Legal Rights of Handicapped Persons: Cases, Materials, and Text* (1980).

Veteran Reserve Corps (VRC)

Formed during the American Civil War, the Veteran Reserve Corps (VRC) was comprised of soldiers moderately to severely disabled in combat or as a result of illness or accident sustained while in service to the Union army. By 1865, the VRC had grown to 762 commissioned officers and 29,852 enlisted men, at least twice as large as the entire U.S. Army before the war. Its men guarded tens of thousands of Confederate POWs, helped repress antidraft and antiblack riots in New York and other cities, formed the honor guard for Lincoln's appearance at Gettysburg, and defended railroads and depots throughout the occupied South.

Soldiers in the VRC became disability rights advocates when they protested that their uniforms—a lighter shade of blue than those of other units—set them apart from their nondisabled comrades. They also took offense at their unit's original name—the Invalid Corps. One Union officer wrote that the "men frequently begged to be sent back to their old regiment in the field rather than remain in garrison at the price of being called invalids." Because of this pressure by its members, the name of the unit was officially changed on 18 March 1864 to the Veterans Reserve Corps.

Although it was not intended that units of the VRC see combat, several regiments did find themselves in battle. The Eighteenth Regiment of the Second Battalion was attacked by Wade Hampton's Confederate raiders in the spring of 1864. (When asked if his men would "stand," the regiment's commanding officer told his superior, "My men are cripples and they can't run.") On 11 July 1864, units of the VRC helped to defend Washington, D.C., from attack by 15,000 Confederate soldiers.

U.S. Provost Marshal General James B. Fry wrote in his report in the summer of 1865 that "the corps was in performance of duties which would otherwise have been necessarily performed by as great a number of able-bodied troops detached from the armies in the field. Its career has been one of usefulness as well as honor." After the war, several of the VRC officers remained in the South and joined the Freedman's Bureau, working to improve conditions for recently emancipated slaves.

See also Disabled American Veterans; Paralyzed Veterans of America.

References Catton, Bruce, *A Stillness at Appomattox* (1953); *War of the Rebellion: A Compilation of the Official Records of the Union and Confederate Armies*, Series 3, Vol. V (1902).

Viscardi, Henry, Jr. (b. 1912)

Henry Viscardi Jr. was an early pioneer fighting to break down the barriers faced by people with physical disabilities wanting to work. In 1952, he wrote about the necessity to get employers "thinking along the lines of *ability* rather than *disability*," stating, "All of us are physically limited. It is just a matter of degree."

Viscardi was the child of Italian immigrants in New York City. Born without legs on 10 May 1912, he spent much of his early childhood at New York's Hospital for Deformities and Joint Diseases. After leaving the hospital, Viscardi was enrolled in the public schools—after strenuous objections from school officials—getting around in a children's wagon or on orthopedic shoes fitted over his stumps. (He was forbidden to use the school's front entrance and also denied classes in music and science). In high school, Viscardi was an honors student and a basketball referee. Enrolling at Fordham University in the Bronx, New York, his first hope was to become a Catholic priest, but he was told that the priesthood was not open to people with disabilities. Again an excellent student, lack of money forced Viscardi to leave Fordham before graduating. Discriminated against because of his disability, he finally found work as a clerk in a law office, where he began to consider a career as an attorney.

At age 27, Viscardi learned to walk using a set of custom-made artificial legs. Viscardi termed this his "second birth." After the attack on Pearl Harbor he volunteered to work for the Red Cross with disabled veterans at the Walter Reed Army Medical Center in Washington, D.C. He was appalled at what he found there: little or no rehabilitation, wooden legs so shoddy they often cracked, and a long waiting list even for these inadequate prostheses and services. "The men got discouraged and nobody did much about it. Then they went home on furlough and the communities finished the job. They got pity, pensions, doles, but no respect." Viscardi not only taught his students how to use their artificial legs but also wrote letters, met with their families, and even traveled to their homes to help with their rehabilitation. The hospital's professional therapists complained, however, that he had no degree, and the Red Cross dismissed him for not doing his paperwork. After his dismissal, amputees at Walter Reed would sneak away from their wards to meet Viscardi on the grounds, where he continued to teach them how to walk, drive, and adjust to life with a disability. Viscardi's work came to the attention of rehabilitation pioneer Howard Rusk, and together they enlisted the help of Eleanor Roosevelt and Congress to put pressure on the military to upgrade its rehabilitation programs.

After the war, Viscardi returned to New York City, where he co-founded Just One Break (JOB) with businessman Orin Lehman, himself disabled, and Howard Rusk. The purpose of JOB was to find jobs for disabled workers and to demonstrate to the business community that people with disabilities could be good employees. With Viscardi as its first director, JOB was re-

Henry Viscardi, 1960.

sponsible for thousands of people with physical disabilities obtaining gainful employment. In 1952, Viscardi took out a personal loan to found and become president of Abilities, Inc., a nonprofit industrial and clerical work center based in a vacant garage in West Hempstead, Long Island. "We didn't teach basket making or weaving blankets, this wasn't a sheltered workshop. We taught electronics, manufacturing, and we paid competitive wages." The project was run by people with disabilities, who also marketed its products. By 1954, Abilities, Inc., was employing 160 disabled workers, and it grew to employ thousands more under its present name, the National Center for Disability Services. In the years since, 50 or more centers in 37 countries have been founded, based upon Viscardi's original idea. Viscardi also established what is now known as the Henry Viscardi School on Long Island, offering quality education to disabled students 20 years before passage of the Education for All Handicapped Children Act of 1975.

Viscardi is the author of eight books, the best known of which is his autobiography,

A Man's Stature (1952), which has been translated into more than 30 languages. He chaired the 1977 White House Conference on Handicapped Individuals and was an advisor to federal vocational rehabilitation director Mary Switzer and others in the rehabilitation field. He was the president of the National Center for Disability Services on Long Island, New York, until 1981, and he has remained active on the center's board of directors.

See also Rusk, Howard; Switzer, Mary; White House Conference on Handicapped Individuals.

Reference Viscardi, Henry, Jr., *A Man's Stature* (1952).

Vocational Rehabilitation, Vocational Rehabilitation Acts and Amendments

The first federal training program for people with disabilities came into existence in response to the needs of thousands of servicemen disabled during World War I. The Smith-Sears Veterans Vocational Rehabilitation Act of 1918 provided federal funds for the instruction of disabled veterans and for monthly living allowances for veterans and their families receiving services supervised by the Federal Board for Vocational Education. Within two years, the idea of vocational rehabilitation was extended to include disabled civilians. The Smith-Fess Civilian Vocational Rehabilitation Act of 1920 appropriated federal money to the states for the development of programs for "any person who, by reason of a physical defect or infirmity, whether congenital or acquired by accident, injury, or disease, is . . . totally or partially incapacitated for remunerative occupation; the term 'rehabilitation' shall be construed to mean the rendering of a person disabled fit to engage in a remunerative occupation." These work-related definitions of disability and rehabilitation were to have tremendous impact on the subsequent development of programs and services. Taken together, the Vocational Rehabilitation Acts of 1918 and 1920 represented an unprecedented commitment on the part of the government to economic independence for people with disabilities.

Over the following decades, this commitment was enhanced and codified through a variety of amendments to the original acts. Congress in the World War Veterans Act of 1924 established the United States Veterans Bureau, giving it the responsibility to work with the Department of Labor "to provide for the placement of rehabilitated persons in suitable or gainful occupations." It expanded eligibility for services to include veterans with "neuropsychiatric or tubercular ailments" as well as blindness and other conditions, "whether such ailments or diseases are due to military service or otherwise." Vocational rehabilitation for civilians was given permanent status by the Social Security Act of 1935. Each state and territory developed and funded its own rehabilitation programs, with matching funds and standards provided by the federal government. The programs served as an impetus for research into rehabilitation, the development of assistive technology, and the training of rehabilitation professionals at universities and colleges. The LaFollette-Barden Act of 1943 expanded the services offered, extended them to adolescents, and established the federal Office of Vocational Rehabilitation (OVR).

The scope and size of vocational rehabilitation programs were again dramatically expanded in the 1950s. Mary Switzer, appointed director of the federal OVR in 1950, oversaw the passage of the Vocational Rehabilitation Amendments of 1954. Testimony before Congress that year indicated that there were "approximately 2 million disabled individuals in the United States . . . who could be returned to useful work and places of respect in their communities" but were unable to do so because of a "backlog which has accumulated over the years, in part because the available rehabilitative services and facilities have never been adequate to serve more than a fraction of those who might have been helped." Annual federal-state expenditures for vocational rehabilitation during the 1950s amounted to roughly $30 million, serving slightly more than 60,000 people a year, while it was estimated that "each year approximately 250,000 persons [were] disabled by disease, accidents, or other causes." The 1954 amendments greatly expanded the ability of the OVR to fund both government and private nonprofit rehabilitation agencies. By this time, Congress had also broadened the definition of vocational rehabilitation to include various medical services, prosthetic devices, and programs to rehabilitate mentally disabled people, migrant workers, disadvantaged youth, and families of disabled persons.

Until the 1970s, the vocational rehabilitation system was managed almost entirely by nondisabled people, who often shared society's ableist views on the supposed limitations of people with disabilities. Furthermore, the system still reached only a small fraction of those needing services. Entire categories of individuals, for example, people who were blind or quadriplegic, were excluded because they were considered "infeasible," that is, too disabled to work. Women and people of color were far less likely to receive services than white, middle-class men. Finally, vocational rehabilitation did not address the discrimination faced by people with disabilities at the workplace and in the community, nor did it mandate the removal of architectural, transportation, and other access barriers, which were often more of a problem for potential workers than the nature of their particular disability.

The Rehabilitation Act of 1973 was intended to address these issues. The word *vocational* was dropped from the title of the act to indicate a move away from previous, employment-based definitions of disability and rehabilitation, while Title V, particularly Section 504, dealt for the first time with ableism and discrimination. A few people with significant disabilities were appointed to positions of power within the rehabilitation hierarchy, for example, Ed Roberts became head of the Department of Rehabilitation in California in 1975, and Elmer Bartels took the same position in Massachusetts in 1979. Nevertheless, the under-funded and over-bureaucratized rehabilitation system continues to be a major frustration for many disabled people. The complaints of Billy Golfus, in his film *When Billy Broke His Head* (1995) are typical. Golfus reports that his counselor "never got [him] one job interview in eight years." Instead of trying to assist Golfus to resume his broadcasting career, interrupted by brain injury, his state agency recommended that he learn to polish lenses "at four dollars an hour."

By the 1990s, rehabilitation agencies in the 50 states and the territories were providing services to approximately 950,000 people.

See also Bartels, Elmer C.; Rehabilitation Act of 1973; Roberts, Edward V.; Section 504 of the Rehabilitation Act of 1973; Switzer, Mary.

References Bartels, Elmer C., "Employment and the Public Vocational Rehabilitation Program: Impact of the ADA," in Lawrence O. Gostin and Henry A. Beyer, eds., *Implementing the Americans with Disabilities Act* (1993); Berkowitz, Edward D., *Disabled Policy: America's Programs for the Handicapped* (1987); Berkowitz, Monroe, William G. Johnson, and Edward H. Murphy, *Public Policy toward Disability* (1976); Golfus, Billy, *When Billy Broke His Head . . . and Other Tales of Wonder* (1995).

Voting Accessibility for the Elderly and Handicapped Act of 1984

It was the intent of Congress, in passing the Voting Accessibility for the Elderly and Handicapped Act of 1984, "to promote the fundamental right to vote by improving access for handicapped and elderly individuals to registration facilities and polling places for Federal elections." The act required accessibility to apply to people using wheelchairs and that such aids as large-type instructions and telecommunications devices be provided for people with sensory disabilities. The act gave responsibility for ensuring access to the chief election officer of each state. The act is severely flawed, however, in that there is no "cause of action" allowing individuals to sue, nor are there penalties for failure to comply.

Wade, Cheryl Marie (b. 1948)

Cheryl Marie Wade, the first director of Wry Crips: Disabled Women's Theater, is a poet and performance artist in the San Francisco Bay area. She was born on 4 March 1948 in Vallejo, California. She received her B.A. in 1980 and her M.A. in 1982, both from the University of California at Berkeley.

Wade began her career as a performance artist at age 37, writing poetry and skits for Wry Crips. Her work focused on her own experiences as a woman with a disability, and it often lampooned common myths and fears about disability. "Mine are the hands of your bad dreams," begins one of her poems, as she waves her disabled hands at the audience. In 1988, Wade cofounded the AXIS Dance Troupe and, in 1989, founded her own Gnarly Bones Productions, both in the San Francisco area. Wade has also been a columnist for the *Disability Rag & Resource*.

See also Disability Culture; Wry Crips: Disabled Women's Theater.

Walker, Sylvia

Sylvia Walker is the director of the Research and Training Center for Access to Rehabilitation and Economic Opportunity at Howard University in Washington, D.C. She is nationally known for her research relating to minority persons with disabilities and was appointed by President Clinton in 1995 to serve as vice chair of the President's Committee on Employment of People with Disabilities.

Walker was born in Far Rockaway, New York, and prefers that her birthdate not be published. She received her Ed.D. in special education/administration and international education from Teachers College, Columbia University in New York City.

She has conducted research and training projects in South America and Africa and has taught at Hunter College in New York City and the University of Cape Coast in Ghana, West Africa. She is currently professor of special education in the School of Education and the Graduate School of Arts and Sciences at Howard University. Her work has appeared in *Future Frontiers in the Employment of Minority Persons with Disabilities*, published by the President's Committee on Employment of People with Disabilities in 1991, and the *Howard University Research and Training Center 1995 Sourcebook for Access to Multicultural Federal Programs* (1995), among other publications.

See also Multicultural Issues, Minority Persons with Disabilities.

Warm Springs, Georgia

Warm Springs, Georgia, is most often remembered because of its association with Franklin Delano Roosevelt, who established the rehabilitation center there in the mid-1920s. Less widely known is that the program at Warm Springs was conceived and, in large part, controlled by people with disabilities. As such, it played a role in setting the stage for the disability rights movement of the 1960s and 1970s. Hugh Gregory Gallagher, in *FDR's Splendid Deception* (1985), describes how, "for a generation, Warm Springs was a community of the handicapped." Activist Fred Fay, a resident of Warm Springs shortly after his spinal cord injury in 1961, remembers that "it was an early model of what a community of disabled people could be like."

The hot mineral baths at Warm Springs were recommended to Roosevelt as a possible aid to his paralysis due to polio, and he first visited the area on 3 October 1924.

Roosevelt thought the waters there did him good, and he said so in a nationally syndicated article. Although it would be eight years before his election as president, Roosevelt had already been assistant secretary of the Navy, a New York state senator, and the vice-presidential candidate of the Democratic Party. Because of this celebrity, Roosevelt's bout with polio and his attempt to recover from the paraplegia it caused were a public drama. Soon, hundreds of "polios" were writing to him, some even coming to Warm Springs unannounced, with nowhere to stay. Roosevelt, together with local hotel owner Tom Loyless, set about making Warm Springs accessible to people using wheelchairs.

From there, Roosevelt organized a rehabilitation program centered on the mineral baths, but with great emphasis on enabling each participant to be as self-reliant as possible. People with disabilities themselves were seen as the best strategists and trainers on how to cope with a disability. They worked in groups of similarly disabled people to brainstorm solutions to problems in day-to-day living. They organized parties, went to the movies, joined clubs, and had relationships. The Warm Springs Polio Rehabilitation Center was a program unlike any other of the time, what Lorenzo Milam, another Warm Springs alumnus, called "the most magnificent of rehabilitation facilities in the United States."

Roosevelt became the center's director in 1926, and, in its first years, he provided most of its funding. Warm Springs became the premier post-polio facility in the world, and Eleanor Roosevelt would later claim that her husband nearly abandoned his political dreams for a career in rehabilitation. Roosevelt died at Warm Springs on 12 April 1945.

The center was bought by the state of Georgia in 1974. It is now called the Roosevelt Warm Springs Institute for Rehabilitation.

See also Roosevelt, Franklin Delano.

References Gallagher, Hugh Gregory, *FDR's Splendid Deception* (1985); Gould, Tony, *A Summer Plague: Polio and Its Survivors* (1995).

Waxman, Barbara Faye (b. 1955)

Barbara Faye Waxman is known for her work on the sexual and reproductive rights of disabled people. The first to write about hate crimes against people with disabilities, she has pushed for the federal and local governments to track violence committed against people because they are disabled.

Waxman was born on 1 April 1955 in Los Angeles, California. She graduated with a B.A. in psychology from California State University in Northridge in 1978. From 1978 to 1984, she was the disability program director for Planned Parenthood in Los Angeles, and, from 1985 to 1993, a disability policy consultant on issues of sexuality, reproductive health, and family life. In 1993, she became the director of the Americans with Disabilities Act (ADA) Training and Technical Assistance Project of the California Family Planning Council. Waxman has lectured widely, has made numerous media appearances, and has been a member of a variety of boards and organizations, including the California Committee on the Sexual Rights of Persons with Developmental Disabilities and the Center for Women's Policy Studies in Washington, D.C.

Waxman is an outspoken critic of assisted suicide and the use of genetic screening to abort fetuses with disabilities. Among her published works are *Intimacy and Disability* (with J. Levin, Institute for Information Studies, 1982), "The Politics of Sex and Disability" (with Anne Finger, in *Disability Studies Quarterly*, 1989), and "It's Time To Politicize Our Sexual Oppression" (*Disability Rag & Resource*, March/April 1991). In "Hatred: The Unacknowledged Dimension in Violence against Disabled People" (1991), she maintains that people with disabilities "face a pattern of oppressive social treatment and hatred, much as women face misogyny, gay men and lesbians face homophobia, Jews face anti-Semitism and people of color face racism."

Waxman's advocacy became personal when she decided to marry. Waxman, who uses a ventilator and personal assistance services (PAS), was told that she would lose her Medi-Cal (Medicaid) coverage if she married and continued to work. Her choices were: stay single; marry and quit her job; or marry, work, and lose her ventilator and PAS. After several years of personal and legal advocacy, Medi-Cal granted the couple a waiver, and Waxman was married on 28 July 1996.

See also Disincentives; Euthanasia and Assisted Suicide; Glen Ridge Case; Hate Crimes and Violence against People with Disabilities; Sexuality and Disability.

References Waxman, Barbara Faye, "Hatred: The Unacknowledged Dimension in Violence against Disabled People," *Sexuality and Disability* (October/November 1991): 185–199; ———, "It's Time to Politicize Our Sexual Oppression," in Barrett Shaw, ed., *The Ragged Edge: The Disability Experience from the Pages of the First Fifteen Years of* The Disability Rag (1994).

Western Law Center for Disability Rights

Founded in 1975 as the Western Center on Law and the Handicapped, the Western Law Center for Disability Rights represents low-income individuals who have been discriminated against because of their disability. The center litigates both individual and "impact cases" that have the potential for expanding the rights of all Americans with disabilities. The center organizes seminars for lawyers in specific areas of disability law, sponsors conferences on disability rights, is a source of information on the Americans with Disabilities Act of 1990, encourages attorneys to do pro bono disability rights work, and prepares amicus curiae briefs in disability rights cases of national significance.

The center is a nonprofit organization, located on the campus of the Loyola Law School in Los Angeles.

Westside Center for Independent Living (WCIL)

The Westside Center for Independent Living (WCIL) was incorporated in 1976 as one of nine independent living centers sponsored by Ed Roberts after he was appointed director of California's Department of Rehabilitation. As one of the earliest and largest independent living centers in the nation, it has played a leading role both in California and national disability rights politics.

The impetus for WCIL came when Douglas A. Martin, then a Ph.D. candidate at the University of California in Los Angeles, met Ed Roberts on the streets of Berkeley, California. Martin was impressed by the Center for Independent Living at Berkeley, and Roberts convinced him to found a center in Los Angeles. Martin, together with other activists such as Sherman Clark, Sandra Burnett, and Linda Knipps, began in 1975 to make plans for the Westside Center. The articles of incorporation were signed on 30 March 1976, and WCIL was due to open in the fall with Clark as WCIL's first executive director. These plans were delayed when Clark died at the end of August and the building leased by the WCIL was gutted by fire on Labor Day. An emergency meeting of the organizers was held at Clark's wake, where it was decided that Martin would become WCIL's first executive director. From September 1976 to April 1977, the WCIL shared space at the Los Angeles headquarters of United Cerebral Palsy Associations, Inc., until its own building was ready for occupancy.

In its first years, much of WCIL's advocacy focused on removing the disincentives faced by individuals with disabilities wanting to work. As an example, Martin had to work without pay, since accepting a salary would have put his disability benefits, including his health insurance, in jeopardy. WCIL worked to introduce Section 1619 into the Social Security Amendments Act of 1980, which became the basis of the Employment Opportunities for Disabled Americans Act of 1986. WCIL activists were also involved in the 1977 Department of Health, Education and Welfare (HEW) demonstrations to put pressure on the Carter administration to issue regulations implementing Section 504 of the Rehabilitation Act of 1973.

WCIL activists advocated for transportation and architectural access, the construction of curb-cuts, and the development of a statewide architectural access code in California.

Today, WCIL is a nonresidential, nonprofit corporation with the goal of enabling people with disabilities and seniors in the Los Angeles community to live more independently. Over the years, WCIL has assisted more than 30,000 people toward this goal. It remains a cross-disability organization, staffed primarily by people with disabilities and seniors.

See also Disincentives; Employment Opportunities for Disabled Americans Act of 1986; Independent Living, Independent Living Movement; Martin, Douglas A.; Roberts, Edward V.

Wheelchair Basketball
See Sports and Athletics.

Wheelchairs

The basic design for the manual wheelchair in use today was registered with the U.S. Patent Office in 1869, although some form of wheelchair has probably existed since the invention of the wheel. In 1909, a folding model was patented that became standard among mobility-disabled Americans. Although an improvement over previous models, this wheelchair was still awkward, fragile, and cumbersome during travel. Designers tended to see wheelchairs as "medical equipment" for use by "invalids" who would not be doing much traveling anyway.

This view began to change in 1937, when Herbert A. Everest and Harry C. Jennings patented a design with an X-frame that could be folded and packed into a car trunk. Everest had become paraplegic as a result of a mining accident in 1918, and he contacted his engineer friend Jennings out of frustration with the wheelchairs then available. They founded Everest & Jennings (E&J) in Los Angeles. By the late 1960s, E&J held a virtual monopoly in the domestic wheelchair market. Control of the company had by this time passed into the hands of nondisabled managers. E&J failed to improve on its designs, ignoring the complaints of consumers who found their chairs too bulky and too expensive. Critics also charged that E&J actively sought to squelch its competition. In 1977 the U.S. Justice Department filed an antitrust suit, which was settled in 1979.

The rapid expansion of wheelchair sports in the 1970s, particularly racing, was a major impetus to improvements in wheelchair design. Racers and innovators such as Robert Hall, Marty Ball, Gary Kerr, Jim Knaub, Jim Martinson, Randy Wicks, and others custom designed and built chairs that were a radical improvement over the existing models. These chairs were not available to the general public, but they demonstrated how much room for improvement remained in standard wheelchair design.

The development of the "Quickie" was another major breakthrough. This new model reminded users of a racing bike: simple and sleek, weighing half as much as other manual wheelchairs. The Quickie was the brainchild of Marilyn Hamilton, an athlete who became paraplegic after a hang-gliding accident in 1978, along with Jim Okamoto and Don Helman, experts in designing high performance vehicles. Like Everest, Hamilton was frustrated with the wheelchairs available to her, and she enlisted her engineer friends to come up with something better. In 1979, they started a business in Helman's 600-square-foot shed. Immediately popular with wheelchair athletes, the Quickie soon caught on with the general wheelchair-using public. In 1986, the company was acquired by Sunrise Medical in southern California and named Quickie Designs, Inc., which is now the world's largest manufacturer of lightweight wheelchairs.

Power wheelchairs, using wet or dry cell electric batteries, are used by people with more severe disabilities, such as quadriplegia caused by spinal cord injury or multiple sclerosis. Although these wheelchairs are

A standard wheelchair from the early twentieth century.

necessarily heavier and more cumbersome than light-weight manual chairs, here too the trend has been toward lighter weight and greater durability. With the tightening of public health funding and private health insurance benefits, however, access to wheelchairs remains a major problem for people with disabilities. Particularly in the developing world, the scarcity of durable and affordable wheelchairs prevents millions of people from participating in their societies.

See also Assistive Technology; Health Care Access; Hotchkiss, Ralf.

Wheeled Mobility Center
See Hotchkiss, Ralf David.

Wheels of Justice
In early 1990, there were indications that Congress might not pass the Americans with Disabilities Act (ADA), or that it might delay or amend it so as to be less effective. In response to this threat, American Disabled for Attendant Programs Today (ADAPT) (at that time, American Disabled for Accessible Public Transit) organized Wheels of Justice, a series of demonstrations designed to put pressure on Congress to pass the ADA.

Wheels of Justice was the largest cross-disability event of its kind to date. More than 700 people gathered in Washington, D.C., where, on 12 March, they marched from the White House to the Capitol to listen to speeches by disability rights advocates such as Justin Dart Jr., Evan Kemp Jr., James Brady, I. King Jordan, and Mike Auberger. Auberger, at the foot of the Capitol steps, told the crowd, "We will not permit these steps to continue to be a barrier to prevent us from the equality that is rightfully ours." This was the call to begin "the crawl-up," as people left their wheelchairs to make their way up the 78 steps into the Capitol building.

The next day, more than 200 demonstrators occupied the Capitol rotunda, meeting with House Speaker Tom Foley (D–WA), House Minority Leader Robert Michel (R–IL), and ADA sponsor Rep. Steny Hoyer (D–MD). When Foley and Michel would not commit to passing an ADA without limiting amendments, the group began chanting and was asked to leave. Police arrested 104 demonstrators. On 14 March, ADAPT demonstrators occupied the office of Rep. Bud Shuster (R–PA), identified as one of the leading opponents of the ADA, after Shuster refused to meet with them. Another 64 demonstrators were arrested.

The subsequent trials, held Thursday and Friday of that same week, were used by the arrested activists to educate the court and the media. In their statements to the judge, people described the discrimination they had experienced because of their disabilities. Some of the demonstrators were given light sentences, others were given heavy fines and long probations, which proved to be a problem when it was discovered that the local probation office was not wheelchair accessible.

See also American Disabled for Attendant Programs Today; Americans with Disabilities Act of 1990; Auberger, Mike.

White, Ryan
See Ryan White Comprehensive AIDS Resources Emergency (CARE) Act of 1990.

White House Conference on Handicapped Individuals
The 1974 amendments to the Rehabilitation Act of 1973 called for a conference to be convened to review federal policy toward people with disabilities. Some 1,500 delegates and 1,500 alternates met at the Sheraton Park Hotel in Washington, D.C., 23–27 May 1977, with Henry Viscardi Jr. as chair. This meeting marked the first time that a significant number of disabled people were invited by the federal government to provide input into the policies that affected their lives, which unsettled many rehabilitation professionals.

"Sometimes I am amazed at the number of providers who still believe that disabled persons do not possess the mental capacity to speak for themselves," conference executive director Jack F. Smith remarked at the time.

The conference had an official and an unofficial outcome. Officially, conference delegates passed 142 resolutions, calling for more consumer involvement in rehabilitation programs, a comprehensive health insurance program, establishment of a federal coordinating center and clearinghouse on disability programs, the end of Social Security disincentives, and much more. Most significantly, it called for the federal government to fully enforce existing disability rights law and for Congress to amend the Civil Rights Act of 1964 and the Voting Rights Act of 1965 to include people with mental and physical disabilities. This recommendation is seen by Viscardi and others as the first call for an Americans with Disabilities Act (ADA). The conference also sparked the creation of city, county, and state commissions on handicapped affairs across the country.

Unofficially, the conference was a catalyst for the national disability rights movement. The Department of Health, Education and Welfare (HEW) demonstrations to demand regulations implementing Section 504 of the Rehabilitation Act had occurred just one month before, and delegates used the conference as an opportunity to establish national connections. Many returned home inspired to found or expand their own local organizations.

See also Pfeiffer, David; Viscardi, Henry, Jr.

Wilke, Harold H. (b. 1914)

The Reverend Harold H. Wilke is one of the first Americans with a severe disability to serve as a parish minister. In the past 50 years, he has preached at more than 1,000 local congregations in the United States and abroad, including churches in Hiroshima and Johannesburg. A social activist, clergyman, author, and teacher, Wilke's work has been of tremendous im-

portance in making organized religion, particularly Protestant Christianity, more accessible to people with disabilities. He is the founder and leader of the Healing Community in Claremont, California and a founding director of the National Organization on Disability. He was instrumental in establishing the National Organization on Disability Religion and Disability Program in 1985.

Wilke was born without arms on 10 December 1914 in Washington, Missouri. He was encouraged from early age to be independent, and he learned to dress, write, and drive with his feet. He began his seminary training prior to World War II, earning a travel-study award that enabled him to attend Eden Theological Seminary in St. Louis, the University of Chicago, and Union Theological Seminary in New York. A student of Reinhold Niebuhr and Paul Tillich, Wilke dedicated his life to social activism. Seeking to be ordained in the Evangelical and Reformed Church (now the United Church of Christ, or UCC), Wilke had first to overcome the ableist attitudes of those in the church hierarchy.

"Clergy and laity alike discouraged Wilke to consider pastoral ministry," writes his biographer Robert Pietsch. "'How will you be able to baptize? Conduct the Eucharist?' Wilke, not to be deterred, demonstrated that by touching his lips from baptismal font to the person's forehead, the sacrament could be fulfilled." Wilke was ordained in 1939, and he began his ministry at the Chapel University Church in Columbia, Missouri. While there, he ordained the first woman to become a minister in his denomination and edited the first issues of *Social Action*, soon to become the UCC's premier publication. During World War II, Wilke was a hospital chaplain while finishing his master's of sacred theology from Harvard University and Andover Newton Seminary in Massachusetts. After the war, Wilke moved to Crystal Lake, Illinois, where he was a minister at St. Paul Church while he completed his doctorate at the University of Chicago.

Harold Wilke is presented with a ceremonial pen following President Bush's signing of the ADA, the landmark civil rights legislation for people with disabilities, on 26 July 1990. Wilke, who is armless, accepts the pen with his foot.

Wilke became a national leader in his denomination, moving to New York City to found the Commission on Religion and Health within the UCC General Synod. He became its first executive director in 1955 and worked to open the ministry to women and people with disabilities. Beginning in the 1950s, Wilke was also active in the civil rights movement, participating in marches organized by the Reverend Martin Luther King Jr. Wilke's first arrest had been during the 1930s at an anti-Nazi demonstration in New York City; he was later arrested at civil rights, antiwar and antiapartheid demonstrations. In the 1970s, Wilke founded the National Committee on Church and Disability, and he organized the first "Access Sabbath-Sunday" (worship services to promote the participation of people with disabilities in religion and society) in 1976. Wilke's interest

in the spiritual aspects of disability and rehabilitation led, during this period, to the founding of the Healing Community, helping local congregations to explore these issues.

Wilke is also an internationally known speaker and writer. His address at the United Nations in 1980, "The Whole Family of God," opened the International Year of Disabled Persons. On 26 July 1990, Wilke delivered the invocation at the signing of the Americans with Disabilities Act (ADA) at the White House. Among Wilke's books are *Greet the Man* (1945), *Strengthened with Might* (1952), *Creating the Caring Congregation* (1980), and *The Open Congregation* (1980).

See also National Organization on Disability; Religion.
References Pietsch, Robert, "Becoming the Kingdom of God: Building Bridges between Religion,

Secular Society, and Persons with Disabilities: The Ministry of Harold Wilke," *Journal of Religion in Disability & Rehabilitation* (1996); Wilke, Harold, *Greet the Man* (1945).

Williams, Boyce Robert (b. 1910)

Boyce Robert Williams is the man most responsible for the development of vocational rehabilitation services for Americans who are deaf and hard of hearing. From 1945 until 1983, he designed and managed groundbreaking programs at the federal Office of Vocational Rehabilitation (OVR) (renamed the Rehabilitation Services Administration, or RSA, in 1967) that vastly expanded educational and employment opportunities for deaf Americans.

Williams was born on 29 August 1910 in Racine, Wisconsin, and became totally deaf after an attack of spinal meningitis at age 17. He received a B.A. in mathematics from Gallaudet College in Washington, D.C., in 1932 and took a position at the Wisconsin School for the Deaf in Delavan (which he had briefly attended) in 1933. From 1935 to 1945, he was a teacher and then (after 1937) director of vocational training at the Indiana School for the Deaf in Indianapolis. Williams received his master's in education from Columbia University in 1940.

Williams was hired by the federal OVR in 1945 to develop programs for deaf and hard-of-hearing people. He used his position to facilitate working relationships between the various national organizations working on deafness issues, including the National Association of the Deaf, the National Fraternal Society of the Deaf, and the Conference of American Instructors of the Deaf. These relationships, writes Edna P. Adler in her entry on Williams in the *Gallaudet Encyclopedia of Deaf People and Deafness* (1987), "laid the groundwork for the hundreds of national, state, regional, and community conferences and workshops addressing issues pertinent to the rehabilitation of deaf people that have taken place since.

"Promoting better understanding of deaf adults and their needs, problems, and capabilities was always the single greatest thrust of Williams's work. He repeatedly stressed their normal intelligence, strength, and mobility as considerations in their job placement. . . . Also, even though his own speech was good, he acted as a strong proponent of expert manual communication [sign language] among service delivery professionals."

After the appointment of Mary E. Switzer as commissioner of the OVR in 1950, she and Williams worked together for the next 20 years to foster groundbreaking research into the status and needs of deaf Americans and numerous innovative programs, including the National Theatre of the Deaf, the Registry of Interpreters for the Deaf, and Captioned Films for the Deaf. Adler describes how, "in doing this important work, [Williams] saw to it that deaf people were fully involved in decision-making and planning. . . . Deaf people recall those early workshops as 'walking in trails of glory.'" One crucial aspect of Williams' work was, as he put it, "the rapid materialization of effective deaf leadership." An OVR grant to the San Fernando Valley State College enabled the school to offer management training for deaf teachers and service providers, educating them to become the directors of the agencies and schools where they had previously been employed.

Williams is also an internationally recognized expert on rehabilitation services for deaf people, traveling to Europe, Asia, and Africa to foster research development. He has played a key role in the World Federation of the Deaf, working with Frederick Schreiber at the National Association for the Deaf to bring its international conference to Washington, D.C., in 1976. Williams has also been active in numerous American organizations of deaf people, including the Gallaudet College Alumni Association.

Williams retired from the RSA in 1983, becoming Powrie Vaux Doctor Chair of Deaf Studies at Gallaudet University from 1983 to 1984.

See also Vocational Rehabilitation; Switzer, Mary Elizabeth.

References Moore, Matthew, and Robert Panara, *Great Deaf Americans, 2d edition* (1996); Van Cleve, John V., ed., *Gallaudet Encyclopedia of Deaf People and Deafness*, Vol. 3 (1987).

Williams, Robert (b. 1957)

Robert Williams is a poet, writer, and advocate for people with disabilities that affect their ability to speak. He was born on 23 February 1957 in Willimantic, Connecticut, and graduated from George Washington University in Washington, D.C., in May 1983 with a B.A. in urban affairs. He was a staff assistant on the U.S. Senate Subcommittee on the Handicapped from 1981 to 1982 and, from 1984 to 1988, served as a program analyst at the Pratt Monitoring Program for the District of Columbia Association for Retarded Citizens, becoming the program's deputy director from 1988 to 1990. He oversaw the closing of Forest Haven, the District of Columbia's institution for people with developmental disabilities, while developing community support services for its former residents. From 1990 to 1993, he was also a policy associate for United Cerebral Palsy Associations, Inc., and an advocate for passage of the Americans with Disabilities Act of 1990 (ADA). From 1990 to 1991, he was the president of Hear Our Voices, an organization of people who rely on augmentive communication devices, and he is a former vice president of the Association for Persons with Severe Handicaps (TASH). Williams was co-chair of the Personal Assistance Services (PAS) Task Force of the Consortium for Citizens with Disabilities from 1991 to 1993. In 1993, President Clinton appointed Williams to his current position as commissioner of the Administration on Developmental Disabilities at the U.S. Department of Health and Human Services, the first person with a developmental disability to hold that post.

Williams is also a poet and writer. His first book of poetry, *In a Struggling Voice* (1989), chronicles his experiences as a person with cerebral palsy.

See also Administration on Developmental Disabilities.

Willowbrook State School

On 17 March 1972, a group of disability rights attorneys and parents, together with the New York Association for Retarded Children, filed a lawsuit against New York State, hoping to put an end to the abuses suffered by the residents at the Willowbrook State School. Willowbrook had by then become a symbol of the horrors of institutionalization. During the next ten years, the residents of Willowbrook and their advocates would prove that even the most severely disabled people can, with the proper support, live and prosper in the community.

From its opening in April 1951, Willowbrook's thousands of residents were subject to neglect and abuse. Various accounts from the 1950s and 1960s cite widespread malnutrition. Medical care was cruelly inadequate, with reports of children's wounds left untreated so long they became maggot infested and of deadly diseases spread by improper sanitation. Within four years of its opening, Willowbrook held 3,600 residents in a space designed for 2,950; by 1963, the number had grown to 6,000. The facility was also chronically understaffed. A 1964 investigation by the New York state legislature noted the "vile stench" inside the institution and "the crude way of life" it inflicted on its residents, but its report was not released to the public. In 1965, a series of deaths, including that of a 10-year-old boy scalded to death by faulty plumbing and that of a 12-year-old boy strangled while in restraints, led to a grand jury investigation. That same year, Sen. Robert F. Kennedy (D–NY), visiting Willowbrook, told the press that it was "less comfortable and cheerful than the cages in which we put animals in a zoo." Budget cuts by the New York state legislature in 1971, along with a freeze on staff hiring, only made matters worse. Yet, throughout this time, Willowbrook passed every accreditation inspection of the American Association on Mental Deficiency, the organization of physicians specializing in the treatment of mental retardation.

Robert Williams, commissioner of the federal Administration on Developmental Disabilities at the U.S. Department of Health and Human Services.

The turning point came with the appointment of Dr. William Bronston to the Willowbrook staff in 1970. Bronston had a long history of political activism, and he was impressed both by Wolf Wolfensberger's advocacy of "normalization" and by Richard Koch's emphasis on keeping disabled children out of institutions. He first tried to reform Willowbrook by bringing his concerns to the institution director, who responded by transferring Bronston to a ward where conditions were even more abysmal. Bronston then tried to organize the direct care workers to improve conditions, but most were afraid of losing their jobs. A few, however, responded, particularly Dr. Michael Wilkens and social worker Elizabeth Lee. One of the residents, Bernard Carabello, began writing letters to the local press. Parents too, who had felt stigmatized both for having disabled children and for institutionalizing them, began to protest conditions at the facility. The administration responded first by trying to ban meetings between dissident staff and parents and then by firing Wilkens and Lee. (Bronston, an employee for more than a year, had civil service protection). Wilkens and Lee called Geraldo Rivera, a reporter for ABC-TV. His film footage—of naked residents lying in filth, walls smeared with feces, and floors covered with urine—was broadcast on 6 January 1972 and caused a national furor. Angry parents organized demonstrations, while the Federation of Parents' Organizations for the New York State Mental Institutions, with a chapter at Willowbrook, demanded that a grand jury be convened to indict facility officials for criminal neglect.

The Willowbrook story caught the attention of Bruce Ennis, an attorney who had specialized in prisoners' rights cases. Ennis had served as co-counsel with Morton Birnbaum in *Donaldson v. O'Connor* (eventually heard by the U.S. Supreme Court as *O'Connor v. Donaldson*, 1975) and was a co-founder of the Mental Health Law Project (now the Judge David L. Bazelon Center for Mental Health Law).

Ennis, along with co-counsels Robert Feldt and Anita Barrett, agreed to represent the Willowbrook parents and residents in a class action suit (*New York ARC v. Rockefeller*, 1973). They produced dozens of witnesses and hundreds of pages of testimony. Typical testimony is this account by pediatrician Mary Stewart Goodwin, who visited Willowbrook on 30–31 March 1972: "Door of seclusion room opened by request. . . . Barefoot 17-year-old girl in dingy loose gown standing by the door—pale, pasty appearance. . . . Has been in seclusion for 7 years; heavily tranquilized, teeth extracted long ago because 'she bit someone.'" A couple who went to Willowbrook to visit their child found "her ear bitten off, part of her nose torn off. . . ." Ennis asked the federal court for "emergency relief . . . necessary to protect the lives, physical health, safety and well-being of the residents." "It is our position," Ennis told the court, "that Willowbrook . . . in many respects is worse than a prison." He concluded that "there is probably no more dangerous place to live in New York City than the back wards of Willowbrook."

Judge Orrin Judd of the Federal Court of the Eastern District of New York granted the emergency relief, detailing specific improvements the state needed to make in staffing, sanitation, clothing, and medical care. In May 1975, Judge John R. Bartels approved a consent decree that ordered the state to reduce the population from 5,400 to no more than 250 by 1981, and he appointed a board to monitor compliance. In their history of "the Willowbrook wars," David J. Rothman and Sheila M. Rothman report that, "from 1976 to 1982, 2600 of 5400 residents entered living arrangements in the community that, with a handful of exceptions, were decent, safe, and even habilitative." The emptying of Willowbrook, they conclude, demonstrated that "the cost of delivering good community care is no more expensive than . . . running bad institutions" (1984). As of 30 September 1983, 50 percent of "the Willowbrook class" was living in the community, with many of the others transferred to other facilities. One obvious implication, as the Rothmans point out, is that, "if the retarded are able to live with dignity in group homes, it should be possible to design alternatives for the elderly and frail to uncaring, congregate, and profit-minded nursing homes. Indeed, it should be possible to arrange for many among them to remain at home and out of nursing homes (or even hospitals) altogether" (1984).

See also The Arc; Bronston, William; Deinstitutionalization; *O'Connor v. Donaldson; Pennhurst State School v. Halderman.*

Reference Rothman, David, and Sheila Rothman, *The Willowbrook Wars: A Decade of Struggle for Social Change* (1984).

With the Power of Each Breath: A Disabled Women's Anthology

Dedicated to "disabled women everywhere," *With the Power of Each Breath: A Disabled Women's Anthology* explores, through poetry, fiction, and autobiographical essays, the experience of being a disabled woman. Published by the Cleis Press in 1985, the anthology features the work of writers such as Anne Finger, Cheryl Marie Wade, and Victoria Ann Lewis, on topics ranging from living with a hidden disability, abuse of women with disabilities, and wheelchair basketball to "Orthodox Handicapable Chicken Soup." The anthology has become a standard text of the women's disability rights movement, helping to introduce disability issues to feminists, and feminism to the disability rights movement.

See also Lewis, Victoria Ann; Wade, Cheryl Marie; Women with Disabilities.

Reference Browne, Susan E., Debra Connors, and Nanci Stern, eds., *With the Power of Each Breath: A Disabled Women's Anthology* (1985).

Women with Disabilities

Psychologist Michelle Fine and sociologist Adrienne Asch describe the situation of women with disabilities as "sexism without the pedestal," while sociologists Mary Jo Deegan and Nancy A. Brooks refer to "the double handicap" of ableism and sexism.

The result of this double oppression, as Charlene Poch DeLoach points out in her entry on women in the *Encyclopedia of Disability and Rehabilitation* (1995), is that, "compared to other women in this society, women with disabilities are more often unemployed, receive lower salaries, and are less likely to marry than persons of either gender who do not have disabilities, or men who do."

Disabled feminists have complained that nondisabled feminists have been insensitive to their concerns. Rannveig Traustadottir notes how "issues of importance to women with disabilities have, for the most part, been ignored by the disability rights movement as well as the women's movement" (1990). One notable exception has been the nondisabled lesbian community, which Traustadottir reports "to be more accepting than the women's movement in general." This may be due, in part, to the multiple oppressions experienced by lesbians—who face sexism and homophobia—and specific developments such as the campaign to free Sharon Kowalski, a disabled lesbian incarcerated in a nursing home because of both her disability and her sexuality.

Disabled women have also been marginalized within the disability rights and independent living movements, despite the contributions of such leaders as Helen Keller, Judith Heumann, Judi Chamberlin, Mary Jane Owen, and Patrisha Wright. Deborah McKeithan, founder of Handicapped Organized Women, told an interviewer in 1988 that "men have a monopoly on the national leadership roles" in these movements. Similar discrimination has occurred within the realm of disability sports. It was not until 1974, for example, that the first Women's National Wheelchair Basketball Tournament was held, almost three decades after the first wheelchair basketball games were played in the United States.

Very little by or about women with disabilities had been published before the 1980s. Materials about the sexual problems of spinal cord injured people, for example,

Mentor Mary Ann Bradley (left) talks with Chrissy Correia of Partners for Disabled Youth in 1993. Prior to the 1980s very little by or about women with disabilities had been published. Many argue that issues crucial to women with disabilities have been ignored by both the disability rights movement and the women's movement.

most often discussed male issues such as achieving and maintaining erections; studies of employment discrimination focused almost exclusively on the experiences of men. Issues of concern to women, such as abortion, contraception and reproductive rights, pregnancy and motherhood, and sexual and domestic violence, were rarely mentioned. This situation changed in 1981 with the publication of Jo Campling's *Images of Ourselves: Women with Disabilities Talking* and Yvonne Duffy's *All Things Are Possible*. These books were followed by *Women and Disability: The Double Handicap* (1985), *With the Power of Each Breath* (1985), *With Wings: An Anthology of Literature by and about Women with Disabilities* (1987), and *Disabled, Female and Proud!* (1988).

Among the issues of importance to women with disabilities are: marriage and relationships, motherhood, sexuality, sexual abuse and domestic violence, education, rehabilitation and employment, drug and alcohol dependence, and the youth and beauty culture.

Marriage and Relationships. As DeLoach noted, women with disabilities are less likely than either disabled men or nondisabled women to be married or to be in long-term relationships. In addition, many women who become disabled while in a relationship report being abandoned by their husbands or lovers. By contrast, men who become disabled are less likely to be abandoned by their wives or female lovers, perhaps because women are socialized to be caretakers and nurturers.

Motherhood. Traustadottir describes how there is a "widespread belief that women with disabilities cannot and should not bear and raise children." This stereotype "has made it difficult for pregnant women with disabilities to find doctors who will accept them" and has led to abuses such as the mass institutionalization and forced sterilization of developmentally disabled women of reproductive age. Disabled mothers are more likely than nondisabled mothers to lose custody of their children in divorce proceedings or to social service agencies. Services to help severely disabled women to parent their children, such as personal assistance services and accessible day care, are underfunded or nonexistent.

Sexuality. Women with physical disabilities are stereotyped as asexual, while women with cognitive and psychiatric disabilities are seen as "oversexed" and dangerous. As a result, women with disabilities are often denied sex education and contraception. These stereotypes can also result in lowered self-esteem and in difficulty finding lovers and entering into sexual relationships.

Sexual Abuse and Domestic Violence. Women and girls with disabilities are more likely to be sexually abused or exploited than nondisabled females, particularly if they live in an institution. Women with disabilities are also at equal, if not greater, risk of abuse and battering and are less likely to be in a position to leave their abusers. Nevertheless, until recently, rape crisis centers and battered women shelters were usually inaccessible, and progress to remove architectural and attitudinal barriers by law enforcement, medical, and social service agencies has often been slow.

Education. Disabled women, according to Traustadottir, "are five times as likely as women without disabilities to have less than eight years of formal education." A statistical study by disability rights advocate/researcher Frank Bowe in 1984 found that only 16 percent of disabled women had any college education, as compared to 31 percent of nondisabled women and 28 percent of disabled men. Women with disabilities who were able to enter college were often encouraged, much more so than nondisabled women, to go into a "nurturing" and traditionally women's field such as social work or rehabilitation (although nursing and teaching were generally closed to them).

Rehabilitation and Employment. Studies indicate that women are less likely to receive rehabilitation and less likely to be served by programs such as supported employment than disabled men. No matter what level of training, education, or rehabilitation they attain, disabled women are less likely to be employed than men with comparable disabilities. Like disabled men, many disabled women face a "chrome ceiling," a level above which they are not permitted to rise.

Drug and Alcohol Dependence. Women with disabilities are at equal, if not greater, risk than nondisabled women for drug and alcohol dependence. Yet, prior to the 1980s, there were virtually no programs geared specifically for disabled women, and few mainstream programs were accessible. The situation, though slowly changing, is still woefully inadequate to meet the needs of disabled women who are also drug or alcohol dependent.

The Youth and Beauty Culture. Women and girls in our society are under tremendous pressure to conform to standards of physical attractiveness well-nigh impossible to achieve. Disabled women, whose bodies are shaped or function differently, are seen by nondisabled society as being "deformed" and ugly. Writer/therapist Connie Panzarino sees a direct link between this ableism and the mass media's manipulation of our standards of beauty and worth. "Each time you look in the mirror and say to yourself, 'I'm too fat,' or 'my skin is ugly,' or 'I'm too skinny,' you are committing ableism."

In response to this history of oppression and exclusion, women with disabilities have been among the most active (if often unacknowledged) workers for disability rights. A variety of local and national organizations, including the Project on Women and Disability in Boston, the Domestic Violence Initiative for Women with Disabilities in Denver, and the DisAbled Women's Network of Canada, have been organized by and for women with disabilities. Such women have also created a vibrant counter-culture, including the theater of Wry Crips; the prose of Jean Stewart; the poetry of Leslie Donovan, Muriel Rukeyser, and Adrienne Rich; the comedy of Geri Jewell; and music, dance, and art.

See also Abortion and Reproductive Rights; Callo, Tiffany; DisAbled Women's Network (DAWN) of Canada; Forced Sterilization; Handicapped Organized Women; Kowalski, Sharon, and Thompson, Karen; Parenting; Project on Women and Disability; Rape/Sexual and Domestic Violence; Sexuality and Disability; Stewart, Jean; *With the Power of Each Breath*; Womyn's Braille Press; Wry Crips.

References Asch, Adrienne S., and Michelle Fine, *Women with Disabilities: Essays in Psychology, Culture, and Politics* (1988); Bowe, Frank, *Disabled Women in America: A Statistical Report Drawn from the Census Data* (1984); Browne, Susan E., Debra Connors, and Nanci Stern, *With the Power of Each Breath: A Disabled Women's Anthology* (1985); Deegan, Mary Jo, and Nancy A. Brooks, *Women and Disability: The Double Handicap* (1985); Duffy, Yvonne, *All Things Are Possible* (1981); Grobe, Jeanine, ed., *Beyond Bedlam: Contemporary Women Psychiatric Survivors Speak Out* (1995); Saxton, Marsha, and Florence Howe, *With Wings: An Anthology of Literature by and about Women with Disabilities* (1987); Traustadottir, Rannveig, *Women with Disabilities: Issues, Resources, Connections* (1990).

Womyn's Braille Press

The Womyn's Braille Press was founded in 1980 by six blind women in Minneapolis who wanted to make feminist and women's literature available to people who are blind or use alternate media. In its 13 years of operation, the press transcribed more than 800 titles into braille or onto tape for subscribers in the United States, Canada, Europe, Australia, and Israel.

"There was nothing available to blind women who wanted to read work by other women, particularly feminist and lesbian literature," said co-founder Marj Schneider in a 1996 interview. "The mainstream Braille outlets weren't addressing that need at all." Subscribers to the press were able to borrow or purchase books and tapes, or to borrow with an option to purchase. The press also published a newsletter featuring articles on topics of interest to blind women, and it advocated for pas-

sage of the Americans with Disabilities Act of 1990.

Although never officially dissolved, the press ceased most of its activities after 1993. Its collection is currently housed at the Bureau of Braille and Talking Book Services in Daytona Beach, Florida, and titles are available through the National Library Service of the Library of Congress.

See also Braille; Women with Disabilities.

Workers' Compensation

The Industrial Revolution dramatically increased the number of people injured in the workplace. In response, progressive activists, beginning in the late 1890s, pushed state governments to pass workers' compensation legislation. Workers' compensation programs are administered by the states but underwritten by private insurance companies, and they are funded by premiums collected from employers and employees. They provide coverage for medical treatment of illness or injury and an income based upon the worker's salary prior to the onset of the disability. By 1915, 35 states had a workers' compensation program; that figure rose to 43 by 1919.

One aspect of workers' compensation that is problematic to disability rights activists is that it defines disability as the inability to work. People receiving workers' compensation traditionally have had little incentive or opportunity to be retrained or rehabilitated so they could return to the workplace. Workers' compensation in some instances has acted, then, as a work disincentive, at odds with the goals of other state and federal disability programs such as vocational rehabilitation.

See also Disincentives; Vocational Rehabilitation.
Reference Berkowitz, Edward D., *Disabled Policy: America's Programs for the Handicapped* (1987).

World Institute on Disability (WID)

The World Institute on Disability (WID) was created in independent living pioneer Ed Roberts' home at a 1983 meeting between Roberts, activist Judith Heumann, and Joan Leon, Roberts' assistant at the California Department of Rehabilitation. WID, based in Oakland, California, describes itself today as "an international center for the study of public policy, research, and training on disability." WID staff travel around the world to meet with disability activists and professionals, as well as government officials, educators, business and community leaders, and the media.

Internationally, WID has been particularly active in Eastern Europe and Russia, and in linking American and Eastern European activists. For example, receiving funds through a U.S. Agency for International Development (AID) grant, WID helped to sponsor Ralf Hotchkiss of the Wheeled Mobility Center to travel to Russia to help establish three wheelchair production projects. The project in Novosibirsk, Siberia, was part of a larger effort to address access and disability discrimination in Russia. WID-sponsored partnerships are also active in the Czech Republic and Poland. WID also hosts visits to the United States by foreign activists and service providers, for example, tours by rehabilitation specialists from El Salvador.

Some two-thirds of WID's work addresses U.S. domestic issues, such as health care access, personal assistance services, transportation, technology and communications access, and other issues. WID research is used by disability activists in other organizations as they lobby and organize for social change. WID's many publications include *Attending to America: Personal Assistance for Independent Living* (1987); *Measuring the Health Insurance Needs of Persons with Disabilities and Persons with Chronic Illness* (1988); and *Building the Framework: Telecommunications & Persons with Disabilities* (1994). WIDNET, its international computer service, offers online users updated information on U.S. and overseas disability policy.

See also Heumann, Judith E.; Hotchkiss, Ralf David; Personal Assistance Services; Roberts, Edward V.

Wright, Patrisha A. (b. 1949)

Patrisha A. Wright is known as "the General" who coordinated the campaign to enact the Americans with Disabilities Act of 1990 (ADA). She has been director of governmental affairs in Washington, D.C., for the Disability Rights Education and Defense Fund (DREDF) since 1980.

Wright was born on 1 February 1949 in Bridgeport, Connecticut. She earned a master's degree in health services administration from Antioch University in Yellow Springs, Ohio in 1976. In the mid-1970s, while living in California, she established community programs for people with cerebral palsy and cognitive disabilities. Wright was directing the graduate program in the Psychology of Physical Disability and Health Services Administration for Antioch's San Francisco campus in 1977, when disabled activists began their demonstrations to force Department of Health, Education and Welfare (HEW) Secretary Califano to sign regulations implementing Section 504 of the Rehabilitation Act of 1973. When she realized that most of her students were participating in the sit-in at the San Francisco HEW offices, Wright suspended classes and joined them. She traveled to Washington, D.C., with demonstration leaders Kitty Cone, Judith Heumann, and others, serving as a strategist and assistant to the group. This experience led her not only to understand disability as a civil rights issue but also to accept and acknowledge her own visual disability. Wright has been committed to advancing the civil rights of people with disabilities ever since.

In 1979, Wright participated in creating DREDF. Following the election of President Ronald Reagan in 1980, Wright and DREDF Directing Attorney Arlene Mayerson went to Washington to open DREDF's Governmental Affairs office. Initially housed rent-free at the Disability Rights Center, Mayerson and Wright became the driving force behind the introduction of disability rights to the traditional national disability organizations, the

Reagan administration, and Congress. Washington disability lobbyists at that time were generally rehabilitation professionals, not disability rights activists, and not themselves disabled. This "Washington disability establishment" had never before experienced such an aggressive assault on their long-held beliefs about people with disabilities.

Wright and other DREDF activists plotted a strategy to defend and advance disability rights, using community education, tough legal analysis, and access to decision makers in the Reagan and Bush administrations provided by the Disability Rights Center director Evan Kemp Jr. Along with Kemp, Wright played a central role in the campaign to halt Reagan administration plans to gut the regulations implementing the Education for All Handicapped Children Act of 1975 and Section 504 of the Rehabilitation Act of 1973. Working with DREDF attorneys, Wright was also pivotal in passage of the Handicapped Children's Protection Act of 1986 and the Civil Rights Restoration Act of 1987.

In 1988, when proposed amendments to the Fair Housing Act failed to include protection for people with disabilities, Wright enlisted the support of the Leadership Conference on Civil Rights (LCCR), on whose executive committee she served. Wright, working with LCCR, DREDF's legal experts, and other housing advocates, convinced the act's congressional sponsors to require that new multifamily housing be constructed with the "adaptable housing" features developed by Ronald Mace at Barrier Free Environments. Wright also played a pivotal role during the early days of the AIDS epidemic, promoting the acceptance of HIV/AIDS as a disability by both traditional disability groups and Congress. She was instrumental in developing the AIDS lobby, and she fought against discriminatory policies advocated by some members of Congress.

Wright is best known for her role as the principal strategist of the campaign for passage of the ADA. In this effort, she brought together lawyers representing all of the major disability organizations, while the grassroots campaign included thousands of activists from the broadest coalition of disability groups ever assembled, including previously underrepresented constituencies such as people with drug and alcohol dependency, people with HIV/AIDS, and psychiatric survivors. Wright, urging people with disabilities to "wake up to . . . the discrimination we all accept as part of our lives," called on them to keep "discrimination diaries" to "educate yourselves and Congress." More than 25,000 such diaries were presented to Congress. Publicly and privately Wright advanced a strategy of "united we stand, divided we fall."

Wright has received numerous awards for her work, including the Distinguished Service Award from President Bush and the Dole Foundation Award from Sen. Robert Dole. Wright is the first person with a disability to receive the Hubert H. Humphrey Civil Rights Award from the Leadership Conference on Civil Rights.

Wright divides her time between DREDF's Washington, D.C., and Berkeley, California, offices. She also travels internationally to promote equal citizenship and civil rights for people with disabilities.

See also Americans with Disabilities Act of 1990; Civil Rights Restoration Act of 1987; Dart, Justin, Jr.; Disability Rights Education and Defense Fund (DREDF); Fair Housing Amendments Act of 1988; Kemp, Evan, Jr.; Mayerson, Arlene B.; *Smith v. Robinson*.

Wry Crips: Disabled Women's Theater

Wry Crips describe themselves as "disabled women actors, writers, theater technicians, and poets, making art from the truth of our lives." The company is known for its satire and political humor, for its radical take on disability and disability rights, and for its cross-disability inclusiveness. "Our strength is that we are a group and that we give each other support. It helps us proclaim the power of our disabilities."

Wry Crips, founded in the summer of 1985, is based in Oakland, California, and is a sponsored project of the San Francisco Women's Centers.

See also Disability Culture; Women with Disabilities.

Wyatt v. Stickney 503 F.2d 1305 (1974)

In 1970, the aunt and guardian of Ricky Wyatt, a cognitively disabled man living at the Bryce Hospital in Tuscaloosa, Alabama, initiated a class action suit on behalf of her nephew and other institution residents. The case was expanded in August 1971 to include residents at Partlow State School and Hospital, also in Tuscaloosa. The resulting decisions, rendered in 1971 and 1972 by Judge Frank Johnson of the U.S. District Court for the Middle District of Alabama, North Division, and then upheld by the Federal Appeals Court for the Fifth Circuit in 1972 and 1974, affirmed the constitutional right of people in residential state schools "to receive such individual treatment as (would) give each of them a realistic opportunity to be cured or to improve his or her mental condition." It was a crucial victory for disability rights activists and attorneys advocating for deinstitutionalization.

Conditions at the Partlow School, as at other such facilities across the country, were brutal and appalling. A congressional report documented how "retarded persons [were] . . . tied to their beds at night in the absence of sufficient staff to care for them; toilet paper was locked up to avoid additional cleanup work. One patient was regularly confined in a straightjacket for 9 years, as a result of which she lost the use of both arms." In his 1971, decision, Judge Johnson defined minimum treatment standards that both Bryce and Partlow had to meet, including specific criteria for admissions policies, staff numbers and training, residents' right to education and medical treatment and "habilitation," and the use

of medication. This ruling represented an unprecedented expansion of the role of the federal courts in the management of a state facility for people with disabilities. Judge Johnson also called for the creation of an independent monitoring committee to implement the details of his judgment.

In May 1972, Alabama Governor George Wallace filed an appeal of Johnson's decisions to the U.S. Court of Appeals for the Fifth Circuit. A panel of judges, ruling in November 1974, essentially affirmed Judge Johnson's decisions. The court ruled that people with cognitive and/or physical disabilities, housed in state "schools" or institutions, had a constitutional right to treatment. The court also held that federal courts could indeed intervene to ensure that this constitutional right was secured and that they could, as Judge Johnson had, set standards and monitor their implementation.

Wyatt was a landmark decision with far-reaching implications. The attorneys in *Wyatt*—George Dean, Charles Halpern, and Bruce Ennis—would use the precedent set by Judge Johnson to argue their case in *New York ARC v. Rockefeller* (1973) (the Willowbrook case in New York). The *Wyatt* case, together with the federal decisions in *O'Connor v. Donaldson* (1975) and *Halderman v. Pennhurst* (1978), meant that people with disabilities could no longer be segregated from society without treatment, education, or any hope of an end to their institutionalization. As one federal judge put it, "a tolerable living environment is now guaranteed by law." The *Wyatt* litigation itself continued into the 1990s, with state officials continuing to file motions to loosen or remove altogether standards set by the federal courts.

See also Deinstitutionalization; *Halderman v. Pennhurst*; *O'Connor v. Donaldson*; Willowbrook State School.

References Burgdorf, Robert L., *The Legal Rights of Handicapped Persons: Cases, Materials, and Text* (1980); Scheerenberger, R. C., *A History of Mental Retardation: A Quarter Century of Progress* (1987).

Yeh, John
See Deaf President Now
Campaign.

Ziegler Magazine (Matilda Ziegler Magazine for the Blind)
First published in March 1907, the *Matilda Ziegler Magazine for the Blind* was the country's first general interest periodical available to blind people who could read by touch. Originally printed in braille, New York Point, and Moon Type (a system of embossed lettering), today the *Ziegler Magazine* reaches 10,000 readers in braille and on tape.

Founded by Walter G. Holmes, a Tennessee journalist who was also the magazine's first editor, and philanthropist Electa Matilda Ziegler, who provided the funding, the magazine served as a source of news and social contact in an era before television and radio, when other newspapers and magazines were inaccessible to blind readers. It became, in the words of its second editor, Howard Liechty, "a bulletin board, an information bureau, a buyer's guide, a suggestion box, a personnel and agency directory, a mutual assistance club, a commodity exchange, an advertising medium, a rehabilitation and vocational guidance and placement agent, a self-improvement association, a soap-box platform and, unwittingly, sometimes even a marriage bureau."

In 1910, Congress passed a bill to allow the magazine to be mailed without postage. This waiver was needed because braille materials were up to 30 times more expensive to produce, and far bulkier and thus more expensive to mail, than printed matter. The waiver has since been expanded into the "Free Matter for the Blind and Handicapped" postal rating.

See also Braille.
Reference Koestler, Frances A., *The Ziegler Magazine Story* (1992, 1995).

Zola, Irving Kenneth (1935–1994)

Irving Kenneth Zola, sociologist, college professor, and founder of the Boston Self Help Center, is known for his books and articles on the disabled experience. A prolific writer and respected scholar, he has written works ranging from autobiographical accounts of life with a disability to academic treatises and studies of disability policy in the United States and around the world.

Zola was born on 24 January 1935. He was raised in Boston, where he contracted polio as a young man. He graduated from Boston Latin High School in 1954 and received a B.A. from Harvard in 1956. He received his doctorate at Harvard's Department of Social Relations in 1962.

Although starting his professional career as a research sociologist at Masschusetts General Hospital in Boston, Zola moved to Brandeis University in Waltham, Massachusetts, in 1963. He remained at Brandeis for the rest of his life, serving for many years as the chair of the Sociology Department. He was a consultant in residence on disability issues to the World Health Organization and to the Netherlands Institute of Preventive Health. In addition to founding the Boston Self Help Center and Greenhouse, a mental health clinic, Zola was also a founder of the Society for Disability Studies (now at Suffolk University in Boston) and Community Works, a fund-raising collective of small, grassroots organizations working for social change. He was a founder and, for many years, editor of *Disability Studies Quarterly*, and he served on the editorial boards of more than 20 other journals.

Zola's best-known book is *Missing Pieces: A Chronicle of Living with a Disability*. Published in 1982, the book describes his experiences while visiting Het Dorp, a community in the Netherlands designed by the Dutch government expressly (and exclusively) for people with disabilities. Zola began the visit as a sociologist, curious to see how segregation, as opposed to the American push toward integration, had worked for the Dutch disability community. The book turned into an account of his own personal odyssey, as Zola confronted the meaning of disability in his own life while recounting the stories of the people he met at Het Dorp.

Other titles by Zola include *Ordinary Lives: Voices of Disability and Disease*, an anthology of poetry and prose published in 1982, which he edited; *Independent Living for Physically Disabled People* (with Nancy M. Crewe), published in 1987; and articles, short stories, and poetry. His work earned him numerous awards, including the N. Neal Pike Prize for Service to the Handicapped in 1989. Zola was a member of the Clinton administration's transition team in 1992–1993.

An exponent of "disability pride," Zola believed that, "until we own our disability as an important part, though not necessarily all, of our identity, any attempt to create a meaningful pride, social movement or culture is doomed." He died on 1 December 1994 at age 59.

See also Boston Self Help Center; Disability Pride; *Disability Studies Quarterly*; Society for Disability Studies.

Reference Zola, Irving Kenneth, *Missing Pieces: A Chronicle of Living with a Disability* (1982).

Zukas, Hale J. (b. 1943)

Hale J. Zukas is one of the founders of the Center for Independent Living in Berkeley, California. He was born on 31 May 1943 in Los Angeles. Enrolling at the University of California at Berkeley in the mid-1960s, he became a member of the Rolling Quads and one of the founders and leaders of the Physically Disabled Students' Program. He left Berkeley with a B.A. in mathematics, graduating with distinction in 1971.

Zukas was the coordinator of community affairs at the Center for Independent Living from its inception until 1982. During this time, he became an expert on the various benefits programs for disabled and elderly people, particularly Supplemental Security Income (SSI) and In-Home Supportive Services (IHSS). He also became a leading advocate for the elimination of architectural and transportation barriers, pressuring local governments to install curb-cuts and curb ramps, and advising transit operators and other public and private organizations on how to remove barriers to people with disabilities.

In 1983, Zukas became a public policy analyst at the World Institute on Disability in Oakland, California, where he is now director of research. In this capacity, he has become an internationally recognized authority on such topics as the need for personal assistance services (PAS), accessible mass transportation, the elimination of architectural barriers, and disability-related statistics. Zukas is also a consultant for numerous agencies and organizations, including the National Science Foundation and the Federal Highway Administration. Also in 1983, Zukas became the vice chair of the U.S. Architectural and Transportation Barriers Compliance Board, where he had been a member of the Standards, Research, and Technical Assistance Committee since 1979. He is the author of *Attending to America: Report of the National Survey of Attendant Services Programs in the United States* (1987), *CIL History* (1976), and various articles and reports.

See also Center for Independent Living; World Institute on Disability.

Chronology

1817   The American School for the Deaf is founded in Hartford, Connecticut. This is the first school for disabled children anywhere in the Western Hemisphere.

1832   The Perkins School for the Blind in Boston admits its first two students, the sisters Sophia and Abbey Carter.

1841   Dorothea Dix begins her work on behalf of people with disabilities incarcerated in jails and poorhouses.

1847   The *American Annals of the Deaf* begins publication at the American School for the Deaf in Hartford, Connecticut.

1848   The first residential institution for people with mental retardation is founded by Samuel Gridley Howe at the Perkins Institution in Boston. During the next century, hundreds of thousands of developmentally disabled children and adults will be institutionalized, many for their entire lives.

1854   The New England Gallaudet Association of the Deaf is founded in Montpelier, Vermont.

1860   Simon Pollak demonstrates the use of braille at the Missouri School for the Blind.

The *Gallaudet Guide and Deaf-Mutes' Companion* becomes the first publication in the United States aimed at a disabled readership.

1861   Helen Adams Keller is born in Tuscumbia, Alabama.

1862   The Veterans Reserve Corps is formed by the U.S. Army. After the war, many of its members join the Freedman's Bureau to work with recently emancipated slaves.

1864   The enabling act giving the Columbia Institution for the Deaf and Dumb and Blind the authority to confer college degrees is signed by President Abraham Lincoln, making it the first college in the world expressly established for people with disabilities. A year later, the institution's blind students are transferred to the Maryland Institution at Baltimore, leaving the Columbia Institution with a student body made up entirely of deaf students. The institution would eventually be renamed Gallaudet College, and then Gallaudet University.

1869 The first wheelchair patent is registered with the U.S. Patent Office.

1878 Joel W. Smith presents his Modified Braille to the American Association of Instructors of the Blind. The association rejects his system, continuing to endorse instead New York Point, which blind readers complain is more difficult to read and write. What follows is a "War of the Dots" in which blind advocates for the most part prefer Modified Braille, while sighted teachers and administrators, who control funds for transcribing, prefer New York Point.

1880 The International Congress of Educators of the Deaf, at a conference in Milan, Italy, calls for the suppression of sign languages and the firing of all deaf teachers at schools for the deaf. This triumph of oralism is seen by deaf advocates as a direct attack upon their culture.

The National Convention of Deaf-Mutes meets in Cincinnati, Ohio, the nucleus of what will become the National Association of the Deaf (NAD). The first major issue taken on by the NAD is oralism and the suppression of American Sign Language.

1883 Sir Francis Galton in England coins the term *eugenics* to describe his pseudo-science of "improving the stock" of humanity. The eugenics movement, taken up by Americans, leads to passage in the United States of laws to prevent people with various disabilities from moving to this country, marrying, or having children. In many instances, it leads to the institutionalization and forced sterilization of disabled people, including children. Eugenics campaigns against people of color and immigrants lead to passage of "Jim Crow" laws in the South and legislation restricting immigration by southern and eastern Europeans, Asians, Africans, and Jews.

1887 Anne Sullivan meets Helen Keller for the first time in Tuscumbia, Alabama.

1890s–1920 Progressive activists push for the creation of state Workers' Compensation programs. By 1913, some 21 states have established some form of Worker's Compensation; the figure rises to 43 by 1919.

1901 The National Fraternal Society of the Deaf is founded by alumni at the Michigan School for the Deaf in Flint. It becomes the world's only fraternal life insurance company managed by deaf people. Through the first half of the century, it advocates for the rights of deaf people to purchase insurance and to obtain drivers' licenses.

1902–1903 Helen Keller, the first deaf-blind person to matriculate at college, publishes her autobiography, *The Story of My Life*, in a serial form in *Ladies' Home Journal* in the latter part of 1902, as a book in 1903.

1907 The first issue of the *Matilda Ziegler Magazine for the Blind* is published.

1908 Clifford Beers publishes *A Mind That Found Itself*, an exposé of conditions inside state and private mental institutions.

1909 The New York Public School System adopts Modified, or American, Braille for use in its classes for blind children, after public hearings in which blind advocates call for abandoning New York Point.

The National Committee for Mental Hygiene is founded by Clifford Beers in New York City.

The first folding wheelchairs are introduced for people with mobility disabilities.

1911 Congress passes a joint resolution (P.R. 45) authorizing the appointment of a federal commission to investigate the subject of workers' compensation and the liability of employers for financial compensation to disabled workers.

1912 Henry H. Goddard publishes *The Kallikak Family*, the best-seller purporting to link disability with immorality and alleging that both are tied to genetics. It advances the agenda of the eugenics movement, which in pamphlets such as *The Threat of the Feeble Minded* creates a climate of hysteria allowing for massive human rights abuses of people with disabilities, including institutionalization and forced sterilization.

1918 The Smith-Sears Veterans Vocational Rehabilitation Act establishes a federal vocational rehabilitation program for disabled soldiers.

1920 The Fess-Smith Civilian Vocational Rehabilitation Act is passed, creating a vocational rehabilitation program for disabled civilians.

1921 The American Foundation for the Blind is founded. Helen Keller becomes its principal fund-raiser, (Robert Irwin becomes director of research in 1922, executive director in 1929.)

1927 Franklin Roosevelt co-founds the Warms Springs Foundation at Warms Springs, Georgia. The Warm Springs facility for polio survivors becomes a model rehabilitation and peer counseling program.

The U.S. Supreme Court, in *Buck v. Bell*, rules that the forced sterilization of people with disabilities is not a violation of their constitutional rights. The decision removes the last restraints for eugenists advocating that people with disabilities be prohibited from having children. By the 1970s, some 60,000 disabled people are sterilized without their consent.

1929 Seeing Eye establishes the first dog-guide school for blind people in the United States.

1932 "The Treaty of London" standardizes American and English braille.

Disabled American Veterans is chartered by Congress to represent disabled veterans in their dealings with the federal government.

1933 Franklin Delano Roosevelt, the first seriously physically disabled person ever to be elected as a head of government, is sworn into office as president of the United States. He continues his "splendid deception," choosing to minimize his disability in response to the ableism of the electorate.

1935 Congress passes and President Roosevelt signs the Social Security Act, establishing federal old-age benefits and grants to the states for assistance to blind individuals and disabled children. The act also extends the already existing vocational rehabilitation programs established by earlier legislation.

The League of the Physically Handicapped is formed in New York City to protest discrimination against people with disabilities by federal relief programs. The group organizes sit-ins, picket lines, and demonstrations, and it travels to Washington, D.C., to protest and meet with officials of the Roosevelt administration.

1936 Passage of the Randolph Sheppard Act establishes a federal program for employing blind vendors at stands in the lobbies of federal office buildings.

1937 Herbert A. Everest and Harry C. Jennings patent a design for a folding wheelchair with an X-frame that can be packed into a car trunk. They found Everest & Jennings (E & J), which eventually becomes the largest manufacturer of wheelchairs in the United States.

1938 Passage of the Fair Labor Standards Act leads to an enormous increase

1938 (cont.) in the number of sheltered workshop programs for blind workers. Although intended to provide training and job opportunities for blind and visually disabled workers, it often leads to exploitation of workers at sub-minimum wages in poor conditions.

1940 The National Federation of the Blind is formed in Wilkes-Barre, Pennsylvania, by Jacobus tenBroek and other blind advocates. It advocates for "white cane laws" and input by blind people into programs for blind clients, among other reforms.

The American Federation of the Physically Handicapped is founded by Paul Strachan as the nation's first cross-disability, national political organization. It pushes for an end to job discrimination and lobbies for passage of legislation calling for a National Employ the Physically Handicapped Week, among other initiatives.

1942–1944 Henry Viscardi begins his work as an American Red Cross volunteer, training disabled soldiers to use their prosthetic limbs. His work at Walter Reed Army Medical Center in Washington, D.C., draws the attention of Howard Rusk and Eleanor Roosevelt, who protest when Viscardi's program is terminated by the Red Cross and the military.

1943 Congress passes the Vocational Rehabilitation Amendments, known as the LaFollette-Barden Act, adding physical rehabilitation to the goals of federally funded vocational rehabilitation programs and providing funding for certain health care services.

1944 Howard Rusk is assigned to the U.S. Army Air Force Convalescent Center in Pawling, New York, where he begins a rehabilitation program for disabled airmen. First dubbed "Rusk's folly" by the medical establishment, rehabilitation medicine becomes a new medical specialty.

1945 The Blinded Veterans Association (BVA) is formed in Avon, Connecticut.

President Harry Truman signs Public Law 176, a joint congressional resolution calling for the creation of an annual National Employ the Handicapped Week.

Boyce R. Williams is hired by the federal Office of Vocational Rehabilitation as Consultant for the Deaf, the Hard of Hearing, and the Speech Impaired. He begins close to four decades of work at OVR, designing and implementing educational and vocational programs for deaf Americans.

1946 Congress enacts the Hospital Survey and Construction Act, also known as the Hill-Burton Act, authorizing federal grants to the states for the construction of hospitals, public health centers, and health facilities for rehabilitation of people with disabilities.

The Cerebral Palsy Society of New York City is established by parents of children with cerebral palsy. This is the first chapter of what will become the United Cerebral Palsy Associations, Inc.

The National Mental Health Foundation is founded by conscientious objectors who served as attendants at state mental institutions during World War II. It works to expose the abusive conditions at these facilities and becomes an early impetus in the push for deinstitutionalization.

1947 Paralyzed Veterans of America (PVA) is founded at the Birmingham Hospital in Van Nuys, California, by Fred Smead, Randall Updyke, and other delegates from Veterans Administration hospitals across the country.

The first meeting of the President's Committee on National Employ the Physically Handicapped Week is held in Washington, D.C. Its publicity campaigns, coordinated by state and local committees, emphasize the competence of people with disabilities and use movie trailers, billboards, and radio and television ads to convince the public that it's "good business to hire the handicapped."

Harold Russell wins two Academy Awards for his role in *The Best Years of Our Lives*.

1948   The National Paraplegia Foundation is founded by members of the Paralyzed Veterans of America, as the civilian arm of their growing movement. Foundation chapters in many cities and states take a leading role in advocating for disability rights.

The disabled students' program at the University of Illinois at Galesburg is officially established. Founded and directed by Timothy Nugent, the program moves to the campus at Urbana-Champaign, where it becomes a prototype for disabled student programs and then independent living centers across the country.

We Are Not Alone (WANA), a mental patients' self-help group, is organized at the Rockland State Hospital in New York City.

1949   The first Annual Wheelchair Basketball Tournament is held in Galesburg, Illinois. Wheelchair basketball, and other sports, become an important part of disability lifestyle and culture over the next several decades.

Timothy Nugent founds the National Wheelchair Basketball Association.

The National Foundation for Cerebral Palsy is chartered by representatives of various groups of parents

of children with cerebral palsy. Renamed the United Cerebral Palsy Associations, Inc., in 1950, it becomes, together with the Association for Retarded Children, a major force in the parents' movement of the 1950s and thereafter.

1950   The Social Security Amendments of 1950 establish a federal-state program to aid the permanently and totally disabled (APTD). This is a limited prototype for later federal disability assistance programs such as Social Security Disability Insurance.

The Association for Retarded Children of the United States (later renamed the Association for Retarded Citizens and then The Arc) is founded in Minneapolis by representatives of various state associations of parents of mentally retarded children.

Mary Switzer is appointed director of the federal Office of Vocational Rehabilitation.

1951   Howard Rusk opens the Institute of Rehabilitation Medicine at New York University Medical Center. Staff at the Institute, including people with disabilities, begin work on such innovations as electric typewriters, mouthsticks, and improved prosthetics, as adaptive aids for people with severe disabilities.

1952   The President's Committee on National Employ the Physically Handicapped Week becomes the President's Committee on Employment of the Physically Handicapped, a permanent organization reporting to the president and Congress.

Henry Viscardi takes out a personal loan to found Abilities, Inc., a jobs training and placement program for people with disabilities.

1954   The U.S. Supreme Court, in *Brown v. Board of Education of Topeka*, rules

**1954
(cont.)** that separate schools for black and white children are inherently unequal and unconstitutional. This pivotal decision becomes a catalyst for the African-American civil rights movement, which in turn becomes a major inspiration to the disability rights movement.

Congress passes the Vocational Rehabilitation Amendments, authorizing federal grants to expand programs available to people with physical disabilities. Mary Switzer, director of the Office of Vocational Rehabilitation, uses this authority to fund more than 100 university-based rehabilitation-related programs.

The Social Security Act of 1935 is amended by Pub. Law 83 - 761, which includes a "freeze" provision for workers who are forced by disability to leave the work force. This protects their benefits when they retire by not counting the years between the time they cease working and their retirement, thus freezing their retirement benefits at their predisability level.

1955 Harold Wilke becomes the founder and first executive director of the Commission on Religion and Health within the United Church of Christ General Synod in New York City. In this capacity he works to open religious life and the ministry to women and people with disabilities.

1956 Congress passes the Social Security Amendments of 1956, which creates the Social Security Disability Insurance (SSDI) program for disabled workers aged 50 to 64.

Accent on Living begins publication.

1957 The First National Wheelchair Games in the United States are held at Adelphi College in Garden City, New York.

Little People of America is founded in Reno, Nevada, to advocate on behalf of dwarfs or little people.

Gunnar Dybwad is named executive director of the Association for Retarded Children.

1958 Congress passes the Social Security Amendments of 1958, extending Social Security Disability Insurance benefits to the dependents of disabled workers.

Gini Laurie becomes editor of the *Toomeyville Gazette* at the Toomey Pavilion polio rehabilitation center. Eventually renamed the *Rehabilitation Gazette*, this grassroots publication becomes an early voice for disability rights, independent living, and cross-disability organizing, and it features articles by disabled writers on all aspects of the disability experience.

The American Federation of the Physically Handicapped is dissolved at a convention in Grand Rapids, Michigan. Participants organize the National Association of the Physically Handicapped, Inc., to take its place.

1960 The first Paralympic Games, under the auspices of the International Paralympic Committee (IPC) are held in Rome, Italy.

Congress passes the Social Security Amendments of 1960, eliminating the restriction that disabled workers receiving Social Security Disability Insurance benefits be aged 50 or older.

1961 The American Council of the Blind is formally organized.

President Kennedy appoints a special President's Panel on Mental Retardation, to investigate the status of people with mental retardation and develop programs and reforms for its improvement.

The American National Standards Institute, Inc. (ANSI) publishes *American Standard Specifications for Making Buildings Accessible to, and Usable by, the Physically Handicapped*. This landmark document becomes the basis for all subsequent architectural access codes.

1962 The President's Committee on Employment of the Physically Handicapped is renamed the President's Committee on Employment of the Handicapped, reflecting its increased interest in employment issues affecting people with cognitive disabilities and mental illness.

Edward V. Roberts becomes the first severely disabled student at the University of California at Berkeley.

1963 President Kennedy, in an address to Congress, calls for a reduction, "over a number of years, and by hundreds of thousands, [in the number] of persons confined" to residential institutions, and he asks that methods be found "to retain in and return to the community the mentally ill and mentally retarded, and there to restore and revitalize their lives through better health programs and strengthened educational and rehabilitation services." Though not labeled such at the time, this is a call for deinstitutionalization and increased community services.

Congress passes the Mental Retardation Facilities and Community Health Centers Construction Act, authorizing federal grants for the construction of public and private nonprofit community mental health centers.

South Carolina passes the first statewide architectural access code.

John Hessler joins Ed Roberts at the University of California at Berkeley; other disabled students follow. Together they form the Rolling Quads to advocate for greater access on campus and in the surrounding community.

1964 The Civil Rights Act is passed, outlawing discrimination on the basis of race in public accommodations and employment, as well as in federally assisted programs. It will become a model for subsequent disability rights legislation.

Robert H. Weitbrecht invents the "acoustic coupler," forerunner of the telephone modem, enabling teletypewriter messages to be sent via standard telephone lines. This invention makes possible the widespread use of teletypewriters for the deaf (TDDs, now called TTYs), offering deaf and hard-of-hearing people access to the telephone system.

1965 Medicare and Medicaid are established through passage of the Social Security Amendments of 1965. These programs provide federally subsidized health care to disabled and elderly Americans covered by the Social Security program. The amendments also change the definition of disability under the Social Security Disability Insurance program, from "of long-continued and indefinite duration" to "expected to last for...not less than 12 months."

Vocational Rehabilitation Amendments of 1965 are passed, authorizing federal grants for the construction of rehabilitation centers, expanding existing vocational rehabilitation programs, and creating the National Commission on Architectural Barriers to Rehabilitation of the Handicapped.

William C. Stokoe, Carl Croneberg, and Dorothy Casterline publish *A Dictionary of American Sign Language on Linguistic Principles*, establishing the legitimacy of American Sign Language and beginning the move away from oralism.

1965
(cont.)
The Autism Society of America is founded by parents of children with autism in response to the lack of services, discrimination against children with autism, and the prevailing view of medical "experts" that autism is a result of poor parenting, as opposed to neurological disability.

Congress establishes the National Technical Institute for the Deaf at the Rochester Institute of Technology in Rochester, New York.

1966
Frederick C. Schreiber becomes the executive secretary of the National Association of the Deaf.

President Johnson establishes the President's Committee on Mental Retardation.

Christmas in Purgatory, by Burton Blatt and Fred Kaplan, is published, documenting the appalling conditions at state institutions for people with developmental disabilities.

1967
The National Theatre of the Deaf is founded with a grant from the federal Office of Vocational Rehabilitation.

1968
The Architectural Barriers Act is passed, mandating that federally constructed buildings and facilities be accessible to people with physical disabilities. This act is generally considered to be the first ever federal disability rights legislation.

1969
Niels Erk Bank-Mikkelsen from Denmark and Bengt Nirje from Sweden introduce the concept of normalization to an American audience at a conference sponsored by the President's Committee on Mental Retardation, helping to provide the conceptual framework for deinstitutionalization. Their remarks, and those of others, are published in *Changing Patterns in Residential Services for the Mentally Retarded*.

Silent News is founded by Julius and Harriet Wiggins as a newspaper for deaf people.

1970
The Insane Liberation Front is organized in Portland, Oregon.

The Developmental Disabilities Services and Facilities Construction Amendments are passed. They contain the first legal definition of developmental disabilities and authorize grants for services and facilities for the rehabilitation of people with developmental disabilities and state "DD Councils."

Nursing home resident Max Starkloff founds Paraquad in St. Louis.

Disabled in Action is founded in New York City by Judith Heumann, after her successful employment discrimination suit against the city's public school system. With chapters in several other cities, it organizes demonstrations and files litigation on behalf of disability rights.

The Physically Disabled Students Program (PDSP) is founded by Ed Roberts, John Hessler, Hale Zukas, and others at the University of California at Berkeley. With its provisions for community living, political advocacy, and personal assistance services, it becomes the nucleus for the first Center for Independent Living, founded two years later.

Congress passes the Urban Mass Transportation Assistance Act, declaring it a "national policy that elderly and handicapped persons have the same right as other persons to utilize mass transportation facilities and services." Passage of the act has little impact, however, as the law contains no provision for enforcement.

1971
The Mental Patients' Liberation Front is founded in Boston, and the Mental Patients' Liberation Project is founded in New York City.

The National Center for Law and the Handicapped is founded at the University of Notre Dame in South Bend, Indiana, becoming the first legal advocacy center for people with disabilities in the United States.

The U.S. District Court for the Middle District of Alabama hands down its first decision in *Wyatt v. Stickney*, ruling that people in residential state schools and institutions have a constitutional right "to receive such individual treatment as (would) give them a realistic opportunity to be cured or to improve his or her mental condition." Disabled people can no longer simply be locked away in "custodial institutions" without treatment or education. This decision is a crucial victory in the struggle for deinstitutionalization.

The Caption Center is founded at WGBH Public Television in Boston, and it begins providing captioned programming for deaf viewers.

The Fair Labor Standards Act of 1938 is amended to bring people with disabilities other than blindness into the sheltered workshop system. This measure leads to the establishment, in coming years, of an enormous sheltered workshop system for people with cognitive and developmental disabilities.

1972 The U.S. District Court for the District of Columbia, in *Mills v. Board of Education*, rules that the District of Columbia cannot exclude disabled children from the public schools. Similarly, the U.S. District Court for the Eastern District of Pennsylvania, in *PARC v. Pennsylvania*, strikes down various state laws used to exclude disabled children from the public schools. These decisions will be cited by advocates during the public hearings leading to passage of the Education for All Handicapped Children Act of 1975. *PARC* in particular sparks

numerous other right-to-education lawsuits and inspires advocates to look to the courts for the expansion of disability rights.

The Center for Independent Living (CIL) is founded in Berkeley, California. Generally recognized as the world's first independent living center, the CIL sparks the worldwide independent living movement.

Passage of the Social Security Amendments of 1972 creates the Supplemental Security Income (SSI) program. The law relieves families of the financial responsibility of caring for their adult disabled children. It consolidates existing federal programs for people who are disabled but not eligible for Social Security Disability Insurance.

The Houston Cooperative Living Residential Project is established in Houston, Texas, becoming a model, along with the Center for Independent Living in Berkeley, for subsequent independent living programs.

The Judge David L. Bazelon Center for Mental Health Law is founded in Washington, D.C., to provide legal representation and to advocate for the rights of people with mental illness.

The Legal Action Center, with offices in Washington, D.C., and New York City, is founded to advocate for the interests of people who are alcohol or drug dependent. Today, it also works on behalf of people with HIV/AIDS.

Paralyzed Veterans of America, the National Paraplegia Foundation, and Richard Heddinger file suit to force the Washington Metropolitan Area Transit Authority to incorporate access into their design for a new, multibillion dollar subway system in Washington, D.C. Their eventual victory becomes a landmark in the struggle for accessible public mass transit.

1972
(cont.)
Wolf Wolfensberger et al. publish *The Principle of Normalization in Human Services*, expanding the theory of normalization and bringing it to a wider American audience.

The Network Against Psychiatric Assault is organized in San Francisco.

The parents of residents at the Willowbrook State School in Staten Island, New York, file suit (*New York ARC v. Rockefeller*) to end the appalling conditions at that institution. A television broadcast from the facility outrages the general public, which sees the inhumane treatment endured by people with developmental disabilities. This press exposure, together with the lawsuit and other advocacy, eventually moves thousands of people from the institution into community-based living arrangements.

Demonstrations are held by disabled activists in Washington, D.C., to protest the veto of what will become the Rehabilitation Act of 1973 by President Richard M. Nixon. Among those organizing demonstrations in Washington and elsewhere are Disabled in Action, Paralyzed Veterans of America, the National Paraplegia Foundation, and other groups.

Madness Network News begins publication in San Francisco.

1973
The first handicap parking stickers are introduced in Washington, D.C.

The first Conference on Human Rights and Psychiatric Oppression is held at the University of Detroit.

Passage of the Federal-Aid Highway Act authorizes federal funds to provide for construction of curb-cuts.

Passage of the Rehabilitation Act of 1973 marks the greatest achievement of the disability rights movement thus far. The act—particularly Title V and, especially, Section 504—for the first time, confronts discrimination against people with disabilities. Section 504 prohibits programs receiving federal funds from discriminating against "otherwise qualified handicapped" individuals and sparks the formation of "504 workshops" and numerous grassroots organizations. Disability rights activists seize on the act as a powerful tool and make the signing of regulations to implement Section 504 a top priority. Litigation arising out of Section 504 will generate such central disability rights concepts as "reasonable modification," "reasonable accommodation," and "undue burden," which will form the framework for subsequent federal law, especially the Americans with Disabilities Act of 1990.

The Architectural and Transportation Barriers Compliance Board is established under the Rehabilitation Act of 1973 to enforce the Architectural Barriers Act of 1968.

The Consortium for Citizens with Disabilities is organized to advocate for passage of what will become the Developmentally Disabled Assistance and Bill of Rights Act of 1975 and the Education for All Handicapped Children Act of 1975.

1974
The first U.S. National Wheelchair Basketball Tournament is held, as well as the first National Wheelchair Marathon.

The Boston Center for Independent Living is founded.

Halderman v. Pennhurst is filed in Pennsylvania on behalf of the residents of the Pennhurst State School & Hospital. The case, highlighting the horrific conditions at state "schools" for people with mental retardation, becomes an important precedent in the battle for deinstitutionalization, establishing a right to community services for people with developmental disabilities.

The first convention of People First is held in Salem, Oregon. People First becomes the largest U.S. organization composed of and led by people with cognitive disabilities.

The first Client Assistance Projects (CAPs) are established to act as advocates for clients of state vocational rehabilitation agencies.

North Carolina passes a statewide building code with stringent access requirements drafted by access advocate Ronald Mace. This code becomes a model for effective architectural access legislation in other states. Mace founds Barrier Free Environments to advocate for accessibility in buildings and products.

1975   The first convention of the American Association of the Deaf-Blind is held in Cleveland.

Congress enacts the Community Services Act, creating the Head Start program, with the stipulation that at least 10 percent of program openings be reserved for disabled children.

Congress passes the Developmentally Disabled Assistance and Bill of Rights Act, providing federal funds to programs serving people with developmental disabilities and outlining a series of rights for those who are institutionalized. The lack of an enforcement mechanism within the bill and subsequent court decisions, will, however, render this portion of the act virtually useless to disability rights advocates.

The Education for All Handicapped Children Act (Pub. Law 94-142) is passed, establishing the right of children with disabilities to a public school education in an integrated environment. The act is a cornerstone of federal disability rights legislation. In the next two decades, millions of disabled children will be educated under its provisions, radically changing the lives of people in the disability community.

The American Coalition of Citizens with Disabilities is founded. It becomes the preeminent national cross-disability rights organization of the 1970s, pulling together disability rights groups representing blind, deaf, physically disabled, and developmentally disabled people. It hires Frank Bowe as its first executive director, who begins a major study of the current status of Americans with disabilities.

The Association of Persons with Severe Handicaps (TASH) is founded by special education professionals responding to *PARC v. Pennsylvania* (1972) and subsequent right-to-education cases. The organization will eventually call for the end of aversive behavior modification and the closing of all residential institutions for people with disabilities.

The Atlantis Community is founded in Denver as a group housing program for severely disabled adults who, until that time, had been forced to live in nursing homes.

The U.S. Supreme Court, in *O'Connor v. Donaldson*, rules that people cannot be institutionalized against their will in a psychiatric hospital unless they are determined to be a threat to themselves or to others.

Mainstream: Magazine of the Able-Disabled begins publication in San Diego.

The first Parent and Training Information Centers are founded to help parents of disabled children to exercise their rights under the Education for All Handicapped Children Act of 1975.

Chronology

1975
(cont.)
Edward Roberts becomes the director of the California Department of Rehabilitation. He moves to establish nine independent living centers all across that state, based on the model of the original Center for Independent Living in Berkeley. The success of these centers demonstrates that independent living can be replicated and eventually results in the founding of hundreds of independent living centers all over the world.

The Western Center on Law and the Handicapped is founded in Los Angeles.

1976
Passage of an amendment to the Higher Education Act of 1972 provides services to physically disabled students entering college.

The Transbus group, made up of Disabled in Action of Pennsylvania, the American Coalition of Citizens with Disabilities, United Cerebral Palsy Associations, and others, and represented by the Public Interest Law Center of Philadelphia, files suit (*Disabled in Action of Pennsylvania, Inc. v. Coleman*) to require that all buses purchased by public transit authorities receiving federal funds meet Transbus specifications, making them wheelchair accessible.

Disabled in Action pickets the United Cerebral Palsy telethon in New York City, calling telethons "demeaning and paternalistic shows which celebrate and encourage pity."

The Coalition of Provincial Organizations of the Handicapped is founded in Winnipeg, Canada, later becoming the Council of Canadians with Disabilities.

The Disability Rights Center is founded in Washington, D.C. Sponsored by Ralph Nader's Center for the Study of Responsive Law, it specializes in consumer protection for people with disabilities, joining the Justice Department in antitrust

action against the Everest & Jennings company.

The Westside Center for Independent Living in founded in Los Angeles as one of the first nine independent living centers established by Ed Roberts and the California Department of Rehabilitation.

1977
President Jimmy Carter appoints Max Cleland to head the U.S. Veterans Administration, making Cleland the first severely disabled (as well as the youngest) person to fill that position.

Disability rights activists in ten cities stage demonstrations and occupations of the offices of the federal department of Health, Education and Welfare (HEW) to force the Carter administration to issue regulations implementing Section 504 of the Rehabilitation Act of 1973. The demonstrations galvanize the disability community nationwide, particularly the San Francisco action, which lasts nearly a month. On 28 April, HEW Secretary Joseph Califano signs the regulations.

The White House Conference on Handicapped Individuals brings together 3,000 disabled people to discuss federal policy toward people with disabilities. This first ever gathering of its kind results in numerous recommendations and acts as a catalyst for grassroots disability rights organizing.

Passage of the Legal Services Corporation Act Amendments adds financially needy people with disabilities to the list of those eligible for publicly funded legal services.

The U.S. Court of Appeals for the Seventh Circuit, in *Lloyd v. Regional Transportation Authority*, rules that individuals have a right to sue under Section 504 of the Rehabilitation

Act of 1973 and that public transit authorities must provide accessible service. The U.S. Court of Appeals for the Fifth Circuit, in *Snowden v. Birmingham-Jefferson County Transit Authority*, undermines this decision by ruling that authorities need provide access only to "handicapped persons other than those confined to wheelchairs."

1978 Fiesta Educativa, Inc., is founded in Los Angeles by Hispanic parents of children with disabilities.

Adaptive Environments Center is founded in Boston.

Disability rights activists in Denver stage a sit-in demonstration, blocking several Denver Regional Transit Authority buses, to protest the complete inaccessibility of that city's mass transit system. The demonstration is organized by the Atlantis Community and is the first action in what will be a years-long civil disobedience campaign to force the Denver Transit Authority to purchase wheelchair lift–equipped buses.

Title VII of the Rehabilitation Act Amendments of 1978 establishes the first federal funding for independent living and creates the National Council of the Handicapped under the U.S. Department of Education.

On Our Own: Patient Controlled Alternatives to the Mental Health System is published. Written by Judi Chamberlin, it becomes a standard text of the psychiatric survivor movement.

The National Center for Law and the Deaf is founded in Washington, D.C.

Handicapping America, by Frank Bowe, is published. The book is a comprehensive review of the policies and attitudes denying equal citizenship to people with disabilities,

and it becomes a standard text of the general disability rights movement.

1979 The U.S. Olympic Committee organizes its Handicapped in Sports Committee.

The U.S. Supreme Court, in *Southeastern Community College v. Davis*, rules that, under Section 504 of the Rehabilitation Act of 1973, programs receiving federal funds must make "reasonable modifications" to enable the participation of otherwise qualified disabled individuals. This decision is the Court's first ruling on Section 504, and it establishes reasonable modification as an important principle in disability rights law.

Marilyn Hamilton, Jim Okamoto, and Don Helman produce their "Quickie" lightweight folding wheelchair, revolutionizing manual wheelchair design.

The Disability Rights Education and Defense Fund (DREDF) is founded in Berkeley, California, becoming the nation's preeminent disability rights legal advocacy center and participating in much of the landmark litigation and lobbying of the 1980s and 1990s.

The National Alliance for the Mentally Ill is founded in Madison, Wisconsin, by parents of persons with mental illness.

Self Help for Hard of Hearing People, Inc., is founded in Bethesda, Maryland, by Howard "Rocky" Stone.

1980 Congress passes the Social Security Amendments, with Section 1619 designed to address work disincentives within the Social Security Disability Insurance and Supplemental Security Income programs. Other provisions mandate a review of Social Security recipients, leading to the termination of benefits of hun-

1980
(cont.)
dreds of thousands of people with disabilities.

Congress passes the Civil Rights of Institutionalized Persons Act, authorizing the U.S. Justice Department to file civil suits on behalf of residents of institutions whose rights are being violated.

The first issue of the *Disability Rag & Resource* is published in Louisville, Kentucky.

Disabled Peoples' International is founded in Singapore, with the participation of advocates from Canada and the United States.

The Womyn's Braille Press is founded in Minneapolis to make women's and feminist literature available in braille and on tape.

1981
The International Year of Disabled Persons begins with speeches before the United Nations General Assembly. During the year, governments are encouraged to sponsor programs bringing people with disabilities into the mainstream of their societies.

In an editorial in the *New York Times*, Evan Kemp Jr. attacks the Jerry Lewis National Muscular Dystrophy Association Telethon, writing that "the very human desire for cures...can never justify a television show that reinforces a stigma against disabled people."

Publication of *Images of Ourselves: Women with Disabilities Talking* by Jo Campling and *All Things Are Possible* by Yvonne Duffy highlights the concerns of women with disabilities.

1981–
1983
The newly elected Reagan administration threatens to amend or revoke regulations implementing Section 504 of the Rehabilitation Act of 1973 and the Education for All Handicapped Children Act of 1975. Disability rights advocates, led by Patrisha Wright at the Dis-

ability Rights Education and Defense Fund (DREDF) and Evan Kemp Jr. at the Disability Rights Center, respond with an intensive lobbying effort and a grassroots campaign that generates more than 40,000 cards and letters. After three years, the Reagan administration abandons its attempts to revoke or amend the regulations.

1981–
1984
The Reagan administration terminates the Social Security benefits of hundreds of thousands of disabled recipients. Advocates charge that these terminations are an effort to reduce the federal budget and often do not reflect any improvement in the condition of those being terminated. A variety of groups, including the Alliance of Social Security Disability Recipients and the Ad Hoc Committee on Social Security Disability, spring up to fight these terminations. Several disabled people, in despair over the loss of their benefits, commit suicide.

1982
National Black Deaf Advocates is founded.

The parents of "Baby Doe" in Bloomington, Indiana, are advised by their doctors to deny a surgical procedure to unblock their newborn's esophagus, because the baby has Down syndrome. Although disability rights activists try to intervene, Baby Doe starves to death before legal action can be taken. The case prompts the Reagan administration to issue regulations calling for the creation of "Baby Doe squads" to safeguard the civil rights of disabled newborns.

The Telecommunications for the Disabled Act mandates telephone access for deaf and hard-of-hearing people at important public places, such as hospitals and police stations, and that all coin-operated phones be hearing aid–compatible by 1 January 1985. It also calls for state subsidies for production and distribution of TTDs (telecommunications devices for the deaf), more commonly referrred to as TTYs.

The National Council on Independent Living is formed to advocate on behalf of independent living centers and the independent living movement.

1983　The Disabled Children's Computer Group (DCCG) is founded in Berkeley, California.

Ed Roberts, Judy Heumann, and Joan Leon found the World Institute on Disability in Oakland, California.

American Disabled for Accessible Public Transit (ADAPT) is organized at the Atlantis Community headquarters in Denver, Colorado. For the next seven years ADAPT conducts a civil disobedience campaign against the American Public Transit Association (APTA) and various local public transit authorities to protest the lack of accessible public transportation.

The National Council on the Handicapped issues a call for Congress to "act forthwith to include persons with disabilities in the Civil Rights Act of 1964 and other civil and voting rights legislation and regulations."

The United Nations expands the International Year of Disabled Persons into the International Decade of Disabled Persons, to last from 1983 to 1992.

Sharon Kowalski is disabled by a drunk driver near Onamia, Minnesota. Her parents, discovering that she is a lesbian, refuse to allow her to return home to her lover Karen Thompson, instead keeping her in a nursing home. Thompson's eight-year struggle to free Kowalski becomes a focus of disability rights advocates and leads to links between the lesbian and disability rights communities.

The Job Accommodation Network (JAN) is founded by the President's Committee on Employment of the Handicapped to provide information to businesses with disabled employees.

1984　The Baby Jane Doe case, like the 1982 Bloomington Baby Doe case, involves an infant being denied needed medical care because of her disability. The case results in litigation argued before the U.S. Supreme Court in *Bowen v. American Hospital Association*, and in passage of the Child Abuse Prevention and Treatment Act Amendments of 1984.

George Murray becomes the first wheelchair athlete to be featured on the Wheaties cereal box.

The U.S. Supreme Court rules, in *Irving Independent School District v. Tatro*, that school districts are required under the Education for All Handicapped Children Act of 1975 to provide intermittent catheterization, performed by the school nurse or a nurse's aide, as a "related service" to a disabled student. School districts can no longer refuse to educate a disabled child because they might need such a service.

The National Council of the Handicapped becomes an independent federal agency.

Congress passes the Social Security Disability Reform Act in response to the complaints of hundreds of thousands of people whose Social Security disability benefits have been terminated. The law requires that payment of benefits and health insurance coverage continue for terminated recipients until they have exhausted their appeals and that decisions by the Social Security Administration to terminate benefits be made only on the basis of "the weight of the evidence" in a particular recipient's case.

1984
(cont.) The Voting Accessibility for the Elderly and Handicapped Act mandates that polling places be accessible or that ways be found to enable elderly and disabled people to exercise their right to vote. Advocates find that the act is difficult, if not impossible, to enforce.

1985 Wry Crips, a radical disability theatre group, is founded in Oakland, California.

The U.S. Supreme Court rules, in *Burlington School Committee v. Department of Education*, that schools must pay the expenses of disabled children enrolled in private programs during litigation under the Education for All Handicapped Children Act of 1975, if the courts rule such placement is needed to provide the child with an appropriate education in the least restrictive environment.

The U.S. Supreme Court rules, in *City of Cleburne v. Cleburne Living Center*, that localities cannot use zoning laws to prohibit group homes for people with developmental disabilities from opening in a residential area solely because its residents are disabled.

Gini Laurie founds the International Polio Network, based in St. Louis, Missouri, and begins advocating for recognition of postpolio syndrome.

The National Association of Psychiatric Survivors is founded.

1986 The Air Carrier Access Act is passed, prohibiting airlines from refusing to serve people simply because they are disabled, and from charging them more for airfare than nondisabled travelers.

The National Council on the Handicapped issues *Toward Independence*, a report outlining the legal status of Americans with disabilities, documenting the existence of dis-

crimination and citing the need for federal civil rights legislation (what will eventually be passed as the Americans with Disabilities Act of 1990).

Concrete Change, a grassroots organization advocating for accessible housing, is organized in Atlanta, Georgia.

The Employment Opportunities for Disabled Americans Act is passed, allowing recipients of Supplemental Security Income and Social Security Disability Insurance to retain benefits, particularly medical coverage, even after they obtain work. The act is intended to remove the disincentives that keep many disabled people unemployed.

The Protection and Advocacy for Mentally Ill Individuals Act is passed, setting up protection and advocacy agencies for people who are in-patients or residents of mental health facilities.

The Society for Disability Studies is founded.

The Rehabilitation Act Amendments of 1986 define supported employment as a "legitimate rehabilitation outcome."

1987 The Alliance for Technology Access is founded in California by the Disabled Children's Computer Group and the Apple Computer Office of Special Education.

Marlee Matlin wins an Oscar for her performance in *Children of a Lesser God*.

The AXIS Dance Troupe is founded in Oakland, California.

The DisAbled Women's Network (DAWN) is founded in Winnipeg, Canada.

The U.S. Supreme Court, in *School Board of Nassau County, Fla. v.*

Arline, outlines the rights of people with contagious disease under Title V of the Rehabilitation Act of 1973. It establishes that people with infectious diseases cannot be fired from their jobs "because of prejudiced attitudes or ignorance of others." This ruling is a landmark precedent for people with tuberculosis, HIV/AIDS, and other infectious diseases or disabilities, and for people, such as individuals with cancer or epilepsy, who are discriminated against because others fear they may be contagious.

The Association of Late Deafened Adults (ALDA) is founded in Chicago.

1988 Students at Gallaudet University in Washington, D.C., organize a week-long shut-down and occupation of their campus to demand selection of a deaf president, after the Gallaudet Board of Trustees appoints a nondeaf person as president of the university. On 13 March, the Gallaudet administration announces that I. King Jordan will be the university's first deaf president.

Deaf Life begins monthly publication in Rochester, New York.

The Technology-Related Assistance Act for Individuals with Disabilities (the "Tech Act") is passed, authorizing federal funding to state projects designed to facilitate access to assistive technology.

The Fair Housing Amendments Act adds people with disabilities to those groups protected by federal fair housing legislation, and it establishes minimum standards of access and adaptability for newly constructed multiple-dwelling housing.

The National Council on the Handicapped issues *On the Threshold of Independence* and a first draft of the Americans with Disabilities Act (ADA), which is introduced into

Congress by Rep. Tony Coelho and into the Senate by Sen. Lowell Weicker. The Congressional Task Force on the Rights and Empowerment of Americans with Disabilities is created by Rep. Major R. Owens and co-chaired by Justin Dart Jr. and Elizabeth Boggs. The task force begins building grassroots support for passage of the ADA.

Congress overturns President Ronald Reagan's veto of the Civil Rights Restoration Act of 1987. The act undoes the Supreme Court decision in *Grove City College v. Bell* and other decisions limiting the scope of federal civil rights law, including Section 504 of the Rehabilitation Act of 1973.

The U.S. Supreme Court, in *Honig v. Doe*, affirms the "stay put rule" established under the Education for All Handicapped Children Act of 1975, under which school authorities cannot expel or suspend or otherwise move disabled children from the setting agreed upon under the child's Individualized Education Program (IEP) without a due process hearing.

The National Parent Network on Disabilities is established as an umbrella organization for the Parent Training and Information Centers.

1989 The federal appeals court, in *ADAPT v. Skinner*, rules that federal regulations requiring that transit authorities spend only 3 percent of their budgets on access are arbitrary and discriminatory.

The original version of the Americans with Disabilities Act, introduced into Congress the previous year, is redrafted and reintroduced. Disability organizations across the country advocate on its behalf, with Patrisha Wright as "general" and Marilyn Golden, Liz Savage, Justin Dart Jr., and Elizabeth Boggs as principal coordinators of this effort.

Chronology

1989
(cont.)
The Center for Universal Design (originally the Center for Accessible Housing) is founded by Ronald Mace in Raleigh, North Carolina.

Mouth: The Voice of Disability Rights begins publication in Rochester, New York.

The President's Committee on Employment of the Handicapped is renamed the President's Committee on Employment of People with Disabilities.

1990
Altered States of the Arts is founded.

The Wheels of Justice campaign in Washington, D.C., organized by American Disabled for Accessible Public Transit (ADAPT), brings hundreds of disabled people to the nation's capital in support of the Americans with Disabilities Act. ADAPT activists occupy the Capitol rotunda, and are arrested when they refuse to leave.

The Americans with Disabilities Act is signed by President George Bush on 26 July in a ceremony on the White House lawn witnessed by thousands of disability rights activists. The law is the most sweeping disability rights legislation in history, for the first time bringing full legal citizenship to Americans with disabilities. It mandates that local, state, and federal governments and programs be accessible, that businesses with more than 15 employees make "reasonable accommodations" for disabled workers, that public accommodations such as restaurants and stores make "reasonable modifications" to ensure access for disabled members of the public. The act also mandates access in public transportation, communication, and in other areas of public life.

The Autism National Committee is founded.

The Committee of Ten Thousand is founded to advocate for people with hemophilia, and their family members, who have been infected with HIV/AIDS through tainted blood products.

The Ryan White Comprehensive AIDS Resources Emergency Act is passed to help localities cope with the burgeoning HIV/AIDS epidemic.

With passage of the Americans with Disabilities Act, American Disabled for Accessible Public Transit (ADAPT) changes its focus to advocating for personal assistance services and changes its name to American Disabled for Attendant Programs Today.

The Education for All Handicapped Children Act is amended and renamed the Individuals with Disabilities Education Act (IDEA).

1991
Jerry's Orphans stages its first annual picket of the Jerry Lewis Muscular Dystrophy Association Telethon.

1993
The American Indian Disability Legislation Project is established to collect data on Native American disability rights laws and regulations.

Communication Unbound, by Douglas Biklen, is published, leading to a great increase in the use of Facilitated Communication. The method becomes controversial when it results in accusations of physical and sexual abuse by teachers, caretakers, and family members of people with communication disabilities.

The Glen Ridge case comes to trial in New Jersey, and three men are convicted of sexual assault and conspiracy, and a fourth of conspiracy, for raping a 17-year-old mentally disabled woman. The case highlights the widespread sexual abuse of people with developmental disabilities.

Robert Williams becomes commissioner of the Administration on Developmental Disabilities, the first developmentally disabled person to hold that post.

1994   The final federal appeals court ruling in *Holland v. Sacramento City Unified School District* affirms the right of disabled children to attend public school classes with nondisabled children. The ruling is a major victory in the ongoing effort to ensure enforcement of the Individuals with Disabilities Education Act.

1995   Justice for All is founded in Washington, D.C.

When Billy Broke His Head . . . and Other Tales of Wonder premiers on PBS. The film is, for many, a first-time introduction to the concept of disability rights and the disability rights movement.

The American Association of People with Disabilities is founded in Washington, D.C.

The U.S. Court of Appeals for the Third Circuit, in *Helen L. v. Snider*, rules that the continued publicly funded institutionalization of a disabled Pennsylvania woman in a nursing home, when not medically necessary, and where the state of Pennsylvania could offer her the option of home care, is a violation of her rights under the Americans with Disabilities Act of 1990. Disability rights advocates hail this ruling as a landmark decision regarding the rights of people in nursing homes to personal assistance services, allowing them to live at home.

Sandra Jensen, a member of People First, is denied a heart-lung transplant by the Stanford University School of Medicine because she has Down syndrome. After pressure from disability rights activists, administrators there reverse their decision, and, in January 1996, Jensen becomes the first person with Down syndrome to receive a heart-lung transplant.

1996   Congress passes legislation eliminating more than 150,000 disabled children from the Social Security rolls, as well as individuals who are alcohol or drug dependent.

Not Dead Yet is formed by disabled advocates to oppose Jack Kevorkian and the proponents of assisted suicide for people with disabilities. The Supreme Court agrees to hear several right-to-die cases, and disability rights advocates redouble their efforts to prevent a resurgence of "euthanasia" and "mercy killing" as practiced by the Nazis against disabled people during World War II. Of particular concern are calls for the "rationing" of health care to people with severe disabilities and the imposition of "Do Not Resuscitate" (DNR) orders for disabled people in hospitals, schools, and nursing homes.

Sen. Robert Dole becomes the first person with a visible disability since Franklin Roosevelt to run for president of the United States. Unlike Roosevelt, he publicly acknowledges the extent of his disability. He is defeated by incumbent Bill Clinton.

Georgia voters elect disabled candidate Max Cleland to the U.S. Senate.

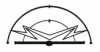

Bibliography

Albrecht, Gary L., editor. *The Sociology of Physical Disability and Rehabilitation*. Pittsburgh: University of Pittsburgh Press, 1976.

Allen, Robert S. "Testimony." *Valor* (August 1950): 18.

Altmeyer, Arthur J. *The Formative Years of Social Security*. Madison: University of Wisconsin Press, 1966.

American Council of the Blind. *Annual Report 1993*. Washington, DC: American Council of the Blind, 1994.

American Disabled for Attendant Programs Today. "DC Action a Huge Success." *Incitement* (Spring 1990): 3–4.

———. "National Highlights of a Decade of ADAPT Actions." Unpublished manuscript, 1995.

American Printing House for the Blind, Inc. *Annual Report: July 1, 1992–June 30, 1993*. Louisville, KY: American Printing House for the Blind, 1994.

Amundson, R. "Disability, Handicap, and the Environment." *Journal of Social Philosophy*. Vol. 23, No. 1 (1993): 105–117.

"Animal Quarantine May Violate ADA." *Silent News*. Vol. 28, No. 8 (August 1996): 11.

"Another Loss: Howie the Harp, 42." *Disability Rag & Resource*. Vol. 16, No. 3 (May/June 1995): 26.

Armstrong, David F. "Deep Roots: The Historical Context for Gallaudet's Birth and Growth." *Gallaudet Today*. Vol. 17, No. 3 (Spring 1987): 10–17.

Arnold, Jean. Interview. 8 July 1996.

Asch, Adrienne S. "Has the Law Made a Difference?: What Some Disabled Students Have To Say." In Dorothy Kerzner Lipsky and Alan Gartner, editors. *Beyond Special Education: Quality Education for All*. Baltimore: Paul H. Brookes Publishing Co., 1989.

———. "The Human Genome and Disability Rights." *Disability Rag & Resource* (January/February 1994): 12–15.

———. Interview. 22 September 1996.

Asch, Adrienne S., and Michelle Fine. "Disability beyond Stigma: Social Interaction, Discrimination, and Activism." *Journal of Social Issues*. Vol. 44, No. 1 (Spring 1988): 3–21.

———. *Women with Disabilities: Essays in Psychology, Culture and Politics*. Philadelphia: Temple University Press, 1988.

Association of Persons with Severe Handicaps (TASH). *TASH's Structure, Purpose, History and Program*, 1995.

Atkins, B. J., and G. N. Wright. "Vocational Rehabilitation of Blacks: The Statement. The Response, The Comment." *Journal of*

Rehabilitation. Vol. 46, No. 2 (April/May/June 1980): 40–46.

Auberger, Michael. "ADA Now: Mike Auberger's Address to the Wheels of Justice Marchers at the Nation's Capitol Monday 3/12/90." *Incitement* (Spring 1990): 7.

Averill, Clarence. Interview. 19 September 1996.

Backman, Eric. "Is the Movement Racist?" *Mainstream*. Vol. 18, No. 8 (May 1994): 24–31.

Bahan, Ben. "Total Communication: Total Farce." In Sherman Wilcox, editor. *American Deaf Culture*. Burstonsville, MD: Linstok Press, 1989.

———. "Who's Itching To Get into Mainstreaming?" In Sherman Wilcox, editor. *American Deaf Culture*. Burstonsville, MD: Linstok Press, 1989.

Bajema, Carl Jay, editor. *Eugenics: Then and Now*. Stroudsburg, PA: Dowden, Hutchinson and Ross, 1976.

Baker, Ann. "Doors, Hearts Opened to Ex-Mental Patients." *St. Paul Pioneer Press and Dispatch* (18 October 1985): 4C.

Baker, Charlotte, and Carol Padden. *American Sign Language: A Look at Its History, Structure, and Community*. Silver Spring, MD: T. J. Publishers, 1978.

Baldwin, Stephen C. *Pictures in the Air: The Story of the National Theatre of the Deaf*. Washington, DC: Gallaudet University Press, 1993.

Ballard, Joseph, Bruce Ramirez, and Kathy Zantal-Wiener. *Public Law 94-142. Section 504, and Public Law 99-457: Understanding What They Are and Are Not*. Reston, VA: Council for Exceptional Children, 1987.

Barnes, Sandra. *Who's Who in Entertainment, Second Edition, 1992–1993*. Wilmette, IL: Reed Publishing Co., 1992.

Barrier Free Environments. *The Accessible Housing Design File*. New York: Van Nostrand Reinhold, 1991.

"Barriers Persist." *Out-Line*. Vol. 10. No. 24 (14 February 1984).

Bartels, Elmer C. "Employment and the Public Vocational Rehabilitation Program: Impact of the ADA." In Lawrence O. Gostin

and Henry A. Beyer, editors. *Implementing the Americans with Disabilities Act: Rights and Responsibilities of All Americans*. Baltimore: Paul H. Brookes Publishing Co., 1993.

Bartlett, Katharine T., and Judith Welch Wegner, editors. *Children with Special Needs*. New Brunswick, NJ: Transaction Books, 1987.

Batiste, Gerald. Interview. 27 March 1996.

Bazelon Center for Mental Health Law. *What Does Fair Housing Mean to People with Disabilities?* Washington, DC, 1994.

Becker, Elle Freidman. *Female Sexuality following Spinal Cord Injury*. Bloomington, IL: Accent Special Publications, 1978.

Becker, Jaimie. Interview. 29 July 1996.

Beers, Clifford Wittington. *A Mind That Found Itself*. Garden City, NY: Doubleday and Company, 1908, 1965.

Berkowitz, Edward D. *Disabled Policy: America's Programs for the Handicapped*. Cambridge, New York, and Port Chester: Cambridge University Press, 1987.

Berkowitz, Monroe, William G. Johnson, and Edward H. Murphy. *Public Policy toward Disability*. New York: Praeger, 1976.

Best, Harry. *Deafness and the Deaf in the United States*. New York: Macmillan, 1943.

Betenbaugh, Helen R. "ADA and the Religious Community: The Moral Case." *Journal of Religion in Disability & Rehabilitation*. Vol. 2, No. 4 (1996): 47–69.

Beyer, Henry A. "A Free Appropriate Public Education." *Western New England Law Review*. Vol. 5, No. 3 (Winter 1983): 363–390.

Bibow, Martin. "The Winning Technology." *New Mobility*. Vol. 7, No. 35 (August 1996): 34–38.

Biklen, Douglas. *Communication Unbound*. New York: Columbia University Teachers College Press, 1993.

———. "Why Parents and Children with Disabilities Should Have the Right To Use Facilitated Communication." *Exceptional Parent*. Vol. 25, No. 7 (July 1995): 48–50.

Biklen, Douglas, Nina Saha, and Chris Kliewer. "How Teachers Confirm the Authorship of Facilitated Communication: A Portfolio Approach." *Journal of the Associa-*

tion for Persons with Severe Handicaps. Vol. 20, No. 1 (1995): 45–56.

Bishop, Mary. "An Elite Said Their Kind Wasn't Wanted: How Social Judgements of the Day Forced Sterilizations." *Roanoke Times & World News* (26 June 1994): E-1, E-5.

Blank, Wade. Interview. 22 December 1993.

Blair, William, and Dana Davidson. "Religion." In *Encyclopedia of Disability and Rehabilitation*, Arthur E. Dell Orto and Robert P. Marinelli, editors. New York: Simon & Schuster Macmillan, 1995.

Blatt, Burton, and Fred Kaplan. *Christmas in Purgatory*. Allyn and Bacon, Inc., 1966.

Blumberg, Lisa. "Eugenics vs. Reproductive Choice." *Disability Rag & Resource* (January/February 1994): 3–11.

Boatner, Maxine Tull. *Voice of the Deaf: A Biography of Edward Miner Gallaudet*. Washington, DC: Public Affairs Press, 1959.

Bogdan, Robert. *Freak Show: Presenting Human Oddities for Amusement and Profit*. Chicago: University of Chicago Press, 1988.

Bogdan, Robert, and Steven J. Taylor. *Inside Out: The Social Meaning of Mental Retardation*. Toronto: University of Toronto Press, 1982.

Bolte, Bill. "Bree Walker: TV Anchor Pays the Price for Coming Out of the Cripple Closet." *Mainstream*. Vol. 16, No. 3 (November 1991): 12–17.

———. "Hollywood's New Blackface: Just Spray 'em with Chrome." *Mainstream*. Vol. 17, No. 6 (March 1993): 25–32.

———. "A Matter of Hiring: Are Disabled People in Positions of Power Pulling Up the Ramps To Keep the Rest of Us Out?" *Mainstream*. Vol. 18, No. 2 (October 1993): 20–23.

Boston Center for Independent Living (BCIL). *20th Anniversary Banquet*. Boston: BCIL, 6 October 1994.

———. *Annual Report 1994*. Boston: BCIL, 1995.

Bowe, Frank G. *Handicapping America: Barriers to Disabled People*. New York: Harper and Row, 1978.

———. *Rehabilitating America*. New York: Harper and Row, 1980.

———. *Disabled Women in America: A Statistical Report Drawn from Census Data*. Washington, DC: President's Committee on Employment of the Handicapped, 1984.

———. *Changing the Rules*. Silver Spring, MD: T. J. Publishers, 1986.

———. "Section 504: 10 Years Later." *American Rehabilitation*. Vol. 13, No. 2 (April/May/June 1987): 2–3, 23–24.

———. *Approaching Equality: Education of the Deaf*. Silver Spring, MD: T. J. Publishers, 1991.

———. Correspondence. 4 March 1995, 30 August 1996.

Bower, Jo. "HIV & Disability: Worlds Apart or Worlds Together?" *Disability Rag & Resource* (March/April 1994): 8–14.

Braddock, David. "Community Mental Health and Mental Retardation Services in the United States: A Comparative Study of Resource Allocation." *American Journal of Psychiatry*. Vol. 149, No. 2 (February 1992): 175–183.

———. "Foreword." In Gunnar Dybwad and Hank Bersani Jr., editors. *New Voices: Self-Advocacy by People with Disabilities*. Cambridge, MA: Brookline Books, 1996.

Brand, Teresa. "Opinion." *Silent News*. Vol. 28, No. 9 (September 1996): 2.

Brandt, Anthony. *Reality Police*. New York: William Morrow and Company, 1975.

Breggin, Peter R., and Ginger Ross Breggin. *The War against Children: How the Drugs, Programs and Theories of the Psychiatric Establishment Are Threatening America's Children with a Medical 'Cure' for Violence*. New York: St. Martin's Press, 1994.

Brightman, Alan J., editor. *Ordinary Moments: The Disabled Experience*. Syracuse, NY, 1985.

Bristo, Marca. Interview. 15 March 1995.

Bronston, William. Interview. 8 September 1995.

Brown, Bruce M. "Second Generation: West Coast." *American Rehabilitation*. Vol. 3, No. 6 (July/August 1978): 23–30.

Brown, Dale. "Leadership: Some Views and

Perspectives from the Top." *Mainstream.* Vol. 12, No. 11 (May 1988): 13.

Brown, Dale S., and Vargo, John. "Bibliography of Resources on Universal Design." *Journal of Rehabilitation.* Vol. 59, No. 3 (July/August/September 1993): 8–11.

Brown, Steven E. "Super Duper: The (Unfortunate) Ascendancy of Christopher Reeve and the Cure-All for the 1990s." *Mainstream.* Vol. 21, No. 2 (October 1996): 28–31.

Brown, Susan E., Debra Connors, and Nancy Stern, editors. *With the Power of Each Breath.* Pittsburgh, San Francisco: Cleis Press, 1985.

Bruce, Robert V. *Bell: Alexander Graham Bell and the Conquest of Solitude.* Boston: Little, Brown and Company, 1973.

Brummel, Susan. *People with Disabilities and the National Information Infrastructure: Breaking Down Barriers, Building Choice.* Washington, DC: U.S. General Services Administration, 1994.

Buckman, Danielle F. "Women with Disabilities at Mid-Life." *Disability Rag & Resource.* Vol. 16, No. 4 (July/August 1995): 19–21.

Burgdorf, Robert L., Jr. *The Legal Rights of Handicapped Persons: Cases, Materials, and Text.* Baltimore: Paul H. Brookes Publishing Co., 1980.

———. "Equal Access to Public Accommodations." *Milbank Quarterly.* Vol. 69, Supplement 1/2 (1991): 183–213.

———. *Disability Discrimination in Employment Law.* Washington, DC: Bureau of National Affairs Books, 1995.

———. Interview. 3 October 1996.

Burgdorf, Robert L., Jr., and Christopher Bell. "Eliminating Discrimination against Physically and Mentally Handicapped Persons: A Statutory Blueprint." *Mental and Physical Disability Law Reporter.* Vol. 64, No. 1 (1984).

Burke, Chris, and Jo Beth McDaniel. *A Special Kind of Hero.* New York: Dell Publishing, 1991.

Burns, James MacGregor. *Roosevelt: The Soldier of Freedom.* New York: Harcourt Brace Jovanovich, 1970.

Burson, Bradley. "Dear General—Wherever You Are." *Braille Forum.* Vol. 33, No. 7 (January 1995): 35–36.

Burt, Robert A. "Pennhurst: A Parable." In Robert H. Mnookin, editor. *In the Interest of Children: Advocacy, Law Reform, and Public Policy.* New York: W. H. Freeman and Company, 1985.

Byrd, Todd. "The Way We Were—And Will Be: Measuring the Impact." *Gallaudet Today.* Vol. 18, No. 5 (Summer 1988): 30–31.

Byron, Peg. "Health Insurance Conspiracy: How Doctors, Insurers, and Hospitals Have Left Us in Critical Condition." *Ms.* (September/October 1992): 40–45.

Byzek, Josie. "The Company Town: Its Decline and Fall, Its Resurrection." *Mouth: The Voice of Disability Rights.* Vol. 5, No. 5 (January/February 1995): 16–19.

———. "Stephanie Says: An Interview with Stephanie Thomas." *Mouth: The Voice of Disability Rights.* Vol. 6, No. 2 (July/August 1995): 6–7, 46–47.

———. "Chair Trumps Cane." *Mouth: The Voice of Disability Rights.* Vol. 7, No. 4 (November/December 1996): 14–15.

———. "Judi Says: An Interview with Judi Chamberlin." *Mouth: The Voice of Disability Rights.* Vol. 7, No. 4 (November/December 1996): 10–13.

Callahan, John. *Don't Worry, He Won't Get Far on Foot.* New York: Vintage Books, 1989.

———. *Do What He Says! He's Crazy!!!* New York: Quill, 1992.

Campbell, Philippa, editor. *Use of Aversive Procedures with Persons Who Are Disabled: An Historical Review and Critical Analysis.* Seattle: The Association for Persons with Severe Handicaps, 1987.

Campling, J., editor. *Images of Ourselves: Women with Disabilities Talking.* London: Routledge & Kegan Paul, 1981.

Campos, Art. "Pioneer in Independence for Disabled People Dies." *Sacramento Bee* (13 May 1993): B-1.

Cannon, Dennis. "Design for All Persons: The Architectural Barriers Act and Public Transit." *Journal of Rehabilitation.* Vol. 55, No. 2 (April/May/June 1989): 10–12.

Capozzi, David M., and Dennis J. Cannon. "Transportation Accessibility." In Arthur E. Dell Orto and Robert P. Marinelli, editors. *Encyclopedia of Disability and Rehabilitation.* New York: Simon & Schuster Macmillan, 1995.

Carling, Paul J. "Access to Housing: Cornerstone of the American Dream." *Journal of Rehabilitation.* Vol. 55, No. 3 (July/August/ September 1989): 6–8.

Carney, Nell C. "Seventy Years of Hope, Seventy Years of Success." *Journal of Rehabilitation.* Vol. 56, No. 4 (October/November/ December 1990): 6–7.

Caroom, Ilene. "Court Approves Exclusion of Assistance Dog from Emergency Room." *Partner's Forum: International Association of Assistance Dog Partners.* Vol. 2, No. 4 (Winter 1995): 1.

Catton, Bruce. *A Stillness at Appomattox.* Garden City, NY: Doubleday and Company, 1953.

Cecere, Michael S., Martin F. Payson, and Meryl R. Kaynard. "AIDS in the Workplace: Are AIDS Sufferers Handicapped under Federal and State Laws?" *Trial.* Vol. 22 (December 1986): 40–42+.

Chamberlin, Judi. *On Our Own: Patient-Controlled Alternatives to the Mental Health System.* New York: Hawthorn Books, 1978.

———. "Psychiatric Survivors: Are We Part of the Disability Rights Movement?" *Disability Rag & Resource.* Vol. 16, No. 2 (March/April 1995): 1, 4–9.

———. Interview. 23 May 1996.

———. "The Ex-Patients' Movement: Where We've Been and Where We're Going." *Journal of Mind and Behavior.* Vol. 11, Nos. 3–4 (Summer/Autumn 1990).

Chappell, John A., Jr. Interview. 2 June 1995.

Charleston, James. "Religion and Disability, a World View." *Disability Rag & Resource.* Vol. 14, No. 5 (September/October 1993): 14–16.

Cheever, Raymond C. "The *ACCENT* Story." *ACCENT on People...Who Happen To Have a Physical Disability.* Bloomington, IL: ACCENT, 1995.

"Chicago Shock Jock Revives Freak Shows." *Mouth: The Voice of Disability Rights.* Vol. 7,

No. 2 (July/August 1996): 5.

Chong, Curtis. *Computer Science Update.* Minneapolis: National Federation of the Blind, Summer 1995.

Christiansen, John B., and Sharon N. Barnartt. *Deaf President Now! The 1988 Revolution at Gallaudet University.* Washington, DC: Gallaudet University Press, 1995.

Clarke Institution for Deaf Mutes. *Annual Reports: 1878–1885.* Vols. 11–18. Northampton, MA: Metcalf & Co., 1885.

Clay, Julie, Carol Locust, Tom Seekins, et al. *American Indian Disability Legislation Project: Findings of a National Survey of Tribal Governments.* Missoula, MT: Montana University Affiliated Rural Institute on Disabilities, 1995.

Cleland, Max. *Strong at the Broken Places.* New York: Berkeley Books, 1980.

"Cochlear Implants: The Final Putdown?" *Disability Rag & Resource.* Vol. 7, No. 2 (March/April 1986): 1, 4–6.

Coelho, Tony. "The New Chairman of the President's Committee for the Employment of People with Disabilities" (an interview with Tony Coelho). *Enable Georgia* (Fall 1994): 27–31.

———. "Epilepsy Gave Me a Mission." *Epilepsy Association of Greater Greensboro Newsletter* (November 1995): 6–7.

Cohen, Abby. "Accessible Child Care: Who Does the ADA Protect and What Does It Require?" *Mainstream.* Vol. 18, No. 7 (April 1994): 18–21.

Cohen, Leah Hager. *Train Go Sorry: Inside a Deaf World.* Boston, New York: Houghton Mifflin Company, 1994.

Coleman, Diane, and Carol Gill. Testimony before the Constitution Subcommittee of the Judiciary Committee of the U.S. House of Representatives. 29 April 1996.

Conley, Ronald, and John Noble Jr. "Workers' Compensation Reform: Challenge for the 80s." *American Rehabilitation.* Vol. 3, No. 3 (January/February 1978): 19–26.

Consortium for Citizens with Disabilities Health Task Force. "Principles for Health Care Reform from a Disability Perspective." Washington, DC: Consortium for Citizens with Disabilities, 1993.

Consortium for Citizens with Disabilities Task Force on Personal Assistance Services. "Recommended Federal Policy Directions on Personal Assistance Services for Americans with Disabilities." Washington, DC: Consortium for Citizens with Disabilities, October 1991, May 1992.

Consortium for Citizens with Disabilities Housing Task Force. "Opening Doors: Recommendations for a Federal Policy To Address the Housing Needs of People with Disabilities." Washington, DC: Consortium for Citizens with Disabilities Housing Task Force and the Technical Assistance Collaborative, Inc., June 1996.

Cook, Timothy M. "The Friendly Skies?" *Mainstream*. Vol. 11, No. 7 (November 1986): 34.

———. "The Americans with Disabilities Act: The Move to Integration." *Temple Law Review*. Vol. 64, No. 2 (1991).

Cooke, Annmarie. "Jean L. Driscoll." *Mainstream*. Vol. 17, No. 9 (June/July 1993): 20–21.

Corbet, Barry. *Options: Spinal Cord Injury and the Future*. Denver: A. B. Hirschfeld Press, 1980.

———. "Billy Golfus' Righteous Surprise." *New Mobility* (January/February 1995): 42–44.

Corcoran, Paul J., with Frederick A. Fay, Elmer C. Bartels, and Robert McHugh. *The BCIL Report: A Summary of the First Three Years of the Boston Center for Independent Living, Inc.* Boston: Health, Education and Welfare, Office of Human Development; Rehabilitation Services Administration, 1977.

———. The Henry B. Betts Award 1994 Nomination Form.

Coudroglou, Aliki, and Dennis L. Poole. *Disability, Work, and Social Policy: Models for Social Welfare*. New York: Springer Publishing Company, 1984.

Council of Canadians with Disabilities. *Annual Report 1994–1995*. Winnipeg, Canada: Council of Canadians with Disabilities, 1996.

Covington, George A. "Crippling Images: Educating the Vice President." *Ability Magazine* (Fall 1992): 4–6.

———. "Shattering the Myth of Super Crip." *Home Health Dealer* (March/April 1994): 109–111.

Crewe, Nancy M., and Irving Kenneth Zola, editors. *Independent Living for Physically Disabled People*. San Francisco: Jossey-Bass Publishers, 1987.

Cunningham, Amy. "Blind Loyalty." *Baltimore Magazine* (July 1992).

Dart, Justin, Jr. Interview. 8 June 1995, 28 June 1996.

"Deaf Man's Hearing Restored by Implant." *Silent News*. Vol. 28, No. 9 (September 1996): 29.

Deegan, M. J., and N. A. Brooks, editors. *Women and Disability: The Double Handicap*. New Brunswick, NJ: Transaction Books, 1985.

Dietl, Dick. "FDR's Living Memorial in Warm Springs, Ga.: A $61.5 Million Tribute Coming True." *Journal of Rehabilitation*. Vol. 51, No. 3 (July/August/September 1985): 13–18.

———. "The Phoenix: From the Ashes and Looking to the Ultimate Barrier: Our Own Attitude." *Journal of Rehabilitation*. Vol. 49, No. 3 (July/August/September 1983): 12–17.

Dell Orto, Arthur E., and Robert P. Marinelli, editors. *Encyclopedia of Disability and Rehabilitation*. New York: Simon & Schuster Macmillan, 1995.

DeLoach, Charlene Poch. "Women in Rehabilitation." In Arthur E. Dell Orto and Robert P. Marinelli, editors. *Encyclopedia of Disability and Rehabilitation*. New York: Simon & Schuster Macmillan, 1995.

Disabled Peoples' International. *DPI Overview*. Winnipeg, Canada: Disabled Peoples' International, 1994.

Donaldson, Kenneth. *Insanity Inside Out*. New York: Crown Publishers, 1976.

Driedger, Diane. "Speaking for Ourselves: A History of COPOH on Its 10th Anniversary." Winnipeg, Canada: Coalition of Provincial Organizations of the Handicapped, 1986.

———. *The Last Civil Rights Movement: Disabled Peoples' International*. New York: St. Martin's Press, 1989.

Drimmer, Frederick. *Very Special People: The Struggles, Loves and Triumphs of Human Oddities.* New York: Bantam Books, 1973.

Driscoll, John V., Bruce Marquis, Paul J. Corcoran, and Frederick A. Fay. "Second Generation: New England." *American Rehabilitation.* Vol. 3, No. 6 (July/August 1978): 17–21.

DuBrow, Arthur L. "Attitudes towards Disability." *Journal of Rehabilitation.* Vol. 31, No. 4 (July/August 1965): 25–26.

Ducharme, Stanley. Interview. 27 June 1984.

Duffy, Yvonne. *All Things Are Possible.* Ann Arbor, MI: A. J. Garvin and Associates, 1981.

Duncan, Janet, and Kathy Hulgin. *Resources on Inclusive Education.* Syracuse, NY: Research and Training Center on Community Integration and Center on Human Policy, 1993.

Durbano, Art, and Sue Avery Brown. "And the Oscar Goes To..." *People* (17 August 1992): 101.

Dybwad, Gunnar. "The Rediscovery of the Family." Keynote address presented at the Sixth Caribbean Congress on Mental Retardation, Nassau, Bahamas, 17–23 August 1980.

———. "From Feeblemindedness to Self-Advocacy: A Half Century of Growth and Self-Fulfillment." Paper presented at the 118th meeting of the American Association on Mental Retardation, 1994.

———. Interview. 12 March 1996.

Dybwad, Gunnar, and Hank Bersani Jr., editors. *New Voices: Self-Advocacy by People with Disabilities.* Cambridge, MA: Brookline Books, 1996.

Eames, Ed, and Toni Eames. *A Guide to Guide Dog Schools.* Fresno, CA: NHES, 1994.

Ebenstein, Barbara. "The Law and Inclusion." *Exceptional Parent.* Vol. 25, No. 8 (September 1995): 40–43.

Edgerton, Robert B., editor. *Lives in Progress: Mildly Retarded Adults in a Large City.* Washington, DC: American Association on Mental Deficiency, 1984.

Edgington, Eugene S. "Colleges and Universities with Special Provisions for Wheelchair Students." *Journal of Rehabilitation.* Vol. 29, No. 3 (May/June 1963): 14–15.

Edwards, Richard L., editor. *Encyclopedia of Social Work: 19th Edition.* Washington, DC: National Association of Social Workers Press, 1995.

Egerton, Marilyn R. Correspondence. 6 April 1995.

Ehman, Joe. "Social Security's New Follies." *Mouth: The Voice of Disability Rights.* Vol. 7, No. 1 (May/June 1996): 6–7.

Eiesland, Nancy L. *The Disabled God: Toward a Liberatory Theology of Disability.* Nashville: Abingdon Press, 1994.

Ennis, Bruce. *Prisoners of Psychiatry: Mental Patients, Psychiatrists, and the Law.* New York: Harcourt Brace Jovanovich, 1972.

Ervin, Michael. "Have Sheltered Workshops Outlived Their Usefulness?" *One Step Ahead—The Resource for Active, Healthy, Independent Living.* Vol. 3, No. 8 (August 1996): 3–4.

———. Interview. 23 August 1996.

———. "Remembering Childhood." *New Mobility.* Vol. 7, No. 36 (September 1996): 32–33.

"F.D.R. Cured!" *Mouth: The Voice of Disability Rights.* Vol. 6, No. 2 (July/August 1995): 39.

Falvey, Mary A., Christine C. Givner, and Christina Kimm. "What Is an Inclusive School?" In R. A. Villa and J. S. Thousands, editors. *Creating an Inclusive School.* Alexandria, VA: Association for Supervision and Curriculum Development, 1995.

Fay, Fred. Interview. 28 February 1994, 21 May 1995.

Feist-Price, Sonja, and Donna Ford-Harris. "Rehabilitation Counseling: Issues Specific to Providing Services to African American Clients." *Journal of Rehabilitation.* Vol. 60, No. 4 (October/November/December 1994): 13–19.

Feldblum, Chai R. "Antidiscrimination Requirements of the ADA." In Lawrence O. Gostin and Henry A. Beyer, editors. *Implementing the Americans with Disabilities Act: Rights and Responsibilities of All Americans.* Baltimore: Paul H. Brookes Publishing Co., 1993.

Feldman, David, and Brian Feldman. "The Effect of a Telethon on Attitudes toward Disabled People and Financial Contributions." *Journal of Rehabilitation*. Vol. 51, No. 3 (July/August/September 1985): 42–45.

Fennell, Donald. Interview. 17 April 1996.

Fenton, Joseph. "Research and Training Centers." *American Rehabilitation*. Vol. 2, No. 4 (March/April 1977): 5.

Ferguson, Philip M. *Abandoned to Their Fate: Social Policy and Practice toward Severely Retarded People in America, 1820–1920*. Philadelphia: Temple University Press, 1994.

Fiedler, Leslie A. *Freaks: Myths and Images of the Secret Self*. New York: Simon & Schuster, 1978.

Fields, Suzanne. "Rape: The Meaning of Consent." *Boston Herald* (22 March 1993): Op. Ed. page.

"Fighting for Equality." *Middlesex News* (4 December 1992): 1.

Fiorito, Eunice K. Interview. 19 September 1996.

Fleming, Mary Bach. "Scoring a Victory for People with Disabilities: Paralympics CEO Andy Fleming." *In Motion: A Publication of the Amputee Coalition of America*. Vol. 5, No. 3 (Summer 1995): 26–30.

Foderaro, Lisa W. "Mentally Ill Gaining New Rights, With the Ill as Their Own Lobby." *New York Times* (14 October 1995): 1, 24.

Francis, Robert A. "The Development of Federal Accessibility Law." *Journal of Rehabilitation*. Vol. 49, No. 1 (January/February/March 1983): 29–32.

"Fred Fay 'Opens Doors' for Others with Disabilities." *Minuteman Chronicle* (21 November1992): 1.

Freedman, Joel. *On Both Sides of the Wall: An In-Depth Look at the Inhumane Conditions in Massachusetts' Psychiatric Hospitals and Schools for the Mentally Retarded*. New York: Vantage Press, 1980.

Frieden, Lex. "IL: Movement and Programs." *American Rehabilitation*. Vol. 3, No. 6 (July/August 1978): 6–7.

———. "Independent Living: Houston Experience." *American Rehabilitation*. Vol. 4, No. 6 (July/August 1979): 23–26.

Frieden, Lex, and Joyce Frieden. "Organized Consumerism at Local Level." *American Rehabilitation*. Vol. 5, No. 1 (September/October 1979): 3–6.

Friedman, Ina. *The Other Victim*. Boston: Houghton-Mifflin, 1990.

Frist, William. "The Reauthorization of the IDEA." *Exceptional Parent*. Vol. 25, No. 12 (December 1995): 46.

Frost-Knappman, Elizabeth. *The ABC-CLIO Companion to Women's Progress in America*. Santa Barbara, CA: ABC-CLIO, 1994.

Funk, Robert J. "In Our Court: Decisions by the Supreme Court Make Clear That It's up to Us To Secure Disability Policy Reform." *Mainstream*. Vol. 10, No. 1 (April 1985): 11–15, 44.

———. "A National Workshop: Washington, D.C., the News Media and Disability Issues." Washington, DC: News Media Education Project, 1988.

———. Interview. 1 June 1995.

Gainer, Kate. "I Was Born Crippled and Black." *Mouth: The Voice of Disability Rights*. Vol. 3, No. 3 (September/October 1992): 31.

Gallagher, Hugh Gregory. *FDR's Splendid Deception*. New York: Dodd, Mead Co., 1985.

———. *By Trust Betrayed: Patients, Physicians, and the License To Kill in the Third Reich*. New York: Henry Holt and Co., 1990.

———. "Tiny Tim Goes to the Paralympics." *New Mobility*. Vol. 7, No. 36 (September 1996): 70.

Gallaudet, Edward Miner. *History of the College of the Deaf 1857–1907*. Washington, DC: Gallaudet College Press, 1983.

Galloway, Donald. Interview. 24 September 1996.

Gannon, Jack R. *Deaf Heritage: A Narrative History of Deaf America*. Silver Spring, MD: National Association of the Deaf, 1981.

———. "The Many Names of Gallaudet." *Gallaudet Today*. Vol. 17, No. 2 (Winter 1987): 35–36.

———. *The Week the World Heard Gallaudet.* Washington, DC: Gallaudet University Press, 1989.

Garfinkel, Irwin, and James D. Wright. "Is Mental Illness a Cause of Homelessness?" In Stuart A. Kirk and Susan D. Einbinder, editors. *Controversial Issues in Mental Health.* Boston: Allyn and Bacon, 1994.

Gartner, Alan, and Tom Joe, editors. *Images of the Disabled, Disabling Images.* New York: Praeger, 1987.

Geer, Sarah. "Public Law 94-142: What's a Parent To Do?" *Gallaudet Today, 1987 Special Legal Review Issue.* Vol. 17, No. 4, 7–15.

Gibbs, Nancy R. "Tragic Tug-of-War." *Time* (22 August 1988): 71.

Gilhool, Thomas K. "The Right to Community Services." In Michael Kindred et al., editors. *The Mentally Retarded Citizen and the Law.* New York: The Free Press, 1976.

———. "The Right to an Effective Education: From Brown to PL 94–142 and Beyond." In Dorothy Kerzner Lipsky and Alan Gartner, editors. *Beyond Special Education: Quality Education for All.* Baltimore: Paul H. Brookes Publishing Co., 1989.

———. "Testimony before the Joint Subcommittee Hearings on 'the Events, Forces and Issues That Triggered Enactment of the Education for All Handicapped Children Act of 1975." Washington, DC, 9 May 1995.

Gill, Carol. "The Pleasure We Take in Our Community . . ." *Disability Rag & Resource.* Vol. 16, No. 8 (September/October 1995): 5.

———. "'Right To Die' Threatens Our Right To Live Safe and Free." *Mainstream.* Vol. 16, No. 5 (March 1992): 32–36.

———. Interview. 8 September 1995.

Gillet, Dexter R. *Tools for Empowerment—A Self-Help Resource Guide for the DisAbled.* Dexter R. Gillet, 1993.

Glenn, M., ed. *Voices from the Asylum.* New York: Harper and Row, 1974.

Gliedman, John, and William Roth. *The Unexpected Minority: Handicapped Children in America.* New York: Harcourt Brace Jovanovich, 1980.

Goette, Tanya, and Jack T. Marchewka.

"Voice Recognition Technology for Persons Who Have Motoric Disabilities." *Journal of Rehabilitation.* Vol. 60, No. 2 (April/May/June 1994): 38–41.

Gold, Steven. "Supreme Court Supports ADA Decision Concerning People in Nursing Homes." *DIA Activist.* Vol. 26, No. 2 (June 1996): 11.

Goldberg, Glenn. Interview. 20 August 1993.

Goldberg, Steven S. *Special Education Law: A Guide for Parents, Advocates, and Educators.* New York: Plenum Press, 1982.

Golden, Marilyn. "Title II—Public Services, Subtitle B: Public Transportation." In Lawrence O. Gostin and Henry A. Beyer, editors. *Implementing the Americans with Disabilities Act: Rights and Responsibilities of All Americans.* Baltimore: Paul H. Brookes Publishing Co., 1993.

———. "Damn Straight We're a Real Movement!" *Disability Rag & Resource.* Vol. 17, No. 2 (March/April 1996): 1, 4–5, 15.

———. "Behind the Scenes of Universal Design." *Disability Rag & Resource.* Vol. 17, No. 4 (July/August 1996): 6–10.

Golden, Marilyn, Linda Kilb, and Arlene Mayerson. *The Americans with Disabilities Act: An Implementation Guide.* Berkeley, CA: The Disability Rights Education and Defense Fund, 1991.

Goldman, Charles D. *Disability Rights Guide: Practical Solutions to Problems Affecting People with Disabilities.* 2d edition. Lincoln, NE: Media Publishing, 1991.

———. "Americans with Disabilities Act: Dispelling the Myths: A Practical Guide to EEOC's Voodoo Civil Rights and Wrongs." *University of Richmond Law Review.* Vol. 27, No. 1 (Fall 1992): 73–101.

Golfus, Billy. "Disconfirmation." *Disability Rag & Resource* (November/December 1989): 1, 4–8.

Goshay, Charita M. "Surviving a Nightmare: Mental-Health Advocate Criticizes Treatment." *Repository Canton, Ohio* (22 October 1992): A-11.

Gostin, Lawrence O., and Henry A. Beyer, editors. *Implementing the Americans with Disabilities Act: Rights and Responsibilities of*

All Americans. Baltimore: Paul H. Brookes Publishing Co., 1993.

Gould, Stephen Jay. "Carrie Buck's Daughter: A Popular, Quasi-Scientific Idea Can Be a Powerful Tool for Injustice." *Natural History* (July 1984): 14–18.

Gould, Tony. *A Summer Plague: Polio and Its Survivors*. New Haven and London: Yale University Press, 1995.

Graden, Hank, Rosemary Lips, and Kenneth Mitchell. "The Campus Scene: Attendants Trained To Aid Handicapped Students. *Journal of Rehabilitation*. Vol. 39, No. 6 (November/December 1973): 11–13.

Grandin, Temple. *Thinking in Pictures and Other Reports from My Life with Autism*. New York: Doubleday and Company, 1995.

Grant, Michael. "Jim Abbott Strikes Out His Doubters." *Mainstream*. Vol. 16, No. 7 (April 1992): 14–17, 20.

Griss, Bob. "Health Insurance at Risk." *Word from Washington* (May/June 1991): 13–16.

———. "HHS Rejects Oregon Medicaid Rationing Plan: Violates ADA." *Word from Washington* (August/September 1992): 3–12.

———. "I Thought I Was Covered: Obstacles to Reimbursement for Consumers Who Supposedly Are Insured." Washington, DC: United Cerebral Palsy Associations, 1993.

Grobe, Jeanine, editor. *Beyond Bedlam: Contemporary Women Psychiatric Survivors Speak Out*. Chicago: Third Side Press, 1995.

Groce, Nora Ellen. *Everyone Here Spoke Sign Language: Hereditary Deafness on Martha's Vineyard*. Cambridge, MA: Harvard University Press, 1985.

———. *The U.S. Role in International Disability Activities: A History and a Look towards the Future: A Study Commissioned by the World Institute on Disability, the World Rehabilitation Fund and Rehabilitation International*. New York: Rehabilitation International, 1992.

Gutestam, Monica. "International Year of Disabled Persons: Seeking Self-Reliance." *UN Chronicle*. Vol. 28, No. 2 (June 1991): 76–77.

Gwin, Lucy. "How Independent Living Got Rolling: An Interview with Ed Roberts." *This Brain Has a Mouth*. Vol. 3, No. 2 (July/August 1992): 8–11.

———. "Murder by Charity." *Mouth: The Voice of Disability Rights*. Vol. 4, No. 3 (September/October 1993): 6–11.

———. "America, the Unvisitable: An Interview with Eleanor Smith of Concrete Change." *Mouth: The Voice of Disability Rights*. Vol. 5, No. 2 (July/August 1994): 20–23.

———. Correspondence. 14 April 1995.

———. "Free at Last, Free at Last, Thank God Almighty and the ADA, We're Free at Last." *Mouth: The Voice of Disability Rights*. Vol. 6, No. 1 (May/June 1995): 4–5, 33–34.

———. "Mouth Rejects Utne Award." *Mouth: The Voice of Disability Rights*. Vol. 7, No. 3 (September/October 1996): 42.

———. "Rae Says: An Interview with Rae Unzicker." *Mouth: The Voice of Disability Rights*. Vol. 5, No. 6 (March/April 1995): 4–5, 46–47.

Hagner, David, and Dale Dileo. *Working Together: Workplace Culture, Supported Employment, and Persons with Disabilities*. Cambridge, MA: Brookline Books, 1993.

Hahn, Harlan. "The Politics of Physical Differences: Disability and Discrimination." *Journal of Social Issues*. Vol. 44, No. 1 (Spring 1988): 39–47.

———. "Toward a Politics of Disability: Definitions, Disciplines and Policies." *Social Science Journal*. Vol. 22 (1985): 87–105.

Hairston, Ernest, and Linwood Smith. *Black and Deaf in America: Are We That Different*. Silver Spring, MD: T. J. Publishers, 1983.

Halamandaris, Val J. "Marvelous Max: A Profile of Max Cleland." *Caring People*. Vol. 5 (Spring 1992).

Hamilton, Kenneth W. *Counseling the Handicapped in the Rehabilitation Process*. New York: The Ronald Press Company, 1950.

Hannaford, Susan. *Living Outside Inside: A Disabled Woman's Experience, Towards a Social and Political Perspective*. Berkeley, CA: Canterbury Press, 1985.

Hasbrouck, Amy. Interview. 7 June 1995.

Heath, Dennis. Interview. 11 June 1996.

Heddinger, Richard W. "The Twelve Year Battle for a Barrier Free METRO." *American Rehabilitation*. Vol. 1, No. 4 (March/April 1976): 7–10.

Hendricks, Deborah J., and Anne E. Hirsh. "The Job Accommodation Network: A Vital Resource for the '90s." *Rehabilitation Education*. Vol. 5 (1991): 1–4.

Herold, Rod, and Carmen Johnson. *Self-Advocacy Organizing: A Self-Advocacy Manual for People with Disabilities*. Boston: Project In Self-Advocacy of the Massachusetts Coalition of Citizens with Disabilities, 1984.

Hershey, Laura. "Pride." *Disability Rag & Resource*. Vol. 12, No. 4 (July/August 1991): 1, 4–5.

———. "Wade Blank, 1940–1993." *Mainstream*. Vol. 17, No. 7 (April 1993): 17–19.

———. "Wade Blank's Liberated Community." In Barrett Shaw, editor. *The Ragged Edge: The Disability Experience from the Pages of the First Fifteen Years of* The Disability Rag. Louisville, KY: Advocado Press, 1994.

Heslinga, K., with A. M. C. M. Schellen and A. Verkuyl. *Not Made of Stone: The Sexual Problems of Handicapped People*. Leyden, the Netherlands: Stafleu's Scientific Publishing Company, 1974.

Hessler, Anthony. Interview. 5 September 1996.

Hessler, Jean. Interview. 12 September 1996.

Hessler, John. "College Education for the Severely Disabled." *American Rehabilitation*. Vol. 1, No. 5 (May/June 1976): 29–33.

Heumann, Judith E. Interview. 29 March 1993.

———. "Lessons for Independence: We've Got the Right IDEA." *Mainstream*. Vol. 20, No. 6 (March 1996): 23–25.

Hillyer, Barbara. *Feminism and Disability*. Norman, OK: University of Oklahoma Press, 1993.

Hockenberry, John. *Moving Violations, A Memoir: War Zones, Wheelchairs, and Declarations of Independence*. New York: Hyperion, 1995.

Hoffman, Susan Thompson, and Inez Fitgerald Storch, editors. *Disability in the United States: A Portrait from National Data*. New York: Springer Publishing Company, 1991.

Hohler, Bob. "Surprise, Anger at BC over Ex-Student's Rape Case in N.J." *Boston Globe* (March 25 1993): 1.

Holcomb, Mabs, and Sharon Wood. *Deaf Women: A Parade through the Ages*. Berkeley, CA: Dawn Sign Press, 1989.

Hollis, M. Alverna. "Religion, Catholic." In John Van Cleve, editor. *Gallaudet Encyclopedia of Deaf People and Deafness*. McGraw-Hill, 1987.

Holmes, Gary E., and Ronald H. Karst. "The Institutionalization of Disability Myths: Impact on Vocational Rehabilitation Services." *Journal of Rehabilitation*. Vol. 56, No. 1 (January/February/March 1990): 20–27.

Hopkins, Thomas. Interview. 6 September 1995.

Horne, Marcia D. *Attitudes toward Handicapped Students: Professional, Peer, and Parent Reactions*. Hillsdale, NJ: Lawrence Erlbaum Associates, 1985.

Hotchkiss, Ralf D. "Ground Swell on Wheels." *Sciences* (July/August 1993): 14–18.

Houppert, Karen. "Baseball Bats and Broomsticks." *Village Voice* (16 March 1993): 29–33.

———. "Glen Ridge Rape Trial: A Question of Consent." *Ms.* (March/April 1993): 86–88.

Howard, Phillip K. *The Death of Common Sense: How Law Is Suffocating America*. New York: Random House, 1994.

Howards, Irving, Henry P. Brehm, and Saad Z. Nagi. *Disability: From Social Problem to Federal Program*. New York: Praeger, 1980.

Hudak, Edward John. "Sex! If You Care about It You Should Read This." *Mainstream*. Vol. 16, No. 7 (April 1992): 34.

Hunter, Richard. Interview. 8 July 1996.

"Implementation of White House Conference Recommendations." *American Rehabilitation*. Vol. 4, No. 3 (January/February 1979): 9–10.

Intergalactic Network of Crazy Folks. "Mad Memoria: Howie the Harp Is Gone." *Dendron*. No. 36 (Spring 1995): 6.

"Irving Zola, Brandeis Professor Who Fought for Rights of Disabled." *Boston Sunday Globe* (4 December 1994): 88.

Irwin, Robert B. *As I Saw It*. New York: American Foundation for the Blind, 1955.

Jacobs, Alice E., and Deborah J. Hendricks. "Job Accommodations for Adults with Learning Disabilities: Brilliantly Disguised Opportunities." *Learning Disability Quarterly*. Vol. 15 (Fall 1992): 274–285.

Janes, Michael. "Unified Sports Gains Momentum at '95 World Games." *Exceptional Parent*. Vol. 25, No. 6 (June 1995): 56–57.

Jarrow, Jane E. "Integration of Individuals with Disabilities in Higher Education: A Review of the Literature." *Journal of Postsecondary Education and Disability*. Vol. 5, No. 2 (Spring 1987): 38–57.

Johnson, Ann Braden, and Richard C. Surles. "Has Deinstitutionalization Failed?" In Stuart A. Kirk and Susan D. Einbinder, editors. *Controversial Issues in Mental Health*. Boston: Allyn and Bacon, 1994.

Johnson, Mark. Interview. 29 May 1996.

Johnson, Mary. "That Fire-in-the-Belly Passion." *Disability Rag & Resource* (July/August 1989): 32.

———. "Myth & Media: Opportunity Lost." *Disability Rag & Resource* (May/June 1990): 30–31.

———. "The Nursing Home Rip-Off." *New York Times* (2 June 1991): Op. Ed. page.

———. "Universal Man: Architect Ron Mace Leads the Way to Design That Includes Everyone." *Mainstream*. Vol. 18, No. 10 (August 1994): 18–27.

———. "Double Jeopardy: African Americans with Disabilities." *New Mobility*. Vol. 7, No. 32 (May 1996): 37–41.

Johnstone, Mary. "In My Opinion: Views about the Gallaudet Revolution." *Gallaudet Today*. Vol. 18, No. 5 (Summer 1988): 26–29.

Jones, Cyndi. "Claim Your Power: Wade Blank 1940–1993." *Mainstream*. Vol. 17, No. 7 (April 1993): 5.

———. "20 Years: We've Come a Long Way . . ." *Mainstream*. Vol. 20, No. 6 (March 1996): 17–21.

———. Interview. 19 September 1996.

Jones, Reginald L., editor. *Reflections on Growing Up Disabled*. Reston, VA: Council of Exceptional Children, 1983.

Kael, Pauline. *5,001 Nights at the Movies: A Guide from A to Z*. New York: Holt, Rinehart and Winston, 1982.

Kaminker, Laura. "The Darker Side of Going for the Gold." *New Mobility*. Vol. 7, No. 35 (August 1996): 26–29.

———. "The Graying of the Games: Where Are the Kids?" *New Mobility*. Vol. 7, No. 35 (August 1996): 22–25.

Kaplan, Deborah. Interview. 2 July 1996.

Karuth, Denise. "If I Were a Car, I'd Be a Lemon." In Alan J. Brightman, editor. *Ordinary Moments: The Disabled Experience*. Baltimore: University Park Press, 1984.

———. Interview. 21 November 1995.

Katz, Ephraim. *The Film Encyclopedia*. New York: Thomas Y. Crowell, 1979.

Katzmann, Robert A. "Transportation Policy." *Milbank Quarterly*. Vol. 69, Supplement 1/2 (1991): 214–235.

Keller, Helen Adams. *The Story of My Life*. Garden City, NY: Doubleday and Company, 1954 edition.

Kemp, Evan, Jr. "Aiding the Disabled: No Pity, Please." *New York Times* (3 September 1981): Op. Ed. page.

———. Interview. 16 September 1991.

Kennedy, Jae. "Policy and Program Issues in Providing Personal Assistance Services." *Journal of Rehabilitation*. Vol. 59, No. 3 (August/September 1993): 17–23.

Kennedy, Michael, with Bonnie Shoultz. *Thoughts about Self-Advocacy*. Syracuse, NY: Center on Human Policy, 1996.

Kidder, Lynn. "They Fought Disabilities and Won." Antioch, California, *Daily Ledger* (2 May 1982): 1.

Killilea, Marie. *Karen*. New York: Dell Publishing Co., 1952.

Kindred, Michael, et al., editors. *The Mentally Retarded Citizen and the Law*. New York: The Free Press, 1976.

Kirk, Stuart A., and Susan D. Einbinder, editors. *Controversial Issues in Mental Health*. Boston, London: Allyn and Bacon, 1994.

Kleinfield, Sonny. *The Hidden Minority*. New York: Atlantic-Little, Brown, 1979.

Klobas, Lauri. "Hollywood." In Sam Maddox, editor. *Spinal Network, the Total Resource for the Wheelchair Community*. Boulder, CO: Spinal Network, 1987.

Kneedler, Rebecca Dailey, with Daniel P. Hallahan and James M. Knauffman. *Special Education for Today*. Englewood Cliffs, NJ: Prentice Hall, 1984.

Knowlen, Barbara. "Tim Cook and Disability Rights Law." *Mouth: The Voice of Disability Rights*. Vol. 4, No. 5 (January/February 1994): 26–27.

Kocher, Meg. "I Would Be This Way Forever." In Alan J. Brightman, editor. *Ordinary Moments*. Syracuse, NY, 1985.

Koestler, Frances A. *The Unseen Minority: A Social History of Blindness in the United States*. New York: David McKay Company, 1976.

————. *The Ziegler Magazine Story: A History of the Matilda Ziegler Magazine for the Blind*. New York: Matilda Ziegler Magazine for the Blind, 1992, 1995.

Kriegel, Leonard. *The Long Walk Home*. New York: Appleton, 1964.

————. *Falling into Life*. San Francisco: North Point Press, 1991.

Kugel, Robert B., and Wolf Wolfensberger, editors. *Changing Patterns in Residential Services for the Mentally Retarded*. Washington, DC: President's Committee on Mental Retardation, 1969.

Kuhl, Stefan. *The Nazi Connection: Eugenics, American Racism, and German National Socialism*. New York, Oxford: Oxford University Press, 1994.

"A Labor of Love: The (Not-So-Secret) History of Deaf Life." *Deaf Life* (July 1993).

LaMay, Colleen. "Ex-Patient Tells Mentally Ill To Run Their Own Lives." *Idaho Statesman* (22 June 1990): 1C–2C.

Lamb, Lynette. "Selecting for Perfection: Is Prenatal Screening Becoming a Kind of Eugenics?" *Utne Reader*. No. 66 (November/December 1994): 26–28.

Lane, Harlan. *The Wild Boy of Aveyron*. Cambridge, MA: Harvard University Press, 1976.

————. *When the Mind Hears: A History of the Deaf*. New York: Random House, 1984.

————. *The Mask of Benevolence: Disabling the Deaf Community*. New York: Alfred Knopf, 1992 and Vintage, 1993.

Lane, Harlan, and F. Philip. *The Deaf Experience: Classics in Language and Education*. Cambridge, MA: Harvard University Press, 1984.

Lane, Nancy J. "Healing of Bodies and Victimization of Persons: Issues of Faith-Healing for Persons with Disabilities." *Disability Rag & Resource*. Vol. 14, No. 3 (September/October 1993).

Lash, Joseph P. *Helen and Teacher: The Story of Helen Keller and Anne Sullivan Macy*. New York: Delacorte Press and Seymour Lawrence, 1980.

Laski, Frank J. "Legal Advocacy, Positive Factor in Rights for Disabled People." *American Rehabilitation*. Vol. 1, No. 5 (May/June 1976): 12–17.

LaSpina, Nadina. "They Don't Want To Be Like Us." *DIA Activist*. Vol. 26, No. 2 (June 1996): 13.

Lathrop, Douglas. "Liberation Man: Neil Marcus Celebrates His Life and Disability as a Work of Theatrical Art." *Mainstream*. Vol. 18, No. 3 (November 1993): 14–17.

Laurie, Gini. *Housing and Home Services for the Disabled: Guidelines and Experiences in Independent Living*. New York: Harper and Row, 1977.

Laurie, Virginia. "Glimpses of Gini and G.I.N.I." *Rehabilitation Gazette*. Vol. 30, No. 1 (January 1990).

Lebovich, William L. *Design for Dignity: Accessible Environments for People with Disabilities*. New York: John Wiley and Sons, 1993.

Leon, Joan. Interview. 15 March 1995.

Levesque, Jack. "A Tribute: Frederick C. Schreiber—The Man." *Interstate*. No. 3 (1979): 6.

Levine, Ervin L., and Elizabeth M. Wexler, *PL 94–142: An Act of Congress*. New York: Macmillan, 1981.

Levine, Karen, and Robert Wharton. "Facilitated Communication: What Parents Should Know." *Exceptional Parent*. Vol. 25, Issue 5 (May 1995): 40–53.

Levine, Robert L. "Steps into Ramps." *DIA*

Activist. Vol. 25, No. 4 (December 1995): 16.

Levy, Chava Willig. *A People's History of the Independent Living Movement*. Lawrence, KS: Research and Training Center on Independent Living at the University of Kansas, 1988.

Lewis, Jerry. "If I Had Muscular Dystrophy." *Parade* (2 September 1990).

Liachowitz, Claire H. *Disability as a Social Construct: Legislative Roots*. Philadelphia: University of Pennsylvania Press, 1988.

"Life, Liberty, and the Pursuit of Happiness!" *Valor*. Vol. 1, No. 2 (August 1950): 1.

Lifton, Robert Jay. *The Nazi Doctors: Medical Killing and the Psychology of Genocide*. New York: Basic Books, 1986.

Lippman, Leopold D. *Right to Education: Anatomy of the Pennsylvania Case and Its Implications for Exceptional Children*. New York: Teachers College Press, 1973.

Lipsky, Dorothy Kerzner, and Alan Gartner, editors. *Beyond Special Education: Quality Education for All*. Baltimore: Paul H. Brookes Publishing Co., 1989.

———. "The Current Situation." In Kerzner and Gartner, editors. *Beyond Special Education: Quality Education for All*. Baltimore: Paul H. Brookes Publishing Co., 1989.

Longmore, Paul K. "A Note on Language and the Social Identity of Disabled People." *American Behavioral Scientist*. Vol. 28, No. 3 (January/February 1985): 419–423.

———. "The Life of Randolph Bourne and the Need for a History of Disabled People." *Reviews in American History* (December 1985): 581–587.

———. "Elizabeth Bouvia, Assisted Suicide and Social Prejudice." *Issues in Law & Medicine*. Vol. 3, No. 2 (Fall 1987): 141–168.

———. "Screening Stereotypes: Images of Disabled People in Television and Motion Pictures." In Alan Gartner and Tom Joe, editors. *Images of the Disabled, Disabling Images*. New York: Praeger, 1987.

———. "Uncovering the Hidden History of People with Disabilities." *Reviews in American History* (September 1987): 355–364.

———. "Crippling the Disabled." *New York Times* (November 26 1988): Op. Ed. page.

———. "Medical Decision Making and People with Disabilities: A Clash of Cultures." *Journal of Law, Medicine & Ethics*. 23 (1995): 82–87.

———. "The Second Phase: From Disability Rights to Disability Culture." *Disability Rag & Resource*. Vol. 16, No. 5 (September/October 1995): 4–11.

———. Interview. 16 May 1996.

Louie, Chun, et al. "The Week That Was—In Photos." *Gallaudet Today*. Vol. 18, No. 5 (Summer 1988): 8–25.

Low, Wendy. "New Clayton Valli Video Makes ASL Poetry Affordable." *Silent News*. Vol. 28, No. 6 (June 1996): B–7.

Luczak, Raymond. *Eyes of Desire: A Deaf Gay and Lesbian Reader*. Los Angeles: Alyson Publications, 1993.

———. *St. Michael's Fall*. Rochester, NY: Deaf Life Press, 1996.

"'Lynchburg Story' Chronicles Untold Story of Sterilization." *Daily Progress* (of Charlottesville, VA) (2 July 1994): C-4.

McCrone, William P. "Senator Tom Harkin: Reflections on Disability Policy." *Journal of Rehabilitation*. Vol. 56, No. 2 (April/May/June 1990): 8–10.

Mace, Ronald L. "Housing." In Arthur Dell Orto and Robert P. Marinelli, editors. *Encyclopedia of Disability and Rehabilitation*. New York: Simon & Schuster Macmillan, 1995.

———. Interview. 17 September 1996.

McGarry, Bill. "Cruising the Internet." *Exceptional Parent*. Vol. 24, No. 6 (June 1994): 39–44.

McGhehey, M. A., editor. *School Law for a New Decade*. Topeka, KS: National Organization on Legal Problems of Education, 1981.

———. *School Law in Changing Times*. Topeka, KS: National Organization on Legal Problems of Education, 1982.

McKnight, John. "Control: Out of Our Hands...Into Their Pockets." *Mouth: The Voice of Disability Rights*. Vol. 5, No. 5 (January/February 1995): 28–29.

Macurdy, Allan H. "The Americans with Disabilities Act: Time for Celebration, or Time for Caution?" *Boston University Public Interest Law Journal*. Vol. 1, No. 1 (Winter 1991): 21–38.

Maddox, Sam. "Christopher Reeve: Making Sense out of Chaos." *New Mobility*. Vol. 7, No. 35 (August 1996): 58–66, 104–105.

———. *Spinal Network: The Total Resource for the Wheelchair Community*. Boulder, CO: Spinal Network, 1988.

Maine Consumer and Technology Training Exchange, Maine Department of Education. *Theater without Limits: Making Performances Accessible*. Portland, ME: Very Special Arts, Maine, 1994.

"Marlee Matlin To Host Second Season of *People in Motion*." *Silent News*. Vol. 28, No. 4 (April 1996): 34.

Marshall, Helen E. *Dorothea Dix: Forgotten Samaritan*. New York: Russell and Russell, 1937.

Martin, Douglas A. "A Call for Reform: Current Disability Health and Benefits Program Penalize Recipients." *Mainstream*. Vol. 18, No. (5 February 1994): 36–39.

———. Interview. 26 June 1996.

Martin, Edwin W. "The Golden Age of Special Education." *Exceptional Parent*. Vol. 26, No. (6 June 1996): 62–66.

Martin, Rosemary M. *People with Multiple Chemical Sensitivity: A New Social Policy for NASW*. Minneapolis: Minnesota Chapter, National Association of Social Workers, 1995.

Massie, Willman A. "The Evolution of Standards for Sheltered Workshops." *Journal of Rehabilitation*. Vol. 34, No. 3 (May/June 1968): 32–33.

Mathews, Jay. *A Mother's Touch: The Tiffany Callo Story*. New York: Henry Holt and Company, 1992.

Matson, Floyd. *Walking Alone and Marching Together: A History of the Organized Blind Movement in the United States, 1940–1990*. Baltimore: National Federation of the Blind, 1990.

Mayerson, Arlene. "The History of the ADA: A Movement Perspective." In Lawrence O. Gostin and Henry A. Beyer, editors. *Implementing the Americans with Disabilities Act: Rights and Responsibilities of All Americans*. Baltimore: Paul H. Brookes Publishing Co., 1993.

Mayeux, Nancy. "Dwarf Tossing and Dwarf Bowling Now Illegal in Florida." *LPA Today* (September 1989): 4–8.

Medgyesi, Victoria. "Candidate Callahan." *New Mobility*. Vol. 7, No. 35 (September 1996): 76–81.

———. *No More B.S.* Clarkston, WA: People First of Washington, 1992.

Meister, Joan. Interview. 28 March 1996.

Mendelsohn, Steve. "Silence on the Psychiatric Holocaust." In Barrett Shaw, editor. *The Ragged Edge: The Disability Experience from the Pages of the First Fifteen Years of The Disability Rag*. Lousiville, KY: Advocado Press, 1994.

Metzger, Linda, editor. *Contemporary Authors: New Revision Series*. Detroit: Gale Research Company, 1982, 1984.

Mezey, Susan Gluck. *No Longer Disabled: The Federal Courts and the Politics of Social Security Disability*. New York: Greenwood Press, 1988.

Miggims, Charles. "The Workshop Movement Today." *Journal of Rehabilitation*. Vol. 31, No. 1 (January/February 1965): 20.

Milam, Lorenzo Wilson. *The Cripple Liberation Front Marching Band Blues*. San Diego: Mho & Mho Works, 1984.

———. *Crip Zen: A Manual for Survival*. San Diego: Mho & Mho Works, 1993.

Mnookin, Robert H. *In the Interest of Children: Advocacy, Law Reform, and Public Policy*. New York: W. H. Freeman and Company, 1985.

Molnar, Michele. "Whose Words Are They Anyway? Controversy Rages over Facilitated Communication." *Mainstream*. Vol. 18, No. 3 (November 1993): 18–22.

Moore, John W. "On the Case: At a Time When President Bush's Civil Rights Stance Is Being Questioned, the Equal Employment Opportunity Commission Has Initiated an Aggressive Crackdown on Workplace Discrimination." *National Journal* (2 March 1991): 501–504.

Moore, Matthew S., and Levitan, Linda. *For Hearing People Only: Answers to Some of the Most Commonly Asked Questions about the Deaf Community*. Rochester, NY: Deaf Life Press, 1992.

Moore, Matthew S., and Panara, Robert. *Great Deaf Americans, The Second Edition*. Rochester, NY: Deaf Life Press, 1996.

Moore, Nancy T. "Carrying on the Work: A Newly Established Institute Honors Frederick C. Schreiber." *Gallaudet Today*. Vol. 18, No. 2 (Winter 1987–1988): 18–19.

Moore, Teresa. "Edward Roberts—Advocate for Disabled." *San Francisco Chronicle* (15 March 1995).

Morgan, Sharon R. *Abuse and Neglect of Handicapped Children*. Boston: Little, Brown and Company, 1987.

Moritz, Charles, editor. *Current Biography Yearbook 1990*. New York: H. W. Wilson Company, 1991.

Morris, Jenny, editor. *Able Lives: Women's Experience of Paralysis*. London: The Women's Press, 1989.

"Mothers from Hell: An Interview with Mary-Louise Pasutti." *Mouth: The Voice of Disability Rights*. Vol. 4, No. 5 (January/February 1994): 18–21, 34–35

Mouth: The Voice of Disability Rights. You Choose. Rochester, NY: Free Hand Press, 1995

Murphy, Robert F. *The Body Silent*. New York: Henry Holt and Company, 1987.

Murphy, Stephen T., and Patricia M. Rogan. *Closing the Shop: Conversion from Sheltered to Integrated Work*. Baltimore: Paul H. Brookes Publishing Co., 1995.

National Council on the Handicapped. *Toward Independence: An Assessment of Federal Laws and Programs Affecting People with Disabilities—With Legislative Recommendations*. Washington, DC: National Council on the Handicapped, U.S. Government Printing Office, 1986.

———. *On the Threshold of Independence: A Report to the President and to the Congress of the United States*. Washington, DC: National Council on the Handicapped, 1988.

National Institute of Handicapped Research, Office of Special Education and Rehabilitative Services. *The Influence of Parental Disability on Children*. Pamphlet. Washington, DC: U.S. Department of Education, January 1982.

National Spinal Cord Injury Association. "Vivienne S. Thomson, May 9, 1933 to June 25, 1994." *Spinal Cord Injury Life* (Summer/Fall 1994): 8.

National Spinal Cord Injury Foundation. *National Resource Directory*. Newton Upper Falls, MA: National Spinal Cord Injury Foundation, 1979.

Neisser, Arden. *The Other Side of Silence: Sign Language and the Deaf Community in America*. New York: Alfred A. Knopf, 1983.

Nelson, Jack A., editor. *The Disabled, the Media, and the Information Age*. Westport, CT: Greenwood Press, 1994.

Nelson, Nathan. *Workshops for the Handicapped in the United States: An Historical and Developmental Perspective*. Springfield, IL: Charles C. Thomas, 1971.

Nemeth, Mary, and Bart Johnson. "Nobody Has the Right To Play God: A Woman Goes to Court over Her Forced 1959 Sterilization." *Maclean's*. Vol. 108, No. 26 (26 June 1995): 17.

Newman, Patricia. "Handicapped Concerns." *American Rehabilitation*. Vol. 3, No. 3 (January/February 1978): 8.

Norden, Martin F. *The Cinema of Isolation: A History of Physical Disability in the Movies*. New Brunswick, NJ: Rutgers University Press, 1994.

Nugent, Timothy J. Interview. 13 September 1996.

Obermann, C. Esco. "The Challenge of the Last 40 Years in Vocational Rehabilitation." *Journal of Rehabilitation*. Vol. 32, No. 1 (January/February 1966): 21.

O'Brien, Mark. "Identity Squared." *Disability Rag & Resource*. Vol. 16, No. 5 (September/October 1995): 9.

O'Brien, Shawn Casey. "A Little History." *Uprising: Unique People's Voting Project* (Fall 1995): 7–8.

O'Day, Bonnie. Interview. 25 March 1996.

Oliphant, Thomas. "A Law To Protect the

Disabled." *Boston Globe.* (20 August 1989): A-23.

Olsen, Gary W., editor. *A Kaleidoscope of Deaf America.* Silver Spring, MD: National Association of the Deaf, 1984.

Osmanczyk, Edmund Jan. *The Encyclopedia of the United Nations and International Relations.* New York: Taylor and Francis, 1990.

Oswald, Barbara. Interview. 1 March 1995.

Owen, Mary Jane. "David B. Gray, Ph.D.: Disability Leadership at the Top." *Mainstream.* Vol. 11, No. 2 (May 1986): 9–14.

———. "PVA Leads the Way on Airline Legislation." *Mainstream.* (November 1986): 6–7.

———. "On the Scene—'Wired, Yeah, You're Wired.'" *Horizons* (June 1996).

———. Interview. 6 June 1996.

Pace, Eric. "Irving Kenneth Zola Dies at 59; Sociologist Aided the Disabled." *New York Times* (2 December 1994): D-22.

Packard, Robert T. *Encyclopedia of American Architecture, Second Edition.* New York: McGraw-Hill, 1995.

Padden, Carol, and Tom Humphries. *Deaf in America: Voices from a Culture.* Cambridge, MA: Harvard University Press, 1988.

Panzarino, Connie. *The Me in the Mirror.* Seattle: Seal Press, 1994.

Parent, Wendy S., Mark L. Hill, and Paul Wehman. "From Sheltered to Supported Employment Outcomes: Challenges for Rehabilitation Facilities." *Journal of Rehabilitation.* Vol. 55, No. 4 (October/November/December 1989): 51–57.

Parry, John, editor. *Mental Disability Law: A Primer.* Washington, DC: Commission on the Mentally Disabled, American Bar Association, 1984.

Patterson, Jeanne Boland, and Frank Woodrich. "The Client Assistance Projects: 1974–1984." *Journal of Rehabilitation.* Vol. 52, No. 4 (October/November/December 1986): 49–52.

Pelka, Fred. "Disability Rights in Zimbabwe." *Mainstream.* Vol. 14, No. 3 (October 1989): 21–23.

———. "Who Is Evan Kemp and What Is

He Doing Sitting on the Top of the EEOC?" *Mainstream.* Vol. 16, No. 3 (November 1991): 30–37.

———. "Trauma Time: Disability Issues Must Be a Litmus Test for Evaluating the Validity of any Proposal for Health Care Reform." *Mainstream.* Vol. 17, No. 6 (March 1993): 35–41.

———. "Personal Assistance Services: A Critical Element of Health Care Reform." *Mainstream.* Vol. 17, No. 7 (April 1993): 25–31.

———. "Ed Roberts, 1939–1995: Father of Independent Living." *Mainstream.* Vol. 19, No. 8 (May 1995): 24–29.

———. "Rape: Sexual Abuse of Persons with Disabilities Is Considered by Some To Be an Epidemic, but Few Voices from Our Community Are Raised in Outrage. Why?" *Mainstream.* Vol. 18, No. 3, 24–33.

Percy, Stephen L. "The ADA: Expanding Mandates for Disability Rights." *Intergovernmental Perspective* (Winter 1993): 11–14.

———. *Disability, Civil Rights, and Public Policy: The Politics of Implementation.* Tuscaloosa, AL: University of Alabama Press, 1989.

Perske, Robert. *Unequal Justice?: What Can Happen When Persons with Retardation or Other Developmental Disabilities Encounter the Criminal Justice System.* Nashville: Abingdon Press, 1991.

———. *Deadly Innocence?* Nashville: Abingdon Press, 1995.

Pfeiffer, David. Correspondence. 13 August 1996.

———. Interview. 5 September, 6 September 1996.

Phillips, William R. F., and Janet Rosenberg, editors. *Changing Patterns of Law: The Courts and the Handicapped.* New York: Arno Press, 1980.

Piastro, Dianne. "Telethons: Where Do We Go from Here?" *Disability Rag & Resource.* Vol. 16, No. 4 (July/August 1995): 24–25.

Pickens, Donald K. *Eugenics and the Progressives.* Nashville: Parthenon Press, Vanderbilt University Press, 1968.

Bibliography

Pietsch, Robert. "Becoming the Kingdom of God: Building Bridges between Religion, Secular Society, and Persons with Disabilities: The Ministry of Harold Wilke." *Journal of Religion in Disability & Rehabilitation*. Vol. 2, No. 4 (1996): 15–25.

Platt, Mary Frances. "'I'm a Radical Crip,' Not a 'Disabled Woman.'" *Sojourner: The Women's Forum* (June 1995): 8–9.

Pohlmann, Kenneth E. "Federal State Programs for the Physically Handicapped." *Valor* (September 1956): 6–7.

Polman, Stoney M. Interview. 16 April 1996.

Pompkins, Joanne. Interview. 12 September 1996.

Porter, Roy. *A Social History of Madness: The World through the Eyes of the Insane*. New York: E. P. Dutton, 1989.

Preiser, Wolfgang E., et al., editors. *Design Intervention: Toward a More Human Architecture*. New York, 1990.

"President Honors Concordian's Fight for the Disabled." *Concord Journal* (12 November 1992).

President's Committee on Employment of People with Disabilities. *Job Accommodation Network: U.S. Annual Report October 1, 1993 through September 30, 1994*. Morgantown, WV: West Virginia University, 1994.

President's Committee on Employment of the Handicapped. "A Survey of State Laws To Remove Barriers." Washington, DC: President's Committtee on Employment of the Handicapped, August 1973.

———. "The President's Committee, a Forty Year Chronicle." In *1987 Annual Meeting of the President's Committee on Employment of the Handicapped*. Washington, DC: President's Committee on Employment of the Handicapped, 1987.

Prouty, Robert, and K. Charlie Lakin, editors. *Residential Services for Persons with Developmental Disabilities: Status and Trends through 1994*. Minneapolis: Research and Training Center on Community Living, 1995.

"Rachel Wins." *Mainstream*. Vol. 18, No. 10 (August 1994): 11.

Rainbow Alliance of the Deaf. Correspondence. 24 May 1995.

Reed, Heidi, and Hartmut Teuber. Correspondence. December 1996.

Reiskin, Julie. "Suicide: Political or Personal?" In Barrett Shaw, editor. *The Ragged Edge: The Disability Experience from the Pages of the First Fifteen Years of* The Disability Rag. Louisville, KY: Advocado Press. 1994.

Riekenhof, Lottie L. *The Joy of Signing: The New Illustrated Guide for Mastering Sign Language and the Manual Alphabet*. Springfield, MO: Gospel Publishing House, 1978.

Roberts, Edward V. "Independent Living Movement Promotes Self-Determination for Disabled Individuals." *Mainstream*. Vol. 10, No. 1 (April 1985): 23–27, 50.

———. "How Independent Living Got Rolling." *This Brain Has a Mouth*. Vol. 3, No. 2 (July/August 1992): 9–11.

Roberts, Zona. Interview. 12 September 1996.

Romano, Frank. "White House Conference Report Presented." *American Rehabilitation*. Vol. 3, No. 5 (May/June 1978): 4–5.

———. Interview. 5 September 1996.

Rothman, David, and Sheila Rothman. *The Willowbrook Wars: A Decade of Struggle for Social Change*. New York: Harper and Row, 1984.

Rothstein, Laura F. *Disabilities and the Law* (formerly, *Rights of Physically Handicapped Persons*). Colorado Springs, CO: Shepard's/McGraw-Hill, Inc., 1992.

Rubenfeld, Phyllis. Interview. 20 July 1995.

Rueda, Robert, and Irene Martinez. "Fiesta Educativa: One Community's Approach to Parent Training in Developmental Disabilities for Latino Families." *Journal of the Association for Persons with Severe Handicaps*. Vol. 17, No. 2 (1992): 95–103.

Ruffner, Robert H. "504 and the Media: Legitimizing Disability." *American Rehabilitation*. Vol. 13, No. 2 (April/May/June 1987): 4–7, 25.

Rusk, Howard A. *A World To Care For: The Autobiography of Howard A. Rusk, M.D.* New York: Random House, 1972.

Russell, Harold. Interview. 20 June 1995.

Russell, Harold, with Victor Rosen. *Victory in My Hands*. New York: Creative Age Press, 1949.

Sackett, Susan. *The Hollywood Reporter Book of Box Office Hits*. New York: Billboard Books, 1990.

Salladay, Robert. "Cal's Edward V. Roberts Gave Dignity to Disabled." *Oakland Tribune* (15 March 1995): A-11.

Samuel, Allen T., Jr. "New Horizons: Wagner O'Day Amendments." *Journal of Rehabilitation*. Vol. 39, No. 1 (January/February 1973): 23, 48.

Sands, Jim. *Common Barriers: Toward an Understanding of AIDS and Disability*. Vancouver, British Columbia: The British Columbia Coalition of the Disabled, December 1988.

Saxton, Marsha. "A Peer Counseling Training Program for Disabled Women." *Journal of Sociology and Social Welfare*. Vol. 8, No. 2 (July 1981): 8, 334–346.

———. "The Disabled Women's Community Responds to 'A Private Matter.'" *Roll Call* (August/Septmember 1992): 8, 18.

———. "What's at Stake? The Right To Bear Young: The Earl Hearing." *Disability Rag & Resource*. Vol. 14, No. 3 (May/June 1993): 3–5.

Saxton, Marsha, et al. *Ableism*. Brookline, MA: Boston Self Help Center, 1995.

Saxton, Marsha, and Florence Howe, editors. *With Wings: An Anthology of Literature by and about Women with Disabilities*. New York: The Feminist Press at the City University of New York, 1987.

Scheerenberger, R. C. *Deinstitutionalization and Institutional Reform*. Springfield, IL: Charles C. Thomas, 1976.

———. *A History of Mental Retardation: A Quarter Century of Progress*. Baltimore: Paul H. Brookes Publishing Co., 1987.

Schein, Jerome D. *A Rose for Tomorrow: Biography of Frederick C. Schreiber*. Silver Spring, MD: National Association of the Deaf, 1981.

———. *At Home among Strangers*. Washington, DC: Gallaudet University Press, 1989.

Schein, Jerome D., and Marcus Welk. *The Deaf Population of the United States*. Silver Spring, MD: National Association of the Deaf, 1974.

Schneider, Marjorie. Interview. 1 April 1996.

Schrauder, Betsy, and Jeannine Villing, editors. *Proceedings of the Supreme Court Davis Decision: Implications for Higher Education and Physically Disabled Students*. Detroit: Wayne State University, 1979.

Scotch, Richard. *From Good Will to Civil Rights: Transforming Federal Disability Policy*. Philadelphia: Temple University Press, 1984.

Scott, Mildred. "Notes on NEPH Week." In *1987 Annual Meeting of the President's Committee on Employment of the Handicapped*. Washington, DC: President's Committee on Employment of People with Disabilities, 1987.

Sege, Irene. "He Will Not Go Gentle." *Boston Globe* (27 June 1995): 53, 58.

Shapiro, Joseph P. "Disabled and Free at Last." *U.S. News & World Report* (17 May 1993): 50–52.

———. *No Pity: People with Disabilities Forging a New Civil Rights Movement*. New York: Times Books, 1993, 1994.

Shaw, Barrett. "Eugenics Then & Now." *Disability Rag & Resource* (January/February 1994): 23–25.

———. Correspondence. 3 April 1995.

———, editor. *The Ragged Edge: The Disability Experience from the Pages of the First Fifteen Years of* The Disability Rag. Louisville, KY: Advocado Press, 1994.

Shelman, Ralph. Interview. 17 April 1996.

Shilts, Randy. *And the Band Played On: Politics, People, and the AIDS Epidemic*. New York: St. Martin's Press, 1987.

Shirer, William L. *Berlin Diary*. New York: Alfred A. Knopf, 1941.

Shrout, Richard Neil. *Resource Directory for the Disabled*. New York, Oxford: Facts on File, 1991.

Skelley, Richard V. *Insuring Health Care for People with Disabilities*. Columbus, OH: The Ohio Developmental Disabilities Planning Council, 1990.

Smilovitz, Robert. "A Brief History of Pennhurst 1908–1926: Compiled from

Superintendents' Documents." Unpublished Manuscript, 1974.

Smith, Eleanor. "Visitability: A Revolution in Housing Development." *Mainstream*. Vol. 18, No. 10 (August 1994): 28–34.

Sobsey, Dick. *Violence and Abuse in the Lives of People with Disabilities: The End of Silent Acceptance?* Baltimore: Paul H. Brookes Publishing Co., 1994.

Sontag, Ed, and Norris G. Haring. "The Professionalization of Teaching and Learning for Children with Severe Disabilities: The Creation of TASH." *Journal of the Association for Persons with Severe Handicaps*. Vol. 21, No. 1 (1996): 39–45.

"Special Writings." *Disability Rag & Resource*. Vol. 10, No. 2 (March/April 1989): 25.

Spungin, Susan J. *Braille Literacy: Issues for Blind Persons, Families, Professionals, and Producers of Braille*. New York: American Foundation for the Blind, 1989.

Stainback, Susan, and William Stainback. *Integration of Students with Severe Handicaps in the Regular Classroom*. Reston, VA: Council for Exceptional Children, 1985.

———, editors. *Curriculum Considerations in Inclusive Classrooms*. Baltimore: Paul H. Brookes Publishing Co., 1992.

Starr, Paul. *The Social Transformation of American Medicine: The Rise of a Sovereign Profession and the Making of a Vast Industry*. New York: Basic Books, 1982.

Stewart, Jean. *The Body's Memory*. New York: St. Martin's Press, 1989.

Stothers, William G. Correspondence. 12 June 1995.

———. "Jay Rochlin." *Mainstream*. Vol. 20, No. 10 (August 1996): 19.

———. "Organ Donor Bill." *Mainstream*. Vol. 20, No. 10 (August 1996): 16.

Strachan, Paul A. "The National Conference on Placement of Severely Handicapped." *Valor* (July 1952): 15–16.

Strauss, Karen Peltz. "Signs of Progress: Federal Legislation." *Gallaudet Today*. Vol. 17, No. 4 (1987 Legal Review): 21–25.

———. "Title IV—Telecommunications." In Lawrence O. Gostin and Henry A. Beyer,

editors. *Implementing the Americans with Disabilities Act: Rights and Responsibilities for All Americans*. Baltimore: Paul H. Brookes Publishing Co., 1993.

Strohkendl, Horst, editor, with Armand Thiboutot. *The 50th Anniversary of Wheelchair Basketball*. New York and Münster, Germany: Waxman, 1996.

Stuckey, Kenneth A. *Samuel Gridley Howe*. Watertown, MA: Perkins School for the Blind, 1994.

Suazo, Antonio C. "On Workshops and Government." *Journal of Rehabilitation*. Vol. 31, No. 1 (January/February 1965): 47–49.

Swindlehurst, Wayne I. Interview. 3 October 1996.

Szasz, Thomas. *The Myth of Mental Illness*. New York: Hoeber-Harper, 1961.

———. *The Manufacture of Madness*. New York: Dell, 1970.

Task Force on the Rights and Empowerment of Americans with Disabilities. *From ADA to Empowerment: The Report of the Task Force on the Rights and Empowerment of Americans with Disabilities*. Washington, DC, 1990.

Technical Assistance for Parent Programs (TAPP). "The TAPP Network." *Coalition Quarterly*. Vol. 7, No. 1 (Winter 1989–1990).

Tempel, Linda A. Correspondence. 22 July 1996.

TenBroek, Jacobus, and Floyd W. Matson. *Hope Deferred: Public Welfare and the Blind*. Berkeley, CA: University of California Press, 1959.

Thiboutot, Armand. Interview. 4 September 1996.

Thomas, Clayton L., editor. *Taber's Cyclopedic Medical Dictionary, 15th Edition*. Philadelphia: F. A. Davis Co., 1985.

Thompson, Karen. Interview. 30 September 1995.

Thompson, Karen, and Julie Andrzejewski. *Why Can't Sharon Kowalski Come Home?* San Francisco: Spinsters/Aunt Lute, 1988.

Thompson, William C. "Media and the Myth of Mobility." *American Rehabilitation*. Vol. 5, No. 3 (January/February 1980): 12–14.

Thomson, Mildred. *Prologue: A Minnesota*

Story of Mental Retardation Showing Changing Attitudes and Philosophies prior to September 1, 1959. Minneapolis: Gilbert Publishing Company, 1963.

Thoreson, Richard. "Disability Viewed in Its Cultural Context." *Journal of Rehabilitation.* Vol. 30, No. 1 (January/February 1964): 12–13.

Thornburgh, Dick. "The Americans with Disabilities Act: What It Means to All Americans." *Boston University Public Interest Law Journal.* Vol. 1, No. 1, 15–20.

Thornburgh, Ginny. "For the Love of Peter." *Guideposts: A Practical Guide to Successful Living,* October 1993.

"Tony Coelho: The New Chairman of the President's Committee for the Employment of People with Disabilities." *Enable Georgia* (Fall 1994).

Traustadottir, Rannveig. *Women with Disabilities: Issues, Resources, Connections.* Syracuse, NY: Center on Human Policy, 1990.

Treanor, Richard Bryant. *We Overcame: The Story of Civil Rights for Disabled People.* Falls Church, VA: Regal Direct Publishing, 1993.

Treese, Joel D., editor. *Biographical Directory of the American Congress 1774–1996.* Alexandria, VA: CQ Staff Directories, Inc., 1997.

Trent, James W., Jr., *Inventing the Feeble Mind: A History of Mental Retardation in the United States.* Berkeley, CA: University of California Press, 1994.

Trombley, Stephen. *The Right To Reproduce: A History of Coercive Sterilization.* London: Weidenfeld and Nicolson, 1988.

Turnbull, H. Rutherford, III. *Free Appropriate Public Education: The Law and Children with Disabilities.* Third Edition. Denver, CO: Love Publishing Company, 1990.

Turnbull, H. Rutherford, III, and Ann P. Turnbull. *Parents Speak Out: Then and Now.* Columbus, OH: Charles E. Merrill Publishing Company, 1985, 1978.

Tuttle, Cheryl G., and Gerald A. Tuttle, editors. *Challenging Voices: Writings by, for and about Individuals with Learning Disabilities.* Los Angeles: Lowell House, 1995.

Tutu, Desmond. "As Much a Moral Issue as Apartheid Ever Was." *Disability International* (Spring 1995): 32–34.

Tyor, Peter L., and Leland V. Bell. *Caring for the Retarded in America: A History.* Westport, CT: Greenwood Press, 1985.

United States Code Congressional and Administrative News. St. Paul, MN: West Group, 1953–.

United States Code Congressional and Administrative Service (2 volumes). St. Paul, MN: West Publishing Company, 1952.

United States Code Congressional Service (13 volumes). St. Paul, MN: West Publishing Company, 1942–1951.

United States Commission on Civil Rights. *Civil Rights Issues of Handicapped Americans: Public Policy Implications.* Washington, DC: U.S. Government Printing Office, 1980.

"U.S. Settles 2 Complaints of Bias against Disabled." *Boston Globe* (August 30 1996): A-21.

Unzicker, Rae. E. Interview. 4 October 1995.

Val, Sarah E. Correspondence. 22 February 1995.

Valentine, Victoria. "Being Black and Deaf: Coping in Both Communities." *Emerge: Black America's Newsmagazine.* Vol. 7, No. 3 (December/January 1996): 56–61.

Van Biema, David. "AIDS: In One Community, Silence Equals Death." *Time* (4 April 1994): 76–77.

Van Cleve, John V., and Barry A. Crouch. *A Place of Their Own: Creating the Deaf Community in America.* Washington, DC: Gallaudet University Press, 1989.

Van Cleve, John V., editor. *Gallaudet Encyclopedia of Deaf People and Deafness* (3 volumes). New York: McGraw-Hill, 1987.

Vaughan, C. Edwin. *The Struggle of Blind People for Self-Determination: The Dependency-Rehabilitation Conflict: Empowerment in the Blindness Community.* Springfield, IL: Charles C. Thomas, 1993.

"Victory in Landmark 'Full Inclusion' Case." *Disability Rights and Defense Fund News* (September 1994): 1.

Villa, R. A., and J. S. Thousands. *Creating an Inclusive School.* Alexandria, VA: Association for Supervision and Curriculum Development, 1995.

Viscardi, Henry, Jr. *A Man's Stature*. New York: The John Day Company, 1952.

———. *Give Us the Tools: A History of Abilities, Inc*. New York: Paul Erickson, 1959.

———. Interview. 25 September 1996.

Wade, Cheryl Marie. "Other Voices: Creating Crip Text." *Disability Rag & Resource*. Vol. 16, No. 4 (July/August 1995): 34–37.

———. "Flying Solo." *Disability Rag & Resource*. Vol. 16, No. 5 (September/October 1995): 28–38.

Wadleigh, Jonathan. "Major Legal Victory: Class Action Certified; $160 Million Offered by Armour and Baxter." *Common Factor: The Voice of the Committee of Ten Thousand*. Issue 9 (September 1994): 1, 4, 34–36.

Walker, Martha Lentz. *Beyond Bureaucracy: Mary Elizabeth Switzer and Rehabilitation*. New York: University Press of America, 1985.

Walls, Richard T., and Denetta L. Dowler. "Information Resources." In Arthur E. Dell Orto and Robert P. Marinelli, editors. *Encyclopedia of Disability and Rehabilitation*. New York: Simon & Schuster Macmillan, 1995.

Walter, Vickie. "Inside the Madness: An Unusual Exhibit Depicts the Nazi Persecution of Deaf People." *Gallaudet Today*. Vol. 18, No. 2 (Winter 1987–1988): 6–11.

———. "Off and Running: Gallaudet's New President Takes the Helm." *Gallaudet Today*. Vol. 18, No. 5 (Summer 1988): 3–7.

War of the Rebellion: A Compilation of the Official Records of the Union and Confederate Armies. Washington, DC: U.S. War Department, 1902.

Watson, Sara D. "An Alliance at Risk: The Disability Movement and Health Care Reform." *American Prospect* (Winter 1993).

Watson, Sara, and O'Day, Bonnie. "Movement Leadership." *Disability Studies Quarterly*. Vol. 16, No. 1 (Winter 1996): 26–30.

Waxman, Barbara Faye. "Hatred: The Unacknowledged Dimension in Violence against Disabled People." *Journal of Sexuality and Disability*. Vol. 9. No. 3 (October/November 1991): 261–271.

———. "Hate." *Disability Rag & Resource*. Vol. 13, No. 3 (May/June 1992): 4–7.

Weber, Mark C. "Towards Access, Accountability, Procedural Regularity and Participation: The Rehabilitation Act Amendments of 1992 and 1993." *Journal of Rehabilitation*. Vol. 60, No. 3 (July/August/September 1994): 21–25.

Weiss, Nancy R. *The Application of Aversive Procedures to Individuals with Developmental Disabilities: A Call to Action*. Seattle: The Association for Persons with Severe Handicaps, 1991.

Welch, Jane. "Unique College Program for the Severely Handicapped." *Journal of Rehabilitation*. Vol. 30, No. 6 (November/December 1964): 34–35.

Welch, Polly, editor. *Strategies for Teaching Universal Design*. Boston: Adaptive Environments Center, 1995.

West, Jane. "The Evolution of Disability Rights." In Lawrence O. Gostin and Henry A. Beyer, editors. *Implementing the Americans with Disabilities Act: Rights and Responsibilities of All Americans*. Baltimore: Paul H. Brookes Publishing Co., 1993.

———, editor. *Implementing the Americans with Disabilities Act*. Cambridge, MA: Blackwell Publishers, 1996.

"White House Conference Report." *American Rehabilitation*. Vol. 2, No. 1 (September/October 1976): 30–31.

Whitten, E. B. "A New Legislative Milestone for the Handicapped." *Journal of Rehabilitation*. Vol. 31, No. 6 (November/December 1965): 10–12.

Wilcox, Sherman, editor. *American Deaf Culture: An Anthology*. Burtonsville, MD: Linstok Press, 1989.

Wilke, Harold. *Greet the Man*. Cleveland: Pilgrim Press, 1945.

Wilkerson, Arnold M. "The Sheltered Workshop Movement: Management or Muddlement?" *Journal of Rehabilitation*. Vol. 31, No. 2 (March/April 1965): 20–22.

Williamson, David R. "Men and Women Wheelchair Sports Continues Growth and Popularity." *American Rehabilitation*. Vol. 4,

No. 1 (September/October 1978): 25–29.

Wills, Garry. "What Makes a Good Leader?" *Atlantic Monthly* (April 1994): 63–80.

Wilson, Dorothy Clarke. *Stranger and Traveller: The Story of Dorothea Dix, American Reformer.* Boston: Little, Brown and Company, 1975.

Winefield, Richard. *Alexander Graham Bell—Edward Miner Gallaudet: Never the Twain Shall Meet—The Communications Debate.* Washington, DC: Gallaudet University Press, 1987.

Winston, Charlie, editor. *America's Telability Media.* Columbia, MO: National Telability Media Center, 1995.

Witte, Edwin E. *The Development of the Social Security Act.* Madison, WI: University of Wisconsin Press, 1962.

Wolfe, Kathi. "The Bible and Disabilities: From 'Healing' to the 'Burning Bush.'" *Disability Rag & Resource.* Vol. 14, No., 3 (September/October 1993): 9–10.

———. "Springtime for Hitler." In Barrett Shaw, editor. *The Ragged Edge: The Disability Experience from the Pages of the First Fifteen Years of The Disability Rag.* Louisville, KY: Advocado Press, 1994.

———. "Tony Coelho." *Mainstream.* Vol. 18, No. 8 (May 1994): 51–55.

———. "Heroes and Holy Innocents: In Portraying Disabled People, Hollywood Hasn't Got a Clue." *Utne Reader* (January/February 1996): 24–26.

Wolfensberger, Wolf. *The Princple of Normalization in Human Services.* Toronto: National Institute on Mental Retardation, 1972.

———. *The Origin and Nature of Our Institutional Models.* Syracuse: Human Policy Press, 1975.

Woodward, John R. "How CILs Succeed." *This Brain Has a Mouth.* Vol. 3, No. 2 (July/August 1992): 13–15.

———. "When CILs Fail." *This Brain Has a Mouth.* Vol. 3, No. 2 (July/August 1992): 16–17, 34.

———. "Your Right To Squawk." *Mouth: The Voice of Disability Rights.* Vol. 4, No. 5 (January/February 1994): 8–11, 38–39.

World Institute on Disability. "Resolution on Personal Assistance Services." Passed by the participants of the International Personal Assistance Services Symposium convened 29 September to 1 October 1991 in Oakland, California.

———. *Impact! World Institute on Disability SemiAnnual Report.* Oakland, CA: World Institute on Disability, 1994.

Wright, Patrisha. Interview. 1 October 1996.

Wright, Tennyson J., and Paul Leung, editors. *The Unique Needs of Minorities with Disabilities: Setting an Agenda for the Future.* Conference proceedings co-sponsored by the National Council on Disability and Jackson State University, Jackson Mississippi. Washington, DC: National Council on Disability, 1992.

Ysseldyke, James E., Bob Algozzine, and Martha L. Thurlow. *Critical Issues in Special Education.* Boston: Houghton-Mifflin, 1992.

Zames, Freida. Interview. 12 June 1996.

Ziegler, Martha. "Parent Advocacy and Children with Disabilities: A History." *OSERS News in Print* (Summer 1995): 4–6.

Zinman, Sally. "The Legacy of Howie the Harp Lives On." *National Empowerment Center Newsletter* (Spring/Summer 1995): 1, 9.

———. "Howard Geld, 42, Advocate, Activist and Friend." *Rights Tenet* (Summer 1995): 2.

Zinn, Harlan. *Media Stereotypes of Mental Illness, Their Role in Promoting Stigma, and Advocacy Efforts To Overcome Such Stereotypes and Stigma.* New York: National Stigma Clearinghouse, 1995.

Zola, Irving Kenneth. *Missing Pieces: A Chronicle of Living with a Disability.* Philadelphia: Temple University Press, 1982.

———. "The Language of Disability—Dilemmas of Practice and Politics." Paper presented to the 85th annual meeting of the American Anthropological Association in Philadelphia, Pennsylvania, on 4 December 1986.

Zukas, Hale. "CIL History." Berkeley, CA: Center for Independent Living, March 1979. Unpublished manuscript.

Illustration Credits

Index

Index

Index

Index